BOLLINGEN SERIES XLIII

Map of the World

From MS. C (Atif Effendi 1936). Cf. pp. 108 and 110, below

IBN KHALDÛN

THE MUQADDIMAH

An Introduction to History

TRANSLATED FROM THE ARABIC BY

FRANZ ROSENTHAL

IN THREE VOLUMES

1

CONTENTS

VOLUME ONE

The Muqaddimah
The Introduction and Book One
of the World History, entitled Kitâb al-'Ibar,
of Ibn Khaldûn

Contents: Volume One

Book One of the *Kitâb al-ʿIbar*

Chapter II: Bedouin civilization, savage nations and tribes and their conditions of life, including several basic and explanatory statements 247

VOLUME TWO

Chapter IV: Countries and cities, and all other forms of sedentary civilization. The conditions occurring there. Primary and secondary considerations in this connection 233

Chapter V: On the various aspects of making a living, such as profit and the crafts. The conditions that occur in this connection. A number of problems are connected with this subject

VOLUME THREE

LIST OF ILLUSTRATIONS

PLATES

VOLUME ONE

FRONTISPIECE. Map of the World, from MS. C (Atif Effendi 1936, fols. 21*b*–22*a* of the Arabic pagination).

P: Courtesy of Dr. Paul A. Underwood. The key to the map is to be found following p. 110.

following p. xciv

I. Autograph of Ibn Khaldûn (upper left corner), from MS. C (Atif Effendi 1936).

following p. 356

IIa. The Reception Hall of Khosraw in 1869.

P: From an unidentified drawing. Courtesy of Herzfeld Archive, Smithsonian Institution, Washington, D. C.

IIb. The Reception Hall of Khosraw at the beginning of this century.

P: Professor E. Herzfeld. Courtesy of Herzfeld Archive, Smithsonian Institution, Washington, D. C.

IIIa. The Roman Bridge in Córdoba.

P: Mrs. Elizabeth S. Ettinghausen.

VOLUME THREE

FIGURES

VOLUME ONE

VOLUME THREE

TRANSLATOR'S NOTE TO THE SECOND EDITION

This new printing permits the insertion of just a comparatively few, negligible changes, the only major one being the additional bibliography provided by Professor Walter J. Fischel, beginning on 3:512. Where an empty space beckoned, brief references, marked by an asterisk, have occasionally been added. This has happened rarely and quite haphazardly. Some useful items had to be omitted simply because of lack of space. No discrimination or judgment is intended by either the inclusion or the omission of those many things that would have a claim to a hearing. The review by G. Levi Della Vida, in *Oriente Moderno,* XXXVIII (1958), pp. 1005–7, has been utilized for several corrections not individually acknowledged. It has not been possible to include the new changes in the index.

July 1966 F. R.

In the second printing of the second edition (1980), for reasons of economy, only limited textual revisions could be made (see vol. 1, p. 202, n. 288; p. 203, n. 290; vol. 3, p. 30, n. 289; p. 229, n. 966; p. 241, n. 992) and certain mechanical modifications have been undertaken: the colored frontispieces are now given in black and white, some of the folding illustrations have been reduced in order to fit a single page, and the large folding plate formerly placed in a pocket at the end of Volume 3 has been reduced and bound into the book.

F. R.

ACKNOWLEDGMENTS

OVER the many years that this work has been in preparation, the translator's labors, of necessity solitary because of the very nature of scholarship, have found manifold encouragement, and help has been forthcoming whenever he needed it and wherever he asked for it.

When I first tried to obtain manuscript material from Turkey, the late Dr. J. K. Birge proved most helpful in bridging the geographical distance. Later on, in the summer of 1952, when I was able to visit Turkey and spend two and a half months doing research in its beautiful libraries, all the courtesy and help that a foreigner could ever hope for were extended to me. If I refrain from mentioning the names of individual library officials, it is the better to emphasize the deep gratitude that I feel to all of them. Also, I wish to express my thanks to the many other libraries, both in this country and abroad, that I have had the privilege of using at one time or another, profiting from the selfless devotion of their staffs.

Dr. Walter J. Fischel, of the University of California, kindly offered a bibliography of books and articles dealing with Ibn Khaldûn, which he has prepared in the course of his studies, for inclusion in this publication. His offer was gratefully accepted, to the vast benefit, I am sure, of future students of Ibn Khaldûn.

The photographs of manuscript pages reproduced in these volumes were obtained through the good offices of Dr. Paul A. Underwood. Some of them, in particular the color photographs, were taken by Dr. Underwood himself; they attest not only to his excellence as a photographer but also to his generosity in helping a colleague not known to him personally. With his unrivaled knowledge of all the material relics of Muslim civilization, Dr. Richard Ettinghausen came again to my aid by providing me with illustrations of Islamic art objects and monuments. To Dr. George C. Miles, the world's outstanding authority on Muslim coins, I owe the illustrations that give point to Ibn Khaldûn's discussion of the history of Muslim coinage.

I am, needless to say, deeply grateful to the Bollingen Foundation, which made possible the appearance of these volumes. Editorial help, for which authors are rarely grateful, was given by members of the staff of the Foundation, who, for some time, were ably seconded by Dr. Ilse Lichtenstaedter, with her profound knowledge of Arabic studies. Mr. Edwin S. Seldon's editorial work on my English text was of much value.

The debt of gratitude that a translator always owes to the original author will, I hope, be repaid in this instance by a wider appreciation of Ibn Khaldûn's achievement and his extraordinary contribution to human knowledge. On my own behalf, I feel constrained, at the conclusion of this long work, to quote a remark attributed to Plato by Arabic authors. I believe that it can do much to encourage and sustain a scholar when the magnitude of his task makes him wonder whether his time and labor are being well spent:

"Do not try to do whatever you do in a hurry, but try to do it well; for people will not ask how long it took a man to do a particular piece of work, but they will ask how well he did it."

F. R.

New Haven, summer 1957

ABBREVIATIONS AND SYMBOLS

(The use of abbreviations has been avoided as much as possible, but most works cited in the footnotes are provided with full bibliographical data only on their first occurrence in each volume. Thereafter, reference is by short title, with volume and page numbers referring to the edition already cited. The first occurrence of each work can be located with the help of the Index, at the end of Vol. 3.)

A, B̤, etc.	Sigla used to denote Ibn Khaldûn MSS, described on pp. xc ff., below.
Autobiography	MUḤAMMAD TÂWÎT AṬ-ṬANJÎ (ed.). *at-Ta'rîf bi-Ibn Khaldûn wa-riḥlatuhû gharban wa-sharqan.* Cairo, 1370 [1951].
Bombaci	A. BOMBACI, "Postille alla traduzione De Slane della *Muqaddimah* di Ibn Ḫaldûn," *Annali dell' Istituto Universitario Orientale di Napoli,* N.S. III (1949), 439–72.
Bulaq	NAṢR AL-HÛRÎNÎ (ed.). *Ibn Khaldûn: Muqaddimah.* Bulaq, 1274 [1857].
Concordance	A. J. WENSINCK, J. P. MENSING, *et alii. Concordance et Indices de la tradition musulmane.* Leiden, 1936——.
EI	*Encyclopaedia of Islam.* Leiden and London, 1913–34. (A new edition began to appear in 1954.)
EI Supplement	———. *Supplement.* Leiden and London, 1938.
GAL	C. BROCKELMANN. *Geschichte der arabischen Literatur.* Weimar, 1898; Berlin, 1902.
GAL, Suppl.	———. ———. *Supplementbände.* Leiden, 1937–42.
GAL (2nd ed.)	———. ———. Leiden, 1943–49.

Handbook	A. J. WENSINCK. *A Handbook of Early Muhammadan Tradition*. Leiden, 1927.
'Ibar	IBN KHALDÛN. *Kitâb al-'Ibar wa-dîwân al-mubtada' wa-l-khabar*. Bulaq, 1284 [1867/68].
de Slane (tr.)	W. M. DE SLANE (tr.). *Ibn Khaldoun: Histoire des Berbères et des dynasties musulmanes de l'Afrique septentrionale*. Algiers, 1852–56.
Issawi	C. ISSAWI (tr.). *An Arab Philosophy of History: Selections from the Prolegomena of Ibn Khaldun of Tunis (1332–1406)*. London, 1950.
Paris edition	E. QUATREMÈRE (ed.). *Prolégomènes d'Ebn-Khaldoun*. Vols. XVI–XVIII of the *Notices et Extraits des manuscrits de la Bibliothèque Impériale* (Académie des Inscriptions et Belles-Lettres). Paris, 1858.
( )	Contextual sense supplied. Cf. p. cxii, below.
	Translator's interpolations.
< >	MS supplied.
* *	Asterisks enclose passages for which variant (usually, earlier) texts are translated at the foot of the page, in italic.

TRANSLATOR'S INTRODUCTION

Ibn Khaldûn's Life

WRITING the biography of Ibn Khaldûn would not seem to be a particularly difficult task, for he left posterity an autobiography which describes the events of his life in great detail and presents the historical background clearly. He supports his statements with many documents quoted literally. In fact, Ibn Khaldûn's description of his own life is the most detailed autobiography in medieval Muslim literature. It gives us an accurate knowledge of events in the author's life such as is available, before modern times, for but few historical personalities.

Until recently, Ibn Khaldûn's autobiography was known only in a recension that broke off at the end of the year 1394,[1] but now its continuation has been discovered and is available in a carefully annotated edition.[2] It brings the account down to the middle of the year 1405, less than a year before Ibn Khaldûn's death.

In 1382 the fifty-year-old scholar and statesman left his native northwest Africa never to return. For the period before this date, Ibn Khaldûn's autobiographical statements can be supplemented by a perfunctory biographical note incorporated by his friend Ibn

---

[1] Cf. *'Ibar*, VII, 379–463. The text, which is very unsatisfactory, was reprinted in the margin of an edition of the *Muqaddimah* published in Cairo, 1322/1904. Showing that in the autograph manuscript of Ibn Khaldûn's *Lubâb al-Muḥaṣṣal*, the vocalization *muqaddamah* is occasionally used, Fr. Luciano Rubio makes a rather strong case for reading *Muqaddamah*, instead of *Muqaddimah*. Cf. *La Ciudad de Dios*, CLXII (1950), 171–78. No completely vocalized occurrence of the word—which would decide the question—is known to me from the old MSS of the *Muqaddimah*. I feel certain that both forms are equally possible, and that the problem is a very minor one.

[2] The complete autobiography was edited by Muḥammad Tâwît aṭ-Ṭanjî and published under the title *at-Ta'rîf bi-Ibn Khaldûn wa-riḥlatuhû gharban wa-sharqan* [Biography of Ibn Khaldûn and Report on his Travel(s) in the West and in the East] (Cairo, 1370/1951). In his footnotes aṭ-Ṭanjî supplies ample bibliographical references concerning the personalities Ibn Khaldûn mentions in the *Autobiography*.

al-Khaṭîb in his *History of Granada.*[3] Written in general terms of praise, it lacks any critical appreciation of its subject. There exists another biography of Ibn Khaldûn which a Western writer, Ismâ'îl b. Yûsuf b. al-Aḥmar, inserted in an anthology of contemporary poets, entitled *Nathîr al-jumân.* The writer, a member of the ruling family of Granada, died about the same time as Ibn Khaldûn. It can be assumed that he relied on Western authorities for the earlier period of Ibn Khaldûn's life. Unfortunately, the text of this biography is not yet available.[4]

For Ibn Khaldûn's later years, when he participated in the flourishing literary life of Mameluke Egypt, the biographical sources are more varied. Biographies of Ibn Khaldûn were composed by his pupils and admirers; nor could his enemies disregard him when writing the biographical history of the period. The latter present another view of his personality, and though their statements have to be taken with reservations, they help us to understand it better.[5]

Ibn Khaldûn's own great work, especially the *Muqaddimah,* is another important source for his biography. Written in a much more personal style than most medieval works, the *Muqaddimah* sharply outlines his own personal philosophy and provides insights into the workings of his mind.

---

[3] The *History of Granada,* entitled *al-Iḥâṭah fî akhbâr Gharnâṭah,* was published in Cairo, 1319/1901, but the two volumes which appeared do not contain Ibn Khaldûn's biography. My knowledge of the work is based upon al-Maqqarî, *Nafḥ aṭ-ṭîb* (Cairo, 1304/1886–87), IV, 6 ff. Al-Maqqarî may be assumed to have given a rather complete and literal quotation of Ibn al-Khaṭîb's text. Al-Maqqarî's contemporary, Aḥmad Bâbâ, *Nayl al-ibtihâj* (Cairo, 1351/1932, in the margin of Ibn Farḥûn, *Dîbâj*), p. 169, also quotes, if rather briefly, from Ibn al-Khaṭîb's biography of Ibn Khaldûn. Cf. also al-Ghuzûlî, *Maṭâli'* (Cairo, 1299–1300/1881–83), I, 275.

The volume of the *Iḥâṭah* that contains Ibn Khaldûn's biography is preserved in the Escorial, No. 1674 of the recent catalogue. M. Casiri, *Bibliotheca Arabico-Hispana Escurialensis* (Madrid, 1760–67), II, 105, referred briefly to it, mentioning the list of Ibn Khaldûn's works (cf. p. xliv, below). It is strange that this list, as quoted here, includes a reference to Ibn Khaldûn's "*History of the Arabs* in five volumes."

[4] References to it are found in the editor's notes to the *Autobiography,* p. 67 (n. 1) and index, p. 439.

[5] At present, we know most of these biographies only in excerpts quoted by as-Sakhâwî (1427/28–1497), in his *Ḍaw' al-lâmi'* (Cairo, 1353–55/1934–36), IV, 145–49. A collection of all biographical accounts, as preserved in MSS and printed texts or as reconstructed from quotations, would be of great help for the study of Ibn Khaldûn's life.

This abundance of biographical source material has enabled modern scholars at various times to write Ibn Khaldûn's life and to present the data in a factually correct form to which little can be added. These modern biographies vary greatly in length. Among the longest are de Slane's account in the Introduction to his translation of the *Muqaddimah,* largely a literal translation of the *Autobiography,*[6] and that by M. A. Enan, in his *Ibn Khaldûn, His Life and Work.*[7] There has been no recent treatment *in extenso* of Ibn Khaldûn's early life (down to 1382), but his Egyptian period is the subject of two masterly studies by W. J. Fischel, "Ibn Khaldûn's Activities in Mamlûk Egypt (1382–1406)" [8] and *Ibn Khaldûn and Tamerlane.*[9]

In its outlines, Ibn Khaldûn's life thus is quite clearly known. However, the modern student who would like to know much more about him, discovers that his questions can only be answered by conjecture, if at all. Considering the excellence of the source material, at least as judged by external criteria, the deficiencies in our knowledge must be ascribed to the internal character of the available information. It is true that no amount of material will ever fully satisfy a biographer, but in Ibn Khaldûn's case there are particular reasons why a fully satisfactory account of his life is virtually impossible of achievement. In the first place, Ibn Khaldûn considered only such events in his life worth recording as were especially remarkable, the most unusual achievements of an exceptional person. Thus he did not pay much attention to the kind of data so dear to modern psychological biographers. He does not speak about his childhood. His family is mentioned only because family considerations often influenced the course of his wanderings and because it was afflicted by unusual misfortunes. All his ordinary activities are passed over in silence. Ibn Khaldûn would probably have denied that this kind of data has any heuristic value. He would

[6] W. M. de Slane had previously published this biographical account in *Journal asiatique,* III 4 (1844), 5–60, 187–210, 291–308, 325–53.

[7] Published in Lahore in 1941 and subsequently reprinted there. Enan's work is a translation from the Arabic. A second edition of the Arabic work appeared recently. There is, of course, an ever-growing number of Arabic studies of Ibn Khaldûn's life and work.

[8] In *Semitic and Oriental Studies Presented to William Popper* (University of California Publications in Semitic Philology, No. 11) (Berkeley & Los Angeles, 1951), pp. 103–24.

[9] Berkeley & Los Angeles: University of California Press, 1952.

have doubted the validity of the modern biographer's claim that experiences which he shared with all his contemporaries contributed to the formation of his individual personality; he would have doubted that recording them might help future generations of scholars to understand him better.

Another difficulty that confronts Ibn Khaldûn's biographer is not unconnected with this attitude. Patient scholarly research has succeeded in gaining a picture in broad outline of the environment in which Ibn Khaldûn grew up and spent his life. Yet, all our sources together do not yield enough detailed information to allow us to understand fully his position in it for, in spite of his importance, he was but a minor element in the over-all picture. R. Brunschvig's outstanding historical synthesis, *La Berbérie orientale sous les Ḥafṣides*,[10] contributes greatly to our understanding of the historical factors of Ibn Khaldûn's era. But through no avoidable fault of its own, the work cannot yet answer all the questions modern students raise concerning Ibn Khaldûn's development as a historical personality. Just as the autobiography does not disclose all the facets of his being, other medieval historians grossly neglected other important factors. They do not fully reveal the true character of certain events in which Ibn Khaldûn was actively or passively involved. Hardly ever do they give precise information about his contemporaries. The rulers, statesmen, and scholars with whom he had to deal are not described with sufficient clarity for us to be able to assess the true meaning of his relationship to them.

Thus there are still many questions that cannot be answered, and Ibn Khaldûn cannot as yet be made the subject of an "interesting" biography in the modern sense. A biographical sketch prefacing an edition or translation of the author's work, however, is subject to less exacting specifications. Primarily, it should fulfill two purposes. First, it should acquaint the reader sufficiently well with the leading facts of the author's life. This purpose, I believe, can be amply fulfilled in Ibn Khaldûn's case. Secondly, it should set forth the historical conditions that enabled the author to develop his genius. Where Ibn Khaldûn and the *Muqaddimah* are concerned, we must often enough rely on conjecture and inference, but the thought that it is always difficult, if not impossible, adequately to

---

[10] Published in Paris as Vols. VIII (1940) and XI (1947) of the "Publications de l'Institut d'Etudes Orientales d'Alger."

account for intellectual greatness, may be of some consolation to us here.

Ibn Khaldûn belonged to a clan of South Arabian origin. Khaldûn, from whom the family name was derived, is believed to have immigrated to Spain in the eighth century, in the early years of the Muslim conquest. He settled in Carmona, a small city situated within the fateful triangle that Córdoba, Sevilla, and Granada form; in that small area much Spanish Muslim history of general European significance took place over the centuries. Khaldûn's "children"—that is, his descendants—left Carmona to settle in Sevilla. We do not know the exact date, but it is probable that the Khaldûn family had already taken residence there in the eighth century.

According to Ibn Khaldûn's own memory, only ten generations of forebears separated him from the founder of his family. These are too few generations to span a period of seven hundred years, even if one doubts the validity of Ibn Khaldûn's theory that there are three generations to a century. Ibn Khaldûn's own genealogy was obviously defective. It is worthy of note that a descendant of (the first) Khaldûn had in the eleventh century reckoned about nine generations from the founder down to his own time.[11]

Ibn Khaldûn's knowledge of his more remote ancestors is remarkably limited, considering the great prominence that his family enjoyed for centuries. All his information was based upon works published by Spanish historians. At least two of these works, by Ibn Ḥayyân and Ibn Ḥazm, have been preserved to the present day. Apparently there existed no written history or private archives in the Khaldûn family itself; such records as may have existed might have been lost when the family left Spain in the first half of the thirteenth century.

Historically, the most prominent among Ibn Khaldûn's relatives was a certain Kurayb. He revolted against the Umayyad ruler at some time near the end of the ninth century, and succeeded in establishing a quasi-independent patrician government in Se-

[11] Cf. *Autobiography*, pp. 3 f. Quoting Ibn Ḥazm, Ibn Khaldûn relates the genealogy of one Abû l-Faḍl, a descendant of Kurayb b. Khaldûn. Kurayb's pedigree as given in the *Autobiography* is defective; see Ibn Ḥazm's original text, *Jamharah*, ed. E. Lévi-Provençal (Cairo, 1948), p. 430, and also *'Ibar*, II, 244 f. It is, of course, by no means certain that Abû l-Faḍl's and Kurayb's pedigree was accurately traced in any of the sources.

villa, which lasted for over a decade. He was killed in 899.[12] Ibn Khaldûn, however, was unable to determine the exact relationship between himself and this Kurayb. If one can believe in the accuracy of the pedigree Ibn Khaldûn recorded, their only common ancestor was the first Khaldûn.

While Ibn Khaldûn's Arab descent has occasionally been questioned, it has also been considered a major influence in forming his outlook on life and on history. Neither point of view has anything to recommend it. Ibn Khaldûn's claim to Arab descent through the male line cannot reasonably be doubted, though he may have had Berber and Spanish blood in his veins as well. Decisive in itself is the fact that he believed himself to be of Arab descent, a circumstance that, in a sense, conferred title of nobility. However, even if Ibn Khaldûn was proud of his ancient Arab lineage, there is no indication that it colored his historical views or influenced his reactions to his environment differently than his peers and contemporaries. In fact, it would seem that not his Arab descent, but his Spanish origin was the crucial factor in his intellectual development and outlook, as will be shown below.

The disaster Kurayb met with at the end of the ninth century must have involved a large part, if not all, of the Khaldûn clan. But its position in Sevilla was soon re-established in its former eminence. In the middle of the eleventh century,[13] the Banû Khaldûn are said to have been the intellectual and political leaders of the city.

In 449 [1057/58], there died in Sevilla Abû Muslim 'Amr ('Umar?) b. Aḥmad Ibn Khaldûn, a pupil of the great scientist Maslamah al-Majrîṭî. He was himself, we are told, a great scientist.[14] He was a sixth generation descendant, at the very least, of

---

[12] Cf. R. Dozy, *Histoire des Musulmans d'Espagne* (2d ed.; Leiden, 1932), II, 40 ff., 80 ff. Cf. also *'Ibar*, IV, 135 f.

[13] Cf. Ibn Ḥayyân as quoted in the *Autobiography*, p. 5.

[14] See note 643 to Ch. VI, below.

We have one reference to a certain Ibn Khaldûn from the twelfth century, probably a member of the famous Khaldûn family. This one is described as a haughty poet in a couplet by Ibn Kisrâ al-Mâlaqî (d. A.D. 1206/7, or 1207/8), quoted by al-Kutubî, *Fawât al-Wafayât* (Cairo, 1951), I, 261:

> You overbearing poet whose ancestor is Khaldûn:
> You are not satisfied with being vinegar (*khall*),
> but also want to be mean (*dûn*).

* Cf. also Ibn Sa'îd, *'Unwân al-murqiṣât* (Algiers, 1949), p. 32.

Kurayb's brother Muḥammad. Ibn Khaldûn had occasion to mention him in the *Muqaddimah*. No other scholar among Ibn Khaldûn's ancestors and relatives is known by name, but there can be no doubt that most of them were highly educated men. It was a condition of leadership in their city, and that some of them excelled in religious and legal, if not in worldly learning, is certain.

The political leadership in Sevilla, in fact, belonged to the Banû Khaldûn together with some other noble families. Sovereignty over the city was vested in a nominal ruler, but actual control of Sevilla's affairs was exercised by these great families from their fortified rural seats and imposing residences in town. In the early thirteenth century, the realm of the Spanish Almohads crumbled. The Christians encroached more and more closely upon the triangle of Córdoba-Sevilla-Granada. By that time, the Khaldûn family and the other patricians of Sevilla held completely independent control through domination of the city council; but they failed to heed the call sent out around the year 1232 by Muḥammad b. Yûsuf Ibn al-Aḥmar, founder of the Naṣrid dynasty in Granada, to rally to the Muslim cause and help form a united front against the infidel "abomination." The Banû Khaldûn, realizing the city's precarious situation, had decided to leave even before the actual fall of Sevilla in 1248, and crossed over to the safety of northwest Africa, where they were not without friends.

The early decision to leave Sevilla appears to have been strongly motivated by their support of the rising cause of the Almohad Ḥafṣids in Africa. A certain Ibn al-Muḥtasib, related by marriage to the Khaldûn family, had given to the founder of the Ḥafṣid dynasty, Abû Zakarîyâ' Yaḥyâ (1228–49), a slave girl who in time became the honored mother of some of Abû Zakarîyâ''s sons. Now, this Ibn al-Muḥtasib was the maternal grandfather of Ibn Khaldûn's great-great-grandfather. Thus, from the start, the Banû Khaldûn had good connections with the most powerful group in northwestern Africa. In addition, they can be assumed to have had other associations there which they were able to use to good advantage and through which they gained influential positions as soon as they arrived. Marriages and personal cleverness added other important friends.

The refugees from Spain who came over and settled in northwestern Africa in ever growing numbers constituted a group apart, an elite group at that.[15] The *Muqaddimah* frequently mentions the great contributions made by Spanish refugees to the cultural life of northwestern Africa and stresses the superiority of Spain and the originality of its civilization.[16] This shows that Ibn Khaldûn, more than a century after his family had left Spain, still considered himself to some extent a member of that glorious civilization. Though as a Muslim he felt at home everywhere within the vast realm of Islam, he preserved throughout his life a deep and sincere affection for northwest Africa, the country of his birth, for the "homeland" where, according to the poet, "the amulets are first attached" to the child. He always felt a certain responsibility for the political fate of northwestern Africa and took an active interest in it long after he had left. His true spiritual home, however, was Spain.

This background helps to explain the ease with which Ibn Khaldûn shifted his loyalties throughout his life. No matter how high his own position or that of his ancestors before him at one or another northwest African court, no matter how close he was to a ruler, he did not feel bound by "group feeling," as he might have called it, or by the ties of a common cultural heritage. He considered the ruler his employer, and his position a job to be done, neither more nor less. But his basic loyalty to Spain and its civilization had a much more far-reaching effect on Ibn Khaldûn's personality and work than these transient ties. It gave him a remarkable detachment with respect to the historical events that took place before his eyes. In a sense, it enabled him to view them as an impartial observer, even when he was deeply involved personally. This peculiar division in Ibn Khaldûn's physical and spiritual ties seems to have been the decisive factor in his ability to abstract general reflections about history from observed facts, in his ability, that is, to write the *Muqaddimah*.

The ancestor of Ibn Khaldûn among the members of the Khaldûn family who went to northwestern Africa, was al-Ḥasan b. Muḥammad, his grandfather's grandfather. Al-Ḥasan went first to Ceuta, the city of northwestern Africa which is closest to Spain, and customarily the first stopping place for refugees from Spain. He then went on to Mecca, which suggests that he may have used

[15] Cf. R. Brunschvig, *La Berbérie orientale*, II, 155 f.
[16] See 2:24, 290, 350 f., 386 f., and 3:302, below.

his intention to perform the pilgrimage as an excuse for leaving Sevilla. Upon his return from Mecca, he joined the Ḥafṣid ruler Abû Zakarîyâ' in Bône, using his relationship to the above-mentioned Ibn al-Muḥtasib as an introduction. He received a pension and fiefs. Thus, the intimate relationship of the Khaldûn family with the Ḥafṣid house started auspiciously. It continued to bring high honors and, as a corollary, wealth to all of Ibn Khaldûn's forebears.

His immediate ancestors were affected by the vicissitudes that befell individual members of the Ḥafṣid dynasty. However, through good luck and intelligent politics, they usually managed to stay on the winning side. Their places of residence changed with the requirements of court life. For most of the time they seem to have resided in Tunis.

Al-Ḥasan is said to have died during the reign of Abû Zakarîyâ'. His son Abû Bakr Muḥammad, Ibn Khaldûn's great-grandfather, attained the very important position of manager of financial affairs (*ṣâḥib al-ashghâl*),[17] or, as we might say, minister of finance. He was captured and killed during Ibn Abî 'Umârah's revolt against the Ḥafṣids, around the year 1283.[18] It has recently become known that Abû Bakr was the author of a handbook for government secretaries,[19] which he wrote in his youth during Abû Zakarîyâ''s reign. Though not a *Fürstenspiegel* in the true sense, it belongs to a type of works that, according to Ibn Khaldûn's own statement, was one of the main sources of inspiration for the *Muqaddimah.*

Ibn Khaldûn's grandfather, also named Muḥammad, was satisfied with the minor position of deputy doorkeeper [20] to the Ḥafṣid rulers. According to his grandson, they held him in high esteem, and his personal influence was great. Moreover, in later life he himself refused higher positions offered him. After having twice performed the pilgrimage to Mecca, he lived a retired life and devoted himself to pious studies. He died at a very advanced age in 737 [1336/37].

---

[17] See 2:16 and 24, below.

[18] Cf. R. Brunschvig, *La Berbérie orientale*, I, 84 ff.

[19] Cf. E. Lévi-Provençal (the owner of the MS), "Un Recueil de lettres officielles almohades," in *Hespéris*, XXVIII (1941), 1–80, esp. 12 ff.

[20] For the office of doorkeeper, see below, 2:14 ff. Ibn Khaldûn also speaks of his grandfather in *'Ibar*, VI, 300 f., 304, 311; de Slane (tr.), II, 384 f., 394, 409.

Under his influence, his son Muḥammad, Ibn Khaldûn's father, also pursued a scholarly career. He achieved a respectable knowledge of the Qur'ân and jurisprudence and had a good foundation in grammar and poetry. He died in the terrible epidemic of 1348–49. His son, who was seventeen years old when his father died, has noted a few remarks of his father in the *History*.[21] As was customary, the father saw to it that his children received a good education, and he participated himself in their instruction. The love of scholarship and contemplation evident in Ibn Khaldûn's father and grandfather combined in their famous offspring with a reawakening of the high political ambitions that had gripped many generations of the first Khaldûn's descendants. Thus was produced the admirable combination of scholar and statesman that we find in Ibn Khaldûn.

Ibn Khaldûn, Abû Zayd, was born in Tunis on Ramaḍân 1, 732 [May 27, 1332]. His given name was 'Abd-ar-Raḥmân, his ethnic denomination al-Ḥaḍramî, derived from Ḥaḍramawt, the ancestral home of his clan in South Arabia. The scholarly title of his later years was Walî-ad-dîn, "Guardian of the Religion." We know that he had two brothers: an elder brother, Muḥammad, whose fellow student he was, and Yaḥyâ, one year his junior, who, like Ibn Khaldûn, was to become a high-ranking politician and an accomplished historian.[22]

Ibn Khaldûn provides a disproportionate amount of information about his education and the personalities of his teachers.[23] This was in keeping with traditional Muslim biographical practice, for this science, which had been created to satisfy the demands of legal and religious scholars for exact data concerning their authorities, attributed great importance to the names of a scholar's teachers. In Ibn Khaldûn's autobiography, references to his teachers' Spanish origin or to their close connections with Spain occur with regularity. Very few among them fail to fall into this category.

His early education followed customary lines. He studied the Qur'ân and the Qur'ânic sciences under the guidance of Muḥammad b. Sa'd b. Burrâl. He learned Arabic under his father and a number of other scholars whose names are given as Muḥammad b. al-'Arabî al-Ḥaṣâ'irî, Muḥammad b. ash-Shawwâsh az-Zarzâlî,

---

[21] *'Ibar*, VI, 197, 292; de Slane (tr.), II, 104, 365. See also 2:222, below.

[22] Cf. *GAL*, II, 241; *Suppl.*, II, 340.

[23] Most of these men are known to us mainly through Ibn Khaldûn. When he does not say much about one of them, there probably was little to say.

Aḥmad b. al-Qaṣṣâr, and Muḥammad b. Baḥr. The last-named also instructed Ibn Khaldûn in poetry; he may have been responsible for planting the seeds of Ibn Khaldûn's unusual understanding of poetry which is so evident in the discussion of poetry in the last chapters of the *Muqaddimah*.

Traditions (*ḥadîth*) and jurisprudence were more advanced subjects. Ibn Khaldûn's teachers in these fields, therefore, included some better-known names, such as Shams-ad-dîn Muḥammad b. Jâbir b. Sulṭân al-Wâdiyâshî (1274–1348), for the traditions, and Muḥammad b. 'Abdallâh al-Jayyânî, Muḥammad al-Qaṣîr, as well as the famous Muḥammad b. 'Abd-as-Salâm al-Hawwârî (1277/78–1348/49),[24] for jurisprudence.

Childhood influences are largely unconscious, and usually the child's reception of them is passive. The most decisive period for the intellectual development of a young man is the years between fifteen and twenty-five. During these years the youth completes his education and begins his career, giving his life a direction which later can hardly undergo basic change. Often, this time of growth from childhood to manhood passes without violent transitions; but when great historical events occur during it, they may play havoc with the ordinary course of development. It was of the greatest significance for Ibn Khaldûn's future that these decisive years of his life fell in the period from 1347 to 1357, a time of extraordinary upheaval in the history of northwest Africa.

The position of the Ḥafṣid dynasty in Tunis, never stable, had become increasingly insecure before Ibn Khaldûn's birth and during his childhood. This instability may have been one of the reasons why his father and grandfather preferred lives of quiet retirement to active participation in political life. But in the period between 1347 and 1357, Ḥafṣid rule over Tunis suffered its worst eclipse. For a time it all but disappeared. However, it recovered in due course and by 1370 entered upon another flourishing era.

In 1347, the Merinid ruler of Fez, Abû l-Ḥasan, since 1337 master of the 'Abd-al-Wâdid state of Tlemcen, conquered Tunis. In the following year, after suffering a severe setback at Kairouan (al-Qayrawân)[25] at the hands of the Arab tribes of the region, he was obliged to withdraw again from Tunis. However, for some time the political situation of the Ḥafṣids remained precarious.

[24] Cf. also *GAL*, I, 306.

[25] See also 3:264 and 471 ff., below.

Abû 'Inân, Abû l-Ḥasan's son and successor, succeeded in another attack on Tunisia in 1357, but his victory almost immediately came to naught. After Abû 'Inân's death in 1358, only the usual squabbles of northwest African politics presented minor and temporary obstacles to a speedy Ḥafṣid recovery. Nature played her part among the events that influenced Ibn Khaldûn's destiny, adding the Black Death, the terrible plague that struck Tunis in 1348–49 with unabated fury, to the man-made disturbances.[26]

The Merinid conquest of 1347 brought to Tunis a great number of famous scholars in the retinue of Abû l-Ḥasan. The adolescent Ibn Khaldûn found among them men who inspired him with their scholarship, and who became his *shaykhs*, the masters and teachers who exercised decisive influence upon his intellectual development. Their scholarly fame was probably well deserved, though we can only judge from hearsay; only a few isolated remarks and scarcely any of their written works have come down to us. Ibn Khaldûn took as his teachers Muḥammad (b. 'Alî) b. Sulaymân as-Saṭṭî, 'Abd-al-Muhayman b. Muḥammad al-Ḥaḍramî (1277/78–1349), and, above all, Muḥammad b. Ibrâhîm al-Âbilî (1282/83–1356),[27] whom Ibn Khaldûn considered his principal master. Al-Âbilî's departure from Tunis, later on, was one of the reasons for Ibn Khaldûn to leave his native city.

There were other famous scholars in Abû l-Ḥasan's company, such as young 'Abdallâh b. Yûsuf b. Riḍwân al-Mâlaqî,[28] who was of about Ibn Khaldûn's age, Muḥammad b. Muḥammad b. aṣ-Ṣabbâgh, and Muḥammad b. Aḥmad b. Marzûq (d. 781 [1379/80]), with whom Ibn Khaldûn did not always remain on good terms. Ibn Khaldûn, however, did not regard these men as his teachers.

The great plague carried away many of Ibn Khaldûn's *shaykhs* and he lost both his parents at this time. Ibn Khaldûn's only reference to his mother is this mention of her death. He was left, it would seem, without the guidance he needed. His elder brother

---

26 See also Ibn Khaldûn's account in the *Muqaddimah*, p. 64, below.

27 As aṭ-Ṭanjî states in the *Autobiography*, p. 33, this is the correct form of the name, and the original home of al-Âbilî was Ávila in northern Spain. Forms like Abboli, Âbulî, etc. are not correct; cf. H. P. J. Renaud in *Hespéris*, XXV (1938), 18–20, 25; G. Marçais, *La Berbérie musulmane et l'Orient au Moyen Age* (Paris, 1946), p. 300. Al-Âbilî is quoted, 2:197 and 339, below. He also furnished material for the *'Ibar:* see, for instance, VII, 91 f., 95, 96, 232; de Slane (tr.), III, 369, 376 f., 379 f.; IV, 167 f.

28 * F. Rosenthal, *The Muslim Concept of Freedom* (Leiden, 1960), p. 44.

Muḥammad became head of the family. Ibn Khaldûn could hardly have foreseen that a bright future was in store for the Ḥafṣids in Tunis; had he done so, he might have stayed on there and weathered the storm. He would have passed his life in Tunis as a member of the patrician Khaldûn family—and perhaps, in that case, he would never have written the *Muqaddimah.* As it was, he was conscious only of the dearth of scholarship there and of the bleak political outlook of the moment. The government and the Ḥafṣid ruler were under the control of Ibn Tâfrâgîn.[29] The twenty-year-old Ibn Khaldûn was made *Ṣâḥib al-'alâmah,* Master of the Signature, an important court position. His service consisted of writing the words "Praised be God" and "Thanks are due to God" in large letters between the opening formula and the text of official documents.[30] The office of the *'alâmah* does not seem to have included any definite executive or administrative functions, but its holder became privy to all important government business, enabling him to act in an advisory capacity. Thus, Ibn Khaldûn was started upon a government career, but he did not cherish the prospect of staying in Tunis. Neither the new and promising position nor his elder brother's disapproval prevented him from absconding, in 1352, from the Tunisians' camp during their campaign against the people of Constantine led by a Ḥafṣid rival of the Tunisian ruler.

With the help of the Khaldûn family's many scholarly and political connections everywhere in northwestern Africa, Ibn Khaldûn slowly made his way west. Abû 'Inân, the new Merinid ruler, was no less a friend of scholarship than his father Abû l-Ḥasan had been,[31] and his star as the leading personality among northwest African rulers was rapidly rising. Ibn Khaldûn met him in the summer of 1353.[32] He spent the winter of 1353/54 in Bougie, at this time in the hands of a high Merinid official, and in 1354 he accepted Abû 'Inân's invitation to come to Fez and join the circle of scholars he was gathering around himself for study and teaching.

---

[29] See also 3:427 ff., below.

[30] On the *'alâmah,* cf. E. Lévi-Provençal in *Hespéris,* XXVIII (1941), 17 ff.; R. Brunschvig, *La Berbérie orientale,* II, 61 ff. See also 2:26 f. and 62 f., below.

[31] We are told that Abû 'Inân carried a library with him on his expeditions. Cf. Ibn Farḥûn, *Dîbâj* (Cairo, 1351/1932), p. 283.

[32] Cf. *'Ibar,* VII, 291; de Slane (tr.), IV, 300.

In Fez, Ibn Khaldûn completed his education in lively association with the scholars who lived there or passed through. He had contact with the Qur'ân scholar Muḥammad b. aṣ-Ṣaffâr. He encountered the powerful personality of Muḥammad b. Muḥammad al-Maqqarî, who, like other great Muslim scholars, considered it improper to reveal the date of his birth and who died at the end of 1357 or the beginning of 1358.[33] There was Muḥammad b. Aḥmad al-'Alwî (1310/11–1369/70) who, according to rumor, had instructed Muḥammad b. 'Abd-as-Salâm, one of Ibn Khaldûn's teachers in Tunis, in the highly suspect subjects of philosophy and science. Among them were also the little-known judge Muḥammad b. 'Abd-ar-Razzâq and Muḥammad b. Yaḥyâ al-Barjî (1310/11–1384). Upon Ibn al-Khaṭîb's request, Ibn Khaldûn wrote down some of al-Barjî's poetry so it could be incorporated with the poet's biography in Ibn al-Khaṭîb's *History of Granada.*[34] In Fez, Ibn Khaldûn enjoyed the opportunity of meeting the physician and astrologer Ibrâhîm b. Zarzar whom later, in 1364, he met again at the court of Pedro the Cruel in Sevilla.[35] In Fez, he also saw the *sharîf* Muḥammad b. Aḥmad as-Sabtî (1297/98–1359) shortly before his death, and in 1355 he met there for the first time the famous scholar Abû l-Barakât Muḥammad b. Muḥammad al-Ballafîqî (d. 1370),[36] whom he quotes several times [37] in the *Muqaddimah.* At that time, and again later, in 1361,[38] he studied Mâlik's *Muwaṭṭa'* with him, and, as Ibn Khaldûn's Egyptian student, the great Ibn Ḥajar, reports,[39] always held al-Ballafîqî in the highest respect.

In medieval Muslim civilization the development of a scholar was a long-drawn-out process and, in a sense, his education con-

---

[33] Cf. Ibn al-Khaṭîb, *al-Iḥâṭah,* II, 164 f.

[34] *Ibid.*, II, 220 f.

[35] Cf. *Autobiography,* p. 85. In 1356, Abû 'Inân called Ibn Zarzar to Morocco a second time, but he did not come. Cf. W. J. Fischel, *Ibn Khaldûn and Tamerlane,* pp. 80 f.; M. M. Antuña in *al-Andalus,* I (1933), 144 (n. 1).

[36] Cf. H. P. J. Renaud in *Hespéris,* XXV (1938), 27. For the vocalization Ballafîqî, see *Autobiography,* p. 61, and the vocalization indicated in MSS. C and D of the *Muqaddimah,* as well as in the verse quoted by Ibn al-Khaṭîb, *al-Iḥâṭah,* II, 116. The form appears to refer to a place name composed with "villa," perhaps Villavega? * S. Gilbert in *al-Andalus,* XXVIII (1963), 381 ff.

[37] See 2:459 and 3:269 and 407 f., below.

[38] Cf. *Autobiography,* p. 305.

[39] Cf. Ibn Ḥajar, *ad-Durar al-kâminah* (Hyderabad, 1348–50/1929–31), IV, 155–57.

tinued throughout his life. Accomplished scholars would attend the classes and lectures of their colleagues whenever they wished to profit from them. In this way Ibn Khaldûn used every opportunity that offered itself to study with fellow scholars. In this respect his residence in Granada during the years 1363–65 seems to have been especially profitable, but even during his most unsettled years, such as the time he spent in Biskra in 1370–71, he found a scholar from whom he gained information which he later incorporated in the *Muqaddimah*.[40]

However, Ibn Khaldûn's formative period reached its conclusion during the years he stayed in Fez with Abû 'Inân. From his seventeenth year onwards, his schooling could hardly be called formal or continuous. Possibly it was this haphazard education as much as his particular intellectual endowment that explains why he did not become an outstanding specialist in any one field. Some of the aspersions later cast on his learning by his enemies may be discounted, but the *Muqaddimah* itself clearly shows that Ibn Khaldûn had neither the desire nor the equipment to make original contributions of note to any of the established disciplines. He was endowed with that rarer gift, a deep insight into the essentials of the accumulated knowledge of his time, and he possessed the ability to express this gift clearly and forcefully. This gift helped to place his "new science" upon firm foundations.

Neither in his *Autobiography* nor in the *Muqaddimah*, nor in any other parts of his *History*, does Ibn Khaldûn mention any scholarly works written before the *Muqaddimah*. The *Autobiography* contains many specimens of his letters and of his occasional poetry—types of literary exercise requiring great skill and a wide range of literary knowledge. They were acclaimed in his own age and would suffice to establish the reputation of a man of letters quite as well as any other kind of publication. In the *Autobiography*, however, Ibn Khaldûn does not state that he had published any collections of this type before, and only one later work is mentioned, namely, the description of northwestern Africa that he wrote for Timur (Tamerlane) in 1401. In the eyes of Ibn Khaldûn this document, an official pamphlet despite its great length, hardly qualified as a true work of scholarship; moreover, it was probably never published.

---

[40] See p. 238 and 3:196, below.

It is strange that Ibn Khaldûn mentions no publications by his pen except his great historical work. His silence could be taken to mean that he actually did not publish anything at all during his earlier, very active, years. However, we have the word of his older contemporary and close friend, Ibn al-Khaṭîb,[41] that Ibn Khaldûn did publish some works long before he started on the *Muqaddimah.* Ibn al-Khaṭîb says:

He wrote an original commentary on the *Burdah,*[42] in which he showed his wide ability, his understanding of many things, and his great knowledge.

He abridged a good deal of the books of Averroes.

He put together a useful composition on logic for the Sultan,[43] in the days when he studied the intellectual disciplines.

He abridged the *Muḥaṣṣal* of the imam Fakhr-ad-dîn ar-Râzî.[44] When I first met him,[45] I jokingly said to him: "You owe me something, for you have abridged my *Muḥaṣṣal.*" [46]

He wrote a book on calculation (elementary arithmetic).

At the time of writing,[47] he has begun to write a commentary on a *rajaz* poem I composed on the principles of jurisprudence. What he has (done) already is so perfect that it cannot be surpassed.

---

[41] Muḥammad b. 'Abdallâh, 713–776 [1313–1374]. Cf. *GAL,* II, 260 ff.; *Suppl.,* II, 372 ff. His "History of Granada" has already been quoted several times as an important source of information for Ibn Khaldûn and his time. Ibn Khaldûn quotes from his friend repeatedly in the *Muqaddimah.* However, mention of "Ibn al-Khaṭîb" or "the imam al-Khaṭîb" refers to the great philosopher Fakhr-ad-dîn ar-Râzî; see n. 44 to this Introduction and n. 246 to Ch. III of the *Muqaddimah,* below. The quotation from Ibn al-Khaṭîb that follows is based on al-Maqqarî, *Nafḥ aṭ-ṭîb,* IV, 11; cf. n. 3, above.

[42] This is the famous poem in praise of Muḥammad written by al-Bûṣîrî in the thirteenth century. Cf. *GAL,* I, 264 ff.; *Suppl.,* I, 467 ff. Ibn Khaldûn considered a copy of the *Burdah* a suitable present for Timur. Cf. *Autobiography,* p. 377; W. J. Fischel, *Ibn Khaldûn and Tamerlane,* p. 41.

[43] Abû 'Inân? However, M. Mahdi, *Ibn Khaldûn's Philosophy of History* (London, 1957), p. 42, thinks of Muḥammad V of Granada.

[44] See n. 41, above, and p. 402, below. Aḥmad Bâbâ, *Nayl al-ibtihâj,* p. 169, who also quotes Ibn al-Khaṭîb in this connection, has, incorrectly, *al-Maḥṣûl,* which is another famous work by Fakhr-ad-dîn ar-Râzî.

[45] This would be at the time of Ibn al-Khaṭîb's arrival in Fez in 1359/60.

[46] Since Fakhr-ad-dîn ar-Râzî was commonly known in Ibn Khaldûn's circle as Ibn al-Khaṭîb, Ibn al-Khaṭîb claimed the work of his namesake as his own.

[47] The *History of Granada* contains references to events as late as 1373. However, the work had been published prior to that date. Ibn al-Khaṭîb mentioned a copy of the work in a letter addressed to Ibn Khaldûn, dated January 24, 1368; cf. *Autobiography,* p. 121. One would like to think that Ibn Khaldûn worked on this commentary during his stay in Granada in 1363–64.

(Ibn al-Khaṭîb then praises the prose, both rhymed and unrhymed, of Ibn Khaldûn's official writings and speaks about his promising bid for recognition as a poet.)

For any ordinary scholar in his early thirties, this would be a respectable list of publications; however, it does not contain any distinguished work. To compose a commentary on the *Burdah* was a beginner's exercise, never much more. None of the other works mentioned, all of which were textbooks, required, or (probably) displayed, much originality. Nevertheless, had Ibn Khaldûn been an ordinary scholar he would almost certainly have referred, in the appropriate chapters of the *Muqaddimah*, to his abridgment of the *Muḥaṣṣal* or to his book on elementary arithmetic. His failure to mention these earlier works, possibly because of his own low regard for them, shows his rare and wholly admirable restraint. Since some of them were abridgments or brief handbooks, he may have felt an aversion to them later in his life; for he came to consider brief handbooks as detrimental to scholarship and said so in the *Muqaddimah* (Sect. 35 of Ch. VI).

Very recently, Ibn Khaldûn's abridgment of the *Muḥaṣṣal*, entitled *Lubâb al-Muḥaṣṣal fî uṣûl ad-dîn*, has come to light. Long buried in the great Library of the Escorial, Ibn Khaldûn's autograph manuscript of the work, completed on Ṣafar 29, 752 [April 27, 1351], when Ibn Khaldûn was not yet nineteen years old, has been edited by Fr. Luciano Rubio and was published in Tetuán in 1952. The abridgment was what we would call a long and learned term paper, written for his teacher al-Âbilî, with whom he had been studying the *Muḥaṣṣal*. It shows that young Ibn Khaldûn had mastered the intricate philosophical speculations of the *Muḥaṣṣal* and Naṣîr-ad-dîn's commentary on it to an astonishing degree, even though his work was a beginner's exercise.[47a]

During his stay at the Merinid court in Fez during the years 1354–62, Ibn Khaldûn was already married; indeed, it seems most likely that he married while still in Tunis. His wife was a daughter of Muḥammad b. al-Ḥakîm (d. 1343), the great Ḥafṣid general and minister of war, member of a noble and scholarly family.[48] Ibn Khaldûn mentions that he had children by her. When he went to Spain, in the fall of 1363, he sent his wife and children to Con-

[47a] M. Mahdi, *op. cit.*, p. 297, refers to a hitherto unknown work of Ibn Khaldûn on Sufism.

[48] Cf. R. Brunschvig, *La Berbérie orientale*, I, 155 ff. He also was very wealthy, as appears from the amount of personal property confiscated from him by the ruler on one occasion. See p. 368, below.

stantine to stay with his wife's brothers, since he did not want to take them with him before he was settled there. Later on, they followed him to Spain. As a result of his frequent changes of domicile, Ibn Khaldûn had often to repeat this family arrangement. He was deeply devoted to his family, but was frequently separated from them for long periods of time. More than once, they were in great danger and held as hostages, while Ibn Khaldûn himself was safe and far away.

It is not known whether Ibn al-Ḥakîm's daughter was Ibn Khaldûn's only wife, though probably she remained his principal one as long as she lived. We hear, incidentally, of the birth of another son, which must have taken place about the year 1370,[49] but we do not know whether Ibn al-Ḥakîm's daughter was the mother, though nothing would contradict this assumption. According to one source, his wife and his five daughters perished in 1384 when a tragic accident befell Ibn Khaldûn's family on the journey from Tunis to Egypt, and only his two sons, Muḥammad and 'Alî, reached Egypt safely.[50] Ibn Khaldûn does not mention the circumstances of the tragedy in his *Autobiography*, so that this account can hardly be trusted in all its details. But its reference to only one wife may indicate that it was Ibn al-Ḥakîm's daughter who perished.

Possibly Ibn Khaldûn married again later in Egypt. The only positive statement to this effect was made in connection with aspersions on Ibn Khaldûn's private life; [51] therefore, it may not be true. But during his interview with Timur, too, he referred to his family in Egypt,[52] but it is doubtful whether this reference can be taken literally. However, it is most likely that he did marry again, a course perfectly proper and almost obligatory upon him in accordance with Muslim custom.

It seems extremely doubtful that any of Ibn Khaldûn's children survived him. If so, and especially had they been sons, some incidental information about them would almost certainly have been found. According to the *Autobiography*, a son of his was a secretary

---

[49] Cf. *Autobiography*, pp. 209 ff.

[50] The source for this report is Ibn Qâḍî Shuhbah. Cf. *Autobiography*, p. 259 (n. 3).

[51] Cf. as-Sakhâwî, *aḍ-Ḍaw' al-lâmi'*, IV, 146.

[52] Cf. *Autobiography*, p. 379; W. J. Fischel, *Ibn Khaldûn and Tamerlane*, p. 43.

to the ruler of Morocco in 1398/99, but the text of the passage and its interpretation are rather uncertain.[53]

This is practically all we know of Ibn Khaldûn's personal life, and it is hardly enough to satisfy our legitimate curiosity. Even this limited knowledge we owe solely to Ibn Khaldûn's inability to keep from mentioning his family altogether when he recounted the great events of his life and career. Thus, in spite of his unconscious tendency to minimize family influence, we glimpse something of how strong and significant it may have been in reality.

At Abû 'Inân's court in Fez, Ibn Khaldûn was a member of the ruler's circle of scholars. As such, he had the duty of attending public prayers in Abû 'Inân's company. But soon Abû 'Inân tried to draw Ibn Khaldûn into government affairs. Towards the end of the year 1355, he was asked to serve as the ruler's secretary with the task of recording Abû 'Inân's decisions on the petitions and other documents submitted to him. Ibn Khaldûn did not relish the idea of performing this job, because, he said, he "had never seen his ancestors do a thing like that." It seemed to him beneath his own and his family's dignity to hold a clerical position, even a very high one. The Banû Khaldûn were used to occupying advisory, administrative, or executive positions.

At any rate, Ibn Khaldûn's official employment did not last long. With the Ḥafṣid Abû 'Abdallâh who was at that time in Fez, he had begun a friendship which was to prove sincere and lasting. However, this friendship aroused Abû 'Inân's suspicion, and led to Ibn Khaldûn's imprisonment on February 10, 1357. Abû 'Inân shortly thereafter embarked upon his conquest of Tunisia, and it is easy to infer why he considered it advisable to withhold freedom of movement from a Tunisian who was on good terms with the Ḥafṣid family.

Ibn Khaldûn's prison term lasted for twenty-one months. He was released only when Abû 'Inân died, on November 27, 1358. For a young man eager to build a career, this must have seemed a long time of enforced inactivity, but it probably gave him the leisure to continue his scholarly pursuits.

With Abû 'Inân's death, the power of the Merinid dynasty

[53] Cf. *Autobiography*, pp. 369 ff. Fischel, *op. cit.*, p. 34, reads "birthplace" instead of "son," and refers the equally doubtful "secretary" to Ibn Khaldûn himself. However, as he explains himself, Ibn Khaldûn speaks of Morocco in the context and thus cannot mean his birthplace.

collapsed. Except for a brief period of recovery under an energetic ruler some years later, the Merinid realm was to undergo a fate that Ibn Khaldûn describes often and graphically in the *Muqaddimah.* The rulers became mere figureheads controlled by prime ministers who exercised the actual power, an atmosphere ideal for the mushroom-like growth of little kingmakers. Each of the higher state officials selected his favorite candidate from among the members of the dynasty and tried to promote him. Ibn Khaldûn himself participated enthusiastically in this game, and he seems to have been inferior to none in the art of political maneuvering. Later in life he often complained of the "intrigues" that had brought about his misfortunes and had so frequently obliged him to change his place of residence. Although we feel sympathetically inclined towards one of the great personalities of all times, and naturally disposed to discount criticism of him, we have to acknowledge the disconcerting, if not surprising, fact that the intrigues against him of which Ibn Khaldûn complained were merely countermeasures to his own.

The candidate whose side Ibn Khaldûn supported after Abû 'Inân's death was Abû Sâlim. This proved a good choice, for Abû Sâlim became the ruler of Morocco in July of 1359. As a reward for his support, Ibn Khaldûn was made his secretary of state. Near the end of Abû Sâlim's reign, he was entrusted with the *maẓâlim*, that is, with jurisdiction over complaints and crimes not covered by Muslim religious law.[54] This was Ibn Khaldûn's first legal position, albeit connected with law and the judiciary only in the European sense of these terms. In Islam, it was a long way from the secular judicial *maẓâlim* duties, delegated by the ruler, to the powerful position of judge. Ibn Khaldûn enjoyed his new function; he modestly remarked that he performed it well. But it did not last long, for Abû Sâlim perished in the autumn of 1361 in the course of a revolt organized by civilian and military officials.

In the meantime, the 'Abd-al-Wâdids had regained control over Tlemcen. Farther east, in Bougie, Constantine, and Tunis, the Ḥafṣids were re-establishing their positions. By contrast, politics in Fez were rather disturbed. Ibn Khaldûn, therefore, wished to leave Fez and hoped to find a more secure and promising field of

[54] For the *maẓâlim*, cf. E. Tyan, *Histoire de l'organization judiciaire en pays d'Islam* (Annales de l'Université de Lyon, Droit, III[4]) (Paris, 1938–43), II, 141 ff. See also pp. 455 f., below.

activity elsewhere. However, the government in Fez feared that he might use his knowledge of northwest African politics to its detriment and tried to detain him. He finally made a deal with the Fâsî authorities and was permitted to leave on the condition that he would not remain in northwestern Africa but go to Spain. Thus, he left Fez and traveled, via Ceuta, to Granada, the only important Muslim state left in the Iberian peninsula. He arrived in Granada December 26, 1362.

Granada was prepared to give Ibn Khaldûn a royal welcome. As Abû Sâlim's secretary of state, Ibn Khaldûn had given a friendly reception to Muḥammad V of Granada (1354–59 and 1362–91) when the latter had come to Fez as a fugitive from his native country, accompanied by his prime minister, the great scholar and writer Ibn al-Khaṭîb, mentioned earlier. Through Ibn Khaldûn's active interest, Muḥammad V had been enabled to re-establish his rule over Granada. For these past services, Ibn Khaldûn was now rewarded with the ruler's confidence and munificence and by the friendship of Ibn al-Khaṭîb. In 1364, he was put in charge of a mission sent to Pedro the Cruel, King of Castilla, for the purpose of ratifying a peace treaty between Castilla and the Muslims. Thus, Ibn Khaldûn had an opportunity to visit Sevilla, the city of his ancestors. The Christian ruler honored him highly, offering to take him into his service and to restore his family's former property to him. Ibn Khaldûn declined; but, it may be noted, he had no word of indignation for an offer the acceptance of which would have involved betraying his religion. Nor did he at this time censure the infidel, as, much later in his *Autobiography*, he was to censure the infidels of the East.

In the cultured atmosphere of Granada Ibn Khaldûn felt secure enough to bring his family over from Constantine. Soon, however, he saw danger signs on the horizon. He sensed that Ibn al-Khaṭîb was becoming displeased at his growing influence in the court. Yet, he desired to avoid an open break with him. As a matter of fact, he remained on the best of terms with Ibn al-Khaṭîb and retained throughout his life the greatest respect for the latter's literary abilities. The personal contact of the two men, however, was interrupted. It appears that Ibn Khaldûn actually saw Ibn al-Khaṭîb only once again after their Granada association. This was during Ibn al-Khaṭîb's unhappy stay in Fez shortly before his assassination in 1374.

Under the circumstances, Ibn Khaldûn was glad to receive an invitation from his old friend, the Ḥafṣid Abû 'Abdallâh, who had gained control over Bougie in June, 1364. Asked to come and be his prime minister, Ibn Khaldûn gladly accepted the invitation. On leaving Granada he received expressions of great regret and a very flattering letter of thanks written by Ibn al-Khaṭîb in the name of Muḥammad V, and dated February 11, 1365. He arrived in Bougie the following month and was there given a rousing reception.

Ibn Khaldûn apparently tried his best to further Abû 'Abdallâh's cause. However, Abû l-'Abbâs, Abû 'Abdallâh's cousin, at this time the ruler of Constantine, was destined to restore the Ḥafṣid dynasty. Abû 'Abdallâh was not successful in the military defense of his regime. After his first defeat, Ibn Khaldûn volunteered for the dangerous task of collecting taxes from the Berber tribes in the mountains of Bougie. The money was badly needed to maintain Abû 'Abdallâh's rule. But after the latter's death in May, 1366, Ibn Khaldûn did not feel inclined to cast his lot with Abû 'Abdallâh's children. Realizing the hopelessness of their situation, he took the sensible step of going over to Abû l-'Abbâs in order to salvage as much of his own position as possible.

The next eight or nine years were the most precarious ones in Ibn Khaldûn's stormy career. But they were also those in which he played an important independent role in the political life of northwestern Africa. Soon after he had gone over to Abû l-'Abbâs, he felt his position vis-à-vis that ruler to be uncertain and wanted to withdraw. He eventually succeeded in overcoming Abû l-'Abbâs' reluctance to give him permission to leave. Thereupon he resumed his old connections with the Riyâḥ-Dawâwidah Arabs, begun when he left Tunis in 1352, and settled in Biskra. Soon, the news reached him that his brother Yaḥyâ, who was subsequently to become for a number of years his close associate, had been imprisoned by Abû l-'Abbâs. This act convinced him of the hopelessness, at least for the time being, of his position with that prince.

The political pattern in northwestern Africa for the next few years was a simple one. On the one side, we find Abû Ḥammû, who was the 'Abd-al-Wâdid ruler of Tlemcen, and the Ḥafṣid ruler of Tunis. Opposed to them were an 'Abd-al-Wâdid pretender to the rule over Tlemcen, and Abû l-'Abbâs, the Ḥafṣid ruler of Constantine and Bougie. In this situation, the attitude of the Arab tribes was the decisive factor. They could swing the victory to one side or the other, and here Ibn Khaldûn had considerable influence.[55]

Abû Ḥammû of Tlemcen was married to a daughter of Abû 'Abdallâh of Bougie, Ibn Khaldûn's former friend and master. Abû Ḥammû now approached Ibn Khaldûn and asked him to enter his service. For his part, Ibn Khaldûn seems to have considered Abû Ḥammû his most promising choice for future employment. However, he was reluctant to follow Abû Ḥammû's uncertain destiny. Even in March, 1368, after receiving a most pressing and flattering invitation to become Abû Ḥammû's prime minister, he preferred to maintain a cautious, waiting attitude. He sent his brother Yaḥyâ, who had been released, to Tlemcen, but himself remained in the region of Biskra. The reasons he gave for refusing Abû Ḥammû's offer were that he was disgusted with the snares and pitfalls of high office and that he had neglected scholarship for too long. Indeed, during these years, Ibn Khaldûn's feeling of bitterness toward political life—he once called it [56] "the morass of politics"—and his desire for the peace and quiet of scholarly research, found more and more frequent expression. Ibn Khaldûn fully realized how difficult it is to withdraw from the higher levels of politics once one has attained them.[57] He, for one, never succeeded in keeping out of public life except for rather brief periods, because the particular gifts he possessed and the services he was eminently qualified to render were always in great demand. Although, when his political fortunes were at their lowest ebb, he fervently asserted his desire for a scholar's life in peaceful retirement, to the very last he always surrendered easily to the temptations of power and a political career.

His reluctance to join Abû Ḥammû was proved by subsequent events to have been justified. A new element appeared on the northwest African political scene when a temporary recovery of the Merinid power was made under the leadership of 'Abd-al-'Azîz, the young and energetic new ruler of Fez (1366–72). His march on Tlemcen, in 1370, made Abû Ḥammû's position there untenable for the time being. In April of the same year, Ibn Khaldûn met

[55] For the events of this period, see also G. Marçais, *Les Arabes en Berbérie du XIe au XIVe siècle* (Constantine & Paris, 1913), pp. 310 ff.

[56] Cf. *Autobiography*, p. 143.

[57] See 2:99 ff., below.

with Abû Ḥammû. But he seems to have felt that 'Abd-al-'Azîz's victorious progress made it unsafe for him to stay in northwestern Africa, especially in view of his own strained relations with the Merinids ever since he had left Fez following Abû Sâlim's death. Consequently, he decided to cross over to Spain, but the attempt to escape did not succeed. Stranded at the port of Hunayn, which is situated halfway between the modern towns of Beni Saf and Nemours, he was captured by a detachment of 'Abd-al-'Azîz's troops. 'Abd-al-'Azîz seems to have feared that his departure to Spain would inaugurate an attempt by Ibn Khaldûn's group to secure Spanish intervention in northwestern Africa. Brought before the Merinid ruler, Ibn Khaldûn was hard put to it to explain his earlier attitude towards the Merinids and to soothe 'Abd-al-'Azîz with assurances that Bougie would be an easy conquest. When Ibn Khaldûn left the ruler's presence he was not sure whether he would escape with his life. He was, therefore, greatly relieved when his confinement lasted only for one night and he was set free the next morning. He went to El-Eubbad (al-'Ubbâd), near Tlemcen, the sanctuary of the great mystic and saint Abû Madyan, and firmly decided to devote his future to study and teaching.

A few weeks later, Ibn Khaldûn was pressed into the service of 'Abd-al-'Azîz, who wanted to exploit the scholar's connections with the Arab tribes and hoped he could win them over to the Merinid side. Ibn Khaldûn did not feel in a position to refuse 'Abd-al-'Azîz's request. Also, perhaps, he was not unaware of the opportunity for a change of scene and for freeing himself to some degree from direct Merinid supervision. Thus, he left for Biskra August 4, 1370, and again took a hand in Arab tribal politics, though he may not have been overactive in his employer's behalf. After two full years of this life, he was summoned by 'Abd-al-'Azîz to Fez. He left Biskra with his family September 11, 1372.

While on the way to Fez only a few days later, the news of 'Abd-al-'Azîz's death reached him. He decided to continue his journey nevertheless, only to be held up by Bedouins acting on the instigation of Abû Ḥammû. He escaped only with the greatest difficulty, and reached Fez in October or November. The confusion reigning in Fez made it impossible for him to obtain a satisfactory and sufficiently secure position. While biding his time, he may have had some leisure for scholarly pursuits; but he had to look for a more promising place to live, and again he turned to Spain, hoping to find a refuge there. His friend, Ibn al-Khaṭîb, now an exile in Fez, had been replaced as prime minister in Granada by Ibn Zamrak,[58] another famous littérateur, whom Ibn Khaldûn had known when he, like Ibn al-Khaṭîb now, was a refugee in Fez during the reign of Abû Sâlim. However, Ibn Khaldûn encountered a number of difficulties in realizing his plan. The relations between Fez and Granada were at this time strained almost to the point of war, and the Fâsî government tried to prevent his departure by every means. Sometime in 1374, probably in the fall, he finally succeeded in getting away, but his family was not permitted to join him. The government in Fez even went so far as to persuade the ruler of Granada to extradite him. He was returned to northwest Africa, but through the intervention of a friend managed to go from Hunayn, where he was landed, to Abû Ḥammû who once again was in control of Tlemcen. Ibn Khaldûn took up his residence in nearby al-'Ubbâd. Here his family was able to join him on March 5, 1375.

After the experiences of these nine years, Ibn Khaldûn was thoroughly tired of politics and the dangers of public life. Thus, when Abû Ḥammû asked him to head a political mission to the Dawâwidah Arabs, he seized the opportunity it offered to seek freedom from governmental service. After leaving Tlemcen, he stopped among the Awlâd 'Arîf, the leading family of the Suwayd branch of the Arab Zughbah tribes, and had his family brought to him. The Awlâd 'Arîf permitted the whole family to live under their protection in Qal'at Ibn Salâmah, a castle and village in the province of Oran granted to them by Abû 'Inân, the Merinid of Fez in whose reign Ibn Khaldûn had completed his studies almost twenty years before. There, Ibn Khaldûn spent over three years in comfort and quiet, and started to write his *History* of the world. In November of 1377, he tells us,[59] "I completed its Introduction (*Muqaddimah*) in that remarkable manner to which I was inspired by that retreat, with words and ideas pouring into my head like cream into a churn, until the finished product was ready." It was to take Ibn Khaldûn four more years, together with an opportunity to use the libraries in Tunis, before he completed his great historical work.

More will be said about the *Muqaddimah* in the following

[58] Cf. *GAL*, II, 259; 2d ed., II, 336; *Suppl.*, II, 370.
[59] Cf. *Autobiography*, p. 229.

pages. The other parts of the monumental *History* (*Kitâb al-'Ibar*) certainly deserve more careful study and discussion than they have so far received, though this is not the place for an exhaustive analysis of the work. But we may, at least, stress the fact that, in general, Ibn Khaldûn's achievement has not been judged fairly. On the contrary, a good deal of direct and indirect abuse has been heaped upon the *'Ibar*. This began when Ibn Ḥajar, Ibn Khaldûn's famous student, saw fit to remark that his teacher's knowledge of the eastern part of the Muslim world and its history was not too precise [60]—a statement which, though to some degree correct, is so obvious and of so little real significance that one wishes that Ibn Ḥajar had not made it. In modern times, scholars have often expressed the opinion that the *'Ibar* does not reflect the historical and sociological insights of the *Muqaddimah*.

The last two volumes of the seven-volume work deal with the history of the Muslim West. To this day, these two volumes are the most important source we possess for northwest African and Berber history. As such, they are indispensable. It is, however, more important to know that they clearly reflect Ibn Khaldûn's great gifts as a researcher and writer. A good deal of the material they contain is based upon knowledge carefully collected at first-hand. The historical presentation is as clear and interesting as the Muslim taste in historiography—which runs to excessively detailed reporting of facts—permitted.

Volumes II to V of the *'Ibar* (of which the *Muqaddimah* constitutes volume I), belong to a different category. They deal with events of the pre-Islamic world and with Arab and Eastern Muslim history. Occasionally, though rarely, they contain information for which they appear to be our principal source, such as the account of the Arab tribes in Syria.[61] In general, however, these volumes contain little material for which we do not have older or more accurate sources. This could hardly be otherwise, considering the character of Muslim historiography and the abundant material at our disposal. However, in his treatment of pre-Islamic history, a matter that Muslim historians have always known imperfectly, Ibn Khaldûn has the merit of having consulted unusual sources. In

---

[60] Cf. F. Rosenthal, *A History of Muslim Historiography* (Leiden, 1952), p. 420. Cf. also Ibn Khaldûn himself, p. 65, below.

[61] Cf. *'Ibar*, V, 436 f. A résumé of the information appears later in Vol. VI of the *'Ibar*. See p. 269, below.

particular, he was eager to use more than one source, whenever possible.[62] He compared the sources at his disposal and tried to exercise as much critical judgment with regard to them as the meagerness and confusing character of the information permitted.

The pages on Muslim history have to be judged by different criteria. Here the decisive factor is the method used by Ibn Khaldûn in selecting and abridging the historical material at his disposal. Much investigation and study are needed before a definite judgment on his achievement in this respect can be given. However, Ibn Khaldûn seems to have done whatever was humanly possible with considerable ability, avoiding the chitchat and incredible tales that he easily might have been tempted to use.

Ibn Khaldûn does not deserve the reproach that the descriptive part of his history fails to measure up to the high standards set by the theories of the *Muqaddimah.* His discussion of contemporary northwest African history, dealing largely with material he had himself observed, is obviously guided by the insights into tribal politics which he expressed in the *Muqaddimah.* The larger, more urbanized and centralized eastern Muslim region presented much more complex problems. Ibn Khaldûn possessed only written sources for its history and was almost completely unacquainted with its contemporary reality when he wrote. To apply the general reflections of the *Muqaddimah* to individual events so remote and unfamiliar to him, would have been an almost hopeless task and, moreover, would have required a forbidding amount of space. It was for this reason that Ibn Khaldûn put his theoretical reflections in the form of an introduction. Incidentally, in doing so, he merely followed the example of many earlier Muslim historians who also relegated their general historical theories to the introductions of their respective works. However, they usually did so in a manner infinitely more restricted than that of Ibn Khaldûn.

Meanwhile, the author of the *Muqaddimah* was beginning to grow restless in his seclusion at Qal'at Ibn Salâmah. Indeed, it is hard to visualize this active man of affairs, long accustomed to the company of scholars and the great of his time, living out the prime

---

[62] Cf. G. Levi Della Vida, "La traduzione araba delle Storie di Orosio," in *Miscellanea Giovanni Galbiati* (Fontes ambrosiani, No. 27) (Milan, 1951), III, 185–203, esp. 203. Spanish translation in *al-Andalus,* XIX (1954), 257–93.

of his life in a place where there was little to learn and even less to do. When he fell gravely ill, his realization of his loneliness and isolation became acute. Upon recovery, he decided to leave Qal'at Ibn Salâmah and, thinking of the work still to be done on his *History*, wished he could be near large libraries, such as were to be found in Tunis.[63]

By this time, the Ḥafṣid Abû l-'Abbâs had been master of Tunis and the mightiest ruler in all of northwestern Africa for seven years. Ibn Khaldûn's first, unfortunate encounter with him had happened eleven years ago. Thus, it was natural that Ibn Khaldûn should now turn his eyes in that direction. The most promising approach was also clearly indicated. Ibn Khaldûn addressed Abû l-'Abbâs as a scholar who wanted to do research in Tunis and as a native who desired to see the town of his birth and the graves of his parents once more. His petition was successful. Abû l-'Abbâs, respecting Ibn Khaldûn's famous family name, graciously permitted him to come to Tunis. Early in the winter of 1378, Ibn Khaldûn left Qal'at Ibn Salâmah. On his way, he met Abû l-'Abbâs, who was on a military expedition. He arrived in Tunis in November or December, 1378.

Once he had again settled down in his old home, Ibn Khaldûn began to encounter difficulties with many people, both scholars and courtiers. As Ibn Khaldûn tells the story, it was because he enjoyed Abû l-'Abbâs' favor that he aroused the envy of the ruler's entourage. In view of their past conflict, however, it would seem more likely that Abû l-'Abbâs was reluctant to promote Ibn Khaldûn. The courtiers, moreover, were themselves interested in having Ibn Khaldûn under the ruler's supervision, and, as far as we know, had no fear that Ibn Khaldûn could use his close association to influence him. Thus, while there certainly was animosity against Ibn Khaldûn in court circles, it probably was not due to his alleged success in winning Abû l-'Abbâs' favor.

Ibn Khaldûn started teaching in Tunis and met with opposition from the great jurist Ibn 'Arafah al-Warghamî (1316–1401).[64] Ibn 'Arafah was sixteen years older than Ibn Khaldûn; he had studied under the same teachers, but it had taken him longer to

[63] There is very little precise information on libraries in Tunisia at this period. Cf. R. Brunschvig, *La Berbérie orientale*, II, 367 f. There must also have existed many private collections in Tunis.

[64] Cf. *GAL*, II, 247; *Suppl.*, II, 347.

mature as a scholar. He had slowly achieved eminence in the Muslim world as the leading representative of Mâlikite jurisprudence. When he saw that his students preferred Ibn Khaldûn's classes to his own, he deeply resented the presence of the brilliant intruder who, for his part, may have failed to establish a suitably deferential relationship with the older man. The situation as described by Ibn Khaldûn, is, of course, a common one in university life, and while we may hesitate to apportion exact degrees of guilt to one side or the other, neither the fact of this rivalry nor its unfortunate effect upon Ibn Khaldûn's situation in Tunis can be doubted. For the rest of his life Ibn 'Arafah never changed his opinion of Ibn Khaldûn. Much later, probably in either 1390/91 or 1393/94[65] when he stopped in Egypt in the course of his pilgrimage, he grimly denounced Ibn Khaldûn's fitness as a jurist and stated sarcastically that he had lost all respect for the office of judge now that Ibn Khaldûn had become one.[66] It has been shrewdly suggested that Ibn 'Arafah's opposition to Ibn Khaldûn may have had a deeper meaning, that it symbolized the opposition of formal Muslim jurisprudence to the stirrings of a new spirit faintly noticeable in Ibn Khaldûn's thinking.[67] Be this as it may, there were more concrete motives to determine Ibn 'Arafah's attitude towards Ibn Khaldûn during his years in Tunis.

When Abû l-'Abbâs went on another of his military expeditions, Ibn Khaldûn was obliged to accompany him, for the ruler feared that if he were left alone in Tunis, Ibn Khaldûn would intrigue against him. Ibn Khaldûn resented this interruption of his life and work. To make matters worse, he had presented Abû l-'Abbâs with a copy of the completed *History*, but this work did not contain the customary panegyric (on the reign of the ruler who commissioned it or supported its author) with which Muslim historians were wont to end their works. Ibn Khaldûn suspected that his failure to have included such a panegyric was used to cast suspicion upon his loyalty to Abû l-'Abbâs. Finally, in October of 1382, when Abû l-'Abbâs was getting ready another military expedition, Ibn Khaldûn feared he was again to be forced to accompany it, and decided to leave. He seized the opportunity offered by the presence of a ship in the harbor of Tunis, ready to sail for

[65] Cf. as-Sakhâwî, *aḍ-Ḍaw' al-lâmi'*, IX, 240–42.
[66] *Ibid.*, IV, 146.
[67] Cf. R. Brunschvig, *La Berbérie orientale*, II, 391.

Alexandria, to ask Abû l-'Abbâs for permission to make the pilgrimage to Mecca. This was the age-old pretext for Muslims in public life who felt insecure and wanted to remove themselves from the political scene. The permission was granted, and October 24, 1382, Ibn Khaldûn sailed for Alexandria. His family remained in Tunis, possibly because he had first to find a means of livelihood abroad, or because Abû l-'Abbâs may not have allowed them to leave with him. They would be valuable hostages in the event Ibn Khaldûn turned west instead of east and decided to play a part, once again, in the history of northwestern Africa or Spain.

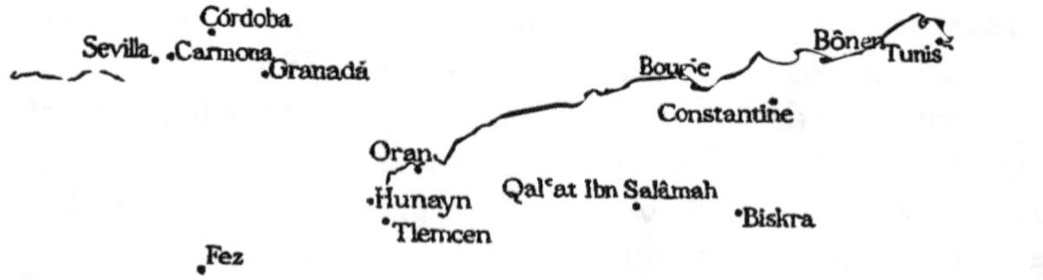

Ibn Khaldûn's Maghrib and Southern Spain

However, Ibn Khaldûn sailed eastward, and thereafter his only contacts with the West were by correspondence or through travelers.[68] After more than forty days at sea, he reached Alexandria December 8, 1382. He did not then go on to Mecca, but settled in Egypt where, except for occasional travels in the East, including an eventual pilgrimage, he remained for the rest of his life.

If Ibn Khaldûn had seriously entertained the idea of going on the pilgrimage at that critical juncture of his career, he gave it up for the time being. On January 6, 1383, he moved to Cairo, the fame of which had already reached him while he was still in the West. Egypt under the Mamelukes was prosperous and comparatively stable politically. To Ibn Khaldûn Cairo's size, the innumerable people it contained, and its importance as the center of Islam surpassed his anticipations.[69] The city's crowded streets, its splendid buildings, its magnificent and splendidly equipped colleges, and the eternal beauty of the Nile aroused his excitement and enthusiasm. However, his most urgent task was to find a

[68] See p. lxiv, below.
[69] See 3:315, below.

position which would allow him to stay in Egypt. Great as his personal qualifications undeniably were, his career in the West had been greatly facilitated by his family connections, by his relationship with many important people there, and by the numerous helpful friendships that were his birthright. A sizable number of his countrymen lived in Egypt, and Ibn Khaldûn presumably consulted them; later on, his own house was to become a center for visitors from northwestern Africa. Yet, in building up a position for himself in Egypt, he had to rely mainly on his own resources, his personality, abilities, scholarship, and experience of public life. His success in Egypt is proof, if such were needed, of his personal qualities.

Fortunately for Ibn Khaldûn, al-Malik aẓ-Ẓâhir Barqûq had become Egypt's ruler shortly before his arrival. In beginning his reign, he presumably was trying to attract new personalities to enlarge and improve the quality of his entourage. Ibn Khaldûn soon gained the new ruler's esteem and confidence. Only once did a passing disturbance interrupt their good relations, which lasted until Barqûq's death in 1399. Ibn Khaldûn reciprocated Barqûq's favor by the gesture of renaming the *History* in his honor *aẓ-Ẓâhirî*, using Barqûq's royal title.[70] Throughout his life, Ibn Khaldûn never ceased to speak of Barqûq with gratitude and affection.

Another fortunate circumstance helped Ibn Khaldûn in Egypt. Almost immediately upon arrival, he was able, in some way unknown, to establish connections with a high-ranking and very influential Turkish official, Alṭunbughâ al-Jûbânî (d. 1390), who was instrumental in introducing him to Barqûq and into the proper Egyptian circles. He was to spend the remaining twenty-three years of his life in a variety of highly respected positions, becoming at different times professor, college president, and judge. In his youth Ibn Khaldûn may have regarded such positions as somewhat beneath his ambitions and the family tradition, but they were in keeping with the development of his personality and the course of his career, as well as appropriate activities for his declining years.

Intellectual communication between the western and the eastern parts of the Muslim world was poor, even if certain con-

---

[70] See p. xci, below. The name *aẓ-Ẓâhirî*, however, did not remain attached to the work.

tacts existed in Ibn Khaldûn's time.[71] So recent a work as his *History* could hardly have been widely known or appreciated in Egypt at the time of his arrival. While still in Tunis, he may have sent a few presentation copies to Egyptian scholars, or, more likely, when he came to Cairo he may have given copies to a few scholars likely to be interested in the work. Nor could his previous publications, if they had reached Egypt at all, have gained a great reputation for the author. But his wide and ready knowledge and, above all, his mastery of literary Arabic, must have made an immediate impression on the persons he met. He was given an opportunity to hold courses at al-Azhar University, and, when it became open, Barqûq appointed him to the professorship of Mâlikite jurisprudence in the Qamḥîyah College.

Ibn Khaldûn began teaching in the Qamḥîyah College on March 19, 1384.[72] The inaugural lecture he delivered on that occasion, as well as two other inaugural lectures given in connection with subsequent appointments to professorships, are preserved in the *Autobiography*. These inaugural lectures are extremely valuable documents of Muslim academic life. The Qamḥîyah lecture comprised an encomium on the Turks and Barqûq, and a statement as to the spirit in which Ibn Khaldûn intended to discharge his professorial duties. The Ẓâhirîyah inaugural lecture was delivered at a newly established institution and therefore followed slightly different lines. It had as its exclusive theme the praise of Barqûq, particularly as builder of the Ẓâhirîyah College. The most important lecture of the three was given at Ṣurghatmishîyah College. It began, as was customary, with an encomium on Barqûq and a statement as to the spirit in which Ibn Khaldûn approached his task. It then turned into a scholarly discussion of Mâlik's *Muwaṭṭa'*, with biography of its author, an account of the origin of the work, and the history of its transmission. On these three academic occasions, a distinguished audience of officials was greatly impressed by Ibn Khaldûn's skillful presentation of his subject.

All of Ibn Khaldûn's teaching positions were officially in the religious sciences. There can be little doubt that he mainly taught jurisprudence and traditions. But he also lectured on the *Muqad-*

[71] See, in particular, 2:350, below.
[72] Cf. *Autobiography*, p. 279 (n. 3).

dimah,[73] and he probably had some liberty to teach historical subjects of his own choosing, if he desired. During all the years in Egypt, he kept working on the *Muqaddimah*, improving it, and bringing his *History* up to date.

The Qamḥîyah professorship was a good position, but Ibn Khaldûn was soon called to a more important task. On August 8, 1384, Barqûq appointed him Chief Mâlikî Judge of Egypt. Custom required the individual nominated to a judgeship to pretend to refuse the appointment, and Ibn Khaldûn went through the required motions. Still sensitive to the lure of public life, he gladly accepted the new honor; for, while the professorship gave him prestige, the judgeship meant both prestige and power. Five times more he was called upon to be a judge, and on all these occasions he seems to have welcomed the opportunity for official activity that the judgeship offered. It must have been gratifying to him at the end to die in office. Fully conscious of the importance of his position, he fulfilled his legal functions with dignity and severity; his adversaries charged him with being intolerably overbearing while in office, yet willing to please everybody while out of office.[74]

At the beginning of his career as judge, Ibn Khaldûn appears to have assumed the role of reformer—a rather puzzling metamorphosis for a man with his outlook on life, a realist by both temperament and experience. Moreover, Ibn Khaldûn must have known beforehand that to attempt reforms of long-established customs would make enemies for himself. He must certainly have realized that he could not succeed in introducing reforms in a foreign country without "group feeling" (*'aṣabîyah*) to sustain him in his efforts. Apparently he was actuated not so much by a conscious scheme of reform as by the urge to do his job well. This is why he proceeded against the corruption and bribery which were rampant among notaries and clerks, and tried to weed out incompetent muftis and ignorant legal advisers. Among the latter were many countrymen of his from the West who had settled in Egypt and set themselves up as experts in Mâlikite jurisprudence.

As a result of these efforts, he remained less than a year in the judgeship. His will to fight was broken by a great personal misfortune, the loss of his family. As soon as he had obtained the full professorship at the Qamḥîyah College, he had set in motion the

[73] See p. cv, below.
[74] Cf. as-Sakhâwî, *aḍ-Ḍaw' al-lâmi'*, IV, 146.

international machinery necessary to bring to Cairo his loved ones whom he had been forced to leave behind in Tunis. In a letter dated April 8, 1384, Barqûq approached Abû l-'Abbâs of Tunis in this matter, and his intervention was successful. But the ship carrying Ibn Khaldûn's family and some fine horses intended as a gift from Abû l-'Abbâs to Barqûq, was wrecked near the harbor of Alexandria [75] in October/November, 1384, and everyone, it seems, was lost.[76]

Relieved from the judgeship, Ibn Khaldûn again turned to teaching. He was appointed professor of Mâlikite jurisprudence in the Ẓâhirîyah College and Mausoleum which Barqûq had just built and named after his own royal title. He was now securely established in Egypt and could think of undertaking the long-postponed pilgrimage to Mecca. Ibn Khaldûn left Cairo on September 29, 1387, and returned eight months later, compensated for the hardships of the journey by contact with the interesting people he had met. Soon after his return, in January, 1389, he was made professor of the science of traditions in the Ṣurghatmishîyah College, and in April of the same year, when the presidency of the Baybars Institute became vacant, he was, in addition, appointed president of that institution.

The year 1389 also witnessed a revolt against Barqûq in Egypt. For a time he was deprived of his throne, but was able to regain control and re-entered Cairo February 2, 1390. During that period, Ibn Khaldûn, together with the other Egyptian legal authorities, had issued a legal opinion against Barqûq; but they claimed to have been forced to do so. Ibn Khaldûn's relationship with Barqûq seems to have been somewhat clouded for a time, and Barqûq, at the urging of an interested third party, deprived Ibn Khaldûn of the presidency of the Baybars Institute. That there was no real break between the two men is shown by the fact that Ibn Khaldûn retained his professorship and, on May 21, 1399, regained the Mâlikite judgeship. One month later, Barqûq died and was succeeded by his ten-year-old son, Faraj.

Ibn Khaldûn was confirmed in his position under the new ruler. In 1400, he visited Damascus in the company of Faraj. On the way back to Egypt, he made a pilgrimage to the holy cities of Palestine,

[75] Cf. *Autobiography*, p. 339; *'Ibar*, V, 480.
[76] See p. xlvi, above.

Jerusalem, Bethlehem, and Hebron. On his return to Egypt, he found another aspirant to his judgeship trying, by influence and bribery, to remove him and to be appointed in his place—intrigues such as, Ibn Khaldûn claims, led to his removal from office on later occasions also. His rival was successful, and replaced him as Mâlikite judge on September 5, 1400.

The Tatar hordes under Timur were by then knocking at the Syrian gateway to Egypt, and the Egyptian army under Faraj had to move against them. Ibn Khaldûn, though still out of office, was asked to accompany the ruler on this expedition, and reluctantly agreed. The expedition left Egypt in November, 1400, and reached besieged Damascus a month later. During the first week of 1401, Faraj and his advisers, informed of a revolt then being planned in Egypt, decided to return. In the beleaguered city a difference of opinion arose between the military and civilian authorities as to the best course to take. While the military authorities wanted to hold out, the civilian authorities, that is, the judges and jurists in Damascus, including such temporary residents as Ibn Khaldûn, thought it best to surrender. Their treasonable weakness, which perhaps may be excused by the seeming hopelessness of the situation, won out. They escaped unscathed, but had to watch the betrayed city being sacked and ravaged by the Tatar hordes. To later generations, though not to the contemporary Damascenes, there was a compensating element in the debacle: the civilian authorities' lack of courage provided Ibn Khaldûn with a chance to meet Timur face to face and to leave posterity a vivid account of their historic meeting.

When the Damascus judges first approached Timur, he asked them about Ibn Khaldûn and expressed the wish to see him. Since the military authorities were still in control of the city gates, Ibn Khaldûn could not leave the city by way of them. Thus, he had to have himself lowered by ropes from the walls of Damascus and, January 10, 1401, got in touch with Timur. His personal association with the world conqueror extended to the end of February of that year. Ibn Khaldûn's main concern, on the occasion of their interviews, was to obtain the safety of his colleagues and himself. At the same time, he was fully conscious of meeting in Timur one of the great makers of history. Timur, for his part, had in mind the advantage to his future plans of grandiose world conquest, of having a man of Ibn Khaldûn's background and experience attached to his court. In particular, he desired to avail himself of Ibn Khaldûn's intimate, firsthand knowledge of the western portion of the Muslim world, a qualification that Barqûq, too, had considered a most valuable asset.

For Ibn Khaldûn had kept his connections with the West alive, and even showed his northwest African origin outwardly by dressing in the style of that region. While in Egypt, he did many favors for Western friends, such as presenting a poem by a Western littérateur to Barqûq, and procuring books in Egypt for a Spanish scholar unable to buy them himself. He informed interested statesmen in the West of his own doings and of the political situation in Egypt. In turn, he tried, through pilgrims and travelers as well as through correspondents, to obtain political information from the West, ostensibly for bringing his *History* up to date, but partly for political purposes. Thus, he was especially useful as an adviser on diplomatic relations between Egypt and the West, whether concerning the exchange of presents or the proper reception due a Western pilgrim of high rank passing through Egypt.[77]

Timur's interest in Ibn Khaldûn's knowledge of the West appears to have been of a more aggressive character. He inquired about the geography of the area and asked Ibn Khaldûn to write a detailed description of it to be translated into Mongol for the use of himself and his military advisers. Ibn Khaldûn complied with the request by writing a long paper on the subject. However, as soon as he was safely back in Egypt, he wrote another, also rather lengthy document, a letter addressed to "the ruler of northwestern Africa," presumably, the Merinid in Fez.[78] In it, he supplied his addressee with a history of the Tatars and a careful and well-balanced estimate of Timur's personality. Obviously, he felt a twinge of conscience at having given Timur information dangerous to the future well-being and independence of the country of his youth. By informing the northwest Africans of the character of the Tatar menace, he intended to neutralize the potentially harmful results of his previous action.

---

[77] Cf. W. J. Fischel in *Semitic and Oriental Studies Presented to William Popper*, pp. 115–17.

[78] If a son of Ibn Khaldûn was actually present at the court of Fez (see n. 53, above), it would have been natural for Ibn Khaldûn to address himself to the Merinid.

If Timur actually thought of attaching Ibn Khaldûn to his staff, he did not press the matter. Ibn Khaldûn was able to obtain Timur's permission to leave and return to Egypt. On his way to the coast via Ṣafad, he was robbed by tribesmen, but when he reached the coast he was able to board a passing vessel which carried him to Gaza. Without having the faintest premonition of the significance of this encounter, Ibn Khaldûn met on board an ambassador of Bâyazîd Yıldırım, the Ottoman ruler of Asia Minor, a power destined to become far more important for the future of Ibn Khaldûn's world and work than the great conqueror whom he had just left. It is only just to observe that the chances of Yıldırım's survival, in the precarious position in which he found himself at that moment, would have seemed remote to any observer just then.

In March, 1401, Ibn Khaldûn reached Egypt after an absence of six months. Except for the dates of his appointments to and dismissals from the judgeship, we know very little about these last five years of his life. He was appointed judge for the third time in April, 1401, deposed at the beginning of March, 1402, reappointed again in July, 1402, and deposed in September, 1403. His next appointment came on February 11, 1405, and this time his tenure of office lasted to the end of May, 1405. His last appointment came in March, 1406, and only a few days later, on Wednesday, March 17, 1406, death suddenly relieved him of the office. He was buried in the Sufi cemetery outside Cairo's Naṣr Gate.

As is so often the case with men of genius, Ibn Khaldûn's actions and aspirations were simple and uncomplicated. With great single-mindedness he endeavored to acquire leadership in the organization of his society and to master the intellectual development of humanity at its contemporary level. His background and upbringing had taught him to consider these the most desirable achievements in this world, and, by and large, he was able to realize them. Recognizing that all means were necessary and therefore justified, Ibn Khaldûn's actions to achieve the first goal were ruthless and opportunistic. Recognizing further that the more enduring achievement of intellectual leadership is largely incompatible with the search for worldly success,[79] he strove to strike a sound balance between the active and the contemplative aspects of his personality. Aided by great ability and endurance, as well as by

[79] See 3:308 ff., below.

circumstances that, though harsh, were favorable to his aspirations, he became the great thinker and doer he set out to be.

In the realm of intellectual achievement, the greatest hopes he may reasonably have harbored were eventually fulfilled. His contemporaries, it is true, and the generations immediately following, refused to recognize or to appreciate the stirrings of a new spirit apparent in his work. But his labors had considerable influence upon the first generation of his pupils, including such men as al-Maqrîzî and Ibn Ḥajar, and, through them, in turn, upon such pupils of theirs as as-Sakhâwî. These and many other great scholars throughout the fifteenth century profited from Ibn Khaldûn's historical teaching.[80] It may well be said that the great and active interest in historical studies noticeable during that period was stimulated by him. Moreover, a new interest in the independent theoretical discussion of historiography may be observed at that time. Ibn Khaldûn's great example may well have started this trend, though it did not continue along the lines he suggested.

The great period of the rediscovery of Ibn Khaldûn began as early as the sixteenth century and gained momentum in the seventeenth. At the beginning of the latter century, al-Maqqarî, a scholar from northwestern Africa, made considerable use of Ibn Khaldûn's work.[81] But for the true understanding of Ibn Khaldûn, a people was needed who, like the Romans, were mainly concerned

---

[80] Al-Fâsî, the historian of Mecca (1373–1429), quoted the *History* of Ibn Khaldûn in his *'Iqd*, and around 1425 a certain Muḥammad b. Aḥmad b. Muḥammad Ibn az-Zamlakânî incorporated excerpts from Ibn Khaldûn's *History* in his *Tadhkirah*, of which a MS is preserved in Cairo (Egyptian Library, Taymûr, *adab* 604). Ibn az-Zamlakânî tells us that he used a MS of the *History* deposited in the Mu'ayyadîyah Library in Cairo.

As-Suyûṭî (1445–1505), through his teacher Ibn Ḥajar, knew of Ibn Khaldûn's theory about three generations spanning a century; cf. *Naẓm al-'iqyân*, ed. P. K. Hitti (New York, 1927), p. 171. Al-Qalqashandî (1355–1418) quoted Ibn Khaldûn repeatedly; see nn. 504 and 546 to Ch. III, below.

A late fifteenth-century work, in which Ibn Khaldûn's discussion of politics and political ethics was abridged from the *Muqaddimah*, would be interesting to know. This was the *Badâ'i' as-silk fî ṭabâ'i' al-mulk* by Muḥammad b. 'Alî b. Muḥammad b. al-Azraq; cf. al-Maqqarî, *Analectes*, ed. R. Dozy *et al.* (Leiden, 1855–61), I, 940. Ibn al-Azraq is referred to by as-Sakhâwî, *aḍ-Ḍaw' al-lâmi'*, XI, 234, but his biography, which should appear in *Ḍaw'*, VIII, 205, is missing, apparently owing to an omission in the printed edition.

[81] His contemporary Aḥmad Bâbâ also knew Ibn Khaldûn's *Autobiography*; see 3:395, below, and *Nayl al-ibtihâj*, pp. 170, 243 ff.

with politics and therefore concentrated their intellectual interests upon history. Such a people were the Ottoman Turks, whose scholars and statesmen vied with each other in their interest in Ibn Khaldûn's work and ideas. They included such men as Weysi (Wissi) Effendi,[82] Ṭâshköprüzâdeh (1495–1561),[83] Ḥâjjî Khalîfah (1609–57), Ṭab'î Bey (*ca.* 1670),[84] Na'îmâ (1688/89–1716),[85] and many others of the eighteenth century and later. Their activities, so far as they concerned Ibn Khaldûn, constitute an important segment of Turkish intellectual history and ought to be studied as such. Nor should we forget the men, often little known or anonymous, who brought numerous manuscripts of Ibn Khaldûn's work to Turkey and had them copied for their own study.

At the beginning of the nineteenth century, European scholars joined with the Turks in studying Ibn Khaldûn. Many ideas discussed in the European West long after Ibn Khaldûn's time were found, amazingly enough, not to be as new as had been thought, but to have been known, in their rudiments at least,[86] to the northwest African of the fourteenth century who founded a "new science" in his *Muqaddimah.*

[82] See p. xciv, below.

[83] Mentioned by A. Z. Velidi Togan, *Tarihde Usul* (Istanbul, 1950), p. 170, as an author familiar with Ibn Khaldûn's work; no further information is supplied.

According to A. Adnan Adıvar, "Ibn Haldûn," in *Islâm Ansiklopedisi* (Istanbul, 1950), V, 740, Ibn Khaldûn had been a subject of notice in the encyclopaedia composed by Muḥammad b. Aḥmad al-'Ajamî, a professor in Istanbul who died in 1550. Cf. *GAL*, II, 453.

[84] Cf. F. Babinger, *Die Geschichtsschreiber der Osmanen* (Leipzig, 1927), p. 212.

[85] Cf. A. Z. Velidi Togan, p. 171, following Z. F. Fındıkoğlu & H. Z. Ülken, *Ibn Haldun* (Istanbul, 1940). Fındıkoğlu has published another article on the subject of Turkish students of Ibn Khaldûn, in *Mélanges Fuad Köprülü* (Istanbul, 1953), pp. 153–63.

[86] Ibn Khaldûn has been claimed as the forerunner of a great many Western scholars, both major and minor. A. Schimmel, *Ibn Chaldun* (Tübingen, 1951), p. xvii, lists Machiavelli, Bodin, Vico, Gibbon, Montesquieu, Abbé de Mably, Ferguson, Herder, Condorcet, Comte, Gobineau, Tarde, Breysig, and W. James. He has been compared with Hegel, and there is hardly any thinker with whom he might not be compared. Such comparisons may help to evaluate the intellectual stature of the person with whom Ibn Khaldûn is compared; certainly they suggest a lesson in scholarly humility. But they do not contribute much to our understanding of Ibn Khaldûn.

The *Muqaddimah*

THE ORIGINAL "introduction" (*muqaddimah*) to Ibn Khaldûn's great *History* covers only a few pages (below, pp. 15–68). As is customary in Muslim historical works, these introductory pages contain a eulogy of history. This is followed by a discussion, illustrated with historical examples, of errors historians have committed and the reasons for them. One of these is a principal reason why even great historians occasionally err, namely, their ignorance of changes in the environment within which history unfolds. The remainder of what is now called the *Muqaddimah* originally constituted the first book of the *History*, and was designed to prove this thesis. It was intended to elucidate the fundamental principles of all history, which determine the true historian's reconstruction of the past.

However, during its author's lifetime the original introduction and the first book became an independent work known under the title of *Muqaddimah*. In the 1394 edition of his *Autobiography*, Ibn Khaldûn speaks of the first book of his *History* in this way. At the same time, the table of contents prefixed to our oldest manuscripts of the *Muqaddimah* states that "this first book went by the name of *Muqaddimah* until (that name) came to be a characteristic proper name for it." Thus, it is not surprising that, in a late addition to the *Muqaddimah* itself, Ibn Khaldûn refers to it as the *Muqaddimah* [87] and that he gave lectures exclusively devoted to it.[88] To all later ages, *Muqaddimah* was the title almost universally used.

With respect to its literary form, the *Muqaddimah* would not seem to deserve unqualified praise.[89] Like the last two volumes of

[87] See 2:124, below. In the colophon at the end of Ch. III, A speaks of the "end of the first half of the *Muqaddimah*," and in the colophon at the end of Ch. IV, D speaks of the chapter as the "fourth chapter of the *muqaddimah* of the *History*." See also p. 10, l. 11, below.

[88] See p. cv, below.

[89] For opinions on the style and language of the *Muqaddimah*, see also p. cxi, below.

the History, it is Ibn Khaldûn's original creation in the main; it is not influenced by the literary character of its sources, as is frequently the case in Muslim historical writing and as is the case with the middle volumes of Ibn Khaldûn's work. The *Muqaddimah* was written in the precise, cultured speech that was used in academic discussion by Ibn Khaldûn, his friends, and his contemporaries in the Muslim West. This language is as much, or as little, down-to-earth as the formal speech of the educated anywhere in the world tends to be. Both the language and the style of the *Muqaddimah* clearly reflect the discursive manner of the academic lecturer, concerned primarily with an audience that is listening to him, and driving his points home viva voce. A large segment of Muslim literature was influenced in style and content by classroom needs; thus, it became customary and easy for an author to use the lecture style even when not writing for school use or for a listening audience. This was the case when Ibn Khaldûn wrote the *Muqaddimah*, quite apart from the consideration that he used the work later as a textbook for lectures.

Another factor to make for prolixity was Ibn Khaldûn's use of a new terminology that was largely his own. Since the reader, or listener, could not be assumed to be acquainted with it, it required constant repetition and redefinition. In addition, there was the old problem of proper cross-referencing which the manuscript literature prior to the invention of printing was never able to solve.[90] Since it was difficult to refer to some previous statement briefly and unambiguously, it always seemed safer for an author to repeat the same information as often as his exposition might require. In consequence, Ibn Khaldûn's style often appears to be redundant. It may even be said that the *Muqaddimah* could easily be reduced to about half its size and would then be a much more readable work, especially to readers unable to savor the richness of the original language or unwilling to follow all the nuances and subtle variations in the workings of a great scholar's mind.

Nevertheless, as a glance at the Table of Contents shows, the *Muqaddimah* is logically organized and follows its subject rigorously through to the end. The work begins with man's physical environment and its influence upon him, and his nonphysical characteristics. This is followed by a discussion of primitive social

[90] Cf. F. Rosenthal, *The Technique and Approach of Muslim Scholarship* (Analecta Orientalia, No. 24) (Rome, 1947), pp. 37 ff.

organization, the character of leadership in it, and the relationship of primitive human societies with each other, as well as their relationship to the higher, urban form of society. Then the government of the state, the highest form of human social organization, is discussed in general and that of the caliphate, the special Muslim case, in particular; this part includes a discussion of how changes come about in the dynasties charged with the administration of a given state. Then the author turns to urban life as the most developed form of human association and civilization. Finally, much space is devoted to higher civilization, to commerce, the crafts, and the sciences, considered both as conditions and consequences of urban life and, as such, indispensable for the understanding of history. A better form of presentation for Ibn Khaldûn's ideas and material could hardly be imagined.

As a scholarly craftsman, Ibn Khaldûn proves his mettle in miniature sketches of the historical development of the various crafts and sciences. His information, based upon his teachers' instruction, was rather restricted, especially in comparison with the vast amount of Arabic literature from all periods that the modern scholar has at his disposal. For the early epochs of Muslim literature, Ibn Khaldûn usually depended upon the traditional information contained in a few classics, without attempting to verify it, and he did not hesitate to jump from the oldest times directly to periods nearer his own. The results, therefore, often seem superficial and rather arbitrary to modern scholarship. They are, however, deceptively convincing, even though they do not always stand up to the scrutiny of a much later stage of scholarship, and thus testify to the insight, vigor, and skill of Ibn Khaldûn.

Another measure of Ibn Khaldûn's scholarly craftsmanship is the way he handles the quotations that he inserts in his work. They run the gamut from reliability to unreliability, from doubly checked, exact quotations to vague and inaccurate allusions from memory. At the one extreme, for instance, is the text of Ṭâhir's long *Epistle* to his son.[91] Ibn Khaldûn first quoted it from Ibn al-Athîr's *History*. Then he checked and corrected it, although, it seems, rather haphazardly, against the text quoted in the *Annals* by aṭ-Ṭabarî, whom he rightly held in the highest esteem.[92] The

[91] See 2:139 ff., below.

[92] Cf. *Autobiography*, p. 373; W. J. Fischel, *Ibn Khaldûn and Tamerlane*, pp. 37 f.

Annals do, in fact, contain the original text of Ṭâhir's *Epistle,* which Ibn al-Athîr had taken over into his work. Whenever Ibn Khaldûn doubted the reliability of his manuscript source for a quotation, he had no illusions about the matter, nor did he leave his readers in the dark.[93]

At the other extreme, there are general references that profess to indicate the contents of a work but fail to do so correctly. One such is the reference to a book by Ibn 'Arabî.[94] There are references that cannot be located, at least not at the place cited. These were clearly quotations from memory,[95] and even the best-trained memory cannot always be trusted. The circumstances under which the *Muqaddimah* was composed in the seclusion of Qal'at Ibn Salâmah, explain, of course, such lapses; but Ibn Khaldûn certainly had many opportunities later on to correct other quotations, as he corrected that of Ṭâhir's *Epistle,* and yet he failed to do so.

Further, there are summary references to a number of sources for the same subject, none of them quite accurate. There are quotations that reproduce their source exactly, and others that render the meaning of the source correctly but take some liberty in the wording, mainly by shortening the original. In general, Ibn Khaldûn most frequently used this last procedure, which the nature of his material demanded, in particular, in the historical presentation.

While the form of the *Muqaddimah* and the scholarly details of its composition are not without significance for the proper appreciation of the work and its author, its main interest is as a contribution to human thought. Brief summary of the contents hardly does it justice. Much of its value lies in the light it sheds upon details in Ibn Khaldûn's political, sociological, economic, and philosophic thinking. The complete text as provided in the following pages is a better guide to the meaning of the work than any summary presentation. Therefore, only a few leading ideas of Ibn Khaldûn's system are here singled out for remark.

The center of Ibn Khaldûn's world is man, in the same sense that for most Muslim historians and philosophers he is the center of speculation.

Greek geography as it had been transmitted to the Muslims

[93] See 3:183, below.

[94] See 2:187 ff., below.

[95] See, for instance, nn. 110, 1489, and 1502 to Ch. vi, below.

taught that man is dependent on his physical environment; it must provide physical conditions that enable him to sustain life. The extreme north and the extreme south are too cold or too hot for human beings to exist there. The best conditions are offered in the middle regions of the earth between its northern and southern extremes. The physical environment also influences man's character, his appearance, and his customs, in accordance with differences in the climate and fertility of given areas.[96]

Beyond man, there is the supernatural, which has many different manifestations. It extends from the sublime realm of the omnipotent, omniscient, and eternal Muslim Deity—for the supreme oneness and intellectuality of Graeco-Muslim philosophy had become hardly distinguishable from the monotheistic God—down to the most primitive magic and superstition. Ibn Khaldûn sincerely believed in the reality of all the supernatural's manifestations. Muslim religious tradition firmly supported him in this attitude; not only belief in the divine aspect of the supernatural, but also belief in magic, were parts of the religious credo, as the Qur'ân and alleged facts of Muḥammad's life both attest. The famous *Risâlah* of Ibn Abî Zayd al-Qayrawânî, a brief textbook on Mâlikite jurisprudence, for instance, presupposes the reality of sorcery, the evil eye, and the divinatory power of dreams. On the other hand, it repudiates astrology as being incompatible with Islam.[97] Ibn Khaldûn studied this work in his youth and almost certainly must have known it by heart.

---

[96] Cf. Ptolemy *Tetrabiblos* [Quadripartitum] ii. 2; ed. and tr. F. E. Robbins (Loeb Classical Library) (Cambridge, Mass. & London, 1940), pp. 120 f.

A. von Kremer, "Ibn Chaldun und seine Kulturgeschichte der islamischen Reiche," in *Sitzungs-Berichte der k. Akademie der Wissenschaften zu Wien*, XCIII (1879), 589 ff., referred to al-Jâḥiẓ in this connection. Cf. also al-Kindî, *Fî l-ibânah 'an al-'illah al-fâ'ilah al-qarîbah li-l-kawn wa-l-fasâd*, ed. M. 'A. Abû Rîdah in *Rasâ'il al-Kindî al-falsafîyah* (Cairo, 1369/1950), I, 224 ff.

From a later period one may, for instance, compare Rashîd-ad-dîn, *Ta'rîkh al-Ghâzânî* (photostat of an Istanbul MS in the Egyptian Library in Cairo, *ta'rîkh* 1889, p. 41): "In each zone there must be people who dwell in towns and people who dwell in deserts off by themselves, especially in countries where there are gardens and meadows and much water and splendid pastures and where there is no equal distribution of cultivated areas (*'imârât*)."

[97] Cf. Ibn Abî Zayd, *Risâlah*, ed. L. Bercher (Bibliothèque arabe-française) (3d ed.; Algiers, 1949), pp. 320 ff. Two of Ibn Khaldûn's early teachers, al-Wâdiyâshî and Ibn 'Abd-as-Salâm, taught him the *Risâlah*; cf. as-Sakhâwî, *aḍ-Ḍaw' al-lâmi'*, IX, 241.

However, despite his belief in the reality of the supernatural, Ibn Khaldûn relegated its influence to a realm outside of, or beyond, the ordinary course of human affairs. Magic and sorcery existed for him, though he contended that much fraud and sleight of hand enter into their actual practice, as he knew from his own experience and from hearsay. Astrology and alchemy, on the other hand, do not exist; their claims can be disproved by rational arguments. Notwithstanding the reality of some of the black arts, they do not interfere in the processes of human history and are in no way able to do so.

Similarly, Ibn Khaldûn restricted the influence of the Divine to the extraordinary in human affairs. It may manifest itself occasionally in psychological attitudes; for instance, psychological factors can be more decisive for the outcome of a battle than numbers and equipment. However, the divine influence on human affairs shows itself mainly in an unusual, rare "extra push," in the added impetus to greatness that it may provide. Religious fervor and the appearance of prophets, who, incidentally, cannot succeed in this world without concrete political support, can intensify and accelerate political movements. History offers instances of this, the most prominent one being the phenomenal, superhuman success of Islam.

Thus, supernatural influence upon human affairs in one way or another was for Ibn Khaldûn an established, indubitable fact. However, he thought of it as out of the ordinary and not as a necessity in the historical drama, the processes of which may go on unfolding without ever being disturbed by it. In this sense, Ibn Khaldûn's philosophy can be called secular, as scholars have occasionally described it. His secularism does not imply, however, any opposition to the supernatural world, let alone disavowal of it; to him its existence was as certain as anything observed by means of his senses. In his mind the only matter for inquiry was the degree of relationship between man and the supernatural. The civilization in which Ibn Khaldûn lived was permeated with a tradition of mysticism many centuries old. Ibn Khaldûn was inclined to consider constant and active contact with the Divine to be primarily the prerogative of the individual, and to acknowledge no more than a casual relationship between the supernatural and the forms of human social organization.

To explain the origins of human social organization, man's

first step in his historical career, Ibn Khaldûn adopted a theory that Muslim philosophy had already, fairly generally, accepted. As he himself tells us,[98] the view had developed in discussion of a particular religious problem, namely, that of the necessity of prophecy. But it is characteristic of the working of his mind, that Ibn Khaldûn generalized and secularized the applicability of this deeply pessimistic theory. Man, with his God-given power of thinking, is acknowledged to be at the pinnacle of an ascending world order which progresses from minerals, plants, and animals toward human beings. Basically, however, man is an animal, and human organization starts from the realization that, if left to his own animal instincts, man would eat man.[99]

Ibn Khaldûn found this theory expounded in two great works by Avicenna, the *Kitâb ash-Shifâ'* and its abridged version, the *Kitâb an-Najâh*.[100] A full elaboration appeared in the large philosophical encyclopedia compiled by the thirteenth-century writer ash-Shahrazûrî. In all probability, this work was never available to Ibn Khaldûn. Nonetheless, since ash-Shahrazûrî's statement is close to the spirit of Ibn Khaldûn's thinking, it is worth quoting here. As in Avicenna's works, the theory of the origins of human social organization is presented in the form of premises for proving the existence of prophecy: [101]

(1) The individual human being cannot accomplish all the things that are necessary for his livelihood, unless he has co-operation from someone else. He needs food, clothing, shelter, and weapons, not only for himself, but also for his wives, his children, his servants, and his dependent

---

[98] See p. 79 and 2:417, below.

[99] A Mâlikite scholar of northwestern Africa, al-Qâbisî, quotes the seventh-century Ibn Mas'ûd as saying, "Men need three things: (1) a ruler to decide their differences, for without one, each would eat the other. . . ." Cf. A. F. al-Ahwânî, *at-Ta'lîm fî ra'y al-Qâbisî* (Cairo, 1364/1945), p. 270.

[100] Cf. M. Horten, *Die Metaphysik Avicennas* (Halle & New York, 1907), pp. 673 f., for the *Kitâb ash-Shifâ'*; and Avicenna, *Kitâb an-Najâh* (Rome, 1593), p. 84. For references from Greek and Arabic literature in this connection, see D. Santillana, *Istituzioni di diritto musulmano malichita* (Rome, [1926]–38), I, 10 (n. 57). A brief statement by Ibn Taymîyah along the same lines, from his *Ḥisbah fî l-Islâm* (Cairo, 1318/1900–1901), p. 3, was also quoted in connection with Ibn Khaldûn by H. A. R. Gibb, "The Islamic Background of Ibn Khaldûn's Political Theory," in *Bulletin of the School of Oriental Studies*, VII (1933), 23–31.

[101] As-Shahrazûrî, *ash-Shajarah al-ilâhîyah*, quoted from the Istanbul MS, Topkapusaray, Ahmet III, 3227, fol. 501*a*.

relatives. All the things mentioned are technical matters. In order to learn them, a man by himself would require a longer time than the time he could keep alive without these things. Assuming that he could (somehow manage) to live (on his own), it would be (only) with great difficulty and trouble. He would not be able to obtain the various kinds of intellectual perfection (that are the goal of humanity). Thus, of necessity there must exist a group the members of which co-operate to acquire many different crafts and (technical) skills. In this way, each individual accomplishes something from which his fellow men can profit. Full co-operation will (in this way) materialize, and the life of the human species and of other animal species will reach perfection. . . . The sages called this social organization "urbanization" (*tamaddun*, from Greek πόλις, town). Therefore, they said "man is political by nature." (This is to be understood) in the sense that he needs this kind of social organization in order to live, to provide for his own livelihood, to improve his situation in this world, and to perfect his soul for the next world.

(II) The proper order of such social organization, which is political and based upon co-operation, can materialize only when there exists mutual intercourse governed by justice among the people, because (otherwise) each individual would want all the needed benefits for himself and would come to grief in conflict with the others competing with him for them. . . .

(III) This religious law must have (as its founder) a person who lays down all these general norms. . . .

In contrast to ash-Shahrazûrî, Ibn Khaldûn does not consider religious inspiration a requirement for the person charged with keeping people from devouring each other. Any individual in a position to exercise a restraining influence upon his fellow men will do; besides, on the highest moral plane, there exist individuals with native ability for such a role in society. A person with such restraining influence upon others is called *wâzi'* by Ibn Khaldûn. The term, and the idea implied, is borrowed from the literature of traditions (of the Prophet and the early Muslims). According to this literature, al-Ḥasan (al-Baṣrî), upon being appointed judge, had remarked that people cannot do without *wâzi'*s; one of the explanations for *wâzi'* in this context is "the ruler and his men who keep the people apart." [102]

[102] Cf. Majd-ad-dîn Ibn al-Athîr, *Nihâyah* (Cairo, 1322/1904), IV, 221; *Lisân al-'Arab* (Bulaq, 1300–1308/1882–90), X, 270. Another of the traditions quoted in these works reads: "The restraining influence of the government is more widely effective than that of the Qur'ân." Ascribed to the caliph

The ability to think, God's special gift to man, is the particular human quality or innate gift that enables human beings to co-operate. Among the other animals, co-operation can be observed only on a very restricted scale. As a rule they are stronger than man, because they possess sharp teeth, claws, etc. To compensate man for lacking this type of physical endowment, he was given the ability to think, and his hands serve him as skillful instruments for executing his ideas.

As soon as several human beings, with their God-given power of thinking, begin to co-operate with each other and to form some kind of social organization, *'umrân* results. *'Umrân* (translated here as "civilization") is one of the key terms in Ibn Khaldûn's system. It is derived from a root which means "to build up, to cultivate," and is used to designate any settlement above the level of individual savagery. In Ibn Khaldûn's time and place, ruins left by many great and prosperous cities attested to the prior existence of high civilization; it could be seen that large agglomerations of human beings had been stopped in their growth and expansion by geographical factors. Thus, Ibn Khaldûn naturally arrived at the idea (which, incidentally, seems to be by and large correct) that progress in civilization is in direct proportion to the number of people co-operating for their common good. Thus, *'umrân* ac-

---

'Uthmân, this remark appears as early as the ninth-century *Kitâb al-Kuttâb* of 'Abdallâh al-Baghdâdî, ed. D. Sourdel in *Bulletin d'Etudes Orientales* (Damascus), XIV (1954), 142. Its application to political theory was discussed in the tenth century by Muḥammad b. Yûsuf al-'Âmirî in his *I'lâm bi-manâqib al-Islâm* (MS, Istanbul, Ragib 1463, fol. 18*b*). Cf. *The Islamic Quarterly*, III (1956), 51. In the work of a Spanish author known to Ibn Khaldûn, Ibn Bassâm, the remark is ascribed to al-Ḥasan b. Abî l-Ḥasan al-Baṣrî (d. *ca.* 728). Cf. his *Dhakhîrah* (Cairo, 1361/1942), I², 9. The *waza'ah* (pl. of *wâzi'*) function as a kind of truant officers sent after mischievous boys in a story from the *Kitâb al-Aghânî* (Bulaq, 1285/1868), XVIII, 124. Cf. also ash-Sharîshî, *Sharḥ al-Maqâmât* (Cairo 1306/1889), I, 143.

For the person who has the restraining influence in himself, earlier authors did not use the root *wz'* but similar roots such as *w'ẓ* and *zjr;* cf. al-Jâḥiẓ, *Bukhalâ'* (Cairo, 1948), p. 173; tr. C. Pellat (Beirut & Paris, 1951), p. 274; and al-Mâwardî, *al-Aḥkâm as-sulṭânîyah* (Cairo, 1298/1881), Ch. XVI, p. 180. Al-Mâwardî says that scholars have a restraining influence in themselves (*zâjir min nafsihî*) which prevents them from sitting down in seats belonging to more distinguished and deserving scholars. According to a tradition quoted by al-Ghazzâlî, *Iḥyâ'* (Cairo, 1352/1933), III, 10, the possession of a restraining influence in one's heart (*wâ'iẓ min qalbihî*) is a gift of God. *Zâjir min nafsihî*, in connection with teachers, is also used by Ibn Khaldûn, p. 452, l. 12, below.

quired the further meaning of "population," and Ibn Khaldûn frequently uses the word in this sense. Wherever people are co-operating with each other, no matter on how limited a scale, there is *'umrân*. When the number of these people increases, a larger and better *'umrân* results. This growth in numbers, with a corresponding progress in civilization, finally culminates in the highest form of sedentary culture man is able to achieve; it declines from this peak when the number of co-operating people decreases.

The two fundamentally different environments in which all human co-operation takes place and the forms of social organization develop, were distinguished by Ibn Khaldûn as "desert, desert life" (*badâwah,* cf. Bedouins) and "town, sedentary environment." The literal translation of *badâwah* and cognate words by "desert (Bedouins)" requires some explanation, as it only partially expresses the concept Ibn Khaldûn had in mind when he used these words. Ibn Khaldûn was familiar with the essential characteristics of nomadism, and often stressed the detriment to higher civilization inherent in the Bedouin way of life. In this connection, he used *badâwah* to express the concept of nomadism. However, in Arabic as spoken outside the Arabian peninsula, the term *badâwah* was applied to the largely sedentary rural people living at some distance from the great population centers, and Ibn Khaldûn preferably used it in this sense. Thus, by referring to "desert, Bedouins" and "settled area, sedentary urban people," Ibn Khaldûn did not consciously make a distinction between nomadism and sedentary life as sociological phenomena. He simply grouped together nomads and (sedentary) backwoods people, on the one hand, and contrasted them with sedentary urban people as inhabitants of large population centers, on the other. Ibn Khaldûn's "Bedouins" were not, as a rule, nomads living in the desert, but dwelt chiefly in villages, and practiced agriculture and animal husbandry for a livelihood. It must also not be forgotten that, in Ibn Khaldûn's experience, the term "urban population" did not have the same meaning as it has today. Cities in his day permitted, and required, a good deal of agricultural activity. In Ibn Khaldûn's thinking, the sociological distinction amounts to no more than a quantitative distinction as to the size and density of human settlements.

The question arises: What causes differences in the size of human settlements? If all the elements in nature existed in the same quantity and strength, none greater or lesser, stronger or weaker, than another, there would be no mixture, no creation nor generation. Correspondingly, did all human beings share equally the urge and need for co-operation, there would be no difference in the quality or size of the resulting human social organizations. There must be some factor that causes such differences as do exist, some incitement for the desire for co-operation to exist on a larger scale among some human beings than among others. Only thus can large states have originated.

That some such factor exists, Ibn Khaldûn recognized and called *'aṣabîyah* "group feeling." [103] Arab lexicographers correctly connect the term with the word *'aṣabah* "agnates." Thus, it originally signified something like "making common cause with one's agnates." [104] However, in Ibn Khaldûn's mind the term appears to have been associated with the related words *'iṣâbah* and Qur'ânic *'uṣbah,* both meaning "group" in a more general sense.[105] The group with which a human being feels most closely connected is primarily that of his relatives, the people with whom he shares a common descent. But as a feeling and a state of mind the *'aṣabîyah* can also be shared by people not related to each other by blood ties but by long and close contact as members of a group.

Ibn Khaldûn's use of the term is noteworthy because it has been much used in Muslim literature in a different meaning. Islam generally condemned *'aṣabîyah* as a quality and state of mind. It is traditionally considered to mean "bias," or, more specifically, blind support of one's group without regard for the justice of its cause.[106] As such, any show of *'aṣabîyah* is depreciated as an atavistic survival of the pagan, pre-Islamic mentality. Ibn Khaldûn, of course, was fully aware of this customary usage. In a *locus classicus* [107] he discriminates between an objectionable pagan *'aṣabîyah* and "the na-

---

[103] There has been considerable discussion among modern scholars as to the meaning of *'aṣabîyah.* We may mention here only F. Gabrieli, "Il concetto della 'aṣabiyyah nel pensiero storico di Ibn Ḫaldûn," in *Atti della R. Accademia delle scienze di Torino, Classe di scienze morali, storiche e filologiche,* LXV (1930), 473–512; and, most recently, H. Ritter, "Irrational Solidarity Groups, a Socio-Psychological Study in Connection with Ibn Khaldûn," in *Oriens,* I (1948), 1–44.

[104] Cf. *Lisân al-'Arab,* II, 96.

[105] See p. 263, below, and F. Gabrieli, p. 474 (n. 1).

[106] The historian aṭ-Ṭabarî also uses the term in the meaning of "tribal unrest." Cf. his *Annales,* ed. M. J. de Goeje *et al.* (Leiden, 1879–1901), III, 624; Glossary, p. CCCLXIV.

[107] *'Ibar,* III, 3. See also pp. 414 f., below.

tural *'aṣabîyah* that is inseparable (from human beings). The latter is the affection a man feels for a brother or a neighbor when one of them is treated unjustly or killed. Nothing can take it away. It is not forbidden (by Muslim religious law). On the contrary, it is something desirable and useful in connection with the holy war and with propaganda for Islam."

There are a few passages in other writers where *'aṣabîyah* is similarly spoken of as a praiseworthy quality. Thus, from his own reading, Ibn Khaldûn knew that on one occasion the historian Ibn al-Athîr employed *'aṣabîyah* in the meaning of "giving helpful group support to anyone who needed and claimed it." [108] He was also aware that *'aṣabîyah* could be applied to praiseworthy emotions, e.g. patriotism, in which case, as Ibn al-Khaṭîb had said,[109] *'aṣabîyah* was then inoffensive to either religion or worldly rank. Still, it cannot as yet be determined just how original and daring Ibn Khaldûn was when he gave the term the positive meaning he did. It is uncertain to what degree he may have followed the example of the intellectual circle in which he moved, and whose backing he received. Jurisprudence stressed the privileged position agnates had in many respects, but it remains to be seen whether the juridical literature ever discussed the abstract concept of *'aṣabîyah* in this context. Possibly, Ibn Khaldûn got some support from this quarter.[110] At any rate, so far as our present knowledge goes, it seems that his use of the term *'aṣabîyah* in so positive a sense is his most original single intellectual contribution to the *Muqaddimah*.

Preponderance of *'aṣabîyah* renders one group superior to others; it also determines leadership within a given group. The leading or ruling element within one or more groups will be that person or, more frequently, that family, the importance and rami-

---

[108] Cf. *'Ibar*, V, 237, following Ibn al-Athîr, *Kâmil* (Cairo, 1302/1885), XI, 49, *anno* 541.

[109] Ibn al-Khaṭîb, *al-Iḥâṭah*, I, 7, and cf. also I, 100. A similar application of *'aṣabîyah* is found in al-Mubashshir, *Mukhtâr al-ḥikam* (Madrid, 1958), p. 41. Cf. F. Rosenthal, "Arabische Nachrichten über Zenon den Eleaten," in *Orientalia*, N.S. VI (1937), 33 f. Further examples of *'aṣabîyah* in connection with praiseworthy aspirations are found in Yâqût, *Irshâd*, ed. Margoliouth (E. J. W. Gibb Memorial Series, No. 6) (Leiden & London, 1907–27), I, 77; II, 157; (Cairo, 1355–57), II, 129; V, 155; however, in such cases, *ta'aṣṣub* is often used. * Al-Qifṭî, *Inbâh*, II, 242; aṣ-Ṣafadî, *Wâfî*, IV, 335.

[110] Cf. D. Santillana, *Istituzioni di diritto musulmano malichita*, II, 514: ". . . *'aṣabah* 'agnates,' derived from *'aṣaba*, 'to surround, fortify,' because, as the jurists say, the agnates surround a man and give him strength."

fications of whose blood relationships give them the strongest and most natural claim to control of the available *'aṣabîyahs*. And no group can retain its predominance, nor any leader his dominant position in the group, when their former *'aṣabîyah* is no longer there to support them.

The leader who controls an *'aṣabîyah* of sufficient strength and importance may succeed in founding a dynasty and in winning *mulk,* "royal authority," for himself and his family. In Ibn Khaldûn's vocabulary, the word for both "dynasty" and "state" is *dawlah,* although the idea of "state" also finds approximate expression in the occasional use of such terms as *amr* and *kalimah.*[111] In Ibn Khaldûn's view of history, according to which the whole world and everything in it depends upon man, there is no room for an abstract concept of "the state." A state exists only in so far as it is held together and ruled by individuals and the group which they constitute, that is, the dynasty. When the dynasty disappears, the state, being identical with it, also comes to an end.

According to Ibn Khaldûn, the described process of the formation of states does not apply to the early Muslim state. Early Muslim history, with its concept of a pure, unworldly type of state, represented by the first four caliphs, must be considered an exception to the law of *'aṣabîyah* that governs the formation of states in general. However, this particular case represents one of the rare interventions of the supernatural in human affairs. Therefore, Ibn Khaldûn was able to follow the orthodox Muslim view of early Islamic history (and of the recurrence of the early conditions at a later date in the days of the Mahdî as well), and felt justified in dealing extensively with the caliphate and its institutions, even though they were, for him, entirely atypical.

Since the founding of a dynasty or state involves large numbers of people, it is, of necessity, linked to the most developed stage of *'umrân,* that in which it becomes *ḥaḍârah* "sedentary culture." A dynasty requires large cities and towns and makes their existence possible; in turn, they permit the development of luxury. Accord-

[111] *Amr* is a word of many meanings, the principal ones being "command" and "matter." *Kalimah* means "word." In this context, the meaning of either word would seem to be something like "the whole business." *Kalimah* is commonly used in Muslim literature in this sense. It may have gained this meaning from "word" coming to mean "thing," a transition in meaning known from other Semitic languages. Therefore, *kalimah* has usually been translated in the following pages "the whole thing."

ing to the philosophic ideas mentioned above as to the origins of man's social organization, all human activities are undertaken to enable the individual to preserve his life and to secure his livelihood. To that end, each man has to contribute his labor, which is his only basic capital, to satisfy the fundamental needs of his group. When there is a large number of human beings, a large amount of labor, even an excess supply of it, becomes available. A certain amount of labor may then be channeled into the production of things and the provision of services that are scarcely necessities but may be called "conveniences." Finally, the available pool of excess manpower is large enough to permit the cultivation of crafts that serve no actual need but are concerned with mere luxuries.[112] Once this stage in the development of civilization is reached, man is able to develop the sciences which, although they do not produce any material object or immediate gain, nonetheless constitute fulfillment of mankind's higher and truly human aspirations in the domains of the spirit and the intellect.

This development towards luxury carries its own penalty with it in the form of causing degeneration. The pristine simplicity and rudeness of manners (often called "desert life" and "desert attitude") that flourished in small human organizations, become corroded.[113] Obviously, Ibn Khaldûn had a lingering and rather

---

[112] Ibn Khaldûn's three steps: necessities, conveniences, and luxuries, correspond to Vico's six steps: "Men first feel necessity, then look for utility, next attend to comfort, still later amuse themselves with pleasure, thence grow dissolute in luxury, and finally go mad and waste their substance." Cf. G. Vico, *The New Science*, tr. T. G. Bergin and M. H. Fisch (Ithaca, N. Y., 1948), p. 70. Cf. also Ibn Khaldûn's five stages in the life of dynasties, pp. 353 ff., below.

[113] Again, Vico (*loc. cit.*) agrees with Ibn Khaldûn: "The nature of peoples is first crude, then severe, then benign, then delicate, finally dissolute."

Al-Mubashshir b. Fâtik, whose *Mukhtâr al-ḥikam*, an anthology of the sayings of the ancient sages, was very popular in Spain—if not in Ibn Khaldûn's time, at any rate a century earlier—attributes the following saying to Plato (No. 400 of Plato's sayings, quoted from the edition of the *Mukhtâr* prepared by me = ed. Badawî [Madrid, 1958], p. 176):

"Great dynasties are tough of nature at the beginning, able to cope with realities and obedient to God and civil authority. Later on, towards the end of their course [?], when the security of the people has been assured, the latter begin to participate in the well-being that has been prepared for them. Then, submerged in the life of abundance and ease which the dynasty has made possible, they give themselves over to luxury and no longer come to the support (of the regime when it needs them). They are so affected by this course of events that eventually they lack the power to defend themselves against

sentimental admiration for "the good old days" when Arab civilization was imbued with the desert attitude. However, he fully recognized the superiority of sedentary culture, the goal of all of man's efforts to become civilized, and was resigned to the inevitability of the development leading to and past it.

The principal victim of this inevitable tendency towards luxury is state and dynasty. Like an individual, the dynasty is endowed with a natural span of life. It runs its full course in three generations—"from shirt-sleeves to shirt-sleeves," so to speak. It passes from obscurity through power and wealth back into obscurity. Three interrelated factors produce this development and accelerate the eventual "senile decay" of the dynasty: indulgence in luxury, loss of *'aṣabîyah*, and financial trouble.[114] The desire of the ruling group to gain exclusive control over all the sources of power and wealth brings about strained relations and, eventually, a fatal estrangement between the dynasty and the men whose *'aṣabîyah* supports and maintains it. Its members thus come to need military support from outside sources, and must have money to procure it. Further, their growing addiction to luxurious habits also requires more and more money. To raise the needed sums, they must increase the tax load and try to open up new sources of revenue. Finally, the point of diminishing returns is reached in tax collections and other schemes for securing added revenues.

As a jurist, Ibn Khaldûn was naturally much interested in questions of government finance and business matters. The Muslim legal and economic literature in our possession clearly reflects the great practical importance assigned these questions in juridical activity. Yet, this literature is dominated by theoretical considera-

attack. When this has occurred, the power of the dynasty crumbles at the first assault. Dynasties are like fruits: too firm to be eaten at the beginning, they are of middling quality as they grow riper. Once they are fully ripened they taste good, but now they have come as close as fruits can come to rottenness and change."

[114] Cf. the saying ascribed to Plato in al-Mubashshir b. Fâtik, *Mukhtâr al-ḥikam*, No. 148 of Plato's sayings; cf. H. Knust, *Mittheilungen aus dem Eskurial* (Bibliothek des Litterarischen Vereins in Stuttgart, No. 141) (Tübingen, 1879), p. 224 ed. Badawî (Madrid, 1958), p.149:

"Dynasties begin young, grow to adulthood, and pass into their dotage. When the dynasty's income is greater than the ruler and his followers merit, the dynasty is young and promises to endure. When the income becomes equal to the need, the dynasty has reached self-contained adulthood. And when the income falls below what is needed, the dynasty has entered upon its second childhood."

tions and is greatly inclined to follow traditional forms. It is far from containing complete information about the innumerable aspects of financial and economic life that occupied the day-by-day attention of lawyers and jurists and were discussed in academic legal circles. Written formulations of legal questions were largely obliged to follow theoretical lines; practical economic and financial matters were not considered worthy of being treated in books. Thus, Ibn Khaldûn's attention to practical questions in a literary work showed admirable boldness. He succeeded in giving a picture of the role of capital and labor in society that not only does credit to his acumen, but bears witness to the high level the legal circles of his time had reached in their understanding of these matters.

In the course of its rapid progress toward senility and final collapse, the dynasty loses control of its own destiny. Often the ruler becomes a ruler in name only, controlled by some outsider who is not a member of the dynasty but who wields the actual power. However, there are limitations to the outsider's sway since no *'aṣabîyah* ("group feeling") sustains him. Thus, as a rule, he is unable to take over complete authority; eventually he may supersede the dynasty by founding one of his own. To achieve this, however, the challenging person or group must be fired and propelled by possession of a new *'aṣabîyah.*

All dynastic history moves in circles. As it approaches senility, the dynasty slowly shrinks inwards from its borders toward its center, under the persistent pressure of the new "outside" leader and his group. Eventually, the ruling dynasty collapses. The new leader and his group thereupon constitute a new dynasty, which takes power—only to suffer, in three more generations, the fate of its predecessors.

Here, another problem arises. How, under these conditions, can the survival of any higher civilization be explained? In the first place, there is the great and inevitable attraction of a higher civilization for people on a lower level. Defeated peoples always show a strong tendency towards imitating the customs of their conquerors in every detail. While still struggling against the ruling dynasty, and during the first period of their power after having displaced it, the less civilized groups take over some of the advantages of civilization that the ruling dynasty had possessed. Thus, they do not start completely afresh, and some of the gains of the older civilization, at least, are preserved. Ibn Khaldûn's answer to the problem of how all higher civilization is preserved lies in the word *malakah* "habit." *Malakah* is a loan-translation of the Greek ἕξις, which also was translated into the Latin *habitus*, from which our "habit" is derived.[115] Through continuous repetition, an individual may master a craft or a science, thus making it his "habit." This even explains the knowledge of the Arabic language with which the Arabs of former times were born, but which had to be acquired as a "habit" by later generations. Once a person has acquired the "habit" of a craft or science, it is difficult, if not impossible, for him to master another; but mastery of the first habit remains with him permanently. Since the acquisition of habits is a matter of education, they can be passed on to others who aspire to them, provided that proper methods of education and instruction are known and that their exercise does not lapse during political upheavals. Thus, we have an explanation for the survival of past civilizations, though it may manifest itself only in minor remnants and in certain customs and practices that can be recognized as cultural survivals only by the trained observer.

In Ibn Khaldûn's orthodox Muslim environment, it was believed that human intellectual power was always constant and capable of producing the highest civilization at any given time. Therefore, Ibn Khaldûn could hardly have assumed that steady progress in human civilization was possible or even necessary. There was, however, another widespread popular notion in his time. Nations of earlier times were believed to have been better endowed physically for achieving a high and materially splendid civilization than contemporary nations. Ibn Khaldûn felt compelled to refute this notion as emphatically as possible. In his opinion it was merely the decay of political organization and the power of government that gave his contemporaries the impression that the civilization of their day was inferior to that of the past. In fact, in Ibn Khaldûn's thinking, there could be no essential difference between the faculties and achievements of former and contemporary generations, for political and cultural life was moving in never-ending, always repeated circles.

After this brief survey of some leading ideas in the *Muqaddimah*, we may ask what the sources are from which Ibn Khaldûn

[115] Cf. S. Munk, *Mélanges de philosophie juive et arabe* (Paris, 1859), p. 450 (n. 1). The same word *malakah* is also used by Ibn Khaldûn in a different meaning as a technical term, "rulership." See p. 383, below.

drew inspiration and information for his comprehensive picture of human society. He himself acknowledged his great indebtedness to the Muslim literature of political administration and the *Fürstenspiegel.* In particular, he referred to al-Mâwardî's *Aḥkâm as-sulṭânîyah,* a rather theoretical compilation of basic data on political law and administration, and to the *Fürstenspiegel* of the Spaniard aṭ-Ṭurṭûshî, a mediocre achievement compared with other works of its kind but still containing much relevant material. Ibn Khaldûn's references to these two works seem to be from memory: he certainly was familiar with their contents, but he may not have looked into them for some years when he composed the *Muqaddimah.* In addition to this type of works whose general influence he rightly stressed, Ibn Khaldûn often indicates the sources from which he derived specific pieces of information.

Much of his material and many of his best ideas Ibn Khaldûn owed to his juridical training. In particular, discussions of legal matters with his teachers, fellow students, and colleagues must have contributed greatly to his knowledge. A search for other works in which the material of such oral discussions might have been preserved would not, presumably, be too successful. For, as stated before, Muslim juridical literature is predominantly theoretical in spirit and traditional in form; furthermore, manuscript literature in general is selective and reluctant to admit new disciplines or topics. Each new written work must repeat all or nearly all of the material previously known, else that material would be lost. For all these reasons, we should not expect to find many echoes of the oral exchange of ideas between Ibn Khaldûn and his friends, or among lawyers of other periods, in the legal literature.

Moreover, owing to well-known historical circumstances, the amount of Arabic literature from Spain and northwest Africa still extant is proportionally much smaller than that of the Muslim East. We know very little of the Western writings of Ibn Khaldûn's time or from the period immediately preceding.[116] Under these circumstances, we should perhaps be justified in assuming that practically every matter of detail found in the *Muqaddimah* was probably not original with Ibn Khaldûn, but had been previously expressed elsewhere. Even his characterization of *'aṣabîyah* as a positive factor in society, or his demand for knowledge of social

[116] A considerable proportion of the surviving literature is very imperfectly known and has yet to be published.

conditions as prerequisite to the historian's correct evaluation of historical information, although seemingly original ideas, may have been inspired by a source yet to be rediscovered.

Our evidence does not permit us to attribute a great amount of originality to Ibn Khaldûn so far as the details of his work are concerned. Yet, he was right when he claimed that the *Muqaddimah* was profoundly original and constituted a new departure in scholarly research. Its originality in the intellectual sense is obvious. The *Muqaddimah* re-evaluates, in an altogether unprecedented way, practically every single individual manifestation of a great and highly developed civilization. It accomplishes this both comprehensively and in detail in the light of one fundamental and sound insight, namely, by considering everything as a function of man and human social organization.

How Ibn Khaldûn conceived this idea is a question that will probably never be answered, at least not until we learn much more about the workings of the minds of exceptionally gifted individuals. The circumstances of his life gave him the external qualifications needed for the writing of a work like the *Muqaddimah,* and there were other factors that created a favorable atmosphere for its production. It is true that Ibn Khaldûn used comparatively few direct examples from contemporary history. This fact becomes still more apparent if one compares the *Muqaddimah* with Machiavelli's *Il Principe* (though the two works are so different in scope and outlook that they should hardly be mentioned in the same breath). The *Principe* is full of events its author had witnessed in his own time, while Ibn Khaldûn was more used to deductive than to inductive reasoning. Moreover, as an active politician, he probably felt it necessary to exercise the greatest care in interpreting contemporary events while the chief actors were still alive or while their power remained with their descendants. However, he had wide political experience and a happy ability to view the contemporary political happenings of northwestern Africa with the detachment of a spiritual foreigner, forever comparing them in his own mind with the greatness of his own Spanish homeland.[117]

But surely there must have been others, perhaps many others, who were similarly situated, and yet did not write a *Muqaddimah.*

[117] See p. xxxvi, above. It may be noted that Ibn Khaldûn had a very low opinion of Abû Bakr, the Ḥafṣid during whose reign he was born, and did not trouble to conceal it.

As it is, we can hardly do better than to state simply that here was a man with a great mind, who combined action with thought, the heir to a great civilization that had run its course, and the inhabitant of a country with a living historical tradition—albeit reduced to remnants of its former greatness—who realized his own gifts and the opportunities of his historical position in a work that ranks as one of mankind's important triumphs.

The Textual History of the *Muqaddimah*

1. MANUSCRIPTS

THE TEXT of the *Muqaddimah* is very well attested and documented. Few, if any, works written before modern times can boast of being as well represented by manuscripts. Four manuscripts written during Ibn Khaldûn's lifetime exist in Turkey alone. Two undated ones also exist, which were written, at the latest, shortly after his death. Manuscripts written during an author's lifetime may, of course, contain an inferior text, but in this particular case the quality of the old manuscripts is, in general, very high. One of them (A) is a copy presented to the library of the ruler of Egypt, apparently by Ibn Khaldûn himself. Another (B) was written under Ibn Khaldûn's eye by his proven amanuensis (who may also have been a friend and admirer). A third copy (C) bears testimony to its accuracy in Ibn Khaldûn's own hand.

All these manuscripts have the same textual value that, in the period after the invention of printing, would be ascribed to a book printed under its author's supervision. There may be occasional mistakes, but a carefully written manuscript usually compares favorably with a printed text. Most manuscripts of this type may be confidently regarded as authentic copies of the text, and any factual mistakes or miswritings they contain may be considered the author's own.

Under these circumstances, we should expect the variant readings to be comparatively few and insignificant. Collation shows this to be, indeed, the case. There do exist a great number of very considerable variations among the texts, but these are not variant readings in the ordinary sense. They are additions and corrections made by Ibn Khaldûn at different periods of his life. The existence of such extensive emendations demonstrates in a fascinating manner that the medieval author worked much as his modern colleague does. Once the text of the *Muqaddimah* is established with the help of the extant manuscripts, the principal result will be found to be the light it throws upon the history of the text in the hands of its author.

In translating the *Muqaddimah* a certain amount of duplication is unavoidably caused by the existence of an earlier and a later text. Though it would be desirable to translate all variations of the different texts known to have been seen by the author, such an undertaking is impracticable, if not impossible, for a work as long as the *Muqaddimah*. But the manuscript evidence of the *Muqaddimah* also shows that, basically, the text of the work is well established and utterly reliable for purposes of translation.

The excellent quality of the Arabic text of the *Muqaddimah* has often been doubted by Western scholars, but it is an indisputable fact. Such textual difficulties as do occur would not, in any case, be cleared up by a complete collation of manuscripts. In preparing this translation, I have therefore collated only some of the outstanding ones. An exhaustive utilization of all the manuscripts can be expected in the forthcoming edition of the *Muqaddimah* by Muḥammad Tâwît aṭ-Ṭanjî, who has already published the text of Ibn Khaldûn's *Autobiography*.[118] Since aṭ-Ṭanjî has traveled widely in search of *Muqaddimah* manuscripts, his edition will surely make it possible to elucidate their interrelationship and to clear up the many problems connected with their history.

The following remarks should be considered as entirely provisional, pending the appearance of aṭ-Ṭanjî's edition. Earlier scholars who have dealt with the manuscripts of Ibn Khaldûn[119] have often had to rely upon incomplete or secondhand information, and therefore their statements are sometimes more than a bit confused. In order to avoid this danger so far as is within my abilities, I have restricted myself to manuscripts that I have seen myself, with the single exception of the Fez manuscript. Needless to say, my remarks are subject to such revision as a more thorough

---

118 See n. 2, above.

119 Pioneer work was done by N. Schmidt in *Journal of the American Oriental Society*, XLVI (1926), 171–76; M. Plessner in *Islamica*, IV (1931), 538–42; and Claude Cahen in *Revue des études islamiques*, X (1936), 351 f. The important listing of *Muqaddimah* MSS in *GAL*, II, 245; 2d ed., II, 316; *Suppl.*, II, 343, must also be mentioned. For MSS and editions of Ibn Khaldûn's work, one may further compare G. Gabrieli, "Saggi di bibliografia e concordanza della Storia d'Ibn Ḫaldûn," in *Rivista degli studi orientali*, X (1924), 169–211. * Cf. Badawî, *Mu'allafât Ibn Khaldûn* (Cairo, 1962).

study of the manuscripts than I was able to undertake may one day make possible.

During my stay in Turkey in the summer of 1952, I consulted the following manuscripts of the *Muqaddimah:*

LIBRARY WHERE LOCATED (*In Istanbul unless otherwise noted*)	MS DESIGNATION
Süleymaniye	Esad 2418
	Damad Ibrahim 863
	Reis el-küttap (=Aşir I) 679
	Halet Eff. 617
Nuru Osmaniye	3423
	3424
	3065
	3066
	3067
	3069
	3070
Topkapusaray	Ahmet III, 3042
Atif Effendi	1936
Ragib Paşa	978
Murad Molla	Hamidiye 982
Millet Library	Hekimoğlu Ali Paşa 805
University Library	MS. ar. 2743
Orhan Cami, Bursa (Brussa)	Hüseyin Celebi 793 [120]

The large number of manuscripts of the *Muqaddimah* in Turkey reflects the great interest of the Ottoman Turks.[121] From this point of view, practically all the manuscripts are of considerable historical import. Here, however, only the oldest and best manuscripts will be briefly described. The letters in the margin are the sigla by which the manuscripts will be designated whenever they are referred to.

A (1) MS. Damad Ibrahim 863. The manuscript contains 433 folios and is not dated. It clearly seems to have been written by the same hand that wrote MS. Damad Ibrahim 867, which contains the

[120] Another MS of the *Muqaddimah* in Turkey (which I was unable to examine) is at Gülşehri, in the library of Kara Vezir Mehmet Paşa. Cf. *Une liste des manuscrits choisis parmi les bibliothèques de Kayseri, Akşehir, Bor, Gülşehri, Nevşehir, Niğde, Ürgüp, publiée à l'occasion du XXII. Congrès International des Orientalistes* (Istanbul, 1951), p. 11.

[121] See p. lxvii, above.

sixth part of the *'Ibar*. The latter manuscript is dated Ṣafar 4, 797 [November 29, 1394]. The scribe gives his name as 'Abdallâh b. Ḥasan b. Shihâb, a name strangely similar to that of the scribe of our manuscript B of the *Muqaddimah*. But the handwriting is entirely different, so that there is no possibility that the scribes could be identical; this seems anyhow unlikely.

As in some other manuscripts, the text of A is distributed over two parts with separate title pages and tables of contents. Part One contains the beginning, up to and including chapter three, while Part Two contains the rest of the work.

The title page informs us that the manuscript was written for the library of Ibn Khaldûn's patron, the Mameluke ruler al-Malik aẓ-Ẓâhir, with the given name of Barqûq (1382–99).[122] In the manuscript (fols. 7*b* ff.), the work itself is dedicated to Barqûq in a long and sincerely affectionate dedication. Ibn Khaldûn even changes its title to include the name of his benefactor: *aẓ-Ẓâhirî fî l-'ibar bi-akhbâr al-'Arab wa-l-'Ajam wa-l-Barbar*; also, at the end of the first part (fol. 235*a*) and at the end of the second part, reference is again made to the new title *aẓ-Ẓâhirî*. This is further evidence that the manuscript was written during Barqûq's lifetime. It is less easy to understand why manuscript B, which was also written during Barqûq's life, makes no mention either of the title *aẓ-Ẓâhirî* or of the dedication of the work to him. On the other hand, it is not difficult to see why the manuscript sent to Fez refrained from advertising Ibn Khaldûn's renaming of the work.

Manuscript A, the oldest of the preserved manuscripts, is not the best among them. Both B and C are superior to it. A appears to have been written by a professional copyist. The text is nonetheless reliable and comes as close to being the equivalent of a published edition of a modern author as any work of the manuscript age. A copy of A formed the basis of Quatremère's edition of the *Muqaddimah*, which thus has the most solid basis that the great French scholar, almost a hundred years ago, could have hoped for.

(2) Another manuscript, written in 798 [1396], is the famous copy of the *Muqaddimah* at Fez. For a long time there has been a sort of mystery around it that is only now beginning to be solved. Much has been written about it in the scholarly literature. Brief

---

122 See pp. lix ff., above.

reference may be made to it here, though I have not seen it myself.

The manuscript forms part of a complete copy of the *'Ibar* that Ibn Khaldûn sent as a *waqf* donation to the Qarawîyîn Mosque in Fez. Al-Maqqarî, in 1629/30, in his voluminous biography of Ibn al-Khaṭîb, mentioned that he had seen and used the eight-volume copy of the *'Ibar* in the Qarawîyîn Mosque in Fez and that a notation in Ibn Khaldûn's own handwriting was on it.[123]

In the second quarter of the nineteenth century, J. Gråberg af Hemsö heard about the existence of an "autograph copy" of the *Muqaddimah* in the Qarawîyîn Mosque. However, he was unable to gain access to it.[124]

A copy of the manuscript was apparently used in Naṣr al-Hûrînî's Bulaq edition of 1274 [1857], but nothing definite can be added in this connection at the present time.

In his *Catalogue des livres arabes de la Bibliothèque de la Mosquée d'El-Qarouiyîne* (Fez, 1918), A. Bel listed as No. 1266 a manuscript of the *'Ibar* with a *waqf* notice in Ibn Khaldûn's handwriting but failed to say whether No. 1270, which he listed as containing the *Muqaddimah*, belonged to the same set or not.[125] Following up Bel's lead, in 1923 E. Lévi-Provençal was able to publish the photograph of a *waqf* deed, dated Ṣafar 21, 799 [November 24, 1396], which he found at the beginning of Volume v of the *'Ibar.*[126] The same page also contained a notation in Ibn Khaldûn's hand: "Praised be God! That which is attributed to me (here) is correct. Written by 'Abd-ar-Raḥmân b. Muḥammad b. Khaldûn." E. Lévi-Provençal was also shown a copy of Volume III of the *'Ibar*. However, he was unable to obtain any information as to the *Muqaddimah* manuscript of this set. The scribe of the manuscripts seen was 'Abdallâh b. al-Ḥasan Walad al-Fakhûrî, who also copied manuscript B.

In 1930, G. Bouthoul stated that he had examined a two-volume copy of the *Muqaddimah* in Fez. It was, he said, written in Maghribî script and contained poems in the vulgar language at the end, some of which had been composed by Ibn Khaldûn in his youth.[127] These statements have not been verified. In his reprint of

[123] Cf. al-Maqqarî, *Nafḥ aṭ-ṭîb*, IV, 14.

[124] Cf. his *Notizia intorno alla famosa opera istorica di A'bd-er-Rahman Ibnu Khaldûn*, nuova edizione (Florence, 1846), pp. 8 f.

[125] H. P. J. Renaud reproduced a short passage from this MS, without comment. See 3:123 (n. 616), below.

[126] In *Journal asiatique*, CCIII (1923), 161–68.

[127] Cf. G. Bouthoul, *Ibn-Khaldoun, sa philosophie sociale* (Paris, 1930), p. 92.

de Slane's translation of the *Muqaddimah*, Bouthoul published, as a frontispiece to Volume III (Paris, 1938), a reproduction of the *waqf* notice which, he said, ". . . appears at the front of the copy of the *Prolegomena.*" However, the photograph turns out to be merely another shot of the same page that had been reproduced before by E. Lévi-Provençal.

There are, however, other indications that the copy of the *Muqaddimah* from Ibn Khaldûn's *waqf* set of the *'Ibar* is, in fact, preserved in Fez. Recently, A. J. Arberry informed me that he was shown a two-volume copy in Fez. (* However, I was assured in Fez in 1963 that the *Muqaddimah* is lost.)

(3) MS. Yeni Cami 888. The manuscript contains 273 large folios. One folio, comprising 3:449, l. 20, to 3:454, l. 17 of this translation, is missing. **B**

The manuscript is dated Jumâdâ I 10, 799 [February 9, 1397]. The scribe was 'Abdallâh b. Ḥasan b. al-Fakhkhâr, who also copied the Fez set and the Aya Sofya and Topkapusaray copies of Ibn Khaldûn's *Autobiography*. He copied manuscript B from a manuscript "crowned" with the handwriting of the author, who had also added some marginal notes and additions to it, all of which he copied. We are further told that Ibn Khaldûn himself read most of this manuscript copy. His "reading" may have been no more than perfunctory. There can be no doubt, however, as to the excellence of Ibn al-Fakhkhâr's work.

The manuscript is not divided into two parts. The table of contents at the beginning covers the whole work. Ibn Khaldûn's additions to the original manuscript from which B was copied, occasionally have not been incorporated in the body of the text of B, but are written on separately inserted slips of paper. It may be noted that one event mentioned on an inserted slip occurred less than a year before B was copied. (See note 157 to Ch. III, below.)

(4) MS. Atif Effendi 1936. The text of the *Muqaddimah* covers 303 folios. The manuscript breaks off with fol. 302*b*, corresponding to 3:413 (n. 1620), below; it is continued by another hand for a few lines, and then concludes with Ibn Khaldûn's subscription from the end of the *Muqaddimah*. Between fols. 129*b* and 130*a*, one quire of the manuscript has been copied in a later hand on seven additional leaves numbered 130*a*–136*b*, to replace a missing portion of the original. This situation is indicated, in Arabic, at the bottom **C**

left of fol. 129*b:* "From here on, one quire is missing. We hope that God will restore it in the original." This is followed by a notation in Turkish: "In the handwriting of the late Weysi (Wissi) Effendi," the famous littérateur who lived from 1561 to 1628.[128] He purchased the manuscript in Cairo on April 7, 1598, a note on the title page informs us.

The first flyleaf of the manuscript contains the following notation: ". . . I happened to read this book, the first volume of the *Kitâb al-'Ibar fî akhbâr al-'Arab wa-l-'Ajam wa-l-Barbar*. I have found it full of many useful notes and numerous ingenious observations. No previous (work) contains as many interesting remarks or is so rich a treasure-trove of novel, useful notes. The excellence of its composition as well as its order and arrangement show the author's perfect scholarship and his pre-eminence over his contemporaries in learning and the transmission of knowledge. I wrote these lines realizing the great importance of the book, as a testimony to its author, God give him the opportunity to enjoy it and similar (works), by [?] the Prophet and his family! These lines were written by the weak slave (of God), Muḥammad b. Yûsuf b. Muḥammad al-Isfîjâbî, on Saturday, Sha'bân 24, 804 [April 29, 1402]."

In the upper left-hand corner of the title page appears the following note in Maghribî writing:

> This is the draft of the *Muqaddimah* of the *Kitâb al-'Ibar fî akhbâr al-'Arab wa-l-'Ajam wa-l-Barbar*. The contents are altogether scientific[129] and form a kind of artistic preface to the historical work. I have collated and corrected it. No manuscript of the *Muqaddimah* is more correct than this one. Written by the author of the work, 'Abd-ar-Raḥmân Ibn Khaldûn, God give him success and in His kindness forgive him.

The note is framed by a gold border, the work of some later owner of the manuscript, who has also called attention to the autograph of Ibn Khaldûn in a note of his own.[130]

---

[128] Cf. F. Babinger, *Die Geschichtsschreiber der Osmanen*, pp. 152–54.

[129] That is, in contrast to historical information based upon tradition.

[130] This was not unusual. Other bibliophiles proud of their treasures made sure that the association value of a MS would not be overlooked. In Istanbul, for instance, a MS copy of Maskawayh's *Jâwîdhân Khiradh* (Library Feyzullah, 1587) contains the note of a former owner or student to the effect that it had been studied in the year 583 [1187] by Mas'ûd b. Mawdûd b. Zengi, atabek of Mosul from 1176 to 1193.

I. Autograph of Ibn Khaldûn (upper left corner)

From MS. C (Atif Effendi 1936)

The title page contains fifteenth-century notes of sales. Some concern the Ṭantadâ'î family. It seems that Badr-ad-dîn Ḥasan aṭ-Ṭantadâ'î, a blind scholar who lived from about 1400 to 1483 [131] bought the manuscript in 1465. He must have given it away while he was still alive, for in 1479 his son Bahâ'-ad-dîn Muḥammad purchased it from his brothers Aḥmad and Yaḥyâ. Further information about the manuscript may be gleaned from the title page—the story of its purchase by Weysi (Wissi) Effendi mentioned above, for instance. One of the owners' notes is dated in the year 1665/66. Another, dated in 1705/6, is that of a Mecca judge, but there is no reason to believe that the manuscript was at that time in Mecca. The judge may have been a resident of Istanbul.

The verso of the title page contains the table of contents for the entire work, since (like manuscript B) manuscript C is not divided into two parts. At the top, we find the following notation: "Completion of the writing of the book, 804 [1401/2]"

There can be no doubt that C was written during Ibn Khaldûn's lifetime. However, until recently, the problem of whether the note in his handwriting is genuine may well have arisen, for until then the only authentic specimen of Ibn Khaldûn's handwriting available for comparison was the two lines in Maghribî handwriting in the Fez manuscript. Similarity between them and the writing in C is not striking, although there are a number of points of similarity. Other probable autographs of Ibn Khaldûn (recently reproduced by W. J. Fischel in his *Ibn Khaldûn and Tamerlane*, pp. 8 f., 11, and by aṭ-Ṭanjî in his edition of the *Autobiography*) are all written in a good Eastern hand and are therefore of no help for establishing the authenticity of the note in Maghribî writing in C. The problem has now been decided by H. Ritter's [132] publication of eleven lines in Ibn Khaldûn's Western handwriting from the *Tadhkirah al-jadîdah* of his pupil Ibn Ḥajar. These lines indubitably are in the same hand as that of C. Only a scribe well acquainted with Ibn Khaldûn's handwriting, using it as a model, could have forged the specimen in C. This, however, is most unlikely and need not be considered seriously. The autograph manuscript of Ibn Khaldûn's *Lubâb al-Muḥaṣṣal* (cf. p. xlv, above) is of comparatively little help in this connection. The script as it appears on the specimens from the

[131] Cf. as-Sakhâwî, *aḍ-Ḍaw' al-lâmi'*, III, 94 f.

[132] Cf. H. Ritter, "Autographs in Turkish Libraries," in *Oriens*, VI (1953), 83 and pl. XVII.

middle and the end of the manuscript reproduced in the edition, is not strikingly similar to the one used in C or in the note published by Ritter, nor is it markedly different. But it should be noted that the *Lubâb al-Muḥaṣṣal* was written from forty-four to fifty years earlier than the other two documents, and Ibn Khaldûn's signatures definitely look alike in all cases.

The fact that Ibn Khaldûn continued using his Western handwriting in Egypt does not necessarily dispose of the genuineness of the specimens in Eastern script. We do not know whether Ibn Khaldûn's early education included a course in Eastern handwriting, but he probably used the Eastern script rarely, if ever, before he went to Egypt. However, it may have been much easier to wear Western dress in the East (as Ibn Khaldûn did) than to attempt to use the Western script there. Ibn Khaldûn himself tells us [133] that the Western script was difficult for Egyptians to read; on one occasion, as a favor to a Western poet, he had one of the latter's poems transcribed in the Eastern script for presentation to Barqûq. Although in this case, Ibn Khaldûn presumably did not do the actual copying himself, yet it seems almost certain that, on many occasions, he considered it advisable to use the Eastern handwriting in Egypt. In particular, when making notes on a copy of one of his works written in the Eastern script, he may have preferred to use it. There are obvious traces of Western calligraphic style in the presumed specimens of Ibn Khaldûn's Eastern handwriting, especially in the forms of *ṣ* and *ḍ*.[134] However, if Ibn Khaldûn did not have considerable previous experience in writing an Eastern hand before coming to Egypt—and this seems doubtful—it is remarkable that a man past fifty succeeded so well in changing his accustomed style.[135] It may thus be that the presumed specimens of his Eastern hand were not written by him after all.

The text of C contains many of the additions and corrections

[133] Cf. *Autobiography*, p. 271.

[134] Cf. William Wright (ed.), *The Palaeographical Society, Facsimiles of Manuscripts and Inscriptions* (*Oriental Series*) (London, 1875–83), pl. LXXXIV: "Ibn Khaldûn's own hand is that of a Maghribî who has trained himself to write in the Egyptian fashion."

[135] Another famous scholar from the Muslim West, Ibn Sayyid-an-nâs (cf. *GAL*, II, 71 f.; *Suppl.*, II, 77), who, however, was born in Cairo, is said to have had a good knowledge of both the Egyptian and the Maghribî scripts. Cf. Ibn Ḥajar, *ad-Durar al-kâminah*, IV, 209. Cf. also the handwriting in the autograph of Ibn Sa'îd (see below, 3:445), described by F. Trummeter, *Ibn Sa'îd's Geschichte der vorislamischen Araber* (Stuttgart, 1928), p. 21.

that constitute the later stages of the text of the *Muqaddimah.* Most of them were written by the writer of the entire manuscript. Unfortunately, the name of the scribe is not given; but, of course, he was a person other than Ibn Khaldûn.

How are we to interpret the historical data just reviewed? The most likely explanation, which, however, still involves guesswork, seems to be as follows. Manuscript C was copied in 804 [1401/2] from an early text of the *Muqaddimah,* presumably Ibn Khaldûn's own copy. The additions and corrections found in it were transferred verbatim to C by the same scribe.[136] Ibn Khaldûn had indicated on his copy the year 804 as the date when he had stopped working on the *Muqaddimah* (for the time being, at least). Later in the same year, al-Isfîjâbî, probably the first owner of C, affixed his admiring note at the beginning of the work, after reading it.

Manuscript C was used in later centuries as model for other copies. For example, Nuru Osmaniye 3424, which was copied by a certain Mehmet Muezzinzade for 'Alî Pasha (d. 1716)[137] and which is dated Rabî' I 4, 1127 [March 10, 1715], has the same lacuna at the end as C. The same is true of the manuscript which in Quatremère's edition was referred to as A,[138] though it remains to be seen whether that manuscript was copied from our manuscript C directly or indirectly. The manuscript Hamidiye 982 contains a note to the effect that it was collated with the Atif Effendi manuscript, that is, with C, by a certain Ḥâjj 'Abd-ar-Razzâq in 1177 [1763/64]. (Cf. below, p. xcix.)

(5) MS. Hüseyin Celebi 793 in Bursa (Brussa). This manuscript was noted in *Une Liste des manuscrits choisis parmi les bibliothèques de Bursa, publiée à l'occasion du XXII. Congrès International des Orientalistes* (Istanbul, 1951), p. 49. The catalogue number and the date of the manuscript are not, however, correctly designated on this list. Dr. Ahmed Ateş first called my attention to this manuscript. **D**

The manuscript contains 239 folios. It is dated Wednesday, Sha'bân 8, 806 [February 20, 1404]. The name of the scribe is

[136] Passages that appear as marginal additions in C are occasionally found incorporated in the texts of A and B.

[137] Cf. *EI, s.v.* "'Alî Pasha Dâmâd."

[138] See pp. c f., below. This MS has the additions that appear in the MS. Ragib Paşa but not in C or any other of the available MSS. See p. xcix, below.

given as Ibrâhîm b. Khalîl as-Sa'dî ash-Shâfi'î al-Miṣrî. On its title page it has an owner's note dated in the year 850 [1446/47], written by Yaḥyâ b. Ḥijjî ash-Shâfi'î, of the famous family of scholars. Starting early as a student and bibliophile, he was only twelve or thirteen years old when he wrote the note in manuscript D. He died in 888 [1483].[139] Ibn Ḥijjî's note would seem to make it practically certain that D was, indeed, written in 806, and is not a later copy of the manuscript written in that year, as might well be possible otherwise. For it must be pointed out that D, despite its date, is not an exceptionally good manuscript but contains a number of omissions and a great many other mechanical mistakes.

Manuscript D clearly was based on C, or was derived from the archetype from which C itself was copied. This origin is indicated, for instance, where D inserts a meaningless *man yaqṣidu* after *ghayrîyah* at Vol. III, p. 68, line 6, of the Paris edition (in this translation, 3:86, l. 19, below). In C a mark after *ghayrîyah* indicates that a marginal note is to be added at this place. However, *man yaqṣidu* does not belong there. It is to be inserted after *wa-qaṣd* in line 15 (3:87, l. 5, below), where the fact that it was omitted is indicated by another omission mark after *wa-qaṣd.* The intended marginal note to *ghayrîyah* apparently was never written.

Manuscript D had subsequently a rather curious history. The original colophon of the year 806 was frequently included in later copies, and these copies were mistaken for the original.[140] Thus, Nuru Osmaniye 3423 has been mistaken for the manuscript of 806, but script and paper exclude the possibility that it was written in the fifteenth century. In fact, its similarity to Nuru Osmaniye 3424, mentioned above, p. xcvii, dates it in the early eighteenth century.

Another copy of D is the manuscript Hekimoğlu Ali Paşa 805, which has a flyleaf notation to the effect that it was written in 1118 [1706/7] for one Abû l-Khayr Aḥmad. The second part of the manuscript Halet Effendi 617 is likewise a copy of D.

E (6) MS. Ahmet III, 3042, Vol. I. The manuscript contains 297 folios. It is not dated but has an owner's note of the year 818

[139] Cf. as-Sakhâwî, *aḍ-Ḍaw' al-lâmi'*, X, 252–54.

[140] The dependence of other MSS on D can easily be checked with the help of the omissions in D, as, for instance, the passage from 3:420 (n. 1649) to 3:426 (n. 1680), below.

[1415/16] in the name of one Muḥammad b. ʻAbd-ar-Raḥmân aḍ-Ḍârib. Consequently, it must have been written in or before that year. The manuscript is important because (apart from the basic text of C) it is the only old manuscript available that contains an early form of the text of the *Muqaddimah.*

Another volume found under the same catalogue number contains Ibn Khaldûn's personal copy of the *Autobiography.*[141] It was written out by Ibn al-Fakhkhâr (cf. above, p. xciii). However, if my memory does not deceive me, manuscript E is in a different hand.

(7) MS. Halet Effendi 617 consists of two parts, in 235 and 181 folios, respectively. The second part has already been mentioned as a copy of D. The first part, however, dates back to the fifteenth century. It has an owner's note in the name of a Muḥammad b. Muḥammad b. al-Qûṣawî (?), dated 853 [1449].

(8) MS. Ragib Paşa 978 contains 382 folios. It is of recent date, no earlier than the early eighteenth century. The note of a reader who tried to collate and correct the manuscript is dated in [1]153 [1740/41]. One of the marginal notes in the manuscript refers to az-Zurqânî, the commentator of Mâlik's *Muwaṭṭa'*, who died in 1122 [1710].

This manuscript, the text of which has yet to be studied, is interesting because it contains occasional marginal notes originating from a manuscript written by a certain al-Qaṭarî, claimed by him to have been copied from "the original manuscript." This Qaṭarî evidently was the Abû ṣ-Ṣalâḥ Muḥammad al-Ḥanafî al-Qaṭarî who wrote the manuscript Nuru Osmaniye 3066, dated Monday, Dhû l-Qa'dah 14, 1082 [March 13/14, 1672]. In another Nuru Osmaniye manuscript, 3065, which the same scribe finished on Sunday, Dhû l-Qa'dah 30, 1101 [September 4(?), 1690], he was described as an imam and preacher of the Jâmiʻ al-Wazîr (Mosque of the Wazîr) in the Border City (*thaghr*) of Jidda. However, there is no further information about "the original manuscript" that al-Qaṭarî claimed to have used. Judging from such passages as those below, p. 192 (n. 260), and p. 230 (n. 349), it cannot have been C, unless in its present state C has not preserved all the inserted slips it once contained. (Cf. above, p. xcvii [n. 138].)

[141] Cf. aṭ-Ṭanjî's introduction to his edition of the *Autobiography*, pp. 10 f.

2. EDITIONS

Editions of the *Muqaddimah* are as numerous as manuscripts. The work is studied in the schools and colleges of the Arab countries. At least in recent years, it seems that each year produces a new reprint of the text, but most of these editions are worthless. A constantly increasing number of misprints disfigures them. It would be reassuring, though not particularly instructive, to review all these editions and investigate their interdependence. Since I have been unable to do this, my remarks are restricted to such observations as I can make about editions in my private possession. The rare Paris edition is not among these but is, of course, well represented in the great libraries.

Publication and translation of small portions of the *Muqaddimah* before 1857–58 are associated with such names as Hammer-Purgstall and Silvestre de Sacy. Today, their works have little more than bibliographical interest, and full listing may, therefore, be reserved as a task for the compiler of the complete bibliography of Ibn Khaldûn, which has been needed for so long. In the meantime, de Slane's observations, in the introduction to his translation of the *Muqaddimah* (Vol. I, pp. cxv–cxvi — see p. cviii, below), and those by G. Gabrieli (see note 119, above) suffice. Cf. now W. J. Fischel's bibliography, pp. 483 ff. of Vol. 3, below, as well as the one by H. Pérès in *Studi orientalistici in onore di Giorgio Levi Della Vida* (Rome, 1956), II, 304–29.

(1) The first complete scholarly European edition of the *Muqaddimah* was brought out by Etienne Marc Quatremère in Paris in 1858, under the title of *Prolégomènes d'Ebn-Khaldoun*. It was printed by Firmin Didot Frères in three volumes, figuring as Volumes XVI, XVII, and XVIII of the *Notices et Extraits des manuscrits de la Bibliothèque Impériale*, published by the Académie des Inscriptions et Belles-Lettres. Quatremère had died only the year before at the age of seventy-five, regretted as a scholar of great merits but also, it seems, one who was at odds with his colleagues and with the world in general.

Quatremère did not live to publish an introduction to his edition. According to W. M. de Slane, the French translator of the *Muqaddimah*, Quatremère based his text on four manuscripts, presently located as follows. Quatremère's manuscript A, dated 1146

[1733], is in the Bibliothèque Nationale, catalogued as No. 1524 of the Arabic manuscripts. MS. B, dated 1151 [1738], is in Munich as No. 373 in Aumer's catalogue.[142] MS. C, a copy made in 1835/36 of the Damad Ibrahim manuscript referred to above (pp. xc ff.) by the letter A, is now in the Bibliothèque Nationale, catalogued as No. 1517. MS. D, the oldest manuscript among the four used by Quatremère and dated 1067 [1656/57], is No. 5136 among the Arabic manuscripts of the Bibliothèque Nationale.[143]

On the surface, the manuscript basis of Quatremère's edition seems rather shaky. However, Quatremère was fortunate in being able to use a copy of the oldest extant manuscript (our A), which, apparently, was very reliable. His good fortune extended further, in that among his manuscripts he discovered the last and most complete text of the *Muqaddimah* as it came from Ibn Khaldûn's pen. Thus, he was able to offer in his edition a good complete text. The only exception to this statement concerns some particularly difficult passages such as the poems at the end of the *Muqaddimah*, where Quatremère's edition fails us completely. That his edition includes a good number of minor misprints may be blamed, in part, on the fact that the printing firm chosen by Quatremère did not specialize in printing long Arabic texts. However, few printed editions of Arabic texts are free from misprints. The misprints in Quatremère's edition, though numerous, do not amount to much as a major shortcoming of his edition. The principal reproach to be laid against him is that he neglected to indicate textual differences and variant readings among his manuscripts, as accurately and carefully as we could wish. These may have seemed of small importance to him, and they often are; however, he made it difficult for later scholars to judge the quality of his work correctly.

As a matter of fact, Quatremère's edition has often been maligned unfairly, and still is undervalued at the present time. The

[142] The MS belonged to Quatremère personally; his large library was acquired by the then King of Bavaria for his library in Munich.

No. 654 of Aumer's catalogue contains a very few excerpts from the *Muqaddimah*. Strangely enough, Aumer remarks that this MS agrees with Quatremère's MS. A. For the possibility that Quatremère's A is a copy of the Atif Effendi MS. C, see p. xcvii, above.

[143] Cf. E. Blochet, *Catalogue des manuscrits arabes des nouvelles acquisitions* (Paris, 1925). Of course, this MS was no new acquisition, but in de Slane's catalogue of the Arabic MSS in Paris it was mentioned only in the Table de Concordances as No. 742 *i*—corresponding to No. 5076 of the handwritten catalogue.

editor's negligence in indicating manuscript variants is part of the reason. The obvious fact that the manuscripts used were of recent date has also aroused mistrust. However, it should be stated bluntly that much of the unfair treatment meted out to Quatremère's work must be laid at the door of William MacGuckin de Slane, the French translator of the *Muqaddimah*. With an unusual pettiness, such as betrays some personal grudge, de Slane went so far as to note even the most minor and obvious misprints in Quatremère's edition, and treated them as major, damning blunders in the footnotes to his translation. He left no doubt as to how poorly he regarded Quatremère's work, and de Slane was supported in this view by Dozy, who wrote an influential review of the translation. In his review, R. Dozy brushed Quatremère's edition aside as a product of the scholar's senility. Between them, de Slane and Dozy set the stage for an unfriendly reception of Quatremère's work. It has been more for this reason, than for any more solidly based one, that doubts concerning the quality of Quatremère's text have been voiced and demands for a new edition raised. While a new edition will mean a great step forward, it will not expose major factual defects in Quatremère's text.

(2) While Quatremère's edition was still in press, an Egyptian edition of the *Muqaddimah* appeared, which had been printed at Bulaq near Cairo. Finished in Ṣafar, 1274 [September/October, 1857], it was printed in a very large format and succeeded in compressing the entire text to 316 pages. The editor was Naṣr al-Hûrînî (d. 1874),[144] an Egyptian scholar of considerable merit. Although it was intended to form the first volume of a complete edition of the *'Ibar*, only the *Muqaddimah* was published at this time.

To judge by occasional marginal notes, al-Hûrînî apparently used two manuscripts, which he called the Fez and the Tunis manuscripts. Of course, there is no consistent indication of variant readings. Al-Hûrînî often corrected the text according to his own judgment, a fact de Slane noted in the introduction to his translation (pp. cix f.). Indeed, it seems that in practically all instances where the Bulaq edition diverges from the manuscripts that have come to my attention, we have to reckon with free corrections by the editor. Sometimes his text gives the impression of being superior, but this superiority lacks documentary confirmation. Only

[144] Cf. *GAL*, II, 489 f.; *Suppl.*, II, 726.

in a few passages, as, for instance, 3:235 and 3:446 (n. 1813), below, do we find indisputable instances of a superior text in the Bulaq edition. Thus, the text of the Bulaq edition may usually be disregarded even where it is tempting to rely on its *lectio facilior*. Final judgment on it, however, should be postponed until the entire manuscript evidence has been thoroughly investigated.

However, Bulaq has some importance of its own by virtue of the fact that it provides the earliest text of the *Muqaddimah* presently available in printed form, with the fewest number of the author's later corrections and additions. The Tunis manuscript preserves Ibn Khaldûn's original dedication to the Ḥafṣid ruler. The Fez manuscript appears to go back to Ibn Khaldûn's donation copy (see pp. xci ff. above). In these respects the Bulaq edition supplements the Paris edition which represents a much later stage of the text of the *Muqaddimah.*

(3) Ten years later, in 1284 [1867/68], the complete text of the *'Ibar* was published in Bulaq in seven volumes. The first volume contains the *Muqaddimah* in 534 pages. The text is identical with that published previously and even retains al-Hûrînî's notes. However, it may be noted that in the chapter on letter magic, the new edition contains the magical table between pp. 436 and 437, and some of the material on magic that had been omitted from the first Bulaq text (pp. 255–57). So far as the quality of the text of the rest of the *'Ibar* is concerned, it clearly leaves much to be desired.[145]

(4) All later Oriental reprints, so far as I know, are based upon the Bulaq text and take no cognizance of the Paris edition. One very successful reprint of this sort was undertaken in Beirut in 1879 (and published early in 1880). I have before me a second, identical edition of the year 1886.

The technically very ambitious project of publishing a fully

[145] For partial editions and translations of sections of the *'Ibar* other than the *Muqaddimah,* cf. *GAL,* II, 245; *Suppl.,* II, 343 f.

A concordance of pages of de Slane's edition of the *Histoire des Berbères,* his translation of it, and Vols. VI and VII of the Bulaq edition, has been provided by G. Gabrieli in *Rivista degli studi orientali,* X (1924), 169–211. A reprint of de Slane's translation of the *Histoire des Berbères* was undertaken under the supervision of P. Casanova (Paris, 1925, 1927, and 1934), but did not go beyond Vol. III. The pagination of the reprint is the same as that of the first edition. (Vol. IV was published in Paris in 1956, without the bibliography originally promised.)

Cf. further, O. A. Machado, "La historia de los Godos según Ibn Jaldûn," in *Cuadernos de Historia de España* (Buenos Aires), I–II (1944), 139–55.

vocalized edition of the *Muqaddimah, in usum scholarum*, was also undertaken in Beirut.[146] I have before me a photomechanical reproduction of the vocalized Beirut edition. This reproduction was put together in the Printing Ḥouse of Muṣṭafâ Muḥammad in Cairo, and although it is not dated, it must be about twenty to twenty-five years old. The "publisher" does not indicate the origin of his text but states on the title page that he is reserving all rights for himself and that his edition has been checked by a committee of scholars against a number of manuscripts!

The long chapter on letter magic is omitted in my copy, as are all the long dialect poems and some of the *muwashshaḥahs* and *zajals* at the close of the *Muqaddimah*. In addition, the vocalized text is slightly censored, omitting comments that appear to reflect adversely upon Christianity (p. 480 and 3:82, below), as well as remarks dealing with sexual matters (2:295, below). The difficult and exhausting task of vocalizing the entire text of the *Muqaddimah* has been fairly successfully executed. However, the text as such is unusually poor, shot through with mistakes and marred by many omissions.

There are many other Egyptian reprints of the *Muqaddimah*. Some of these do not follow the Beirut edition, but the Bulaq text. In this way each has perpetuated itself in successive reprint editions marked by increasing numbers of mistakes. I have before me editions of 1327 [1909] and 1348 [1930], as well as one very recent reprint of the Beirut text, undated but printed in Cairo, that is an especially outrageous insult to the noble art of printing.

(5) Some editions of brief excerpts of the *Muqaddimah* are mentioned below, p. cix. See also footnote 31 to Ibn Khaldûn's Introduction.

(6) The plans of aṭ-Ṭanjî for a critical edition of the *Muqaddimah* were mentioned above, p. lxxxix.

3. GRADUAL GROWTH OF THE TEXT

Before passing on to the translations, a word may be said about the gradual growth of the text of the *Muqaddimah*. From the

---

[146] According to some old notes of mine, which I am at present unable to check, the vocalized text appeared simultaneously with the unvocalized Beirut edition. However, Gabrieli, *op. cit.*, states that the first vocalized edition appeared in 1900.

available evidence, as presented in the preceding pages, it is possible to draw the following picture of the history of the text in Ibn Khaldûn's hands.

Ibn Khaldûn himself informs us that he wrote the *Muqaddimah* during a period of five months ending in the middle of the year 779 [November, 1377]; see 3:480, below. He was far from any large library, and had to rely largely on his memory and notes. He then went to Tunis, where he had access to the books he needed to consult, and there he finished the entire *History*. He presented a copy to the Ḥafṣid Abû l-'Abbâs of Tunis (1370–94).[147] It is possible that one of the manuscripts on which the Bulaq edition was based contains this oldest text. But none of the available manuscripts or editions has it. The earliest texts at present available are those of the Bulaq edition and manuscript E, but since they already contain indications of Ibn Khaldûn's stay in Egypt, they can be no earlier than 1382.

Ibn Khaldûn's habit of correcting and expanding the *History* continued while he was in Egypt. In one particular case it is expressly stated that Ibn Khaldûn lectured on the *Muqaddimah* in Egypt.[148] He probably devoted more time to his work when he was out of office than when he was judge, but he never ceased trying to improve the *Muqaddimah* or collecting additional material for it, even when in office.[149] He was constantly reading pertinent material and even had Egyptian Bedouins recite poetry to him (3:438 f., below). But it seems that, primarily, the material for his additions and corrections derived from his lectures on the *Muqaddimah* and other subjects. This would explain why the sections dealing with traditions and jurisprudence—subjects on which he lectured ex officio and in which his students were professionally interested—show the most numerous traces of larger and smaller revisions.

It would be wrong to consider the successive stages of the text of the *Muqaddimah* as "recensions" in the proper sense of the term. For instance, Ibn Khaldûn never changed the passages where he speaks of himself as still being in the Maghrib. His additions and corrections were jotted down unsystematically in a long-

---

[147] See p. lvii, above.

[148] Cf. F. Rosenthal, *A History of Muslim Historiography*, p. 40, quoting as-Sakhâwî, *aḍ-Ḍaw' al-lâmi'*, VIII, 233.

[149] See p. cvi, below.

drawn-out process, much as a modern author might add notes in the margins of his published works.

Ibn Khaldûn's corrections rectify obvious mistakes committed earlier, as, for instance, in his treatment of the division of the earth into zones (pp. 111 ff., below). Or, in the case of quotations, they supply a better text obtained with the help of some new source: an example is Ṭâhir's *Epistle* to his son.[150] Ibn Khaldûn had already corrected his original quotation from Ibn al-Athîr with the help of aṭ-Ṭabarî by the time A was written, and C still preserves the marginal corrections which later copyists entered in the body of the text.

The table of contents at the beginning of the work, which treats the *Muqaddimah* as an independent work,[151] must nonetheless have been added by the author at an early stage, for it appears already in A. Ibn Khaldûn also adds quotations from works he has come across in further reading, as a sort of afterthought. Or, he expands and changes the text, because it no longer seems to express adequately or fully the ideas he has in mind. A minor instance of this kind of correction (or revision) can be found in a passage where Ibn Khaldûn thought it advisable to tone down a strong expression of monistic mysticism (2:398, below). The most prominent emendations in the text of the work are of this kind, although there are not a great many of them. An outstanding example of Ibn Khaldûn's concern for clear expression is the very considerable enlargement of his introductory remarks to the sixth chapter, dealing with the sciences (2:411 ff., below). The earliest text in which the expanded version occurs is manuscript C, so it must have entered the text of the *Muqaddimah* between 1397 and 1402. This interval may perhaps be further restricted to the period between 1397 and 1399, because Ibn Khaldûn was thereafter extremely busy with official duties. However, it should not be forgotten that, even while on official business, Ibn Khaldûn found time to study. In fact, the last-dated entry in the *Muqaddimah* refers to reading accomplished during his stay in Damascus in the spring of 802 [1400] (2:229 f., below); and he found time to insert the note bearing upon it in manuscript C.

A later stage, the latest we know of, in fact, is represented by the Bursa manuscript D of 806 [1404]. It shows that Ibn Khaldûn

150 See pp. lxx ff., above, and 2:139 ff., below.
151 See p. lxviii, above.

was still working on his book two years before his death. Characteristic of this stage in the development of the text of the *Muqaddimah* was his replacement of a distich near the end with another very beautiful one (3:478, below). It shows that Ibn Khaldûn retained his fine appreciation of poetry up to a time of life when many men, and especially men of affairs, no longer give much thought to it.[152]

That most of Ibn Khaldûn's additions and corrections were incorporated into the body of the text in the manuscripts written during his lifetime is shown by manuscript D. This process did not always come off without mishaps, as a striking example below (pp. 365 f.) indicates.

In general, it is possible to show at what stage in the textual history of the *Muqaddimah* almost any addition or correction was made by Ibn Khaldûn. Undoubtedly, if a manuscript of the pre-Egyptian "recension" of the work were to become available, still greater precision would be attained. The history of the text of the *Muqaddimah* offers a classical example of how an author's variant readings originate and how they influence the traditional appearance of his work.

4. PREVIOUS TRANSLATIONS

(1) The first complete translation of the *Muqaddimah* ever published was a Turkish version. In the year 1730 Pirizade Effendi (1674–1749) translated the *Muqaddimah* from the beginning through the fifth chapter. This Turkish text was published in Cairo in 1275 [1859],[153] in a lithographed edition of 617 pages in large format; the translation ended on p. 522. On the remaining pages, the work was completed by a reproduction of the Arabic text based on the first Bulaq edition. A few pages on Ibn Khaldûn's

---

[152] For the *'Ibar*, the latest date to be found in the Bulaq text is 796 [1394]; cf. *'Ibar*, V, 508; VI, 9. The Bulaq text of *'Ibar*, VI, 200, refers to the year 799, but this appears to be a misprint, since de Slane's translation, II, 110, gives 796. It would, however, seem probable that MSS of the *'Ibar* with additions of a later date exist.

[153] F. Babinger, *Die Geschichtsschreiber der Osmanen*, pp. 282 f., mentions an edition (Bulaq, 1274) of 626 pp. I have no further information about it. M. Mostafa Ziada refers to a Turkish translation of the *Muqaddimah* made for Muḥammad 'Alî of Egypt [?]. Cf. *Middle Eastern Affairs*, IV (1953), 267.

life serve as introduction, compiled by Ahmet Jevdet Effendi, later Pasha (1822–95). The latter also translated the remaining sixth chapter of the *Muqaddimah*, which was published in Istanbul in 1277 [1860/61],[154] accompanied by copious explanatory notes.

(2) A complete French translation, under the title of *Prolégomènes historiques, d'Ibn Khaldoun*, was published by William MacGuckin de Slane on the basis of Quatremère's edition and with comparison of the Paris manuscripts used by Quatremère, the first Bulaq edition, and the Turkish translation (in part). The three volumes appeared in Paris in the years 1862, 1865, and 1868, as Vols. XIX to XXI of the *Notices et Extraits des manuscrits de la Bibliothèque Impériale*.

De Slane did an altogether admirable job of presenting a highly readable and, in the main, accurate translation of the work. The "freedom" of his version has often been unjustly censured, for it was intentional, and a "free" translation is perfectly legitimate for a work with the stylistic character of the *Muqaddimah*. There are occasional mistakes of translation, some of them caused by the difficulty of the subject matter and the language, others of a sort that might easily have been avoided. Explanatory footnotes are sparse, and de Slane usually did not bother to indicate the sources for his statements. However, the concluding words of R. Dozy's review of de Slane's work still stand: "Rarely has so difficult a book been translated so well." [155]

A photomechanical reproduction of de Slane's translation was published in Paris in 1934–38, with a brief preface by G. Bouthoul. Important corrections to the translation were provided by R. Dozy in the review by him which appeared in *Journal asiatique*, XIV[6] (1869), 133–218. More recently, a number of valuable corrections were published by A. Bombaci, "Postille alla traduzione De Slane della *Muqaddimah* di Ibn Ḫaldûn," in *Annali dell'Istituto Universitario Orientale di Napoli*, N.S. III (1949), 439–72.

For many years after the publication of de Slane's translation, scholars, almost to a man, relied on it for their quotations from the *Muqaddimah*. The occasional exceptions have been noted in foot-

[154] According to Babinger, this is the third volume of a complete edition of the Turkish translation, begun in 1275 [1858/59]. I am familiar only with the volume containing the sixth chapter. For the work on the *'Ibar* by 'Abd-al-Laṭîf Ṣubḥî Pasha (1818–1886), published in Istanbul in 1276 [1859/60], cf. Babinger, pp. 368–70.

[155] In *Journal asiatique*, XIV[6] (1869), 218.

notes to this translation at the appropriate passages. Only in recent years have fresh translations of comparatively large sections of the *Muqaddimah* begun to be made.[156]

(3) In English, there are a few brief passages in R. A. Nicholson, *Translations of Eastern Poetry and Prose* (Cambridge, 1922). Recently, a rather large selection of brief excerpts was published by Charles Issawi, under the title of *An Arab Philosophy of History* (London, 1950).

(4) The book by Erwin Rosenthal, entitled *Ibn Khalduns Gedanken über den Staat* (Munich and Berlin, 1932), consists largely of excerpts from the *Muqaddimah,* in German translation. A large volume of selections in German translation was published by A. Schimmel in Tübingen in 1951, under the title of *Ibn Chaldun: Ausgewählte Abschnitte aus der muqaddima.*

(5) A short selection of Arabic passages with accompanying French translation was published by G. Surdon and L. Bercher under the title of *Recueil de textes de sociologie et de droit public musulman contenus dans les "Prolégomènes" d'Ibn Khaldoun,* "Bibliothèque de l'Institut d'Etudes Supérieures Islamiques d'Alger," No. 6 (Algiers, 1951). The translators profess their particular concern for bringing out the basically juridical flavor of Ibn Khaldûn's terminology.

5. THE PRESENT TRANSLATION

A work such as the *Muqaddimah,* modern in thought yet alien in language and style, may be presented to the modern reader in one of three ways. It may be translated as literally as the second language permits. The translator may go farther and use modern phraseology and style. Or, finally, the work may be recast and given the form it would have had it been written by a contemporary author in the second language.

If a translation is to impress the modern reader with the full worth and significance of the original, the last-mentioned approach would seem to be the ideal one. Realizing this, scholars have frequently chosen to publish selected and rearranged passages of the *Muqaddimah.* However, a complete rewriting in this manner, besides being hardly practicable, would almost necessarily produce a

---

156 For early partial translations, see p. c, above.

subjective interpretation of the *Muqaddimah*, and thereby obscure Ibn Khaldûn's thought.

The second approach to translation was what de Slane attempted. It, too, has pitfalls. One is the danger of distorting the author's ideas by modernizing them, and thereby attributing to him thoughts that were utterly foreign to him. Moreover, a work dealing with a great variety of subjects, and the *Muqaddimah* is certainly such a work, depends to a great extent in its formal and intellectual organization upon the threads of association that the author's particular terminology and way of expression provide.

The drawback of any completely literal translation is obvious: it may easily be incomprehensible to the general reader. Further, a literal translation often entirely perverts the literary character of the original. It is transformed from a literary product using the normal and accepted forms of its own language into a work rendered strained and unnatural by not conforming to the style of the language into which it was translated.

The present translation was begun in the belief that a mixture of the literal and modernizing types of rendering would produce the most acceptable result. Yet, it must be confessed that with each successive revision, the translator has felt an irresistible urge to follow ever more faithfully the linguistic form of the original.

The literalness of the present version is intended to reduce to a minimum the amount of interpretation always necessary in any translation. The reader unfamiliar with the Arabic original ought to be encumbered by no more than an unavoidable minimum of subjective interpretation. Moreover, Ibn Khaldûn's particular terminology, which he evolved with great pains for his "new science," had to be preserved as far as possible; to some degree, it must have impressed his contemporary readers as unusual. Therefore, at least the outstanding terms, such as *'umrân*, *'aṣabîyah*, *badâwah*, were preserved in the translation by rather artificial loan renderings ("civilization," "group spirit," "desert life or attitude"). This involved the occasional occurrence of expressions such as "large civilization." But any other procedure would irrevocably have destroyed the essential unity of Ibn Khaldûn's work, which is one of its main claims to greatness.[157] For the sake

157 It seems regrettable, and in some ways definitely misleading, that it was not possible to give a uniform translation to such commonly used words as *nasab* "descent, pedigree, lineage, family," *sirr* "secret," *fann* "branch,"

of literalness, an attempt has been made to translate passages that are repeated in the original, in identical or nearly identical words, in the same fashion each time. However, since such repetitions occur frequently in the text of the *Muqaddimah*, the attempt probably remained unsuccessful, or, at best, only partly successful. Some modernizing tendency remains in the translation but it chiefly affects syntactical and stylistic features, and only very rarely the vocabulary.

Ibn Khaldûn's contemporaries praised the literary quality of the *Muqaddimah* highly. Ibn Khaldûn himself, in a poetical dedication of his *History*, used rather exuberant language in speaking of the linguistic perfection of his work:

> I tamed rude speech. It may be said that
> Refractory language becomes in (my work) amenable to the words I utter.[158]

This self-praise was, of course, a routine authors had to follow in the past when the advertising methods of the modern publishing business were as yet unknown. But others chimed in with their praise. The style of the *Muqaddimah* was said to be "more brilliant than well-strung pearls and finer than water fanned by the zephyr." It was called a "Jâḥiẓian" style, reminiscent of the verbal fireworks of al-Jâḥiẓ, the celebrated model of good Arabic style.[159] All these testimonies may have been rather perfunctory; still, they certainly have some basis in fact. It is true, as has often been remarked, that Ibn Khaldûn did not always adhere strictly to the accepted norms and rules of classical Arabic, which were artificial to him and remote from the speech habits of his time. But Ibn Khaldûn's long, rolling, involved sentences, his skillful and yet restrained application of rhetorical figures, and his precise use of a large, though not farfetched, vocabulary make it indeed a pleasure to read the *Muqaddimah*, or to hear it read aloud.[160]

---

and many others. In quite a few cases, as, for instance, in the case of *sulṭân* "government, authority, ruler, Sultan," it may seem advisable to add the Arabic at each occurrence. I decided against such a procedure, and only very rarely will the reader find an Arabic word added in brackets in the text of the translation.

[158] Cf. *Autobiography*, p. 240, l. 10.

[159] Cf. F. Rosenthal, *A History of Muslim Historiography*, p. 419 (n. 7).

[160] See pp. lxviii f., above.

However, the modern translator's agreement with such positive appraisals of the linguistic and stylistic qualities of the *Muqaddimah* is somewhat forced. For, alas! all the factors that enhance the beauty of the work in its original language and justified the admiration of Ibn Khaldûn's contemporaries, are so many thorns in the translator's flesh. His long sentences have constantly to be broken up into smaller units, and the cohesiveness of the author's style is thereby loosened. In keeping with a common stylistic feature of Arabic speech, Ibn Khaldûn could repeat pronouns through whole pages, thus confronting his translator with the task of supplying the appropriate nouns. Ibn Khaldûn also was extremely fond of a threefold *parallelismus membrorum*, another source of embarrassment to the translator. The ordinary twofold parallelism, well known from the Bible, is difficult enough to translate, an imitation of the threefold one practically impossible. Sometimes, one word or phrase may do as a translation of all three members, but more often than not, the threefold parallelism can only be broken up into seemingly redundant phrases. Another stylistic feature is a kind of inversion by means of which later elements of a story are given first, and the earlier elements are given later, in a sentence introduced by "after." This can be brilliant in Arabic but is most often unpalatable in modern English translation (although it would have been somewhat more acceptable in another age, in the eighteenth century, for instance).

The large number of parentheses (in the translation) is the result of the need for clarifying stylistic changes. These parentheses have been used in order to indicate to the reader that in these passages the translator has added something that is not literally found in the Arabic text. They may be disregarded, and the text enclosed by them should be considered an integral part of the context. In a few cases, however, the words in parentheses serve another purpose, namely, that of explaining the preceding words.

In the choice of explanatory footnotes the translator has more leeway. Ibn Khaldûn's own ideas and the way he expressed them offer no particular difficulties to the understanding. But the numerous passages where technical details are discussed or earlier authors are quoted sorely try the translator's knowledge of words and things. Incidentally, Ibn Khaldûn himself is on record as admitting that he did not quite understand the text he copied (at

2:224 and 3:183, below). Like many other Arabic works, the *Muqaddimah* contains some passages where it obviously was much easier for the author to copy his source than it is for the translator to find out the meaning of the text copied. In general, where the translator has succeeded in understanding Ibn Khaldûn's text correctly, very little in the way of added explanation is necessary.

However, historical understanding and interpretation of the work pose greater problems. The *Muqaddimah* was composed nearly at the end of the intellectual development of medieval Islam, and the work covers practically all its aspects. A well-nigh incalculable number of notes and excursuses would be required if one were to comment on the historical significance of Ibn Khaldûn's statements and put each of them in proper perspective. Nearly a century ago de Slane felt that he could provide unlimited notes and explanations to his translation (cf. his introduction, p. ii), but he refrained from doing so for the sake of brevity. In the end, he did very little indeed in the way of annotation.[161] Since his time, the material that has a sound claim to consideration in the notes has grown immeasurably. A hundred years ago, very few printed Arabic texts existed, and nearly all the pertinent information was still buried in manuscripts. Even nowadays, when a good part of Arabic literature has become available in printed form, it is often necessary, in connection with the *Muqaddimah*, to refer to manuscripts. In fact, our knowledge has outgrown the stage where the historical problems of a work like the *Muqaddimah*, considered in its entirety, can be elucidated by means of footnotes. The important task of interpretation must be left to monographs on individual sections of the text, a scholarly labor that has been attempted so far only on a very small scale.[162] In the notes to this translation, the major problem has been one of selection, that of providing references that give the fullest possible information in easily accessible form.

In some respects, it has been possible to be briefer than de Slane. Nowadays, many of Ibn Khaldûn's examples from political history no longer require comment, nor, from the point of view of

---

[161] See p. cviii, above.

[162] Cf., for instance, the article by Renaud quoted below, n. 616 to Ch. VI. For earlier attempts in this direction by S. van den Bergh, J.-D. Luciani, and H. Frank, see nn. 1, 263, and 464 to Ch. VI.

modern historiography and sociology, does the acceptability of Ibn Khaldûn's historical interpretations have to be argued.[163]

A reference to C. Brockelmann, *Geschichte der arabischen Literatur,* where authors and works of literature are concerned, makes it possible to dispense with further references, save, perhaps, for very recent bibliographical material, which has been carefully examined before inclusion. The *Encyclopaedia of Islam* and that splendid time-saving tool, the *Concordance et Indices de la tradition musulmane,* were also, in many cases, considered sufficient as guides to further study.

Apart from obvious references of this kind, and a certain amount of necessary philological comment,[164] the selection of notes has been guided by one dominant consideration. Works that Ibn Khaldûn himself knew, knew about, or may reasonably be supposed to have known or known about, have been emphasized. Knowledge of Ibn Khaldûn's sources is of immeasurable assistance in better understanding his historical position and significance. While a very small start in this direction could be made in the footnotes to this translation, I am convinced that this kind of comment should be given preference over any other.

When I had completed my version, I compared it with the previous translations as carefully as possible, giving particular attention to de Slane's. I have not considered it necessary to acknowledge de Slane's help whenever I have corrected mistakes of my own. Nor have I felt it necessary to signal passages where I think de Slane erred. The reader ignorant of Arabic may be slightly puzzled when he observes the divergencies, often considerable, between this translation and that of de Slane. Nonetheless, my hope is that he will put greater reliance in the present translation, although its recent origin, of course, is no guarantee of its correctness.

[163] The total number of "mistakes" of one kind or another in the *Muqaddimah* is astonishingly small. Vico's *La scienza nuova,* by comparison, is full of wrong and outdated statements; cf. the translation by T. G. Bergin and M. H. Fisch (Ithaca, N. Y., 1948), p. VIII. Naturally, Vico was handicapped by his age's predilection for learned information. The desire to show off one's learning led to committing many blunders, but also prepared the soil for a tremendous growth of true learning, such as the prudent and staid civilization of Ibn Khaldûn would never have contemplated.

[164] Variant readings of the MSS have, however, not been indicated with any degree of consistency. Cf. p. lxxxix, above.

Rendering proper names is a minor problem in all translations from the Arabic, as here. Arabic proper names can easily be transcribed, and the method of transcription employed here needs no special comment. However, foreign proper names, and especially place names in northwestern Africa (the Maghrib), make for complications. European place names, Spanish ones most notably, have been translated into their accepted English or current native form. Place names from the East are given in transcription, except when a generally accepted English form exists. There may, however, be differences of opinion as to what constitutes a generally accepted English form. Thus, some of the proper names as well as generally known Arabic terms retained in the translation have been deprived of their macrons or circumflexes, while others, with perhaps an equal claim to such distinction, have been left untouched; as a rule, preference has been given to accurate transcription. With a very few exceptions, place names from northwestern Africa have been given in what may be considered the most widely used and acceptable of the various French forms; usually, a transcription of the Arabic form has been added. In the case of Berber names, we will know how Ibn Khaldûn pronounced them, once a study of the manuscripts of the *'Ibar* has been made. For the time being, we know his pronunciation only in those cases where the manuscripts of the *Muqaddimah* and the *Autobiography* indicate it, and his pronunciation has, of course, been followed. In modern scholarly literature, there seems to be little agreement on the finer points of the transcription of ancient Berber tribal and personal names.

Much more might be said about technical details arising out of the present translation. However, if they were wrongly handled, mere knowledge of that fact would not repair the harm done to, nor, if they were correctly applied, increase by itself the usefulness of, the translation of what has been called with little, if any, exaggeration, "undoubtedly the greatest work of its kind that has ever yet been created by any mind in any time or place." [165]

[165] A. J. Toynbee, *A Study of History* (2d ed.; London, 1935), III, 322.

THE MUQADDIMAH

The Introduction and Book One

of the World History, entitled Kitâb al-ʿIbar,

of Ibn Khaldûn

IN THE NAME OF GOD, THE MERCIFUL, THE COMPASSIONATE. PRAY, O GOD, FOR OUR LORD MUḤAMMAD AND HIS FAMILY AND THE MEN AROUND HIM.

THE SERVANT of God who needs the mercy of God who is so rich in His kindness, 'Abd-ar-Raḥmân b. Muḥammad b. Khaldûn al-Ḥaḍramî—God give him success!—says: [1]

Praised be God! He is powerful and mighty. In His hand, He holds royal authority and kingship.[2] His are the most beautiful names and attributes. His knowledge is such that nothing, be it revealed in secret whispering or (even) left unsaid, remains strange to Him. His power is such that nothing in heaven and upon earth is too much for Him or escapes Him.

He created us from the earth as living, breathing creatures. He made us to settle [3] on it as races and nations. From it, He provided sustenance and provisions for us.

---

[1] These words are written in Maghribî script in B and C. MSS written later in Ibn Khaldûn's life are more effusive. A already has: "The *Shaykh*, jurist, imam, (religious) scholar, chief judge, Walî-ad-dîn 'Abd-ar-Raḥmân b. Khaldûn—God lengthen his life—has said. . . ." C adds in the margin: "This is the Muslim Judge, Walî-ad-dîn Abû Zayd al-Mâlikî." D reads: "Our Lord and Master, the servant of God who needs God, Walî-ad-dîn, the Muslim Judge, Abû Zayd 'Abd-ar-Raḥmân b. Khaldûn al-Ḥaḍramî al-Mâlikî —God lengthen his days and strengthen his judgments and repair all his powers [cf. n. 145, below] and seal his actions with good deeds in His excellence and and generosity, for He is likely and able to do that, and He 'has power over everything'—has said. . . ."

[2] These terms (*mulk* and *malakût*) are commonly used to refer to the natural and supernatural worlds, respectively.

[3] The root *'mr*, from which *'umrân* "civilization" is derived, is used here. It is the purpose of the *khuṭbah* "invocation" of Arabic works to summarize

The wombs of our mothers and houses are our abode.
I, 2 Sustenance and food keep us alive. Time wears us out. Our lives' final terms, the dates of which have been fixed for us in the book (of destiny), claim us. But He lasts and persists. He is the Living One who does not die.

Prayer and blessings upon our Lord and Master, Muḥammad, the Arab [4] prophet, whom Torah and Gospel have mentioned and described; [5] him for whose birth the world that is was (already) in labor before Sundays were following upon Saturdays in regular sequence and before Saturn and Behemoth had become separated; [6] him to whose truthfulness pigeon and spider bore witness.[7]

---

the main theme of the work, and this is what Ibn Khaldûn attempts to do here in two paragraphs.

The word "races," Arabic *jîl*, may also mean "generations." It is occasionally translated by "groups." See p. 249, l. 2, below.

[4] Bulaq adds "illiterate."

[5] In the medieval polemics between Muslims and Christians and Muslims and Jews, an important subject of discussion was the references to Muḥammad that, according to Muslim theologians, could be found in Scripture. Cf., for instance, Maimonides, *Epistle to Yemen*, ed. and tr. A. S. Halkin and B. Cohen (New York, 1952), p. VIII; J. Horovitz in *EI*, *s.v.* "Tawrât"; W. M. Watt, "His Name is Aḥmad," in *The Muslim World*, XLIII (1953), 110–17.

[6] Muḥammad existed prior to time and space, if not in body at least in soul and through the divine light of prophecy, which, as something divine, was also primeval. The (Neo-Platonic, mystic, Shî'ah) theory of the primeval prophetic light was common in orthodox Islam long before Ibn Khaldûn's time and had been spread mainly through the medium of Sufism. Cf. T. Andrae, *Die Person Muhammeds in Lehre und Glauben seiner Gemeinde* (Stockholm, 1917), pp. 313 ff.; L. Massignon in *EI*, *s.v.* "Nûr Muḥammadî."

Saturn occupies the seventh heaven and, therefore, represents the most remote distance. Cf. W. Hartner in *EI*, *s.v.* "Zuḥal."

Al-Bah(a)mût is the Biblical Behemoth of Job 40:15, which Jewish tradition identified with Leviathan. Some commentators of Qur'ân 68.1 (1) (cf. al-Bayḍâwî and the references given by de Slane) identify the mythological fish upon which the earth rests with Behemoth.

[7] When Muḥammad left Mecca to go to Medina, he stayed in a cave for some time. Meccans who went after him saw that two pigeons had built a nest over the entrance to the cave, and/or a spider had spread a web over it. They concluded that no one could have used the cave recently. This famous legend, which is mentioned by the commentaries on Qur'ân 9.40 (40), is of rather late origin and was considered with some suspicion even by medieval biographers of the Prophet. Cf. Ibn Kathîr, *Bidâyah* (Cairo, 1351–58/1932–40), III, 181 f.

(Prayer and blessings) also upon his family and the men around him who by being his companions [8] and followers gained wide influence and fame and who by supporting him found unity while their enemies were weakened through dispersion. Pray, O God, for him and them, for as long as Islam shall continue to enjoy its lucky fortune and the frayed rope of unbelief shall remain cut! Give manifold blessings (to him and them)!

[8] *Ṣuḥbatihî*, as in B and D. A, C, and E have *maḥabbatihî* "loving him."

(FOREWORD)

HISTORY is a discipline widely cultivated among nations and races. It is eagerly sought after. The men in the street, the ordinary people, aspire to know it. Kings and leaders vie for it.

Both the learned and the ignorant are able to understand it. For on the surface history is no more than information about political events, dynasties, and occurrences of the remote past, elegantly presented and spiced with proverbs. It serves to entertain large, crowded gatherings and brings to us an understanding of human affairs. (It shows) how changing conditions affected (human affairs), how certain dynasties came to occupy an ever wider space in the world, and how they settled the earth until they heard the call and their time was up.

The inner meaning of history, on the other hand, involves speculation and an attempt to get at the truth, subtle explanation of the causes and origins of existing things, and deep knowledge of the how and why of events. (History,) therefore, is firmly rooted in philosophy. It deserves to be accounted a branch of (philosophy).[9]

The outstanding Muslim historians made exhaustive collections of historical events and wrote them down in book
I, 3 form. But, then, persons who had no right to occupy themselves with history introduced into those books untrue gossip which they had thought up or freely invented, as well as false, discredited reports which they had made up or embellished. Many of their successors followed in their steps and

[9] Cf. Bombaci, p. 441.

passed that information on to us as they had heard it. They did not look for, or pay any attention to, the causes of events and conditions, nor did they eliminate or reject nonsensical stories.

Little effort is being made to get at the truth. The critical eye, as a rule, is not sharp. Errors and unfounded assumptions are closely allied and familiar elements in historical information. Blind trust in tradition is an inherited trait in human beings. Occupation with the (scholarly) disciplines on the part of those who have no right is widespread. But the pasture of stupidity is unwholesome for mankind. No one can stand up against the authority of truth, and the evil of falsehood is to be fought with enlightening speculation. The reporter merely dictates and passes on (the material). It takes critical insight to sort out the hidden truth; it takes knowledge to lay truth bare and polish it so that critical insight may be applied to it.

Many systematic historical works have been composed, and the history of nations and dynasties in the world has been compiled and written down. But there are very few (historians) who have become so well known as to be recognized as authorities, and who have replaced the products of their predecessors by their own works. They can almost be counted on the fingers of the hands; they are hardly more numerous than the vowels in grammatical constructions (which are just three). There are, for instance, Ibn Isḥâq; [10] aṭ-Ṭabarî; [11] Ibn al-Kalbî; [12] Muḥammad b. ʻUmar al-Wâqidî; [13] Sayf b. ʻUmar al-Asadî; [14] al-Masʻûdî,[15] and other famous (histo-

[10] Muḥammad b. Isḥâq, author of the famous biography (*sîrah*) of Muḥammad. He died in 150 or 151 [A.D. 767/68]. Cf. *GAL*, I, 134 f.; *Suppl.*, I, 205 f.

[11] Muḥammad b. Jarîr, author of the *Annales*, 224/25–310 [839–923]. Cf. *GAL*, I, 142 f.; *Suppl.*, I, 217 f.

[12] Hishâm b. Muḥammad, d. 204 or 206 [819/20 or 821/22]. Cf. *GAL*, I, 138 ff.; *Suppl.*, I, 211 f.

[13] The biographer of Muḥammad and historian of early Islam, 130–207 [747–823]. Cf. *GAL*, I, 135 f.; *Suppl.*, I, 207 f.

[14] He died in 180 [796/97]. Cf. *GAL*, *Suppl.*, I, 213 f.

[15] ʻAlî b. al-Ḥusayn, d. 345 or 346 [956 or 957]. Cf. *GAL*, I, 143 ff.; *Suppl.*, I, 270 f.

rians) who are distinguished from the general run (of historians).

It is well known to competent persons and reliable experts that the works of al-Mas'ûdî and al-Wâqidî are suspect and objectionable in certain respects.[16] However, their works have been distinguished by universal acceptance of the information they contain and by adoption of their methods and their presentation of material. The discerning critic is his own judge as to which part of their material he
I, 4 finds spurious, and which he gives credence to. Civilization, in its (different) conditions, contains (different) elements to which historical information may be related and with which reports and historical materials may be checked.

Most of the histories by these (authors) cover everything because of the universal geographical extension of the two earliest Islamic dynasties [17] and because of the very wide selection of sources of which they did or did not make use. Some of these authors, such as al-Mas'ûdî and historians of his type, gave an exhaustive history of the pre-Islamic dynasties and nations and of other (pre-Islamic) affairs in general. Some later historians, on the other hand, showed a tendency toward greater restriction, hesitating to be so general and comprehensive. They brought together the happenings of their own period and gave exhaustive historical information about their own part of the world. They restricted themselves to the history of their own dynasties and cities. This was done by Ibn Ḥayyân, the historian of Spain

[16] Ibn Khaldûn's Egyptian pupil, Ibn Ḥajar, is a good witness as to the partisan objections of theologians against the historians mentioned. Al-Mas'ûdî's works are out of circulation (*ṭâfiḥah*), because he was a Shî'ah and Mu'tazilah, and the Spaniard Ibn Diḥyah (cf. *GAL*, I, 310 ff.; *Suppl.*, I, 544 f.) thought very little of him. Cf. Ibn Ḥajar, *Lisân al-Mîzân* (Hyderabad, 1329–31/1911–13), IV, 224 f. Al-Wâqidî is often considered an untruthful transmitter of historical traditions and ignorant of pre-Islamic history. Ash-Shâfi'î declared all his writings to be lies. Cf. al-Khaṭîb al-Baghdâdî, *Ta'rîkh Baghdâd* (Cairo, 1349/1931), III, 14 ff.; and Ibn Ḥajar, *Tahdhîb* (Hyderabad, 1325–27/1907–9), IX, 363 ff.

[17] That is, the Umayyads and the 'Abbâsids.

and the Spanish Umayyads,[18] and by Ibn ar-Raqîq, the historian of Ifrîqiyah and the dynasty in Kairouan (al-Qayrawân).[19]

The later historians were all tradition-bound and dull of nature and intelligence, or, (at any rate) did not try not to be dull. They merely copied [20] the (older historians) and followed their example. They disregarded the changes in conditions and in the customs of nations and races that the passing of time had brought about. Thus, they presented historical information about dynasties and stories of events from the early period as mere forms without substance, blades without scabbards, as knowledge that must be considered ignorance, because it is not known what of it is extraneous and what is genuine. (Their information) concerns happenings the origins of which are not known. It concerns species the genera of which are not taken into consideration, and whose (specific) differences are not verified.[21] With the information they set down they merely repeated historical material which is, in any case, widely known, and followed the earlier historians who worked on it. They neglected the importance of change over the generations in their treatment of the (historical material), because they had no one who could interpret it for them. Their works, therefore, give no explanation for it. When they then turn to the description of I, 5
a particular dynasty, they report the historical information about it (mechanically) and take care to preserve it as it had been passed on down to them, be it imaginary or true. They

[18] Ḥayyân b. Khalaf, 377–469 [987/88–1076]. Cf. *GAL*, I, 338; *Suppl.*, I, 578; and see below, 3:364. B and C change the correct *Ibn* Ḥayyân in the margin to Abû Ḥayyân.

[19] Ibrâhîm b. al-Qâsim, who lived *ca.* A.D. 1000. Cf. *GAL*, I, 155; *Suppl.*, I, 229, 252; see also below, 1:360 and 3:363.

Ifrîqiyah reflects the name of the Roman province of Africa. This geographical term is commonly used by Ibn Khaldûn (cf. p. 130, below) and has been retained in the translation.

[20] Literally, "wove on the loom." Cf., for instance, n. 1444 to Ch. VI, below.

[21] For these terms of logic, see below, 3:142, 145, and 272, for example. Cf. Bombaci, p. 441.

do not turn to the beginning of the dynasty. Nor do they tell why it unfurled its banner and was able to give prominence to its emblem, or what caused it to come to a stop when it had reached its term. The student, thus, has still to search for the beginnings of conditions and for (the principles of) organization of (the various dynasties). He must (himself) investigate why the various dynasties brought pressures to bear upon each other and why they succeeded each other. He must search for a convincing explanation of the elements that made for mutual separation or contact among the dynasties. All this will be dealt with in the Introduction to this work.

Other historians, then, came with too brief a presentation (of history). They went to the extreme of being satisfied with the names of kings, without any genealogical or historical information, and with only a numerical indication of the length of reigns.[22] This was done by Ibn Rashîq in the *Mîzân al-'amal,*[23] and by those lost sheep who followed his method. No credence can be given to what they say. They are not considered trustworthy, nor is their material considered worthy of transmission, for they caused useful material to be lost and damaged the methods and customs acknowledged (as sound and practical) by historians.

When I had read the works of others and probed into the recesses of yesterday and today, I shook myself out of that drowsy complacency and sleepiness. Although not much of a writer,[24] I exhibited my own literary ability as well as I could, and, thus, composed a book on history. In (this book) I lifted the veil from conditions as they arise in the various generations. I arranged it in an orderly way in chapters

---

[22] For the so-called "dust letters" mentioned here as used for numerical indication, see n. 882 to Ch. vi, below.

[23] Ḥasan b. Rashîq, 390 to 456 or 463 [1000 to 1064 or 1070/71]. Cf. *GAL,* I, 307; *Suppl.,* I, 539 f. Ibn Khaldûn's reference to the *Mîzân al-'amal* was apparently copied by Ḥâjjî Khalîfah, *Kashf aẓ-ẓunûn,* ed. Flügel (Leipzig & London, 1835–58), VI, 285. The *Mîzân al-'amal* is not preserved.

[24] Literally, "I bargained on my own for authorship though I was bankrupt. . . ."

dealing with historical facts and reflections. In it I showed how and why dynasties and civilization originate. I based the work on the history of the two races that constitute the population of the Maghrib at this time and people its various regions and cities, and on that of their ruling houses, both long- and short-lived, including the rulers and allies they had in the past. These two races are the Arabs and the Berbers. They are the two races known to have resided in the Maghrib for such a long time that one can hardly imagine I, 6
they ever lived elsewhere, for its inhabitants know no other human races.

I corrected the contents of the work carefully and presented it to the judgment of scholars and the elite. I followed an unusual method of arrangement and division into chapters. From the various possibilities, I chose a remarkable and original method. In the work, I commented on civilization, on urbanization, and on the essential characteristics of human social organization, in a way that explains to the reader how and why things are as they are, and shows him how the men who constituted a dynasty first came upon the historical scene. As a result, he will wash his hands of any blind trust in tradition. He will become aware of the conditions of periods and races that were before his time and that will be after it.

I divided the work into an introduction and three books:

> The Introduction deals with the great merit of historiography, (offers) an appreciation of its various methods, and cites errors of the historians.
>
> The First Book deals with civilization and its essential characteristics, namely, royal authority, government, gainful occupations, ways of making a living, crafts, and sciences, as well as with the causes and reasons thereof.
>
> The Second Book deals with the history, races, and dynasties of the Arabs, from the beginning of creation down to this time. This will include references to such

famous nations and dynasties contemporaneous with them,[25] as the Nabataeans,[26] the Syrians, the Persians, the Israelites, the Copts, the Greeks, the Byzantines, and the Turks.

The Third Book deals with the history of the Berbers and of the Zanâtah who are part of them; with their origins and races; and, in particular, with the royal authority and dynasties in the Maghrib.

I, 7 Later on, there was my trip to the East, in order to find out about the manifold illumination it offers and to fulfill the religious duty and custom of circumambulating the Ka'bah and visiting Medina, as well as to study the systematic works and tomes on (Eastern) history. As a result, I was able to fill the gaps in my historical information about the non-Arab (Persian) rulers of those lands, and about the Turkish dynasties in the regions over which they ruled. I added this information to what I had written here (before in this connection). I inserted it into the treatment of the nations of the various districts and rulers of the various cities and regions that were contemporary with those (Persian and Turkish) races. In this connection I was brief and concise and preferred the easy goal to the difficult one. I proceeded from general genealogical (tables) [27] to detailed historical information.

Thus, (this work) contains an exhaustive history of the world. It forces stubborn stray wisdom to return to the fold. It gives causes and reasons for happenings in the various dynasties. It turns out to be a vessel for philosophy, a receptacle for historical knowledge. The work contains the

---

[25] Since the pre-Islamic Arabs are considered to have existed since the beginning of the world, all the nations of the world may be said to have been their contemporaries.

[26] The Nabataeans, according to Muslim belief, were the pre-Islamic population indigenous to the 'Irâq. The ancient Syrians, as well as the Nabataeans, include the ancient Mesopotamians.

[27] Bulaq and E have *al-asbâb* "general causes," but the reading *al-ansâb* seems preferable. The genealogical tables are the ones which Ibn Khaldûn regularly adds to the historical description of peoples and dynasties in the *'Ibar*.

history of the Arabs and the Berbers, both the sedentary groups and the nomads. It also contains references to the great dynasties that were contemporary with them, and, moreover, clearly indicates memorable lessons to be learned from early conditions and from subsequent history. Therefore, I called the work "Book of Lessons and Archive of Early and Subsequent History, Dealing with the Political Events Concerning the Arabs, Non-Arabs, and Berbers, and the Supreme Rulers Who Were Contemporary with Them." [28]

I omitted nothing concerning the origin of races and dynasties, concerning the synchronism of the earliest nations, concerning the reasons for change and variation in past periods and within religious groups, concerning dynasties and religious groups, towns and hamlets, strength and humiliation, large numbers and small numbers, sciences and crafts, gains and losses, changing general conditions, nomadic and sedentary life, actual events and future events, all things ex- I, 8
pected to occur in civilization. I treated everything comprehensively and exhaustively and explained the arguments for and causes of it(s existence).

[28] In Arabic: *Kitâb al-ʿIbar wa-dîwân al-mubtada' wa-l-khabar fî ayyâm al-ʿArab wa-l-ʿAjam wa-l-Barbar wa-man ʿâṣarahum min dhawî as-sulṭân al-akbar*. The exact meaning of the title, especially of the words *dîwân al-mubtada' wa-l-khabar*, translated here by "Archive of Early and Subsequent History," has given rise to much speculation. A recent discussion is that of R. Köbert in *Orientalia*, N.S. XV (1946), 150–54. The different suggestions are conveniently summarized by Fischel, *Ibn Khaldûn and Tamerlane*, p. 25 (n. 32). Closest to the correct understanding was Silvestre de Sacy in his *Chrestomathie arabe* (Paris, 1826), II, 290.

Al-mubtada' and *al-khabar* placed next to each other are grammatical terms which refer to the subject and predicate of a nominal sentence. The subject of a nominal sentence comes at the beginning and the predicate usually at the end. The sense in which Ibn Khaldûn wants "beginning" and "end" to be understood here is made amply clear by the preceding sentence (as well as by the whole *Muqaddimah*). In the preceding sentence, *mubtada' al-aḥwâl wa-mâ baʿdahû min al-khabar*, translated here by "early conditions and subsequent history," refers to the "early conditions," the beginnings of human social and political organization, which come first like the subject of a nominal sentence; "subsequent history" (*khabar*) follows upon them as the predicate of a nominal sentence follows its subject. The grammatical connection is conceived by Ibn Khaldûn as a logical connection, suggesting a causal nexus between "early beginnings" and "subsequent history."

As a result, this book has become unique, as it contains unusual knowledge and familiar if hidden wisdom. Still, after all has been said, I am conscious of imperfection when (I look at) the scholars of (past and contemporary) times.[29] I confess my inability to penetrate so difficult a subject. I wish that men of scholarly competence and wide knowledge would look at the book with a critical, rather than a complacent eye, and silently correct and overlook the mistakes they come upon. The capital of knowledge that an individual scholar has to offer is small. Admission (of one's shortcomings) saves from censure. Kindness from colleagues is hoped for. It is God whom I ask to make our deeds acceptable in His sight. He suffices me. He is a good protector.[30]

[29] *Ahl al-'uṣûr*. For this expression, cf. *Autobiography*, p. 297, and below, 2:463 (*a'immat al-a'ṣâr*).

[30] Cf. Qur'ân 3.173 (167). In some MSS, a dedication addressed to a particular patron follows here.

INTRODUCTION

The excellence of historiography.—An appreciation of the various approaches to history.—A glimpse at the different kinds of errors to which historians are liable. Something about why these errors occur.[31]

IT SHOULD BE KNOWN that history is a discipline that has a great number of (different) approaches. Its useful aspects are very many. Its goal is distinguished.

(History) makes us acquainted with the conditions of past nations as they are reflected in their (national) character. It makes us acquainted with the biographies of the prophets and with the dynasties and policies of rulers. Whoever so desires may thus achieve the useful result of being able to imitate historical examples in religious and worldly matters.

The (writing[32] of history) requires numerous sources and greatly varied knowledge. It also requires a good speculative mind and thoroughness. (Possession of these two qualities) leads the historian to the truth and keeps him from slips and errors. If he trusts historical information in its plain transmitted form and has no clear knowledge of the principles resulting from custom, the fundamental facts of politics, the nature of civilization, or the conditions governing human social organization, and if, furthermore, he does not evaluate remote or ancient material through comparison 1, 9

[31] The following four pages were translated by R. A. Nicholson, *Translations of Eastern Poetry and Prose* (Cambridge, 1922), pp. 176–79. The Arabic text, down to p. 56, l. 30, of this translation, was edited with notes and a glossary by D. B. Macdonald, *A Selection from the Prolegomena of Ibn Khaldûn* (Semitic Study Series, No. 4) (Leiden, 1905; repr. 1948).

[32] Nicholson supplies "student" instead of "writing."

with near or contemporary material, he often cannot avoid stumbling and slipping and deviating from the highroad of truth. Historians, Qur'ân commentators and leading transmitters have committed frequent errors in the stories and events they reported. They accepted them in the plain transmitted form, without regard for its value. They did not check them with the principles underlying such historical situations, nor did they compare them with similar material. Also, they did not probe (more deeply) with the yardstick of philosophy, with the help of knowledge of the nature of things, or with the help of speculation and historical insight. Therefore, they strayed from the truth and found themselves lost in the desert of baseless assumptions and errors.

This is especially the case with figures, either of sums of money or of soldiers, whenever they occur in stories. They offer a good opportunity for false information and constitute a vehicle for nonsensical statements. They must be controlled and checked with the help of known fundamental facts.

For example, al-Mas'ûdî and many other historians report that Moses counted the army of the Israelites in the desert.[33] He had all those able to carry arms, especially those twenty years and older, pass muster. There turned out to be 600,000 or more. In this connection, (al-Mas'ûdî) forgets to take into consideration whether Egypt and Syria could possibly have held such a number of soldiers. Every realm may have as large a militia as it can hold and support, but no more. This fact is attested by well-known customs and familiar conditions. Moreover, an army of this size cannot march or fight as a unit. The whole available territory would be too small for it. If it were in battle formation, it would extend two, three, or more times beyond the field of vision.

---

[33] Cf. al-Mas'ûdî, *Murûj adh-dhahab* (Paris, 1861–77), I, 93 f.; IV, 20. Al-Mas'ûdî refers briefly to the number of Israelites. According to al-Bakrî, *Kitâb al-masâlik wa-l-mamâlik* (MS. Nuru Osmaniye, 3034, fol. 47*a*), Moses left Egypt with 620,000 men able to carry arms, not counting those under ten and over sixty years of age. The exact number 603,550 found in Num. 1:46, was also known to the Arabs; cf., for instance, Ibn Kathîr, *Bidâyah*, I, 321, where the printed text gives 603,555.

How, then, could two such parties fight with each other, or one battle formation gain the upper hand when one flank does not know what the other flank is doing! The situation at the present day testifies to the correctness of this statement. The past resembles the future more than one (drop of) water another. I, 10

Furthermore, the realm of the Persians was much greater than that of the Israelites. This fact is attested by Nebuchadnezzar's victory over them. He swallowed up their country and gained complete control over it. He also destroyed Jerusalem, their religious and political capital. And he was merely one of the officials of the province of Fârs.[34] It is said that he was the governor of the western border region. The Persian provinces of the two 'Irâqs,[35] Khurâsân, Transoxania, and the region of Derbend on the Caspian Sea [36] were much larger than the realm of the Israelites. Yet, the Persian army did not attain such a number or even approach it. The greatest concentration of Persian troops, at al-Qâdisîyah, amounted to 120,000 men, all of whom had their retainers. This is according to Sayf [37] who said that with their retainers they amounted to over 200,000 persons. According to 'Â'ishah and az-Zuhrî,[38] the troop concentration with which Rustum advanced against Sa'd at al-Qâdisîyah amounted to only 60,000 men, all of whom had their retainers.

Then, if the Israelites had really amounted to such a number, the extent of the area under their rule would have been larger, for the size of administrative units and provinces under a particular dynasty is in direct proportion to the size

---

[34] Al-Mas'ûdî, *Murûj adh-dhahab*, I, 117, describes him as governor of the 'Irâq and the Arabs for the Persian King (King of Fârs). Cf. also aṭ-Ṭabarî, *Annales*, I, 646.

[35] That is, Mesopotamia and northwestern Persia adjacent to it.

[36] Cf. W. Barthold in *EI*, *s.v.* "Derbend." For the "Gates" and Derbend, see also p. 155, below.

[37] See p. 7, above. For the numbers of the participants in this battle, see also p. 321, below.

[38] Muḥammad b. Muslim, who died between 123 and 125 [740 and 742/43]. Cf. *GAL*, I, 65; *Suppl.*, I, 102.

of its militia and the groups that support the (dynasty), as will be explained in the section on provinces in the first book.[39] Now, it is well known that the territory of the (Israelites) did not comprise an area larger than the Jordan province and Palestine in Syria and the region of Medina and Khaybar in the Ḥijâz.[40] Also, there were only three generations [41] between Moses and Israel, according to the best-informed scholars. Moses was the son of Amram, the son of Kohath (*Qâhat* or *Qâhit*), the son of Levi (*Lêwî* or
I, *11* *Lâwî*),[42] the son of Jacob who is Israel-Allâh. This is Moses' genealogy in the Torah.[43] The length of time between Israel and Moses was indicated by al-Mas'ûdî when he said: "Israel entered Egypt with his children, the tribes, and their children, when they came to Joseph numbering seventy souls. The length of their stay in Egypt until they left with Moses for the desert was two hundred and twenty years. During those years, the kings of the Copts, the Pharaohs, passed them on (as their subjects) one to the other." [44] It is improbable that the descendants of one man could branch out into such a number within four generations.[45]

It has been assumed that this number of soldiers applied to the time of Solomon and his successors. Again, this is improbable. Between Solomon and Israel, there were only eleven generations, that is: Solomon, the son of David, the son of Jesse, the son of Obed (*'Ûbidh*, or *'Ûfidh*), the son of Boaz (*Bâ'az*, or *Bû'iz*), the son of Salmon, the son of Nahshon, the son of Amminadab (*'Ammînâdhâb*, or *Ḥammînâdhâb*), the son of Ram, the son of Hezron (*Ḥaḍ/ṣrûn*,

[39] See pp. 327 ff., below.

[40] See also p. 474, below.

[41] The early text, as represented by Bulaq, had the statement (later corrected by Ibn Khaldûn) that there were four generations between Moses and Jacob. Amram is made the son of Izhar, the son of Kohath. Cf. also, for instance, ath-Tha'labî, *Qiṣaṣ al-anbiyâ'*, at the beginning of the chapter on Moses.

[42] The MSS state that the *L* of Levi should have either *i* or *a*, as indicated above. * For Israel-Allâh, cf. aṭ-Ṭabarî, I, 442.

[43] Exod. 6:16 ff.

[44] The quotation is not, apparently, to be found in al-Mas'ûdî.

[45] On population increase, see also *'Ibar*, V, 506.

or *Ḥasrûn*), the son of Perez (*Bâras*, or *Bayras*), the son of Judah, the son of Jacob. The descendants of one man in eleven generations would not branch out into such a number, as has been assumed. They might, indeed, reach hundreds or thousands. This often happens. But an increase beyond that to higher figures [46] is improbable. Comparison with observable present-day and well-known nearby facts proves the assumption and report to be untrue. According to the definite statement of the Israelite Stories,[47] Solomon's army amounted to 12,000 men, and his horses [48] numbered 1,400 horses, which were stabled at his palace. This is the correct information. No attention should be paid to nonsensical statements by the common run of informants. In the days of Solomon, the Israelite state saw its greatest flourishing and their realm its widest extension.

Whenever [49] contemporaries speak about the dynastic armies of their own or recent times, and whenever they engage in discussions about Muslim or Christian soldiers, or when they get to figuring the tax revenues and the money spent by the government, the outlays of extravagant spenders, and the goods that rich and prosperous men have in stock, they are quite generally found to exaggerate, to go beyond the bounds of the ordinary, and to succumb to the temptation of sensationalism. When the officials in charge are questioned about their armies, when the goods and assets *1, 12*

[46] Literally, "to higher powers of ten" (*'uqûd*). Cf. also J. Ruska, *Der Islam*, X (1920), 87 ff. Somewhat different, Bombaci, p. 441.

[47] Cf. I Kings 10:26. As a rule, Muslim scholars gave an unpleasant connotation to the term "Israelite Stories," as mere fiction presented as history. Cf. F. Rosenthal, *A History of Muslim Historiography*, p. 417.

[48] *Muqrabât* is an adjective used in connection with horses and camels. Ibn Khaldûn uses the word commonly for good riding (or race) horses; see 2:358, below, and *'Ibar*, V, 473, 479 f., 501; VI, 289, 394; VII, 36. The vocalization *muqrabât*, as against *muqarrabât*, is confirmed by a verse of Ibn Khaldûn's in the *Autobiography*, p. 73, l. 4. Regardless of what the original derivation of the term may have been (cf. *Lisân al-'Arab*, II, 158; Ibn Hudhayl, *La Parure des cavaliers*, ed. L. Mercier [Paris, 1922], p. 29; tr. by the same [Paris, 1924], p. 110), Ibn Khaldûn seems to have connected it with the form *qarraba*, in the meaning of "to present" (noble horses as a gift). This is shown by *'Ibar*, V, 499, last line.

[49] Cf. Issawi, p. 29.

of wealthy people are assessed, and when the outlays of extravagant spenders are looked at in ordinary light, the figures will be found to amount to a tenth of what those people have said. The reason is simple. It is the common desire for sensationalism, the ease with which one may just mention a higher figure, and the disregard of reviewers and critics. This leads to failure to exercise self-criticism about one's errors and intentions, to demand from oneself moderation and fairness in reporting, to reapply oneself to study and research. Such historians let themselves go and made a feast of untrue statements. "They procure for themselves entertaining stories in order to lead (others) astray from the path of God." [50] This is a bad enough business.

It [51] may be said that the increase of descendants to such a number would be prevented under ordinary conditions which, however, do not apply to the Israelites. (The increase in their case) would be a miracle in accordance with the tradition which said that one of the things revealed to their forefathers, the prophets Abraham, Isaac, and Jacob, was that God would cause their descendants to increase until they were more numerous than the stars of heaven and the pebbles of the earth. God fulfilled this promise to them as an act of divine grace bestowed upon them and as an extraordinary miracle in their favor. Thus, ordinary conditions could not hinder (such an event), and nobody should speak against it.

Someone might come out against this tradition (with the
I, *13* argument) that it occurs only in the Torah which, as is well known, was altered by the Jews. (The reply to this argument would be that) the statement concerning the alteration (of the Torah by the Jews) is unacceptable to thorough scholars and cannot be understood in its plain meaning, since custom prevents people who have a (revealed) religion from dealing with their divine scriptures in such a manner. This was men-

---

[50] Qur'ân 31.6 (5).

[51] The following three paragraphs are found in the margin of C (and in MS. Nuru Osmaniye, 3424), but appear neither in the earlier texts nor in D.

tioned by al-Bukhârî in the *Ṣaḥîḥ*.[52] Thus, the great increase in numbers in the case of the Israelites would be an extraordinary miracle. Custom, in the proper meaning of the word, would prevent anything of the sort from happening to other peoples.

It is true that a (co-ordinated battle) movement in (such a large group) would hardly be possible, but none took place, and there was no need for one. It is also true that each realm has its particular number of militia (and no more). But the Israelites at first were no militiamen and had no dynasty. Their numbers increased that much, so that they could gain power over the land of Canaan which God had promised them and the territory of which He had purified for them. All these things are miracles. God guides to the truth.

The [53] history of the Tubba'Ꞌs, the kings of the Yemen and of the Arabian Peninsula, as it is generally transmitted, is another example of silly statements by historians. It is said that from their home in the Yemen, (the Tubba'Ꞌs) used to raid Ifrîqiyah and the Berbers of the Maghrib. Afrîqus b. Qays b. Ṣayfî, one of their great early kings who lived in the time of Moses or somewhat earlier,[54] is said to have raided Ifrîqiyah. He caused a great slaughter among the Berbers. He gave them the name of Berbers when he heard

---

[52] For Muḥammad b. Ismâ'îl al-Bukhârî, 194–256 [810–870], and his famous canonical collection of prophetical traditions, see *GAL*, I, 157 ff.; *Suppl.*, I, 260 ff. I do not know which passage of the *Ṣaḥîḥ* Ibn Khaldûn may have had in mind here. Al-Bukhârî certainly believed in the alteration of the Torah by the Jews. Perhaps Ibn Khaldûn was recalling the often-quoted tradition that the Muslims should neither believe nor disbelieve statements concerning the Torah made by Jews and Christians; cf. J. Horovitz in *EI*, *s.v.* "Tawrât."

[53] The whole discussion of South Arabian history appears in C on an inserted sheet.

[54] The historical reports on ancient South Arabian history were no less confusing for Ibn Khaldûn than they are for us. He tried to deal with them critically in *'Ibar*, II, 50 ff. Cf. below, pp. 296 and 360. For the legendary eponym of Africa, one may also compare al-Balâdhurî, *Futûḥ al-buldân*, ed. M. J. de Goeje (Leiden, 1866), p. 229; (Pseudo-)Ibn Hishâm, *Tîjân* (Hyderabad, 1347/1928–29), pp. 407 ff. Ibn Ḥazm, *Jamharat ansâb al-'Arab* (Cairo, 1948), p. 461, calls Ḥimyar-Berber connections lies existing only in the imagination of Yemenite historians.

their jargon and asked what that "*barbarah*" was.[55] This gave them the name which has remained with them since that time. When he left the Maghrib, he is said to have concentrated some Ḥimyar tribes there. They remained there and mixed with the native population. Their (descendants) are the Ṣinhâjah and the Kutâmah. This led aṭ-Ṭabarî, al-Jurjânî,[56]
I, *14* al-Mas'ûdî, Ibn al-Kalbî,[57] and al-Bayhaqî[58] to make the statement that the Ṣinhâjah and the Kutâmah belong to the Ḥimyar. The Berber genealogists do not admit this, and they are right. Al-Mas'ûdî also mentioned that one of the Ḥimyar kings after Afrîqus, Dhû l-Adh'âr, who lived in the time of Solomon, raided the Maghrib and forced it into submission. Something similar is mentioned by al-Mas'ûdî concerning his son and successor, Yâsir.[59] He is said to have reached the Sand River[60] in the Maghrib and to have been unable to find passage through it because of the great mass of sand. Therefore, he returned.

Likewise, it is said that the last Tubba',[61] As'ad Abû Karib, who lived in the time of the Persian Kayyanid king

---

[55] Cf. also aṭ-Ṭabarî, *Annales*, I, 516; *'Ibar*, II, 51; VI, 89, 93 f.; de Slane (tr.), I, 168, 176.

[56] 'Alî b. 'Abd-al-'Azîz, d. 392 [1002]. Cf. *GAL*, *Suppl.*, I, 199. Cf. also *'Ibar*, VI, 93; de Slane (tr.), I, 175.

[57] See p. 7, above, and *'Ibar*, VI, 90; de Slane (tr.), I, 170.

[58] Al-Bayhaqî's *Kitâb al-Kamâ'im* is one of the principal sources for Ibn Sa'îd's (see 3:445, below) account of pre-Islamic history. Cf. F. Trummeter, *Ibn Sa'îd's Geschichte der vorislamischen Araber*, p. 62; *GAL*, *Suppl.*, I, 558. Ibn Sa'îd, in turn, was one of Ibn Khaldûn's sources. However, the identity of the author of the *Kamâ'im* is not certain. It has been suggested that he was the historian and littérateur 'Alî b. Zayd, 499–565 [1106–1169] (*GAL*, I, 324; *Suppl.*, I, 557 f.), but we are well informed about his literary output, and no *Kitâb al-Kamâ'im* appears in the list of his works.

[59] Al-Mas'ûdî mentions Afrîqus and his brother Dhû l-Adh'âr, and in another context speaks of the Sand River; cf. *Murûj adh-dhahab*, II, 224, 151; I, 369. But the story of Yâsir (whose name is occasionally spelled Nâshir, incorrectly) and the Sand River appears in aṭ-Ṭabarî, *Annales*, I, 684 ff.

[60] On the legendary Wâdî as-Sabt (the "Sabbath River" of the Jewish Sambation legends) in the West, where sand flows like water, see G. Ferrand, "Le *Tuḥfat al-albâb* de Abû Ḥâmid al-Andalusî al-Ġarnâṭî," in *Journal asiatique*, CCVII (1925), 48, 252. Cf. also Ibn al-Athîr, *Kâmil*, I, 118 f.

[61] Or rather, "the second"? Ḥamzah al-Iṣfahânî, *Annales*, ed. Gottwaldt (St. Petersburg & Leipzig, 1844–48), I, 125, calls him *al-awsaṭ*, "the middle Tubba'," but *al-âkhir* is, of course, found elsewhere. Cf. Ibn Hishâm, *Sîrah*, ed. Wüstenfeld (Göttingen, 1858–60), I, 12.

Yastâsb,[62] ruled over Mosul and Azerbaijan. He is said to have met and routed the Turks and to have caused a great slaughter among them. Then he raided them again a second and a third time. After that, he is said to have sent three of his sons on raids, (one) against the country of Fârs, (one) against the country of the Soghdians, one of the Turkish nations of Transoxania, and (one) against the country of the Rûm (Byzantines).[63] The first brother took possession of the country up to Samarkand and crossed the desert into China. There, he found his second brother who had raided the Soghdians and had arrived in China before him. The two together caused a great slaughter in China and returned together with their booty. They left some Ḥimyar tribes in Tibet. They have been there down to this time. The third brother is said to have reached Constantinople. He laid siege to it and forced the country of the Rûm (Byzantines) into submission. Then, he returned.

All this information is remote from the truth. It is rooted in baseless and erroneous assumptions. It is more like the fiction of storytellers. The realm of the Tubba's was restricted to the Arabian peninsula. Their home and seat was Ṣan'â' in the Yemen. The Arabian peninsula is surrounded by the ocean on three sides: the Indian Ocean on the south, the Persian Gulf jutting out of the Indian Ocean to al-Baṣrah
on the east, and the Red Sea jutting out of the Indian Ocean I, *15*
to Suez in Egypt on the west. This can be seen on the map. There is no way from the Yemen to the Maghrib except via Suez. The distance between the Red Sea and the Mediterranean is two days' journey or less. It is unlikely that the distance could be traversed by a great ruler with a large army unless he controlled that region. This, as a rule, is impossible. In that region there were the Amalekites and Canaan in Syria, and, in Egypt, the Copts. Later on, the Amalekites

---

[62] This is how Ibn Khaldûn read the name, as indicated by the vocalization in C. B and D similarly have Yastâsab, and in the passage below, p. 25, D has *f* as the last letter. It should be Bishtâsp = Vishtâspa. The Kayyanids correspond to the historical Achaemenids.

[63] For the eastern expedition of the Tubba's, see Ibn al-Athîr, *Kâmil*, I, 119, and (Pseudo-)Ibn Hishâm, *Tîjân*, pp. 429 ff.

took possession of Egypt, and the Israelites (took possession) of Syria. There is, however, no report that the Tubba's ever fought against one of these nations or that they had possession of any part of this region. Furthermore, the distance from the Yemen to the Maghrib is great, and an army requires much food and fodder. Soldiers traveling in regions other than their own have to requisition grain and livestock and to plunder the countries they pass through. As a rule, such a procedure does not yield enough food and fodder. On the other hand, if they attempted to take along enough provisions from their own region, they would not have enough animals for transportation. So, their whole line of march necessarily takes them through regions they must take possession of and force into submission in order to obtain provisions from them. Again, it would be a most unlikely and impossible assumption that such an army could pass through all those nations without disturbing them, obtaining its provisions by peaceful negotiation. This shows that all such information (about Tubba' expeditions to the Maghrib) is silly or fictitious.

Mention of the (allegedly) impassable Ṣand River has never been heard in the Maghrib, although the Maghrib has often been crossed and its roads have been explored by
I, 16 travelers and raiders at all times and in every direction.[64]
Because of the unusual character of the story, there is much eagerness to pass it on.

With regard to the (alleged) raid of the Tubba's against the countries of the East and the land of the Turks, it must be admitted that the line of march in this case is wider than the (narrow) passage at Suez. The distance, however, is greater, and the Persian and Byzantine nations are interposed on the way to the Turks. There is no report that the Tubba's ever took possession of the countries of the Persians and Byzantines. They merely fought the Persians on the borders of the 'Irâq and of the Arab countries between al-Baḥrayn and al-Ḥîrah, which were border regions common to both

[64] The same argument is used again below, pp. 27 and 75.

nations.[65] These wars took place between the Tubba' Dhû l-Adh'âr and the Kayyanid king Kayqâwûs, and again between the Tubba' *al-Aṣghar* [66] Abû Karib and the Kayyanid Yastâsb (Bishtâsp). There were other wars later on with rulers of the dynasties that succeeded the Kayyanids, and, in turn, with their successors, the Sassanians. It would, however, ordinarily have been impossible for the Tubba's to traverse the land of the Persians on their way to raid the countries of the Turks and Tibet, because of the nations that are interposed on the way to the Turks, because of the need for food and fodder, as well as the great distance, mentioned before. All information to this effect is silly and fictitious. Even if the way this information is transmitted were sound, the points mentioned would cast suspicion upon it. All the more then must the information be suspect since the manner in which it has been transmitted is not sound. In connection with Yathrib (Medina) and the Aws and Khazraj, Ibn Isḥâq [67] says that the last Tubba' traveled eastward to the 'Irâq and Persia, but a raid by the Tubba's against the countries of the Turks and Tibet is in no way confirmed by the established facts. Assertions to this effect should not be trusted; all such information should be investigated and checked with sound norms.[68] The result will be that it will most beautifully be demolished.

God is the guide to that which is correct.

Even [69] more unlikely and more deeply rooted in baseless assumptions is the common interpretation of the following

---

[65] Al-Ḥîrah on the Euphrates was the capital of the Lakhmid buffer state under Persian control. Al-Baḥrayn included the country on the northwestern shore of the Persian Gulf, and not only the islands today known under that name.

[66] "The Younger" Abû Karib is apparently identical with the above-mentioned "last" Tubba', As'ad Abû Karib.

[67] Cf. *'Ibar*, II, 53. Cf. also Ibn Hishâm, *Sîrah*, I, 12 f., where, however, only events dealing with the Tubba''s return from his eastern expedition are dealt with.

[68] Cf. Bombaci, p. 442.

[69] The following story, too, is found in the margin of C, though it appears incorporated in the text of B and D. It is found in Bulaq, but not in A.

verse of the *Sûrat al-Fajr:* "Did you not see what your Lord
I, 17 did with 'Âd—Iram, that of the pillars?"[70]

The commentators consider the word Iram the name of a city which is described as having pillars, that is, columns. They report that 'Âd b. 'Ûṣ b. Iram had two sons, Shadîd and Shaddâd, who ruled after him. Shadîd perished. Shaddâd became the sole ruler of the realm, and the kings there submitted to his authority. When Shaddâd heard a description of Paradise, he said: "I shall build something like it." And he built the city of Iram in the desert of Aden over a period of three hundred years. He himself lived nine hundred years. It is said to have been a large city, with castles of gold and silver and columns of emerald and hyacinth, containing all kinds of trees and freely flowing rivers. When the construction of (the city) was completed, Shaddâd went there with the people of his realm. But when he was the distance of only one day and night away from it, God sent a clamor from heaven, and all of them perished. This is reported by aṭ-Ṭabarî, ath-Tha'âlibî,[71] az-Zamakhsharî,[72] and other Qur'ân commentators. They transmit the following story on the authority of one of the men around Muḥammad, 'Abdallâh b. Qilâbah.[73] When he went out in search of some of his camels, he hit upon (the city) and took away from it as much as he could carry. His story reached Mu'âwiyah, who had him brought to him, and he told the story. Mu'âwiyah sent for Ka'b al-aḥbâr[74] and asked him about it. Ka'b said, "It is Iram, that of the pillars. Iram will be entered in your time by a Muslim who is of a reddish, ruddy

[70] Qur'ân 89.6–7 (5–6). Cf. J. Horovitz, *Koranische Untersuchungen* (Berlin & Leipzig, 1926), p. 89, and, for the following story, A. J. Wensinck in *EI, s.v.* "Iram Dhât al-'Imâd."

[71] See 2:444, below.

[72] See 2:446 f. and 3:338 f., below.

[73] Actually, Ibn Qilâbah is known only for this story; cf. Ibn Ḥajar, *Lisân al-Mîzân,* III, 327, who calls attention to the biography of the man in Ibn 'Asâkir, *Ta'rîkh Dimashq.*

[74] Cf. M. Schmitz in *EI, s.v.,* and, most recently, M. Perlmann in *The Joshua Starr Memorial Volume* (Jewish Social Studies, Publication No. 5) (New York, 1953), pp. 85–99, and *idem, Jewish Quarterly Review,* XLV (1954), 48–58.

color, and short, with a mole at his eyebrow and one on his neck, who goes out in search of some of his camels." He then turned around and, seeing Ibn Qilâbah, he said: "Indeed, he is that man."

No information about this city has since become available anywhere on earth. The desert of Aden where the city is supposed to have been built lies in the middle of the Yemen. It has been inhabited continuously, and travelers and guides have explored its roads in every direction. Yet, no information about the city has been reported. No antiquarian, no I, 18
nation has mentioned it. If (the commentators) said that it had disappeared like other antiquities, the story would be more likely, but they expressly say that it still exists. Some identify it with Damascus, because Damascus was in the possession of the people of 'Âd. Others go so far in their crazy talk as to maintain that the city lies hidden from sensual perception and can be discovered only by trained (magicians) and sorcerers. All these are assumptions that would better be termed nonsense.

All these suggestions proffered by Qur'ân commentators were the result of grammatical considerations, for Arabic grammar requires the expression, "that of the pillars," to be an attribute of Iram. The word "pillars" was understood to mean columns. Thus, Iram was narrowed down in its meaning to some sort of building. (The Qur'ân commentators) were influenced in their interpretation by the reading of Ibn az-Zubayr [75] who read (not 'Âdin with *nûnation* but) a genitive construction: 'Âd of Iram. They then adopted these stories, which are better called fictitious fables and which are quite similar to the (Qur'ân) interpretations of Sayfawayh which are related as comic anecdotes.[76]

---

[75] That is, 'Abdallâh b. az-Zubayr, who is also quoted elsewhere as an authority for Qur'ân readings. Cf. A. Jeffery, *Materials for the History of the Text of the Qur'ân* (Leiden, 1937), pp. 226 ff.

[76] Sayfawayh (or Sîfawayh) is mentioned as early as the tenth century, in the list of famous comedians in Ibn an-Nadîm, *Fihrist*, ed. Flügel (Leipzig, 1871–72), p. 313; (Cairo, 1348/1929–30), p. 435. Cf., further, Ibn al-Jawzî, *Akhbâr al-ḥamqâ wa-l-mughaffalîn* (Cairo, 1347/1928), pp. 81 f., and Ibn

(In fact,) however, the "pillars" are tent poles. If "columns" were intended by the word, it would not be farfetched, as the power of (the people of 'Âd) was well known, and they could be described as people with buildings and columns in the general way. But it would be farfetched to say that a special building in one or another specific city (was intended). If it is a genitive construction, as would be the case according to the reading of Ibn az-Zubayr, it would be a genitive construction used to express tribal relationships, such as, for instance, the Quraysh of Kinânah, or the Ilyâs of Muḍar, or the Rabî'ah of Nizâr. There is no need for such an implausible interpretation which uses for its starting point silly stories of the sort mentioned, which cannot be imputed to the Qur'ân because they are so implausible.

Another fictitious story of the historians, which they all report, concerns the reason for ar-Rashîd's destruction of the Barmecides. It is the story of al-'Abbâsah, ar-Rashîd's sister,
I, 19 and Ja'far b. Yaḥyâ b. Khâlid, his client. Ar-Rashîd is said to have worried about where to place them when he was drinking wine with them. He wanted to receive them together in his company. Therefore, he permitted them to conclude a marriage that was not consummated. Al-'Abbâsah then tricked (Ja'far) in her desire to be alone with him,[77] for she had fallen in love with him. Ja'far finally had intercourse with

---

Ḥajar, *Lisân al-Mîzân*, III, 132 f. This Sayfawayh (or Sîfawayh) should not be confused with the later Egyptian Sîbawayh to whom Ibn Zûlâq devoted the *Kitâb Akhbâr Sîbawayh al-Miṣrî* (Cairo, 1352/1933). Cf. now F. Rosenthal, *Humor in Early Islam* (Leiden, 1956), p. 11.

MSS. B, C, and D clearly indicate a reading Sayqawayh (Sîqawayh) with *q*, but Sayfawayh probably is the correct form.

It may seem strange that a comedian like Sayfawayh should have had anything to do with "Qur'ân interpretations." If Ibn Khaldûn expressed himself correctly, they may have been facetious applications of Qur'ân verses (and traditions), jokes such as we find in the literature on Muslim comedians. Cf. also the story of ar-Rashîd and Ibn Abî Maryam, p. 33, below.

77 The long story as to how the persistent 'Abbâsah finally succeeded, with the connivance of Ja'far's mother, in being united with Ja'far (who did not know that it was she), is told by al-Mas'ûdî, *Murûj adh-dhahab*, VI, 387 ff.

her—it is assumed, when he was drunk—and she became pregnant. The story was reported to ar-Rashîd who flew into a rage.

This story [78] is irreconcilable with al-'Abbâsah's position, her religiousness, her parentage, and her exalted rank. She was a descendant of 'Abdallâh b. 'Abbâs and separated from him by only four generations, and they were the most distinguished and greatest men in Islam after him. Al-'Abbâsah was the daughter of Muḥammad al-Mahdî, the son of Abû Ja'far 'Abdallâh al-Manṣûr, the son of Muḥammad as-Sajjâd, the son of the Father of the Caliphs 'Alî. 'Alî was the son of 'Abdallâh, the Interpreter of the Qur'ân, the son of the Prophet's uncle, al-'Abbâs. Al-'Abbâsah was the daughter of a caliph and the sister of a caliph. She was born to royal power, into the prophetical succession (the caliphate), and descended from the men around Muḥammad and his uncles. She was connected by birth with the leadership of Islam, the light of the revelation, and the place where the angels descended to bring the revelation. She was close in time to the desert attitude of true Arabism, to that simple state of Islam still far from the habits of luxury and lush pastures of sin. Where should one look for chastity and modesty, if she did not possess them? Where could cleanliness and purity be found, if they no longer existed in her house? How could she link her pedigree with (that of) Ja'far b. Yaḥyâ and stain her Arab nobility with a Persian client? His Persian ancestor had been acquired as a slave, or taken as a client, by one of her ancestors, an uncle of the Prophet and noble Qurashite, and all (Ja'far) did was that he together with his father was dragged along (by the growing fame of) the 'Abbâsid dynasty and thus prepared for and elevated to a position of nobility. And how could it be that ar-Rashîd, with his high- I, 20
mindedness and great pride, would permit himself to become related by marriage to Persian clients! If a critical person looks at this story in all fairness and compares al-'Abbâsah

[78] Cf. also *'Ibar*, V, 436 f.; VI, 7. See pp. 269 and 272, below.

with the daughter of a great ruler of his own time, he must find it disgusting and unbelievable that she could have done such a thing with one of the clients of her dynasty and while her family was in power. He would insist that the story be considered untrue. And who could compare with al-'Abbâsah and ar-Rashîd in dignity!

The reason for the destruction of the Barmecides was their attempt to gain control over the dynasty and their retention of the tax revenues. This went so far that when ar-Rashîd wanted even a little money, he could not get it. They took his affairs out of his hands and shared with him in his authority. He had no say with them in the affairs of his realm. Their influence grew, and their fame spread. They filled the positions and ranks of the government with their own children and creatures who became high officials, and thus barred all others from the positions of wazir, secretary, army commander, doorkeeper (*ḥâjib*), and from the military and civilian administration. It is said that in the palace of ar-Rashîd, there were twenty-five high officials, both military and civilian, all children of Yaḥyâ b. Khâlid. There, they crowded the people of the dynasty and pushed them out by force. They could do that because of the position of their father, Yaḥyâ, mentor to Hârûn both as crown prince and as caliph. (Hârûn) practically grew up in his lap and got all his education from him. (Hârûn) let him handle his affairs and used to call him "father." As a result, the (Barmecides), and not the government, wielded all the influence.[78a] Their presumption grew. Their position became more and more influential. They became the center of attention. All obeyed them. All hopes were addressed to them. From the farthest borders, presents and
I, 21 gifts of rulers and amirs were sent to them. The tax money found its way into their treasury, to serve as an introduction to them and to procure their favor. They gave gifts to and

---

[78a] Lit., "the preferred position (ordinarily enjoyed by government and ruler) went from the government to them," or, if *îthâr* should rather be translated "bounty," instead of "preferential position" (cf. 2:274, l. 34, below), "the bounty (ordinarily dispensed by government and ruler). . . ."

bestowed favors upon the men of the ('Alid) Shî'ah [79] and upon important relatives (of the Prophet). They gave the poor from the noble families (related to the Prophet) something to earn. They freed the captives. Thus, they were given praise as was not given to their caliph. They showered privileges and gifts upon those who came to ask favors from them. They gained control over villages and estates in the open country and (near) the main cities in every province.

Eventually, the Barmecides irritated the inner circle. They caused resentment among the elite and aroused the displeasure of high officials. Jealousy and envy of all sorts began to show themselves, and the scorpions of intrigue crept into their soft beds in the government. The Qaḥṭabah family, Ja'far's maternal uncles, led the intrigues against them. Feelings for blood ties and relationship could not move or sway them (the Qaḥṭabah family) from the envy which was so heavy on their hearts. This joined with their master's incipient jealousy, with his dislike of restrictions and (of being treated with) highhandedness, and with his latent resentment aroused by small acts of presumptuousness on the part of the Barmecides. When they continued to flourish as they did, they were led to gross insubordination, as is shown, for instance, by their action in the case of Yaḥyâ b. 'Abdallâh b. Ḥasan b. al-Ḥasan b. 'Alî b. Abî Ṭâlib, the brother of "the Pure Soul" (an-Nafs az-Zakîyah), Muḥammad al-Mahdî, who had revolted against al-Manṣûr.[80]

This Yaḥyâ had been brought back by al-Faḍl b. Yaḥyâ from the country of the Daylam under a safe-conduct of ar-Rashîd written in his own hand. According to aṭ-Ṭabarî,[81]
(al-Faḍl) had paid out a million dirhams in this matter. Ar- I, 22
Rashîd handed Yaḥyâ over to Ja'far to keep him imprisoned in his house and under his eyes. He held him for a while but, prompted by presumption, Ja'far freed Yaḥyâ by his own

[79] In the first case, the 'Alids, rather than the 'Abbâsid Shî'ah, are meant. The latter are meant by "important relatives of the Prophet," though this, too, may be another term for the 'Alids.

[80] See pp. 410 f., below.

[81] *Annales*, III, 614, *anno* 176.

decision, out of respect for the blood of the Prophet's family as he thought, and in order to show his presumption against the government. When the matter was reported to ar-Rashîd, he asked Ja'far about (Yaḥyâ). Ja'far understood and said that he had let him go. Ar-Rashîd outwardly indicated approval and kept his grudge to himself. Thus, Ja'far himself paved the way for his own and his family's undoing, which ended with the collapse of their exalted position, with the heavens falling in upon them and the earth's sinking with them and their house. Their days of glory became a thing of the past, an example to later generations.

Close examination of their story, scrutinizing the ways of government and their own conduct, discloses that all this was natural and is easily explained. Looking at Ibn 'Abdrabbih's report [82] on ar-Rashîd's conversation with his great-granduncle Dâwûd b. 'Alî concerning the destruction of the Barmecides as well as al-Aṣma'î's evening causeries with ar-Rashîd and al-Faḍl b. Yaḥyâ, as mentioned in the chapter on poets in the *'Iqd*,[83] one understands that it was only jealousy and struggle for control on the part of the caliph and his subordinates that killed them. Another factor was the verses that enemies of the Barmecides among the inner circle surreptitiously gave the singers to recite, in the intention that the caliph should hear them and his stored-up animosity against them be aroused. These are the verses:

Would that Hind could fulfill her promise to us
And deliver us from our predicament,
And for once act on her own.
The impotent person is he who never acts on his own.[84]

---

[82] Aḥmad b. Muḥammad, 246–328 [860–940]. Cf. *GAL*, I, 154 f.; *Suppl.*, I, 250 f.; *'Iqd* (Cairo, 1305/1887), III, 24. The edition of the *'Iqd* has Isḥâq b. 'Alî, instead of Dâwûd b. 'Alî.

[83] *'Iqd*, III, 108–11. See also below, 3:411.

[84] The verses are by 'Umar b. Abî Rabî'ah who lived *ca.* A.D. 700. Cf. *GAL*, I, 45 ff.; *Suppl.*, I, 76 f. Cf. P. Schwarz, *Der Diwan des 'Umar Ibn Abi Rebi'a* (Leipzig, 1901), I, 115 (No. 155, ll. 1 f.). Cf. also Ibn al-Athîr, *Kâmil*, VII, 4, *anno* 229.

When ar-Rashîd heard these verses, he exclaimed: "Indeed, I am just such an impotent person." By this and similar methods, the enemies of the Barmecides eventually succeeded I, 23
in arousing ar-Rashîd's latent jealousy and in bringing his terrible vengeance upon them. God is our refuge from men's desire for power and from misfortune.

The stupid story of ar-Rashîd's winebibbing and his getting drunk in the company of boon companions is really abominable. It does not in the least agree with ar-Rashîd's attitude toward the fulfillment of the requirements of religion and justice incumbent upon caliphs. He consorted with religious scholars and saints. He had discussions with al-Fuḍayl b. 'Iyâḍ,[85] Ibn as-Sammâk,[86] and al-'Umarî,[87] and he corresponded with Sufyân.[88] He wept when he heard their sermons. Then, there is his prayer in Mecca when he circumambulated the Ka'bah.[89] He was pious, observed the times of prayer, and attended the morning prayer at its earliest hour. According to aṭ-Ṭabarî and others, he used every day to pray one hundred supererogatory *rak'ahs*.[90] Alternately, he was used to go on raids (against unbelievers) one year and to make the pilgrimage to Mecca the other. He rebuked his jester, Ibn Abî Maryam, who made an unseemly remark to him during prayer. When Ibn Abî Maryam heard ar-Rashîd recite: "How is it that I should not worship Him who created me?" [91] he said: "Indeed, I do not know why."

[85] Died 187 [803]. Cf. *GAL*, *Suppl.*, I, 430.

[86] Muḥammad b. Ṣabîḥ, d. 183 [799/800]. Cf. al-Khaṭîb al-Baghdâdî, *Ta'rîkh Baghdâd*, V, 364–73.

[87] Apparently 'Abdallâh b. 'Abd-al-'Azîz b. 'Abdallâh b. 'Abdallâh b. 'Umar b. al-Khaṭṭâb, d. 184 [800/801]. Cf. Ibn Ḥajar, *Tahdhîb*, V, 302 f. A nephew of this man, 'Ubaydallâh b. 'Umar, was brought by ar-Rashîd to Baghdad (cf. al-Khaṭîb al-Baghdâdî, *Ta'rîkh Baghdâd*, X, 310), but he would not seem to be the one meant here.

[88] Of the two famous Sufyâns, Sufyân ath-Thawrî and Sufyân b. 'Uyaynah, the latter is meant here. He lived from 107 to 198 [725/26 to 814]. Cf. al-Khaṭîb al-Baghdâdî, *Ta'rîkh Baghdâd*, IX, 174–84.

[89] Cf. Ibn al-Athîr, *Kâmil*, VI, 87 f., *anno* 193. Cf. also G. Audisio, *Harun al-Rashid* (New York, 1931), p. 173.

[90] Cf. aṭ-Ṭabarî, *Annales*, III, 740, *anno* 193. A *rak'ah* is a prescribed sequence of motions in prayer.

[91] Qur'ân 36.22 (21).

Ar-Rashîd could not suppress a laugh, but then he turned to him angrily and said: "O Ibn Abî Maryam, (jokes) even during the prayer? Beware, beware of the Qur'ân and Islam. Apart from that, you may do whatever you wish." [92]

Furthermore, ar-Rashîd possessed a good deal of learning and simplicity, because his epoch was close to that of his forebears who had those (qualities). The time between him and his grandfather, Abû Ja'far (al-Manṣûr), was not a long
I, 24 one. He was a young lad when Abû Ja'far died. Abû Ja'far possessed a good deal of learning and religion before he became caliph and (kept them) afterwards. It was he who advised Mâlik to write the *Muwaṭṭa'*, saying: "O Abû 'Abdallâh, no one remains on earth more learned than I and you. Now, I am too much occupied with the caliphate. Therefore, you should write a book for the people which will be useful for them. In it you should avoid the laxity of Ibn 'Abbâs and the severity of Ibn 'Umar,[93] and present (*waṭṭi'*) it clearly to the people." Mâlik commented: "On that occasion, al-Manṣûr indeed taught me to be an author." [94]

Al-Manṣûr's son, al-Mahdî, ar-Rashîd's father, experienced the (austerity of al-Manṣûr) who would not make use of the public treasury to provide new clothes for his family. One day, al-Mahdî came to him when he was in his office discussing with the tailors the patching of his family's worn garments. Al-Mahdî did not like that and said: "O Commander of the Faithful, this year I shall pay for the clothes of the members of the family from my own income." Al-Manṣûr's reply was: "Do that." He did not prevent him from paying himself but would not permit any (public) Muslim money to be spent for it. Ar-Rashîd was very close in

[92] Cf. aṭ-Ṭabarî, *Annales*, III, 743 f.

[93] Ibn 'Abbâs is the 'Abdallâh b. 'Abbâs mentioned above, p. 29, the Prophet's cousin. Ibn 'Umar is 'Abdallâh, a son of the caliph 'Umar, who died in 73 or 74 [692/93 or 693/94]. Cf. K. V. Zetterstéen in *EI, s.v.* " 'Abd Allâh b. 'Umar."

[94] Ibn Khaldûn also refers to this story in his Ṣurghatmishîyah lecture. Cf. *Autobiography*, p. 301. Cf. also Ibn Farḥûn (Cairo, 1351/1932), *Dîbâj*, p. 25.

time to that caliph and to his forebears.[95] He was reared under the influence of such and similar conduct in his own family, so that it became his own nature. How could such a man have been a winebibber and have drunk wine openly? It is well known that noble pre-Islamic Arabs avoided wine. The vine was not one of the plants (cultivated) by them. Most of them considered it reprehensible to drink wine. Ar-Rashîd and his forebears were very successful in avoiding anything reprehensible in their religious or worldly affairs and in making all praiseworthy actions and qualities of perfection, as well as the aspirations of the Arabs, their own nature.

One may further compare the story of the physician I, 25
Jibrîl b. Bukhtîshû' reported by aṭ-Ṭabarî and al-Mas'ûdî.[96] A fish had been served at ar-Rashîd's table, and Jibrîl had not permitted him to eat it. (Jibrîl) had then ordered the table steward to bring the fish to (Jibrîl's) house. Ar-Rashîd noticed it and got suspicious. He had his servant spy on Jibrîl, and the servant observed him partaking of it. In order to justify himself, Ibn Bukhtîshû' had three pieces of fish placed in three separate dishes. He mixed the first piece with meat that had been prepared with different kinds of spices, vegetables, hot sauces, and sweets. He poured iced water over the second piece, and pure wine over the third. The first and second dishes, he said, were for the caliph to eat, no matter whether something was added by him (Ibn Bukhtîshû') to the fish or not. The third dish, he said, was for himself to eat. He gave the three dishes to the table steward. When ar-Rashîd woke up and had Ibn Bukhtîshû' called in to reprimand him, the latter had the three dishes brought. The one with wine had become a soup with small pieces of fish,

---

[95] A, C, and D read *ubûwatihî*, but in B we find *abawayhi* "his parents," or "his two forebears" (?). Translating *wa-ubûwatihî* "and counted him among his forebears" would be possible here, but is hardly correct.

[96] Cf. *Murûj adh-dhahab*, VI, 305 ff., but aṭ-Ṭabarî does not seem to have the story. Cf. also Ibn Abî Uṣaybi'ah, *'Uyûn al-anbâ'*, ed. Müller (Königsberg & Cairo, 1882–84), I, 129.

Jibrîl was an early member of the famous dynasty of physicians. He died in 213 [828/29]. Cf. C. Brockelmann in *EI*, *s.v.* "Bakhtîshû'."

but the two other dishes had spoiled, and smelled differently. This was (sufficient) justification of Ibn Bukhtîshû''s action (in eating a dish of fish that he had prevented the caliph from eating). It is clear from this story that ar-Rashîd's avoidance of wine was a fact well known to his inner circle and to those who dined with him.

It is a well-established fact that ar-Rashîd had consented to keep Abû Nuwâs imprisoned until he repented and gave up his ways, because he had heard of the latter's excessive wine-bibbing.[97] Ar-Rashîd used to drink a date liquor (*nabîdh*), according to the 'Irâqî legal school whose *responsa* (concerning the permissibility of that drink) are well known.[98] But he cannot be suspected of having drunk pure wine. Silly reports to this effect cannot be credited. He was not the man to do something that is forbidden and considered by the Muslims as one of the greatest of the capital sins. Not one of
I, 26 these people (the early 'Abbâsids) had anything to do with effeminate prodigality or luxury in matters of clothing, jewelry, or the kind of food they took. They still retained the tough desert attitude and the simple state of Islam. Could it be assumed they would do something that would lead from the lawful to the unlawful and from the licit to the illicit? Historians such as aṭ-Ṭabarî, al-Mas'ûdî, and others are agreed that all the early Umayyad and 'Abbâsid caliphs used to ride out with only light silver ornamentation on their belts, swords, bridles, and saddles, and that the first caliph to originate riding out in golden apparel was al-Mu'tazz b. al-Mutawakkil, the eighth caliph after ar-Rashîd.[99] The same applied to their clothing. Could one, then, assume any differently with regard to what they drank? This will become still clearer when the nature of dynastic beginnings in desert life and modest circumstances is understood, as we shall

---

[97] For Abû Nuwâs, see *GAL*, I, 75 ff.; *Suppl.*, I, 114 ff.

[98] For the lenient Ḥanafite attitude toward *nabîdh*, see A. J. Wensinck in *EI*, *s.v.* "Nabîdh." Cf. also p. 445, below.

[99] Cf. al-Mas'ûdî, *Murûj adh-dhahab*, VII, 401.

explain it among the problems discussed in the first book, if God wills.[100]

A parallel or similar story is that reported by all (the historians) about Yaḥyâ b. Aktham, the judge and friend of al-Ma'mûn.[101] He is said to have drunk wine together with al-Ma'mûn and to have gotten drunk one night. He lay buried among the sweet basil until he woke up. The following verses are recited in his name:

O my lord, commander of all the people!
He who gave me to drink was unjust in his judgment.
I neglected the cupbearer, and he caused me to be,
As you see me, deprived of intelligence and religion.

The same applies to Ibn Aktham and al-Ma'mûn that applies to ar-Rashîd. What they drank was a date liquor (*nabîdh*) which in their opinion was not forbidden. There can be no question of drunkenness in connection with them. Yaḥyâ's familiarity with al-Ma'mûn was friendship in Islam.
It is an established fact that Yaḥyâ slept in al-Ma'mûn's I, 27
room. It has been reported, as an indication of al-Ma'mûn's excellence and affability, that one night he awoke,[102] got up,

[100] See, for instance, pp. 313 ff., below.

[101] The story is told fully in Ibn 'Abdrabbih, *'Iqd*, III, 313.
Yaḥyâ b. Aktham died in 242 or 243 [847]. Cf. al-Khaṭîb al-Baghdâdî, *Ta'rîkh Baghdâd*, XIV, 191 ff.

[102] Bulaq adds "thirsty." In this case the "vessel" (*inâ'*) mentioned would not be a chamber pot, but a water pitcher. A very similar story of how al-Ma'mûn himself went out for a drink of water and did not disturb Yaḥyâ b. Aktham occurs in al-Itlîdî, *I'lâm an-nâs bi-mâ waqa'a li-l-Barâmikah min Banî l-'Abbâs* (Cairo, 1303/1886), p. 110. Al-Itlîdî adds another story, according to which al-Ma'mûn had gone to urinate and hesitated to call his servants to help him to get ready for the morning prayer, as long as Yaḥyâ did not stir. Thus, it seems hardly possible to decide whether Ibn Khaldûn thought of a water pitcher or a chamber pot. *Inâ'* "urine glass" is found in aṭ-Ṭabarî, *Firdaws al-ḥikmah* (Berlin, 1928), pp. 354 f. An author closer to the time of Ibn Khaldûn, as-Suyûṭî, uses a synonym for *inâ'*, *wi'â'*; cf. as-Suyûṭî, *Tanbî'at al-ghabî bi-tabri'at Ibn al-'Arabî*, Istanbul MS, Laleli, 3645, fol. 162a. For another version of the story, cf. as-Sulamî, *Âdâb aṣ-ṣuḥbah*, ed. M. J. Kister (Oriental Notes and Studies, No. 6) (Jerusalem, 1954), p. 57.

and felt around for the chamber pot. He was afraid to wake Yaḥyâ b. Aktham. It also is an established fact that the two used to pray together at the morning prayer. How does that accord with drinking wine together! Furthermore, Yaḥyâ b. Aktham was a transmitter of traditions. He was praised by Ibn Ḥanbal [103] and Judge Ismâ'îl.[104] At-Tirmidhî [105] published traditions on his authority. The *ḥadîth* expert al-Mizzî mentioned that al-Bukhârî transmitted traditions on Yaḥyâ's authority in works other than the *Jâmi' (aṣ-Ṣaḥîḥ)*.[106] To vilify Yaḥyâ is to vilify all of these scholars.

Furthermore, licentious persons accuse Yaḥyâ b. Aktham of having had an inclination for young men. This is an affront to God and a malicious lie directed against religious scholars. (These persons) base themselves on storytellers' silly reports, which perhaps were an invention of Yaḥyâ's enemies, for he was much envied because of his perfection and his friendship with the ruler. His position in scholarship and religion makes such a thing impossible. When Ibn Ḥanbal was told about these rumors concerning Yaḥyâ, he exclaimed: "For God's sake, for God's sake, who would say such a thing!" He disapproved of it very strongly. When the talk about Yaḥyâ was mentioned to Ismâ'îl, he exclaimed: "Heaven forbid that the probity (*'adâlah*) [107] of such a man should cease to exist because of the lying accusations of envious talebearers." [108] He said: "Yaḥyâ b. Aktham is inno-

[103] Aḥmad b. Muḥammad b. Ḥanbal, the founder of the Ḥanbalite school of jurisprudence, 164–241 [780–855]. Cf. *GAL*, I, 181 ff.; *Suppl.*, I, 309 f.

[104] Ismâ'îl b. Isḥâq, the Mâlikite judge. Cf. 3:13, below.

[105] Muḥammad b. 'Îsâ, d. 279 [892], author of one of the authoritative collections of traditions. Cf. *GAL*, I, 161 f.; *Suppl.*, I, 267 f.

[106] The *Tahdhîb al-Kamâl* of Yûsuf b. 'Abd-ar-Raḥmân al-Mizzî, 654–742 [1256–1341] (cf. *GAL*, II, 64; *Suppl.*, II, 66 f.), was not available, but see Ibn Ḥajar, *Tahdhîb*, XI, 180. In al-Bukhârî's *Ta'rîkh* (Hyderabad, 1360——/ 1941——), IV², 263, we find only Yaḥyâ's name, without any further information.

[107] *'Adâlah* is a common term of Muslim jurisprudence and political science for which in this translation the word "probity" was chosen. It means possession of the moral qualifications that make a person acceptable for high office and for serving as a witness, that is, for exercise of his duties as a citizen. See also p. 395 and n. 388 to Ch. III, below.

[108] Cf. al-Khaṭîb al-Baghdâdî, *Ta'rîkh Baghdâd*, XIV, 200, l. 13.

cent in the eyes of God of any such relationship with young men (as that) of which he is accused. I got to know his most intimate thoughts and found him to be much in fear of God. However, he possessed a certain playfulness and friendliness that might have provoked such accusations." Ibn Ḥibbân mentioned him in the *Thiqât*.[109] He said that no attention I, 28
should be paid to these tales about him because most of them were not correct.

A similar story is the one about the basket reported by Ibn 'Abdrabbih, author of the *'Iqd*, in explanation of how al-Ma'mûn came to be al-Ḥasan b. Sahl's son-in-law by marrying his daughter Bûrân.[110] One night, on his rambles through the streets of Baghdad, al-Ma'mûn is said to have come upon a basket that was being let down from one of the roofs by means of pulleys and twisted cords of silk thread. He seated himself in the basket and grabbed the pulley, which started moving. He was taken up into a chamber of such-and-such a condition—Ibn 'Abdrabbih described the eye- and soul-filling splendor of its carpets, the magnificence of its furnishings, and the beauty of its appearance. Then, a woman of extraordinary, seductive beauty is said to have come forth from behind curtains in that chamber. She greeted al-Ma'mûn and invited him to keep her company. He drank wine with her the whole night long. In the morning he returned to his companions at the place where they had been awaiting him. He had fallen so much in love with the woman that he asked her father for her hand. How does all this accord with al-Ma'mûn's well-known religion and learning, with his imitation of the way of life of his forefathers, the right-guided ('Abbâsid) caliphs, with his adoption of the way of life of those pillars of Islam, the (first) four caliphs, with his respect for the religious scholars, or his observance in his prayers and

[109] I consulted the MS. Ahmet III, 2995 (of the Topkapusaray in Istanbul) of the work on reliable transmitters (*Thiqât*) by Ibn Ḥibbân, 274–354 [887/88–965] (cf. *GAL*, I, 164; *Suppl.*, I, 273 f.), but it does not go as far as Yaḥyâ. For the remarks of Ibn Ḥibbân and the statement of Ismâ'îl, see Ibn Ḥajar, *Tahdhîb*, XI, 181.

[110] Cf. *'Iqd*, III, 356–63. Cf. also below, pp. 348 f.

legal practice of the norms established by God! How could it
be correct that he would act like (one of those) wicked
scoundrels who amuse themselves by rambling about at
I, 29 night, entering strange houses in the dark, and engaging in
nocturnal trysts in the manner of Bedouin lovers! And how
does that story fit with the position and noble character of
al-Ḥasan b. Sahl's daughter, and with the firm morality and
chastity that reigned in her father's house!

There are many such stories. They are always cropping up in the works of the historians. The incentive for inventing and reporting them is a (general) inclination to forbidden pleasures and for smearing the reputation of others. People justify their own subservience to pleasure by citing men and women of the past (who allegedly did the same things they are doing). Therefore, they often appear very eager for such information and are alert to find it when they go through the pages of (published) works. If they would follow the example of the people (of the past) in other respects and in the qualities of perfection that were theirs and for which they are well known, "it would be better for them,"[111] "if they would know."[112]

I once criticized a royal prince for being so eager to learn to sing and play the strings. I told him it was not a matter that should concern him and that it did not befit his position. He referred me to Ibrâhîm b. al-Mahdî[113] who was the leading musician and best singer in his time. I replied: "For heaven's sake, why do you not rather follow the example of his father or his brother? Do you not see how that activity prevented Ibrâhîm from attaining their position?" The prince, however, was deaf to my criticism and turned away.

[111] Qur'ân 3.110 (106); 4.46 (49), 66 (69); 47.21 (23); 49.5 (5).

[112] Qur'ân 2.102 (96), 103 (97); 16.41 (43); 29.41 (40), 64 (64); 68.33 (33).

[113] The son of the caliph al-Mahdî, who was for a short time considered by some groups as caliph. 162–224 [779–839]; cf. *GAL, Suppl.*, I, 223, and below, pp. 325 f. and 433 f., and 3:341.

Further silly information which is accepted by many historians concerns the 'Ubaydid(-Fâṭimids), the Shî'ah caliphs in al-Qayrawân and Cairo.[114] (These historians) deny their 'Alid origin and attack (the genuineness of) their descent from the imam Ismâ'îl, the son of Ja'far aṣ-Ṣâdiq. They base I, 30
themselves in this respect on stories that were made up in favor of the weak 'Abbâsid caliphs by people who wanted to ingratiate themselves with them through accusations against their active opponents and who (therefore) liked to say all kinds of bad things about their enemies. We shall mention some such stories in our treatment of the history of (the 'Ubaydid-Fâṭimids). (These historians) do not care to consider the factual proofs and circumstantial evidence that require (us to recognize) that the contrary is true and that their claim is a lie and must be rejected.

They all tell the same story about the beginning of the Shî'ah dynasty. Abû 'Abdallâh *al-Muḥtasib*[115] went among the Kutâmah urging acceptance of the family of Muḥammad (the 'Alids). His activity became known. It was learned how much he cared for 'Ubaydallâh al-Mahdî and his son, Abû l-Qâsim. Therefore, these two feared for their lives and fled the East, the seat of the caliphate. They passed through Egypt and left Alexandria disguised as merchants. 'Îsâ an-Nawsharî, the governor of Egypt and Alexandria, was informed of them. He sent cavalry troops in pursuit of them, but when their pursuers reached them, they did not recognize them because of their attire and disguise. They escaped into

[114] The question of the 'Alid origin of the Fâṭimids and their early history was loaded with political "dynamite" for many centuries after the Fâṭimid dynasty had ceased to exist. In some respects, it is still of importance today. Cf. the works of W. Ivanow: *Ismaili Tradition Concerning the Rise of the Fatimids* (Islamic Research Association Series, No. 10) (Oxford, 1942), and *The Alleged Founder of Ismailism* (The Ismaili Society Series, No. 1) (Bombay, 1946). Cf. also F. Rosenthal, *A History of Muslim Historiography*, p. 335.

[115] Abû 'Abdallâh ash-Shî'î, through whose efforts the Fâṭimids became rulers of northwestern Africa, is said to have been *muḥtasib* (cf. pp. 462 f., below) in al-Baṣrah, if it was not his brother Abû l-'Abbâs who held that office. Cf. *'Ibar*, III, 362; IV, 31 f., 204 f. See also below, 2:133.

the Maghrib. Al-Mu'taḍid [116] ordered the Aghlabid rulers of Ifrîqiyah in al-Qayrawân as well as the Midrârid rulers of Sijilmâsah to search everywhere for them and to keep a sharp lookout for them. Ilyasa', the Midrârid lord of Sijilmâsah, learned about their hiding place in his country and detained them, in order to please the caliph. This was before the Shî'ah victory over the Aghlabids in al-Qayrawân. Thereafter, as is well known, the ('Ubaydid-Fâṭimid) propaganda spread successfully throughout Ifrîqiyah and the Maghrib,
I, 31 and then, in turn, reached the Yemen, Alexandria and (the rest of) Egypt, Syria and the Ḥijâz. The ('Ubaydid-Fâṭimids) shared the realm of Islam equally with the 'Abbâsids. They almost succeeded in penetrating the home country of the 'Abbâsids and in taking their place as rulers. Their propaganda in Baghdad and the 'Irâq met with success through the amir al-Basâsîrî, one of the Daylam clients who had gained control of the 'Abbâsid caliphs. This happened as the result of a quarrel between al-Basâsîrî and the non-Arab amirs.[117] For a whole year, the ('Ubaydid-Fâṭimids) were mentioned in the Friday prayer from the pulpits of Baghdad. The 'Abbâsids were continually bothered by the ('Ubaydid-Fâṭimid) power and preponderance, and the Umayyad rulers beyond the sea (in Spain) expressed their annoyance with them and threatened war against them. How could all this have befallen a fraudulent claimant to the rulership, who was (moreover) considered a liar? [118] One should compare (this account with) the history of the Qarmaṭian.[119] His genealogy was, in fact, fraudulent. How completely did his propaganda

---

[116] Rather, his son and successor al-Muktafî. The event related took place in the year 293 [905/6], after the death of al-Mu'taḍid. Cf. Ibn 'Idhârî, *al-Bayân al-Mughrib*, ed. G. S. Colin and E. Lévi-Provençal (Leiden, 1948–51), I, 140. But see also below, p. 46, and *'Ibar*, III, 360; IV, 31.

[117] This refers to events at the beginning of the Saljûq rule under Tughrilbek, that took place in the period from December, 1058, to 1060. Cf. also *'Ibar*, III, 463 f.

[118] Cf. *'Ibar*, III, 360.

[119] The "Qarmaṭian" was the supposed founder of the sect, a certain Ḥamdân, who lived in the second half of the ninth century. Cf. L. Massignon in *EI*, *s.v.* "Ḳarmaṭians."

disintegrate and his followers disperse! Their viciousness and guile soon became apparent. They came to an evil end and tasted a bitter fate. If the 'Ubaydid(-Fâṭimids) had been in the same situation, it would have become known, even had it taken some time.

> Whatever qualities of character a man may have,
> They will become known, even if he imagines they are concealed from the people.[120]

The ('Ubaydid-Fâṭimid) dynasty lasted uninterruptedly for about two hundred and seventy years. They held possession of the place where Ibrâhîm (Abraham) had stood[121] and where he had prayed, the home of the Prophet and the place where he was buried, the place where the pilgrims stand and where the angels descended (to bring the revelation to Muḥammad). Then, their rule came to an end. During all that time, their partisans showed them the greatest devotion and love and firmly believed in their descent from the imam Ismâ'îl, the son of Ja'far aṣ-Ṣâdiq. Even after the dynasty had gone and its influence had disappeared, people still came forward to press the claims of the sect. They proclaimed the names of young children, descendants of (the 'Ubaydid-Fâṭimids), whom they believed entitled to the caliphate. They I, 32 went so far as to consider them as having actually been appointed to the succession by preceding imams. Had there been doubts about their pedigree, their followers would not have undergone the dangers involved in supporting them. A sectarian does not manipulate his own affairs, nor sow confusion within his own sect, nor act as a liar where his own beliefs are concerned.

It is strange that Judge Abû Bakr al-Bâqillânî,[122] the great

---

[120] This verse is quoted from near the end of Zuhayr's *Mu'allaqah;* cf. 3:397 and 410, below. Cf. J. Hausherr, *Die Mu'allaka des Zuhair* (Berlin, 1905), p. 35.

[121] That is, the *Maqâm Ibrâhîm* in the Sanctuary in Mecca.

[122] Muḥammad b. aṭ-Ṭayyib, d. 403 [1013]. Cf. *GAL,* I, 197; *Suppl.,* I, 349. In Ibn Khaldûn's circle, he was esteemed one of the greatest of ancient eastern Mâlikites, and he is, therefore, often quoted in the *Muqaddimah.*

speculative theologian, was inclined to credit this unacceptable view (as to the spuriousness of the 'Ubaydid-Fâṭimid genealogy), and upheld this weak opinion. If the reason for his attitude was the heretical and extremist Shî'ism of (the 'Ubaydid-Fâṭimids, it would not be valid, for his denial of their 'Alid descent) does not invalidate [123] (the objectionable character of) their sectarian beliefs, nor would establishment of their ('Alid) descent be of any help to them before God in the question of their unbelief. God said to Noah concerning his sons: "He does not belong to your family. It is an improper action. So do not ask me regarding that of which you have no knowledge." [124] Muḥammad exhorted Fâṭimah in these words: "O Fâṭimah, act (as you wish). I shall be of no help to you before God." [124a]

When a man comes to know a problem or to be certain about a matter, he must openly state (his knowledge or his certainty). "God speaks the truth. He leads (men into) the right way." [125] Those people (the 'Ubaydid-Fâṭimids) were constantly on the move because of the suspicions various governments had concerning them. They were kept under observation by the tyrants, because their partisans were numerous and their propaganda had spread far and wide. Time after time they had to leave the places where they had settled. Their men, therefore, took refuge in hiding, and their (identity) was hardly known, as (the poet) says:

Recent publications in connection with al-Bâqillânî include the edition of his *Kitâb at-Tamhîd* by al-Khuḍayrî and Abû Rîdah (Cairo, 1366/1947), who contribute much biographical material, and G. E. von Grunebaum, *A Tenth-Century Document of Arabic Literary Criticism* (Chicago, 1950). An edition of his *Inṣâf* appeared in Cairo in 1369/1950. Al-Bâqillânî's work against the Fâṭimids was entitled *Kashf al-asrâr wa-hatk al-astâr*. Cf. Ibn Kathîr, *Bidâyah*, XI, 346; the edition of the *Tamhîd* cited above, p. 259 (n. 3). That al-Ghazzâlî based his *Mustaẓhirî* upon al-Bâqillânî's *Kashf* has been denied by I. Goldziher, and, indeed, Goldziher's study of the *Mustaẓhirî* has no indication that the work dealt with the 'Alid descent of the Fâṭimids. Cf. I. Goldziher, *Streitschrift des Ġazâlî gegen die Bâṭinijja-Sekte* (Leiden, 1916), pp. 15 f.

[123] The phrase used here means "to push back." Cf. 3:49, below.

[124] Qur'ân 11.46 (48). [124a]* Cf. *Concordance*, V, 15, ll. 64 f.

[125] Qur'ân 33.4 (4).

If you would ask the days what my name is, they would not know,
And where I am, they would not know where I am.[126] I, 33

This went so far that Muḥammad, the son of the imam Ismâ'îl, the ancestor of 'Ubaydallâh al-Mahdî, was called "the Concealed (Imam)." [127] His partisans called him by that name because they were agreed on the fact he was hiding out of fear of those who had them in their power. The partisans of the 'Abbâsids made much use of this fact when they came out with their attack against the pedigree of (the 'Ubaydid-Fâṭimids). They tried to ingratiate themselves with the weak ('Abbâsid) caliphs by professing the erroneous opinion that (the 'Alid descent of the 'Ubaydid-Fâṭimids was spurious). It pleased the 'Abbâsid clients and the amirs who were in charge of military operations against the enemies of the ('Abbâsids). It helped them and the government to make up for their inability to resist and repel the Kutâmah Berbers, the partisans and propagandists [128] of the 'Ubaydid(-Fâṭimids), who had taken Syria, Egypt, and the Ḥijâz away from (the 'Abbâsids). The judges in Baghdad eventually prepared an official statement denying the 'Alid origin (of the 'Ubaydid-Fâṭimids).[129] The statement was witnessed by a number of prominent men, among them the Sharîf ar-Raḍî [130] and his

[126] The verse is ascribed by some authors to Abû Nuwâs. Cf. al-Âmidî, *al-Mu'talif wa-l-mukhtalif* (Cairo, 1354/1935–36), p. 94, and ar-Râghib al-Iṣfahânî, *Muḥâḍarât* (Cairo, 1287/1870), I, 171. However, it does not appear in Abû Nuwâs' *Dîwân* (Cairo, 1898). Ibn Buṭlân, *Da'wat al-aṭibbâ'*, at the beginning, ascribes it to al-Ḥusayn b. Hâni' (*leg.* Abû l-Ḥasan b. Hâni').

The first line may be read in the passive: "If the days were asked. . . ." The text found in Ibn Buṭlân has a variant reading requiring this translation.

[127] See also p. 412, below.

[128] C and D read "representatives of the dynasty."

[129] Cf. B. Lewis, *The Origins of Ismâ'îlism* (Cambridge, 1940), pp. 60 f. The earliest published source so far known for the text of the affidavit is Ibn al-Jawzî, *Muntaẓam* (Hyderabad, 1357——/1938——), VII, 255. Ibn Khaldûn's list of signers corresponds much more closely to that in Ibn al-Athîr, *Kâmil*, IX, 98, *anno* 402, and VIII, 10, *anno* 296, than to that in Ibn al-Jawzî.

[130] Muḥammad b. al-Ḥusayn, 359–406 [969/70–1015]. Cf. *GAL*, I, 82; *Suppl.*, I, 131 f.

brother al-Murtaḍâ,[131] and Ibn al-Baṭḥâwî.[132] Among the religious scholars (who also witnessed the document) were Abû Ḥâmid al-Isfarâyinî,[133] al-Qudûrî,[134] aṣ-Ṣaymarî,[135] Ibn al-Akfânî,[136] al-Abîwardî,[137] the Shî'ah jurist Abû 'Abdallâh b. an-Nu'mân,[138] and other prominent Muslims in Baghdad. The event took place one memorable [139] day in the year 402 [1011] in the time of al-Qâdir. The testimony (of these witnesses) was based upon hearsay, on what people in Baghdad generally believed. Most of them were partisans of the 'Abbâsids who attacked the 'Alid origin (of the 'Ubaydid-Fâṭimids). The historians reported the information as they had heard it. They handed it down to us just as they remembered it. However, the truth lies behind it. Al-Mu'taḍid's [140] letter concerning 'Ubaydallâh (addressed) to the Aghlabid
I, 34 in al-Qayrawân and the Midrârid in Sijilmâsah, testifies most truthfully to the correctness of the ('Alid) origin of the ('Ubaydid-Fâṭimids), and proves it most clearly. Al-Mu'taḍid (as a very close relative) was better qualified than anyone else to speak about the genealogy of the Prophet's house.[141]

Dynasty and government serve as the world's market

---

[131] 'Alî b. al-Ḥusayn, 355–436 [966–1044/45]. Cf. Ibn al-Jawzî, *op. cit.*, VIII, 120 ff.

[132] Ibn al-Athîr expressly states that he was an 'Alid, but I have no further information about the man.

[133] Aḥmad b. Muḥammad, 345–406 [956/57–1016]. Cf. Ibn al-Jawzî, *op. cit.*, VII, 277 f.

[134] Aḥmad b. Muḥammad, 362–428 [972/73–1037]. Cf. *GAL*, I, 174 f.; *Suppl.*, I, 295 f.

[135] Abû 'Abdallâh al-Ḥusayn b. 'Alî, 351–436 [962/63–1045]. Cf. Ibn al-Jawzî, *op. cit.*, VIII, 119.

[136] Abû Muḥammad 'Abdallâh b. Muḥammad, 316 or 320 to 405 [928/29 or 932 to 1014]. Cf. Ibn al-Jawzî, *op. cit.*, VII, 273.

[137] Abû l-'Abbâs Aḥmad b. Muḥammad, d. 425 [1034]. Cf. Ibn al-Jawzî, *op. cit.*, VIII, 80 f.

[138] Muḥammad b. Muḥammad b. al-Mu'allim, d. 413 [1022]. Cf. Ibn al-Jawzî, *op. cit.*, VIII, 11 f.

[139] See note 162 to Ch. III, and p. 450, below.

[140] See n. 116, above.

[141] Cf. R. Dozy, *Journal asiatique*, XIV 6 (1869), 149 f., and *Supplément aux dictionnaires arabes*, II, 380 f.

place,[142] attracting to it the products of scholarship and craftsmanship alike. Wayward wisdom and forgotten lore turn up there. In this market stories are told and items of historical information are delivered. Whatever is in demand on this market is in general demand everywhere else. Now, whenever the established dynasty avoids injustice, prejudice, weakness, and double-dealing, with determination keeping to the right path and never swerving from it, the wares on its market are as pure silver and fine gold. However, when it is influenced by selfish interests and rivalries, or swayed by vendors of tyranny and dishonesty, the wares of its market place become as dross and debased metals. The intelligent critic must judge for himself as he looks around, examining this, admiring that, and choosing this.

A similar and even more improbable story is one privately discussed by those who attack the ('Alid) descent of Idrîs b. Idrîs b. 'Abdallâh b. Ḥasan b. al-Ḥasan b. 'Alî b. Abî Ṭâlib, who became imam after his father in Morocco.[143] They hint at the punishable crime of adultery by insinuating that the unborn child left after the death of the elder Idrîs was in fact the child of Râshid, a client of the Idrîsids. How stupid of these God-forsaken men! They should know that the elder Idrîs married into the Berber tribes and, from the time he came to the Maghrib until his death, was firmly rooted in desert life. In the desert, no such thing could remain a secret. I, 35
There are no hiding places there where things can be done in secret. The neighbors (if they are women) can always see and (if they are men) always hear what their women are doing, because the houses are low and clustered together without

[142] Cf. below, 2:102 and 287, and also 2:352. As early as the ninth century, Ibn Qutaybah quoted Abû Ḥâzim as saying to Sulaymân b. 'Abd-al-Malik: "The government serves as a market place to which whatever is in demand with (the government) is brought." Cf. Ibn Qutaybah, *'Uyûn al-akhbâr* (Cairo, 1343–49/1925–30), I, 2.

[143] Ibn Khaldûn speaks of the Idrîsids of Fez in *'Ibar*, IV, 12 ff. Cf. also below, p. 411.

space between them. Râshid was entrusted with the stewardship of all the women after the death of his master, upon the recommendation of friends and partisans of the Idrîsids and subject to the supervision of them all. Furthermore, all Moroccan Berbers agreed to render the oath of allegiance to the younger Idrîs as his father's successor. They voluntarily agreed to obey him. They swore that they were willing to die for him, and they exposed themselves to mortal danger protecting him in his wars and raids. Had they told each other some such scandalous story or heard it from someone else, even a vengeful enemy or scandal-mongering rebel, some of them at least would have refused to do those things. No, this story originated with the 'Abbâsid opponents of the Idrîsids and with the Aghlabids, the 'Abbâsid governors and officials in Ifrîqiyah.

This happened in the following manner. When the elder Idrîs fled to the Maghrib after the battle of Fakhkh,[144] al-Hâdî sent orders to the Aghlabids to lie in wait and keep a sharp watch out for him. However, they did not catch him, and he escaped safely to the Maghrib. He consolidated his position, and his propaganda was successful. Later on, ar-Rashîd became aware of the secret Shî'ah leanings of Wâḍiḥ,
I, 36 the 'Abbâsid client and governor of Alexandria, and of his deceitful attitude in connection with the escape of Idrîs to the Maghrib, and (ar-Rashîd) killed (Wâḍiḥ). Then, ash-Shammâkh, a client of (ar-Rashîd's) father, suggested to ar-Rashîd a ruse by means of which to kill Idrîs. (Ash-Shammâkh) pretended to become his adherent and to have broken with his 'Abbâsid masters. Idrîs took him under his protection and admitted him to his private company. Once, when Idrîs was alone, ash-Shammâkh gave him some poison and thus killed him. The news of his death was received by the

[144] A locality near Mecca where 'Alids in revolt were defeated in 169 [786]. Cf., for instance, Abû l-Faraj al-Iṣfahânî, *Maqâtil aṭ-Ṭâlibîyîn* (Cairo, 1368/1949), pp. 434 ff.; Ibn al-Athîr, *Kâmil*, VI, 38, *anno* 169; *'Ibar*, III, 215 f. Ibn al-Athîr states that it is uncertain whether it was al-Hâdî or ar-Rashîd who killed Wâḍiḥ, who was postmaster general and chief of the intelligence service in Egypt.

ʿAbbâsids most favorably, since they hoped that it would cut the roots and blunt the edge of the ʿAlid propaganda in the Maghrib. News of the unborn child left after Idrîs' death had not (yet) reached them. Thus, it was only a brief moment until the (ʿAlid) propaganda reappeared. The Shîʿah was successful in the Maghrib, and Shîʿah rule was renewed through Idrîs, Idrîs' son. This was a most painful blow to the ʿAbbâsids. Weakness and senility had already taken hold of the Arab dynasty. No longer could (the ʿAbbâsids) aspire to the control of remote regions. Far away as the elder Idrîs was in the Maghrib, under the protection of the Berbers, ar-Rashîd had just enough power, and no more, to poison him with the help of a ruse. Therefore, the ʿAbbâsids now had recourse to their Aghlabid clients in Ifrîqiyah. They asked them to heal the dangerous breach caused by (the Idrîsids), to take measures against the woe that threatened to befall the dynasty from that direction, and to uproot (the Idrîsids) before they could spread. Al-Ma'mûn and the succeeding caliphs wrote to the Aghlabids to this effect. However, the Aghlabids were also too weak (to control) the Berbers of Morocco, and might better have tried to embarrass their own rulers as (the Idrîsids embarrassed them), because the power of the caliphate had been usurped by non-Arab slaves, who diverted *I, 37*
to their own purposes its entire control and authority [145] over men, taxes, and functionaries. It was as the contemporary (ʿAbbâsid) poet described it: [146]

A caliph in a cage
Between Waṣîf and Bughâ:
He says what they tell him,
Like a parrot.

---

[145] *An-naqḍ wa-l-ibrâm,* literally "the untwisting and twisting." Cf. n. 1, above: "all his powers," and below, p. 379, l. 21. Cf. also H. Lammens, *Etudes sur le siècle des Omayyades* (Beirut, 1930), p. 4.

[146] The verses are quoted by al-Masʿûdî, *Murûj adh-dhahab,* VII, 325, with reference to the caliph al-Mustaʿîn, who was one of those dominated by the Turkish generals Waṣîf and Bughâ.

The Aghlabid amirs, therefore, were afraid of possible intrigues and tried all kinds of excuses. Sometimes, they belittled the Maghrib and its inhabitants. At other times, they tried to arouse fear of the power of Idrîs and his descendants who had taken his place there. They wrote the 'Abbâsids that he was crossing the borders of his territory. They included his coins among their gifts, presents, and tax collections, in order to show his growing influence and to spread terror about his increasing power, to magnify (the dangers) which would lie in attacking and fighting him, as they were being asked to do, and to threaten a change in allegiance if they were forced to that. Again, at other times, they attacked the descent of Idrîs with the (afore-mentioned) lie, in order to harm him. They did not care whether the accusation was true or not. The distance (from Baghdad) was great, and, weak-minded as the 'Abbâsid children and their non-Arab slaves were, they took anybody's word and listened to anybody's noise. They went on in this manner until the Aghlabid rule came to an end.

The nasty remark (about the Idrîsid genealogy) then became known to the mob. Some slanderers listened eagerly to it, using it to harm the Idrîsids when there were rivalries. Why do such God-forsaken men stray from the intentions of the religious law, which knows no difference between definite (fact) and (mere) guess? [146a] Idrîs was born in his father's
I, 38 bed, and "the child belongs to the bed." [147] It is a (Muslim) article of faith that the descendants of Muḥammad are above any such thing (as adultery). God removed every turpitude from them and cleansed them. Idrîs' bed is free of all uncleanliness and all turpitude. This is decided in the Qur'ân.[148] Whoever believes the contrary confesses his guilt and invites unbelief.

I have refuted the accusation against Idrîs here at length,

[146a] In a case like this, involving the crime of throwing suspicion upon someone's sexual morality.

[147] This is a Prophetic tradition. Cf. *Handbook*, p. 43*b*; D. Santillana, *Istituzioni di diritto musulmano*, I, 193.

[148] Cf. Qur'ân 33.33 (33).

in order to forestall doubts and strike out against the envious. I heard the story with my own ears from a man who was hostile to (the Idrîsids) and attacked their descent with this lying invention. In his self-deception, he passed on the story on the authority of certain historians of the Maghrib who had turned their backs on Muḥammad's descendants and were skeptical concerning their ancestors. But the situation (of the Idrîsids) is above all that and not susceptible of such a (taint). (No space should be devoted to refuting such an accusation, since) to deny a fault where (the existence of) a fault is impossible is (in itself) a fault.[149] However, I did defend them here in this world and, thus, I hope that they will defend me on the Day of Resurrection.

It should be known that most of those who attack the ('Alid) descent of (the Idrîsids) are themselves persons who claim to be descendants of Muḥammad or pretend to be connected with his descendants, and who envy the descendants of Idrîs. The claim to (Muḥammadan) descent is a great title to nobility among nations and races in all regions. Therefore, it is subject to suspicion. Now, both in their native Fez and in the other regions of the Maghrib, the descent of the Idrîsids is so well known and evident that almost no one can show or hope to show as well-established a pedigree. It is the result of continuous transmission by the more recent nations and generations on the authority of the older preceding ones. The Idrîsids count the house of their ancestor Idrîs, the founder and builder of Fez, among their I, 39
houses. His mosque is adjacent to their quarter and streets. His sword is (suspended) unsheathed atop the main minaret of their residence. There are other relics of his which have been attested to many times in an uninterrupted tradition, so that the tradition concerning them is almost as valuable as direct observation (as to its reliability). Other descendants of Muḥammad can look at these signs which God gave to the Idrîsids. They will see the Muḥammadan nobility of the Idrîsids enhanced by the majesty of the royal authority their

[149] See also 3:54, below.

ancestors exercised in the Maghrib. They will realize that they themselves have nothing of the sort and that they do not measure up even halfway to any one of the Idrîsids. They will also realize that those who claim to be Muḥammad's descendants but do not have such testimonies to confirm their claim as the Idrîsids have, may at best find their position conceded (as possibly true), because people are to be believed with regard to the descent they claim for themselves,[150] but there is a difference between what is known and what is mere guess, between what is certain and what is merely conceded as possibly true.

When they realize these facts, they are choked in their own spittle (which they swallow in impotent jealousy). Their private envy causes many of them to wish that they could bring down the Idrîsids from their noble position to the status of ordinary, humble persons. Therefore, they have recourse to spite and persistent malevolence and invent erroneous and lying accusations such as the one discussed. They justify themselves by the assumption that all guesses are equally probable. They ought to (prove) that! We know of no descendants of Muḥammad whose lineage is so clearly and obviously established as that of the descendants of Idrîs of the family of al-Ḥasan. The most distinguished Idrîsids at this time are the Banû 'Imrân in Fez. They are descendants of Yaḥyâ al-Jûṭî b. Muḥammad b. Yaḥyâ al-'Addâm b. al-
I, 40 Qâsim b. Idrîs b. Idrîs. They are the chiefs of the 'Alids there. They live (at the present time) in the house of their ancestor Idrîs. They are the leading nobility of the entire Maghrib. We shall mention them in connection with the Idrîsids, if God wills.[151] They are the descendants of 'Imrân b.

---

[150] Cf. Bombaci, p. 442, and below, p. 54.

[151] In *'Ibar*, IV, 15, l. 25, Ibn Khaldûn mentions only Yaḥyâ al-'Addâm. *Al-'Addâm* is the form indicated in the MSS of the *Muqaddimah*.

The pedigree of the Banû 'Imrân which follows is added in the margin of C and incorporated in the text of D.

Ibn Ḥazm, *Jamharat ansâb al-'Arab*, p. 44, refers to the first Yaḥyâ (al-'Addâm) as Yaḥyâ al-Jûṭî. Ibn Ḥazm, *loc. cit.*, l. 10, also refers to Yaḥyâ b. Ibrâhîm b. Yaḥyâ (al-Jûṭî).

Muḥammad b. al-Ḥasan b. Yaḥyâ b. ʻAbdallâh b. Muḥammad b. ʻAlî b. Muḥammad b. Yaḥyâ b. Ibrâhîm b. Yaḥyâ al-Jûṭî. The chief of their (house) at this time is Muḥammad b. Muḥammad b. Muḥammad b. ʻImrân.

To these wicked statements and erroneous beliefs one may add the accusations that weak-minded jurists in the Maghrib leveled against the imam al-Mahdî, the head of the Almohad dynasty.[152] He was accused of deceit and insincerity when he insisted upon the true oneness of God and when he complained about the unjust people before his time. All his claims in this respect were declared to be false, even down to his descent from the family of Muḥammad, which his Almohad followers accept. Deep down in their hearts it was envy of al-Mahdî's success that led the jurists to declare him a liar. In their self-deception, they thought that they could compete with him in religious scholarship, juridical decisions, and religion. He then turned out to be superior to them. His opinion was accepted, what he said was listened to, and he gained a following. They envied this success of his and tried to lessen his influence by attacking his dogmas and declaring his claims to be false. Furthermore, they were used to receive from al-Mahdî's enemies, the Lamtûnah kings (the Almoravids), a respect and an honor they received from no one else, because of the simple religion (of the Almoravids). Under the I, 41
Lamtûnah dynasty, religious scholars held a position of respect and were appointed to the council, everybody according to his influence among his people in his respective village. The scholars, therefore, became partisans (of the Almoravids) and enemies of their enemies. They tried to take revenge on al-Mahdî for his opposition to them, his censure of them, and his struggle against them. This was the result of their partisanship for the Lamtûnah and their bias in favor of the Lamtûnah dynasty. Al-Mahdî's position was different from theirs. He did not share their beliefs. What else could

[152] Ibn Khaldûn dealt with the beginning of the Almohads in *ʻIbar,* VI, 225 ff.; de Slane (tr.), II, 161 ff.

be expected of a man who criticized the attitude of the ruling dynasty as he did and was opposed in his efforts by its jurists? He called his people to a holy war against them. He uprooted the dynasty and turned it upside down, despite its great strength, its tremendous power, and the strong force of its allies and its militia. Followers of his killed in the struggle were innumerable. They had sworn allegiance to him until death. They had protected him from death with their own lives. They had sought nearness to God by sacrificing themselves for the victory of the Mahdî's cause as partisans of the enterprise that eventually gained the upper hand and replaced the dynasties on both shores.[153] (Al-Mahdî himself) remained always frugal, retiring, patient in tribulation, and very little concerned with the world to the last; he died without fortune or worldly possessions. He did not even have children, as everybody desires but as one often is deceived in desiring. I should like to know what he could have hoped to obtain by this way of life were it not (to look upon) the face of God,
I, 42 for he did not acquire worldly fortune of any kind during his lifetime. Moreover, if his intention had not been good, he would not have been successful, and his propaganda would not have spread. "This is how God formerly proceeded with His servants." [154]

The (jurists') disavowal of (al-Mahdî's) descent from Muḥammad's family is not backed up by any proof. Were it established that he himself claimed such descent, his claim could not be disproved, because people are to be believed regarding the descent they claim for themselves.[155] It might be said that leadership over a people is vested only in men of their own skin. This is correct, as will be mentioned in the first [156] chapter of this book. But [157] al-Mahdî exercised leadership over all the Maṣmûdah. They agreed to follow him and be guided by him and his Harghah group, and,

[153] I.e., northwestern Africa and Spain.
[154] Qur'ân 40.85 (85).
[155] Cf. p. 52, above.
[156] *Leg.* "second." Cf. p. 273, below.
[157] Cf. Bombaci, pp. 442 f.

eventually, God gave complete success to his propaganda. In this connection, it must be realized that al-Mahdî's power did not depend exclusively on his Fâṭimid descent, and the people did not follow him on that account (only). They followed him because of their Harghah-Maṣmûdah group feeling and because of his share in that group feeling which was firmly rooted in him. (Al-Mahdî's) Fâṭimid descent had become obscured and knowledge of it had disappeared from among the people, although it had remained alive in him and his family through family tradition. His original (Fâṭimid) descent had, in a way, been sloughed off, and he had put on the skin of the Harghah-Maṣmûdah and thus appeared as one of their skin. The fact that he was originally of Fâṭimid descent did not harm him with regard to his group feeling, since it was not known to the members of the group. Things like that happen frequently once one's original descent has become obscured.

One might compare (with the above) the story of 'Arfajah and Jarîr concerning the leadership of the Bajîlah.[158] 'Arfajah I, 43
had belonged to the Azd but had put on the skin of the Bajîlah so successfully that he was able to wrangle with Jarîr over the leadership before 'Umar, as has been reported. This example makes one understand what the truth is like.

God is the guide to that which is correct.

Lengthy discussion of these mistakes has taken us rather far from the purpose of this work. However, many competent persons and expert historians slipped in connection with such stories and assertions, and they stuck in their minds. Many weak-minded and uncritical persons learned these things from them, and even (the competent historians) themselves accepted them without critical investigation, and thus (strange stories) crept into their material. In consequence, historiography became nonsensical and confused, and its students fumbled around. Historiography came to be considered a domain of the common people. Therefore, today, the scholar

[158] Cf. p. 268 and 2:39, below.

in this field needs to know the principles of politics, the (true) nature of existent things, and the differences among nations, places, and periods with regard to ways of life, character qualities, customs, sects, schools, and everything else. He further needs a comprehensive knowledge of present conditions in all these respects. He must compare similarities or differences between the present and the past (or distantly located) conditions. He must know the causes of the similarities in certain cases and of the differences in others. He must be aware of the differing origins and beginnings of (different) dynasties and religious groups, as well as of the reasons and incentives that brought them into being and the circumstances and history of the persons who supported them. His goal must be to have complete knowledge of the reasons for every happening, and to be acquainted with the origin of every event. Then, he must check transmitted information
I, 44 with the basic principles he knows. If it fulfills their requirements, it is sound. Otherwise, the historian must consider it as spurious and dispense with it. It was for this reason alone that historiography was highly considered by the ancients, so much so that aṭ-Ṭabarî, al-Bukhârî, and, before them, Ibn Isḥâq and other Muslim religious scholars, chose to occupy themselves with it. Most scholars, however, forgot this, the (real) secret of historiography, with the result that it became a stupid occupation. Ordinary people as well as (scholars) who had no firm foundation of knowledge, considered it a simple matter to study and know history, to delve into it and sponge on it. Strays got into the flock, bits of shell were mixed with the nut, truth was adulterated with lies.

"The final outcome of things is up to God." [159]

A [160] hidden pitfall in historiography is disregard for the fact that conditions within the nations and races change with the change of periods and the passing of days. This is a sore affliction and is deeply hidden, becoming noticeable only

[159] Qur'ân 31.22 (21).
[160] Cf. Issawi, pp. 29–33.

after a long time, so that rarely do more than a few individuals become aware of it.

This is as follows. The condition of the world and of nations, their customs and sects, does not persist in the same form or in a constant manner. There are differences according to days and periods, and changes from one condition to another. This is the case with individuals, times, and cities, and, in the same manner, it happens in connection with regions and districts, periods and dynasties.

"This is how God formerly proceeded with His servants." [161]

The old Persian nations, the Syrians, the Nabataeans, the Tubba's, the Israelites, and the Copts, all once existed. They all had their own particular institutions in respect of dynastic and territorial arrangements, their own politics, crafts, languages, technical terminologies, as well as their own ways of dealing with their fellow men and handling their cultural institutions. Their (historical) relics testify to that. They were I, 46
succeeded by the later Persians, the Byzantines, and the Arabs. The old institutions changed and former customs were transformed, either into something very similar, or into something distinct and altogether different. Then, there came Islam with the Muḍar dynasty. Again, all institutions underwent another change, and for the most part assumed the forms that are still familiar at the present time as the result of their transmission from one generation to the next.

Then, the days of Arab rule were over. The early generations who had cemented Arab might and founded the realm of the Arabs, were gone. The power was seized by others, by non-Arabs like the Turks in the east, the Berbers in the west, and the European Christians [162] in the north. With their [162a] passing, entire nations ceased to exist, and institutions and customs changed. Their glory was forgotten, and their power no longer heeded.

---

[161] Qur'ân 40.85 (85).
[162] Literally, "Franks."
[162a] The pronoun presumably refers to the Arabs.

The widely accepted reason for changes in institutions and customs is the fact that the customs of each race depend on the customs of its ruler. As the proverb says: "The common people follow the religion of the ruler."[163]

When politically ambitious men overcome the ruling dynasty and seize power, they inevitably have recourse to the customs of their predecessors and adopt most of them. At the same time, they do not neglect the customs of their own race. This leads to some discrepancies between the customs of the (new) ruling dynasty and the customs of the old race.

The new power, in turn, is succeeded by another dynasty, and customs are further mixed with those of the new dynasty. More discrepancies come in, and the discrepancy between the new dynasty and the first one is much greater (than that between the second and the first one). Gradual increase in the degree of discrepancy continues. The eventual result is an altogether distinct (set of customs and institutions). As long
I, 46 as there is this continued succession of different races to royal authority and government, discrepancies in customs and institutions will not cease to occur.

Analogical reasoning and comparison are well known to human nature. They are not safe from error. Together with forgetfulness and negligence, they sway man from his purpose and divert him from his goal. Often, someone who has learned a good deal of past history remains unaware of the changes that conditions have undergone. Without a moment's hesitation, he applies his knowledge (of the present) to the historical information and measures the historical information by the things he has observed with his own eyes, although the difference between the two is great. Consequently, he falls into an abyss of error.

This may be illustrated by what the historians report concerning the circumstances of Al-Ḥajjâj.[164] They state that his father was a schoolteacher. At the present time, teaching is a

[163] Cf. p. 300 and 2:123, 306, below. *Dîn* "religion" is here used in the more general sense of "way of doing things." Cf. Ibn Qutaybah, *'Uyûn al-akhbâr*, I, 2.

[164] Al-Ḥajjâj b. Yûsuf, the great governor of the 'Irâq (*ca.* 660–714). Cf. H. Lammens in *EI*, *s.v.* "al-Ḥadjdjâdj."

craft and serves to make a living. It is a far cry from the pride of group feeling. Teachers are weak, indigent, and rootless. Many weak professional men and artisans who work for a living aspire to positions for which they are not fit but which they believe to be within their reach. They are misled by their desires, a rope which often slips from their hands and precipitates them into the abyss of ruinous perdition. They do not realize that what they desire is impossible for men like them to attain. They do not realize that they are professional men and artisans who work for a living. And they do not know that at the beginning of Islam and during the (Umayyad and 'Abbâsid) dynasties, teaching was something different. Scholarship, in general, was not a craft in that period. Scholarship was transmitting statements that people had heard the Lawgiver (Muḥammad) make. It was teaching religious matters that were not known, by way of oral transmission. Persons of noble descent and people who shared in the group feeling (of the ruling dynasty) and who directed the affairs of Islam were the ones who taught the Book of I, 47
God and the Sunnah of the Prophet, (and they did so) as one transmits traditions, not as one gives professional instruction. (The Qur'ân) was their Scripture, revealed to the Prophet in their midst. It constituted their guidance, and Islam was their religion, and for it they fought and died. It distinguished them from the other nations and ennobled them. They wished to teach it and make it understandable to the Muslims. They were not deterred by censure coming from pride, nor were they restrained by criticism coming from arrogance. This is attested by the fact that the Prophet sent the most important of the men around him with his embassies to the Arabs, in order to teach them the norms of Islam and the religious laws he brought. He sent his ten companions [165] and others after them on this mission.

Then, Islam became firmly established and securely

[165] The *'asharah al-mubashsharah*, the ten early Muslims to whom Paradise was guaranteed. Cf. A. J. Wensinck, *Handwörterbuch des Islam* (Leiden, 1941), *s.v.* "al-'Ashara 'l-mubashshara." They were the first four caliphs, Ṭalḥah, az-Zubayr, 'Abd-ar-Raḥmân b. 'Awf, Sa'd b. Abî Waqqâṣ, Sa'îd b. Zayd, and Abû 'Ubaydah b. al-Jarrâḥ.

rooted. Far-off nations accepted Islam at the hands of the Muslims. With the passing of time, the situation of Islam changed. Many new laws were evolved from the (basic) texts as the result of numerous and unending developments. A fixed norm was required to keep (the process) free from error. Scholarship came to be a habit.[166] For its acquisition, study was required. Thus, scholarship developed into a craft and profession. This will be mentioned in the chapter on scholarship and instruction.[167]

The men who controlled the group feeling now occupied themselves with directing the affairs of royal and governmental authority. The cultivation of scholarship was entrusted to others. Thus, scholarship became a profession that served to make a living. Men who lived in luxury and were in control of the government were too proud to do any teaching. Teaching came to be an occupation restricted to weak individuals. As a result, its practitioners came to be despised by the men who controlled the group feeling and the government.

Now, Yûsuf, the father of al-Ḥajjâj, was one of the lords
I, 48 and nobles of the Thaqîf, well known for their share in the Arab group feeling and for their rivalry with the nobility of the Quraysh. Al-Ḥajjâj's teaching of the Qur'ân was not what teaching of the Qur'ân is at this time, namely, a profession that serves to make a living. His teaching was teaching as it was practiced at the beginning of Islam and as we have just described it.

Another illustration of the same (kind of error) is the baseless conclusion critical readers of historical works draw when they hear about the position of judges and about the leadership in war and the command of armies that judges (formerly) exercised. Their misguided thinking leads them to aspire to similar positions. They think that the office of judge

166 Cf. p. lxxxiv, above.

167 That is, the sixth chapter of the *Muqaddimah*, beginning at 2:411, below. Cf. esp. n. 2 to Ch. VI as well as 2:426 and passages such as that at 2:444, below.

at the present time is as important as it was formerly. When they hear that the father of Ibn Abî 'Âmir, who had complete control over Hishâm, and that the father of Ibn 'Abbâd, one of the rulers of Sevilla, were judges,[168] they assume that they were like present-day judges. They are not aware of the change in customs that has affected the office of judge, and which will be explained by us in the chapter on the office of judge in the first book.[169] Ibn Abî 'Âmir and Ibn 'Abbâd belonged to Arab tribes that supported the Umayyad dynasty in Spain and represented the group feeling of the Umayyads, and it is known how important their positions were. The leadership and royal authority they attained did not derive from the rank of the judgeship as such, in the present-day sense that (the office of judge constitutes an administrative rank). In the ancient administrative organization, the office of judge was given by the dynasty and its clients to men who shared in the group feeling (of the dynasty), as is done in our age with the wazirate in the Maghrib. One has only to consider the fact that (in those days judges) accompanied the army on its summer campaigns and I, 49
were entrusted with the most important affairs, such as are entrusted only to men who can command the group feeling needed for their execution.

Hearing such things, some people are misled and get the wrong idea about conditions. At the present time, weak-minded Spaniards are especially given to errors in this respect. The group feeling has been lost in their country for many years, as the result of the annihilation of the Arab dynasty in Spain and the emancipation of the Spaniards from the control of Berber group feeling. The Arab descent has been remembered, but the ability to gain power through group feeling and mutual co-operation has been lost. In fact, the (Spaniards) came to be like (passive) subjects,[170] without

[168] Al-Manṣûr died in 392 [1002]. Cf. E. Lévi-Provençal in *EI*, *s.v.* "Al-Manṣûr Ibn Abî 'Âmir." The 'Abbâdids ruled Sevilla during the eleventh century.

[169] Cf. pp. 452 ff., below.

[170] *Ra'âyâ* (raia, rayah) "cattle," then "subjects." See also p. 383, below.

any feeling for the obligation of mutual support. They were enslaved by tyranny and had become fond of humiliation, thinking that their descent, together with their share in the ruling dynasty, was the source of power and authority. Therefore, among them, professional men and artisans are to be found pursuing power and authority and eager to obtain them. On the other hand, those who have experience with tribal conditions, group feeling, and dynasties along the western shore, and who know how superiority is achieved among nations and tribal groups, will rarely make mistakes or give erroneous interpretations in this respect.

Another illustration of the same kind of error is the procedure historians follow when they mention the various dynasties and enumerate the rulers belonging to them. They mention the name of each ruler, his ancestors, his mother and father, his wives, his surname, his seal ring, his judge, doorkeeper, and wazir. In this respect, they blindly follow the tradition of the historians of the Umayyad and 'Abbâsid dynasties, without being aware of the purpose of the historians of those times. (The historians of those times) wrote
I, 50 their histories for members of the ruling dynasty, whose children wanted to know the lives and circumstances of their ancestors, so that they might be able to follow in their steps and to do what they did,[171] even down to such details as obtaining servants from among those who were left over from the (previous) dynasty [172] and giving ranks and positions to the descendants of its servants and retainers. Judges, too, shared in the group feeling of the dynasty and enjoyed the same importance as wazirs, as we have just mentioned. Therefore, the historians of that time had to mention all these things.

Later on, however, various distinct dynasties made their appearance. The time intervals became longer and longer.

---

[171] Literally, "wove on their loom." Cf. p. 9, above, and n. 1444 to Ch. vi, below.

[172] Cf. Bombaci, p. 443.

Historical interest now was concentrated on the rulers themselves and on the mutual relationships of the various dynasties in respect to power and predominance. (The problem now was) which nations could stand up (to the ruling dynasty) and which were too weak to do so. Therefore, it is pointless for an author of the present time to mention the sons and wives, the engraving on the seal ring, the surname, judge, wazir, and doorkeeper of an ancient dynasty, when he does not know the origin, descent, or circumstances of its members. Present-day authors mention all these things in mere blind imitation of former authors. They disregard the intentions of the former authors and forget to pay attention to historiography's purpose.

An exception are the wazirs who were very influential and whose historical importance overshadowed that of the rulers. Such wazirs as, for instance, al-Ḥajjâj, the Banû Muhallab, the Barmecides, the Banû Sahl b. Nawbakht, Kâfûr al-Ikhshîdî, Ibn Abî ʿÂmir, and others should be mentioned. There is no objection to dealing with their lives or referring to their conditions for in importance they rank with the rulers.

An additional note to end this discussion may find its place here.

History refers to events that are peculiar to a particular age or race. Discussion of the general conditions of regions, races, and periods constitutes the historian's foundation. I, 51
Most of his problems rest upon that foundation, and his historical information derives clarity from it. It forms the topic of special works, such as the *Murûj adh-dhahab* of al-Masʿûdî. In this work, al-Masʿûdî commented upon the conditions of nations and regions in the West and in the East during his period (which was) the three hundred and thirties [the nine hundred and forties]. He mentioned their sects and customs. He described the various countries, mountains, oceans, provinces, and dynasties. He distinguished between Arabic and non-Arabic groups. His book, thus, became the basic refer-

ence work for historians, their principal source for verifying historical information.

Al-Mas'ûdî was succeeded by al-Bakrî [173] who did something similar for routes and provinces, to the exclusion of everything else, because, in his time, not many transformations or great changes had occurred among the nations and races. However, at the present time—that is, at the end of the eighth [fourteenth] century—the situation in the Maghrib, as we can observe, has taken a turn and changed entirely. The Berbers, the original population of the Maghrib, have been replaced by an influx of Arabs, (that began in) the fifth [eleventh] century. The Arabs outnumbered and overpowered the Berbers, stripped them of most of their lands, and (also) obtained a share of those that remained in their possession. This was the situation until, in the middle of the eighth [fourteenth] century, civilization both in the East and the West was visited by a destructive plague which devastated nations and caused populations to vanish.[174] It swallowed up many of the good things of civilization and wiped them out. It overtook the dynasties at the time of their senility, when
I, 52 they had reached the limit of their duration. It lessened their power and curtailed their influence. It weakened their authority. Their situation approached the point of annihilation and dissolution. Civilization decreased with the decrease of mankind. Cities and buildings were laid waste, roads and way signs were obliterated, settlements and mansions became empty, dynasties and tribes grew weak. The entire inhabited world changed. The East, it seems, was similarly visited, though in accordance with and in proportion to (the East's more affluent) civilization. It was as if the voice of existence in the world had called out for oblivion and restriction, and the world had responded to its call. God inherits the earth and whomever is upon it.

---

[173] The geographer, 'Abdallâh b. Muḥammad, 432–487 [1040/41–1094]. Cf. *GAL*, I, 476; *Suppl.*, I, 875 f. He is repeatedly quoted by Ibn Khaldûn. A new edition of al-Bakrî's geographical dictionary, *Mu'jam mâ sta'jam*, appeared in Cairo in 1945–51. His *Routes and Provinces* (*al-Masâlik wa-l-mamâlik*) is still unpublished except for some sections.

[174] Cf. p. xl, above.

When there is a general change of conditions, it is as if the entire creation had changed and the whole world been altered, as if it were a new and repeated creation, a world brought into existence anew. Therefore, there is need at this time that someone should systematically set down the situation of the world among all regions and races, as well as the customs and sectarian beliefs that have changed for their adherents, doing for this age what al-Mas'ûdî did for his. This should be a model for future historians to follow. In this book of mine, I shall discuss as much of that as will be possible for me here in the Maghrib. I shall do so either explicitly or implicitly in connection with the history of the Maghrib, in conformity with my intention to restrict myself in this work to the Maghrib, the circumstances of its races and nations, and its subjects and dynasties, to the exclusion of any other region.[175] (This restriction is necessitated) by my lack of knowledge of conditions in the East and among its nations, and by the fact that secondhand information would not give the essential facts I am after. Al-Mas'ûdî's I, *53*
extensive travels in various countries enabled him to give a complete picture, as he mentioned in his work. Nevertheless, his discussion of conditions in the Maghrib is incomplete. "And He knows more than any scholar." [176] God is the ultimate repository of (all) knowledge. Man is weak and deficient. Admission (of one's ignorance) is a specific (religious) duty. He whom God helps, finds his way (made) easy and his efforts and quests successful. We seek God's help for the goal to which we aspire in this work. God gives guidance and help. He may be trusted.

It remains for us to explain the method of transcribing non-Arabic sounds whenever they occur in this book of ours:

It should be known that the letters (sounds) [177] of speech,

---

[175] Ibn Khaldûn soon changed his mind and added the history of the East to his work at a very early stage in its preparation.

[176] Qur'ân 12.76 (76).

[177] The written symbol is considered to be identical with the sound indicated by it.

as will be explained later on,[178] are modifications of sounds that come from the larynx. These modifications result from the fact that the sounds are broken up in contact with the uvula and the sides of the tongue in the throat, against the palate or the teeth, and also through contact with the lips. The sound is modified by the different ways in which such contact takes place. As a result, the letters (sounds) sound distinct. Their combination constitutes the word that expresses what is in the mind.

Not [179] all nations have the same letters (sounds) in their speech. One nation has letters (sounds) different from those of another. The letters (sounds) of the Arabs are twenty-eight, as is known. The Hebrews are found to have letters
I, *64* (sounds) that are not in our language. In our language, in turn, there are letters (sounds) that are not in theirs. The same applies to the European Christians, the Turks, the Berbers, and other non-Arabs.

In order to express their audible letters (sounds), literate Arabs [180] chose to use conventional letters written individually separate, such as *'*, *b*, *j*, *r*, *ṭ*, and so forth through all the twenty-eight letters. When they come upon a letter (sound) for which there is no corresponding letter (sound) in their language, it is not indicated in writing and not clearly expressed. Scribes sometimes express it by means of the letter which is closest to it in our language, the one either preceding or following it.[181] This is not a satisfactory way of indicating a letter (sound) but a complete replacement of it.

Our book contains the history of the Berbers and other non-Arabs. In their names and in some of their words, we

---

[178] Apparently the remarks immediately following are meant.

[179] Cf. Issawi, pp. 156 f. Cf. also *'Ibar*, VII, 7; de Slane (tr.), III, 188 ff.

[180] Actually, the term Ibn Khaldûn uses carries the connotation of "(pre-Islamic) Jewish and Christian Arabs." He thinks first of the originators of Arabic orthography and then refers to the way in which, in his opinion, literate (Muslim) Arabs later expressed sounds not found in Arabic.

[181] The way Ibn Khaldûn expresses himself, this would seem to refer to the position of letters in the written alphabet, and not to their articulation. It should, of course, refer to the latter. Again, the notions of letters and sounds are confused.

came across letters (sounds) that did not correspond with our written language and conventional orthography. Therefore, we were forced to indicate such sounds (by special signs). As we said, we did not find it satisfactory to use the letters closest to them, because in our opinion this is not a satisfactory indication. In my book, therefore, I have chosen to write such non-Arabic letters (sounds) in such a way as to indicate the two letters (sounds) closest to it, so that the reader may be able to pronounce it somewhere in the middle between the sounds represented by the two letters and thus reproduce it correctly.

I derived this idea from the way the Qur'ân scholars write sounds that are not sharply defined, such as occur, for instance, in *aṣ-ṣirâṭ* according to Khalaf's reading.[182] The *ṣ* is 1, 55
to be pronounced somehow between *ṣ* and *z*. In this case, they spell the word with *ṣ* and write a *z* into it.[183] They thus indicate a pronunciation somewhere in the middle between the two sounds.[184]

In the same way, I have indicated every letter (sound) that is to be pronounced somehow in the middle between two of our letters (sounds). The Berber *k*, for instance, which is pronounced midway between our clear *k* and *j* (*g*) or *q*, as, for instance, in the name Buluggîn, is spelled by me with a *k* with the addition of one dot—from the *j*—below, or one dot or two—from the *q*—on top of it.[185] This indicates that the

---

[182] Khalaf b. Hishâm, one of the seven Qur'ân readers, d. 229 [843/44]. Cf. T. Nöldeke, F. Schwally, G. Bergsträsser, and O. Pretzl, *Geschichte des Qorâns* (Leipzig, 1909–38), III, 182. His reading of *aṣ-ṣirâṭ* applies to Qur'ân 1.6 (5).

[183] For this spelling (صز) in Berber words, see, for instance, pp. 128 f., 2:49, 197, and 3:129, below.

[184] In the ninth century, a transcription alphabet was invented by Aḥmad b. aṭ-Ṭayyib as-Sarakhsî. Cf. P. Kraus, *Jâbir Ibn Ḥayyân* (Mémoires de l'Institut d'Egypte, Nos. 44–45) (Cairo, 1942–43), II, 245 (n. 2). However, we do not know what it looked like.

[185] Instances for the spelling ڮ are quite frequent. Cf., for instance, "Gawgaw," p. 119, below. Examples for ڭ and ݢ may be found in the spelling of Wangârah in C; cf. p. 119, below.

Arabic *jîm* was pronounced in Egypt according to its ancient Semitic sound value *g*, but Ibn Khaldûn was not thinking of the Egyptian pronunciation when he referred to it in this context, but rather of the generally

sound is to be pronounced midway between *k* and *j* (*g*) or *q*. This sound occurs most frequently in the Berber language. In the other cases, I have spelled each letter (sound) that is to be pronounced midway between two letters (sounds) of our language, with a similar combination of two letters. The reader will thus know that it is an intermediate sound and pronounce it accordingly. In this way, we have indicated it satisfactorily. Had we spelled it by using only one letter (sound) adjacent to it on either side,[185a] we would have changed its proper pronunciation to the pronunciation of the particular letter (sound) in our own language (which we might have used), and we would have altered the way people speak. This should be known.

God gives success.

---

recognized fact of the similarity of *j*, *q*, and *k* as pronounced in the various Arabic dialects. On the pronunciation of *q*, cf. the discussion below, 3 : 348 ff.

The references to *q* in this sentence appear in the margin of C.

Another transcription sign ڟ (*ṭ* with the two dots of *t*) is used for European *t*, as, for instance, in *Angalatirrah* (England). It also appears in *Ṭatar*.

[185a] That is, using either *k* or *j* (*q*) to express the *g* sound, as, for instance, in the case of *Buluggîn*.

Book One of the

Kitâb al-ʿIbar

The nature of civilization. Bedouin I, 56
and settled life, the achievement of superiority,
gainful occupations, ways of making a living, sciences,
crafts, and all the other things that affect
(civilization). The causes
and reasons thereof.

IT[1] SHOULD be known that history, in matter of fact, is information about human social organization, which itself is identical with world civilization. It deals with such conditions affecting the nature of civilization as, for instance, savagery and sociability, group feelings, and the different ways by which one group of human beings achieves superiority over another. It deals with royal authority and the dynasties that result (in this manner) and with the various ranks that exist within them. (It further deals) with the different kinds of gainful occupations and ways of making a living, with the sciences and crafts that human beings pursue as part of their activities and efforts, and with all the other institutions that originate in civilization through its very nature.

Untruth naturally afflicts historical information. There are various reasons that make this unavoidable. One of them is partisanship for opinions and schools. If the soul is impartial in receiving information, it devotes to that information the share of critical investigation the information deserves, and its truth or untruth thus becomes clear. However, if the soul is infected with partisanship for a particular opinion or sect, it accepts without a moment's hesitation the information that is agreeable to it. Prejudice and partisanship obscure I, 57
the critical faculty and preclude critical investigation. The result is that falsehoods are accepted and transmitted.

Another reason making untruth unavoidable in historical

[1] Cf. Issawi, pp. 26 f., and J. Sauvaget, *Historiens arabes* (Paris, 1946), pp. 138–42.

information is reliance upon transmitters. Investigation of this subject belongs to (the theological discipline of) personality criticism.[2]

Another reason is unawareness of the purpose of an event. Many a transmitter does not know the real significance of his observations or of the things he has learned about orally. He transmits the information, attributing to it the significance he assumes or imagines it to have. The result is falsehood.

Another reason is unfounded assumption as to the truth of a thing. This is frequent. It results mostly from reliance upon transmitters.

Another reason is ignorance of how conditions conform with reality.[2a] Conditions are affected by ambiguities and artificial distortions. The informant reports the conditions as he saw them, but on account of artificial distortions he himself has no true picture of them.

Another reason is the fact that people as a rule approach great and high-ranking persons with praise and encomiums. They embellish conditions and spread the fame (of great men). The information made public in such cases is not truthful. Human souls long for praise, and people pay great attention to this world and the positions and wealth it offers. As a rule, they feel no desire for virtue and have no special interest in virtuous people.

Another reason making untruth unavoidable—and this one is more powerful than all the reasons previously mentioned—is ignorance of the nature of the various conditions arising in civilization. Every event (or phenomenon), whether (it comes into being in connection with some) essence or (as the result of an) action, must inevitably possess a
I, 58 nature peculiar to its essence as well as to the accidental conditions that may attach themselves to it. If the student knows the nature of events and the circumstances and requirements

[2] "Personality criticism" (*al-jarḥ wa-t-taʿdîl*) is concerned with investigating the reliability or unreliability of the transmitters of traditions. Ibn Khaldûn often has occasion to refer to it; see, for instance, p. 76 and 2:160 ff., 447 ff., below.

[2a] Cf. n. 379 to Ch. 1, below.

in the world of existence, it will help him to distinguish truth from untruth in investigating the historical information critically. This is more effective in critical investigation than any other aspect that may be brought up in connection with it.

Students often happen to accept and transmit absurd information that, in turn, is believed on their authority. Al-Mas'ûdî,[3] for instance, reports such a story about Alexander. Sea monsters prevented Alexander from building Alexandria. He took a wooden container in which a glass box was inserted, and dived in it to the bottom of the sea. There he drew pictures of the devilish monsters he saw. He then had metal effigies of these animals made and set them up opposite the place where building was going on. When the monsters came out and saw the effigies, they fled. Alexander was thus able to complete the building of Alexandria.

It is a long story, made up of nonsensical elements which are absurd for various reasons. Thus, (Alexander is said) to have taken a glass box and braved the sea and its waves in person. Now, rulers would not take such a risk.[4] Any ruler who would attempt such a thing would work his own undoing and provoke the outbreak of revolt against himself, and (he would) be replaced by the people with someone else. That would be his end. People would not (even) wait one moment for him to return from the (dangerous) risk he is taking.

Furthermore, the jinn are not known to have specific forms and effigies. They are able to take on various forms. The story of the many heads they have is intended to indicate ugliness and frightfulness. It is not meant to be taken literally.

All this throws suspicion upon the story. Yet, the element in it that makes the story absurd for reasons based on I, 59
the facts of existence is more convincing than all the other

[3] Cf. al-Mas'ûdî, *Murûj adh-dhahab*, II, 425 ff. The story goes back ultimately to the snake (dragon) that frightened the workmen who built Alexandria. Cf. Pseudo-Callisthenes, *Historia Alexandri Magni*, ed. Kroll (Berlin, 1926), p. 32.

[4] *Gharar* "risk" is a legal term, used mainly in connection with commercial matters. In this context it implies unlawful gambling.

(arguments). Were one to go down deep into the water, even in a box, one would have too little air for natural breathing. Because of that, one's spirit [5] would quickly become hot. Such a man would lack the cold air necessary to maintain a well-balanced humor of the lung and the vital spirit. He would perish on the spot. This is the reason why people perish in hot baths when cold air is denied to them. It also is the reason why people who go down into deep wells and dungeons perish when the air there becomes hot through putrefaction, and no winds enter those places to stir the air up. Those who go down there perish immediately. This also is the reason why fish die when they leave the water, for the air is not sufficient for (a fish) to balance its lung. (The fish) is extremely hot, and the water to balance its humor is cold. The air into which (the fish) now comes is hot. Heat, thus, gains power over its animal spirit, and it perishes at once. This also is the reason for sudden death,[6] and similar things.

Al-Mas'ûdî reports another absurd story, that of the Statue of the Starling in Rome.[7] On a fixed day of the year, starlings gather at that statue bringing olives from which the inhabitants of Rome get their oil. How little this has to do with the natural procedure of getting oil!

Another absurd story is reported by al-Bakrî. It concerns the way the so-called "Gate City" was built.[8] That city had a

---

[5] The "vital spirit" which, according to Galenic and Muslim medicine, was believed to originate in the left cavity of the heart. See also pp. 210, 329, and 2:136, 374, below.

[6] *Maṣ'ûq* may refer to death by lightning, but also includes other kinds of inexplicable sudden death. Cf. *Lisân al-'Arab*, XII, 66.

[7] Cf. al-Mas'ûdî, *Murûj adh-dhahab*, IV, 94. The story of the Statue of the Starling was mentioned before al-Mas'ûdî by Ibn Khurradâdhbih, *Kitâb al-Masâlik wa-l-mamâlik*, tr. M. J. de Goeje (Bibliotheca Geographorum Arabicorum, No. 6) (Leiden, 1889), p. 88. Many other geographers refer to it; cf. J. Marquart, *Osteuropäische und ostasiatische Streifzüge* (Leipzig, 1903), pp. 260 ff.; and, more recently, M. J. Deny, "La Légende de l'eau des sauterelles et de l'oiseau qui détruit ces insectes," *Journal asiatique*, CCII (1923), 325. Marquart sought the origin of the story in a popular etymology for the Capitol: Campidoglio > *campo d'oglio* "olive oil field."

[8] Al-Bakrî's *Masâlik* contains a brief reference to the "Copper City." Cf. MS. Nuru Osmaniye, 3034, fol. 186*a*; Laleli, 2144, fol. 58*a*. This refer-

circumference of more than a thirty days' journey and had ten thousand gates. Now, cities are used for security and protection, as will be mentioned.[9] Such a city, however, could not be controlled and would offer no security or protection.

Then, there is also al-Mas'ûdî's story of the "Copper City." [10] This is said to be a city built wholly of copper in the desert of Sijilmâsah which Mûsâ b. Nuṣayr [11] crossed on his raid against the Maghrib. The gates of (the Copper City) are said to be closed. When the person who climbs the walls of the city in order to enter it, reaches the top, he claps his hand and throws himself down and never returns. All this is an absurd story. It belongs to the idle talk of storytellers. The desert of Sijilmâsah has been crossed by travelers and guides. They have not come across any information about such a city.[12] All the details mentioned about it are absurd, I, 60

ence does not appear in W. M. de Slane, *Description de l'Afrique septentrionale* (2d ed.; Algiers, 1913). None of the available texts says anything about a "Gate City." A village called *Dhât al-abwâb*, which, however, is different from the one mentioned here, is referred to by al-Bakrî in *Mu'jam mâ sta'jam*, p. 218. Cf. also below, 2:245.

[9] Cf. 2:237 f., below.

[10] Ibn Khaldûn refers to *Murûj adh-dhahab*, IV, 95. However, he adds some details to al-Mas'ûdî's very brief statement, from his own knowledge of the famous story. An earlier contemporary of al-Mas'ûdî gives it in considerable detail: Ibn al Faqîh, *Kitâb al-buldân* (Bibliotheca Geographorum Arabicorum, No. 5) (Leiden, 1885), pp. 71 (n. *g*), 88 ff., quoted by Yâqût, *Mu'jam al-buldân*, ed. Wüstenfeld, IV, 455 ff., and other geographers. In the eleventh century, the theologian al-Khaṭîb al-Baghdâdî studied it in monograph form under the title of "The Story of the Bronze City and the Leaden Cupola." Cf. Yûsuf al-'Ashsh, *al-Khaṭîb al-Baghdâdî* (Damascus, 1945), p. 109. Cf. also G. Ferrand in *Journal asiatique*, CCVII (1925), 61 ff. Through its inclusion in *The Arabian Nights*, the story has become familiar to Western readers.

Instead of "Copper City," the city is referred to as "Bronze City" by al-Mas'ûdî and elsewhere. The word "bronze" (*ṣufr*) is at times wrongly translated as "brass." Cf. M. Aga-Oglu, "A Brief Note on the Islamic Terminology for Bronze and Brass," *Journal of the American Oriental Society*, LXIV (1944), 218–32. The vacillation between "Bronze City" and "Copper City" is due to the fact that the Arabic words for bronze and copper were often used interchangeably without regard to their precise meaning. Cf. G. Levi Della Vida, "The 'Bronze Era' in Muslim Spain," *Journal of the American Oriental Society*, LXIII (1943), 183 (n. 7).

[11] The great general (A.D. 640–716/17) who completed the conquest of the Muslim West. Cf. E. Lévi-Provençal in *EI*, *s.v.* "Mûsâ b. Nuṣair."

[12] The same argument occurs above, pp. 24 and 27.

(if compared with) the customary state of affairs. They contradict the natural facts that apply to the building and planning of cities. Metal exists at best in quantities sufficient for utensils and furnishings. It is clearly absurd and unlikely that there would be enough to cover a city with it.

There [13] are many similar things. Only knowledge of the nature of civilization makes critical investigation of them possible. It is the best and most reliable way to investigate historical information critically and to distinguish truth and falsehood in it. It is superior to investigations that rely upon criticism of the personalities of transmitters. Such personality criticism should not be resorted to until it has been ascertained whether a specific piece of information is in itself possible, or not. If it is absurd, there is no use engaging in personality criticism. Critical scholars consider absurdity inherent in the literal meaning of historical information, or an interpretation not acceptable to the intellect, as something that makes such information suspect. Personality criticism is taken into consideration only in connection with the soundness (or lack of soundness) of Muslim religious information,
I, 61 because this religious information mostly concerns injunctions in accordance with which the Lawgiver (Muḥammad) enjoined Muslims to act whenever it can be presumed that the information is genuine. The way to achieve presumptive soundness is to ascertain the probity (*'adâlah*) and exactness of the transmitters.

On the other hand, to establish the truth and soundness of information about factual happenings, a requirement to consider is the conformity (or lack of conformity of the reported information with general conditions). Therefore, it is necessary to investigate whether it is possible that the (reported facts) could have happened. This is more important than, and has priority over, personality criticism. For the correct notion about something that ought to be [14] can be derived

[13] Cf. Issawi, pp. 34 f.

[14] Referring to the injunctions of the religious law.

For this paragraph, one should compare what Ibn Khaldûn says in *'Ibar,*

only from (personality criticism), while the correct notion about something that was can be derived from (personality criticism) and external (evidence) by (checking) the conformity (of the historical report with general conditions).

If[15] this is so, the normative method for distinguishing right from wrong in historical information on the grounds of (inherent) possibility or absurdity, is to investigate human social organization, which is identical with civilization. We must distinguish the conditions that attach themselves to the essence of civilization as required by its very nature; the things that are accidental (to civilization) and cannot be counted on; and the things that cannot possibly attach themselves to it. If we do that, we shall have a normative method for distinguishing right from wrong and truth from falsehood in historical information by means of a logical demonstration that admits of no doubts. Then, whenever we hear about certain conditions occurring in civilization, we shall know what to accept and what to declare spurious. We shall have a sound yardstick with the help of which historians may find the path of truth and correctness where their reports are concerned.

Such[16] is the purpose of this first book of our work. (The subject) is in a way an independent science. (This science) has its own peculiar object—that is, human civilization and social organization. It also has its own peculiar problems—that is, explaining the conditions that attach themselves to the essence of civilization, one after the other. Thus, the situation is the same with this science as it is with any other I, 62
science, whether it be a conventional[17] or an intellectual one.

It should be known that the discussion of this topic is something new, extraordinary, and highly useful. Pene-

---

II, 116: "In connection with happenings that can be referred to sensual perception, the information transmitted by a single informant (*khabar al-wâḥid*) is sufficient, if its soundness appears probable."

[15] Cf. R. A. Nicholson, *Translations of Eastern Poetry and Prose*, pp. 179 f.

[16] Cf. Issawi, pp. 36 f.

[17] "Conventional" is used here in the sense of the more common "traditional."

trating research has shown the way to it. It does not belong to rhetoric, one of the logical disciplines (represented in Aristotle's *Organon*), the subject of which is convincing words by means of which the mass is inclined to accept a particular opinion or not to accept it.[18] It is also not politics, because politics is concerned with the administration of home or city in accordance with ethical and philosophical requirements, for the purpose of directing the mass toward a behavior that will result in the preservation and permanence of the (human) species.

The subject here is different from that of these two disciplines which, however, are often similar to it. In a way, it is an entirely original science. In fact, I have not come across a discussion along these lines by anyone. I do not know if this is because people have been unaware of it, but there is no reason to suspect them (of having been unaware of it). Perhaps they have written exhaustively on this topic, and their work did not reach us.[19] There are many sciences. There have been numerous sages among the nations of mankind. The knowledge that has not come down to us is larger than the knowledge that has. Where are the sciences of the Persians that 'Umar ordered wiped out at the time of the conquest! [20] Where are the sciences of the Chaldaeans, the Syrians, and the Babylonians, and the scholarly products and results that were theirs! Where are the sciences of the Copts, their predecessors! The sciences of only one nation, the Greek, have come down to us, because they were translated through al-Ma'mûn's efforts. (His efforts in this direction)
I, 63 were successful, because he had many translators at his disposal and spent much money in this connection. Of the sciences of others, nothing has come to our attention.

[18] Cf. 3:368, below.

[19] In later Muslim scholarship, it was considered disrespectful to suggest that earlier scholars knew less than oneself or than other, more recent men. Cf., for instance, F. Rosenthal, "Al-Asṭurlâbî and as-Samaw'al on Scientific Progress," *Osiris*, IX (1950), 563.

[20] See 3:114 ff., below, where 'Umar's alleged action and al-Ma'mûn's translating activities are discussed again.

The accidents involved in every manifestation of nature and intellect deserve study. Any topic that is understandable and real requires its own special science. In this connection, scholars seem to have been interested (mainly) in the results (of the individual sciences). As far as the subject under discussion is concerned, the result, as we have seen, is just historical information. Although the problems it raises are important, both essentially and specifically, (exclusive concern for it) leads to one result only: the mere verification of historical information. This is not much. Therefore, scholars might have avoided the subject.

God knows better. "And you were given but little knowledge."[21]

In the field under consideration here, we encounter (certain) problems, treated incidentally by scholars among the arguments applicable to their particular sciences, but that in object and approach are of the same type as the problems (we are discussing). In connection with the arguments for prophecy, for instance, scholars mention that human beings cooperate with each other for their existence and, therefore, need men to arbitrate among them and exercise a restraining influence.[22] Or, in the science of the principles of jurisprudence, in the chapter of arguments for the necessity of languages, mention is made of the fact that people need means to express their intentions because by their very nature, cooperation and social organization are made easier by proper expressions.[23] Or, in connection with the explanation that laws have their reason in the purposes they are to serve, the jurists mention that adultery confuses pedigrees and destroys the (human) species; that murder, too, destroys the human species; that injustice invites the destruction of civilization with the necessary consequence that the (human) species will I, 64
be destroyed.[24] Other similar things are stated in connection

[21] Qur'ân 17.85 (87).

[22] Cf. p. lxxv, above, and 2:417, below.

[23] Cf., for instance, al-Âmidî, *al-Iḥkâm fî uṣûl al-aḥkâm* (Cairo, 1914), I, 16 f. Ibn Khaldûn was well acquainted with this author's works.

[24] Cf. also 2:295, below.

with the purposes embedded in laws. All (laws) are based upon the effort to preserve civilization. Therefore, (the laws) pay attention to the things that belong to civilization. This is obvious from our references to these problems which are mentioned as representative (of the general situation).

We also find a few of the problems of the subject under discussion (treated) in scattered statements by the sages of mankind. However, they did not exhaust the subject. For instance, we have the speech of the Môbedhân before Bahrâm b. Bahrâm in the story of the owl reported by al-Mas'ûdî.[25] It runs: "O king, the might of royal authority materializes only through the religious law, obedience toward God, and compliance with His commands and prohibitions. The religious law persists only through royal authority. Mighty royal authority is accomplished only through men. Men persist only with the help of property. The only way to property is through cultivation.[26] The only way to cultivation is through justice. Justice is a balance set up among mankind. The Lord set it up and appointed an overseer for it, and that (overseer) is the ruler."

There also is a statement by Anôsharwân[27] to the same effect: "Royal authority exists through the army, the army through money, money through taxes, taxes through culti-

---

[25] Cf. *Murûj adh-dhahab*, II, 169 ff. Môbedh (< *magupat*) is the title of the Zoroastrian priest. Môbedhân actually is the Persian plural of the word. Cf. also 2:104 f., below.

In an abbreviated form, the speech is quoted as made by 'Abdallâh b. Ṭâhir (cf. 2:139, below), in Ibn Abî Ḥajalah at-Tilimsânî, *Sukkardân as-sulṭân* (Cairo, 1317/1899, in the margin of al-'Âmilî, *Mikhlâh*), p. 86.

[26] '*Imârah*, from the same root as '*umrân*, and practically identical with it. Cf. al-Mubashshir b. Fâtik, *Mukhtâr al-ḥikam*, No. 3 of the sayings of Seth: "If a ruler thinks that he can amass property through injustice, he is wrong, for property can be amassed only through cultivation of the soil ('*imârat al-arḍ*)." Cf. the Spanish translation published by H. Knust, *Mittheilungen aus dem Eskurial*, p. 82.

[27] Cf. al-Mas'ûdî, *Murûj adh-dhahab*, II, 210. Anôsharwân is the celebrated Sassanian ruler Khosraw I, A.D. 531–579. A shortened form of the saying is quoted anonymously by Ibn Qutaybah, '*Uyûn al-akhbâr* (Cairo, 1343–49/1925–30), I, 9. A similarly shortened form is ascribed to 'Alî in a marginal note in one of the MSS of the *Secretum Secretorum*; cf. Badawî's edition (cited below, n. 29), p. 128 (n. 1).

vation, cultivation through justice, justice through the improvement of officials, the improvement of officials through the forthrightness of wazirs, and the whole thing in the first place through the ruler's personal supervision of his subjects' condition and his ability to educate them, so that he may rule them, and not they him."

In the *Book on Politics* that is ascribed to Aristotle and has wide circulation, we find a good deal about (the subject which is under discussion here). (The treatment,) however, is not exhaustive, nor is the topic provided with all the arguments it deserves, and it is mixed with other things. In the book, (the author) referred to such general (ideas) [28] as we have reported on the authority of the Môbedhân and Anôsharwân. He arranged his statement in a remarkable circle that he discussed at length. It runs as follows: [29] "The I, 65

[28] C and D: *al-kullîyât*. B: *al-kalimât* "words."

[29] The pseudo-Aristotelian *Politics*, which Ibn Khaldûn also quotes below, p. 235 and 2:48, is better known as *Sirr al-asrâr* "Secretum Secretorum." The work is supposed to have been translated from the Greek by Yaḥyâ b. al-Biṭrîq; cf. *GAL*, I, 203; 2d ed., I, 221 f.; *Suppl.*, I, 364. It had even greater success in European languages than in Arabic.

The Arabic text has recently been published by 'Abd-ar-Raḥmân Badawî, *Fontes Graecae doctrinarum politicarum Islamicarum* (Cairo, 1954), I, 65–171. A modern English translation of the Arabic was prepared by Ismâ'îl 'Alî and A. S. Fulton, and published in Vol. V of the works of Roger Bacon, ed. R. Steele (Oxford, 1920). Cf. M. Plessner, *Orientalistische Literaturzeitung*, XXVIII (1925), 912 ff. An edition and French translation were prepared by P. Sbath but have remained unpublished. Cf. P. Sbath, *Al-Fihris* (Cairo, 1938), I, 9 (n. 4).

The passage quoted appears at the end of the third chapter dealing with justice. Cf. pp. 126–28 of Badawî's ed., and Roger Bacon, *ed. cit.*, V, 226; cf. also pp. LII f. and 126. Cf., further, M. Steinschneider, "Die arabischen Übersetzungen aus dem Griechischen," in *Zwölftes Beiheft zum Centralblatt für Bibliothekswesen* (Leipzig, 1893), p. 82. A fifteenth-century English rendering may be found in R. Steele, *Three Prose Versions of the Secreta Secretorum* (Early English Text Society, Extra Series No. 74) (London, 1898), p. 207.

Among other Arabic authors who quote this passage, mention may be made of Ibn Juljul [tenth century] (cf. Badawî, *op. cit.*, p. 37 of the introd.), and al-Mubashshir b. Fâtik [eleventh century], *Mukhtâr al-ḥikam*, at the end of the chapter on Aristotle. Ibn Juljul, in turn, was quoted by Ibn Abî Uṣaybi'ah, *'Uyûn al-anbâ'*, ed. Müller, I, 66 f. Ibn Abî Uṣaybi'ah shows the eight sentences inscribed along the sides of an octagon. Cf. also R. Blachère's translation of Ṣâ'id al-Andalusî, *Kitâb Ṭabaqât al-umam* (Paris, 1935), p. 68. There are quite a few minor variations in the text as it appears

world is a garden the fence of which is the dynasty. The dynasty is an authority through which life is given to proper behavior. Proper behavior is a policy directed by the ruler. The ruler is an institution supported by the soldiers. The soldiers are helpers who are maintained by money. Money is sustenance brought together by the subjects. The subjects are servants who are protected by justice. Justice is something familiar,[30] and through it, the world persists. The world is a garden . . ."—and then it begins again from the beginning. These are eight sentences of political wisdom. They are connected with each other, the end of each one leading into the beginning of the next. They are held together in a circle with no definite beginning or end. (The author) was proud of what he had hit upon and made much of the significance of the sentences.

When our discussion in the section on royal authority and dynasties [31] has been studied and due critical attention given to it, it will be found to constitute an exhaustive, very clear, fully substantiated interpretation and detailed exposition of these sentences. We became aware of these things with God's help and without the instruction of Aristotle or the teaching of the Môbedhân.

The statements of Ibn al-Muqaffa' [32] and the excursions on political subjects in his treatises also touch upon many of the problems of our work. However, (Ibn al-Muqaffa') did not substantiate his statements with arguments as we have

---

in the various sources. Cf. now Fu'âd Sayyid's edition of Ibn Juljul, *Les Générations des médecins et des sages* (Cairo, 1955), p. 26.

The MSS of the *Muqaddimah* usually leave an empty space for insertion of the circle in which the saying is to be inscribed. The drawing is executed in B and C. The artistically executed drawing of an inscribed octagon reproduced here comes from an Istanbul MS of the *Secretum,* Reis el-küttap (Aşir I), 1002, fol. 121*b*. (Cf. Frontispiece, Vol. 2.)

[30] *Ma'lûf* "familiar" may here possibly mean "harmonious." Arabic *ta'lîf* translates Greek ἁρμονία. Cf., for instance, P. Kraus and R. Walzer, *Galeni Compendium Timaei Platonis* (Corpus Platonicum Medii Aevi, Plato Arabus 1) (London, 1951), p. 106.

[31] Cf. pp. 313 ff., below.

[32] 'Abdallâh b. al-Muqaffa', d. 142 [759/60]. Cf. *GAL,* I, 151 f.; *Suppl.,* I, 233 ff. Cf. also below, 3:393.

done. He merely mentioned them in passing in the (flowing) prose style and eloquent verbiage of the rhetorician.

Judge Abû Bakr aṭ-Ṭurṭûshî [33] also had the same idea in the *Kitâb Sirâj al-Mulûk*. He divided the work into chapters that come close to the chapters and problems of our work. However, he did not achieve his aim or realize his intention. He did not exhaust the problems and did not bring clear proofs. He sets aside a special chapter for a particular problem, but then he tells a great number of stories and traditions and he reports scattered remarks by Persian sages such as Buzurjmihr [34] and the Môbedhân, and by Indian sages, as well as material transmitted on the authority of Daniel, Hermes, and other great men. He does not verify his statements or clarify them with the help of natural arguments. The work is merely a compilation of transmitted material similar to sermons in its inspirational purpose. In a way, aṭ-Ṭurṭûshî aimed at the right idea, but did not hit it. He did not realize his intention or exhaust his problems. I, 66

We, on the other hand, were inspired by God. He led us to a science whose truth we ruthlessly set forth.[35] If I have succeeded in presenting the problems of (this science) exhaustively and in showing how it differs in its various aspects and characteristics from all other crafts, this is due to divine guidance. If, on the other hand, I have omitted some point, or if the problems of (this science) have got confused with something else, the task of correcting remains for the discerning critic, but the merit is mine since I cleared and marked the way.

God guides with His light whomever He wants (to guide).[36]

---

[33] Muḥammad b. al-Walîd, *ca.* 451 to 520 or 525 [1059 to 1126 or 1131]. Cf. *GAL*, I, 459; *Suppl.*, I, 829 f. Cf. also above, p. lxxxv.

[34] The wazir of Khosraw I Anôsharwân who appears in Arabic literature and is the chief representative of Persian wisdom.

[35] Ibn Khaldûn here uses two proverbial expressions for truthful information. They are: "Juhaynah has the right information," and "He gave me the true age of his camel."

[36] Cf. Qur'ân 24.35 (35).

In [37] this book, now, we are going to explain such various aspects of civilization that affect human beings in their social organization, as royal authority, gainful occupation, sciences, and crafts, (all) in the light of various arguments that will show the true nature of the varied knowledge of the elite and the common people, repel misgivings, and remove doubts.

I, 67 We say that man is distinguished from the other living beings by certain qualities peculiar to him, namely: (1) The sciences and crafts which result from that ability to think which distinguishes man from the other animals and exalts him as a thinking being over all creatures.[38] (2) The need for restraining influence and strong authority, since man, alone of all the animals, cannot exist without them. It is true, something has been said (in this connection) about bees and locusts. However, if they have something similar, it comes to them through inspiration,[39] not through thinking or reflection. (3) Man's efforts to make a living and his concern with the various ways of obtaining and acquiring the means of (life). This is the result of man's need for food to keep alive and subsist, which God instilled in him, guiding him to desire and seek a livelihood. God said: "He gave every thing its natural characteristics, and then guided it." [40] (4) Civilization. This means that human beings have to dwell in common and settle together in cities and hamlets for the comforts of companionship and for the satisfaction of human needs, as a result of the natural disposition of human beings toward co-operation in order to be able to make a living, as we shall explain. Civilization may be either desert (Bedouin) civilization as found in outlying regions and mountains, in hamlets (near suitable) pastures in waste regions, and on the fringes of sandy deserts. Or it may be sedentary

---

[37] Cf. R. A. Nicholson, *Translations of Eastern Poetry and Prose*, pp. 180 f.

[38] Cf. 2:411 ff., below.

[39] Arabic uses the same word (*waḥy*) for Prophetical "inspiration" and for what we would translate in this context as "instinct." The "inspiration" of bees is mentioned in Qur'ân 16.68 (70).

[40] Qur'ân 20.50 (52).

civilization as found in cities, villages, towns, and small communities that serve the purpose of protection and fortification by means of walls. In all these different conditions, there are things that affect civilization essentially in as far as it is social organization.

Consequently,[41] the discussion in this work falls naturally under six chapter headings:

(1) On human civilization in general, its various kinds, and the portion of the earth that is civilized. *I, 68*

(2) On desert civilization, including a report on the tribes and savage nations.

(3) On dynasties, the caliphate, and royal authority, including a discussion of government ranks.

(4) On sedentary civilization, countries, and cities.

(5) On crafts, ways of making a living, gainful occupations, and their various aspects. And

(6) On the sciences, their acquisition and study.

I have discussed desert civilization first, because it is prior to everything else, as will become clear later on. (The discussion of) royal authority was placed before that of countries and cities for the same reason. (The discussion of) ways of making a living was placed before that of the sciences, because making a living is necessary and natural, whereas the study of science is a luxury or convenience.[42] Anything natural has precedence over luxury. I lumped the crafts together with gainful occupations, because they belong to the latter in some respects as far as civilization is concerned, as will become clear later.

God gives success and support.

---

[41] Cf. Issawi, p. 26.

[42] Cf. above, p. lxxxi, and below, p. 249.

Chapter I

HUMAN CIVILIZATION IN GENERAL

FIRST PREFATORY DISCUSSION

HUMAN[1] SOCIAL ORGANIZATION is something necessary. The philosophers expressed this fact by saying: "Man is 'political' by nature."[2] That is, he cannot do without the social organization for which the philosophers use the technical term "town" (*polis*).

This is what civilization means. (The necessary character 1, 69
of human social organization or civilization) is explained by the fact that God created and fashioned man in a form that can live and subsist only with the help of food. He guided man to a natural desire for food and instilled in him the power that enables him to obtain it.

However, the power of the individual human being is not sufficient for him to obtain (the food) he needs, and does not provide him with as much food as he requires to live. Even if we assume an absolute minimum of food—that is, food enough for one day, (a little) wheat, for instance—that amount of food could be obtained only after much preparation such as grinding, kneading, and baking. Each of these three operations requires utensils and tools that can be provided only with the help of several crafts, such as the crafts of the blacksmith, the carpenter, and the potter. Assuming that a man could eat unprepared grain, an even greater number of operations would be necessary in order to obtain the grain: sowing and reaping, and threshing to separate it from the husks of the ear. Each of these operations requires a number of tools and many more crafts than those just mentioned. It is beyond the power of one man alone to do all that, or (even) part of it, by himself. Thus, he cannot do without a combination of many powers from among his fellow beings,

---

[1] Cf. Issawi, pp. 99 f. [2] See p. lxxv, above, and 2:417, below.

if he is to obtain food for himself and for them. Through co-operation, the needs of a number of persons, many times greater than their own (number), can be satisfied.

Likewise, each individual needs the help of his fellow beings for his defense, as well. When God fashioned the natures of all living beings and divided the various powers
I, 70 among them, many dumb animals were given more perfect powers than God gave to man. The power of a horse, for instance, is much greater than the power of man, and so is the power of a donkey or an ox. The power of a lion or an elephant is many times greater than the power of (man).

Aggressiveness is natural in living beings. Therefore, God gave each of them a special limb for defense against aggression. To man, instead, He gave the ability to think, and the hand. With the help of the ability to think, the hand is able to prepare the ground for the crafts. The crafts, in turn, procure for man the instruments that serve him instead of limbs, which other animals possess for their defense. Lances, for instance, take the place of horns for goring, swords the place of claws to inflict wounds, shields the place of thick skins, and so on. There are other such things. They were all mentioned by Galen in *De usu partium*.[3]

The power of one individual human being cannot withstand the power of any one dumb animal, especially not the power of the predatory animals. Man is generally unable to defend himself against them by himself. Nor is his (unaided) power sufficient to make use of the existing instruments of defense, because there are so many of them and they require so many crafts and (additional) things. It is absolutely necessary for man to have the co-operation of his fellow men. As long as there is no such co-operation, he cannot obtain any food or nourishment, and life cannot materialize for him, because God fashioned him so that he must have food if he is to live. Nor, lacking weapons, can he defend himself.
I, 71 Thus, he falls prey to animals and dies much before his time.

[3] At the beginning of the work, ed. C. G. Kühn (Leipzig, 1821–33), III, 2. See also below, 3:149.

Under such circumstances, the human species would vanish. When, however, mutual co-operation exists, man obtains food for his nourishment and weapons for his defense. God's wise plan that man(kind) should subsist and the human species be preserved will be fulfilled.

Consequently, social organization is necessary to the human species. Without it, the existence of human beings would be incomplete. God's desire to settle the world with human beings and to leave them as His representatives on earth [4] would not materialize. This is the meaning of civilization, the object of the science under discussion.

The afore-mentioned remarks have been in the nature of establishing the existence of the object in (this) particular field. A scholar in a particular discipline is not obliged to do this, since it is accepted in logic that a scholar in a particular science does not have to establish the existence of the object in that science.[5] On the other hand, logicians do not consider it forbidden to do so. Thus, it is a voluntary contribution. God, in His grace, gives success.

When [6] mankind has achieved social organization, as we have stated, and when civilization in the world has thus become a fact, people need someone to exercise a restraining influence and keep them apart, for aggressiveness and injustice are in the animal nature of man. The weapons made for the defense of human beings against the aggressiveness

---

[4] Cf. Qur'ân 2.30 (28).

[5] The "object" (*mawḍû'*) of a science is the fundamental elements at its basis, such as quantities (measurements) in geometry, numbers in arithmetic, substances in physics, and so on. The object of Ibn Khaldûn's new science is human social organization, or civilization (cf. p. 77, above). See 3:111 f., below. For the Avicennian basis of this theory, see, for instance, A.-M. Goichon, *Lexique de la philosophie d'Ibn Sînâ* (Paris, 1938), p. 439, and Abû l-Barakât Hibatallâh al-Baghdâdî, *Mu'tabar* (Hyderabad, 1357–58/1938–39), I, 221 ff. These fundamental elements of the individual sciences do not require proof of their existence. The pertinent Aristotelian passage in this connection (*Analytica posteriora* 76b 3 ff.), was quoted by de Slane. However, the Arabic translation, as published by 'Abd-ar-Raḥmân Badawî, *Manṭiq Arisṭû* (Cairo, 1948–49), II, 339, does not use the term *mawḍû'* in this context.

[6] Cf. Issawi, pp. 100 f.

of dumb animals do not suffice against the aggressiveness of man to man, because all of them possess those weapons. Thus, something else is needed for defense against the aggressiveness of human beings toward each other. It could not come from outside, because all the other animals fall short of human perceptions and inspiration. The person who exercises a restraining influence, therefore, must be one of themselves. He must dominate them and have power and authority over them, so that no one of them will be able to attack another.
I, 72 This is the meaning of royal authority.

It has thus become clear that royal authority is a natural quality of man which is absolutely necessary to mankind. The philosophers mention that it also exists among certain dumb animals, such as the bees and the locusts.[7] One discerns among them the existence of authority and obedience to a leader. They follow the one of them who is distinguished as their leader by his natural characteristics and body. However, outside of human beings, these things exist as the result of natural disposition and divine guidance, and not as the result of an ability to think or to administrate. "He gave everything its natural characteristics, and then guided it." [8]

The philosophers go further. They attempt to give logical proof of the existence of prophecy and to show that prophecy is a natural quality of man. In this connection, they carry the argument to its ultimate consequences and say that human beings absolutely require some authority to exercise a restraining influence. They go on to say that such restraining influence exists through the religious law (that has been) ordained by God and revealed to mankind by a human being. (This human being) is distinguished from the rest of mankind by special qualities of divine guidance that God gave him, in order that he might find the others submissive to him and ready to accept what he says. Eventually, the existence of a (restraining) authority among them and over them be-

---

[7] See p. 84, above. [8] Qur'ân 20.50 (52).

comes a fact that is accepted without the slightest disapproval or dissent.

This proposition of the philosophers is not logical, as one can see. Existence and human life can materialize without (the existence of prophecy) through injunctions a person in authority may devise on his own or with the help of a group feeling that enables him to force the others to follow him wherever he wants to go. People who have a (divinely revealed) book and who follow the prophets are few in number in comparison with (all) the Magians [9] who have no (divinely revealed) book. The latter constitute the majority of the world's inhabitants. Still, they (too) have possessed dynasties and monuments, not to mention life itself. They still I, 73
possess these things at this time in the intemperate zones to the north and the south. This is in contrast [10] with human life in the state of anarchy, with no one to exercise a restraining influence. That would be impossible.

This shows that (the philosophers) are wrong when they assume that prophecy exists by necessity. The existence of prophecy is not required by logic. Its (necessary character) is indicated by the religious law, as was the belief of the early Muslims.

God gives success and guidance.

---

[9] "Magians" originally meant the Zoroastrians. In later Islam they were considered as people who followed a kind of prophet but did not have Scriptures like the Christians and the Jews. Thus, they occupied a position somewhere between the latter and polytheists. The term was eventually used to denote the general idea of pagans. Cf. V. F. Büchner in *EI, s.v.* "Madjûs."

[10] For the rather difficult use of *bi-khilâf*, cf. also below, p. 400, l. 15.

SECOND PREFATORY DISCUSSION

The parts of the earth where civilization is found. Some information about oceans, rivers, and zones.[11]

IN[12] THE BOOKS of philosophers who speculated about the condition of the world, it has been explained that the earth has a spherical shape and is enveloped by the element

[11] The material presented on pp. 94–103 represents the common stock of Muslim geographical knowledge, but here (and even more for pp. 116–66) Ibn Khaldûn relies mainly upon the *Nuzhat al-mushtâq*, or, as he occasionally calls it (cf. pp. 97 and 103), the *Book of Roger*, by Muḥammad b. Muḥammad al-Idrîsî, *ca.* A.D. 1099/1100–1162. Cf. *GAL*, I, 477; 2d ed., I, 628; *Suppl.*, I, 876 f. Al-Idrîsî wrote his important geographical work for Roger II of Sicily (1129–1154). It was completed the year Roger died. Although Ibn Khaldûn's basis is the work by al-Idrîsî, he occasionally adds to the information he found there, from his own knowledge.

No reliable text of al-Idrîsî's work has so far been published, nor do we have any translation and commentary of the entire book that would satisfy modern scientific requirements. An abridgment was published in Rome in 1592, and translated by Gabriel Sionita and Ioannes Hesronita in Paris in 1619, under the title of *Geographia Nubensis*. A rough translation of the work was attempted by P. A. Jaubert (Paris, 1836–40).

While the whole work is thus not available in the true sense of the word, there have been a good number of detailed studies of small sections of it, in particular those concerned with the marginal areas to the north. Among the older studies, we may mention R. Dozy and M. J. de Goeje, *Description de l'Afrique et de l'Espagne* (Leiden, 1866); M. Amari and C. Schiaparelli, *L'Italia descritta nel "Libro del Re Ruggiero"* (Atti della Reale Accademia dei Lincei, Ser. 2, Vol. VIII) (Rome, 1883); J. Gildemeister in *Zeitschrift des Deutschen Palästina Vereins*, VIII (1885), 117–45. Some of the recent studies are: O. J. Tallgren-Tuulio and A. M. Tallgren, *Idrîsî, La Finlande et les autres pays Baltiques orientaux* in *Studia Orientalia* (ed. Societas Orientalis Fennica), III (1930); O. J. Tallgren (Tuulio), *Du Nouveau sur Idrîsî*, *ibid.*, VI 3 (1936); W. Hoenerbach, *Deutschland und seine Nachbarländer nach der grossen Geographie des Idrîsî* (Bonner Orientalistische Studien, No. 21) (Stuttgart, 1938); T. Lewicki, *La Pologne et les pays voisins dans le "Livre de Roger" de al-Idrîsî* (Cracow, 1945; Warsaw, 1954); D. M. Dunlop, "Scotland According to al-Idrîsî" in *Scottish Historical Review*, XXVI (1947); W. B. Stevenson, "Idrîsî's Map of Scotland," *ibid.*, XXVII (1948), 202–4;

of water. It may be compared to a grape floating upon water.[13]

The water withdrew from certain parts of (the earth), because God wanted to create living beings upon it and settle it with the human species that rules as (God's) representative over all other beings.[14] One might from this get the impression that the water is below the earth. This is not correct. The natural "below" of the earth is the core and middle of its sphere, the center to which everything is attracted by its gravity. All the sides of the earth beyond that and the water surrounding the earth are "above." When some part of the earth is said to be "below," it is said to be so with reference to some other region (of the earth).

The part of the earth from which the water has withdrawn is one-half the surface of the sphere of the earth. It I, 74
has a circular form and is surrounded on all sides by the element of water which forms a sea called "the Surrounding Sea" (*al-Baḥr al-Muḥîṭ*). It is also called *lablâyah,*[15] with

A. F. L. Beeston, "Idrîsî's Account of the British Isles," *Bulletin of the British Schools of Oriental Studies,* XIII (1950), 265–80, etc.

In this section, particularly, the notes had to be severely restricted. As a rule, no special reference is made to the inaccuracies that were unavoidable in Ibn Khaldûn's and al-Idrîsî's time, regardless of the remarkable geographical information they possessed.

Ibn Khaldûn speaks again briefly about the oceans and zones in the *Autobiography*, pp. 351 ff.

[12] Cf. Issawi, pp. 38 f.

[13] Cf. also p. 110, below. Ibn Khurradâdhbih, in his *Masâlik,* prefers the comparison to an egg yolk swimming in the white. The *Rasâ'il Ikhwân aṣ-ṣafâ'* (Cairo, 1347/1928), I, 114, think of a half egg submerged in water. Al-Idrîsî, too, mentions the comparison with a submerged egg.

[14] Cf. Qur'ân 2.30 (28), etc., and n. 212 to Ch. III, below.

[15] Cf. *'Ibar,* VI, 98; de Slane (tr.), I, 187. Cf. also Ibn 'Idhârî al-Marrâkushî, *al-Bayân al-mughrib,* ed. G. S. Colin and E. Lévi-Provençal (Leiden, 1948–51), I, 6. The editors vocalize the word *al-ablâyuh.* De Slane thought to find here a corruption of *Atlant(ic)*, which seems hardly possible. He compared *πέλαγος, pelagus,* which also is very difficult, though it may be mentioned that the Latin word *pelagus* occurs in connection with Spain in the opening pages of Orosius, whose work was translated into Arabic. *Lablâyah,* as the word is vocalized in B and C, does not look like a Berber word, but may have been derived from the Romance languages—perhaps, *el mare?*

thickening of the second *l*, or *oceanos*.[16] Both are non-Arabic words. It is also called "the Green Sea" and "the Black Sea."

The part of the earth that is free from water (and thus suitable) for human civilization has more waste and empty areas than cultivated (habitable) areas. The empty area in the south is larger than that in the north. The cultivated part of the earth extends more toward the north. In the shape of a circular plane it extends in the south to the equator and in the north to a circular[17] line, behind which there are mountains separating (the cultivated part of the earth) from the elemental water. Enclosed between (these mountains) is the Dam of Gog and Magog. These mountains extend toward the east. In the east and the west, they also reach the elemental water, at two sections (points) of the circular (line) that surrounds (the cultivated part of the earth).

The part of the earth that is free from water is said to cover one-half or less of the sphere (of the earth). The cultivated part covers one-fourth of it. It is divided into seven zones.[18]

The equator divides the earth into two halves from west to east. It represents the length of the earth. It is the longest line on the sphere of (the earth), just as the ecliptic and the equinoctial line are the longest lines on the firmament. The ecliptic is divided into 360 degrees. The geographical degree is twenty-five parasangs, the parasang being 12,000 cubits or
I, *75* three miles, since one mile has 4,000 cubits. The cubit is twenty-four fingers, and the finger is six grains of barley placed closely together in one row.[19] The distance of the

[16] B vocalizes *Ûqyânûs;* A, C, and D *Ûfyânûs.*

[17] C has "straight" in the text; it is crossed out and replaced in the margin by "circular." All the features that Ibn Khaldûn describes here can be easily traced on the map reproduced here, which is identical with the one that Ibn Khaldûn had in front of him when he wrote this section.

[18] *Iqlîm,* Greek κλίμα, "clime."

[19] For Muslim information about the length of the degree, see C. A. Nallino, "Il valore metrico del grado di meridiano secondo i geografi arabi," *Raccolta di scritti editi e inediti* (Rome, 1939–48), V, 408 ff. The value of seventy-five miles is credited by Arabic authors to Ptolemy (Nallino, *ibid.*, pp. 416 ff.). Since an Arabic *mîl* "mile" usually can be considered to be about two kilometers, or one and a quarter English miles—more exactly, according

equinoctial line, parallel to the equator of the earth and dividing the firmament into two parts, is ninety degrees from each of the two poles. However, the cultivated area north of the equator is (only) sixty-four degrees.[20] The rest is empty and uncultivated because of the bitter cold and frost, exactly as the southern part is altogether empty because of the heat. We shall explain it all, if God wills.

Information about the cultivated part and its boundaries and about the cities, towns, mountains, rivers, waste areas, and sandy deserts it contains, has been given by men such as Ptolemy in the *Geography* [21] and, after him, by the author of the *Book of Roger*.[22] These men divided the cultivated area into seven parts which they called the seven zones. The borders of the seven zones are imaginary. They extend from east to west. In width (latitudinal extension) they are identical, in length (longitudinal extension) different. The first zone is longer than the second. The same applies to the second zone, and so on. The seventh zone is the shortest. This is required by the circular shape that resulted from the withdrawal of the water from the sphere of the earth.

According to these scholars, each of the seven zones is divided from west to east into ten contiguous sections. Information about general conditions and civilization is given for each section.

(The geographers) mentioned that the Mediterranean

---

to Nallino, 1973.2 m.—this is far too large a value for the length of a degree. However, the Muslims were familiar with much more accurate data, as Nallino points out; and see also below, p. 113. The figure of seventy-five miles is found, for instance, in al-Mas'ûdî, *Murûj adh-dhahab*, III, 440 f., and in al-Idrîsî. The standard gauge indicated above is derived from al-Idrîsî; cf. also al-Mas'ûdî, *loc. cit.*, and Nallino, *op. cit.*, V, 284.

[20] Cf. p. 105, below. Ibn Khaldûn realized later on that this fact, and, more especially, the theory of the identical latitudinal extension of the different zones mentioned in the next paragraph, were not safely established as he had originally thought. Therefore he added the long discussion below, pp. 112 f. and 114 f.

[21] For knowledge of Ptolemy's *Geography* among the Arabs, cf. Nallino, *op. cit.*, V, 458 ff., and *GAL*, *Suppl.*, I, 382. The seven-zone division is of Greek origin but is not found in Ptolemy. Cf. E. Honigmann, *Die sieben Klimata* (Heidelberg, 1929).

[22] See n. 11, above, and pp. 103 and 116, below.

which we all know branches off from the Surrounding Sea in the western part of the fourth zone. It begins at a narrow
I, 76 straits about twelve miles wide between Tangier and Tarifa, called the Street (of Gibraltar). It then extends eastward and opens out to a width of 600 miles. It terminates at the end of the fourth section of the fourth zone, a distance of 1,160 parasangs from its starting point. There, it is bordered by the coast of Syria. On the south, it is bordered by the coast of the Maghrib, beginning with Tangier at the Straits, then Ifrîqiyah, Barqah, and Alexandria. On the north, it is bordered by the coast of Constantinople, then Venice, Rome, France, and Spain, back to Tarifa at the Street (of Gibraltar) opposite Tangier. The Mediterranean is also called the Roman Sea or the Syrian Sea. It contains many populous islands. Some of them are large, such as Crete, Cyprus, Sicily, Majorca, and Sardinia.[23]

In the north, they say, two other seas branch off from the Mediterranean through two straits. One of them is opposite Constantinople. It starts at the Mediterranean in a narrow straits, only an arrow-shot in width. It flows for a three days' run and touches Constantinople. Then, it attains a width of four miles. It flows in this channel for sixty miles, where it is known as the Straits of Constantinople. Through a mouth six miles wide, it then flows into the Black Sea,[24] and becomes a sea that, from there, turns eastward in its course. It passes the land of Heracleia (in Bithynia) [25] and ends at the country of the Khazars, 1,300 miles from its mouth. Along its two coasts live the Byzantine, the Turkish, the Bulgar (Burjân),[26] and the Russian nations.

I, 77 The second sea that branches off from the two straits of

---

[23] The MSS, with the exception of D, add Denia. Denia was the overlord of the Baleares, but it is strange for Ibn Khaldûn to refer to it as an island. Since Majorca is already mentioned, Denia seems clearly an oversight.

[24] Arabic *Baḥr Nîṭush,* an accepted misreading for "Pontus."

[25] The MSS have the spelling *Hryqlyh.* See also n. 191 to this chapter, below.

[26] Ibn Khaldûn mentions later both *Burjân* and *Bulghâr.* Both refer to the same group. Cf. V. Minorsky, *Ḥudûd al-ʿâlam* (E. J. W. Gibb Memorial Series, N.S. No. 11) (Oxford & London, 1937), p. 423.

the Mediterranean is the Adriatic Sea (Gulf of Venice). It emerges from Byzantine territory at its northern limit. Then, from Sant' Angelo (de' Lombardi), its western boundary extends from the country of the Venetians to the territory of Aquileia, 1,100 miles from where it started. On its two shores live the Venetians, the Byzantines (Rûm), and other nations. It is called the Gulf of Venice (Adriatic Sea).

From the Surrounding Sea, they say, a large and wide sea flows on the east at thirteen degrees north of the equator. It flows a little toward the south, entering the first zone. Then it flows west within the first zone until it reaches the country of the Abyssinians and the Negroes (the Zanj) [27] and Bâb al-Mandeb in the fifth section of (the first zone), 4,500 parasangs from its starting point. This sea is called the Chinese, Indian, or Abyssinian Sea (Indian Ocean). It is bordered on the south by the country of the Negroes (Zanj) and the country of Berbera which Imru'ul-Qays mentioned in his poem.[28] These "Berbers" do not belong to the Berbers who make up the tribes in the Maghrib. The sea is then bordered by the area of Mogadishu, Sufâlah, and the land of al-Wâqwâq,[29] and by other nations beyond which there is nothing but waste and empty areas. On the north, where it starts, it is bordered by China, then by Eastern and Western India (al-Hind and as-Sind), and then by the coast of the Yemen—that is, al-Aḥqâf, Zabîd, and other cities. Where it ends, it is bordered by the country of the Negroes, and, beyond them, the Beja.[30]

Two other seas, they say, branch off from the Indian Ocean. One of them branches off where the Indian Ocean

---

[27] Ibn Khaldûn's definition of the distinction between the Abyssinians and the Zanj is found below, p. 171.

[28] Cf. his *Dîwân*, ed. W. M. de Slane (Paris, 1837), p. 27; (tr.) p. 42. Cf. also *'Ibar*, VI, 199; de Slane (tr.), II, 107.

[29] This is rather an elusive country in Muslim geography. It may be identified with Madagascar, as would seem to apply here, or possibly with the whole east coast of Africa, about which Muslim geographers had no clear idea. It has also been tentatively identified with Sumatra, and even with Japan. Cf. Minorsky, *op. cit.*, p. 278, and below, p. 123.

[30] Arabic *al-Bujah*, as always vocalized in the MSS.

ends, at Bâb al-Mandeb. It starts out narrow, then flows
I, 78 widening toward the north and slightly to the west until it ends at the city of al-Qulzum in the fifth section of the second zone, 1,400 miles from its starting point. This is the Sea of al-Qulzum or Sea of Suez (Red Sea). From the Red Sea at Suez to Fusṭâṭ [31] is the distance of a three days' journey. The Red Sea is bordered on the east by the coast of the Yemen, the Ḥijâz, and Jiddah,[32] and then, where it ends, by Midyan (Madyan), Aila (Aylah), and Fârân.[33] On the west, it is bordered by the coast of Upper Egypt, 'Aydhâb, Suakin, and Zayla' (Zâla'), and then, where it begins, by the country of the Beja. It ends at al-Qulzum. It (would) reach the Mediterranean at al-'Arîsh. The distance between (the Red Sea and the Mediterranean) is a six days' journey. Many rulers, both Muslim and pre-Islamic, have wanted to cut through the intervening territory (with a canal) but this has not been achieved.

The second sea branching off from the Indian Ocean and called the Persian Gulf (the Green Gulf), branches off at the region between the west coast of India and al-Aḥqâf in the Yemen. It flows toward the north and slightly to the west until it ends at al-Ubullah on the coast of al-Baṣrah in the sixth section of the second zone, 440 parasangs from its starting point. It is called the Persian Gulf (Persian Sea). It is bordered on the east by the coast of Western India, Mukrân, Kirmân, Fârs, and al-Ubullah where it ends. On the west, it is bordered by the coast of al-Baḥrayn, the Yamâmah, Oman, ash-Shiḥr, and al-Aḥqâf where it starts. Between the Persian Gulf and al-Qulzum lies the Arabian Peninsula, jutting out from the mainland into the sea. It is surrounded by the Indian Ocean to the south, by the Red
I, 79 Sea to the west, and by the Persian Gulf to the east. It adjoins the 'Irâq in the region between Syria and al-Baṣrah,

---

[31] The mention of Fusṭâṭ shows that, basically, the information presented here goes back to a time before the foundation of Cairo in 969/70.

[32] *Juddah,* as vocalized in the MSS.

[33] That is, the Biblical Paran. Cf. also p. 132, below.

where the distance between (Syria and the 'Irâq) is 1,500 miles. (In the 'Irâq) are al-Kûfah, al-Qâdisîyah, Baghdad, the Reception Hall of Khosraw (at Ctesiphon),[34] and al-Ḥîrah. Beyond that live non-Arab nations such as the Turks, the Khazars, and others. The Arabian Peninsula comprises the Ḥijâz in the west, the Yamâmah, al-Baḥrayn, and Oman in the east, and in the south the Yemen along the coast of the Indian Ocean.

In the cultivated area (of the earth), they say, there is another sea to the north in the land of the Daylam. This sea has no connection with the other seas. It is called the Sea of Jurjân and Ṭabaristân (Caspian Sea). Its length is 1,000 miles, and its width 600. To the west of it lies Azerbaijan and the Daylam territory; to the east of it the land of the Turks and Khuwârizm; to the south of it Ṭabaristân; and to the north of it the land of the Khazars and the Alans.

These are all the famous seas mentioned by the geographers.

They further say that in the cultivated part of (the earth), there are many rivers. The largest among them are four in number, namely, the Nile, the Euphrates, the Tigris, and the River of Balkh which is called Oxus (Jayḥûn).

The Nile begins at a large mountain, sixteen degrees beyond the equator at the boundary of the fourth section of the first zone. This mountain is called the Mountain of the Qumr.[35] No higher mountain is known on earth. Many springs issue from the mountain, some of them flowing into one lake there, and some of them into another lake. From these two lakes, several rivers branch off, and all of them
flow into a lake at the equator which is at the distance of a ten I, 80

[34] For the *Îwân Kisrâ*, to which Ibn Khaldûn repeatedly refers as an impressive monument of pre-Islamic dynasties, see pls., IIa, IIb, below.

[35] Ibn Khaldûn did not accept the reading *qamar* "moon," which, as we know from Ptolemy, is correct. Following Ibn Sa'îd, he read Qumr, considered to be the name of some "Indian" people. Cf. p. 120, below. The vocalization in the MSS seems to be *Qumur*. Cf. Minorsky, *Ḥudûd*, p. 205. For the island of the *Qmr*, meaning Java or the entire Malay Archipelago, see below, p. 123.

days' journey from the mountain. From that lake, two rivers issue. One of them flows due north, passing through the country of the Nûbah and then through Egypt. Having traversed Egypt, it divides into many branches lying close to each other. Each of these is called a "channel." All flow into the Mediterranean at Alexandria. This river is called the Egyptian Nile. It is bordered by Upper Egypt on the east, and by the oases on the west. The other river turns westward, flowing due west until it flows into the Surrounding Sea. This river is the Sudanese Nile.[36] All the Negro nations live along its borders.

The Euphrates begins in Armenia in the sixth section of the fifth zone. It flows south through Byzantine territory (Anatolia) past Malatya to Manbij, and then passes Ṣiffîn, ar-Raqqah, and al-Kûfah until it reaches the Marsh (al-Baṭḥâ') between al-Baṣrah and Wâsiṭ. From there it flows into the Indian Ocean. Many rivers flow into it along its course. Other rivers branch off from it and flow into the Tigris.

The Tigris originates in a number of springs in the country of Khilâṭ, which is also in Armenia. It passes on its course southward through Mosul, Azerbaijan, and Baghdad to Wâsiṭ. There, it divides into several channels, all of which flow into the Lake of al-Baṣrah and join the Persian Gulf. The Tigris flows east of the Euphrates. Many large rivers flow into it from all sides. The region between the Euphrates
I, 81 and the Tigris, where it is first formed, is the Jazîrah of Mosul, facing Syria on both banks of the Euphrates, and facing Azerbaijan on both banks of the Tigris.

The Oxus originates at Balkh, in the eighth section of the third zone, in a great number of springs there. Large rivers flow into it, as it follows a course from south to north. It flows through Khurâsân, then past Khurâsân to Khuwârizm in the eighth section of the fifth zone. It flows into

[36] See the map (following p. 110) for the generally accepted theory as to the common origin of the Nile and the Senegal (or the Niger), and p. 118, below. Cf. J. H. Kramers in *EI, s.v.* "al-Nîl."

Lake Aral (the Lake of Gurganj) which is situated at the foot [north?] of the city of (Gurganj). In length as in width, it extends the distance of one month's journey. The river of Farghânah and Tashkent (ash-Shâsh),[37] which comes from the territory of the Turks, flows into it. West of the Oxus lie Khurâsân and Khuwârizm. East of it lie the cities of Bukhârâ, at-Tirmidh, and Samarkand. Beyond that are the country of the Turks, Farghânah, the Kharlukh,[38] and (other) non-Arab nations.

(All) this was mentioned by Ptolemy in his work and by the Sharîf (al-Idrîsî) in the *Book of Roger*. All the mountains, seas, and rivers to be found in the cultivated part of the earth are depicted on maps and exhaustively treated in geography. We do not have to go any further into it. It is too lengthy a subject, and our main concern is with the Maghrib, the home of the Berbers, and the Arab home countries in the East.

God gives success.

SUPPLEMENTARY NOTE I, 82
TO THE SECOND PREFATORY DISCUSSION

The northern quarter of the earth has more civilization than the southern quarter. The reason thereof.

WE KNOW FROM OBSERVATION and from continuous tradition that the first and the second of the cultivated zones have less civilization than the other zones. The cultivated area in the first and second zones is interspersed with empty

[37] That is, the Syr Darya (Jaxartes). Cf. Minorsky, *Ḥudûd*, p. 72.

[38] Cf. Minorsky, *Ḥudûd*, pp. 268 ff.; *idem*, *Sharaf al-Zamân Ṭâhir Marvazî on China, the Turks, and India* (James G. Forlong Fund, No. 22) (London, 1942), pp. 106 f.; P. Kraus, *Jâbir Ibn Ḥayyân*, II, 75 (nn. 3, 5). While Kharlukh appears to be the correct form, Ibn Khaldûn reads the name as al-Khazlajîyah, or al-Ḥazlajîyah. Cf. also pp. 138, 149, below. On p. 149, MS. C has *kh-z-l-khîyah*.

waste areas and sandy deserts and has the Indian Ocean to the east. The nations and populations of the first and second zones are not excessively numerous. The same applies to the cities and towns there.

The third, fourth, and subsequent zones are just the opposite. Waste areas there are few. Sandy deserts also are few or non-existent. The nations and populations are tremendous. Cities and towns are exceedingly numerous. Civilization has its seat between the third and the sixth zones. The south is all emptiness.

Many philosophers have mentioned that this is because of the excessive heat and slightness of the sun's deviation from the zenith in the south. Let us explain and prove this statement. The result will clarify the reason why civilization in the third and fourth zones is so highly developed and extends also to the fifth, <sixth,> and seventh zones.

We say: When the south and north poles (of heaven) are upon the horizon, they constitute a large circle that divides the firmament into two parts. It is the largest circle (in it) and runs from west to east. It is called the equinoctial line. In astronomy, it has been explained in the proper place that
I, 83 the highest sphere moves from east to west in a daily motion by means of which it also forces the spheres enclosed by it to move. This motion is perceptible to the senses. It has also been explained that the stars in their spheres have a motion that is contrary to this motion and is, therefore, a motion from west to east. The periods of this movement differ according to the different speeds of the motions of the stars.

Parallel to the courses of all these stars in their spheres, there runs a large circle which belongs to the highest sphere and divides it into two halves. This is the ecliptic (zodiac). It is divided into twelve "signs." As has been explained in the proper place, the equinoctial line intersects the ecliptic at two opposite points, namely, at the beginning of Aries and at the beginning of Libra. The equinoctial line divides the zodiac into two halves. One of them extends northward from the equinoctial line and includes the signs from the beginning of Aries to the end of Virgo. The other half extends southward from it and includes the signs from the beginning of Libra to the end of Pisces.

When the two poles fall upon the horizon <which takes place in one particular region> among all the regions of the earth, a line is formed upon the surface of the earth that faces the equinoctial line and runs from west to east. This line is called the equator. According to astronomical observation, this line is believed to coincide with the beginning of the first of the seven zones. All civilization is to the north of it.

The north pole gradually ascends on the horizon of the cultivated area (of the earth) until its elevation reaches sixty-four degrees. Here, all civilization ends. This is the end of
the seventh zone. When its elevation reaches ninety degrees I, 84
on the horizon—that is the distance between the pole and the equinoctial line—then it is at its zenith, and the equinoctial line is on the horizon. Six of the signs of the zodiac, the northern ones, remain above the horizon, and six, the southern ones, are below it.

Civilization is impossible in the area between the sixty-fourth and the ninetieth degrees, for no admixture of heat and cold occurs there because of the great time interval between them. Generation (of anything), therefore, does not take place.

The sun is at its zenith on the equator at the beginning of Aries and Libra. It then declines from its zenith down to the beginning of Cancer and Capricorn. Its greatest declination from the equinoctial line is twenty-four degrees.

Now, when the north pole ascends on the horizon, the equinoctial line declines from the zenith in proportion to the elevation of the north pole, and the south pole descends correspondingly, as regards the three (distances constituting geographical latitude).[39] Scholars who calculate the (prayer) times call this the latitude of a place. When the equinoctial line declines from the zenith, the northern signs of the zodiac

---

[39] This is explained below, pp. 112 and 115.

gradually rise above it, proportionately to its rise, until the beginning of Cancer is reached. Meanwhile, the southern signs of the zodiac correspondingly descend below the horizon until the beginning of Capricorn is reached, because of the inclination of the (two halves of the zodiac) upwards or downwards from the horizon of the equator, as we have stated.

The northern horizon continues to rise, until its northern limit, which is the beginning of Cancer, is in the zenith. This
I, 85 is where the latitude is twenty-four degrees in the Ḥijâz and the territory adjacent. This is the declination from the equinoctial at the horizon of the equator at the beginning of Cancer. With the elevation of the north pole (Cancer) rises, until it attains the zenith. When the pole rises more than twenty-four degrees, the sun descends from the zenith and continues to do so until the elevation of the pole is sixty-four degrees, and the sun's descent from the zenith, as well as the depression of the south pole under the horizon, is the same distance. Then, generation (of anything) stops because of the excessive cold and frost and the long time without any heat.

At and nearing its zenith, the sun sends its rays down upon the earth at right angles. In other positions, it sends them down at obtuse or acute angles. When the rays form right angles, the light is strong and spreads out over a wide area, in contrast to what happens in the case of obtuse and acute angles. Therefore, at and nearing its zenith, the heat is greater than in other positions, because the light (of the sun) is the reason for heat and calefaction. The sun reaches its zenith at the equator twice a year in two points of Aries and Libra. No declination (of the sun) goes very far. The heat hardly begins to become more temperate, when the sun has reached the limit of its declination at the beginning of Cancer or Capricorn and begins to rise again toward the zenith. The perpendicular rays then fall heavily upon the horizon there (in these regions) and hold steady for a long time, if not permanently. The air gets burning hot, even excessively so. The same is true whenever the sun reaches the

zenith in the area between the equator and latitude twenty-four degrees, as it does twice a year. The rays exercise almost as much force upon the horizon there (at this latitude) I, 86
as they do at the equator. The excessive heat causes a parching dryness in the air that prevents (any) generation. As the heat becomes more excessive, water and all kinds of moisture dry up, and (the power of) generation is destroyed in minerals, plants, and animals, because (all) generation depends on moisture.

Now, when the beginning of Cancer declines from the zenith at the latitude of twenty-five degrees and beyond, the sun also declines from its zenith. The heat becomes temperate, or deviates only slightly from (being temperate). Then, generation can take place. This goes on until the cold becomes excessive, due to the lack of light and the obtuse angles of the rays of the sun. Then, (the power of) generation again decreases and is destroyed. However, the destruction caused by great heat is greater than that caused by great cold, because heat brings about desiccation faster than cold brings about freezing.

Therefore, there is little civilization in the first and second zones. There is a medium degree of civilization in the third, fourth, and fifth zones, because the heat there is temperate owing to the decreased amount of light. There is a great deal of civilization in the sixth and seventh zones because of the decreased amount of heat there. At first, cold does not have the same destructive effect upon (the power of) generation as heat; it causes desiccation only when it becomes excessive and thus has dryness added. This is the case beyond the seventh zone. (All) this, then, is the reason why civilization is stronger and more abundant in the northern quarter. And God knows better!

The [40] philosophers concluded from these facts that the region at the equator and beyond it (to the south) was empty. On the strength of observation and continuous tradition, it

[40] Cf. Issawi, pp. 39 f.

was argued against them that (to the contrary) it was culti-
I, 87 vated. How would it be possible to prove this (contention)? It is obvious that the (philosophers) did not mean to deny entirely the existence of civilization there, but their argumentation led them to (the realization) that (the power of) generation must, to a large degree, be destroyed there because of the excessive heat. Consequently, civilization there would be either impossible, or only minimally possible. This is so. The region at the equator and beyond it (to the south), even if it has civilization as has been reported, has only a very little of it.

Averroes [41] assumed that the equator is in a symmetrical position [42] and that what is beyond the equator to the south corresponds to what is beyond it to the north; consequently, as much of the south would be cultivated as of the north. His assumption is not impossible, so far as (the argument of) the destruction of the power of generation is concerned. However, as to the region south of the equator, it is made impossible by the fact that the element of water covers the face of the earth in the south, where the corresponding area in the north admits of generation. On account of the greater amount

---

[41] Muḥammad b. Aḥmad b. Rushd, 520–595 [1126–1198]. Cf. *GAL*, I, 461 f.; *Suppl.*, I, 833 ff.

[42] Translation of *mu'tadil* in the usual way by "temperate" would not seem to be correct here. The word must here be translated by "symmetrical," or the like. This becomes clear from the discussion of Averroes' view of the problem found in L. Gauthier, *Ibn Rochd* (Paris, 1948), pp. 84 ff. Averroes argues against the opinion advanced by Ibn Ṭufayl that the region around the equator was temperate. He maintains that Ibn Ṭufayl misunderstood the word *mu'tadil*, which could mean both "uniform" (symmetrical) and "temperate." Averroes further rejects the idea that the southern part of the earth contains habitable areas comparable to those in the north.

This would seem, in effect, the direct opposite of the opinion Ibn Khaldûn here attributes to Averroes. However, the latter came out elsewhere for the theory of a habitable area in the south, which would be in a symmetrical position with relation to that in the north, as we learn from Gauthier, *ibid.*, pp. 87 f. Consequently, Ibn Khaldûn's report on Averroes here is incomplete —in a way, misleading—but it is not incorrect. Cf. also C. Issawi, *Osiris*, X (1952), 114 f.

The idea that the equator has a temperate climate is also mentioned in al-Bîrûnî, *Chronologie orientalischer Völker*, ed. C. E. Sachau (Leipzig, 1878; 1923), p. 258; tr. by the same (London, 1879), p. 249.

of water (in the south), Averroes' assumption of the symmetrical (position of the equator) thus turns out to be impossible. Everything else follows, since civilization progresses gradually and begins its gradual progress where it can exist, not where it cannot exist.

The assumption that civilization cannot exist at the equator is contradicted by continuous tradition. And God knows better!

After this discussion, we wish to draw a map of the earth, as was done by the author of the *Book of Roger*. Then, we shall give a detailed description of the map.

(Map of the World: see Frontispiece.
Key follows the next page.)[43]

DETAILED DESCRIPTION OF THE MAP[44] I, 88

THIS DESCRIPTION is twofold. There is a detailed description and a general description.

The detailed description consists of a discussion of each country, mountain, sea, and river of the cultivated part of the earth. This discussion will be found in the following section.

---

[43] The map is executed only in C and in MS. Nuru Osmaniye, 3066, fol. 24a. The fact that even important MSS such as A and B do not have a map would seem to show that a special artist was required to draw it, who was not always available.

The map in C, which we have reproduced, is identical in nearly every detail with the map of the world in al-Idrîsî's geographical work. Al-Idrîsî's world map in the Oxford MS is reproduced in K. Miller, *Mappae Arabicae*, Vol. VI (Stuttgart, 1927), pl. II. A drawing of it is to be found, *ibid.*, Vol. V (Stuttgart, 1931), between pp. 160 and 161. The Istanbul MS of al-Idrîsî, Köprülü, 955, contains the map on pp. 4 and 5. Cf. also the map reproduced in G. H. T. Kimble, *Geography in the Middle Ages* (London, 1938), pl. v.

[44] The text of this section is that of C and D, which incorporates Ibn Khaldûn's corrections of earlier oversights. The earlier text is printed in italic type at the foot of the pages that follow. In the later stage of the text, asterisks mark the beginning and end of the paralleled passages. Cf. n. 20, above.

The general description consists of a discussion of the division of the cultivated part of the earth into seven zones, their latitudinal (extension), and the length of their days. Such is the contents of this section.

Let us begin to explain these things. We have mentioned before that the earth floats upon the elemental water like a grape.[45] God's plan for civilization and for the elemental generation of life resulted in making part of (the earth) free of water.

The part that is free of water is said to constitute one-half the surface of the earth. The cultivated part is one-fourth of it. The rest is uncultivated. According to another opinion, the cultivated part is only one-sixth of it. The empty areas of the part which is free of water lie to the south and to the north. The cultivated area in between forms a continuum that stretches from west to east. There is no empty area between the cultivated part and the (Surrounding) Sea in these two directions.

They further said: Across the cultivated part of the earth an imaginary line runs from west to east facing the equinoctial line (of the firmament) in regions where the two poles of the firmament are on the horizon. At this line civilization begins. It extends from there northwards.

Ptolemy said: "As a matter of fact, civilization extends beyond that line to the south." He indicated the latitudinal extension, as will be mentioned.[46]

Isḥâq b. al-Ḥasan al-Khâzinî [47] expresses the opinion that beyond the seventh zone (to the north) there is another civilization. He indicated its latitudinal extension, as we shall

[45] Cf. p. 95, above. [46] See p. 112, below.

[47] The reference to al-Khâzinî appears in the margin of C and is incorporated in the text of D.

Nothing seems to be known about this man. This is very strange, since he was evidently one of the older Muslim scholars, and our information about early Arabic scientists is probably as good as Ibn Khaldûn's. He may have found him quoted in one of the works he consulted. This al-Khâzinî cannot be identical with Abû Ja'far al-Khâzin, because the latter is quoted below, p. 115, for different data.

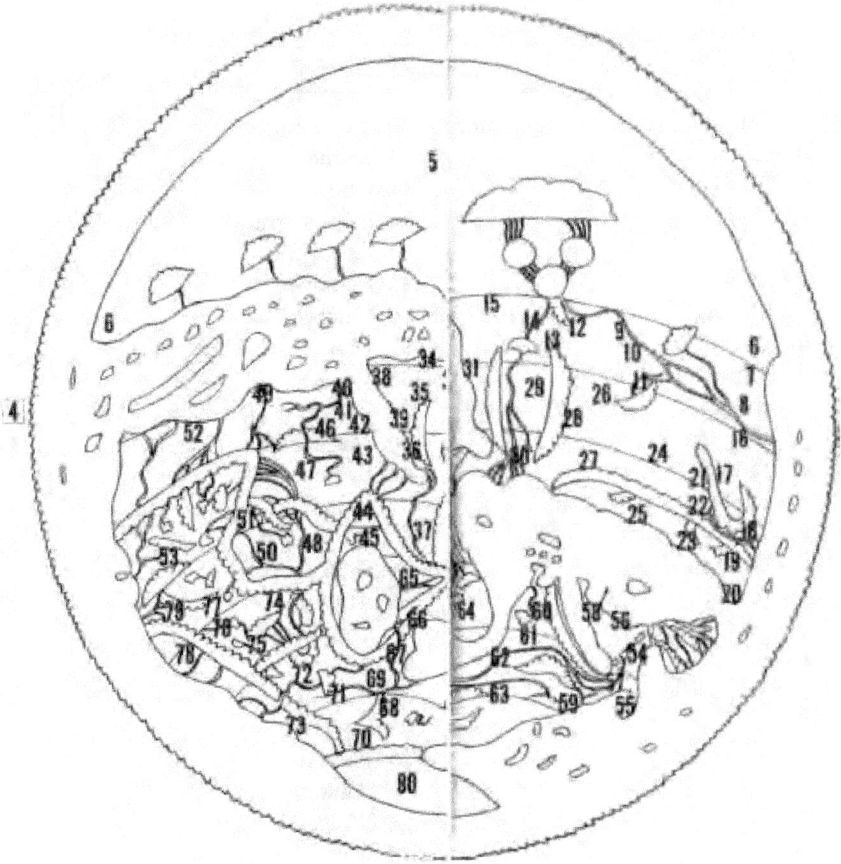
4
5
6
6
7
8
9
10
11
12
13
14
15
16
17
18
19
20
21
22
23
24
25
26
27
28
29
30
31
34
35
36
37
38
39
40
41
42
43
44
45
46
47
48
49
50
51
52
53
54
55
56
58
59
60
61
62
63
64
65
66
67
68
69
70
71
72
73
74
75
76
77
78
79
80

KEY TO THE MAP

1 South
2 West
3 North
4 East
5 Empty beyond the equator
because of the heat
6 Equator
7 Lamlam Country
8 Maghzâwah (Maguzawa?)
9 Kanem [Country
10 Bornu
11 Gawgaw
12 Zaghây
13 at-Tâjuwîn
14 Nubia
15 Abyssinia
16 Ghânah
17 Lamṭah
18 as-Sûs
19 Morocco
20 Tangier
21 Ṣinhâjah
22 Dar'ah
23 Ifrîqiyah
24 Fezzan
25 Jarîd
26 Kawâr
27 Desert of Berenice
28 Inner Oases
29 Upper Egypt
30 Egypt
31 Beja
32 Ḥijâz
33 Syria
34 Yemen
35 Yamâmah
36 al-Baṣrah
37 'Irâq
38 ash-Shiḥr
39 Oman
40 Western India
41 Mukrân
42 Kirmân
43 Fârs
44 *al-Bahlûs*
45 Azerbaijan
46 Desert
47 Khurâsân
48 Khuwârizm
49 Eastern India
50 Tashkent
51 Soghd
52 China
53 Tughuzghuz
54 Gascogne
55 Brittany
56 Calabria
57 France
58 Venice
59 Germany (Alamâniyah)
60 Macedonia
61 Bohemia
62 Jathûliyah
63 Jarmâniyah
64 al-Baylaqân
65 Armenia
66 Ṭabaristân
67 Alans
68 Bashqirs
69 Bulgars
70 Pechenegs
71 Stinking Land
72 Waste Country
73 Magog
74 Ghuzz
75 Türgish
76 Adhkish
77 Khallukh
78 Gog
79 Kimäk
80 Empty in the north
because of the cold

mention.[48] Al-Khâzinî is one of the leading scholars in this craft (geography). I, 89

* Further, the ancient philosophers divided the cultivated part of the earth in the north into seven zones by means of imaginary lines running from west to east. They maintain that these zones have different latitudinal extensions. This will be discussed in detail.

The first zone runs along the equator, north of it. South of it, there is only the civilization to which reference was made by Ptolemy. Beyond that are waste regions and sandy deserts, up to the circle of water which is called the Surrounding Sea. To the north, the first zone is followed, successively, by the second through the seventh zones. (The seventh zone) constitutes the northern limit of civilization. Beyond it are only empty and waste regions, down to the Surrounding Sea as (in the south). However, the empty regions in the south are much larger than those in the north.*

As to latitudes and length of days in the various zones, it should be known that the two poles of the firmament are upon the horizon at the equator in the west and the east.

It should be known that, as was mentioned above, the philosophers divided the cultivated part of the earth into seven parts from south to north. These parts they called zones. The whole of the cultivated area is distributed over these zones. Each zone extends from west to east.

The first zone runs from west to east with the equator as its southern border. Beyond it, there are only waste regions and sandy deserts, and civilization of a sort that, if it actually exists, is more like non-civilization. To the north, the first zone is followed, successively, by the second through the seventh zones. The seventh zone constitutes the northern limit of civilization. Beyond it (to the north) are only empty and waste regions until the Surrounding Sea is reached. The situation is the same here as it is beyond the first zone to the south. However, the empty areas in the north are much smaller than those in the south.

---

[48] See pp. 114 f., below.

The sun there is at the zenith. As we follow the cultivated part of the earth farther and farther north, the north pole ascends slightly, and the south pole descends correspondingly, (at the horizon). Furthermore, the sun moves a corresponding distance from (its zenith at) the equinoctial line. These three distances are equal to each other. Each of them is called geographical latitude. This is well known to the scholars who determine the (prayer) times.

People hold different opinions as to the latitudinal extension (of the cultivated part of the earth) and as to the latitudinal extension (breadth) of the various zones. Ptolemy holds the opinion that the latitudinal extension of the entire cultivated part of the earth is 77½°. The latitudinal extension
I, 90 of the cultivated part beyond the equator to the south is 11°.[48a] Thus, the latitudinal extension of the zones in the north is 66½°. According to him, the first zone extends to 16°;[48b] the second to 20°; the third to 27°; the fourth to 33°; the fifth to 38°; the sixth to 43°; the seventh to 48°.[49]

[48a] According to F. Boll, *Studien über Claudius Ptolemäus* (Leipzig, 1894), pp. 189 f., Ptolemy expressed different opinions as to the extent of the *oikoumenê*. In the *Tetrabiblos*, and apparently also in the *Almagest*, he assumed that it extended to the equator, whereas in the *Geography* he determined it as extending to 16° 25′ S.

[48b] Lit., ". . . the latitudinal extension of the first zone is 16°."

[49] The figures are not Ptolemy's. They ought to be understood as indicating the limits of the zones. Thus, for instance, the second zone is assumed to extend from 16° N to 20° N, and so on. However, the seventh zone should, in this case, extend to 66½°. Obviously, the statement of the preceding sentence, that the latitudinal extension of the northern zones is 66½° is wrong. That figure is the boundary of the cultivated part of the earth. There is cultivation beyond the northern boundary of the seventh zone which, according to this passage, extends to 48° N.

The following computation of the extension of the zones in miles assumes, apparently, that the figures here refer to the extension of the zones in geographical degrees. Still, the figures are quite wrong. They should be: 1,800; 1,333.3; 1,800; 2,200; 2,533.3; 2,866.6; and 3,200. If one corrects the figures for the second and third zones from 2,333 and 2,790 to 1,333 and 1,790 respectively, they are almost correct. However, as the MSS show, Ibn Khaldûn certainly wrote 2,333 and 2,790.

For the latitudes of the zones, see also al-Bîrûnî, *Kitâb at-tafhîm*, ed. and tr. R. R. Wright (London, 1934), p. 138. E. Honigmann's discussion of the extension of the zones according to Arabic geographers does not include late authors such as Ibn Khaldûn. Cf. Honigmann, *Die sieben Klimata*, pp. 163, 180, and 189.

He then determined the degree on the firmament as having a length of 66⅔ miles, (were it to be) measured on the surface of the earth.[50] Thus, the first zone from south to north is 1,067 miles (wide); the second zone, 2,333 miles; the third zone, 2,790 miles; the fourth zone, 2,185 miles; the fifth zone, 2,520 miles; the sixth zone, 2,840 miles, and the seventh zone, 3,150 miles.

* The length of night and day differs in the various zones by reason of the declination of the sun from the equinoctial line and the elevation of the north pole above the horizon. This causes a difference in the arcs of day and night.

At the boundary of the first zone, the longest night—which occurs when the sun enters Capricorn—and the longest day—which occurs when the sun enters Cancer—reach, according to Ptolemy, a maximum of twelve and one-half hours; at the boundary of the second zone, a maximum of thirteen hours; at the boundary of the third zone, a maximum of thirteen and one-half hours; at the boundary of the fourth zone, a maximum of fourteen hours; at the boundary of the 1, 91
fifth zone, a maximum of one half-hour more; at the boundary of the sixth zone, a maximum of fifteen hours; and at the boundary of the seventh zone, a maximum of one half-hour more. For the shortest day and night, there thus remains the difference between the last figure and twenty-four, which is

---

The length of night and day differs in the different zones by reason of the declination of the sun from the equinoctial line and the elevation of the north pole above the horizon. This causes a difference in the arcs of day and night.

At the boundary of the first zone, the longest night—which occurs when the sun enters Capricorn—and the longest day—which occurs when the sun enters Cancer—reach a maximum of thirteen hours. The same is the case at the boundary of the second zone in the north. The length of day there reaches its maximum of thirteen and one-half hours when the sun enters Cancer, the summer tropic. The longest night—when the sun enters Capricorn,

[50] See pp. 96 f., above.

the combined number of hours of day and night, or one complete revolution of the firmament. The difference in the maximum length of night and day in the various zones, consequently, is an evenly distributed, gradual increase of half an hour in each, all the way from the first zone in the south to the last zone in the north.*

Isḥâq b. al-Ḥasan al-Khâzinî maintains that the latitudinal extension of civilization beyond the equator (to the south) is 16° 25′, and the longest night and day there, thirteen hours. The latitudinal extension of the first zone and the

---

the winter tropic—is as long. For the shortest day and night, there thus remains the difference between thirteen and one-half and twenty-four, which is the combined number of hours of day and night, or one complete revolution of the firmament. The same is the case also at the boundary of the third zone in the north, where night and day reach a maximum length of fourteen hours; at the boundary of the fourth zone, where they reach a maximum length of fourteen and one-half hours; at the boundary of the fifth zone, where they reach a maximum length of fifteen hours; at the boundary of the sixth zone, where they reach a maximum length of fifteen and one-half hours; and at the boundary of the seventh zone, where they reach a maximum length of sixteen hours. There, civilization ends. The difference in the maximum length of night and day in the various zones, consequently, is an evenly distributed, gradual increase of half an hour in each, all the way from the first zone in the south to the last zone in the north.

In connection with these zones, "geographical latitude" refers to the distance between the sun at its zenith in a given place and the equinoctial line where it is at the zenith on the equator. It likewise corresponds to the depression of the south pole below the horizon in that particular place, as well as to the elevation of the north pole. As was mentioned before,[51] *these three distances are equal to each other. They are called "geographical latitude."*

---

[51] See p. 105, above.

length of day and night there are the same as beyond the equator (to the south). The second zone extends to 24°,[51a] and the length of its (longest) day and night at its farthest point is thirteen and one-half hours. For the third zone, the figures are 30° and fourteen hours. For the fourth zone, they are 36° and fourteen and one-half hours. For the fifth zone, they are 41° and fifteen hours. For the sixth zone, they are 45° and fifteen and one-half hours. For the seventh zone, they are 48½° and sixteen hours. The latitudinal extension of civilization beyond the seventh zone (to the north) reaches I, 92
from the boundary of the seventh zone to (latitude) 63°, and the length of the (longest) day and night to twenty hours.

Other leading scholars in the discipline, apart from Isḥâq al-Khâzinî, maintain that the latitudinal extension of the cultivated area beyond the equator (to the south) is 16° 27′. The first zone extends to 20° 15′; the second to 27° 13′; the third to 33° 20′; the fourth to 38½°; [52] the fifth to 43°; the sixth to 47° 53′; or, according to another opinion, to 46° 50′; and the seventh to 51° 53′. Civilization beyond the seventh zone extends to 77°.

In Abû Ja'far al-Khâzinî,[53] one of the leading scholars in the discipline, one also finds that the latitudinal extension of the first zone is from 1° to 20° 13′; of the second, to 27° 13′; of the third, to 33° 39′; of the fourth, to 38° 23′; of the fifth, to 42° 58′; of the sixth, to 47° 2′; and of the seventh, to 50° 45′.[54]

This is as much as I know about the different opinions concerning latitudinal extension and length of day and night in the zones and concerning their width as indicated in miles.

God "created everything. Then, He determined it." [55]

[51a] Lit., "The latitudinal extension of the second zone is 24°. . . ."

[52] D adds 20′ (intended to replace ½°?).

[53] Abû Ja'far Muḥammad al-Khâzin (not al-Khâzinî), an astronomer of the tenth century. Cf. *GAL, Suppl.*, I, 387; G. Vajda in *Rivista degli studi orientali*, XXV (1950), 8.

[54] D has what is apparently an error: 55° 40′.

[55] Qur'ân 25.2 (2). The word translated here by "determined" or "gave it its power" is taken by Ibn Khaldûn here to mean "gave it its measurements."

The geographers have subdivided each of the seven zones
I, 93 lengthwise from west to east in ten equal sections. They mention the countries, cities, mountains, and rivers of each section, and the traveling distances between them.

We shall now briefly summarize the best-known countries, rivers, and seas of each section. Our model will be the data set forth in the *Nuzhat al-mushtâq* which al-'Alawî al-Idrîsî al-Ḥammûdî [56] composed for the Christian king of Sicily, Roger, the son of Roger. Al-Idrîsî's family had given up its rule of Málaga, and he had settled at (Roger's) court in Sicily. He composed the book in the middle of the sixth [twelfth] century. He utilized many books by authors such as al-Mas'ûdî, Ibn Khurradâdhbih, al-Ḥawqalî, al-'Udhrî, Isḥâq al-Munajjim,[57] Ptolemy and others.

We shall begin with the first zone and go on from there to the last one.

The first zone

The Eternal Islands (the Canaries) from which Ptolemy began the determination of geographical longitude, are in the west. They are not part of the land mass of the first zone. They lie in the Surrounding Sea. A number of islands constitute them. The largest and best known are three in number. They are said to be cultivated.

---

[56] See n. 11 to this chapter, above. It is obvious that in the following description, Ibn Khaldûn relied upon the sectional maps that accompanied al-Idrîsî's work. They are reproduced in Vol. VI of K. Miller, *Mappae Arabicae.*

[57] The works of all these authors are preserved.

For 'Ubaydallâh b. 'Abdallâh b. Khurradâdhbih, who lived in the first half of the ninth century, see *GAL*, I, 225 f.; *Suppl.*, I, 404.

For Abû l-Qâsim b. Ḥawqal, of the tenth century, see *GAL*, I, 229; *Suppl.*, I, 408. A new edition of his work was made by J. H. Kramers (Leiden, 1938–39).

For Aḥmad b. 'Umar al-'Udhrî, 393–478 [1003–1085], see E. Lévi-Provençal, *La Péninsule Ibérique* (Leiden, 1938), p. xxiv (n. 2); F. Rosenthal, *A History of Muslim Historiography*, p. 409 (n. 4). (A forthcoming edition of al-'Udhrî's work is announced in *Revue de l'Institut des Manuscrits Arabes*, I (1955), 343. It was not known heretofore that the work was preserved.)

For Isḥâq al-Munajjim, whose eleventh century dates are rather uncertain, see *GAL*, *Suppl.*, I, 405; R. Frye in *Journal of Near Eastern Studies*, VIII (1949), 90–97.

We have heard [58] that European Christian ships reached them in the middle of this century, fought with the (inhabitants), plundered them, captured some of them, and sold some of the captives along the Moroccan coast where they I, 94
came into the service of the ruler. After they had learned Arabic, they gave information about conditions on their island. They said that they tilled the soil with horns. Iron was lacking in their country. Their bread [59] was made of barley. Their animals were goats. They fought with stones, which they hurled backwards. Their worship consisted of prostrations before the rising sun. They knew no (revealed) religion and had not been reached by any missionary activity.

These islands can be reached only by chance, and not intentionally by navigation. Navigation on the sea depends on the winds. It depends on knowledge of the directions the winds blow from and where they lead, and on following a straight course from the places that lie along the path of a particular wind. When the wind changes and it is known where a straight course along it will lead, the sails are set for it, and the ship thus sails according to nautical norms evolved by the mariners and sailors [60] who are in charge of sea voyages. The countries situated on the two shores of the Mediterranean are noted on a chart (*ṣaḥîfah*) which indicates the true facts regarding them and gives their positions along the coast in the proper order. The various winds and their paths are likewise put down on the chart. This chart is called the "compass." [61] It is on this (compass) that (sailors) rely on their voyages. Nothing of the sort exists for the Surrounding Sea. Therefore, ships do not enter it, because, were they to lose sight of shore, they would hardly be able to find their I, 95
way back to it. Moreover, the air of the Surrounding Sea and

[58] This information is not from al-Idrîsî. Consequently, the century in which the event mentioned occurred would seem to be that in which Ibn Khaldûn wrote. Cf. R. Hennig, *Terrae Incognitae* (Leiden, 1944–56), III, 248 ff.

[59] *'Aysh*, originally "life."

[60] The distinction between the two terms is approximately that between sailors of the high seas and those of coastal waters.

[61] Arabic *kunbâṣ*.

its surface harbors vapors that hamper ships on their courses. Because of the remoteness of these (vapors), the rays of the sun which the surface of the earth deflects, cannot reach and dissolve them. It is, therefore, difficult to find the way to (the Eternal Islands) and to have information about them.

The first section of the first zone contains the mouth of the Nile which has its origin in the Mountain of the Qumr, as we have mentioned.[62] (This Nile) is called the Sudanese Nile. It flows toward the Surrounding Sea and into it at the island of Awlîl.[63] The city of Sila,[64] Takrûr,[65] and Ghânah [66] are situated along this Nile. At this time, all of them belong to the Mâlî people,[67] a Negro nation. Moroccan merchants travel to their country.

Close to it in the north is the country of the Lamtûnah and of the other groups of the Veiled Berbers (Ṣinhâjah), as well as the deserts in which they roam. To the south of this Nile, there is a Negro people called Lamlam. They are unbelievers. They brand themselves on the face and temples. The people of Ghânah and Takrûr invade their country, capture them, and sell them to merchants who transport them to the Maghrib. There, they constitute the ordinary mass of

[62] See p. 101, above.

[63] The island of Arguin, southeast of Cape Blanco. Cf. R. Hennig, "Die atlantische 'Salzinsel' der arabischen mittelalterlichen Geographen," *Der Islam*, XXVI (1942), 58–63.

[64] De Slane, it seems, thought of Sili on the Black Volta. However, in the absence of further indications as to the situation of the city, this identification is as uncertain as any other that might be suggested.

[65] Senegal Negroes, known today as Tukulor. Cf. M. Delafosse in *EI, s.v.* "Takrûr."

[66] For this once important city in the western Sudan, cf. G. Yver in *EI, s.v.* "Ghâna."

[67] The people of the Mandingo (Malinke) empire. Cf. H. Labouret in *EI, s.v.* "Mali," and *s.v.* "Mandingo."

For information about Ghânah and the Mâlî, Gawgaw, and Takrûr, cf. G. Ferrand, "Le *Tuḥfat al-albâb* de Abû Ḥâmid al-Andalusî al-Ġarnâṭî," *Journal asiatique*, CCVII (1925), 41 f., 243 ff. Cf. also *'Ibar*, VI, 198 ff.; de Slane (tr.), II, 109 ff. Ibn Khaldûn's source here is Ibn Sa'îd. Cf., further, M. Meyerhof in *Proceedings of the Royal Society of Medicine*, XXX (1937), 670 f.; and *idem* in *Journal of the Royal Egyptian Medical Association*, XXIV (1941), 284–86.

slaves. Beyond them to the south, there is no civilization in the proper sense. There are only humans who are closer to dumb animals than to rational beings. They live in thickets and caves and eat herbs and unprepared grain. They frequently eat each other.[68] They cannot be considered human beings. All the fruits of the Negro territory come from fortified villages in the desert of the Maghrib, such as Touat I, 96
(Tawât, Tuwât), Tîgûrârîn,[69] and Ouargla (Wargalân).[70] In Ghânah, an 'Alid king and dynasty are said to have existed. (These 'Alids) were known as the Banû Ṣâliḥ. According to the author of the *Book of Roger*, (Ṣâliḥ) was Ṣâliḥ b. 'Abdallah b. Ḥasan b. al-Ḥasan, but no such Ṣâliḥ is known among the sons of 'Abdallâh b. Ḥasan.[71] At this time the dynasty has disappeared, and Ghânah belongs to the Mâlî ruler.

To the east of this territory, in the third section of the first zone, is the territory of Gawgaw.[72] It lies along a river that has its origin in certain mountains there, flows westward, and disappears in the sand in the second section. The realm of Gawgaw was independent. The Mâlî ruler then gained power over the territory, and it came into his possession. At this time it is devastated as the result of a disturbance that happened there and that we shall mention when we discuss the Mâlî dynasty in its proper place in the history of the Berbers.[73]

To the south of the country of Gawgaw lies the territory of Kânim, a Negro nation.[74] Beyond them are the Wangârah[75] on the border of the (Sudanese Nile) to the north. To the east

---

[68] Cf. p. 168, below.

[69] According to E. Laoust in *Hespéris*, XVIII (1934), 117, this place name is to be connected with Berber *agrur*, meaning "heap of stones," among other things.

[70] Cf. also *'Ibar*, VI, 59, 103; de Slane (tr.), I, 116, 198.

[71] Ibn Khaldûn repeats this information in *'Ibar*, IV, 99, and V, 433.

[72] This is the way the name of this Negro people is vocalized in B and C.

[73] Cf. *'Ibar*, VI, 200; de Slane (tr.), II, 110.

[74] Cf. G. Yver in *EI*, *s.v.* "Kânem."

[75] The spelling is indicated in C. See n. 185 to Ibn Khaldûn's Introduction, above.

of the countries of the Wangârah and the Kânim, there is the country of the Zaghây [76] and the Tâjirah,[77] adjoining the land of the Nûbah in the fourth section of the first zone. The land of the Nûbah is traversed by the Egyptian Nile throughout its course from its beginning at the equator to the Mediterranean in the north.

This Nile originates at the Mountain of the *Qmr*, sixteen degrees above [78] the equator. There are different
I, 97 opinions as to the correct form of the name of this mountain. Some scholars read the name as *qamar* "moon," because the mountain is very white and luminous. Yâqût, in the *Mushtarik*,[79] as well as Ibn Sa'îd,[80] reads *qumr*, with reference to an Indian people.[81]

Ten springs issue from this mountain. Five of them flow into one lake and five into another lake. There is a distance of six miles between the two lakes. From each of the two lakes,

---

[76] Bulaq: Zaghâwah. A seems to have here the wrong form, Zaghânah (!), but later on has Zaghâwah. B has the usual form Zaghâwah, but indicates that the word should be corrected to Zaghây, as we find it in C and D and on the map. See also p. 125, below. Some bibliographical information on the present-day Zaghâwah of the Sudan may be found in H. A. Wieschhoff, *Anthropological Bibliography of Negro Africa* (American Oriental Series, No. 23) (New Haven, 1948), p. 456.

[77] The *r* in the name is attested as Ibn Khaldûn's reading in all texts. The maps of al-Idrîsî have *w* (Tadjoua = Dageou?); cf. M. Reinaud, *Géographie d'Aboulféda* (Paris, 1848–83), II 1, 224.

[78] "Above" and "below" on Arabic maps correspond to south and north. For the southern "orientation" of Arabic maps, see the remarks by G. Ferrand, *Journal asiatique*, CCVII (1925), 88 f., who states that it also occurs in Chinese and some medieval Western maps. Its origin seems to be as obscure as that of our northern orientation. Aristotle *De coelo* 285*b* 22–24, may have served as an inspiration for and justification of both. In the following pages, the words "above" and "below" have as a rule been translated "south" and "north," respectively.

[79] The edition of this work by F. Wüstenfeld (Göttingen, 1846), has an entry *al-qumr*, which, however, does not contain the information Ibn Khaldûn mentions here. Cf. also Yâqût, *Mu'jam al-buldân*, ed. Wüstenfeld (Göttingen, 1866–73), IV, 862, l. 20, where the source of the Nile is said to be in the "land of the *Qmr*."

[80] On this thirteenth-century historian, an important source for Ibn Khaldûn in many respects, see n. 58 to Ibn Khaldûn's Introduction, above, and 3:445 (n. 1810), below.

[81] Cf. p. 101, above.

three rivers come forth. They come together in a swampy [?] lake (*baṭîḥah*) at the foot of which a mountain emerges. This mountain cuts across the lake at the northern end and divides its waters into two branches. The western branch flows westward through the Negro territory, and finally flows into the Surrounding Sea. The eastern branch flows northward through the countries of the Abyssinians and the Nûbah and the region in between. At the boundary of Egypt, it divides. Three of its branches flow into the Mediterranean at Alexandria, at Rosetta,[82] and at Damietta. One flows into a salt lake before reaching the sea.

In the middle of the first zone along the Nile, lie the countries of the Nûbah and the Abyssinians and some of the oases down to Assuan. A settled part of the Nûbah country is the city of Dongola, west of the Nile. Beyond it are 'Alwah[83] and Yulâq.[84] Beyond them, a six days' journey north of Yulâq, is the mountain of the cataracts. This is a mountain which rises to a great height on the Egyptian side but is much less elevated on the side of the country of the Nûbah. The Nile cuts through it and flows down precipitately in tremendous cascades for a long distance. Boats cannot get through. Cargoes from the Sudanese boats are taken off and carried on I, 98
pack animals to Assuan at the entrance to Upper Egypt. In the same way, the cargoes of the boats from Upper Egypt are carried over the cataracts. The distance from the cataracts to Assuan is a twelve day's journey. The oases on the west bank of the Nile there are now in ruins. They show traces of ancient settlement.

In the middle of the first zone, in its fifth section, is the

---

[82] The reference to Rosetta is a later addition in B and C, but is found already in Bulaq and A.

[83] A medieval country in the area of modern Khartum. Cf. J. S. Trimingham, *Islam in the Sudan* (Oxford University Press, 1949), pp. 72 ff. D has Ghalwah, as one finds sometimes.

[84] This is the form in which the name appears in the MSS. It has been read Bilâq, the island of Philae near Assuan, but the indications given here and in al-Idrîsî do not fit that reading.

country of the Abyssinians, through which a river flows, which comes from beyond the equator and [85] flows toward the land of the Nûbah, where it flows into the Nile and so on down into Egypt. Many people have held fantastic opinions about it and thought that it was part of the Nile of the Qumr (Mountain of the Moon). Ptolemy mentioned it in the *Geography*. He mentioned that it did not belong to the Nile.

In the middle of the first zone, in the fifth section, the Indian Ocean terminates. It comes down from the region of China and covers most of the first zone to the fifth section. Consequently, there is not much civilization there. Civilization exists only on the islands in (the Indian Ocean) which are numerous and said to number up to one thousand. (Civilization also exists) on the southern coast of the Indian Ocean, the southernmost limit of the cultivated part of the earth, as also on its northern coast. Of these coasts, the first zone contains only a part of China to the east and the whole of the Yemen in the sixth section of this zone, where two seas branch off northwards from the Indian Ocean, namely, the Red Sea (Sea of al-Qulzum) and the Persian Gulf. Be-
I, 99 tween them lies the Arabian Peninsula, comprising the Yemen, ash-Shiḥr to the east on the shore of the Indian Ocean, the Ḥijâz, the Yamâmah, and adjacent regions which we shall mention in connection with the second zone and the regions farther north.

On the western shore of the Indian Ocean is Zayla' (Zâla'), which is on the boundary of Abyssinia, and the desert plains of the Beja north of Abyssinia, which lie between the mountain of al-'Allâqî [86] in the southernmost part of Upper Egypt and the Red Sea which branches off from the Indian Ocean. North of Zayla' (Zâla') in the northern part of this section is the straits of Bâb al-Mandeb, where the sea that branches off there is narrowed by the promontory of al-Mandeb which juts into the Indian Ocean from south to north

[85] B and C add here (in the margin): "after passing opposite Mogadishu on the southern coast of the Indian Ocean." This is nonsensical.

[86] Cf., for instance, J. S. Trimingham, *op. cit.*, index, *s.v.*

along the west coast of the Yemen for twelve miles. As a result, the sea becomes so narrow that its width shrinks to approximately three miles. This is called Bâb al-Mandeb. Yemenite ships pass it on their way to the coast of Suez near Egypt (Cairo). North of Bâb al-Mandeb are the islands of Suakin and Dahlak. Opposite it to the west are the desert plains of the Beja, a Negro nation, as we have just mentioned. To the east, on the coast of (the straits of Bâb al-Mandeb) is the Tihâmah of the Yemen. It includes the place of Ḥaly b. Ya'qûb.[87]

To the south of Zayla' (Zâla') on the western coast of the Indian Ocean are the villages of Berbera which extend one after the other all along the southern coast of the (Indian Ocean) to the end of the sixth section. There, to the east, the *I, 100*
country of the Zanj adjoins them. Then [88] comes the city of Mogadishu, a very populous city with many merchants, yet nomad in character, on the southern coast of the Indian Ocean. Adjoining it to the east is the country of the Sufâlah on the southern coast in the seventh section of the first zone.

East of the country of the Sufâlah on the southern shore, lies the country of al-Wâqwâq [89] which stretches to the end of the tenth section of the first zone, where the Indian Ocean comes out of the Surrounding Sea.

There are many islands in the Indian Ocean. One of the largest islands is the island of Ceylon (Sarandîb) which is round in shape and has a famous mountain said to be the highest mountain on earth. It lies opposite Sufâlah. Then, there is the island of Java (Malay Archipelago),[90] an oblong island that begins opposite the land of Sufâlah and extends northeastward until it approaches the coasts that constitute China's southern boundary. In the Indian Ocean, to the south China is surrounded by the islands of al-Wâqwâq, and to the

---

[87] For Ḥaly, cf. H. C. Kay, *Yaman* (London, 1892), p. 166; Yâqût, *Mu'jam al-buldân*, II, 327.

[88] This sentence and the first six words of the next appear in the margin of B and C and in the text of D.

[89] See p. 99, above.

[90] On Jazîrat al-Qumr, cf. n. 35 to this chapter, above.

east by the islands of Korea.[91] There are numerous other islands in the Indian Ocean. These islands produce different kinds of perfumes and incense. They also are said to contain gold and emerald mines. Most of their inhabitants are Magians.[92] They have numerous rulers. These islands present remarkable cultural features that have been mentioned by geographers.

The northern coast of the Indian Ocean, in the sixth section of the first zone, is occupied by the whole of the
I, *101* Yemen. On the Red Sea side lie Zabîd, al-Muhjam,[93] and the Tihâmah of the Yemen. Next beyond that is Ṣa'dah, the seat of the Zaydî imams, lying far from the (Indian) Ocean to the south, and from the Persian Gulf to the east. In the region beyond that are the city of Aden and, north of it, Ṣan'â'. Beyond these two cities, to the east, is the land of al-Aḥqâf and Ẓafâr. Next comes the land of Ḥaḍramawt, followed by the country of ash-Shiḥr between the (Indian) Ocean in the south and the Persian Gulf. This part of the sixth section is the only part that is not covered by water in the middle region of the first zone. Apart from it, a small portion of the ninth section is not covered by water, as well as a larger area in the tenth section that includes the southernmost limit of China. One of China's famous cities is the city of Canton.[94] Opposite it to the east are the islands of Korea which have just been mentioned.

This concludes the discussion of the first zone.

The second zone

The second zone is contiguous with the northern boundary of the first zone. Opposite its west(ern limit) in the Sur-

[91] As-Sîlâ. Cf. Minorsky-Marvazî, p. 89. (See n. 38 to this chapter, above.)

[92] See n. 9 to this chapter, above.

[93] Near Zabîd. Cf. Yâqût, *Mu'jam al-buldân*, IV, 692; *'Ibar*, IV, 103.

[94] The MSS have Khânkû. Al-Idrîsî appears to have Khânqû. Therefore, *k* may represent an attempt at interpreting *q* as *g*, possibly under the influence of some recollection of the name of the other Chinese city which the older geographers mention with this one, namely, Khânjû. Cf., for instance, al-Bîrûnî, *Kitâb at-Tafhîm*, p. 143. *Q* in Khânqû is now commonly considered to be a misreading of Khânfû, Canton. Cf. W. Barthold in *EI*, *s.v.* "Khânfû," and Minorsky-Marvazî, pp. 22, 82.

rounding Sea are two of the Eternal Islands, which have been mentioned.

At the southernmost part of the first and second sections of the second zone, there is the land of Qamnûriyah.[95] Then, to the east, there are the southernmost parts of the land of Ghânah. Then, there are the desert plains of the Zaghây Negroes. In the northernmost part, there is the desert of Nîsar.[96] It extends uninterruptedly from west to east. It has stretches of desert which are crossed by merchants on their *1, 102*
way from the Maghrib to the Sûdân country. It includes the desert plains of the Veiled Ṣinhâjah Berbers. There are many subgroups, comprising the Gudâlah,[97] the Lamtûnah, the Massûfah,[98] the Lamṭah, and the Watrîgah. Directly to the east of the waste regions is the land of Fezzan. Then, there are the desert plains of the Azgâr, a Berber tribe, which extend due east in the southernmost part of the third section. This is followed, still in the third section, by part of the country of Kawâr, a Negro nation. Then, there is a portion of the land of at-Tâjuwîn.[99] The northernmost part of the third section is occupied by the remainder of the land of Waddân, followed directly to the east by the land of Santarîyah which is called the Inner Oases.[100]

The southernmost limit of the fourth section is occupied by the remainder of the land of at-Tâjuwîn.

The middle of the fourth section, then, is intersected by Upper Egypt along the banks of the Nile, which flows from its source in the first zone to its mouth at the sea. In this section it passes through two mountain barriers, the Mountain of the Oases in the west, and the Muqaṭṭam in the east. At the southern part of the section lie Esna and Armant. There is a continuous riverbank region up to Assyut and

---

95 Apparently, Kanûri of Bornu.

96 This is the vocalization of the MSS.

97 Bulaq corrects to the well-known Guzûlah. Cf. 2:197, below.

98 Bulaq corrects to the well-known Zanâtah group of Misrâtah.

99 See n. 77 to this chapter, above.

100 For Siwa and its medieval Arabic name Santarîyah, cf. E. Laoust in *EI*, *s.v.* "Sîwa."

Qûṣ, and then to Ṣawl. There, the Nile divides into two branches. The right branch ends up at al-Lâhûn, still in the fourth section. The left branch ends up at Dalâṣ. The region between them is the southernmost part of (Lower) Egypt. East of Mount Muqaṭṭam are the deserts of 'Aydhâb, ex-
I, 103 tending from the fifth section to the Sea of Suez, that is, the Red Sea (Sea of al-Qulzum) which branches off northwards from the Indian Ocean to the south. On the eastern shore of the Red Sea, in the same section, is the Ḥijâz, extending from the Mountain of Yalamlam to Yathrib (Medina). In the middle of the Ḥijâz is Mecca—God honor it!—and on its seashore there is the city of Jiddah, which is opposite 'Aydhâb on the western shore of the Red Sea.

In the sixth section to the west is the Najd, having as its southernmost limit Jurash and Tabâlah,[101] (and extending) up to 'Ukâẓ in the north. North of the Najd, in the sixth section, is the remainder of the Ḥijâz. Directly to the east of (the Najd) lies the country of Najrân and Janad. North of that is the Yamâmah. Directly to the east of Najrân, there is the land of Saba' and Ma'rib, followed by the land of ash-Shiḥr, which ends at the Persian Gulf. This is the other sea that branches off northward from the Indian Ocean, as has been mentioned, and turns westward on its course in the sixth section. The northeastern area of (the sixth section) constitutes a triangle. At its southernmost part is the city of Qalhât, the coast (seaport) of ash-Shiḥr. North of it, on the coast, is the country of Oman, followed by the country of al-Baḥrayn with Hajar, at the end of the (sixth) section.

The southwestern part of the seventh section contains a portion of the Persian Gulf connecting with the other portion of it in the sixth section. The Indian Ocean covers all the southernmost area of the seventh section. There, Western India lies along it, up to the country of Mukrân which belongs to Western India. Opposite it, is the country of aṭ-

[101] Both Jurash and Tabâlah are described as belonging to the Tihâmah and the Yemen.

Ṭawbarân[102] which also belongs to Western India. All of Western India lies in the western part of the seventh section. Western India is separated from Eastern India by stretches of desert, and is traversed by a river (the Indus) which comes I, *104*
from Eastern India and flows into the Indian Ocean in the south. Eastern India begins on the shore of the Indian Ocean. Directly to the east there lies the country of Ballahrâ.[103] North of it is Multân, the home of the great idol.[104] The northernmost part of Eastern India is the southernmost part of the country of Sijistân.

The western part of the eighth section contains the remainder of the country of Ballahrâ that belongs to Eastern India. Directly to the east of it lies the country of Gandhâra.[105] Then, at the southernmost part (of the section), on the shore of the Indian Ocean, there is the country of Malabar (Munîbâr). North of it, in the northernmost part (of the section), there is the country of Kâbul. Beyond (Kâbul) to the east[105a] is the territory of the Kanauj, between inner and outer Kashmir at the end of the zone.

The ninth section, in its western part, contains farthest Eastern India, which extends to the eastern part (of the section) and stretches along its southernmost part up to the tenth section. In the northernmost part here, there is a portion of China. It includes the city of Khayghûn.[106] China then extends over the whole tenth section up to the Surrounding Sea.

---

[102] Also called aṭ-Ṭâbarân. Cf. Ibn Khurradâdhbih, *Kitâb al-Masâlik wa-l-mamâlik*, p. 55 (text); p. 37 (tr.).

[103] Ballahrâ appears to be a royal title (Vallabharâya?). As the name of a country, it seems to refer to the Deccan. Cf. Minorsky, *Ḥudûd*, p. 238; Minorsky-Marvazî, p. 146.

[104] Cf. Minorsky-Marvazî, pp. 48 f., 149.

[105] Al-Qandahâr. Cf. Minorsky, *Ḥudûd*, p. 254; Minorsky-Marvazî, p. 152 (n. 3). Instead of "east," one should read "north."

[105a] The obviously incorrect addition of: "extending to the Surrounding Sea," is eliminated in D. In C it appears as a marginal addition. At the end of the paragraph, "zone" is a mistake for "section."

[106] It has been suggested that this is identical with the above-mentioned Canton (Khayghûn <Khayfûn <Khanfûn <Khanfû [Khânfû]).

I, 105

The third zone

The third zone is contiguous with the northern boundary of the second zone. The first section, about one-third of the way from the southernmost part of the zone, contains the Atlas Mountain[107] which runs from the western part of the first section at the Surrounding Sea to the eastern end of the section. This mountain is inhabited by innumerable Berber nations, as will be mentioned.[108] In the region between this mountain and the second zone, at the Surrounding Sea, there is the *Ribâṭ* (Monastery) Mâssah.[109] East of here are the adjoining countries of (as-)Sûs[110] and Noun (Nûl). Directly to the east of (these countries) is the country of Dar'ah, followed by the country of Sijilmâsah and then by a portion of the desert of Nîsar, the stretch of desert that we mentioned in describing the second zone.

The Atlas Mountain towers over all these countries of the first section. The western region of the Atlas has few passes and roads but near the Moulouya (Malwîyah) River, and from there on to where it ends, the Atlas has a great number of passes and roads. This region contains the Maṣmûdah nations: at the Surrounding Sea the Saksîwah, then the Hintâtah, the Tînmallal, the Gidmîwah,[111] and then the Haskûrah who are the last Maṣmûdah in this area. Then there are the Ẓanâgah[112]—that is, the Ṣinhâjah—tribes. At

[107] Arabic *Daran; Dyrin, Addirin* in classical geographical literature: Strabo xvii. 825; Pliny v. 73. Cf. Pauly-Wissowa, *Realencyclopädie, s.v.* "Durnus," "Dyrin." Daran is to be connected with the pl. *idraren* of Berber *adrar* "mountain." Cf., for instance, G. Mercier, *Journal asiatique*, CCV (1924), 264. Modern Berbers use the form *dren* (*adrar n dren*). Cf. L. Justinard, "Textes Chleuh de l'oued Nfis," in *Mémorial H. Basset* (Paris, 1928), I, 133 (n. 1). Cf. also R. Thouvenot, "La Montagne Marocaine chez Pline l'Ancien," *Hespéris*, XXVI (1939), 118.

[108] In Vol. VI of the *'Ibar*.

[109] Or Mâssat, Mâssât. Cf. also p. 326 and 2:196 f., below.

[110] Cf. E. Lévi-Provençal in *EI*, *s.v.* "al-Sûs al-Akṣâ."

[111] For the *i* vowel in the first syllable, cf. Aḥmad Bâbâ, *Nayl al-ibtihâj*, pp. 140 f.: *al-Jidmîwî*. Cf. also the spelling *Kydmîwah* in *'Ibar*, VI, 228, if the text is correct.

[112] Spelled with *ṣ*, with a *z* written underneath. Cf. p. 67, above, and 2:197, below. Cf., further, *'Ibar*, VI, 205; de Slane (tr.), II, 122; G. S. Colin, *Hespéris*, X (1930), 110.

the boundary of the first section of the third zone, there are some Zanâtah tribes. To the north, Mount Awrâs (L'Aurès), the mountain of the Kutâmah, adjoins (the Atlas). After that, there are other Berber nations which we shall mention in their proper places.

The Atlas Mountain in the western part of the section I, *106*
towers over Morocco to the north of it. In the southern part of (Morocco) lie Marrakech, Aghmât, and Tâdlâ. On the Surrounding Sea there, are the *Ribâṭ* Asfî and the city of Salé (Salâ). East [112a] of the country of Marrakech lie Fez, Meknès, Tâzâ, and Qaṣr Kutâmah.[113] This is the area that is customarily called the Farthest Maghrib (Morocco) by its inhabitants. On the shore of the Surrounding Sea in that region lie Arcila (Aẓîlâ) [114] and Larache (al-'Arâ'ish). Directly to the east of this area, there is the country of the Middle Maghrib whose center is Tlemcen (Tilimsân). On the shores of the Mediterranean there, lie Hunayn,[115] Oran, and Algiers. The Mediterranean leaves the Surrounding Sea at the Straits of Tangier in the western part of the fourth zone,[116] and then extends eastward to Syria. Shortly after it leaves the narrow straits, it widens to the south and to the north and enters the third and fifth zones. This is why many places within the third zone are on the Mediterranean coast, from Tangier up to al-Qaṣr aṣ-ṣaghîr, then Ceuta, the country of Bâdis, and Ghassâsah. Algiers, which comes next, is near Bougie (Bajâyah) on the east. Then, east of Bougie at the boundary of the first section is Constantine, a day's journey from the Mediterranean. South of these places, toward the south of the Middle Maghrib, is the territory of Ashîr, with Mount Tîṭṭerî, followed by Msila (al-Masîlah)

112a Bulaq has "north," and C had "north" in the text, but in the margin we find "north" corrected to "east." "North" is correct, but possibly Ibn Khaldûn himself made the wrong change.

113 Today Alcazarquivir, according to I. S. Allouche, *Hespéris*, XXV (1938), 2.

114 Spelled with *ṣ*, with a *z* written underneath. Cf. above, p. 67.

115 Cf. p. lii, above.

116 *Sic* correctly Bulaq, but A, B, C, and D have "section."

and the Zâb. The center of (the Zâb) is Biskra, north of
1, 107 Mount Awrâs which connects with the Atlas, as has been mentioned. This is the eastern end of the first section.

The second section of the third zone is like the first section in that about one-third of the distance from its southern (limit) lies the Atlas Mountain which extends across this section from west to east and divides it into two portions. The Mediterranean covers one area in the north. The portion south of the Atlas Mountain is all desert to the west. To the east, there is Ghadâmes. Directly to the east (of this portion) is the land of Waddân, the remainder of which is situated in the second zone, as has been mentioned. The portion north of the Atlas Mountain between the Atlas and the Mediterranean contains in the west Mount Awrâs, Tebessa, and Laribus (al-Urbus). On the seacoast is Bône (Bûnah). Directly east of these places lies the country of Ifrîqiyah, with the city of Tunis, then Sousse (Sûsah), and al-Mahdîyah on the seacoast. South of these places and north of the Atlas Mountain, is the country of the Djérid (Jarîd, al-Jarîd), Tozeur (Tûzar), Gafsa (Qafṣah), and Nefzoua (Nafzâwah). Between them and the coast is the city of Kairouan (al-Qayrawân), Mount Ousselat (Ouselet, Waslât), and Sbeïtla (Subayṭilah). Directly east of these places lies Tripoli on the Mediterranean. Facing it in the south are the mountains of the Hawwârah tribes, Dammar (Mount Demmer), and Maqqarah (the city of Maggara), which connect with the Atlas and are opposite Ghadâmes which we mentioned at the end of the southern portion. At the eastern end of the second section lies Suwayqat Ibn Mathkûd [116a] on the sea. To the south are the desert plains of the Arabs in the land of Waddân.

The third section of the third zone is also traversed by the Atlas Mountain, but at the limit (of the section) the Atlas
1, 108 turns northward and runs due north up to the Mediterranean.

[116a] Cf., for instance, W. Hoenerbach, *Das nordafrikanische Itinerar des ʿAbdarî* (Abhandlungen für die Kunde des Morgenlandes, No. 25) (Leipzig, 1940), p. 161.

There, it is called Cape Awthân. The Mediterranean covers the northern part of the third section, so that the land between it and the Atlas narrows. Behind the mountain to the southwest, there is the remainder of the land of Waddân and the desert plains of the Arabs. Then, there is Zawîlat Ibn Khaṭṭâb,[117] followed by sandy deserts and waste regions to the eastern boundary of the section. To the west of the area between the mountain and the sea, there is Sirte (Surt) at the sea. Then, there are empty and waste regions in which the Arabs roam. Then, there is Ajdâbiyah and, where the mountain makes a turn, Barca (Barqah). Next comes Ṭulaymithah (Ptolemais) on the sea. Then, to the east of the mountain, after it makes the turn, are the desert plains of the Hayyib [118] and the Ruwâḥah, which extend to the end of the section.

The southwestern part of the fourth section of the third zone contains the desert of Berenice. North of it is the country of the Hayyib and the Ruwâḥah. Then, the Mediterranean enters this section and covers part of it in a southern direction almost to the southern boundary. Between it and the end of the section, there remains a waste region through which the Arabs roam. Directly to the east of it is the Fayyûm, at the mouth of one of the two branches of the Nile. This branch passes by al-Lâhûn in Upper Egypt, in the fourth section of the zone, and flows into the Lake of the Fayyûm. Directly to the east of (the Fayyûm) is the land of Egypt with its famous city (Cairo), situated on the other branch of the Nile, the one that passes through Dalâṣ in Upper Egypt at the boundary of the second section. This latter branch divides a I, *109*
second time into two more branches below Cairo, at Shaṭṭanawf and Zifta(h).[119] The right branch again divides into two

[117] Of the several Zawîlah in the area mentioned by Yâqût, *Mu'jam al-buldân,* II, 960 f., none, according to Yâqût, is qualified by Ibn Khaṭṭâb. Cf., however, the information given by Ibn Ḥawqal in his geographical work, ed. J. H. Kramers, I, 106.

[118] The doubling of the second consonant is indicated in the MSS, but the vocalization of this name and that of the following Ruwâḥah is uncertain. Some information is found in *'Ibar,* VI, 72 f.; de Slane (tr.), I, 136 f. Cf. also Hoenerbach, *op. cit.,* p. 159.

[119] B and C vocalize *Zaftah.*

other branches at Tarnûṭ.[120] All these branches flow into the Mediterranean. At the mouth of the western branch is Alexandria; at the mouth of the middle branch is Rosetta; and at the mouth of the eastern branch is Damietta. Between Cairo and the Mediterranean coast at these points lies the whole of northern Egypt, which is densely settled and cultivated.

The fifth section of the third zone contains all or most of Syria, as I shall describe it. The Red Sea ends in the southwest (of the section) at Suez, because in its course from the Indian Ocean northward, it turns eventually westward. A long portion of its western extension lies in this section, with Suez at its western end. Beyond Suez, on this part of (the Red Sea), there are the mountains of Paran (Fârân), Mount Sinai (aṭ-Ṭûr), Aila (Aylah) in Midyan (Madyan), and, where it ends, al-Ḥawrâ'.[121] From there, its shoreline turns southward towards the land of the Ḥijâz, as has been mentioned in connection with the fifth section of the second zone.

A portion of the Mediterranean covers much of the northwestern part of the fifth section. On its (coast) lie al-Faramâ [122] and al-'Arîsh. The end of this portion of the Mediterranean comes close to al-Qulzum. The area in between there is narrow. It becomes a kind of gate leading into
I, *110* Syria. West of this gate is the desert plain (at-Tîh), a bare country in which nothing grows, where the Israelites wandered for forty years after they had left Egypt and before they entered Syria, as the Qur'ân tells.[123] In this portion of the Mediterranean, in the fifth section, lies part of the island of Cyprus. The remainder (of Cyprus) lies in the fourth zone, as we shall mention. Along the coastline of that narrow strip of land between the Mediterranean and the Red Sea, are al-'Arîsh, the boundary of Egypt, and Ascalon. Between them, there is a (narrow) strip of land (separating the Mediter-

[120] *Sic* according to the correction suggested by Quatremère. The original *Trwṭ* is corrected in B and C to *Dhrwṭ*. D has *Ḍ* as the first consonant.

[121] Doubtful.

[122] The MSS vocalize *al-Farmâ*.

[123] Cf. Qur'ân 5.26 (29). Cf. pp. 288 and 344, below.

ranean and) the Red Sea. Then, this portion of the Mediterranean turns to the north into the fourth zone at Tripoli and 'Arqah.[124] That is the eastern end of the Mediterranean. This portion of the Mediterranean comprises most of the Syrian coast. East and slightly to the north of Ascalon, is Caesarea. Then, in the same general direction, are Acco, Tyre, Sidon, and 'Arqah. The sea then turns north into the fourth zone.

Opposite these places on the coast of this portion of the Mediterranean, in the fifth section, there is a big mountain which rises from the coast at Aila (Aylah) on the Red Sea. It runs northeastward until it leaves the fifth section. It is called Amanus (al-Lukkâm). It is a kind of barrier between Egypt and Syria. At the one end, near Aila (Aylah), lies al-'Aqabah which the pilgrims pass through on their way from Egypt to Mecca. After it, to the north, is Abraham's tomb at Mount ash-Sharâh [125] which is a continuation of the afore-mentioned Amanus north of al-'Aqabah. It extends due east, and then *I, 111*
turns slightly (to the south). East of there is al-Ḥijr, the land of the Thamûd, Tema (Taymâ'), and Dûmat al-Jandal, the northernmost part of the Ḥijâz. South of it is Mount Raḍwâ.[126] Farther south, there are the castles of Khaybar. Between Mount ash-Sharâh and the Red Sea lies the desert of Tabûk. North of Mount ash-Sharâh is the city of Jerusalem near the Amanus. Then, there is the Jordan and Tiberias. East of it lies the (Jordan) depression (Ghôr, al-Ghawr) [126a] which extends to Adhri'ât and the Ḥawrân. Directly to the east of (the Ḥawrân) is Dûmat al-Jandal which constitutes the end of the Ḥijâz and the fifth section. Where the Amanus turns north at the end of the fifth section is the city of

[124] Or 'Irqah. Cf. G. Wiet in *Journal asiatique,* XI 18 (1921), 112 f.

[125] This mountain is different from Mount as-Sarâh in Arabia, mentioned by the Arab geographers. Ash-Sharâh is apparently identical with the element *Sharâ* occurring in the name of the Nabataean deity Dusares. Cf. also pp. 409 and 420, below, and *'Ibar,* II, 211.

[126] See pp. 407 f., below.

[126a] The description would hardly fit the Jordan depression. On al-Idrîsî's sectional map, the legend *Bilâd al-Ghawr min ash-Sha'm* starts at the Jordan and continues left almost up to Adhri'ât. This explains Ibn Khaldûn's statement.

Damascus, opposite Sidon and Beirut on the coast. The Amanus lies between (Sidon and Beirut, on the one hand), and (Damascus, on the other). Directly east [127] of Damascus and facing it, is the city of Ba'lbakk. Then, there is the city of Emesa at the northern end of the fifth section, where the Amanus breaks off. East of Ba'lbakk and Emesa are the city Palmyra and desert plains extending to the end of the fifth section.

The southernmost part of the sixth section contains the desert plains of the Arab Bedouins, (which are) located to the north of the Najd and the Yamâmah in the area between the Mountain of al-'Arj and aṣ-Ṣammân and extending to al-Baḥrayn and Hajar at the Persian Gulf. In the northernmost part of the sixth section, to the north of the desert plains, lie al-Ḥîrah, al-Qâdisîyah, and the swampy lowlands of the Euphrates. Beyond that to the east is the city of al-Baṣrah. In the northeastern part of the sixth section, the Persian Gulf ends, at 'Abbâdân and al-Ubullah. The mouth of the Tigris is at 'Abbâdân. The Tigris divides into many branches
I, 112 and takes in other branches from the Euphrates. All of them come together at 'Abbâdân and flow into the Persian Gulf. This portion of the Persian Gulf is wide in the southernmost part (of the section). It narrows toward its eastern boundary, and where it ends in the north it (also) is narrow. On the western coast lie the northernmost portion of al-Baḥrayn, Hajar, and al-Aḥsâ'. To the west of this portion of the Persian Gulf, lie al-Khaṭṭ, aṣ-Ṣammân,[128] and the remainder of the land of the Yamâmah.

The eastern coast comprises the shores of Fârs. In their southernmost part, at the eastern end of the sixth section, along a line stretching from the Persian Gulf eastward and

---

[127] It should be north. On al-Idrîsî's sectional map, Ba'lbakk is located northeast of Damascus.

[128] The MSS and editions of the *Muqaddimah* have a final *n*. B and C vocalize *aṣ-Ṣumân*. Ibn Khaldûn may have thought again of the aforementioned aṣ-Ṣammân. The correction aḍ-Ḍimâr, suggested by de Slane in his translation, supplies a locality that would fit into the context (cf. Yâqût, *op. cit.*, III, 479).

beyond it to the south, are the mountains of al-Qufṣ [129] which are in Kirmân. North of Hurmuz on the coast of the Persian Gulf, are Sîrâf and Najîram. In the east, toward the end of the sixth section and north of Hurmuz, is the country of Fârs, comprising, for instance, Sâbûr, Darâbjird, Fasâ, Iṣṭakhr, ash-Shâhijân, and Shîrâz, the principal city. North of the country of Fârs, at the end of the Persian Gulf, lies the country of Khûzistân which includes al-Ahwâz, Tustar, Jundîshâbûr, Susa (as-Sûs), Râmhurmuz, and other cities. Arrajân is on the boundary between Fârs and Khûzistân. To the east of the country of Khûzistân are the Kurdish Mountains, which extend to the region of Iṣfahân. The Kurds live there. They roam beyond the mountains into the country of Fârs. They are called *az-zumûm*.[130]

The southwestern part of the seventh section contains the remainder of the Mountains of al-Qufṣ to which are adjacent in the south and north the countries of Kirmân ⟨and Mukrân⟩. I, *113*
They include the cities of ar-Rûdhân, ash-Shîrajân, Jîruft (Jayruft), Yazdshîr, and al-Fahraj. North of the land of Kirmân is the remainder of the country of Fârs up to the border of Iṣfahân. The city of Iṣfahân lies in the northwest corner of the seventh section. East of the countries of Kirmân and Fârs, there is the land of Sijistân to the south, and the land of Kûhistân to the north. Between Kirmân-Fârs and Sijistân-Kûhistân, in the middle of this section, is the great desert which has few roads because of the difficult terrain. Cities in Sijistân are Bust and aṭ-Ṭâq. Kûhistân belongs to the country of Khurâsân. One of Khurâsân's best known places is Sarakhs,[131] on the boundary of the section.

[129] Kûfich, in its Persian form. Cf. Minorsky, *Ḥudûd*, p. 374.

[130] As indicated by al-Idrîsî and the geographers, this is the plural of *zamm*, meaning "district, habitat." The geographical handbooks often list the word under *r*, but *z* is clearly indicated here and is the correct form. Cf. M. J. de Goeje, *Indices* . . . (Bibliotheca Geographorum Arabicorum, No. 4) (Leiden, 1879), pp. 251 f.; *idem* (ed.), Ibn Khurradâdhbih, *Kitâb al-Masâlik wa-l-mamâlik*, p. 47. In the latter passage, de Goeje refers to Kurdish *zûmah* as the original word. Cf. also H. L. Fleischer, *Kleinere Schriften* (Leipzig, 1888), II, 546.

[131] The MSS add: "and Qûhistân" (or: "and Qûhistân is"). However, Qûhistân is merely the Arabic spelling of Kûhistân.

The eighth section contains, in the southwest, the plains of the Khalaj,[132] a Turkish nation. They adjoin the land of Sijistân in the west and the land of Kâbul of Eastern India in the south. North of these desert plains are the mountains and country of al-Ghûr starting with Ghaznah, the key to India. Where al-Ghûr ends in the north, lies Astarâbâdh. Then, to the north is the country of Herât in the middle of Khurâsân, extending to the boundary of the section. It includes Isfarâyin, Qâshân, Bûshanj, Marw-ar-rûdh, aṭ-Ṭâliqân, and al-Jûzajân. This part of Khurâsân extends to the river Oxus. Khurâsânian places on this river are the city of Balkh to the west,
I, *114* and the city of at-Tirmidh to the east. The city of Balkh was the seat of the Turkish realm.

The Oxus comes from the country of Wakhân in the area of Badakhshân which borders on India, in the southeast corner of this section. It soon turns west to the middle of the section. There, it is called the Kharnâb River. It then turns north, passes Khurâsân, flows due north, and finally flows into Lake Aral in the fifth zone, as we shall mention. In the middle of the eighth section where it turns from the south to the north, five large rivers belonging to the country of Khuttal and Wakhsh [133] flow into it on the east. Other rivers, coming from the Buttam Mountains to the east and north of Khuttal, also flow into it. The Oxus, thus, becomes wider and larger, so much so that no other river equals it in these respects. One of the five rivers flowing into the Oxus is the Wakhshâb,[134] which comes from the country of Tibet that extends over the southeastern portion of this section. It flows toward the northwest. Its course is blocked by a great mountain which runs from the middle of this section in the south to-

[132] B, C, and D vocalize al-Khulkh. Cf. p. 149, below, and esp. the Khûlukh Turks, p. 161, below. It was thought that this people were identical with the Kharlukh, but Minorsky, *Ḥudûd*, pp. 347 f., maintains the distinctive character of the names Khalaj and Kharlukh (Khallukh).

[133] Cf. Minorsky, *Ḥudûd*, p. 359.

[134] *Wakhsh-âb* "River of Wakhsh" is the part of the Amu Darya system that furnished the Greeks with the name of *Oxus*. For the Oxus in history, cf. also J. Markwart, *Wehrot und Arang* (Leiden, 1938).

ward the northeast, and leaves this section close to its northern (boundary) to pass into the ninth section. It crosses the country of Tibet toward the southeast portion of this section. It separates the Turks from the country of Khuttal. It has only one road in the middle of this section to the east. Al-Faḍl b. Yaḥyâ constructed a dam there with a gate in it,[135] I, *115*
like the Dam of Gog and Magog. When the Wakhshâb leaves the country of Tibet and comes up against that mountain, it flows under it for a long distance, until it enters the country of Wakhsh and flows into the Oxus at the border of Balkh. (The Oxus) then sweeps on to at-Tirmidh in the north and flows into the country of al-Jûzajân.

East of the country of al-Ghûr, in the region between (this country) and the Oxus, is the country of al-Bâmiyân, which belongs to Khurâsân. There on the eastern bank of the river is the country of Khuttal, most of which is mountainous, and the country of Wakhsh. This is bordered in the north by the Buttam Mountains, which come from the border of Khurâsân, west of the Oxus, and run eastward. Finally, where they end, a large mountain range begins, behind which lies the country of Tibet and under which there flows the Wakhshâb, as we have stated. (The two mountain ranges) join at the gate of al-Faḍl b. Yaḥyâ. The Oxus passes between them. Other rivers flow into it, among them the river of the country of Wakhsh, which flows into it from the east, below at-Tirmidh in the north.[135a] The Balkhâ River [136] comes from the Buttam Mountains where it starts at al-Jûzajân, and flows into it from the west. On the western bank of this river (Oxus) lies Âmul,[136a] which belongs to Khurâsân. East of this river (Oxus) are the lands of the Soghd and Usrûshanah, which belong to the country of the Turks. East

[135] Cf. Ibn Khurradâdhbih, *Kitâb al-Masâlik wa-l-mamâlik*, p. 34 (text); p. 24 (tr.).

[135a] As the sectional map of al-Idrîsî shows, the Wakhshâb flows into the Oxus south of at-Tirmidh, and the river of the country of Wakhsh north of it.

[136] Identical with the unnamed river mentioned in Minorsky, *Ḥudûd*, p. 71?

[136a] In the fourth zone.

of them is the land of Farghânah, which extends to the eastern end of the section. The entire country of the Turks here is crossed by the Buttam Mountains on the north.

In the western part of the ninth section lies the country of Tibet, up to the middle of the section. In the south is India,
I, 116 and in the east, to the boundary of the section, is China. In the northernmost part of this section, north of the country of Tibet, is the country of the Kharlukh,[137] which belongs to the country of the Turks, extending to the northern boundary of the section. Adjacent to it on the west is the land of Farghânah,[138] and on the east is the land of the Turkish Tughuzghuz,[139] extending to the northeastern end of the section.

The southern part of the tenth section is entirely occupied by the remaining northernmost portion of China. In the north is the remainder of the country of the Tughuzghuz. East of them is the country of the Turkish Kirghiz,[140] extending to the eastern end of the section. North of the land of the Kirghiz is the country of the Turkish Kimäk.[141]

Opposite (the Kirghiz and Kimäk countries), in the Surrounding Sea, lies the Hyacinth (Ruby) Island in the middle of a round mountain that completely blocks access to it. Climbing to the top of the mountain from the outside is extremely difficult. On the island, there are deadly snakes and many pebbles of hyacinth (ruby). The people of that region contrive to mine them with the help of divine inspiration.

The regions in the ninth and tenth sections extending beyond Khurâsân and Khuttal are desert plains where innumerable Turkish nations roam. They are wandering nomads who have camels, sheep, cattle, and horses for breeding, riding, and eating. There are very many, (indeed) in-

---

[137] See n. 38 to this chapter, above, and p. 149, below.

[138] Bulaq adds: "also to the end of the section."

[139] Ibn Khaldûn pronounced the name Bagharghar. However, below, p. 172, he had the form aṭ-Ṭagharghar. For the Tughuzghuz, cf. Minorsky, *Ḥudûd*, pp. 263 ff.

[140] Ibn Khaldûn pronounced the name Kharkhîr, or Khirkhîr. Cf. Minorsky, *Ḥudûd*, pp. 282 ff.; Minorsky-Marvazî, pp. 104 f.

[141] Cf. Minorsky, *Ḥudûd*, pp. 304 ff.; Minorsky-Marvazî, p. 107.

numerable groups. There are Muslims among them in the area adjacent to the Oxus. They make raids on the unbelievers among them, who follow the Magian[142] religion. They sell their captives to their near (neighbors), who export them to Khurâsân, India, and the 'Irâq.

The fourth zone I, 117

The fourth zone is contiguous with the northern part of the third (zone). Its first section, in the west, contains a portion of the Surrounding Sea which, oblong in shape, extends from the southern to the northern boundary of the section. The city of Tangier is situated on it in the south. North of Tangier, the Mediterranean branches off from this portion of the Surrounding Sea in a narrow straits that is only twelve miles wide, Tarifa and Algeciras (lying) to the north of it and Qaṣr al-Majâz[143] and Ceuta to the south of it. It runs east until it reaches the middle of the fifth section of the fourth zone, gradually widening and eventually covering the (first) four sections and most of the fifth section of the fourth zone, as well as adjacent regions of the third and fifth zones, as we shall mention.

The Mediterranean is also called the "Syrian Sea." It contains many islands. The largest of them, from west to east, are Ibiza, Majorca, Minorca, Sardinia, Sicily—which is the largest of them—the Peloponnesos, Crete, and Cyprus. We shall mention each of them in its particular section.

At the end of the third section of the fourth zone and in the third section of the fifth zone, the Adriatic Sea (Straits of the Venetians) branches off from the Mediterranean. It runs in a northern direction, then turns westward in the northern half of the section, and finally ends in the second section of the fifth zone.

At the eastern boundary of the fourth section of the fifth zone, the Straits of Constantinople branches off from the Mediterranean. In the north, it makes a narrow passage only

---

[142] See n. 9 to this chapter, above.

[143] This location is usually thought to be the site of the above-mentioned al-Qaṣr aṣ-ṣaghîr (p. 129), nor can it have been far from it.

an arrow shot in width, extending up to the boundary of the
I, *118* zone and on into the fourth section of the sixth zone, where it turns into the Black Sea, running eastward across the whole of the fifth, and half of the sixth, sections of the sixth zone, as we shall mention in the proper place.

Where the Mediterranean leaves the Surrounding Sea through the Straits of Tangier and expands into the third zone, there remains a small portion of this section south of the Straits. The city of Tangier is situated in it, at the confluence of the two seas. After Tangier comes Ceuta on the Mediterranean, then Tetuán (Tîṭṭâwîn), and Bâdis. The remainder of this section to the east is covered by the Mediterranean, which extends into the third (zone). Most of the cultivated area in this section is north of it and north of the Straits. All this is Spain.

The western part of Spain, the area between the Surrounding Sea and the Mediterranean, begins at Tarifa, at the confluence of the two seas. East of it, on the shore of the Mediterranean, is Algeciras, followed by Málaga, Almuñécar, and Almería. Northwest of these cities and close to the Surrounding Sea, there is Jerez (de la Frontera), followed by Niebla. Opposite these two cities, in the Surrounding Sea, is the island of Cadiz. East of Jerez and Niebla are Sevilla, followed by Écija, Córdoba, and Marbella [?],[144] then Granada, Jaén, and Úbeda, then Guadix and Baza. Northwest of these cities on the Surrounding Sea are Santamaria and Silves. (North)east of these two cities are Badajoz, Mérida, and Évora,[145] followed by Ghâfiq [146] and Trujillo, and then

---

[144] For this geographical name, cf. E. Lévi-Provençal, *La Péninsule Ibérique*, p. 75 (n. 1), and the same scholar's edition of an-Nubâhî, *Histoire des Juges d'Andalousie intitulée Kitab al-Markaba al-'ulya* [*al-Marqabah al-'ulyâ*] (Cairo, 1948), p. 82. However, the MSS definitely indicate *t* and not *b*. It is difficult to assume that Ibn Khaldûn was not familiar enough with the geography of this particular part of Spain to avoid a mistake here. Therefore, de Slane's identification with Montillo cannot be ruled out.

[145] Évora is west of Badajoz and Mérida.

[146] Cf. E. Lévi-Provençal, *La Péninsule Ibérique*, p. 167, where an identification with Guijo, northwest of Pedroche, is suggested, and the edition of an-Nubâhî, p. 238, where Ghâfiq is identified with Belacazar.

Calatrava. Northwest of these cities on the Surrounding Sea, there is Lisbon on the Tajo. East of Lisbon, on the Tajo, are 1, *119*
Santarem and Coria. Then, there is Alcántara. Facing Lisbon on the east, there rises the Sierra (de Guadarrama) which starts in the west there and runs eastward along the northern boundary of the section. It ends at Medinaceli beyond the middle of (the section). Below (at the foot of) the Sierra, is Talavera, east of Coria, followed by Toledo, Guadalajara, and Medinaceli. Where the Sierra begins, in the region between the Sierra and Lisbon, is Coimbra. This is western Spain.

Eastern Spain is bordered by the Mediterranean. Here, Almería is followed by Cartagena, Alicante, Denia, and Valencia, up to Tarragona [147] at the eastern boundary of the section. North of these cities are Lorca and Segura, adjacent to Baza and Calatrava, which belong to western Spain. To the east, then, comes Murcia, followed by Játiva north of Valencia,[148] then Jucar,[149] Tortosa, and [150] Tarragona at the boundary of the section. Then, north of these cities, there are the lands of Chinchilla and Huete, which are adjacent to Segura and Toledo in the west. Northeast of Tortosa, then, is Fraga. East of Medinaceli, there is Calatayud, followed by Saragossa and Lérida at the northeastern end of the section.

The second section of the fourth zone is entirely covered by water, except for a portion in the northwest which includes the remainder of the Pyrenees,[151] the "Mountain of Passes and Roads." It comes there from the boundary of the first section of the fifth zone. It starts at the southeastern 1, *120*
limit of the Surrounding Sea on the boundary of this section, runs southeastward, and enters the fourth zone upon leaving the first section for the second, so that a portion of it falls into the fourth zone. Its passes lead into the adjacent mainland,

---

[147] Bulaq has Tortosa.

[148] This is not correct. "East," as we find in the Paris edition, is no better.

[149] E. Lévi-Provençal, *La Péninsule Ibérique*, p. 126.

[150] "And" seems a necessary correction of Bulaq. The other texts have "north of."

[151] *Jabal al-burtât* "Mountain of the Gates (*porta*)."

which is called the land of Gascogne. It contains the cities of Gerona and Carcassonne. On the shores of the Mediterranean in this portion, is the city of Barcelona, followed by Narbonne.

The sea which covers this section contains many islands, most of which are uninhabited because they are small. In the west, there is the island of Sardinia, and in the east the large island of Sicily. Its circumference is said to be seven hundred miles. It contains many cities, the best known among them being Syracuse, Palermo, Trapani, Mazzara, and Messina. Sicily is opposite Ifrîqiyah. Between Sicily and Ifrîqiyah are the islands of Gozzo and Malta.

The third section of the fourth zone is also covered by the sea, except for three portions in the north. The one in the west belongs to the land of Calabria, the one in the middle to Lombardy, and the one in the east to the country of the Venetians.

The fourth section of the fourth zone is also covered by the sea, as has been mentioned. It contains many islands. Most of them are uninhabited, as is the case in the third section. The inhabited islands are the Peloponnesos, in the northwest, and Crete, which is oblong in shape and stretches from the middle of the section to the southeast.

I, *121* A large triangular area of the fifth section in the southwest is covered by the sea. The western side of (this triangle) goes to the northern boundary of the fifth section. The southern side goes across about two-thirds of the section. There remains at the eastern side of the section a portion of about one-third. Its northern part runs west along the seacoast, as we have stated. Its southern half contains the northernmost region of Syria. It is traversed in the middle by the Amanus. The Amanus eventually reaches the northern end of Syria, where it turns in a northeasterly direction. At the point where it turns, it is called "Chain Mountain." [152] There, it enters the fifth zone. After it turns, it traverses a portion of the Jazîrah

[152] It corresponds to the Taurus. Cf. M. Canard, *Histoire de la dynastie des H'amdanides* (Algiers, 1951), I, 255. For the Durûb, *ibid.*, I, 243.

in an easterly direction. West of where it turns, there rise contiguous mountain ranges. They finally end at an inlet of the Mediterranean, near the northern end of the section. Through these mountains, there are passes which are called ad-Durûb (mountain passes). They lead into Armenia. This section contains a portion of Armenia situated between these mountains and the Chain Mountain.

The southern region, as we have mentioned before, comprises the northernmost region of Syria, and the Amanus extends across it from south to north in the area between the Mediterranean and the boundary of the section. On the seacoast is Anṭarsûs,[153] at the beginning of the section to the south. It borders on 'Arqah and Tripoli which lie on the shore
of the Mediterranean in the third zone. North of Anṭarsûs *I, 122*
is Jabalah, followed by Lattakiyah, Alexandretta, and Selefke. North of these cities is the Byzantine territory.

The Amanus, which lies between the sea and the end of the section, is hugged, in Syria in the southwestern part of the section, by the fortress of Ḥiṣn al-Khawâbî, which belongs to the Ismâ'îlî Assassins who at this time are called Fidâwîs. The fortress (also) is called Maṣyât.[154] It lies opposite Anṭarsûs to the east. On the side opposite this fortress, east of the Amanus, is Salamîyah, north of Emesa. North of Maṣyât, between the mountain and the sea, lies Antioch. Opposite it, east of the Amanus, is al-Ma'arrah, and east of al-Ma'arrah, al-Marâghah. North of Antioch, there is al-Maṣṣîṣah, followed by Adhanah and Ṭarsûs, at the furthest point of Syria. Facing (Antioch), west of the mountain, is Qinnasrîn, followed by 'Ayn Zarbah. Opposite Qinnasrîn, east of the mountain, is Aleppo, and opposite 'Ayn Zarbah is Manbij, the furthest point of Syria.

The area to the right of the Durûb, between them and the Mediterranean, comprises the Byzantine territory

---

[153] I.e., Anṭarṭûs, Antaradus.

[154] For Maṣyât (Maṣyâd, Maṣyâf, Maṣyâb), cf. R. Dussaud, *Topographie historique de la Syrie antique et médiévale* (Bibliothèque archéologique et historique, No. 4) (Paris, 1927), p. 143.

(Anatolia). At this time, it belongs to the Turkomans and is ruled by Ibn Uthmân (the Ottomans).[155] On the shore of the Mediterranean there, are Antalya and al-'Alâyâ.

Armenia, which lies between the Durûb and the Chain Mountain, comprises Mar'ash, Malatya, and Ankara,[155a] up to the northern end of the section. In Armenia, in the fifth section, originate the river Jayḥân and, to the east of it, the river Sayḥân. The Jayḥân flows south until it has traversed
I, *123* the Durûb. It then passes by Ṭarsûs and al-Maṣṣîṣah, then turns northwestward and eventually flows into the Mediterranean south of Selefke. The Sayḥân runs parallel to the Jayḥân. It is opposite Ankara and Mar'ash, traverses the Durûb Mountains, reaches Syria, then passes by 'Ayn Zarbah, then turns away from the Jayḥân, and turns northwestward. It joins the Jayḥân west of al-Maṣṣîṣah.

The Jazîrah, which is surrounded by the portion of the Amanus that turns into the Chain Mountain, contains in the south ar-Râfiqah and ar-Raqqah, followed by Ḥarrân, Sarûj, Edessa, Nisibis, Samosata, and Âmid, north of the Chain Mountain, at the northeastern end of the section. The Euphrates and the Tigris traverse this area in the middle. They originate in the fifth zone, pass southward through Armenia, and cross the Chain Mountain. The Euphrates, then, flows west of Samosata and Sarûj in an easterly direction. It passes west of ar-Râfiqah and ar-Raqqah and on into the sixth section. The Tigris flows east of Âmid and shortly thereafter turns to the east. Then, it soon passes on into the sixth section.

The sixth section of the fourth zone contains the Jazîrah to the west. Immediately east of it is the country of the 'Irâq,

---

[155] When the *Muqaddimah* was being written, the ruling Ottoman was Murâd I b. Orkhan.

[155a] Ibn Khaldûn certainly read Ankara, but this is impossible. Bulaq has al-Ma'arrah, which is equally wrong but shows that Ibn Khaldûn might have had some other reading than Ankara in his earliest text. The sectional maps of al-Idrîsî have the correct reading Zibaṭrah. A misreading Ankara, for Zibaṭrah, which already in the time of al-Idrîsî had been in ruins for centuries, is easily explained.

which terminates near the boundary of the section. At the boundary of the 'Irâq is the Mountain of Iṣfahân which comes from the south of the section and runs in a westerly direction. When it reaches the middle of the northern end of the section, I, *124*
it runs west. Eventually, leaving the sixth section, it joins on its course due west, the Chain Mountain in the fifth section.

The sixth section is divided into two portions, a western and an eastern. The western portion, in the south, contains the point where the Euphrates leaves the fifth section, and, in the north, the point where the Tigris leaves it. As soon as the Euphrates enters the sixth section, it passes Qirqîsiyâ'. There, a (river) branches off from the Euphrates. It flows north into the Jazîrah and disappears there in the ground. Shortly past Qirqîsiyâ', the Euphrates turns south and passes to the west of the Khâbûr and on west of ar-Raḥbah. A (river) branches off there from the Euphrates and flows south. Ṣiffîn lies to the west of it. (This river) then turns east and divides into a number of branches. Some of them pass by al-Kûfah, others by Qaṣr Ibn Hubayrah and al-Jâmi'ayn (al-Ḥillah). Now, in the south of the section all of them enter the third zone and disappear into the ground east of al-Ḥîrah and al-Qâdisîyah. The Euphrates flows directly east from ar-Raḥbah, and passes north of Hît. It then flows south of az-Zâb [155b] and al-Anbâr, and into the Tigris at Baghdad.

When the Tigris leaves the fifth section for the sixth section, it flows due east, opposite the Chain Mountain which connects with the Mountain of al-'Irâq on its course due west, and passes north of Jazîrat Ibn 'Umar. Then it passes Mosul in the same way, and Takrît. It reaches al-Ḥadîthah, turns south, leaving al-Ḥadîthah to the east of it, and likewise the Greater and the Lesser Zâb. It flows directly south I, *125*
and to the west of al-Qâdisîyah. Eventually it reaches Baghdad and joins with the Euphrates. Then it flows south, to the west of Jarjarâyâ, and eventually leaves the section and enters

[155b] This village is mentioned in Ibn Khurradâdhbih, *Kitâb al-Masâlik wa-l-mamâlik*, p. 72 (text), where the editor suggests that it be read ar-Rabb.

the third zone. There it divides into many branches. They unite again and there flow into the Persian Gulf at 'Abbâdân. The region between the Tigris and the Euphrates, before they have come together at Baghdad, is the Jazîrah. Below Baghdad, another river joins the Tigris. It comes from northeast of (the Tigris). It reaches an-Nahrawân opposite Baghdad to the east. Then it turns south and joins with the Tigris before entering the third zone. For the region between this river and the mountains of al-'Irâq and Kurdistân, there remains Jalûlâ' and, east of it at the mountain, Ḥulwân and Ṣaymarah.

The western portion of the section contains a mountain that starts from the Kurdish mountains and runs east toward the end of the section. It is called the Mountain of Shahrazûr. It divides the (western portion) into two subdivisions. The southern subdivision contains Khûnajân, northwest of Iṣfahân. This section is called the country of *al-Bahlûs*.[156] In the middle of the southern subdivision is Nahâwand, and, in the north, Shahrazûr, west of the point where the two mountain ranges meet, and ad-Dînawar (is) on the east, at the boundary of the section. The other subdivision contains part of Armenia, including its principal place, al-Marâghah. The
I, *126* portion of the Mountain of al-'Irâq that faces it is called the Mountain of Bârimmâ.[157] It is inhabited by Kurds. The Greater Zâb and the Lesser Zâb at the Tigris are behind it. At the eastern end of this section lies Azerbaijan, which includes Tabrîz and al-Baylaqân.[158] In the northeast corner of the section is a small portion of [the Black Sea,] the Caspian (Sea of the Khazars).[159]

The seventh section of the fourth zone contains, in the southwest, the largest portion of the country of *al-Bahlûs*, including Hamadhân and Qazwîn. The remainder of it is in the third zone; Iṣfahân is situated there. (*Al-Bahlûs* and

---

[156] This is a corruption of *al-Bahlawîyîn* "Pahlavis (Parthia)," which appeared in the older geographers. Cf. Ibn Khurradâdhbih, *op. cit.*, p. 57 (text); p. 38 (n. 3) (tr.).

[157] Cf. Minorsky, *Ḥudûd*, pp. 202 f.

[158] Cf. Minorsky, *Ḥudûd*, p. 398.

[159] The reference to the Black Sea is out of place here.

Iṣfahân) are surrounded on the south by mountains which come from the west, pass through the third zone, leave it in the sixth section for the fourth zone, and join the eastern portion of the Mountain of al-ʿIrâq, as has been mentioned before. They (also) surround the eastern portion of the country of *al-Bahlûs*. These mountains which surround Iṣfahân run north from the third zone, enter this seventh section, and then inclose the country of *al-Bahlûs* on the east. Below (at the foot of) them, is Qâshân, followed by Qumm. Near the middle of their course, they turn slightly west; then, describing an arc, they run northeastward, and eventually enter the fifth zone. Where they turn (west) and make the circle, ar-Rayy lies to the east. Where they turn (west), another mountain range starts and runs west to the boundary of the seventh section. South of the mountains there is Qazwîn. North of them and alongside the connecting mountains of ar-Rayy, extending in a northeastern direction to the middle of the section and then into the fifth zone, lies the country of I, 127
Ṭabaristân in the region between these mountains and a portion of the Caspian Sea (Sea of Ṭabaristân). From the fifth zone, it enters the seventh section about halfway between west and east. Where the mountains of ar-Rayy turn west, there lie other, connecting mountains. They run directly east and slightly south, and eventually enter the eighth section from the west. Between the mountains of ar-Rayy and these mountains, at their starting point, there remains Jurjân, which includes Bisṭâm.[160] Behind these (latter) mountains, there is a part of the seventh section that contains the remainder of the desert area between Fârs and Khurâsân, to the east of Qâshân. At its farthest point, near these mountains, is Astarâbâdh. On the eastern slopes of these mountains, and extending to the boundary of the section, lies the country of Nîsâbûr, which belongs to Khurâsân. South of the mountains and east of the desert area, lies Nîsâbûr, followed by Marw ash-Shâhijân [161] at the end of the section. North of

[160] Biṣṭâm is in Khurâsân.

[161] Cf. A. Jakoubovsky in *EI Supplement*, *s.v.* "Merw al-Shâhidjân."

it and east of Jurjân, are Mihrajân, Khâzarûn, and Ṭûs, the eastern end of the section. All these places are north of the mountains. Far to the north of them is the country of Nasâ, which is surrounded by barren stretches of desert, in the northeastern corner of the section.

The eighth section of the fourth zone, in the west, contains the Oxus which flows from south to north. On its western bank, there are Zamm [162] and Âmul which belong to Khurâsân, as well as aṭ-Ṭâhirîyah and Gurgânj which belongs to Khuwârizm. The southwest corner of the section is surrounded by the mountains of Astarâbâdh, which were
I, 128 found already in the seventh section. They enter this section from the west and encircle the (southwestern) corner, which includes the remainder of the country of Herât. In the third zone, the mountains pass between Herât and al-Jûzajân, and eventually connect with the Buttam Mountain, as we mentioned there. East of the Oxus in the south of this section, is the country of Bukhârâ, followed by the country of the Soghd, with Samarkand as its principal place. Then comes the country of Usrûshanah, which includes Khujandah at the eastern end of the section. North of Samarkand and Usrûshanah, is the land of Îlâq.[163] North of Îlâq is the land of Tashkent (ash-Shâsh), which extends to the eastern boundary of the section and occupies a portion of the ninth section that in the south includes the remainder of the land of Farghânah.

From this portion of the ninth section, comes the river of Tashkent (Syr Darya). It cuts through the eighth section, and eventually flows into the Oxus where the latter leaves the eighth section in the north for the fifth zone. In the land of Îlâq, a river coming from the ninth section of the third zone, from the borders of Tibet, flows into the river of Tashkent, and before the latter leaves the ninth section, the river of Farghânah flows into it. Parallel to the river of Tashkent lies Mount Jabrâghûn, which starts from the fifth zone, turns

[162] B and C vocalize Zum. B has aẓ-Ẓâhirîyah, instead of aṭ-Ṭâhirîyah.
[163] Cf. Minorsky, *Ḥudûd*, p. 356.

southeast, and eventually enters the ninth section and runs along the borders of the land of Tashkent. Then, it turns in the ninth section, continues along the boundaries of Tashkent and Farghânah, goes on to the southern part of the section, and then enters the third zone. Between the river of Tashkent and the bend of this mountain in the middle of the section, there is the country of Fârâb. Between it and the land of Bukhârâ and Khuwârizm are barren stretches of desert. In I, 129
the northeast corner of this section is the land of Khujandah,[163a] which includes Isbîjâb [164] and Ṭarâz.[165]

The ninth section of the fourth zone, to the west beyond Farghânah and Tashkent, contains the land of the Kharlukh in the south, and the land of the Khallukh [166] in the north. The whole eastern part of the section to its farthest point is occupied by the land of the Kimäk. It extends over the whole tenth section to the Qûfâyâ Mountains [167] which are at the eastern end of the section and lie there on a portion of the Surrounding Sea. They are the Mountains of Gog and Magog. All these nations are Turkish peoples.

The fifth zone

Most of the first section of the fifth zone is covered by water, except a small portion of the south and of the east. In this western region, the Surrounding Sea enters into the fifth, sixth, and seventh zones from the circle it describes around the zones. The portion to the south that is free from water has a triangular shape. It there touches Spain and comprises the remainder of it. It is surrounded on two sides

---

[163a] The reference to Khujandah, which was mentioned before as situated in the southeast of the section, cannot be correct. The sectional maps of al-Idrîsî read Kunjdih. Cf. Minorsky, *Ḥudûd*, p. 119.

[164] Now Sayram.

[165] Talas. Cf. Minorsky, *Ḥudûd*, p. 358.

[166] They are possibly different from the Khalaj (p. 136, above), but, in spite of this passage, they may be identical with the Kharlukh (p. 103, n. 38 to this chapter, and p. 138, above).

[167] O. J. Tallgren (Tuulio), *Studia Orientalia*, VI 3 (1936), 170, suggests an identification of Qûfâyâ with Ptolemy's Ripaia.

by the sea, as if by the two sides of a triangle. It occupies the remainder of western Spain, including Montemayor [168] on the seacoast at the beginning of the section in the southwest. Salamanca is to the east, and Zamora to the north. East of Salamanca, at the southern end, is Ávila, and east of it, the
I, 130 land of Castilla with the city of Segovia. North of it is the land of León and Burgos. Beyond it to the north is the land of Galicia, which extends to the corner of this portion. At the Surrounding Sea there, at the far point of the western side (of the triangle), the portion includes the region of Santiago—that is, (Saint) Jacob.

Of eastern Spain, the triangular portion contains the city of Tudela, at the southern end of the section and to the east of Castilla. To the northeast of Tudela are Huesca and Pamplona directly to the east of (Huesca). West of Pamplona, there is Estella (Qastâllah), followed by Najera [169] in the region between Estella and Burgos. This (triangular) portion contains a large mountain. It faces the sea and the northeast side of the triangle, in close proximity both to it and to the seacoast at Pamplona in the east. We have mentioned before that it connects in the south with the Mediterranean in the fourth zone. It constitutes a barrier for Spain in the north. Its passes are gates leading from Spain to the country of Gascogne, which belongs to the European Christian nations. In the fourth zone, there belong to (Gascogne) Barcelona and Narbonne on the shore of the Mediterranean; north of them, Gerona and Carcassonne; and in the fifth zone, Toulouse, north of Gerona.

The eastern portion of this section has the shape of an oblong triangle with its acute angle beyond the Pyrenees to
I, 131 the east. On the Surrounding Sea, at the top where it connects with the Pyrenees, this portion includes Bayonne. At the end of it, in the northeastern region of the section, is the

[168] Though there are many small Montemayors in Spain, in this region and elsewhere, de Slane's identification with Montemor-o-velho in Portugal is certainly correct.

[169] The MSS indicate *t* instead of *n*, as the first consonant of the name.

land of Poitou, which belongs to the European Christians and extends to the end of the section.

The western region of the second section contains the land of Gascogne. North of it are the lands of Poitou and Bourges.[170] Both countries have been mentioned by us. East of the country of Gascogne lies a portion of the Mediterranean. It projects into this section like a tooth, in an easterly direction. To the west, the country of Gascogne juts out into a gulf of the Mediterranean[?]. At the northern extremity of this portion is the country of Genoa, along which to the north lie the Alps.[171] At their northern limit lies the land of Burgundy. East of the gulf of Genoa, which comes from the Mediterranean, another gulf comes from the same sea. The two gulfs include a portion of land in the shape of a peninsula on which, in the west, lies Pisa, and in the east the great city of Rome, the capital of the European Christians and the residence of the Pope, their highest religious dignitary. It contains magnificent, historically famous buildings, imposing monuments,[172] and gigantic churches. One of the remarkable things at Rome is the river that flows through it from east to west, the bed of which is paved with copper.[173] Rome contains the Church of the Apostles Peter and Paul, who are buried in it. North of the country of Rome is the country of Lombardy, which extends to the boundary of the section. On the eastern shore of the gulf on which Rome is situated, lies Naples. It is adjacent to the country of Calabria, which (also) I, *132*
belongs to the lands of the European Christians. North of it, a portion of the Adriatic Sea (Gulf of Venice) comes into this section from the third section, turns west, and faces north in

[170] Or perhaps Périgueux? If this place and Poitou (and not Poitou and Gascogne) are referred to as mentioned before, it was probably confused by Ibn Khaldûn with Burgos.

[171] Mont Jûn, apparently identical with Mons Jovis, Montjoux, St. Bernard. Cf. W. Hoenerbach, *Deutschland und seine Nachbarländer nach der grossen Geographie des Idrîsî*, p. 38 (n. 45).

[172] For *haykal* meaning "temple, effigy, large object," or "monument," see below, pp. 354, 356 ff., 2:235, 238 ff., 249, 258, 260, 359, and 3:132.

[173] Cf. G. Levi Della Vida in *Journal of the American Oriental Society*, LXIII (1943), 184 ff.

this section, and extends to about one-third of it. A large portion of the country of the Venetians is situated on this portion of the Adriatic Sea, in the south,[174] in the region between (the Adriatic Sea) and the Surrounding Sea. North of it lies the country of Aquileia in the sixth zone.

The third section of the fifth zone contains in the west the country of Calabria, between the Adriatic Sea and the Mediterranean. Part of the mainland in the Mediterranean in the fourth zone forms a portion of land in the shape of a peninsula, between two gulfs that extend due north from the Mediterranean into this section.[175] East of the country of Calabria is the country of the Lombards,[176] along a portion of land formed by the Adriatic Sea and the Mediterranean, of which one end enters the fourth zone and the Mediterranean.

To the east, this section is surrounded by the Adriatic Sea, which belongs to the Mediterranean. It flows due north, then turns west opposite the northern end of the section. Alongside it, a large mountain (range) comes from the fourth zone. It faces it (the sea) and runs parallel to it on its way north, then turns west along it in the sixth zone, and eventually ends opposite a straits in the north of it, in the country of Aquileia, a German (Alamanni) nation, as we shall mention. At this straits and between it and this mountain (range), where the mountains and the sea go off to the north, lies the country of the Venetians. Where the mountains and the sea go off to the west, they border the country of Jarwâsiyâ, and then the country of the Germans (Alamanni),
I, *133* at the end of the straits.

[174] Bulaq corrects the text by adding: "It (the Adriatic Sea) enters from the south." De Slane has the slightly better suggestion that "south" should be understood in the sense of "west." However, a glance at the map shows why Ibn Khaldûn speaks here of Venice as situated south of the Adriatic Sea (even if its location is described differently later on). No case in support of "Surrounding Sea" can be made. It should read "Mediterranean."

[175] This refers to the Gulf of Taranto and the heel of the Italian boot.

[176] According to Hoenerbach, *op. cit.*, p. 31 (n. 28), al-Idrîsî designates by *bilâd ankbarda* "country of the Lombards," the Lombard principalities in Apulia, whereas *anbardiya* "Lombardy" means Lombardy proper.

The fourth section of the fifth zone contains a portion of the Mediterranean which enters it from the fourth zone. (This portion of the sea) is strongly indented by arms of the sea which jut out in a northerly direction and are separated by portions of land in the shape of peninsulas. At the eastern end of the section lies the Straits of Constantinople. (This narrow body of water) comes from this southern part (of the section), flows due north, and eventually enters the sixth zone. There, it immediately turns eastward (and joins) the Black Sea in the fifth section; (the latter also occupies) part of the fourth and sixth sections of the sixth zone, as we shall mention. Constantinople is to the east of this straits at the northern end of the section. It is a large city and was the seat of the Byzantine emperors. There are many stories about the magnificent architectural and other monuments there. The portion of this section between the Mediterranean and the Straits of Constantinople comprises the country of Macedonia, which belonged to the (ancient) Greeks, whose royal authority had its origin there. East of the straits and extending to the end of the section, there is a portion of the land of *Bâṭûs*.[177] This, I believe, is the desert plains where, at the present time, the Turkomans roam. There is (located) the realm of Ibn ʿUthmân (the Ottomans), with its chief city Bursa (Brussa).[178] Before them, it belonged to the Byzantines, from whom it was taken away by other nations, and eventually came into possession of the Turkomans.

The southwestern part of the fifth section of the fifth zone contains the land of *Bâṭûs* (Anatolia). North of it and extending to the boundary of the section, is the country of I, *134*
Amorium. East of Amorium is the Qubâqib (Tokhma Su) [178a] which flows into the Euphrates. It has its source in a mountain there and flows south until it joins the Euphrates, before

[177] In the older geographers, the form was *an-nâṭulûs* "Anatolia." Cf. Ibn Khurradâdhbih, *Kitâb al-Masâlik wa-l-mamâlik*, p. 107.

[178] C and D vocalize *Burṣah.*

[178a] Cf. M. Canard, *Histoire de la dynastie des H'amdanides*, I, 250 f., 262 ff.

the latter leaves this section and crosses over into the fourth zone. West of (the Euphrates), at the (southern) end of the section, the Sayḥân, and west of it, the Jayḥân, originate. Both rivers flow alongside (the Euphrates). They have been mentioned before. East of (the Euphrates) there, the Tigris originates. It always flows alongside (the Euphrates), and eventually joins it at Baghdad. In the southeastern corner of this section, behind the mountain where the Tigris originates, lies Mayyâfâriqîn. The Qubâqib, which we have mentioned, divides this section into two portions. The one covers the southwest and contains the land of *Bâṭûs* (Anatolia), as we have said. The northernmost part of (the land of *Bâṭûs*), the region extending to the northern end of the section and beyond the mountain where the Qubâqib originates, is the land of Amorium, as we have said. The other portion covers the northeastern and southeastern third (of the section). In the south of this the Tigris and Euphrates originate. In the north, there is the country of al-Baylaqân, which adjoins the land of Amorium behind Mount Qubâqib [179] and extends far. At its end, where the Euphrates originates, is Kharshanah.[180] In the northeast corner is a portion of the Black Sea that connects with the Straits of Constantinople.

The sixth section of the fifth zone contains in the southwest the country of Armenia, which extends eastward be-
I, *135* yond the middle of the section. Arzan (Erzerum) is in the southwest (of Armenia). To the north (of it) lie Tiflis and Dabîl. East of Arzan is the city of Khilâṭ, followed by Bardha'ah. In the southeast is the (capital) city of Armenia. There, Armenia, entering the fourth zone, includes al-Marâghah, east of the Mountain of the Kurds which is called Mountain of Bârimmâ, and which has been mentioned before in connection with the sixth section of the fourth zone. In this section, and in the fourth zone, Armenia is bordered to the

[179] "Mount" may be wrong, but Ibn Khaldûn apparently called the mountain where the Qubâqib was supposed to originate "Mount Qubâqib." On al-Idrîsî's sectional map, this mountain is called Jabal Naḏhân (?). The reading is uncertain. Cf. E. Honigmann, *Byzantion*, X (1953), 153.

[180] Cf. Minorsky, *Ḥudûd*, pp. 420 f.

east by the country of Azerbaijan. (Azerbaijan's) easternmost point in this section is Ardabîl, on a portion of the Caspian Sea. The Caspian Sea enters this section from the east from the seventh section, and is called the Sea of Ṭabaristân (Caspian Sea). On its northern shore, in this section, it contains a portion of the country of the Khazars. They are Turkomans. At the northern end of this portion of the Caspian Sea, a mountain range begins and runs due west to the fifth section, crosses it, encircles Mayyâfâriqîn, and enters the fourth zone at Âmid, where it connects with the Chain Mountain in the northernmost part of Syria, and from there (goes on to) connect with the Amanus, as has already been mentioned.

In these mountains in the northern part of this section, there are passes that constitute a sort of gates giving entry from both sides. To the south, is the country of the "Gates," which extends eastward to the Caspian Sea. The city of Derbend,[181] which belongs to this country, lies on the Caspian Sea. In the southwest, the country of the "Gates" adjoins I, *136*
Armenia. East of (the country of the Gates), between it and southern Azerbaijan, is the country of Arran (Ar-Rân),[182] which extends to the Caspian Sea. North of these mountains, there lies a portion of this section comprising in the west the realm of the Sarîr.[183] The northwest corner of that portion, which constitutes the (northwest) corner of the whole section, is also occupied by a small portion of the Black Sea that connects with the Straits of Constantinople. (This) has been mentioned before. This portion of the Black Sea is surrounded by the country of the Sarîr. Trebizond, which belongs to (that country), lies on it. The country of the Sarîr extends between the mountains of the "Gates" and the northern part of the section. It eventually reaches a mountain in the east that constitutes a barrier between it and the land

[181] See n. 36 to Ibn Khaldûn's Introduction, above.

[182] Cf. W. Barthold in *EI, s.v.* "Arran."

[183] The Sarîr have been identified with the Avars. *Sarîr* "throne" is an abridged form for "Master of the Throne," as their ruler was known to the Arabs. Cf. Minorsky, *Ḥudûd*, pp. 447 ff.

of the Khazars. On the far boundary of the (country of the Sarîr), is the city of Ṣûl. Behind this mountain barrier, there is a portion of the land of the Khazars reaching the northeast corner of this section, between the Caspian Sea and the northern end of the section.

The seventh section of the fifth zone is entirely covered in the west by the Caspian Sea, a portion of which protrudes into the fourth zone to the south. On (the shores of) this portion are situated, as we have mentioned in connection with the (fourth zone), the country of Ṭabaristân and the mountains of the Daylam up to Qazwîn. In the west of this portion and connecting with it, there is the small portion that lies in the sixth section of the fourth zone. Connecting with it in the north is the portion that lies in the eastern part of the sixth section above. A part of the northwest corner of this section, where the Volga flows into it, is not covered by the Caspian Sea. In the eastern region of this section there (also) remains a part which is not covered by the Caspian Sea. It consists of
I, *137* desert plains in which the Ghuzz, a Turk nation, roam.—— They are also called the Khûz. (Ghuzz) looks like an Arabization, with *kh* becoming *gh*, and doubling of the *z*.[184]
This part is surrounded by a mountain (range) to the south that enters the eighth section, runs not quite halfway through the western part, turns north, eventually touches the Caspian Sea, hugs it closely all the way through its remaining portion in the sixth zone, then turns at its end, and separates from it. There, it is called Mount Shiyâh.[185] It runs westward to the sixth section of the sixth zone, then turns back south to the sixth section of the fifth zone. It is this end of the mountain (range) that lies in this section between the land of the Sarîr and the land of the Khazars. The land of the Khazars

---

[184] The parenthesis is a marginal note in B and C, and is found incorporated in the text of D. Cf. also the *Autobiography*, p. 358.

The Turkish tribes are again discussed by Ibn Khaldûn, following al-Idrîsî, in *'Ibar*, V, 369 f.

[185] Shiyâh is always indicated in the MSS. *Siyâh*, Persian "black," would be more correct. The Persian form of Mount Shiyâh, Siyâh Kûh, appears below, p. 161.

extends along the slopes of the mountain called Mount Shiyâh in the sixth and seventh sections, as will be mentioned.

The whole eighth section of the fifth zone contains desert plains where the Ghuzz, a Turkish nation, roam. In the southwest is Lake Aral, into which the Oxus flows. Its circumference is three hundred miles. Many rivers flow into it from these desert plains. In the northeast is the Lake of Ghurghûn,[186] a fresh-water lake. Its circumference is four hundred miles. In the northern region of this section stands Mount Murghâr,[187] which means "Snow Mountain," because the snow on it never melts. It lies at the far end of the section. South of the Lake of Ghurghûn there is a mountain of solid I, *138*
stone where nothing grows. It is called Ghurghûn Mountain. The lake is named after it. In the Ghurghûn and Murghâr Mountains north of the lake, innumerable rivers have their origin. They flow into the lake from both sides.

The ninth section of the fifth zone contains the country of the Adhkish,[188] a Turkish nation, west of the country of the Ghuzz, and east of the country of the Kimäk. In the east at its end, (the section) is hugged by the Qûfâyâ Mountains that surround Gog and Magog. They stretch there from south to north, assuming this direction right after entering from the tenth section, which they had, in turn, entered from the end of the tenth section of the fourth zone. There, they border the Surrounding Sea on the northern boundary of the section. They then turn west in the tenth section of the fourth zone and extend almost to the middle of the section. From where they begin to this point, they surround the country of the Kimäk. Entering the tenth section of the fifth zone, they cross it in a westerly direction to its end. South of them remains a portion of that section that stretches west in an oblong shape and contains the end of the country of the Kimäk.

---

186 Lake of Qaraqum?

187 Mugojar Mountains (see Minorsky, *Ḥudûd*, p. 202, and map VII)? Turkish *kar* means "snow."

188 Cf. Minorsky, *Ḥudûd*, p. 347.

The mountains, then, enter the ninth section at its northeastern border, soon turn north, and run due north to the ninth section of the sixth zone, where the Dam (of Gog and Magog) is situated, as we shall mention. There remains the portion that is surrounded by the Qûfâyâ Mountains in the northeast corner of this section. It is oblong in shape and stretches southward. It belongs to the country of Gog.

I, *139* The tenth section of the fifth zone is entirely covered by the land of Gog, except for a portion of the Surrounding Sea which covers part of it in the east from south to north, and except for the portion that the Qûfâyâ Mountains leave in the southwest on their way through the section. Everything else is the land of Gog.

The sixth zone

Half of the first section of the sixth zone is mostly covered by the sea, which stretches eastward in a curving line along the northern part, then runs southward along the eastern part, and ends near the southern part (of the section). A portion of land in this part is not covered by the sea. It is similar in shape to a peninsula, formed by two arms of the Surrounding Sea. It is long and wide. All this is the land of Brittany. At the entrance to it, between those two arms (of the sea) and in the southeast corner of this section, there is the country of Sées which is adjacent to the country of Poitou. (The country of Poitou) has been mentioned before in connection with the first and second sections of the fifth zone.

The second section of the sixth zone is entered by the Surrounding Sea in the west and north. In the northwest, it covers an oblong portion (extending) over more than half (the south-north extension) of (the section),[188a] east of Brittany (which was mentioned) in the first section. (This portion of the sea) connects with the other portion in the north (that extends) from west to east. It widens somewhat in the western half of (the section). There, a portion of the island of
I, *140*

[188a] *Nisfihi*, as in Bulaq and in A, B, C, and D, is the correct reading and requires the above translation.

England is situated. It is a large, far-flung island which contains a number of cities and is the seat of a magnificent realm. The remainder of (England) lies in the seventh zone. South of and adjacent to this western part and the island located there, (and still) in the western half of this section, are the countries of Normandy and Flanders. Then, there is (northern) France in the southwest of this section, and, east of it, the country of Burgundy. All these countries belong to the European Christian nations. The eastern half of the section contains the country of the Germans (Alamanni). The south is taken up by the country of Aquileia, with the country of Burgundy farther north, and then the lands of Lorraine and Saxony. On a portion of the Surrounding Sea in the northeast corner, is the land of Frisia. All these countries belong to the German (Alamanni) nations.

The western part of the third section of the sixth zone contains, in the south, the country of Bohemia,[189] and in the north, the country of Saxony. The eastern part contains, in the south, the country of Hungary, and in the north, the country of Poland. (Hungary and Poland) are separated by the Carpathian Mountains (Balwâṭ). They come from the fourth section, run northwest, and eventually end in the country of Saxony at the boundary of the western half (of this section).

The fourth section of the sixth zone, in the south, contains the country of Jathûliyah,[189a] and, in the north, the country of Russia. They are separated by the Carpathian Mountains, from the beginning of the section in the west to its end in the eastern half. East of the land of Jathûliyah is the country of Jarmâniyah. In the southeast corner, there is the land of Constantinople and the city of Constantinople at the end of the straits coming from the Mediterranean, where it con- I, *141*
nects with the Black Sea. A small portion of the Black Sea

[189] Cf. Hoenerbach, *Deutschland und seine Nachbarländer* . . . , p. 73.

[189a] Lewicki, *La Pologne* . . . , II, 179 f., 39 ff., corrects Jathûliyah to something like Macedonia (Serbia and Bulgaria), and the following Jarmâniyah, which could hardly be Germany, to Rumania, Romania (see n. 531 to Ch. III).

connecting with the straits appears in the southeast corner of the section. The corner between the straits and the Black Sea contains Musannâh [?].[190]

The fifth section of the sixth zone, in the south, contains the Black Sea, stretching due east from the straits at the end of the fourth section. It traverses the whole of this section and part of the sixth section, covering a distance (in length) of 1,300 miles from its beginning and (in width) of 600 miles. Beyond the Black Sea in the south of this section, there remains a piece of the mainland which is oblong in shape and stretches from west to east. The (western portion) of it contains Heracleia[191] on the shore of the Black Sea, (a city) adjacent to the country of al-Baylaqân in the fifth zone. In the east(ern portion) of it is the land of the Alans, with its principal place, Sinope, on the Black Sea. North of the Black Sea in this section is the land of the Bulgars (Burjân),[192] in the west, and in the east the country of Russia. All (these countries) lie on the shores of the Black Sea. The country of Russia surrounds the country of the Bulgars (Burjân), (bordering it) in the east(ern portion) of this section, in the north(ern portion) of the fifth section of the seventh zone, and in the west(ern portion) of the fourth section of the sixth zone.

The sixth section of the sixth zone contains in the west the remainder of the Black Sea, where it turns slightly north. Between the Black Sea and the northern boundary of the section is the country of the Comans.[193] Following the northward direction of the Black Sea, there is the remainder of
I, *142* the country of the Alans, which was at the southern end of the fifth section and which here becomes wider as it extends northwards. In the eastern part of this section, the land of

---

[190] C indicates, however, that the *s* is vowelless. Cf. Minorsky-Marvazî, p. 120, where reference is made to the attempted identifications with Mesemvria and with the Arabic word meaning "dam."

[191] See n. 25 to this chapter, above. Here, the spelling is *Hrqlyh.* In B, this is gained by correction from *Hrqlh.*

[192] See n. 26 to this chapter, above.

[193] Cf. Minorsky, *Ḥudûd*, p. 315.

the Khazars continues, and farther east lies the land of the Burṭâs.[194] In the northeast corner is the land of the Bulgars (Bulghâr). In the southeast corner is the land of Balanjar,[195] which is there traversed by a portion of Mount Shiyâh.[196] These mountains follow (the coast of) the Caspian Sea later on in the seventh section, and, after separating from it, run west across this part (of the sixth section), and enter the sixth section of the fifth zone, where they are linked with the Mountains of the "Gates." The country of the Khazars lies on both sides of them.

The seventh section of the sixth zone contains in the south an area that Mount Shiyâh cuts across, to the western boundary of the section, after leaving the Caspian Sea. It is a portion of the country of the Khazars. East of (the country of the Khazars) is the portion of (the coast of) the Caspian Sea that is traversed by Mount (Shiyâh) in the northeast. Beyond Mount Shiyâh, in the northwest, is the land of the Burṭâs. In the east(ern portion) of the section is the land of the Bashqirs [197] and the Pechenegs,[198] Turkish nations.

The entire southern part of the eighth section of (the sixth zone) is occupied by the land of the Khûlukh Turks.[199] The northern region contains in the west the Stinking Land [200] and, in the east, the land Gog and Magog are said to have laid waste before the Dam was constructed. In this Stinking Land, the Volga, one of the largest rivers in the world, originates. It passes through the country of the Turks and *I, 143*
flows into the Caspian Sea in the seventh section of the fifth zone. The Volga makes many turnings. It originates in a

[194] They have been identified with the Finnish Moksha-Mordva. Cf. Minorsky, *Ḥudûd*, pp. 462 ff.; Minorsky-Marvazî, p. 109; J. Hrbek, *Archiv Orientální*, XXIII (1955), 129.

[195] Cf. A. Zeki Validi Togan, *Ibn Faḍlân's Reisebericht* (Abhandlungen für die Kunde des Morgenlandes, No. 24) (Leipzig, 1939), pp. 68 (n. 2), 191 ff., 298 (n.1).

[196] *Jabal Shiyâh Kû(ya)h.* See n. 185 to this chapter, above.

[197] Cf. Minorsky, *Ḥudûd*, pp. 318 f.

[198] Cf. Minorsky, *Ḥudûd*, pp. 312 ff.; Minorsky-Marvazî, pp. 102 f.

[199] See n. 132 to this chapter, above.

[200] A. Zeki Validi Togan, *op. cit.*, p. 61 (n. 2), suggests that the term originally referred to the color or quality of the soil (black humus).

mountain in the Stinking Land, from which three streams issue and unite to form one river. It flows due west to the boundary of the seventh section of the sixth zone and turns north into the seventh section of the seventh zone, where it flows along the southwestern boundary. It leaves the seventh zone in the sixth section, flows a short distance west, then turns south a second time, and returns to the sixth section of the sixth zone, where a branch comes out of it and flows westward into the Black Sea in that section. (The Volga itself next) passes through a portion of the country of the Bulgars (Bulghâr) in the northeast, leaves the sixth zone in the seventh section to turn south a third time, flows through Mount Shiyâh, traverses the country of the Khazars, and enters the fifth zone in the seventh section. There it flows into the Caspian Sea, in that portion of the southwest corner of the section which is not covered by the sea.

The ninth section of the sixth zone, in the west, contains the country of the Khifshâkh Turks—the Qipchaqs—and the country of the Türgish,[201] who are also Turks. In the east, it contains the country of Magog which is separated from the west by the afore-mentioned surrounding [201a] Qûfâyâ Moun-
I, *144* tains. They start at the Surrounding Sea in the eastern part of the fourth zone, and follow (the Surrounding Sea) to the northern boundary of the zone. There, they leave it and run northwesterly until they enter the ninth section of the fifth zone, where they return to their former due northerly course into the ninth section of (the sixth zone), which they cross from south to north, bearing a little to the west. There, in the middle of (the mountains), is the Dam built by Alexander. The mountains, then, continue due north into the ninth section of the seventh zone, which they traverse from the south on up to the Surrounding Sea in the north. They follow along it from there westward into the fifth section of the seventh zone, where they encounter a portion of the Surrounding Sea to the west.

[201] Cf. Minorsky, *Ḥudûd*, pp. 300 ff.
[201a] Cf. above, p. 158, and below, p. 163.

In the middle of this ninth section is the Dam built by Alexander, as we have said. Correct information about it is found in the Qur'ân. 'Ubaydallâh b. Khurradâdhbih mentioned in his geographical work[202] that al-Wâthiq saw in a dream that the Dam had opened. Frightened, he awakened and sent Salâm (Sallâm) the dragoman to investigate the Dam and to bring back information about it and a description of it, which he did. This is a long story that has nothing to do with the purpose of our work.

The tenth section of the sixth zone is occupied by the country of Magog, extending to the end of (the section). There it borders on a portion of the Surrounding Sea which surrounds (the section) to the east and north. (This portion) is oblong in the north and widens somewhat in the east.

The seventh zone I, *145*

The Surrounding Sea covers most of the seventh zone in the north (from the beginning) to the middle of the fifth section, where it touches the Qûfâyâ Mountains that surround Gog and Magog.

The first and second sections are covered by water, except for the portion not covered by water where the island of England is located, most of which lies in the second section. In the first section, there is a corner of England which extends towards the north. The remainder, with a portion of the sea that encircles it, lies in the second section of the sixth zone. It was mentioned there. The channel connecting England with the mainland is there twelve miles wide. Beyond the island of England, in the north of the second section, is the island of Raslândah,[203] oblong in shape, stretching lengthwise from west to east.

---

[202] Cf. *Kitâb al-Masâlik wa-l-mamâlik*, pp. 162 ff. (text); pp. 124 ff. (tr.). Cf. also F. Rosenthal, *Journal of the American Oriental Society*, LXXI (1951), 138. For Ibn Khurradâdhbih as a source for al-Idrîsî, see n. 57 to this chapter, above.

[203] The vowel of the first syllable is entirely uncertain. Raslândah has been identified with Iceland or Ireland, but is considered an unidentified part of Scotland by W. B. Stevenson, *Scottish Historical Review*, XXVII (1948), 202–4.

Most of the third section of the seventh zone is covered by water, except for an oblong portion in the south that is wider in its eastern part. Here, the land of Poland continues. It was mentioned in connection with the third section of the sixth zone, as lying in the north of it. In the western part of the portion of the sea covering this section, there lies a round, wide (island). It is connected with the mainland by an isthmus in the south, which leads to the land of Poland. North of it is the island of Norway,[204] oblong in shape, which stretches lengthwise from west to east in the north (of the section).

The fourth section of the seventh zone is entirely covered
I, *146* in the north by the Surrounding Sea from the western to the eastern (boundaries of the section). Its southern part is not covered by the sea. To the west, it contains the land of the Finland [?] [205] Turks. To the east lies the country of Tavast,[206] followed by the land of Estonia [?] [207] extending to the eastern boundary of the section. (Estonia) is permanently covered by snow and has little civilization. It borders on the country of Russia in the fourth and fifth sections of the sixth zone.

The fifth section of the seventh zone contains in the west the country of Russia. In the north, (Russia) [207a] extends to where the portion of the Surrounding Sea and the Qûfâyâ Mountains meet, as we have mentioned before. The eastern region of the section contains the continuation of the land of the Comans, which lies on (the shore of) a portion of the Black Sea in the sixth section of the sixth zone. It reaches the Lake of Ṭ–r–m–y [208] in this section. This is a fresh-water

---

[204] Cf. O. J. Tallgren (Tuulio), *Studia Orientalia*, VI 3 (1936), 82 f.

[205] Ibn Khaldûn read *Faymâzak* or the like (perhaps rather, *Qaymâzak*), which suggested something Turkish to him. For the reading Finmârk = Finland, cf. Tallgren, *ibid.*, pp. 119 ff.

[206] Tavastland, Häme. Cf. Tallgren, *ibid.*, pp. 122 ff.

[207] Cf. Tallgren, *ibid.*, pp. 124 f. Ibn Khaldûn's spelling looks like that of Raslândah, in the second section.

[207a] The dots used in C in connection with the verb (*wa-tantahî*) make it certain that Russia (and not the section) is meant. However, the statement is hardly correct. On the sectional map of al-Idrîsî, the "continuation of the land of the Magians" would seem to lie between Russia and the Surrounding Sea.

[208] Tallgren, p. 163, compares Tyrambe, a city on the Sea of Azov, mentioned by Ptolemy v. 8.

lake into which drain many rivers from the mountains south and north of it. In the northeast of this section is the land of the Nabâriyah [209] Turks, which extends to the boundary of the section.

The sixth section of the seventh zone contains in the southwest the continuation of the land of the Comans. In the middle of that region is Lake Gh–n–w–n.[210] This is a fresh-water lake into which drain the rivers from the mountains in the regions east of it. It is constantly frozen because of the severe cold, except for a short while during the summer. East of the country of the Comans is the country of Russia, which started in the northeast of the fifth section of the sixth zone. In the southeast corner of this (the sixth) section, is the I, *147*
remainder of the land of the Bulgars (Bulghâr) that started in the northeastern part of the sixth section of the sixth zone. In the middle of this portion of the land of the Bulgars, there is the point where the Volga makes its first turn to the south, as has been mentioned. The Qûfâyâ Mountains stretch all along the northern boundary of the sixth section from the west to the east.

The seventh section of the seventh zone, in the west, contains the remainder of the land of the Pechenegs, a Turkish nation. Beginning in the northeastern part of the preceding sixth and southwest of this section, it then, in the south, enters the sixth zone. In the east, there is the remainder of the land of the Bashqirs, followed by the remainder of the Stinking Land, which extends to the eastern boundary of the section. The northern boundary of the section is formed by the surrounding Qûfâyâ Mountains stretching (all along it) from the west to the east.

The eighth section of the seventh zone contains in the southwest the continuation of the Stinking Land. East of it is the Sunken [211] Land, a remarkable place. It is an immense

---

[209] Tallgren, pp. 170 ff., reads Biârma, which seems very plausible.

[210] Cf. Minorsky, *Ḥudûd*, pp. 217 f. No identification has been suggested. The MSS seem to have *ʿ-nnûn* or *ʿ-tûn*, but *ʿayn* is certainly not correct.

[211] Lit., "dug."

opening in the earth, so deep that the bottom cannot be reached. The appearance of smoke during the day and of fire at night, which by turns flares up and disappears, leads to the conclusion that the place is inhabited. A river is occasionally seen there. It cuts through it from south to north. In the east of this section is the Waste Country, which borders the Dam. Across the northern limit of the section are the Qûfâyâ
I, 148 Mountains, stretching all along it from the west to the east.

The ninth section of the seventh zone contains in the west the country of the Khifshâkh, that is, the Qipchaqs. It is traversed by the Qûfâyâ Mountains where they turn away from the north (of the section) at the Surrounding Sea and run southeast through the middle (of the section). They then leave (this zone) for the ninth section of the sixth zone and pass across it. There, in the middle of them, is the Dam of Gog and Magog, which we have already mentioned. The eastern part of this section contains the land of Magog, behind the Qûfâyâ Mountains, on the sea. It [211a] is not very wide and is oblong in shape and surrounds it in the east and north.

The tenth section of the seventh zone is entirely covered by the sea.

This finishes the discussion of the world map with the seven zones.

In the creation of heaven and earth and the difference between night and day, there are signs for those who know.[212]

[211a] Grammatically, this pronoun can refer only to the land of Magog, and the second "it" to the sea. However, al-Idrîsî's sectional map shows that it is the sea which is not very wide and oblong in shape and surrounds the land of Magog.

[212] Cf. Qur'ânic verses such as 2.164 (159); 3.190 (187); 45.3–5 (2–4).

THIRD PREFATORY DISCUSSION

The temperate and the intemperate zones. The influence of the air upon the color of human beings and upon many (other) aspects of their condition.

WE[213] HAVE EXPLAINED that the cultivated region of that part of the earth which is not covered by water has its center toward the north, because of the excessive heat in the south and the excessive cold in the north. The north and the south represent opposite extremes of cold and heat. It necessarily follows that there must be a gradual decrease from the extremes toward the center, which, thus, is moderate. The fourth zone is the most temperate cultivated region. The bordering third and fifth zones are rather close to being I, *149* temperate. The sixth and second zones which are adjacent to them are far from temperate, and the first and seventh zones still less so. Therefore, the sciences, the crafts, the buildings, the clothing, the foodstuffs, the fruits, even the animals, and everything that comes into being in the three middle zones are distinguished by their temperate (well-proportioned character). The human inhabitants of these zones are more temperate (well-proportioned) in their bodies, color, character qualities, and (general) conditions.[214] They are found to

[213] Cf. Issawi, pp. 42–46.

[214] Bulaq adds here: "and religions, even including the various (manifestations of) prophecy that are mostly to be found there, in as much as no historical information about prophetic missions in the southern and northern zones has come to our notice. This is because only those representatives of the (human) species who have the most perfect physique and character are distinguished by prophets and messengers. The Qur'ân says [3.110 (106)], 'You are the best

be extremely moderate in their dwellings, clothing, foodstuffs, and crafts. They use houses that are well constructed of stone and embellished by craftsmanship. They rival each other in production of the very best tools and implements. Among them, one finds the natural minerals, such as gold, silver, iron, copper, lead, and tin. In their business dealings they use the two precious metals (gold and silver). They avoid intemperance quite generally in all their conditions. Such are the inhabitants of the Maghrib, of Syria, the two 'Irâqs, Western India (as-Sind), and China, as well as of Spain; also the European Christians nearby, the Galicians,[215] and all those who live together with these peoples or near them in the three temperate zones. The 'Irâq and Syria are directly in the middle and therefore are the most temperate of all these countries.

The inhabitants of the zones that are far from temperate, such as the first, second, sixth, and seventh zones, are also farther removed from being temperate in all their conditions. Their buildings are of clay and reeds. Their foodstuffs are
I, *150* durra and herbs. Their clothing is the leaves of trees, which they sew together to cover themselves, or animal skins. Most of them go naked. The fruits and seasonings of their countries are strange and inclined to be intemperate. In their business dealings, they do not use the two noble metals, but copper, iron, or skins, upon which they set a value for the purpose of business dealings. Their qualities of character, moreover, are close to those of dumb animals. It has even been reported that most of the Negroes of the first zone dwell in caves and thickets, eat herbs, live in savage isolation and do not congregate, and eat each other.[216] The same applies to

group (ever) produced for mankind.' The purpose of this is to have the divine message of the prophets fully accepted."

The available MSS, including E, do not have this passage, which apparently was deleted by Ibn Khaldûn very early as superfluous, in view of such later remarks as those below, pp. 169 and 173.

[215] Bulaq adds: "Romans (Rûm), Greeks. . . ."

[216] See p. 119, above. See also 2:358 f., below.

the Slavs. The reason for this is that their remoteness from being temperate produces in them a disposition and character similar to those of the dumb animals, and they become correspondingly remote from humanity. The same also applies to their religious conditions. They are ignorant of prophecy and do not have a religious law, except for the small minority that lives near the temperate regions. (This minority includes,) for instance, the Abyssinians, who are neighbors of the Yemenites and have been Christians from pre-Islamic and Islamic times down to the present; and the Mâlî, the Gawgaw, and the Takrûr who live close to the Maghrib and, at this time, are Muslims. They are said to have adopted Islam in the seventh [thirteenth] century. Or, in the north, there are those Slav, European Christian, and Turkish nations that have adopted Christianity. All the other inhabitants of the intemperate zones in the south and in the north are ignorant of all religion. (Religious) scholarship is lacking among them. All their conditions are remote from those of I, *151*
human beings and close to those of wild animals. "And He creates what you do not know." [217]

The (foregoing statement) is not contradicted by the existence of the Yemen, the Ḥaḍramawt, al-Aḥqâf, the Ḥijâz, the Yamâmah, and adjacent regions of the Arabian Peninsula in the first and second zones. As we have mentioned,[218] the Arabian Peninsula is surrounded by the sea on three sides. The humidity of (the sea) influences the humidity in the air of (the Arabian Peninsula). This diminishes the dryness and intemperance that (otherwise) the heat would cause. Because of the humidity from the sea, the Arabian Peninsula is to some degree temperate.

Genealogists who had no knowledge of the true nature of things imagined that Negroes are the children of Ham, the son of Noah, and that they were singled out to be black as the result of Noah's curse, which produced Ham's color

[217] Qur'ân 16.8 (8).

[218] See p. 100, above.

and the slavery God inflicted upon his descendants. It is mentioned in the Torah[219] that Noah cursed his son Ham. No reference is made there to blackness. The curse included no more than that Ham's descendants should be the slaves of his brothers' descendants. To attribute the blackness of the Negroes to Ham, reveals disregard of the true nature of heat and cold and of the influence they exercise upon the air (climate) and upon the creatures that come into being in it. The black color (of skin) common to the inhabitants of the first and second zones is the result of the composition of the air in which they live, and which comes about under the influence of the greatly increased heat in the south. The sun is at the zenith there twice a year at short intervals. In (almost) all seasons, the sun is in culmination for a long time. The light of the sun, therefore, is plentiful.[220] People there have (to undergo) a very severe summer, and their skins turn black because of the excessive heat. Something similar hap-
I, 152 pens in the two corresponding zones to the north, the seventh and sixth zones. There, a white color (of skin) is common among the inhabitants, likewise the result of the composition of the air in which they live, and which comes about under the influence of the excessive cold in the north. The sun is always on the horizon within the visual field (of the human observer), or close to it. It never ascends to the zenith, nor even (gets) close to it. The heat, therefore, is weak in this region, and the cold severe in (almost) all seasons. In consequence, the color of the inhabitants is white, and they tend to have little body hair. Further consequences of the excessive cold are blue eyes, freckled skin, and blond hair.

The fifth, fourth, and third zones occupy an intermediate position. They have an abundant share of temperance,[221] which is the golden mean. The fourth zone, being the one

---

[219] Cf. Gen. 9:25. [220] See p. 106, above.

[221] As we can observe throughout this chapter, the same Arabic word is used by Ibn Khaldûn to designate temperateness of climate and living conditions, and the resulting temperance of moral qualities.

most nearly in the center, is as temperate as can be. We have mentioned that before.[222] The physique and character of its inhabitants are temperate to the (high) degree necessitated by the composition of the air in which they live. The third and fifth zones lie on either side of the fourth, but they are less centrally located. They are closer to the hot south beyond the third zone and the cold north beyond the fifth zone. However, they do not become intemperate.

The four other zones are intemperate, and the physique and character of their inhabitants show it. The first and second zones are excessively hot and black, and the sixth and seventh zones cold and white. The inhabitants of the first and second zones in the south are called the Abyssinians, the Zanj, and the Sudanese (Negroes). These are synonyms used to designate the (particular) nation that has turned black. The name "Abyssinians," however, is restricted to those Negroes who live opposite Mecca and the Yemen, and the name "Zanj" is restricted to those who live along the Indian Sea. These names are not given to them because of an (alleged)
descent from a black human being, be it Ham or any one else. I, *153*
Negroes from the south who settle in the temperate fourth zone or in the seventh zone that tends toward whiteness, are found to produce descendants whose color gradually turns white in the course of time. Vice versa, inhabitants from the north or from the fourth zone who settle in the south produce descendants whose color turns black. This shows that color is conditioned by the composition of the air. In his *rajaz* poem on medicine, Avicenna said:

> Where the Zanj live is a heat that changes their bodies
> Until their skins are covered all over with black.
> The Slavs acquire whiteness
> Until their skins turn soft.[223]

---

[222] See p. 167, above.

[223] Cf. the translation of Avicenna's poem by K. Opitz in *Quellen und Studien zur Geschichte der Naturwissenschaften und der Medizin*, VII^{2} (1939), 162, vv. 50–51. The same work appears to have been the subject of a study by H. Jahier and A. Noureddine, in *IVe Congrès de la Fédération des Sociétés*

The inhabitants of the north are not called by their color, because the people who established the conventional meanings of words were themselves white. Thus, whiteness was something usual and common (to them), and they did not see anything sufficiently remarkable in it to cause them to use it as a specific term. Therefore, the inhabitants of the north, the Turks, the Slavs, the Tughuzghuz,[224] the Khazars, the Alans, most of the European Christians, the Gog and Magog are found to be separate nations [225] and numerous races called by a variety of names.

The inhabitants of the middle zones are temperate in their physique and character and in their ways of life. They have all the natural conditions necessary for a civilized life, such as ways of making a living, dwellings, crafts, sciences, political leadership, and royal authority. They thus have had (various manifestations of) prophecy, religious groups,
I, *154* dynasties, religious laws, sciences, countries, cities, buildings, horticulture, splendid crafts, and everything else that is temperate.

Now, among the inhabitants of these zones about whom we have historical information are, for instance, the Arabs, the Byzantines (Rûm), the Persians, the Israelites, the Greeks, the Indians, and the Chinese. When [226] genealogists noted differences between these nations, their distinguishing marks and characteristics, they considered these to be due to their (different) descents. They declared all the Negro inhabitants of the south to be descendants of Ham. They had misgivings about their color and therefore undertook to report the afore-mentioned silly story. They declared all or most of the inhabitants of the north to be the descendants of Japheth, and they declared most of the temperate nations, who in-

de Gynécologie et d'Obstétrique (1952), pp. 50–59, and of a new edition and translation by the same authors, published in 1956.

On the subject of the origin of the black and the white colors of skin, cf. also *Rasâ'il Ikhwân aṣ-ṣafâ'* (Cairo, 1347/1928), I, 233 f.

[224] See n. 139 to this chapter, above.

[225] Bulaq and B have "names."

[226] Cf. Issawi, p. 50.

habit the central regions, who cultivate the sciences and crafts, and who possess religious groups and religious laws as well as political leadership and royal authority, to be the descendants of Shem. Even if the genealogical construction were correct, it would be the result of mere guesswork, not of cogent, logical argumentation. It would merely be a statement of fact. It would not imply that the inhabitants of the south are called "Abyssinians" and "Negroes" because they are descended from "black" Ham. The genealogists were led into this error by their belief that the only reason for differences between nations is in their descent. This is not so. Distinctions between races or nations are in some cases due to a different descent, as in the case of the Arabs, the Israelites, and the Persians. In other cases, they are caused by geographical location and (physical) marks, as in the case of the Zanj (Negroes), the Abyssinians, the Slavs, and the black (Sudanese) Negroes. Again, in other cases, they are caused by custom and distinguishing characteristics, as well as by descent, as in the case of the Arabs. Or, they may be caused by anything else among the conditions, qualities, and features peculiar to the different nations. But to generalize and say I, *155*
that the inhabitants of a specific geographical location in the south or in the north are the descendants of such-and-such a well-known person because they have a common color, trait, or (physical) mark which that (alleged) forefather had, is one of those errors which are caused by disregard, (both) of the true nature of created beings and of geographical facts. (There also is disregard of the fact that the physical circumstances and environment) are subject to changes that affect later generations; they do not necessarily remain unchanged.

This is how God proceeds with His servants.——And verily, you will not be able to change God's way.[227]

---

[227] Cf. Qur'ân 33.62 (62); 35.43 (41); 48.23 (23). The last sentence is also often translated, "You will not find any change in God's way." The translation given in the text appears to represent the meaning as intended by the Prophet. It would be difficult to be certain about Ibn Khaldûn's understanding of the passage. Qur'ân commentators, such as al-Bayḍâwî, combine both translations.

FOURTH PREFATORY DISCUSSION

The influence of the air (climate) upon human character.

WE [228] HAVE SEEN that Negroes are in general characterized by levity, excitability, and great emotionalism. They are found eager to dance whenever they hear a melody.[229] They are everywhere described as stupid. The real reason for these (opinions) is that, as has been shown by philosophers in the proper place, joy and gladness are due to expansion and diffusion of the animal spirit. Sadness is due to the opposite, namely, contraction and concentration of the animal spirit. It has been shown that heat expands and rarefies air and vapors and increases their quantity. A drunken person experiences inexpressible joy and gladness, because the vapor of the spirit in his heart is pervaded by natural heat, which the power of the wine generates in his spirit. The spirit, as a result, expands, and there is joy. Likewise, when those who enjoy a hot bath inhale the air of the bath, so that
I, 156 the heat of the air enters their spirits and makes them hot, they are found to experience joy. It often happens that they start singing, as singing has its origin in gladness.

Now, Negroes live in the hot zone (of the earth). Heat dominates their temperament and formation. Therefore, they have in their spirits an amount of heat corresponding to that in their bodies and that of the zone in which they live. In

[228] Cf. Issawi, pp. 46 f.

[229] Cf. R. Dozy in *Journal asiatique*, XIV 6 (1869), 151, and *Supplément aux dictionnaires arabes*, II, 831*b*. Cf. also A. Mez, *Die Renaissance des Islâms* (Heidelberg, 1922), p. 157. For the theory that expansion and contraction of the animal spirit cause joy or sadness, cf. F. Rosenthal, *Humor in Early Islam*, p. 137.

comparison with the spirits of the inhabitants of the fourth zone, theirs are hotter and, consequently, more expanded. As a result, they are more quickly moved to joy and gladness, and they are merrier. Excitability is the direct consequence.

In the same way, the inhabitants of coastal regions are somewhat similar to the inhabitants of the south. The air in which they live is very much hotter because of the reflection of the light and the rays of (the sun from) the surface of the sea. Therefore, their share in the qualities resulting from heat, that is, joy and levity, is larger than that of the (inhabitants of) cold and hilly or mountainous countries. To a degree, this may be observed in the inhabitants of the Jarîd in the third zone. The heat is abundant in it and in the air there, since it lies south of the coastal plains and hills. Another example is furnished by the Egyptians. Egypt lies at about the same latitude as the Jarîd. The Egyptians are dominated by joyfulness, levity, and disregard for the future. They store no provisions of food, neither for a month nor a year ahead, but purchase most of it (daily) in the market. Fez in the Maghrib, on the other hand, lies inland (and is) surrounded by cold hills. Its inhabitants can be observed to look sad and I, *157* gloomy and to be too much concerned for the future. Although a man in Fez might have provisions of wheat stored, sufficient to last him for years, he always goes to the market early to buy his food for the day, because he is afraid to consume any of his hoarded food.

If one pays attention to this sort of thing in the various zones and countries, the influence of the varying quality of the air upon the character (of the inhabitants) will become apparent. God is "the Creator, the Knowing One." [230]

Al-Mas'ûdî undertook to investigate the reason for the levity, excitability, and emotionalism in Negroes, and attempted to explain it. However, he did no better than to report, on the authority of Galen and Ya'qûb b. Isḥâq al-Kindî, that the reason is a weakness of their brains which

[230] Qur'ân 15.86 (86); 36.81 (81).

results in a weakness of their intellect.[231] This is an inconclusive and unproven statement. "God guides whomever He wants to guide." [232]

---

[231] Cf. al-Mas'ûdî, *Murûj adh-dhahab*, I, 164 f. For the famous ninth-century philosopher al-Kindî, see *GAL*, I, 209 f.; *Suppl.*, I, 372 ff. From among the many recent publications concerning him, we may mention M. 'A. Abû Rîdah, *Rasâ'il al-Kindî al-falsafîyah* (Cairo, 1369–72/1950–53). Cf. also R. Walzer, "The Rise of Islamic Philosophy," *Oriens*, III (1950), 1–19.

[232] Qur'ân 2.142 (136), 213 (209), etc.

FIFTH PREFATORY DISCUSSION

Differences with regard to abundance and scarcity of food in the various inhabited regions ('umrân) *and how they affect the human body and character.*

IT [233] SHOULD BE KNOWN that not all the temperate zones have an abundance of food, nor do all their inhabitants lead a comfortable life. In some parts, the inhabitants enjoy an abundance of grain, seasonings, wheat, and fruits, because the soil is well balanced and good for plants and there is an abundant civilization. And then, in other parts, the land is strewn with rocks, and no seeds or herbs I, *158*
grow at all. There, the inhabitants have a very hard time. Instances of such people are the inhabitants of the Ḥijâz and the Yemen, or the Veiled Ṣinhâjah who live in the desert of the Maghrib on the fringes of the sandy deserts which lie between the Berbers and the Sudanese Negroes. All of them lack all grain and seasonings. Their nourishment and food is milk and meat. Another such people is the Arabs who roam the waste regions. They may get grain and seasonings from the hills, but this is the case only at certain times and is possible only under the eyes of the militia which protects (the hill country). Whatever they get is little, because they have little money. They obtain no more than the bare necessity, and sometimes less, and in no case enough for a comfortable or abundant life. They are mostly found restricted to milk, which is for them a very good substitute for wheat. In spite of this, the desert people who lack grain and season-

[233] Cf. Issawi, pp. 47–49.

ings are found to be healthier in body and better in character than the hill people who have plenty of everything. Their complexions are clearer, their bodies cleaner, their figures more perfect and better, their characters less intemperate, and their minds keener as far as knowledge and perception are concerned. This is attested by experience in all these groups. There is a great difference in this respect between the Arabs and Berbers (on the one hand), and the Veiled (Berbers) [234] and the inhabitants of the hills (on the other). This fact is known to those who have investigated the matter.

As to the reason for it, it may be tentatively suggested that a great amount of food and the moisture it contains generate pernicious superfluous matters in the body, which, in turn, produce a disproportionate widening of the body, as
1, *159* well as many corrupt, putrid humors. The result is a pale complexion and an ugly figure, because the person has too much flesh, as we have stated. When the moisture with its evil vapors ascends to the brain, the mind and the ability to think are dulled. The result is stupidity, carelessness, and a general intemperance. This can be exemplified by comparing the animals of waste regions and barren habitats, such as gazelles, wild cows (*mahâ*), ostriches, giraffes, onagers, and (wild) buffaloes (cows, *baqar*), with their counterparts among the animals that live in hills, coastal plains, and fertile pastures. There is a big difference between them with regard to the glossiness of their coat, their shape and appearance, the proportions of their limbs, and their sharpness of perception.[235] The gazelle is the counterpart of the goat, and the giraffe that of the camel; the onagers and (wild) buffaloes (cows) are identical with (domestic) donkeys and oxen (and cows). Still, there is a wide difference between them. The only reason for it is the fact that the abundance of food in the hills produces pernicious superfluous matters and corrupt humors in the bodies of the domestic animals, the influence

---

[234] Ibn Khaldûn has just mentioned them as belonging to the former group. Cf. A. Schimmel, *Ibn Chaldun*, p. 26 (n. 9).

[235] Cf. pp. 282 f., below.

of which shows on them. Hunger, on the other hand, may greatly improve the physique and shape of the animals of the waste regions.

The same observations apply to human beings. We find that the inhabitants of fertile zones where the products of agriculture and animal husbandry as well as seasonings and fruits are plentiful, are, as a rule, described as stupid in mind and coarse in body. This is the case with those Berbers who have plenty of seasonings and wheat, as compared with those who lead a frugal life and are restricted to barley or durra, such as the Maṣmûdah Berbers and the inhabitants of as-Sûs and the Ghumârah. The latter are superior both intellectually and physically. The same applies in general to the inhabitants of the Maghrib who have plenty of seasonings and fine wheat, I, *160*
as compared with the inhabitants of Spain in whose country butter is altogether lacking and whose principal food is durra. The Spaniards are found to have a sharpness of intellect, a nimbleness of body, and a receptivity for instruction such as no one else has. The same also applies to the inhabitants of rural regions of the Maghrib as compared with the inhabitants of settled areas and cities. Both use many seasonings and live in abundance, but the town dwellers only use them after they have been prepared and cooked and softened by admixtures. They thus lose their heaviness and become less substantial. Principal foods are the meat of sheep and chickens. They do not use butter because of its tastelessness. Therefore the moisture in their food is small, and it brings only a few pernicious superfluous matters into their bodies. Consequently, the bodies of the urban population are found to be more delicate than those of the inhabitants of the desert who live a hard life. Likewise, those inhabitants of the desert who are used to hunger are found to have in their bodies no superfluous matters, thick or thin.

It should be known that the influence of abundance upon the body is apparent even in matters of religion and divine worship. The frugal inhabitants of the desert and those of settled areas who have accustomed themselves to hunger and

to abstinence from pleasures are found to be more religious and more ready for divine worship than people who live in luxury and abundance. Indeed, it can be observed that there are few religious people in towns and cities, in as much as people there are for the most part obdurate and careless, which is connected with the use of much meat, seasonings,
I, *161* and fine wheat. The existence of pious men and ascetics is, therefore, restricted to the desert, whose inhabitants eat frugally. Likewise, the condition of the inhabitants within a single city can be observed to differ according to the different distribution of luxury and abundance.

It can also be noted that those people who, whether they inhabit the desert or settled areas and cities, live a life of abundance and have all the good things to eat, die more quickly than others when a drought or famine comes upon them. This is the case, for instance, with the Berbers of the Maghrib and the inhabitants of the city of Fez and, as we hear, of Egypt (Cairo). It is not so with the Arabs who inhabit waste regions and deserts, or with the inhabitants of regions where the date palm grows and whose principal food is dates, or with the present-day inhabitants of Ifrîqiyah whose principal food is barley and olive oil, or with the inhabitants of Spain whose principal food is durra and olive oil. When a drought or a famine strikes them, it does not kill as many of them as of the other group of people, and few, if any, die of hunger. As a reason for that, it may tentatively be suggested that the stomachs of those who have everything in abundance and are used to seasonings and, in particular, to butter, acquire moisture in addition to their basic constitutional moisture, and (the moisture they are used to) eventually becomes excessive. Then, when (eating) habits are thwarted by small quantities of food, by lack of seasonings, and by the use of coarse food to which it is unaccustomed, the stomach, which is a very weak part of the body and for that reason considered one of the vital parts, soon dries out and contracts. Sickness and sudden death are prompt consequences to the man whose stomach is in this condition. Those who die in famines are victims of their previous habitual state of satiation, not of the hunger that now afflicts them for the first time. In those who are accustomed to thirst [235a] and to doing without seasonings and butter, the basic moisture, which is good for all natural foods, always stays within its proper limits and does not increase. Thus, their stomachs are not affected by dryness or intemperance in consequence of a change of nourishment. As a rule, they escape the fate that awaits others on account of the abundance of their food and the great amount of seasonings in it. I, *162*

The basic thing to know is that foodstuffs, and whether to use or not to use them, are matters of custom. Whoever accustoms himself to a particular type of food that agrees with him becomes used to it. He finds it painful to give it up or to make any changes (in his diet), provided (the type of food) is not something that does not fulfill the (real) purpose of food, such as poison, or alkaloids,[236] or anything excessively intemperate. Whatever can be used as food and is agreeable may be used as customary food. If a man accustoms himself to the use of milk and vegetables instead of wheat, until (the use of them) gets to be his custom, milk and vegetables become for him (his habitual) food, and he definitely has no longer any need for wheat or grains.

The same applies to those who have accustomed themselves to suffer hunger and do without food. Such things are reported about trained (ascetics). We hear remarkable things about men of this type. Those who have no knowledge of things of the sort can scarcely believe them. The explanation lies in custom. Once the soul gets used to something, it becomes part of its make-up and nature, because (the soul) is able to take on many colorings. If through gradual training it has become used to hunger, (hunger) becomes a natural custom of the soul.

The assumption of physicians that hunger causes death is

[235a] *ʿAymah* means, in particular, "thirsting after milk."

[236] Cf. Bombaci, p. 444. *Yattūʿ* may be specifically Euphorbia, but below, p. 183, it is used as a general term for alkaloids taken as cathartics.

I, 163 not correct, except when a person is exposed suddenly to hunger and is entirely cut off from food. Then, the stomach is isolated, and contracts an illness that may be fatal. When, however, the amount of food one eats is slowly decreased by gradual training, there is no danger of death. The adepts of Sufism practice (such gradual abstinence from food). Gradualness is also necessary when one gives up the training. Were a person suddenly to return to his original diet, he might die. Therefore, he must end the training as he started it, that is, gradually.

We personally saw a person who had taken no food for forty or more consecutive days. Our *shaykhs* were present at the court of Sultan Abû l-Ḥasan [237] when two women from Algeciras and Ronda were presented to him, who had for years abstained from all food. Their story became known. They were examined, and the matter was found to be correct. The women continued this way until they died. Many persons we used to know restricted themselves to (a diet of) goat's milk. They drank from the udder sometime during the day or at breakfast.[237a] This was their only food for fifteen years. There are many others (who live similarly). It should not be considered unlikely.

It should be known that everybody who is able to suffer hunger or eat only little, is physically better off if he stays hungry than if he eats too much. Hunger has a favorable influence on the health and well-being of body and intellect, as we have stated. This may be exemplified by the different
I, 164 influence of various kinds of food upon the body. We observe that those persons who live on the meat of strong, large-bodied animals grow up as a (strong and large-bodied) race. Comparison of the inhabitants of the desert with those of settled areas shows this. The same applies to persons who live on the milk and meat of camels. This influences their

[237] The Merinid of Fez who ruled from 1331 to 1351 and was the predecessor of Abû 'Inân, under whom Ibn Khaldûn came to Fez.

[237a] Or, "when breaking their fast." This may be the preferable translation, even though Ibn Khaldûn does not seem to think of ascetics in this passage.

character, so that they become patient, persevering, and able to carry loads, as is the case with camels.[238] Their stomachs also grow to be healthy and tough as the stomachs of camels. They are not beset by any feebleness or weakness, nor are they affected by unwholesome food, as others are. They may take strong (alkaloid) cathartics unadulterated to purify their bellies, such as, for instance, unripe colocynths, *Thapsia garganica*, and Euphorbia. Their stomachs do not suffer any harm from them. But if the inhabitants of settled areas, whose stomachs have become delicate because of their soft diet, were to partake of them, death would come to them instantly, because (these cathartics) have poisonous qualities.

An indication of the influence of food upon the body is a fact that has been mentioned by agricultural scholars[239] and observed by men of experience, that when the eggs of chickens which have been fed on grain cooked in camel dung, are set to hatch, the chicks come out as large as can be imagined. One does not even have to cook any grain to feed them; one merely smears camel dung on the eggs set to hatch, and the chickens that come out are extremely large. There are many similar things.

When we observe the various ways in which food exercises an influence upon bodies, there can be no doubt that hunger also exercises an influence upon them, because two opposites follow the same pattern with regard to exercising an influence or not exercising an influence. Hunger influences I, *165*
the body in that it keeps it free from corrupt superfluities and mixed fluids that destroy body and intellect, in the same way that food influenced the (original) existence of the body.

God is omniscient.

---

[238] This remark occurs in an appendix to L. Mercier's translation of Ibn Hudhayl, *La Parure des cavaliers* (Paris, 1924), p. 355. The author of the appendix, however, is not the fourteenth-century Ibn Hudhayl, or any other old author, but the modern Muḥammad Pasha. Cf. *GAL, Suppl.*, II, 887.

[239] That is, people familiar with works on agriculture such as the *Falâḥah an-Nabaṭîyah;* cf. 3:151 f., below. Cf. also n. 151 to Ch. IV.

SIXTH PREFATORY DISCUSSION

The various types of human beings who have supernatural perception either through natural disposition or through exercise, preceded by a discussion of inspiration and dream visions.

IT SHOULD BE KNOWN that God has chosen certain individuals. He honored them by addressing (them). He created them so that they might know Him. He made them connecting links between Himself and His servants. (These individuals) are to acquaint their fellow men with what is good for them and to urge them to let themselves be guided aright. They are to make it their task to keep (their fellow men) out of the fire of Hell and to show them the path to salvation. The knowledge that God gave these individuals, and the wonders He manifested through their statements, indicated that there exist things beyond the reach of man, that can be learned only from God through the mediation of (these individuals), and that (these individuals themselves) cannot know unless God instructs them in them. Muḥammad said: "Indeed, I know only what God taught me." It should be known that the information they give is intrinsically and necessarily true, as will become clear when the reality of prophecy is explained.

The sign by which this type of human being can be recognized is that, in the state of inspiration, they seem to be removed from those who are present. This is accompanied by a feeling of being choked that looks like swooning or unconsciousness but has nothing to do with either.[239a] In reality, it

[239a] Cf. 2:423, below.

is an immersion in (and) encounter with the spiritual kingdom, the result of perceptions congenial to them but entirely foreign to the (ordinary) perceptions of men. (These extraor- I, *166*
dinary perceptions) are then brought down to the level of human perceptions in the form of some speech sound the person (who receives the revelation) hears and is able to to understand, or in the form of an individual delivering the divine message to him. This state (of remoteness) then leaves him, but he retains the content of the given revelation. When Muḥammad was asked about revelation, he said: "At times, it comes to me like the ringing of a bell. This affects me most. When it leaves me, I have retained what was said. At other times, the angel appears to me in the form of a man. He talks to me, and I retain the things he says." [240] During that (process, the person who receives the revelation) shows inexplicable signs of strain and choking. A tradition says: "There was some anxiety in connection with the revelation that he had to calm." [241] 'Â'ishah said: "The revelation would come to him on very cold days. Nevertheless, when it left him, there was sweat on his forehead." [242] God says in the Qur'ân: "We shall lay upon you a heavy message." [243]

Because the act of receiving revelations leads to such conditions, the polytheists used to accuse the prophets of being possessed (by jinn). They said: "He has a *jinni* as his doubleganger, or companion." The outward appearance of the condition they observed misled them. "He whom God leads astray has no guide." [244]

Another sign by which inspired human beings can be recognized is the fact that (even) before receiving revelations, they are good, innocent, and averse to any blameworthy, sinful action. This is what is meant by *'iṣmah* (immunity from sin and error, infallibility). It looks as if, by nature, they were disposed to avoid and shun blameworthy actions, and as if

[240] Cf. al-Bukhârî, *Ṣaḥîḥ*, ed. Krehl (Leiden, 1862–1908), I, 4.
[241] Cf. *ibid.*, I, 6; IV, 490. Cf. also *Concordance*, III, 78*b*. Cf. p. 201, below.
[242] Cf. al-Bukhârî, *Ṣaḥîḥ*, I, 4.
[243] Qur'ân 73.5 (5).
[244] Qur'ân 13.33 (33); 39.23 (24), 36 (37); 40.33 (35).

such actions were the negation of their very nature. According to (the sound tradition of) the *Ṣaḥîḥ*, when Muḥammad was a young man he carried stones with his uncle al-ʿAbbâs for the restoration of the Kaʿbah. He was carrying them in his cloak, and thus, he was undressed. (As this was unbecoming,) he fell down in a swoon that lasted until he was covered with his cloak.[245] (On another occasion,) he was invited to a wedding party where there was much merrymaking. He fell
I, 167 fast asleep, and slept until the sun rose. Thus, he had nothing to do with the things the others did on that occasion. God kept him from all that. It was his nature. He even avoided food that was considered objectionable. Thus, he never touched onions or garlic. When he was asked about it, he said: "I communicate with One with whom you do not communicate."[246]

Attention should be paid (in this connection) to what Muḥammad told Khadîjah about the revelation when he first experienced it, and she wanted to know what it was like. She asked him to embrace her, and when he did so, it left him. Khadîjah, thereupon, said that it was an angel, and not a devil, meaning that (a devil) would not come close to a woman. She also asked him what garments he liked best (for the angel) to wear during the revelation, and he replied, "White and green ones." Whereupon Khadîjah said that it was an angel, meaning that green and white are the colors of goodness and of the angels. Black, on the other hand, is the color of evil and of the devils. There are other such stories.

Another sign by which (inspired human beings can be recognized) is the fact that they make propaganda for religion and divine worship by means of prayer, almsgiving, and

[245] This does not refer to Muḥammad's decision in the quarrel over the honor of replacing the Black Stone. Legend tells that he had it placed upon a garment and lifted into position by several rival groups. It refers to Muḥammad's carrying ordinary stones to help with the restoration. Cf. al-Bukhârî, *Ṣaḥîḥ*, I, 400. For variations in the story, see, for instance, Ibn Kathîr, *Bidâyah*, II, 287 f., or Ibn Sayyid-an-nâs, *ʿUyûn al-athar* (Cairo, 1356/1937–38), I, 44 f., where we also find the story of the wedding. Cf. also T. Andrae, *Die Person Muhammeds . . .* , pp. 124 ff.; I. Goldziher in *EI*, *s.v.* "ʿIṣma."

[246] Cf. al-Bukhârî, *Ṣaḥîḥ*, I, 219; IV, 440 f. Cf. also *Handbook*, p. 155*b*.

chastity. Khadîjah, as well as Abû Bakr, took that (conduct) as proof of Muḥammad's truthfulness. They did not need any further proof of his mission beyond his conduct and character. According to (the sound tradition of) the *Ṣaḥîḥ*, when Heraclius received the Prophet's letter in which he was asked to become a Muslim, he is said to have called the Qurashites who could be found in his country, among them Abû Sufyân, and to have asked them about Muḥammad's condition. One of the questions he asked concerned the things Muḥammad commanded them to do. Abû Sufyân's reply was: "Prayer, almsgiving, gifts, and chastity." Similar replies were given to all the other questions Heraclius asked. Heraclius' comment was: "If it is all really as you say, he is a prophet and he I, *168*
will take possession of this very ground upon which I am standing." [247] The "chastity" to which Heraclius referred is *'iṣmah* (immunity from sin and error, infallibility). It is worth noting that Heraclius considered *'iṣmah* and propaganda for religion and divine worship as proofs of the genuineness of a prophetical mission, and did not require a miracle. This story, therefore, is proof that these qualities are among the signs of prophecy.

Another sign by which (inspired human beings can be recognized) is the fact that they have prestige among their people. According to (the sound tradition of) the *Ṣaḥîḥ*, God "sent no prophet who did not enjoy the protection of his people." [248] Another recension reads: ". . . who did not enjoy wealth among his people." [249] This is al-Ḥâkim's correction of the two *Ṣaḥîḥs*.[250] According to (the sound tradition of) the *Ṣaḥîḥ*, Abû Sufyân replied to Heraclius' question con-

---

[247] Cf. al-Bukhârî, *Ṣaḥîḥ*, I, 7 f., and, for further references, *Handbook*, p. 97. Cf. also below, 3:42.

[248] Cf. also pp. 322 and 414, below.

[249] Cf. *Concordance*, I, 291*a*. Since the reference to "wealth" was inappropriate in the case of Muḥammad, "wealth" has been explained to mean "great number," or "protection, power, influence."

[250] Abû 'Abdallâh Muḥammad b. 'Abdallâh, al-Ḥâkim an-Nîsâbûrî, 321–405 [933–1014]. Cf. *GAL*, I, 166; *Suppl.*, I, 276 f. Cf. his *Mustadrak 'alâ ṣ-Ṣaḥîḥayn* [of al-Bukhârî and Muslim] (Hyderabad, 1334–42/1915–23), II, 561.

cerning Muḥammad's standing among the Qurashites, (by saying) that he had prestige among them. Whereupon Heraclius said, "Whenever messengers are sent, they have prestige among their people." [251] That means that (such a man) has group feeling and influence which protect him from harm at the hands of unbelievers, until he has delivered the messages of his Lord and achieved the degree of complete perfection with respect to his religion and religious organization that God intended for him.

Another [252] sign by which (inspired human beings can be recognized) is that they work wonders which attest to their truthfulness. "Wonders" [253] are actions the like of which it is impossible for other human beings to achieve. They are, therefore, called "miracles." They are not within the ability of men, but beyond their power. There is a difference of opinion as to how they occur and as to how they prove the truth of the prophets. Speculative theologians base themselves on the doctrine of the "voluntary agent" [254] and say that miracles occur through the power of God, and not through the action of the prophet. The Mu'tazilah maintain that human actions proceed from man himself. Still, miracles do not belong to the type of actions that human beings per-
I, *169* form. According to all (schools), the prophet's place in the performance of miracles is (circumscribed by) the "advance challenge" (*taḥaddî*) [255] which he offers by divine permission.

---

[251] The term *aḥsâb* is used in this story in al-Bukhârî, *Ṣaḥîḥ*, III, 215; *Concordance*, I, 464*b*, ll. 32 f.

[252] The text from here to p. 192, l. 22, is found in C on an inserted slip.

[253] *Khawâriq* are things that "break through" the ordinary course of affairs. *Mu'jizah* is "miracle" in the sense of something done by a prophet in confirmation of his mission. The terms may be used as synonyms, but, in general, "wonders" are considered inferior to "miracles," where both terms occur together.

[254] Cf. 2:372, below, and *Rasâ'il Ikhwân aṣ-ṣafâ'*, III, 319 f.

[255] *Taḥaddî*, literally, means that the prophet seeks the people out, that he "goes to them and challenges them (*taḥaddâhum*)," by announcing his impending miracle and daring them to perform something similar. Ibn Khaldûn explains the term as "the claim made in advance that the miracle will happen in agreement with the prophetic announcement"; cf. 3:100 and 170, below. Instead of "advance challenge," another suitable translation would be "advance information." Already in his *Lubâb al-Muḥaṣṣal* (Tetuán,

That is, the prophet uses the miracles before they occur as proof of the truth of his claims. They thus take the place of an explicit statement from God to the effect that a particular prophet is truthful, and they are definite proof of the truth. An evidential miracle is the combination of a "wonder" and the "advance challenge" (*taḥaddî*) that (announces) it. Therefore, the latter constitutes part of the miracle.

The notion of the speculative theologians (concerning the "voluntary agent") is self-explanatory. (The "voluntary agent") is (just) one. For they hold that "essential" means (being just one).[255a] According to the notion of the speculative theologians, the "advance challenge" (*taḥaddî*) is what makes the difference between (miracles, on the one hand), and acts of divine grace and sorcery (on the other), since (the latter) two need no confirmation of their truthfulness. The "advance challenge" (if it occurs at all in these cases) exists (in them) only by chance.

In the opinion of those who admit the existence of acts of divine grace, if an "advance challenge" (*taḥaddî*) occurs in connection with them, and if it is proof of them, it is proof only of saintliness, which is different from prophecy. This is why Professor Abû Isḥâq[256] and others did not admit the occurrence of wonders as acts of divine grace. They wanted to avoid confusion between the "advance challenge" (*taḥaddî*) of the saint and prophecy. We, however, have (just) shown

---

1952), p. 111, Ibn Khaldûn used the same definition of "miracle" he repeats here at greater length.

For the problem of *taḥaddî* in Muslim theology, see, for instance, al-Bâqillânî, *Tamhîd*, pp. 114, 121 f., 126–29; *idem*, *I'jâz al-Qur'ân* (Cairo, 1315/1898), pp. 116 f.; Imâm al-Ḥaramayn, *Irshâd* (Cairo, 1369/1950), p. 313; Ibn Ḥazm, *Faṣl* (Cairo, 1317–21), V, 2 and 7 f.

[255a] Following de Slane's doubtful suggestions, we might translate the very difficult passage as follows: "Therefore, the latter constitutes part of the miracle, or, to use the expression of speculative theologians, is its specific quality. It is one, for (speculative theologians) hold that (oneness) is the meaning of essential." There are, however, more objections to this translation than to the one given in the text.

[256] Ibrâhîm b. Muḥammad al-Isfarâyinî, d. 418 [1027]. Cf. *GAL*, *Suppl.*, I, 667; Abû l-Muẓaffar al-Isfarâyinî, *at-Tabṣîr fî d-dîn* (Cairo, 1359/1940), p. 119. Cf. also pp. 223, 393, and 3:100, below.

that there is a difference between the two. The "advance challenge" (*taḥaddî*) of a saint is concerned with other things than that of a prophet. There can be no doubt that the report on the authority of Professor Abû Isḥâq is not clear and has often led to denial of (the possibility) that the wonders of the prophets could have been wrought by (saints), on the grounds that each of the two groups has its own kind of wonders.

The Mu'tazilah do not admit the occurrence of acts of divine grace, because wonders do not belong to the actions of man that are customary and allow of no break (in the customary process).

It is absurd to believe that miracles could be produced fraudulently by a liar. According to the Ash'arites, this is absurd because the essential part of a miracle is defined as "confirmation of truthfulness and right guidance." Were a miracle to occur under the contrary conditions, proof would become doubt, guidance misguidance, and, I might add, the
I, *170* confirmation of truthfulness, untruth. Realities would become absurdities, and the essential qualities would be turned upside down. Something, the occurrence of which would be absurd, cannot be possible.[257]

According to the Mu'tazilah, fraudulent miracles are absurd, because it is improper for proofs to turn into doubts and for guidance to turn into misguidance. Such, therefore, could not come from God.

The philosophers hold that wonders are acts of the prophet (who performs them), even though they have no place in the power (of the prophet himself). This is based upon their doctrine that (there exists) an essential and necessary (causality) and that events develop out of each other according to conditions and reasons that (always) come up anew and, in the last instance, go back to the Necessary *per se* that acts *per se* and not by choice. In their opinion, the prophetical soul has special essential qualities which produce wonders, with the help of the power of (the Necessary *per se*)

---

[257] Cf., for instance, al-Isfarâyin , p. 104.

and the obedience of the elements to Him for purposes of generation. (The role of) the prophet (in this process), in their opinion, is that through those qualities that God put into him, he is by nature fitted for being active among (all) created things, whenever he addresses himself to them and concentrates on them. They hold that wonders are wrought by the prophet (himself), whether there is an "advance challenge" (*taḥaddî*) or not. They are evidence of the prophet's truthfulness, in as much as they prove that he is active among the created things, such activity constituting a special quality of the prophetic soul, not because they take the place of a clear assertion of his truthfulness. In their opinion, therefore, (wonders) are no definitive proof (of the prophet's truthfulness), as they are in the opinion of the speculative theologians. "Advance awareness," for them, does not constitute part of the miracle. It does not stand out as the thing that differentiates (miracles) from acts of divine grace. They hold that (miracles) are differentiated from sorcery by the fact that a prophet is by nature fitted for good actions and averse to evil deeds. Therefore, he could not do evil through the wonders he works. The opposite is the case with the sorcerer. All his actions are evil and done for evil purposes.[258] Further, (miracles) are differentiated from acts of divine grace by the fact that the wonders of a prophet are of an unusual character, such as ascending to heaven, passing through solid bodies, I, *171*
reviving the dead, conversing with angels, and flying through the air.[259] The wonders of a saint, on the other hand, are of a lower order, such as making much out of little, speaking about something that will happen in the future, and similar things inferior to the power of action of prophets. A prophet can produce the wonders of saints, but a saint is not able to produce anything like the wonders of prophets. This has been confirmed by the Sufis in what they have written about the mystic path and reported of their ecstatic experiences.

Now that this has been established, it should be known

---

[258] Cf. 3:167, below. [259] Cf. 3:279, below.

that the evidence of the noble Qur'ân, which was revealed to our Prophet, is the greatest, noblest, and clearest miracle. Wonders are as a rule wrought by a prophet separately and apart from the revelation he receives. The miracle comes as evidence for it(s truthfulness). This is obvious. The Qur'ân, on the other hand, is in itself the claimed revelation. It is itself the wondrous miracle. It is its own proof. It requires no outside proof, as do the other wonders wrought in connection with revelations. It is the clearest proof that can be, because it unites in itself both the proof and what is to be proved. This is the meaning of Muḥammad's statement, "Every prophet was given signs likely to provide reassurance for mankind. What I have been given is a revelation that was revealed to me. Therefore, I hope to have the greatest number of followers on the day of resurrection." [259a] He refers to the fact that a miracle which is identical with the revelation (confirmed by it), is of such clarity and force of evidence that it will be found truthful, because of its clarity, by the greatest number of people. Therefore, many are those who consider (the Prophet) truthful and believe. They are the "followers," the nation of Islam.

And God, praised be He, knows better.

I, *172* All [260] this indicates that the Qur'ân is alone among the divine books, in that our Prophet received it directly [261] in the words and phrases in which it appears. In this respect, it differs from the Torah, the Gospel, and other heavenly books. The prophets received them in the form of ideas during the state of revelation. After their return to a human state, they expressed those ideas in their own ordinary words. There-

---

[259a] Cf. al-Bukhârî, *Ṣaḥîḥ*, III, 391; IV, 419.

[260] The text from here to p. 194, l. 3, below, appears (to my knowledge) only in MS. Ragib Paşa 978, fol. 47*a* (and in the Paris edition). In the MS. Ragib Paşa, the text is contained in a marginal note accompanied by the remark: "I found it this way in the manuscript written in the handwriting of the excellent Qaṭarî, following the autograph (*'alâ khaṭṭ*) of the author." Cf. p. xcix, above, and p. 230, below.

[261] *Matlûw* "recited"; cf. pp. 260, 437, and 3:113, 284, below.

fore, those books do not have "inimitability." [262] Inimitability is restricted to the Qur'ân. The other prophets received their books in a manner similar to that in which our Prophet received (certain) ideas that he attributed to God, such as are found in many traditions.[263] The fact that he received the Qur'ân directly, in its literal form, is attested by the following statement of Muḥammad on the authority of his Lord who said: "Do not set your tongue in motion to make haste with (the revelation of the Qur'ân). It is up to us to put it together and to recite it." [264]

The reason for the revelation of these verses was Muḥammad's haste to study the (Qur'ânic) verses, because he feared that he might forget (them), and because he wished to keep the directly and literally revealed text in memory. God guaranteed him that He (Himself) would "keep" it in the following verse: "We revealed the reminder, and we are keeping it." [265] This is the meaning of "keeping" which is peculiar to the Qur'ân. The meaning of it is not what the common people think. (Their opinion) is far off the mark.

Many verses of the Qur'ân show that He directly and literally revealed the Qur'ân, of which every *sûrah* is inimitable. Our Prophet wrought no greater miracle than the Qur'ân and the fact that he united the Arabs in his mission. "If you had expended all the treasures on earth, you would have achieved no unity among them. But God achieved unity among them." [266]

This should be known. It should be pondered. It will then be found to be correct, exactly as I have stated. One should

---

[262] It should not be forgotten that *i'jâz* "inimitability" is formed from the same root as *mu'jizah* "miracle." Both convey the idea of something that ordinary mortals are too weak to achieve, and by which they are confounded.

[263] The *ḥadîth qudsî* "holy traditions." Cf. S. M. Zwemer in *Der Islam*, XIII (1923), 53–65, and L. Massignon, *Essai sur les origines du lexique technique de la mystique musulmane* (2d ed.; Paris, 1954), pp. 135 f. Cf. also 3:88, below.

[264] Qur'ân 75.16 f. (16 f.).

[265] Qur'ân 15.9 (9).

[266] Qur'ân 8.63 (64).

I, *173* also consider the evidence that lies in the superiority of Muḥammad's rank over that of the other prophets and in the exaltedness of his position.

We shall now give an explanation of the real meaning of prophecy as interpreted by many thorough scholars. We shall then mention the real meaning of soothsaying, dream vision, divination, and other supernatural ways of perception. We say:

(*The real meaning of prophecy*)

It [267] should be known that we—May God guide you and us [268]—notice that this world with all the created things in it has a certain order and solid construction. It shows nexuses between causes and things caused, combinations of some parts of creation with others, and transformations of some existent things into others, in a pattern that is both remarkable and endless. Beginning with the world of the body and sensual perception, and therein first with the world of the visible elements, (one notices) how these elements are arranged gradually and continually in an ascending order, from earth to water, (from water) to air, and (from air) to fire. Each one of the elements is prepared to be transformed into the next higher or lower one, and sometimes is transformed. The higher one is always finer than the one preceding it. Eventually, the world of the spheres is reached. They are finer than anything else. They are in layers which are interconnected, in a shape which the senses are able to perceive only through the existence of motions. These motions provide some people with knowledge of the measurements and positions of the spheres, and also with knowledge of the existence of the essences beyond, the influence of which is noticeable in the spheres through the fact (that they have motion).

---

[267] Cf. Issawi, pp. 164 f. For the discussion that follows here, see below, 2:419 ff. and 3:70 ff.

[268] For the use of such formulas to introduce the communication of esoteric knowledge, cf. n. 925 to Ch. vi.

One should then look at the world of creation. It started out from the minerals and progressed, in an ingenious, gradual manner, to plants and animals. The last stage[269] of minerals is connected with the first stage of plants, such as herbs and seedless plants. The last stage of plants, such as palms and vines, is connected with the first stage of animals, I, *174*
such as snails and shellfish which have only the power of touch. The word "connection" with regard to these created things means that the last stage of each group is fully prepared to become the first stage of the next group.

The animal world then widens, its species become numerous, and, in a gradual process of creation, it finally leads to man, who is able to think and to reflect. The higher stage of man is reached from the world of the monkeys, in which both sagacity and perception are found, but which has not reached the stage of actual reflection and thinking. At this point we come to the first stage of man after (the world of monkeys). This is as far as our (physical) observation extends.

Now, in[270] the various worlds we find manifold influences. In the world of sensual perception there are certain influences of the motions of the spheres and the elements. In the world of creation there are certain influences of the motions of growth and perception. All this is evidence of the fact that there is something that exercises an influence and is different from the bodi(ly substances). This is something spiritual. It is connected with the created things, because the various worlds must be connected in their existence. This spiritual thing is the soul, which has perception and causes motion. Above the soul there must exist something else that gives the soul the power of perception and motion, and that is also connected with it. Its essence should be pure perception and absolute intellection. This is the world of the angels. The soul, consequently, must be prepared to exchange humanity for angelicality, in order actually to become part of the angelic species at certain times in the flash of a moment. This

---

269 Lit., "horizon."

270 Cf. Issawi, pp. 170–74.

happens after the spiritual essence of the soul has become perfect in actuality, as we shall mention later on.

I, *175* (The soul) is connected with the stage next to it, as are all the orders of the *existentia*, as we have mentioned before. It is connected both upward and downward. Downward, it is connected with the body. Through (the body, the soul) acquires the sense perceptions by which it is prepared for actual intellection.[271] Upward, it is connected with the stage of the angels. There, it acquires scientific and supernatural perceptions, for knowledge of the things that come into being exists timelessly in the intellections of (the angels). This is in consequence of the well-constructed order of existence mentioned above, which requires that the essences and powers of (the world of existence) be connected with one another.

The human soul cannot be seen, but its influence is evident in the body. It is as if all (the body's) parts, in combination or separately, were organs of the soul and its powers. The powers of action are touching with the hand, walking with the foot, speaking with the tongue, and the total combined motion with the body.

The powers of sensual perception are graded and ascend to the highest power, that is, the power of thinking, for which there exists the term "rational power." Thus, the powers of external sense perception, with the organs of vision, hearing, and all the other (organs), lead up to inward (perception).

The first (inward sense) is the "common sense,"[272] that is, the power that simultaneously perceives all objects of sensual perception, whether they belong to hearing, seeing, touching, or anything else. In this respect, it differs from the power of external sense perception, as the objects of sensual perception do not all crowd upon external sense perception at one and the same time.

The common sense transfers (the perceptions) to the

---

[271] Cf. p. 215, below.

[272] *Al-Ḥiss al-mushtarik:* κοινὴ αἴσθησις. Cf. A.-M. Goichon, *Vocabulaires comparés d'Aristote et d'Ibn Sînâ* (Paris, 1939), p. 7; S. van den Bergh (tr.), *Averroes' Tahafut al-Tahafut* (E. J. W. Gibb Memorial Series, N.S. No. 19) (London, 1954), I, 333 ff.

imagination, which is the power that pictures an object of sensual perception in the soul, as it is, abstracted from all external matter. The organ for the activity of these two powers (common sense and imagination) is the first cavity of the brain. The front part of that cavity is for the common sense, and the back part for the imagination. I, *176*

Imagination leads up to the estimative power [273] and the power of memory. The estimative power serves for perceiving (abstract) ideas that refer to individualities, such as the hostility of Zayd, the friendship of 'Amr, the compassion of the father, or the savagery of the wolf. The power of memory serves as a repository for all objects of perception, whether they are imagined or not. It is like a storehouse that preserves them for the time when they are needed. The organ for the activity of these two powers is the back cavity of the brain. The front part of that cavity is for the estimative power, and the back for the power of memory.

All these powers then lead up to the power of thinking. Its organ is the middle cavity of the brain. It is the power that causes reflection to be set in motion and leads toward intellection. The soul is constantly moved by it, as the result of its constitutional desire to (think). It wants to be free from the grip of power [274] and the human kind of preparedness. It wants to proceed to active intellection by assimilating itself to the highest spiritual group (that of the angels), and to get into the first order of the *spiritualia* by perceiving them without the help of bodily organs. Therefore, the soul is constantly moving in that direction. It exchanges all humanity and human spirituality for angelicality of the highest stage, without the help of any acquired faculty but by virtue of a primary natural disposition that God has placed in it.

As far as this (process) is concerned, human souls are of three kinds. One is by nature too weak to arrive at spiritual

---

[273] Cf. A.-M. Goichon, p. 40, and F. Rahman, *Avicenna's Psychology* (Oxford & London, 1952), pp. 79 ff.

[274] That is, the lower human powers.

I, *177* perception. Therefore, it is satisfied to move downwards toward the perceptions of the senses and imagination and the formation of ideas with the help of the power of memory and the estimative power, according to limited rules and a special order. In this manner, people acquire perceptive and apperceptive [275] knowledge, which is the product of thinking in the body. All this is (the result of the power of) imagination and limited in extent, since from the way it starts it can reach the primary (*intelligibilia*) but cannot go beyond them. Also, if they are corrupt, everything beyond them is also corrupt.[276] This, as a rule, is the extent of human corporeal perception. It is the goal of the perceptions of scholars. It is in it that scholars are firmly grounded.

A (second) kind (of soul), through thinking, moves in the direction of spiritual intellection and (a type of) perception that does not need the organs of the body, because of its innate preparedness for it. The perceptions of this kind of soul extend beyond the primary (*intelligibilia*) to which primary human perception is restricted, and cover the ground of inward observations, which are all intuitive.[277] They are unlimited as to their beginning and their end. They are the perceptions of saints, of men of mystical learning and divine

---

[275] *Taṣawwur* and *taṣdîq*. Cf. A.-M. Goichon, *Lexique de la langue philosophique d'Ibn Sînâ*, pp. 191 ff., 179 f.

[276] Cf. Bombaci, p. 444.

[277] The term *wijdân*, with the adjective *wijdânî*, is used repeatedly by Ibn Khaldûn; see below, pp. 207, 230, 2:48, 3:71 f., 83, 85, 89, 101, 155, 252, 295, and 360. Basically, Ibn Khaldûn's understanding of it corresponds to the one commonly found in philosophical literature. For instance, al-Îjî in his commentary on the *Mukhtaṣar* of Ibn al-Ḥâjib, one of the legal works that Ibn Khaldûn studied in his boyhood, distinguishes five types of perceptions: (1) Internal observations, called *wijdânîyât*, i.e., those not requiring the services of the intellect, such as hunger, thirst, and pain; animals also possess this type of perception. (2) Primary (intellectual) observations. (3) Observations by means of the senses. (4) Observations by experience. And (5) continuous (traditional) knowledge. Cf. al-Îjî, *Sharḥ 'alâ Mukhtaṣar al-Muntahâ li-Ibn al-Ḥâjib* (Constantinople, 1307/1889–90), p. 19.

Ibn Khaldûn thus uses the term for "intuition, observation by means of inner, emotional feeling." It should be noted, however, that he also uses *wijdân* parallel with *wujûd* "existence" in *'Ibar*, V, 437; VI, 7. The meaning of "existing" for *wijdânî* may, for instance, apply below, n. 1027 to Ch. VI. Cf. also 2:340, below.

knowledge. The blessed obtain them after death, in Purgatory (*barzakh*).[278]

A (third) kind (of soul) is by nature suited to exchange humanity altogether, both corporeal and spiritual humanity, for angelicality of the highest stage, so that it may actually become an angel in the flash of a moment, glimpse the highest group within their own stage, and listen to essential speech [279] and divine address during that moment. (Individuals possessing this kind of soul) are prophets. God implanted and I, *178*
formed in them the natural ability to slough off humanity in that moment which is the state of revelation. God freed them from the lets and hindrances of the body, by which they were afflicted as human beings. He did this by means of *'iṣmah* (immunity from sin and error, infallibility) and straightforwardness, which He implanted in them and which gave them that particular outlook, and by means of a desire for divine worship which He centered in them and which converges from all sides toward that goal. They thus move toward the (angelic) stage, sloughing off humanity at will, by virtue of their natural constitution, and not with the help of any acquired faculty or craft.

(The prophets) move in that direction, slough off their humanity, and, once among the highest group (of angels), learn all that may there be learned. They then bring what they have learned back down to the level of the powers of human perception, as this is the way in which it can be transmitted to human beings. At times, this may happen in the form of a noise the prophet hears. It is like indistinct words from which he derives the idea conveyed to him. As soon as the noise has stopped, he retains and understands (the idea). At other times, the angel who conveys (the message) to the prophet appears to him in the form of a man who talks to him, and the prophet comprehends what he says. Learning the message from the angel, reverting to the level of human perception, and understanding the message conveyed to him

---

[278] Cf. M. Schreck in *EI, s.v.* "Barzakh," and 3:69 ff., below.

[279] Cf. 3:39, below.

—all this appears to take place in one moment, or rather, in a flash. It does not take place in time, but everything happens simultaneously. Therefore, it appears to happen very quickly. For this reason, it is called *waḥy* ("revelation"), because the root *wḥy* has the meaning "to hasten."[280]

It should be known that in the judgment of thorough scholars, the first (degree), the state of noise, is that of
I, 179 prophets who are not sent as messengers. The second degree, the state when an angel appears in the form of a man who addresses the prophet, is that of prophets who are sent as messengers. Therefore, it is more perfect than the first (degree). This is the meaning of the tradition in which the Prophet explained revelation, in reply to a question by al-Ḥârith b. Hishâm.[281] Asked how the revelation came to him, Muḥammad replied, "At times, it comes to me like the ringing of a bell. This affects me most. When it leaves me, I have retained what was said. At other times, the angel appears to me in the form of a man. He talks to me, and I retain the things he says." The first (case) affected him more, being the first attempt to advance from potential to actual contact (with the supernatural). Thus, it was somewhat difficult. When the Prophet returned, in this case, to the level of human perceptions, all he retained was auditory (impressions). All others were difficult. When the revelation was repeated and the messages became numerous, contact (with the supernatural) became easy. When the Prophet returned to the level of human perceptions, now all his senses—and especially the clearest sense, that of vision—conveyed (the revelation).

The use of the perfect tense "I have retained" in the first case, and of the present tense "I retain" in the second, is a meaningful stylistic distinction. In both cases, the words that were spoken (during the revelation) came in a disguise. In the first case, they appeared in the form of "noise," which,

---

[280] Etymology is known to be one of the weakest spots in ancient and medieval scholarship. Actually, *wḥy* appears to be related to Aramaic *ḥwy* "to show, inform" and to Palmyrenian words such as *mwḥ'* and *twḥyt*.

[281] Cf. Ibn Ḥajar, *Tahdhîb*, II, 161 f. Cf. also p. 185, above.

according to accepted usage, is something different from speech. Muḥammad indicated that understanding and comprehension followed immediately upon it after it had stopped. He properly used the perfect tense, which is suitable (to signify) what has ended or stopped, in order to indicate comprehension at the moment he perceived that (the noise) had ended and stopped.[282] In the second case, the angel appeared in the form of a man who addressed the Prophet and spoke to him. Comprehension (in this case) ran parallel with speech. Therefore, Muḥammad properly used the present tense, which of necessity expresses renewed (repeated) activity. I, *180*

It should be known that, in general, the state of revelation presents difficulties and pains throughout. This has been indicated in the Qur'ân: [283] "We shall lay upon you a heavy message." 'Â'ishah said: "There was some anxiety in connection with the revelation, with which he had to struggle." She said: "The revelation would come to him on very cold days. Nevertheless, when it left him, there was sweat on his forehead." This is the reason for his well-known remoteness (from sensual perception) and the choking (feeling) when in that condition, of which the Prophet used to speak. The reason, as we have established, is that revelation means leaving one's humanity, in order to attain angelic perceptions and to hear the speech of the soul.[284] This causes pain, since it means that an essence leaves its own essence and exchanges its own stage for the ultimate stage (of the angels). This is the meaning of the choking feeling which Muḥammad referred to in connection with the beginning of revelation in

---

[282] Comprehension, in this case, was an action of the past that happened but once, hence the perfect. Whereas in the other case it was a continuous and repeated action in the past, hence the present. This distinction is, of course, based upon the supposed meaning of Arabic tenses, which do not correspond exactly with English tenses. The Arabic "perfect" is a completed action; the Arabic present/future, for which Arabists use the more correct term "imperfect," may refer to repeated action.

[283] For this quotation from the Qur'ân and the following two traditions, see p. 185, above. Cf. also 3:73, below.

[284] Cf. 3:39, below.

his statement: "And he (Gabriel) choked me until it became too much for me; then he released me. Then he said, 'Read,' and I replied, 'I cannot read.' "[285] He did this a second and a third time, as the tradition tells.

Gradual habituation to (the process of revelation) brings some relief, as compared to how it was before. It is for this reason that the earliest passages, *sûrahs*, and verses of the Qur'ân, revealed to Muḥammad in Mecca, are briefer than those revealed to him in Medina. One may compare the tradition about how the ninth *sûrah* (*Sûrat al-Barâ'ah*) was revealed, during the expedition to Tabûk. The whole of this (long *sûrah*), or most of it, was revealed to Muḥammad while he was riding his camel.[286] Before this, when he was in Mecca, part of one of the shortest *sûrahs* in the latter part of the Qur'ân[287] was revealed on one occasion, and the rest on another occasion. Also, one of the last revelations received in
I, *181* Medina was the "Verse of the Religion,"[288] which is very long. Before this, in Mecca, the verses revealed were short, like those of the *sûrahs* *ar-Raḥmân*, *adh-Dhâriyât*, *al-Muddaththir*, *aḍ-Ḍuḥâ*, and *al-'Alaq*,[289] and similar *sûrahs*. This may serve as criterion for distinguishing the Meccan *sûrahs* and verses from the Medinese. God leads to that which is correct. This is the quintessence of prophecy.

(*Soothsaying*)

Soothsaying (*kahânah*) is also one of the particular qualities of the human soul. This is as follows.

In the previous discussion, we have always stated that the human soul is prepared to exchange its humanity for the spirituality that lies above (humanity). Human beings have an intimation of that (exchange) in prophets who are by

---

[285] Cf. also p. 261, below. [286] Cf. 3:73, below.

[287] The term *al-mufaṣṣal* used by Ibn Khaldûn refers to the *sûrahs* near the end of the Qur'ân, beginning with *sûrah* 49 (or, according to certain other scholars, with some *sûrah* close to it). Cf. as-Suyûṭî, *Itqân* (Cairo, 1317/1899), I, 65 (Ch. 18).

[288] Rather, ". . .Debt," Qur'ân 2.282 (Svetlana Batsieva).

[289] *Sûrahs* 55, 51, 74, 93, and 96, respectively.

nature fitted to achieve it. It has been established that they neither need acquired qualities for that (exchange), nor are they dependent on any help from perceptions, notions (*taṣawwur*), bodily activities, be they speech or motion, or anything else. It is (with them) a natural change from humanity to angelicality in the flash of a moment.

If this is so and if such preparedness exists in human nature, logical classification requires that there must be another kind of human beings, as inferior to the first kind as anything that has something perfect as its opposite, must be inferior to that (perfect) opposite. Independence from all help in (achieving contact with the supernatural) is the opposite of dependence on help in connection with it. They are two very different things.

Now, the classification of the world of existence requires that there must be a kind of human beings fitted by nature for the process of thinking voluntarily under the impulse of their rational power, whenever that power has a desire for it. (But the rational power) is not by nature capable of (the process of supernatural perception). Thus, when its weakness prevents (the rational power) from (contact with the supernatural), it is natural for (the rational power) to get involved I, *182*
with particulars, either of sensual perception or of the imagination, such as transparent bodies, animal bones, speech in rhymed prose, or whatever bird or animal may present itself. (A person whose rational power is thus engaged) attempts to retain such sensual or imaginary perceptions, since he depends on their help in attaining the supernatural perception he desires. They give him a sort of assistance.

The power which in (such persons) constitutes the starting point of supernatural perception is soothsaying. The souls of such persons are inferior by nature and unable to attain perfection. Therefore, they have a better perception of particulars than of universals. They get involved with the former and neglect the latter. Therefore, the power of imagination is [290] most strongly developed in those persons, be-

[290] Cf. J. Blau, *An Adverbial Construction* (Jerusalem, 1977), p. 13.

cause it is the organ of the particulars. (The particulars) completely pervade (the power of the imagination),[291] both in the sleeping and the waking state. They are ever ready and present in it. The power of imagination brings (the particulars) to the attention of (those persons) and serves as a mirror in which they are seen constantly.

The soothsayer is not able to achieve perfection in his perception of the *intelligibilia*, because the revelation he receives is inspired by devils. The highest state this type of person can reach is to achieve disregard for the senses, with the help of rhymed prose and the use of words of an identical structure at the end of successive cola,[292] and (thereby) to attain an imperfect contact of the sort described (with supernatural things). From that motion and the foreign support that accompanies it, his heart receives some inspiration to express itself in words. The soothsayer, thus, often speaks the truth and agrees with reality. Often, however, what he says are falsehoods, because he supplements his deficiency with something foreign to, different from, and incompatible with, his perceptive essence. Thus, truth and falsehood are jumbled together in him, and he is not trustworthy. He often takes refuge in guesses and hypotheses, because, in his self-
I, *183* deception, he desires to have (supernatural) perception and is willing to cheat those who ask him (for information).

Men who use such rhymed prose are distinguished by the name of soothsayers (*kâhin*, pl. *kuhhân*). They rank highest among their kind. Muḥammad said, regarding something of the sort, "This belongs to the rhymed prose of the soothsayers." [293] The use of the genitive construction ("rhymed prose of") indicates that Muḥammad considered rhymed

[291] Cf. (Pseudo-)Majrîṭî, *Ghâyah*, ed. H. Ritter (Leipzig & Berlin, 1933), p. 84.

[292] For *muwâzanah*, a term of literary criticism, see n. 1576 to Ch. vi.

[293] Ibn Khaldûn seems to be thinking of Muḥammad's statement about someone belonging to the brotherhood (*ikhwân*) of the soothsayers. Cf. *Concordance*, I, 35b. Since Muḥammad himself used *saj'* "rhymed prose" in the Qur'ân, there was a tendency among Muslim scholars not to regard it as the exclusive property of soothsayers. See, for example, Majd-ad-dîn Ibn al-Athîr, *Nihâyah*, IV, 43.

prose a distinctive (mark of the soothsayer). He also questioned Ibn Ṣayyâd,[294] in order to find out about him, and he asked him how that thing came to him. Ibn Ṣayyâd replied: "It comes to me in the form of both truth and falsehood." Whereupon Muḥammad said, "You are confused with regard to the matter." He meant that prophecy is characterized by truthfulness and can in no way be affected by falsehood. For prophecy is a direct and independent contact of the essence of the prophet with the most high group (the angels). Because of his weakness, the soothsayer depends on the help of foreign notions (*taṣawwur*). (These foreign notions) enter into his perception and mingle with the perception toward which he aspires. He thus becomes confused by them. So it is that falsehood makes its way to his (door). It is, therefore, impossible (for his activity) to be prophecy.

We have stated that the highest rank of soothsaying is the state in which rhymed prose is used, because the support derived from rhymed prose is lighter than any other support, such as that derived from vision or hearing. Such light support (as is given by the use of rhymed prose) points to nearness of contact and perception and to a certain freedom from weakness.

Some people assume that soothsaying of this type stopped with the time of prophecy, as the result of the stoning of the devils with meteors, in view of the prophetic mission, which occurred in order to keep them away from heavenly information, as is mentioned in the Qur'ân.[295] The soothsayers had received heavenly information from the devils, and now, from the day on which the devils were stoned, soothsaying ceased
to exist. There is no proof for this contention. Soothsayers I, 184
obtain knowledge from their own souls as well as from the devils, as we have established. Furthermore, the verse of the

[294] The story of Ibn Ṣayyâd is found in al-Bukhârî, *Ṣaḥîḥ*, II, 261 f.; IV, 153. Cf. also *Concordance*, II, 61*a*, ll. 12 f. Nothing definite is known about Ibn Ṣayyâd who is said to have become a Muslim and to have died in 63 [682]. Cf. *Lisân al-'Arab*, IV, 251, and G. Levi Della Vida, *Annales de l'Institut d'Etudes Orientales*, XII (Algiers, 1954), p. 27 (n. 60).

[295] Cf. Qur'ân 15.17 ff. (17 ff.); 37.7 ff. (7 ff.).

Qur'ân shows only that the devils were kept away from one particular kind of heavenly information, namely, that connected with the (prophetic) mission. They were not kept from other information. Also, soothsaying stopped only in view of the existence of prophecy. It may afterwards have returned to its former state. This would seem to be an obvious (fact), because all such (supernatural) perceptions are in abeyance at the time of prophecy, just as stars and lamps lose their brilliance beside the sun. Prophecy is the greatest light, in whose presence every other light is obscured or disappears.

Some philosophers think that (soothsaying) exists only in view of prophecy, and then stops.[296] This happens at each occurrence of prophecy. They argue that the existence of prophecy needs a particular constellation that makes it necessary. The perfection of that constellation coincides with the perfection of the particular prophecy to which the constellation has reference. As long as the constellation is imperfect, it requires the existence of some imperfect related element. This is the meaning of "soothsayer," as we have established it. The perfect state of the constellation is preceded by an imperfect one, which requires the existence of one or more soothsayers. When the constellation reaches perfection, the prophet's existence reaches perfection. The constellations that point to the existence of a(n inferior) element such as soothsaying have passed by, and soothsaying ceases to exist.[297] This (theory) is based upon the assumption that any part of a particular constellation must exercise part of the influence that the constellation (in its perfect state) would exercise. This assumption is not fully acceptable. It may be that a particular constellation exercises its influence only when it has taken on its proper form. If some aspects are
I, *185* missing, it may exercise no influence whatever, not even, as they say, a restricted influence.

Soothsayers who are a prophet's contemporaries are aware of the prophet's truthfulness and the significance of his

[296] Cf. also p. 224, below. [297] Cf. Bombaci, p. 445.

miracle, since they derive some intuitive[298] experience from prophecy, such as every human being derives from sleep. Intellectual awareness of this relationship is stronger in the soothsayer than in the sleeper. What prevents soothsayers from acknowledging the truthfulness of the prophet, and causes them to deny (him), is simply their misguided desire to be prophets themselves. This leads them to spiteful opposition. This happened to Umayyah b. Abî ṣ-Ṣalt, who desired to be a prophet. It also happened to Ibn Ṣayyâd, Musaylimah, and others.[299] When faith gains the upper hand and they stop aspiring to become prophets themselves, they make the most faithful of believers. This happened to Ṭulayḥah al-Asadî and Qârib b. al-Aswad.[300] The actions of these two men in the Muslim conquest show that they were faithful believers.

(*Dream visions*)

Real dream vision is an awareness on the part of the rational soul in its spiritual essence, of glimpse(s) of the forms of events. While the soul is spiritual, the forms of events have actual existence in it, as is the case with all spiritual essences. The soul becomes spiritual through freeing itself from bodily matters and corporeal perceptions. This happens to the soul (in the form of) glimpse(s) through the agency of sleep, as we shall mention. Through (these glimpses) (the soul) gains the knowledge of future events that it desires and by means of which it regains the perceptions that (properly) belong to it. When this process is weak and indistinct, the soul applies to it allegory and imaginary pictures, in order to gain (the desired knowledge). Such allegory, then, necessitates interpretation.[301] When, on the

[298] Cf. n. 277 to this chapter, above.

[299] For Umayyah b. Abî ṣ-Ṣalt, a famous poet of Muḥammad's time, cf. *GAL*, I, 27 f.; *Suppl.*, I, 55 f. For Ibn Ṣayyâd, cf. n. 294, above. For the pseudo-prophet Musaylimah, cf. F. Buhl in *EI*, *s.v.* "Musailima."

[300] For the pseudo-prophet Ṭulayḥah, cf. V. Vacca in *EI*, *s.v* "Ṭulaiḥah." For Qârib, cf. Ibn Ḥajar, *Iṣâbah* (Calcutta, 1856–73), III, 434 ff., No. 1164.

[301] *Ta'bîr* specifically is the interpretation of dreams, to which a special discussion is devoted, 3:103 ff., below.

I, 186 other hand, this process is strong, it can dispense with allegory. Then, no interpretation is necessary, because (the process) is then free from imaginary pictures.

The occurrence, in the soul, of such glimpse(s) is caused by the fact that the soul is potentially a spiritual essence, supplemented by the body and the perceptions of (the body). Its essence, thus, eventually becomes pure intellection, and its existence becomes perfect in actuality. The soul, now, is a spiritual essence having perception without the help of any of the bodily organs. However, among the *spiritualia*, it is of a lower species than the angels, who inhabit the highest stage, and who never had to supplement their essences with corporeal perceptions or anything else. The preparedness (for spirituality) comes to (the soul) as long as it is in the body. There is a special kind (of preparedness), such as saints have, and there is a general kind common to all human beings. This is what "dream vision" means.

In the case of the prophets, this preparedness is a preparedness to exchange humanity for pure angelicality, which is the highest rank of *spiritualia*. It expresses itself repeatedly during revelations. It exists when (the prophet) returns to the level of corporeal perceptions. Whatever perception (the prophet) has at that moment is clearly similar to what happens in sleep, even though sleep is much inferior to (revelation).

Because of this similarity, the Lawgiver (Muḥammad) defined dream vision as being the forty-sixth or, according to other recensions, the forty-third, or the seventieth—part of prophecy.[302] None of these (fractions) is meant to be taken literally. They are to indicate the great degree of difference between the various stages (of supernatural perception). This is shown by the reference to "seventy" in one of the

---

[302] Cf. al-Bukhârî, *Ṣaḥîḥ*, IV, 348 ff.; *Concordance*, II, 409*b*, ll. 21 f.; I, 296*b*, last line. Cf. also, for instance, Ibn Abî Zayd, ***Risâlah***, pp. 322, 326. Fractions mentioned by Ibn Ḥazm, ***Faṣl***, V, 20, are one twenty-sixth, one forty-sixth, and one-seventieth. Cf. also 3:103 and 107, below.

recensions. The number "seventy" is used by the Arabs to express (the idea of) a large number.

The reference to "forty-six" has been explained by some scholars as follows. In its beginning, the revelation took the form of dream visions for six months, that is, for half a year. The whole duration of (Muḥammad's) prophecy in Mecca I, *187*
and Medina was twenty-three years. Half a year, thus, is one forty-sixth (of the whole duration of prophecy). This theory cannot be verified. The given (figures) apply only to Muḥammad. How can we know whether they also applied to other prophets? Moreover, this (theory) describes the relationship of prophecy to dream vision in point of time only, and does not consider the true character of dream visions in relation to the true character of prophecy. If our previous remarks were clear, it will be realized that the fraction refers to the relationship between the primary preparedness general to all mankind, and the close preparedness limited to the (prophets) and natural to them.

The remote preparedness is commonly found among human beings. However, there are many obstacles and hindrances that prevent man from translating it into actuality. One of the greatest hindrances is the external senses. God, therefore, created man in such a way that the veil of the senses could be lifted through sleep, which is a natural function of man. When that veil is lifted, the soul is ready to learn the things it desires to know in the world of Truth (*ḥaqq*). At times, it catches a glimpse of what it seeks. Therefore, the Lawgiver (Muḥammad) classified dream visions among "the bearers of glad tidings" (*mubashshirât*). He said, "Nothing remains of prophecy except the bearers of glad tidings." Asked what they were, he said: "A good dream vision, beheld by—or shown to—a good man." [303]

The reason why the veil of the senses is lifted in sleep is as follows.[304] The perceptions and actions of the rational soul

---

[303] Cf. al-Bukhârî, *Ṣaḥîḥ*, IV, 346. Cf. also 3:103, below.

[304] For the following discussion, cf. 3:104 ff., below.

are the result of the corporeal animal spirit. This spirit is a
I, *188* fine vapor which is concentrated in the left cavity of the heart, as stated in the anatomical works of Galen and others.[305] It spreads with the blood in the veins and arteries, and makes sensual perception, motion, and all the other corporeal actions possible. Its finest part goes up to the brain. There, it is tempered by the coldness of (the brain), and it effects the actions of the powers located in the cavities of the brain. The rational soul perceives and acts only by means of that vaporous spirit. It is connected with it. (This connection is) the result of the wisdom of creation which requires that nothing fine can influence anything coarse. Of all the corporeal matters, only the animal spirit is fine. Therefore, it is receptive to the influence of the essence, which differs from it only in respect of corporeality, that is, the rational soul. Thus, through the medium of (the animal spirit), the influence of the rational soul reaches the body.

We have stated before [306] that the perception of the rational soul is of two kinds. There is an external perception through the five senses, and an inward perception through the cerebral powers. All these perceptions divert the rational soul from the perception for which [307] it is prepared by nature, (namely, that) of the essences of the *spiritualia*, which are higher than it.

Since the external senses are corporeal, they are subject to weakness and lassitude as the result of exertion and fatigue, and to spiritual exhaustion through too much activity. Therefore, God gave them the desire to rest, so that perfect perception may be renewed afterwards. Such (rest) is accomplished by the retirement of the animal spirit from all the external senses and its return to the inward sense. This process is supported by the cold that covers the body during the night. Under the influence of the cold of the night, the natural heat repairs to the innermost recesses of the body

[305] Cf. also p. 74, above. [306] Cf. p. 196, above. [307] *Leg. alladhî.*

and turns from its exterior to the interior. It thus guides its vehicle, the animal spirit, into the interior of the body. This is the reason why human beings, as a rule, sleep only at night. I, 189

The spirit, thus, withdraws from the external senses and returns to the inward powers. The preoccupations and hindrances of sensual perception lessen their hold over the soul, and it now returns to the forms that exist in the power of memory. Then, through a process of synthesis and analysis, (these forms) are shaped into imaginary pictures. Most of these pictures are customary ones, because (the soul) has (only) shortly before withdrawn from the conventional objects of sensual perception. It now transmits them to the common sense, which combines all the five external senses, to be perceived in the manner of (those) five senses. Frequently, however, the soul turns to its spiritual essence in concert with the inward powers. It then accomplishes the spiritual kind of perception for which it is fitted by nature. It takes up some of the forms of things that have become inherent in its essence at that time. Imagination seizes on those perceived forms, and pictures them in the customary molds either realistically or allegorically. Pictured allegorically, they require interpretation. The synthetic and analytic activity which (the soul) applies to the forms in the power of memory, before it perceives its share of glimpses (of the supernatural), is (what is called in the Qur'ân) "confused dreams." [308]

According to (the sound tradition of) the *Ṣaḥîḥ*, the Prophet said, "There are three kinds of dream visions. There are dream visions from God, dream visions from the angels, and dream visions from Satan." [309] This threefold

[308] *Aḍghâth al-aḥlâm.* Qur'ân 12.44 (44); 21.5 (5). Cf. also 2:420 and 3:105, below.

[309] The references in the *Ṣaḥîḥ* of al-Bukhârî seem to mention only a twofold division of dreams, those from God and those from Satan. But cf. *Concordance,* I, 296*b*, last line.

Polydore Virgil, who was born in the century in which Ibn Khaldûn died, distinguished in his *De prodigiis* three varieties of dreams: divine, human, and daemonic. Cf. D. Hay, *Polydore Virgil* (Oxford, 1952), p. 41.

division agrees with our preceding statement. Clear dream visions are from God. Allegorical dream visions, which call
1, *190* for interpretation, are from the angels. And "confused dreams" are from Satan, because they are altogether futile, as Satan is the source of futility.

This is what "dream vision" really is, and how it is caused and encouraged by sleep. It is a particular quality of the human soul common to all mankind. Nobody is free from it. Every human being has, more than once, seen something in his sleep that turned out to be true when he awakened. He knows for certain that the soul must necessarily have supernatural perception in sleep. If this is possible in the realm of sleep, it is not impossible in other conditions, because the perceiving essence is one and its qualities are always present. God guides toward the truth.

("*Dream words*")

Note: Most of the (afore-mentioned supernatural perception by means of dream visions) occurs to human beings unintentionally and without their having power over it. The soul occupies itself with a thing. As a result, it obtains that glimpse (of the supernatural) while it is asleep, and it sees that thing. It does not plan it that way.

In the *Ghâyah*[310] and other books by practitioners of magic, reference is made to words that should be mentioned on falling asleep so as to cause the dream vision to be about the things one desires. These words are called by (the magicians) "dream words" (*al-ḥâlûmah*). In the *Ghâyah*, Maslamah mentioned a dream word that he called "the

---

[310] The *Ghâyat al-ḥakîm* ascribed to the famous tenth-century Spanish scientist Maslamah b. Aḥmad al-Majrîṭî. Cf. *GAL*, I, 243; *Suppl.*, I, 431 f. Modern scholarship has shown that the *Ghâyah* (on sorcery) and the *Rutbat al-ḥakîm* (on alchemy) are pseudepigraphical. Ibn Khaldûn makes much use of these works later on in his discussion of the two sciences mentioned. The reference here is to *Ghâyah*, ed. H. Ritter (Studien der Bibliothek Warburg) (Berlin, 1933), pp. 187 ff. The term *ḥâlûmah* "dream word" as such is not mentioned there. It is derived from Aramaic *ḥâlômâ* "dream" (rather than from the Hebrew form *ḥâlôm*). Cf. also M. Plessner in *Der Islam*, XVI (1927), 95.

dream word of the perfect nature." It consists of saying, upon falling asleep and after obtaining freedom of the inner senses and finding one's way clear (for supernatural perception), the following non-Arabic words: *tamâghis ba'dân yaswâdda waghdâs nawfanâ ghâdis.*[311] The person should then mention what he wants, and the thing he asks for will be shown to him in his sleep.

A man is said to have done this after he had eaten but I, *191*
little and done *dhikr* exercises [312] for several nights. A person appeared to him and said, "I am your perfect nature." A question was put to that person, and he gave the man the information he desired.

With the help of these words, I have myself had remarkable dream visions, through which I learned things about myself that I wanted to know. However, (the existence of such dream words) is no proof that the intention to have a dream vision can produce it. The dream words produce a preparedness in the soul for the dream vision. If that preparedness is a strong one, (the soul) [312a] will be more likely to obtain that for which it is prepared. A person may arrange for whatever preparedness he likes, but that is no assurance that the thing for which preparations have been made will actually happen. The power to prepare for a thing is not the same as power over the thing (itself). This should be known and considered in similar cases. God "is wise and knowing." [313]

(*Other types of divination*)

In the human species we find individuals who foretell things before they take place. They have a special natural

[311] These magical words seem to be Aramaic and may have sounded something like this: *Tmaggesh b'eddân swâdh* (?) *waghdhash nawmthâ ghâdhesh,* "You say your incantations at the time of conversation (?), and the accident of sleep happens." The "perfect nature" is also discussed at length by Fakhr-ad-dîn ar-Râzî, *as-Sirr al-maktûm;* cf. 3:164, below. Cf. also H. Ritter, in *Vorträge der Bibliothek Warburg* 1921–1922, pp. 121 f.

[312] Cf. n. 471 to Ch. VI, below.

[312a] Unless one reads *kânat,* instead of *kâna,* the only possible antecedent would be "preparedness," but it ought to be "soul," as indicated above.

[313] Qur'ân 6.18 (18), 73 (73); 34.1 (1).

qualification for it. Through that qualification, they are distinguished from all other human beings. They do not have recourse to a craft for their predictions, nor do they get them with the help of astral influences or anything else. Their forecasts are the necessary result of their natural disposition. Among such people are diviners (*'arrâf*); men who gaze into transparent bodies such as mirrors or bowls of water; men who examine the hearts, livers, and bones of animals; men who draw auguries from birds and wild animals; and men who cast pebbles, grains of wheat, or (date) pits.[314] All these things are found among mankind; no one can deny
I, *192* them or be ignorant of them. Statements concerning supernatural things are also placed upon the tongues of the insane, who are thus able to give information about (supernatural things). Sleeping and dying persons, being about to die or to fall asleep, likewise speak about supernatural things. Men who have followed Sufi training have, as is well known, as acts of divine grace, obtained perceptions of supernatural things.

(*The different kinds of supernatural perception*)

We are now going to discuss all these ways of (supernatural) perception. We are going to start with soothsaying. Then, we shall discuss all the other kinds, one by one. Before that, however, we want to discuss how the human soul, as it exists in all the types of human beings mentioned, is prepared for supernatural perception. This is as follows.

(The soul) is a spiritual essence which, as we have mentioned before, is the only spiritual being that exists potentially. It exchanges potentiality for actuality with the help of the body and (bodily) conditions. This is something everyone can attain to.

Now, everything that exists potentially has matter and form. The form of the soul, through which its existence materializes, is identical with perception and intellection.

[314] Cf. also 2:201, below.

The soul at first exists potentially. It is prepared for perception and for the reception of the universal and particular forms. Its growth and actual existence then materialize through keeping company with the body, through the things to which (the body) accustoms (the soul) when (the former's) sensual perceptions are foisted upon (the latter), and through the universal ideas which (the soul itself) abstracts from the sensual perceptions of the body. It intellectualizes the forms time after time, until perception and intellection become the actual form of the soul. Thus, its essence materializes. The soul, then, is like matter, and, through perception, the forms come to it one after the other in an uninterrupted sequence.

This is why we find that a child in the earliest stages of his growth is unable to achieve the perception which comes *I, 193* to the soul from its essence, either in his sleep or through removal (of the veil of sense perception),[315] or anything else. For the form of the soul, which is its very essence, namely, perception and intellection, has not yet materialized (in the child). Nor has the power of the soul to abstract the universals materialized. Later on, when the essence of (the soul) has materialized in actuality, the soul has two kinds of perception, as long as it remains in the body: one through the organs of the body, for which the soul is enabled by the corporeal perceptions, and the other through its own essence, without any intermediary. The soul is prevented [316] from (the latter kind of perception) by its immersion in the body and the senses, and the preoccupations of (body and senses). By means of corporeal perception, for which the senses were originally created, they always draw the soul to the external. Frequently, however, the soul plunges from the external into the internal. Then, the veil of the body is lifted for a moment, either by means of a quality that belongs to every human being, such as sleep, or by means of a quality that is found only in certain human beings, such as soothsaying or

[315] Arabic *kashf*, a common term of mysticism (and metaphysics), for Ibn Khaldûn a crucial concept in the discussion of these subjects.

[316] Lit., "veiled." Cf. preceding note.

casting (of pebbles, etc.), or by means of exercises such as those practiced by (certain) Sufis who practice the removal (of the veil of sense perception). At such moments, the soul turns to the essences of the highest group (the angels), which are higher than itself. (This is possible) because in (the order of) existence the stages of the soul and the angels are connected with each other, as we established earlier.[317] These essences are spiritual. They are pure perception and intellects in action. They contain the forms and realities of the *existentia*, as was (just) mentioned. Something of those forms is then disclosed in (the soul). It derives some knowledge from them. Frequently, it transmits the perceived forms to the imagination which, in turn, puts them into the customary molds. (The soul,) then, has recourse to sensual perception to explain the things it has perceived, either in their abstract form or in the molds into which (they were put by the imagination). In this way it gives information about them. This is how the preparedness of the soul for supernatural perception must be explained.

I, 194 Let us now return to the explanation we promised, of the various kinds (of supernatural perception). Persons who gaze into transparent bodies, such as mirrors, bowls, or water, and (examine) the hearts, livers, and bones of animals, as well as those who cast pebbles and (date) pits, all belong to the class of soothsayers. Only, they are constitutionally less well fitted for supernatural perception than soothsayers. The soothsayer does not need to make much of an effort in order to lift the veil of sensual perception. They, however, expend much effort to concentrate all sensual perception in one particular sense, the noblest one, which is vision. It is applied exclusively to whatever plain visual object has been (selected for concentration), until the perception about which information is to be given appears. It is often thought that the place where those (who gaze into mirrors) see something, is the surface of the mirror. This is not so. They continue

[317] Cf. p. 196, above.

gazing at the surface of the mirror until it (the surface) disappears. Between their eyes and the mirror appears a veil like a white cloud. In it, forms are pictured, and (these pictures) are the objects they perceive. This gives them the facts of a negative or positive character they wanted to obtain, and they pass on (these facts) as they perceived them. Neither the mirror nor the forms perceived in it are now present to them. A different kind of perception originates in them in (that state). It is a psychic one that has nothing to do with vision. Through it, objects of psychic perception take on shape (for observation) by sensual perception, as is known. Something similar happens to those who examine the hearts and livers of animals, and to those who gaze into water, bowls, and similar things.

Among these people we have observed persons who keep their senses occupied only by means of incense, as well as *I, 195*
incantations, in order to be prepared (for supernatural perception). Then, they tell what they have perceived. They think that they see the forms take on concrete shapes in the air, telling them what they want to know in the form of pictures and allusions. These persons are less remote from sensual perception than the first group. The world is full of remarkable things.

Augury (*zajr*) is talk about supernatural things which originates in some people when a bird or animal appears, and they reflect about it after it has gone. It is a power in the soul that calls for sagacity and the ability to think about (the things of interest) which augurs see or hear. As we mentioned earlier,[318] the power of imagination is strong in augurs, and they exert that power in their researches, while depending on the help given by things they have seen or heard. This gives them some supernatural perception. The power of imagination acts here as it does in sleepers. When the senses are asleep, (the power of imagination) intervenes among the things seen in the waking state, and combines

[318] The reference appears to be to pp. 203 f., above.

them with the products of its own thinking. Thus, the power of imagination brings about vision.

In the insane, the rational soul is but weakly connected with the body, because the humors, as a rule, are corrupt and have a weak animal spirit. Therefore, the soul belonging to (the body of an insane person) is not deeply immersed in the senses. The painful disease of deficiency that affects it keeps it too much occupied. Frequently, it was pushed into attaching itself to (the insane) by some other Satanic spirituality, which clings to them and which (the soul) itself is too weak to keep away. The insane thus become possessed.[318a] When they have become possessed in this manner, either because of the corruption of their constitution as the result of the essential corruption of their soul, or because of the onslaught the Satanic souls make upon them when they are attached to (their bodies), they are totally removed from
I, *196* sensual perception. They perceive a glimpse of the world of their soul. (Their soul) receives the impress of forms which, in turn, are transformed by the imagination. In this condition, they frequently speak without wanting to speak.

(Supernatural) perception in all these (groups) contains truth and falsehood mixed together. For although they may achieve the loss of sensual perception, it is only with the help of foreign notions (*taṣawwur*) that they achieve contact (with the supernatural), as we have established. This leads to untruthfulness, (which is to be found) in these (ways of supernatural) perception.

The diviners (*'arrâf*) somehow enjoy this kind of perception, but they do not have the same contact (with the supernatural). They concentrate their thinking upon the matter in which they are interested and apply guesses and hypotheses to it. They base themselves upon an unfounded assumption as to what basically constitutes contact with, and perception

[318a] For *takhabbaṭa* "to become possessed," cf. Qur'ân 2.275 (276), and A. Spitaler, *Orientalistische Literaturzeitung*, XLVIII (1953), 535.

of, (the supernatural). They claim acquaintance with the supernatural, but in reality (their procedure) has nothing to do with it.

This is the manner in which such (supernatural knowledge) is obtained. Al-Mas'ûdî discussed the subject in his *Murûj adh-dhahab*.[319] He did not hit upon the right explanation. It is evident from his discussion that he was not firmly grounded in the various kinds of (pertinent) knowledge. He merely reports what he learned from people experienced in the subject, and from others.

All the kinds of (supernatural) perception mentioned are found in man. The Arabs used to repair to soothsayers in order to learn about forthcoming events. They consulted them in their quarrels, to learn the truth by means of supernatural perception. Literature contains much information about this matter. In pre-Islamic times, Shiqq, of the tribe of Anmâr b. Nizâr, and Saṭîḥ, of the tribe of Mâzin b. Ghassân,[320] were famous (soothsayers). (The latter) used to fold up like a garment, as he had no bones save for his skull.

A famous story is their interpretation of the dream vision of Rabî'ah b. Naṣr, in which they informed him that the Abyssinians would take possession of the Yemen, that the Muḍar would rule after them, and that the Muḥammadan prophecy would make its appearance among the Quraysh.[321] Another famous story is that of the dream vision of the Môbedhân.[322] Saṭîḥ interpreted it when the Persian emperor (Khosraw) sent 'Abd-al-Masîḥ to him with (the dream). (On that occasion, Saṭîḥ) informed him about the prophecy (of Muḥammad) and the (future) destruction of the Persian realm. All this is well known. 1, *197*

[319] III, 347 ff.

[320] For Shiqq and Saṭîḥ, cf. G. Levi Della Vida in *EI*, *s.v.* "Saṭîḥ." The strange tribal connections of these mythological figures, which make Mâzin a "son" of Ghassân, were found by Ibn Khaldûn in al-Mas'ûdî, *op. cit.*, III, 364. For the dubious tribal genealogy of Shiqq, cf. also Ibn Ḥazm, *Jamharat ansâb al-'Arab*, pp. 365 f.

[321] Cf. Ibn Hishâm, *Sîrah*, pp. 9 ff. Cf. also 2:202, below.

[322] Cf. al-Mas'ûdî, *op. cit.*, I, 217; II, 228. For the Môbedhân, see n. 25 to p. 80, above.

There were also many diviners among the Arabs. They are mentioned by the Arabs in their poems. (One poet) said:

I said to the diviner of the Yamâmah: Cure me,
For if you cure me, you are indeed a physician.[323]

Another poet said:

I promised to give the diviner of the Yamâmah whatever he would ask me for,
And (I promised the same) to the diviner of Najd, if they would cure me (of my love).
But they said: Let God cure you. By God, we have no
Power over (the disease) that you carry around with you in your body.[324]

The "diviner of the Yamâmah" is Riyâḥ b. ʿIjlah,[325] and the "diviner of Najd" is al-Ablaq al-Asadî.

Some people have another way of supernatural perception. It occurs in the stage of transition from waking to sleeping, and is in (the form of unconsciously) speaking about the thing one wants to know and thereby obtaining supernatural knowledge of the matter as desired. This happens only during the transition from waking to sleeping, when one has lost the power to control one's words. Such a person talks as if by innate compulsion. The most he can do is to hear and understand what (he says).

[323] The verse is by ʿUrwah b. Ḥizâm al-ʿUdhrî (*GAL*, *Suppl.*, I, 81 f.), who is also the author of the following two verses. Cf. al-Masʿûdî, *op. cit.*, III, 353, where the name of the poet is not given; Ibn Qutaybah, *Kitâb ash-shiʿr wa-sh-shuʿarâʾ*, ed. M. J. de Goeje (Leiden, 1904), pp. 396 f.; Abû l-Faraj al-Iṣfahânî, *Kitâb al-Aghânî* (Bulaq, 1285/1868), XX, 154 f.; *Lisân al-ʿArab*, XI, 142; * Ibn al-Jawzî, *Dhamm al-hawâ* (Cairo, 1962), pp. 408 ff.

[324] Cf. the preceding note and T. Nöldeke, *Delectus veterum carminum arabicorum* (Berlin, 1890), p. 8. Cf. further al-Masʿûdî, *op. cit.*, VII, 353 f.; *Rasâʾil Ikhwân aṣ-ṣafâʾ*, III, 261; as-Sarrâj, *Maṣâriʿ al-ʿushshâq* (Constantinople, 1301), p. 209 f.; al-Kutubî, *Fawât al-Wafayât* (Cairo, 1951–53), II, 72 f.

[325] This is the vocalization of MSS. B, C, and D. Ibn Khaldûn derived the names from al-Masʿûdî, *op. cit.*, III, 353.

Words of a similar nature come from those who are about to be killed, at the moment when their heads are being severed from their trunks. We have been informed that certain criminal tyrants used to kill their prisoners in order to learn their own future from the words the prisoners would utter when they were about to be killed. It was unpleasant information they received from them. I, *198*

In the *Ghâyah*,[326] Maslamah similarly mentioned that when a human being is placed in a barrel of sesame oil and kept in it for forty days, is fed with figs and nuts until his flesh is gone and only the arteries and sutures [327] of the skull remain, and is then taken out of the oil and exposed to the drying action of the air, he will answer all special and general questions regarding the future that may be asked. This is detestable sorcery. However, it shows what remarkable things exist in the world of man.

There are men who attempt to obtain supernatural perception through exercise. They attempt an artificial (state of) death through self-mortification.[328] They kill all corporeal powers (in themselves), and wipe out all influences of those powers that color the soul in various ways.[329] This is achieved by concentrated thinking, and doing without food for long (periods). It is definitely known that when death descends upon the body, sensual perception and the veil it constitutes disappear, and the soul beholds its essence and its world. (These men) attempt to produce, artificially before death, the experience they will have after death, and to have their soul behold the supernatural.

---

[326] Cf. (Pseudo-)Majrîṭî, *Ghâyah*, pp. 139 f. (See n. 310 to this chapter, above.) A similar magical practice is ascribed to the Ṣâbians of Ḥarrân. Cf. Ibn an-Nadîm, *Fihrist*, p. 321 (of the Flügel ed.); pp. 446 f. (of the Cairo ed.); A. Mez, *Abulḳâsim, ein bagdâder Sittenbild* (Heidelberg, 1902), p. LVII; C. G. Jung, in *Papers from the Eranos Yearbooks* (Bollingen Series XXX), Vol. 2: *The Mysteries* (New York, 1955), pp. 306 f.

[327] Cf. n. 1509 to Ch. VI, below. [328] *Mujâhadah* "exertion."

[329] Bulaq adds: "and nourish the soul with *dhikr* exercises, so that it may grow stronger." Ibn Khaldûn probably omitted this statement, because it belonged rather to Sufism, mentioned below.

Other such people are the men who train themselves in sorcery. They train themselves in these things, in order to be able to behold the supernatural and to be active in the various worlds. Most such live in the intemperate zones of the north and the south, especially in India, where they are
I, *199* called yogis. They possess a large literature on how such exercises are to be done. The stories about them in this connection are remarkable.

The Sufi training is a religious one. It is free from any such reprehensible intentions. The Sufis aspire to total concentration upon God and upon the approach to Him, in order to obtain the mystical experiences [330] of gnosis and Divine oneness. In addition to their training in concentration and hunger, the Sufis feed on *dhikr* exercises [331] by which their devotion to that training can fully materialize. When the soul is reared on *dhikr* exercises, it comes closer to the gnosis of God, whereas, without it, it comes to be a Satanic one.

Whatever supernatural knowledge or activity is achieved by the Sufis is accidental, and was not originally intended. Had it been intentional, the devotion of the Sufis (who intended to have supernatural perception) would have been directed toward something other than God, namely, toward supernatural activity and vision. What a losing business that would have been! In reality, it would have been polytheism. A (Sufi) has said, "Whoever prefers gnosis for the sake of gnosis comes out for the second (stage of being)." Through their devotion, (Sufis) intend (to come near) the Master, and nothing else. If, meanwhile, some (supernatural perception) is obtained, it is accidental and unintentional. Many (Sufis) shun (supernatural perception) when it accidentally happens to them, and pay no attention to it.[332] They want God only for the sake of His essence, and nothing else. It is well known that (supernatural perception) occurs among the (Sufis). They call their supernatural experiences and mind

---

[330] Lit., "taste." Cf. n. 463 to Ch. vi, below.

[331] Cf. n. 471 to Ch. vi, below.

[332] Cf. 3:102 and 179 f., below.

reading "physiognomy" (*firâsah*) and "removal" (of the veil of sense perception, *kashf*). Their experiences of (supernatural) activity they call "acts of divine grace" (*karâmah*). None of these things is unworthy of them. However, Professor Abû Isḥâq al-Isfarâyinî and Abû Muḥammad b. Abî Zayd al-Mâlikî,[333] among others, disapproved of it, in order to avoid any risk of (prophetic) miracles becoming confused with something else. However, the speculative theologians rely on the "advance challenge" (*taḥaddî*) as the distinguishing characteristic of the (prophetic) miracle. This is sufficient. I, 200

According to (the sound tradition of) the *Ṣaḥîḥ*, Muḥammad said, "Among you, there are men who are spoken to, and 'Umar is one of them." [334] The men around Muḥammad, as is well known, had experiences of a sort that confirms the fact (that mystics and pious persons may have some sort of supernatural perception). For instance, there is the story of 'Umar saying, "O Sâriyah, beware of the mountain!" Sâriyah is Sâriyah b. Zunaym. He was the general of a Muslim army in the 'Irâq during the conquest. He had gotten into a battle with the polytheists. He thought of withdrawing. Near him, there was a mountain toward which he was directing himself (and where the enemy was lying in ambush). This came (supernaturally) to 'Umar's attention while he was preaching from the pulpit in Medina. He called out to him: "O Sâriyah, beware of the mountain." Sâriyah heard it, there where he was (in faraway 'Irâq), and he also saw ('Umar) there in person. This story is well known.[335]

Something similar happened to Abû Bakr in connection with his last will, addressed to his daughter 'Â'ishah. He had given her a certain amount of dates from his orchard,

[333] 'Abdallâh ('Ubaydallâh) b. Abî Zayd, 316–386 [928–996]. Cf. *GAL*, I, 177 f.;.*Suppl.*, I, 301 f., one of Ibn Khaldûn's famous and oft-quoted school authorities. Cf. p. 189, above.

[334] Cf. the references in *Handbook*, p. 234*b*, where *muḥaddath* "spoken to" is translated "inspired." Cf. also 2:203, below.

This tradition, as well as the stories of Sâriyah and 'Â'ishah, were also mentioned by al-Ghazzâlî, *Iḥyâ'*, p. 21.

[335] Cf. aṭ-Ṭabarî, *Annales*, I, 2701. Ibn Khaldûn refers to the story again in the *Autobiography*, p. 165.

as a gift, and then, (when he was near death), he suggested to her that she harvest them, so that the (other) heirs would not get them. Then he said, "They are your two brothers and your two sisters." Whereupon 'Â'ishah said, "There is Asmâ', but who is the other?" Abû Bakr replied, "I see that the child in Bint Khârijah's womb is a girl," and so it was. This is mentioned in the *Muwaṭṭa'* in the chapter on gifts that are not permitted.[336]

(The men around Muḥammad) and the pious and exemplary men after them had many similar experiences. How-
1, *201* ever, the Sufis say that such experiences are rare in the time of prophecy, because, in the presence of the prophet, the adept of mysticism cannot continue in his mystic state. They go so far as to say that the adept of mysticism who comes to Medina is deprived of his mystic state, so long as he remains there and until he leaves.

May God provide us with guidance, and may He lead us to the truth.

Among the adepts of mysticism are fools and imbeciles who are more like insane persons than like rational beings. Nonetheless, they deservedly attained stations of sainthood and the mystic states of the righteous. The persons with mystical experience who learn about them know that such is their condition, although they are not legally responsible. The information they give about the supernatural is remarkable. They are not bound by anything. They speak absolutely freely about it and tell remarkable things. When jurists see they are not legally responsible, they frequently deny that they have attained any mystical station, since sainthood can be obtained only through divine worship. This is an error. "God bestows His grace upon whomever He

---

[336] Cf. Mâlik, *Muwaṭṭa'*, in the *Kitâb al-aqḍiyah* (Tunis, 1280/1863–64), p. 299. It is interesting to note how frankly Ibn Khaldûn expresses himself in paraphrasing the case. In the text of the *Muwaṭṭa'*, Abû Bakr makes the suggestion in a very guarded form, and 'Â'ishah, of course, refuses to take advantage of it.

wants to."[337] The attainment of sainthood is not restricted to (the correct performance of) divine worship, or anything else. When the human soul is firmly established as existent, God may single it out for whatever gifts of His He wants to give it. The rational souls of such people are not non-existent, nor are they corrupt, as is the case with the insane. They (merely) lack the intellect that is the basis of legal responsibility. (That intellect) is a special attribute of the soul. It means various kinds of knowledge that are necessary to man and that guide his speculative ability and teach him how to make a living and organize his home. One may say that if he knows how to make a living, he has no excuse left not to accept legal responsibility, so that he may prepare for his life after death. Now, a person who lacks that (special) attribute (of the soul called intellect) still does not lack the soul itself, and has not forgotten his reality. He has reality, I, 202
though he lacks the intellect entailing legal responsibility, that is, the knowledge of how to make a living. This is not absurd. God does not select His servants for gnosis only on the basis of (the performance of) some legal duty.

If this is correct, it should be known that the state of these men is frequently confused with that of the insane, whose rational souls are corrupted and who belong to (the category of) animals. There are signs by which one can distinguish the two groups. One of them is that fools are found devoting themselves constantly to certain *dhikr* exercises and divine worship, though not in the way the religious law requires, since, as we have stated, they are not legally responsible. The insane, on the other hand, have no (particular) devotion whatever.

Another sign is that fools were created stupid, and were stupid from their earliest days. The insane, on the other hand, lose their minds after some portion of their life has passed, as the result of natural bodily accidents. When this happens to them and their rational souls become corrupt, they are lost.

---

[337] Qur'ân 5.54 (59); 57.21 (21); 62.4 (4).

A further sign is the great activity of fools among men. It may be good or bad. They do not have to have permission, because for them there is no legal responsibility. The insane, on the other hand, show no (such) activity.

The course of our discussion caused us to insert the preceding paragraph. God leads toward that which is correct.

(*Other alleged ways of supernatural perception*)

Some people think that there are ways of supernatural perception not involving remoteness from sensual perception. (Such) are the astrologers who believe in astrological indications, consequences of the positions of (stars) in the firmament, influences of (the stars) upon the elements, and results from the tempering of the natures of (the stars) when they look at each other,[338] as well as effects of such tempers upon the air. Astrologers, (as a matter of fact,) have nothing to do with the supernatural. It is all guesswork and conjec-
I, 203 tures based upon (the assumed existence of) astral influence, and a resulting conditioning of the air. (Such guesswork) is accompanied by an additional measure of sagacity enabling scholars to determine the distribution (of astral influence) upon particular individuals in the world, as Ptolemy said. We shall explain the futility of astrology in the proper place, if God wills.[339] If it were established (as a fact), it would, at best, be guessing and conjecturing. It has nothing whatever to do with (the supernatural perception) we have mentioned.

(*Geomancy*)

Other such people include certain men of the common people who, to discover the supernatural and know the future, invented a craft they called "sand writing" (geomancy) [340]

---

[338] Cf. 3:259, below. [339] Cf. 3:258 ff., below.

[340] Arabic *khaṭṭ ar-raml*. Cf. E. Doutté, *Magie et religion dans l'Afrique du Nord* (Algiers, 1908), pp. 377 ff.; O. Rescher in *Der Islam*, IX (1919), 37; P. Tannery, "Le Rabolion," in his *Mémoires scientifiques* (Toulouse & Paris, 1920), IV, 297–411. The section dealing with Arabic geomancy in Tannery's posthumous paper was compiled by B. Carra de Vaux.

after the material one uses for it. This craft consists in forming combinations of dots in four "ranks." (The resulting combinations) differ in that the (four) ranks are made up of different or identical (arrangements) of even or odd. This makes sixteen combinations. For if (all four ranks) hold evens or (all) odds, we have two combinations. If one rank only has an even, we have four combinations. If two ranks have an even, we have six combinations, and if three ranks have an even, we have four combinations. This makes altogether sixteen combinations.[341]

The sand diviners have given different names to the different combinations and classified them as lucky or unlucky, as is done with the stars. For (the sixteen combinations), they have assumed (the existence of) sixteen "houses." They think that the "houses" are natural and that they correspond to the twelve signs of the zodiac and the four cardines. They have attributed to each combination a "house," lucky (or unlucky) influences, and significance with regard to one particular group (of people) in the world of the elements. (The sand diviners) have thus invented a discipline that runs parallel to astrology and the system of astrological judgments. However, the astrological judgments are based upon natural indications, as Ptolemy assumes. The [342] indications

---

341 It follows that these are the figures used in geomancy:

(1) (2) (3) (4) (5) (6) (7) (8) (9) (10) (11) (12) (13) (14) (15) (16)

Instead of the two dots, a line may be used. For the names of the figures in Arabic and the various European languages, see the comparative table in Tannery, *op. cit.*, IV, 410 f.

342 The following discussion, down to p. 132, l. 19, appears in B in the margin and on an inserted slip. It is inserted in the texts of C and D. The older texts, Bulaq, A, and E, and the original text of B, have the following sentence in place of the above sentence: "They are based upon arbitrary conventions and wishful thinking. Nothing about them is proven." Then the text found below, p. 229, ll. 10–22, is given, followed by an explanation of the tradition which reads: " 'And whoever concurs with the writing of that prophet—this is it.' He is right in view of the fact that the writing was supported by the revelation that came to that prophet whose custom it was

of sand writing, on the other hand, are conventional.

1, 204 Ptolemy discussed only nativities and conjunctions which, in his opinion, come within the influence of the stars and the positions of the spheres upon the world of the elements. Subsequent astrologers, however, discussed questions (*interrogationes*), in that they attempted to discover the innermost thoughts [342a] by attributing them to the various houses of the firmament and drawing conclusions concerning them, according to the judgments governing each particular astral house. They are those mentioned by Ptolemy.

It should be known that the innermost thoughts concern psychic knowledge, which does not belong to the world of the elements. They do not come within the influence of the stars or the positions of the spheres, nor do (the stars and the positions of the spheres) give any indications with regard to them. The branch of questions (*interrogationes*) has indeed been accepted in astrology as a way of making deductions from the stars and positions of the spheres. However, it is used where it is not natural for it to be used.

When the sand diviners came, they discontinued use of the stars and the positions of the spheres, because they found it difficult to establish the altitude of stars by means of instruments and to find the adjusted (positions of the) stars by means of calculations. Therefore, they invented their combinations of figures. They assumed that there were sixteen, according to the houses of the firmament and the cardines, and they specified that they were lucky, unlucky, or mixed, like the planets. They limited themselves to the sextile aspect. They made judgments in accordance with the combinations of figures, as is done in the interrogation (branch of astrology). In both cases, the use made (of the data) is not a natural one, as we stated before.

Many city dwellers who had no work, in order to make

---

to have the revelation come to him while he was writing. Were he to take it from the writing without the concurrence of revelation, he would not be right. This is the meaning of the tradition. And God knows better."

[342a] *Ḍamā'ir* "the unconscious."

a living,[343] tried sand divination. They composed works teaching the foundation and principles of sand divination. This was done by az-Zanâtî [344] and others.

Some sand diviners attempt supernatural perception, in that they occupy their senses with study of the combinations I, 205 of figures. They thus reach a state of preparedness, like those who are by nature fitted for preparedness, as we shall mention later on. These men are the noblest class of sand diviners.

In general, they assume that sand writing originated with the prophets of old. They frequently ascribe its invention to Daniel or Idrîs,[345] as is being done with all the crafts. They (also) frequently claim that (sand writing) is enjoined by the religious law. As a proof of this (contention of theirs), they quote the following tradition of Muḥammad: "There was a prophet who wrote, and whoever concurs with his writing—this is it." [346] However, this tradition contains no evidence for the claim that sand writing is enjoined by the religious law, as some people assume. The meaning of the tradition is: "There was a prophet who wrote," that is, the revelation came to him while he was writing. It is not absurd to assume that such was the custom of some prophets, for prophets differ in their ways of perceiving the revelation.

343 The same argument is referred to below, 2:320 and 3:267.

344 Abû 'Abdallâh Muḥammad (b. 'Uthmân?) az-Zanâtî, whose dates appear to be uncertain. Cf. Tannery, *op. cit.*, IV, 300; *GAL*, *Suppl.*, II, 1037 (No. 5), and 1041 (No. 40). He is the great authority on geomancy now as he was in the past, and his works are often reprinted under titles such as *al-Aqwâl al-marḍîyah fî l-aḥkâm ar-ramlîyah* (Cairo, 1326/1908–9) and *Kitâb al-Faṣl fî uṣûl 'ilm ar-raml* (Cairo, 1280/1863–64), etc. Their genuineness remains to be investigated.

345 Like the Biblical Daniel, the Qur'ânic Idrîs is among the most favored names for attributing authorship of magical works. He is probably correctly identified with the Biblical Enoch, and, incorrectly, with Hermes; cf. 2:367 f., below. Cf., for instance, 3:213 (n. 921), below. The following tradition is referred to Idrîs in Ibn Kathîr, *Bidâyah*, I, 99. The sequence "Daniel or Idrîs" is that found in C and D.

346 It may be possible to translate, "and whose writing agrees with (the writing of that prophet). . . ." But the above translation seems preferable, and the difference in meaning is not great. A variant of the tradition is quoted in Majd-ad-dîn Ibn al-Athîr, *Nihâyah*, I, 338. It reads: "and whoever agrees with his writing knows as much as he does."

God said: "We distinguished the messengers (by giving the ones pre-eminence) over the others." [347] When some of them received the revelation, the angel spoke first to them, without any request or motive (on their part). Others had a human motive, resulting from contact with human affairs, in that their people asked them to explain some difficult problem, some obligation of duty, or the like. Therefore, they directed their devotions to the Divine, and in that way God revealed to them what they wanted to know. (Logical) classification here suggests the existence of another division. Revelation may come to a person who is not prepared for it in any way, as in the afore-mentioned instance, or it may come to a person who is prepared for it in some way. In the Israelite stories, it is reported that a prophet was prepared for the
I, 206 coming of the revelation by hearing sweet melodious voices.[348] This report is not established as correct, but it is not improbable. God singles out His prophets and messengers for whatever (favors) He wishes. This [349] was reported to us on the authority of a great Sufi, who attempts to attain remoteness from sensual perception by listening to music. By this means he becomes completely free for his (supernatural) perceptions, in the station he is in, which (it is true) is inferior to prophecy. "And there is nobody among us who does not have a known station." [350]

If this is established and if, as we have mentioned before, certain sand diviners attempt to remove (the veil of sense perception) by occupying their senses with the study of combinations of figures, they may attain intuitive supernatural revelation (*kashf*) through complete freedom from sense perception. They may exchange bodily perceptions for

---

[347] Qur'ân 2.253 (254).

[348] Cf. also the tradition quoted below, 2:401. For the "Israelite Stories," see n. 47 to Ibn Khaldûn's Introduction, above.

[349] The rest of the paragraph is found only in the MS. Ragib Paşa 978, fol. 56*b* (as well as in the Paris edition). The scribe of the MS again states that he derived the note from the MS of al-Qaṭarî. Cf. p. 192, above, and n. 260 to this chapter. Though it did not enter the mainstream of the *Muqaddimah* tradition, it is undoubtedly by Ibn Khaldûn.

[350] Qur'ân 37.164 (164).

spiritual ones—both of which have been explained earlier. This is a kind of soothsaying, of the type of gazing at bones, water, and mirrors, and it distinguishes (these sand diviners) from those who restrict themselves to techniques that achieve supernatural perception by means of sagacity and conjecturing, but who do not relinquish corporeal perception and continue to wander in the realm of guesswork. Some prophets achieved preparedness for being addressed by the angel, in their prophetical station, by writing, exactly as people who are not prophets may achieve preparedness for spiritual perception and the relinquishment of human perception by the same means. In the case of (sand diviners), however, what they achieve is spiritual perception only, whereas prophets achieve an angelic perception by means of divine revelation.

The prophets have nothing to do with the stations of the sand diviners, whose perceptions are based on sagacity and conjecturing. They do not make it part of the religious law I, 207
for any human being to speak about and discuss the supernatural. The statement in the tradition, "And whoever concurs with his writing—this is it," [351] means: He is right, in view of the fact that the writing was supported by the revelation that came to that particular prophet, whose custom it was to have the revelation come to him while he was writing. Or, the tradition may be a compliment and indicate that the prophet had reached a high competence in the use of sand writing—without (implying) the existence of a connection between (revelation) and (sand writing)—because in this way the prophet was prepared for revelation, which, therefore, concurred with (the conclusions reached from sand writing). But were the prophet to take (those conclusions) from the writing alone, without the concurrence of revelation, they would not be right. This is the meaning of the tradition. And God knows better.

The tradition does not indicate that sand writing is enjoined by religious law, nor that it is permissible to practice

[351] Cf. nn. 342 and 346 to this chapter, above.

sand writing to obtain supernatural perception, as sand diviners in the cities do. Some of them may be inclined to this opinion, on the basis that what (any) prophet did is accepted law, and that sand writing, therefore, is enjoined by the religious law according to the principle, held by some, that the religious law of those who came before us is religious law for us. This does not apply in this (case). Law only results when it is enjoined by messengers upon the various nations. This (particular) tradition, however, indicates no(thing of the sort). It indicates only that the particular condition was that of one of the prophets, and it is possible that it was not enjoined as a religious law. Therefore, it would not be a religious law, neither one restricted to the people of (that particular prophet), nor one common to his people and to others. (The tradition) merely indicates that it is a condition that may occur in the instance of a particular prophet, without being generally applicable to mankind. This is all we wanted to make clear here. God gives the correct inspiration.

If, in their self-deception, (sand diviners) want to discover something supernatural, they take paper, or sand, or
I, 208 flour, and form dots in (four) lines [352] in accordance with the number of the four ranks. This is repeated four times. They thus obtain sixteen lines. They then deduct (some) dots in pairs. The remainder, for each line, whether it is even or odd,[353] is put into the rank to which it belongs according to order. This results in four combinations, which they arrange to form one continuous line. From them, they then form four other combinations through horizontal confrontation, by considering each rank, the corresponding combination next to it, and the evens or odds found in it.[354] These, then, make eight combinations, placed along one line. From each pair of

---

[352] That is, heaps of grains. [353] That is, one or two dots.

[354] The rules governing this procedure vary. If there is one dot next to either one or two dots, it may result in one dot for the new combination, and so on, as explained by de Slane, *Les Prolégomènes d'Ibn Khaldoun*, I, 239 (n. 1).

combinations, they then form one combination (to be placed) underneath the (eight), by considering the evens or odds found in each rank of two combinations. Thus, we have four others under (the eight). From these four combinations, they then form two more combinations, which are likewise placed underneath (the four). From these two, they again form one more combination and place it underneath (the two). They then combine this fifteenth combination with the first one and thus form one more combination, which completes the sixteen.[355] Then, they evaluate the whole "writing" in a curious manner, as to the good luck or misfortune required by the various combinations, taking them as they stand, speculating on them, analyzing them, combining them, making deductions as to the various kinds of *existentia*, and so on.

This craft is prevalent in (all) civilized (regions). There exists a literature dealing with it. Outstanding ancient and modern personalities were famous for it. But it is obviously based on arbitrary notions and wishful thinking. The truth that should be present to one's mind is that the supernatural cannot be perceived by any craft at all. The only people who

[355] The procedure described leads to a figure such as we find reproduced (from Western texts) in Tannery, *Mémoires scientifiques*, IV, 345 f. For instance:

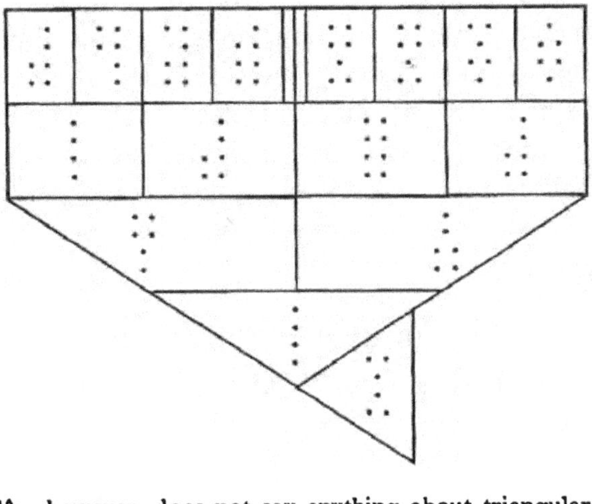

Ibn Khaldûn, however, does not say anything about triangular houses for the last two combinations.

can acquire knowledge of the supernatural are those dis-
I, 209 tinguished human beings who are fitted by nature to return from the world of sensual perception to the world of the spirit. The astrologers, therefore, called all people (able to perceive supernatural knowledge) "Venusians," with reference to Venus, because they assumed that the position of Venus in the nativities of these people indicates their ability to have supernatural perception.

If the person who takes up (sand) writing and similar (practices) is one of those distinguished beings, and if his study of dots, bones, and other things is intended to occupy his senses in order that his soul may return momentarily to the world of the *spiritualia*, then (sand writing) occupies the same position as casting pebbles, examining the hearts of animals, and gazing into transparent mirrors, as we have mentioned.[356] If this is not so, and if knowledge of the supernatural is sought by means of (sand writing), (then) it is meaningless in theory and practice.[357] "God guides whomever He wants to guide." [358]

The sign by which persons who are disposed by nature to supernatural perceptions can be recognized, is this: When these persons devote themselves to acquiring a knowledge of things, they suffer a departure from their natural condition. They yawn and stretch, and show symptoms of remoteness from sensual perception. These (symptoms) vary in intensity according to the different degrees to which they possess this natural disposition. Those in whom this sign is not found have nothing to do with supernatural perception. They are merely trying to spread the falsehoods to which they are committed.

(*The* ḥisâb an-nîm)

There are (other) groups that also lay down certain rules for the discovery of the supernatural. Their rules do not

[356] Cf. p. 216, above. [357] Cf. Bombaci, p. 446.
[358] Qur'ân 2.142 (136), 213 (209), etc.

belong to the first category, that which has to do with the spiritual perceptions of the soul, and also differ from speculations based upon astral influences, as assumed by Ptolemy, as well as from the guesswork and conjecturing with which the diviners work. They are nothing but mistakes which (the I, 210
people who work with them) throw out like snares for weak-minded people. I shall mention only as much of (the subject) as is mentioned in literature and has aroused the interest of distinguished men.

One such rule is the method called *ḥisâb an-nîm.*[359] It is mentioned at the end of the *Politics* which is ascribed to Aristotle. It serves to predict the victor and the vanquished when kings go to war with each other. The procedure is to

[359] The meaning of the word *nîm* (or whatever the consonants *n–y–m* may signify) is not clear. There are many possibilities, none of them convincing. The MSS of the *Muqaddimah* practically never vocalize it (except D, in the passage below, p. 238). Ibn Khaldûn was probably not sure of the pronunciation himself.

The pseudo-Aristotelian *Politics*, or *Secretum secretorum*, contains something quite similar. Cf. the edition of the Arabic text by 'Abd-ar-Raḥmân Badawî, pp. 152 ff., and the English tr. in Roger Bacon, *Opera*, ed. R. Steele, V, pp. LX f. and 250 f. However, no mention whatever is made in the *Secretum* of *ḥisâb an-nîm*. A description not identical with Ibn Khaldûn's, but which comes rather close to it, appears after the *Secretum* in the Istanbul MS, Süleymaniye, 782, fols. 44*b* and 45*b*. There are two sets of letter arrangements in that MS. One, on fol. 45*b*, corresponds to that mentioned by Ibn Khaldûn as going back to Ibn al-Bannâ' (p. 238, below). The other is different from that mentioned by Ibn Khaldûn below, pp. 236 f. (De Slane states that he found a reference to the *ḥisâb an-nîm* in the margin of one of the Paris MSS of the *Secretum*.)

Greek texts dealing with the procedure are ascribed, not to Aristotle but to Pythagoras. Cf. P. Tannery, "Notices sur des fragments d'onomatomancie arithmétique," *Notices et Extraits des Manuscrits de la Bibliothèque Nationale*, XXXI 2 (1886), 231–60, esp. pp. 248 ff. In Arabic tradition, Ptolemy is credited with a book on "Which of two adversaries will be successful"; cf. Ibn an-Nadîm, *al-Fihrist*, p. 268 (of the Flügel ed.); p. 375 (Cairo ed.).

For fifteenth-century Arabic monographs on the "Calculation of Victor and Vanquished," cf. *GAL, Suppl.*, I, 536 (n. 2), and the *Durr al-maṭlûb fî sirr al-ghâlib wa-l-maghlûb* by Yûsuf b. Qorqmâs Amîr al-ḥâjj al-Ḥalabî, which deals with the Aq-Qoyunlu and Qara-Qoyunlu, MS. Nuru Osmaniye, 4901. On fol. 10*b* of the MS, the verses quoted by Ibn Khaldûn are found. They are not found in the MS of the *Secretum* mentioned above. Numerous other manuscripts on the subject are listed, for instance, by G. Vajda, *Index général des manuscrits arabes musulmans de la Bibliothèque Nationale de Paris* (Paris, 1953), p. 359.

add up the numerical total of the letters in the name of each king, according to the system of calculation in which the letters of the alphabet in the sequence *alif, b, j* . . . are given the numerical values of units, tens, hundreds, and thousands from one to a thousand. When that has been done, each total should be divided by nine. The fractional remainder, in both cases, should be kept in mind. The two fractional remainders should be compared. If they are different and both are even or odd numbers, the (king) who has the smaller number will be the victor. If one of them is an even and the other an odd number, the (king) who has the larger number will be the victor. If the two numbers are equal and both even, the object of the inquiry will be the victor. And if both numbers are odd, the (king) who made the inquiry will be the victor. He (Aristotle) reported two verses about this procedure which have wide currency. They are:

> I think, in the case of even or odd numbers (for both), the smaller number will gain the upper hand.
> When the numbers differ (as to being even or odd), the larger number will be the victor.
> The object of the inquiry will be victorious, if the numbers are both equal and even.
> And if they are both equal and odd, the one who made the inquiry will be victorious.

In order to find out what the fractional remainder will be after dividing by nine, a rule has been laid down by (the
I, 211 persons who practice the *ḥisâb an-nîm*), which is well known among them for that purpose. They take the letters that refer to the number one in the four ranks, *alif* for the units, *y* for the tens, *q* for the hundreds, and *sh* for the thousands[360] —there is no number higher than one thousand that can be indicated by letters, because *sh* is the last letter of the alpha-

[360] The use of *sh* for 1,000 is characteristic of the Muslim West. In the East, *gh* is used. Cf. n. 809 to Ch. VI, below.

B says at the end of the sentence that "*gh* is the last letter of the numerical alphabet."

bet(ical arrangement for numerical purposes)—and arrange these four letters in sequence so as to form a word of four consonants: *'yqsh.* Then, they do the same with the letters that designate the number two in the (first) three ranks, omitting the thousands because there are no letters of the alphabet left for them. These three letters are *b* for two, *k* for twenty and *r* for two hundred. Arranged in sequence, they form the word *bkr.* The same is done with the letters that designate the number three, resulting in the word *jls*, and so on through all the letters of the alphabet. This results in nine words, (nine being) the highest unit. The words are: *'yqsh*, *bkr*, *jls*, *dmt*, *hnth*, *wṣkh*, *z'dh*, *ḥfẓ*, and *ṭḍgh*, here arranged according to numerical sequence. Each of them has its own number, one for *'yqsh*, two for *bkr*, three for *jls*, and so on to nine, which belongs to *ṭḍgh*. If they want to divide I, *212* a name by nine, they note in which of these nine words each letter of the name appears, substituting the number (of the word) for each letter (of the name), and adding together all the numbers thus obtained. If the sum is greater than nine, they (deduct nine or a multiple of nine from it and) take the fractional remainder. Otherwise, they take (the sum) as it is. The same thing is then done with the other name, and the two results are compared in the manner indicated above.

The secret of this rule is clear. The fractional remainder in a division by nine is the same in any given multiple of the powers of ten.[361] In a way, (the person making the calculation) just sums up the (unit) number in any given multiple of the powers of ten. The numbers in multiples of higher powers of ten, thus, are like the (corresponding) units. There is no distinction between two, twenty, two hundred, or two thousand.[362] Likewise, three, thirty, three hundred, and three thousand, all are three. The numbers are arranged in such a sequence as to indicate nothing but the (unit) number in

[361] The fractional remainder of 20, 200, or 2,000 divided by 9 is always two; of 30, 300, or 3,000 always three, and so on. Two is also the "(unit) number" of 20, 200, etc.; three of 30, 300, etc.

[362] The editor of Bulaq, Naṣr al-Hûrînî, calls attention to the fact that Ibn Khaldûn had just said that there are no letters expressing numerals higher than 1,000.

any given multiple of the powers of ten. The letters that indicate (the same number in) the different powers of ten, the units, tens, hundreds, and thousands, are combined each in one word. The number of the corresponding word is valid for all the letters it contains, whether they are units, tens, hundreds, or thousands. Thus, the number of the word can be used for all the letters it contains, and all of them are added up, as we have said. This procedure has been common among people for a long time.

Some *shaykhs* we knew personally were of the opinion that the correct thing is to use nine other words in place of those (mentioned). They too represent consecutive (numbers). The
I, 213 procedure of dividing by nine is the same. These words are: *'rb*, *ysqk*, *jzlṭ*, *mdwṣ*, *hf*, *tkhdhn*, *ghsh*, *ḥ'*, *ṭḍẓ*, nine words in all, in numerical sequence. They contain three, four, or two letters, respectively. As one can see, they follow no coherent principle. But our *shaykhs* are transmitting them on the authority of the leading Maghribî scholar in astrology as well as letter magic, Abû l-'Abbâs b. al-Bannâ'.[363] They state on his authority that the use of these words for the division of the *ḥisâb an-nîm* is more correct than that of the words *'yqsh*, (etc.). And God knows better how it may be.

All these ways of perceiving the supernatural are based upon no proof, and are not verifiable. Thorough scholars do not attribute the book that contains the *ḥisâb an-nîm* to Aristotle, because it contains opinions that cannot be verified or proven. This confirms (its spuriousness). The reader should investigate this matter critically, if he is a well-grounded scholar.

(*The* Zâ'irajah)[364]

Another technical rule for alleged discovery of the supernatural is the *zâ'irajah* which is called "*Zâ'irajah* of the

[363] Aḥmad b. Muḥammad [*ca.* 1285–1321]. Cf. *GAL*, II, 255; *Suppl.*, II, 363 f. As a mathematician he is quoted later on by Ibn Khaldûn; cf. 3:121, 123, 137, below. His role as a magician was a legend developed after his death; cf. H. P. J. Renaud in *Hespéris*, XXV (1938), 21.

[364] Cf. 3:182 ff., below. Ibn Khaldûn was initiated into the use of the *zâ'irajah* during his stay in Biskra in 1370/71, at least as far as the question

world." It is attributed to Abû l-'Abbâs as-Sabtî,[365] a very prominent Maghribî Sufi. He lived at the end of the sixth [twelfth] century in Marrakech, during the rule of the Almohad ruler Ya'qûb al-Manṣûr.[366]

The *zâ'irajah* is a remarkable technical procedure. Many distinguished people have shown great interest in using it for supernatural information, with the help of the well-known enigmatic operation that goes with it. For that (purpose), they have been desirous to solve its riddle and uncover its secret. The form of the *zâ'irajah* [367] they use is a large circle that encloses other concentric circles for the spheres, the elements, the created things, the *spiritualia*, as well as other types of beings and sciences. Each circle is divided into sections, the areas of which represent the signs of the zodiac, or the elements, or other things. The lines dividing each section run to the center. They are called chords. Along each chord there are sets of letters that have a conventional (numerical value). Some are *zimâm* ciphers, the same as those used for numerals by government officials and accountants in the contemporary Maghrib. Others are the ordinary *ghubâr* ciphers.[368] Inside the *zâ'irajah*, between the circles, I, *214*

---

that he discusses 3:197 ff., below, is concerned. He discussed it with Jamâl-ad-dîn 'Abd-al-Malik b. 'Abdallâh al-Marjânî. Al-Marjânî himself informs us of this in his work on the *zâ'irajah* which was discovered and discussed by H. P. J. Renaud, "Divination et histoire nord-africaine au temps d'Ibn Khaldûn," *Hespéris*, XXX (1943), 213–21.

The origin of the word *zâ'irajah* has not yet been satisfactorily explained. It has been suggested correctly that it is related to Persian *zâ'icha* "horoscope, astronomical tables," (cf. *zîj*, 3:135 below), but the *r* seems to be an arbitrary addition, possibly by combination with *dâ'irah* "circle"?

365 His name was Muḥammad (Aḥmad) b. Mas'ûd. Cf. *GAL*, *Suppl.*, I, 909. He is a rather shadowy figure, and *GAL* puts him in the late thirteenth century, whereas according to Ibn Khaldûn he lived at the end of the twelfth. Ibn Khaldûn is possibly closer to the truth; cf. nn. 845, 846, to Ch. vi, below. Bulaq adds "Sîdî Aḥmad" to his name, thus confusing him with a famous saint, Aḥmad b. Ja'far, who lived from 540 to 601 [1145/46 to 1204/5]. Cf. M. Ben Cheneb in *EI*, *s.v.* "al-Sabtî." (Cf. also *GAL*, 2d ed., I, 655.)

366 He ruled from 1184 to 1199. Cf. also nn. 845 and 846 to Ch. vi, below.

367 The table was reproduced by Ibn Khaldûn below in connection with his extensive discussion of the *zâ'irajah*. See pls. i and ii and chart in end pocket, Vol. 3.

368 Cf. n. 882 to Ch. vi, below.

are found the names of the sciences and of topics of the created (world).[369] On the back of (the page containing) the circles, there is a table with many squares, fifty-five horizontally and one hundred and thirty-one vertically.[370] Some of the squares are filled in, partly with numbers and partly with letters. Others are empty. The significance of these numbers in their positions is not known, nor are the rules known that govern the distribution of filled and empty squares. The *zâ'irajah* is surrounded by verses in the meter *aṭ-ṭawîl* and rhyming on *-lâ*.[371] They describe the procedure which must be followed to discover the answer to a particular inquiry from the *zâ'irajah*. However, since the verses express their meaning in riddles, they lack clarity. On one side of the *zâ'irajah* is one verse from a poem ascribed to one of the great Western forecasters of future events, the Sevillian scholar, Mâlik b. Wuhayb,[372] who lived during the reign of the Lamtûnah (Almoravids). This is the verse:

I, 215

> A weighty question you have got. Keep, then, to yourself
> Remarkable doubts which have been raised and which
> can be straightened out with diligence.

---

[369] This difficult expression seems to refer to the innermost circle, which contains references to such subjects as horses and warfare.

[370] The tables published in the first volume of the *'Ibar* and in the Turkish translation of the *Muqaddimah*, as well as those in A and E, have only 128.

[371] The verses do not appear on the table, but they are quoted by Ibn Khaldûn below, 3:183 ff.

[372] He lived in the early twelfth century (453–525) [1061–1131]. Cf. *'Ibar*, VI, 228; de Slane (tr.), II, 169. He was a friend of Ibn Bâjjah (Avempace); cf. Ibn Abî Uṣaybi'ah, *'Uyûn al-anbâ'*, II, 63. Cf. also aṣ-Ṣafadî, *Wâfî*, ed. S. Dedering (Damascus, 1953), III, 325 f., and D. M. Dunlop, in *The Islamic Quarterly*, II (1955), 101–4.

B has a marginal note in this place by a Maghribî scholar, Abû l-Faḍl b. al-Imâm, who calls attention to the fact that Mâlik lived before as-Sabtî, the reputed inventor of the *zâ'irajah*. (There seems to be some confusion of *zâ'irajahs* in general, that existed long before, and the particular *Zâ'irajah of the World* discussed here.) The time interval between the two men makes it unlikely that as-Sabtî was the inventor, and its invention should rather be ascribed to Idrîs. (Cf. n. 921 to Ch. vi, below.) The teacher of the writer of the note, a certain Abû l-Qâsim b. Dâwûd as-Salawî (?), maintained this.

The verse is quoted again, 3:211, 214, and 224, below. It occurs also in a *zâ'irajah* ascribed to Ibn 'Arabî; cf. the Princeton MS, 5472 H, fol. 7b.

This is the verse commonly used in attempting to obtain the answer to a question with the help of this or other *zâ'irajahs*. To obtain the answer to a question, the question is written down in unconnected letters and the ascendant as of that day is determined, that is, one of the signs of the zodiac and the degree (of the sign on the horizon). Then, the *zâ'irajah* is consulted, and the particular chord of the *zâ'irajah* that borders the sign of the zodiac of that (particular) ascendant is chosen. This is followed from where it starts to the center, and then on to the circumference of the circle opposite the ascendant. One takes note of all the letters written upon that chord from beginning to end, and of all the numbers written in between. The latter are converted into letters according to their numerical values, transposing all units into tens and all tens into hundreds, and vice versa, as required by the rule governing use of (the *zâ'irajah*). The letters thus obtained are put alongside the letters of the question, and one also adds all the letters and numbers that are upon the chord bordering the sign, three signs from that of the ascendant. (In this case,) one follows it from where it starts to the center, but not beyond it to the circumference. The numbers are converted into letters as before, and added to the other letters. Then, the afore-mentioned verse by Mâlik b. Wuhayb, which is the basis and norm of the procedure, is written down in unconnected letters, and put aside. Then the number of the degree of the ascendant is multiplied by the "base" of the sign (of the zodiac). In the language (used here) the "base" is the sign's distance from the last rank, in contrast to the (meaning of) "base" in the language of astronomers [?], where it is the distance from the first rank.[373] *I, 216*

[373] The word discussed here is *uss* "base." It has a specific meaning in algebra—cf. n. 627 to Ch. VI, below—but still it is difficult to assume that instead of to "astrologers," Ibn Khaldûn refers here to "arithmeticians," even though the word he uses (*ḥussâb*) might mean the latter rather than the former. For the use of *uss* in the *zâ'irajah*, cf. 3:203 ff., below. The only meaning the above definition of the term would seem to suggest is that, in the *zâ'irajah*, *uss* refers to the number of degrees counting back to the beginning of the sign of the ascendant (or to some earlier sign), whereas in

The degree is then multiplied by another number, called the "greatest base" and "principal cycle." The result of these (multiplications) is entered in the squares of the table, following well-known rules and familiar procedures and (using a certain) number of "cycles." Some letters are taken out, others dropped, and the rest matched with what is found among the letters of the verse. Some are transferred to the letters of the question and (the letters) that are with them. Then, these letters are divided by certain numbers called "cycles," and from each "cycle" the letter at which the "cycle" ends, is removed. The (operation) is repeated with the (entire) number of "cycles" specified for that (purpose). The result, finally, is (a number of) unconnected letters which are put together consecutively to form the words of a verse of the same meter and rhyme as the afore-mentioned verse by Mâlik b. Wuhayb, which serves as the basis of the operation. We shall mention all this in the chapter on the sciences, in discussing how a *zâ'irajah* of this kind is used.

We have seen many distinguished people jump at (the opportunity for) supernatural discoveries through (the *zâ'irajah*) by means of operations of this kind. They think that correspondence (in form) between question and answer shows correspondence in actuality. This is not correct, because, as was mentioned before,[374] perception of the supernatural cannot be attained by means of any technique whatever. It is not impossible that there might be a correspondence in meaning, and a stylistic agreement, between question and answer, such that the answer comes out straight and in agreement with the question. It is not impossible that this could be achieved by just such a technique of separating the letters
I, 217 of the question and those of the chord, entering the numbers that come together as the result of the multiplication of fixed numbers in the table, taking out letters from the table and discarding others, operating repeatedly with a given number

astronomy *uss* means the number of degrees to the end of the sign. This, however, is so far mere speculation.

[374] Cf. p. 233, above.

of "cycles," and matching the whole thing with the letters of the verse arranged in sequence. Intelligent persons may have discovered the relationships among these things, and, as a result, have obtained information about the unknown through them. Finding out relationships between things is the secret (means) whereby the soul obtains knowledge of the unknown from the known. It is a way to obtain such knowledge, especially suited to people of (mystical) training. This (training) gives the intellect added power for analogical reasoning and thinking, as has been explained before several times.[375] It is in this sense that *zâ'irajahs* are usually ascribed to people of (mystical) training. This particular *zâ'irajah* is thus ascribed to as-Sabtî. I have come across another one which is ascribed to Sahl b. 'Abdallâh.[376]

It is, indeed, a remarkable operation and a wondrous procedure. As it appears to me, the secret of why the answer comes out in rhymed form is to be explained as the result of matching (the letters of the *zâ'irajah*) with the letters of the verse (by Mâlik b. Wuhayb). This is why the versified answer has the same meter and rhyme. This can be deduced from the fact that we have come across other similar operations in which the matching (of letters) with the verse was omitted. In those cases, the answer did not come out in the form of a verse. This will be shown when the matter is discussed in its proper place.[377]

Many people lack the understanding necessary for belief in the genuineness of the operation and its effectiveness in *I, 218* discovering the object of inquiry. They deny its soundness and believe that it is hocus-pocus. The practitioner, they believe, inserts the letters of a verse he (himself) composes as he wishes, from the letters of question and chord. He follows the described technique, which has no system or norm, and then he produces his verse, pretending that it was the result of an operation that followed an established procedure.

[375] It seems doubtful which passages Ibn Khaldûn has in mind here.
[376] At-Tustarî, a Sufi of the ninth century. Cf. *GAL, Suppl.*, I, 333.
[377] Cf. 3:213 f., below.

This reasoning is baseless and wrong. It is the result of such people's inability to understand the relations between the *existentia* and things that (can be) known, and the differences between the various kinds of perception and intellect. Anyone who has some perception naturally denies (the existence of) anything he is not capable of perceiving. In order to refute this (denial of the genuineness of the operation of the *zâ'irajah*), it is sufficient for us (to refer to the fact) that the technique has been observed in operation and that it has been definitely and intelligently established that the operation follows a coherent procedure and sound norms. No one who has much intelligence and sagacity and has had contact with the (operation of the *zâ'irajah*) would object to this statement. Many an operation with numbers, which are the clearest things in the world, is difficult to grasp, because the (existing) relations are difficult to establish and intricate. This is the case to a much greater degree here, where the relations are so intricate and strange.

Let us mention a problem that will to some degree illustrate the point just stated.

Take a number of dirhams and place beside each dirham three *fals*. Then, take all the *fals* and buy a fowl with them. Then, buy fowls with all the dirhams for the same price that the first bird cost. How many fowls will you have bought?

I, 219 The answer is nine. As you know, a dirham has twenty-four *fals*, three *fals* are one-eighth of a dirham, one is eight times one-eighth. Adding up one-eighth of each dirham buys one fowl. This means eight fowls (for the dirhams), as one is eight times one-eighth.[378] Add another fowl, the one that was bought originally for the additional *fals* and that determined the price of the fowls bought with the dirhams. This makes nine. It is clear how the unknown answer was implied in the relations that existed between the numerical data indicated

[378] In modern symbols, x being the number of fowls, y the number of dirhams:

$$y \cdot 1/8 = 1$$
$$y + y \cdot 1/8 = x$$
$$x = 8 + 1.$$

in the problem. This and similar (things) are at first suspected as belonging to the realm of the supernatural, which cannot be known.

It is thus obvious that it is from the relations existing among the data that one finds out the unknown from the known. This, however, applies only to events occurring in (the world of) existence or in science. Things of the future belong to the supernatural and cannot be known unless the causes for their happening are known and we have trustworthy information about it.

If this is clear, it follows that all the operations of the *zâ'irajah* serve merely to discover the words of the answer in the words of the question. As we have seen, it is a question of producing from a given arrangement of letters another arrangement of letters. The secret here lies in the existence of a relationship between the two (different arrangements of letters). Someone may be aware of it, whereas someone else may not be aware of it. Those who know the existing relationship can easily discover the answer with the help of the stated rules.

From the (conventional) meanings and the combinations of words, the answer may then also indicate a negative or positive (statement) regarding (the object of) the question. This, however, is on another level. It is not on the same I, 220
level (as merely discovering the words of the answer). It implies a conformity of the words to the outside (world).[379] Such knowledge cannot be acquired through those operations. It remains veiled to human beings.

God claims all His knowledge for Himself. "God knows and you do not know." [380]

[379] *Muṭâbaqah* "conformity, agreement," is an important concept in Ibn Khaldûn's epistemology. Cf. also, for instance, 3:251, below.

In another application, the term also plays an important role in Ibn Khaldûn's definition of rhetoric. Cf., for instance, 3:335, below.

[380] Qur'ân 2.216 (213), 232 (232); 3.66 (59); 24.19 (19).

Chapter II

BEDOUIN CIVILIZATION, SAVAGE NATIONS AND TRIBES AND THEIR CONDITIONS (OF LIFE), INCLUDING SEVERAL BASIC AND EXPLANATORY STATEMENTS.[1]

[1] The whole chapter is translated in G. Surdon and L. Bercher, *Recueil de textes de sociologie* (Algiers, 1951), pp. 7–57.

[1] *Both Bedouins and sedentary people are natural groups.*

IT[2] SHOULD BE KNOWN that differences of condition among people are the result of the different ways in which they make their living. Social organization enables them to co-operate toward that end and to start with the simple necessities of life, before they get to conveniences and luxuries.[3]

Some people adopt agriculture, the cultivation of vegetables and grains, (as their way of making a living). Others adopt animal husbandry, the use of sheep, cattle, goats, bees, and silkworms, for breeding and for their products. Those who live by agriculture or animal husbandry cannot avoid the call of the desert, because it alone offers the wide fields, acres, pastures for animals, and other things that the settled *I, 221* areas do not offer.[4] It is therefore necessary for them to restrict themselves to the desert. Their social organization and co-operation for the needs of life and civilization, such as food, shelter, and warmth, do not take them beyond the bare subsistence level, because of their inability (to provide) for anything beyond those (things). Subsequent improvement of their conditions and acquisition of more wealth and comfort than they need, cause them to rest and take it easy. Then, they co-operate for things beyond the (bare) necessities. They use more food and clothes, and take pride in them. They build large houses, and lay out towns and cities for protection. This is followed by an increase in comfort and ease, which leads to formation of the most developed luxury customs. They take the greatest pride in the preparation of food and a fine cuisine, in the use of varied splendid clothes of silk and brocade and other (fine materials), in the construction of ever higher buildings and towers, in elaborate furnish-

---

[2] Cf. Issawi, pp. 80 f. [3] Cf. pp. lxxxi and 85, above.

[4] Cf. G. E. von Grunebaum, "as-Sakkâkî on Milieu and Thought," *Journal of the American Oriental Society*, LXV (1945), 62.

ings for the buildings, and the most intensive cultivation of crafts in actuality. They build castles and mansions, provide them with running water,[5] build their towers higher and higher, and compete in furnishing them (most elaborately). They differ in the quality of the clothes, the beds, the vessels, and the utensils they employ for their purposes. Here, now, (we have) sedentary people. "Sedentary people" means the inhabitants of cities and countries, some of whom adopt the crafts as their way of making a living, while others adopt commerce. They earn more and live more comfortably than
I, 222 Bedouins, because they live on a level beyond the level of (bare) necessity, and their way of making a living corresponds to their wealth.

It has thus become clear that Bedouins and sedentary people are natural groups which exist by necessity, as we have stated.

[2] *The Arabs*[6] *are a natural group in the world.*

We have mentioned in the previous section that the inhabitants of the desert adopt the natural manner of making a living, namely, agriculture and animal husbandry. They restrict themselves to the necessary in food, clothing, and mode of dwelling, and to the other necessary conditions and customs. They do not possess conveniences and luxuries beyond (these bare necessities). They use tents of hair and wool, or houses of wood, or of clay and stone, which are not furnished (elaborately). The purpose is to have shade and shelter, and nothing beyond that. They also take shelter in caverns and caves. The food they take is either little prepared or not prepared at all, save that it may have been touched by fire.[7]

For those who make their living through the cultivation

[5] Cf. also p. 339, below.

[6] As a sociological term, "Arab" is always synonymous with "Bedouin, nomad" to Ibn Khaldûn, regardless of racial, national, or linguistic distinctions.

[7] Ibn Khaldûn was familiar with this phrase for "preparing food in the open fire" through the *ḥadîth* literature. Cf. F. Rosenthal, *A History of Muslim Historiography*, p. 206.

of grain and through agriculture, it is better to be stationary than to travel around. Such, therefore, are the inhabitants of small communities, villages, and mountain regions. These people make up the large mass of the Berbers and non-Arabs.

Those who make their living from animals requiring pasturage, such as sheep and cattle, usually travel around in order to find pasture and water for their animals, since it is better for them to move around in the land. They are called "sheepmen" (*shâwîyah*), that is, men who live on sheep and cattle. They do not go deep into the desert, because they would not find good pastures there. Such people include the Berbers, the Turks and their relatives, the Turkomans and the Slavs,[8] for instance.

Those who make their living by raising camels move I, 223
around more. They wander deeper into the desert, because the hilly [9] pastures with their plants and shrubs do not furnish enough subsistence for camels. They must feed on the desert shrubs and drink the salty desert water. They must move around the desert regions during the winter, in flight from the harmful cold to the warm desert air. In the desert sands, camels can find places to give birth to their young ones. Of all animals, camels have the hardest delivery and the greatest need for warmth in connection with it.[10] (Camel nomads) are therefore forced to make excursions deep (into the desert). Frequently, too, they are driven from the hills by the militia, and they penetrate farther into the desert, because they do not want the militia [11] to mete out justice to them or to

---

[8] Though the Arabic text need not be understood as saying that there exists a relationship between the Slavs and the Turks, it is the most natural construction to understand it that way. It has been shown that Muslim geographers did not always mean precisely Slavs when they spoke about the *Ṣaqâlibah*. (Cf. A. Zeki Validi Togan, *Ibn Faḍlân's Reisebericht*, pp. 295 ff.) However, the above statement should not be taken too literally, and the term used for "relatives" (*ikhwân* "brethren") may perhaps be translated as "companions" or the like, implying no real relationship.

[9] *Tall*, pl. *tulûl* "hills." The expression reflects the situation in northwestern Africa rather than in Arabia.

[10] Cf. p. 265 and 2:353, below, and *'Ibar*, II, 336 f.

[11] Bulaq, apparently by mistake, has "to humiliate them" for the rest of the sentence.

punish them for their hostile acts. As a result, they are the most savage human beings that exist. Compared with sedentary people, they are on a level with wild, untamable (animals) and dumb beasts of prey. Such people are the Arabs. In the West, the nomadic Berbers and the Zanâtah are their counterparts, and in the East, the Kurds, the Turkomans, and the Turks. The Arabs, however, make deeper excursions into the desert and are more rooted in desert life (than the other groups), because they live exclusively on camels, while the other groups live on sheep and cattle, as well as camels.

It has thus become clear that the Arabs are a natural group which by necessity exists in civilization.

God is "the Creator, the Knowing One." [12]

[3] *Bedouins are prior to sedentary people. The desert is the basis and reservoir of civilization and cities.*

We [13] have mentioned that the Bedouins restrict themselves to the (bare) necessities in their conditions (of life) and
I, 224 are unable to go beyond them, while sedentary people concern themselves with conveniences and luxuries in their conditions and customs. The (bare) necessities are no doubt prior to the conveniences and luxuries. (Bare) necessities, in a way, are basic, and luxuries secondary and an outgrowth (of the necessities). Bedouins, thus, are the basis of, and prior to, cities and sedentary people. Man seeks first the (bare) necessities. Only after he has obtained the (bare) necessities, does he get to comforts and luxuries. The toughness of desert life precedes the softness of sedentary life. Therefore, urbanization is found to be the goal of the Bedouin. He aspires to (that goal).[14] Through his own efforts, he achieves what he proposes to achieve in this respect. When he has obtained enough to be ready for the conditions

[12] Qur'ân 15.86 (86); 36.81 (81).
[13] Cf. Issawi, pp. 81 f.
[14] But contrast below, p. 266.

and customs of luxury, he enters upon a life of ease and submits himself to the yoke of the city. This is the case with all Bedouin tribes. Sedentary people, on the other hand, have no desire for desert conditions, unless they are motivated by some urgent necessity [15] or they cannot keep up with their fellow city dwellers.

Evidence for the fact that Bedouins are the basis of, and prior to, sedentary people is furnished by investigating the inhabitants of any given city. We shall find that most of its inhabitants originated among Bedouins dwelling in the country and villages of the vicinity. Such Bedouins became wealthy, settled in the city, and adopted a life of ease and luxury, such as exists in the sedentary environment. This proves that sedentary conditions are secondary to desert conditions and that they are the basis of them.[15a] This should be understood.

All Bedouins and sedentary people differ also among themselves in their conditions (of life). Many a clan is greater than another, many a tribe greater than another, I, 225
many a city larger than another, and many a town more populous (*'umrân*) than another.

It has thus become clear that the existence of Bedouins is prior to, and the basis of, the existence of towns and cities. Likewise, the existence of towns and cities results from luxury customs pertaining to luxury and ease, which are posterior to the customs that go with the bare necessities of life.

[4] *Bedouins are closer to being good than sedentary people.*

The [16] reason for it is that the soul in its first natural state of creation is ready to accept whatever good or evil may ar-

[15] Ibn Khaldûn is probably thinking of political exile and retirement in the country such as he experienced himself when writing the *Muqaddimah.*

[15a] The pronouns are as ambiguous in Arabic as they are in English, and, were it not for the context, would be understood to mean the opposite of what they are intended to mean.

[16] Cf. Issawi, pp. 66 f.

rive and leave an imprint upon it. Muḥammad said: "Every infant is born in the natural state. It is his parents who make him a Jew or a Christian or a Magian." [17] To the degree the soul is first affected by one of the two qualities, it moves away from the other and finds it difficult to acquire it. When customs proper to goodness have been first to enter the soul of a good person and his (soul) has thus acquired the habit of (goodness, that person) moves away from evil and finds it difficult to do anything evil. The same applies to the evil person when customs (proper to evil) have been first to affect him.

Sedentary people are much concerned with all kinds of pleasures. They are accustomed to luxury and success in worldly occupations and to indulgence in worldly desires. Therefore, their souls are colored with all kinds of blameworthy and evil qualities. The more of them they possess, the more remote do the ways and means of goodness become to them. Eventually they lose all sense of restraint. Many of them are found to use improper language in their gatherings
I, 226 as well as in the presence of their superiors and womenfolk. They are not deterred by any sense of restraint, because the bad custom of behaving openly in an improper manner in both words and deeds has taken hold of them. Bedouins may be as concerned with worldly affairs as (sedentary people are). However, such concern would touch only the necessities of life and not luxuries or anything causing, or calling for, desires and pleasures. The customs they follow in their mutual dealings are, therefore, appropriate. As compared with those of sedentary people, their evil ways and blameworthy qualities are much less numerous. They are closer to the first natural state and more remote from the evil habits that have been impressed upon the souls (of sedentary people) through numerous and ugly, blameworthy customs. Thus, they can more easily be cured than sedentary people.

---

[17] Cf., for instance, al-Bukhârî, *Ṣaḥîḥ*, I, 341; *Concordance*, I, 7b, ll. 5 f. Cf. also p. 306, below.

This is obvious. It will later on [18] become clear that sedentary life constitutes the last stage of civilization and the point where it begins to decay. It also constitutes the last stage of evil and of remoteness from goodness. It has thus become clear that Bedouins are closer to being good than sedentary people. "God loves those who fear God." [19]

This is not contradicted by the statement of al-Ḥajjâj to Salamah b. al-Akwaʻ, which is included among the traditions of al-Bukhârî. When al-Ḥajjâj learned that Salamah was going to live in the desert, he asked him, "You have turned back and become an Arab?" Salamah replied, "No, but the Messenger of God permitted me to go (back) to the desert." [20]

It should be known that at the beginning of Islam, the inhabitants of Mecca were enjoined to emigrate, so as to be with the Prophet wherever he might settle, in order to help him and to aid him in his affairs and to guard him. The Arab Bedouins of the desert were not enjoined to emigrate, because the Meccans were possessed of a strong group feeling I, 227
for the Prophet to aid and guard him, such as did not exist among the desert Arabs. The emigrants, therefore, used to express an aversion to "becoming Arabs," that is, (to becoming) inhabitants of the desert upon whom emigration was not obligatory. According to the tradition of Saʻd b. Abî Waqqâṣ, Muḥammad said, when (Saʻd) was ill in Mecca: "O God, give success to the emigration of my companions and do not cause them to turn back." [21] That means, God should enable them to stay in Medina and not to have to leave it, so that they would not have to discontinue the emigration they had begun, and return. It is the same meaning as is implied in the expression "turning back" in connection with any enterprise.

It is (also) said that the (prohibition against "turning

---

[18] Cf. 2:291 ff., below. [19] Qur'ân 3.76 (70); 9.4 (4), 7 (7).

[20] Cf. al-Bukhârî, *Ṣaḥîḥ*, IV, 373; *Concordance*, II, 247*a*, ll. 32 f.; Ibn Ḥajar, *Tahdhîb*, IV, 150 ff.

[21] Cf. al-Bukhârî, *Ṣaḥîḥ*, I, 326; *Concordance*, I, 245*b*, ll. 25 ff.

back") was restricted to the time before the conquest of Mecca, when there was a need for emigration because of the small number of Muslims. After the conquest, when the Muslims had become numerous and strong, and God had guaranteed His Prophet inviolability (*'iṣmah*), emigration was no longer necessary. Muḥammad said: "There is no emigration after the conquest." [22] This has been interpreted as meaning that the injunction to emigrate was no longer valid for those who became Muslims after the conquest. It has also been interpreted (to mean) that emigration was no longer obligatory upon those who had become Muslims and had emigrated before the conquest. (At any rate,) all agree that emigration was no longer necessary after the Prophet's death, because the men around Muḥammad had by then dispersed and spread in all directions. The only thing that remained was the merit of living in Medina, which constituted emigration.

Thus, al-Ḥajjâj's statement to Salamah, who went to live in the desert: "You have turned back and become an Arab?" is a reproach to Salamah for giving up his residence in Medina. It contains an allusion to the words of the afore-mentioned prayer of the Prophet: "Do not cause them to turn back." The words, "You have become an Arab?" are a reproach, as they imply that Salamah had become one of the
I, 228 Arabs who did not emigrate. In his reply, Salamah denied both insinuations. He said that the Prophet had permitted him to go to the desert. This was a special (permission) in Salamah's case, exactly as, for instance, the testimony of Khuzaymah [23] and Abû Burdah's [24] lamb were special to the

---

[22] Cf. the references in *Handbook*, p. 98*b*.

[23] Khuzaymah b. Thâbit's testimony was counted by the Prophet as that of two men. Cf. *Concordance*, III, 198*b*, l. 4; al-Bukhârî, *Ta'rîkh*, II[1], 188; Ibn Sa'd, *Ṭabaqât*, ed. E. Sachau *et al.* (Leiden, 1905–40), IV[2], 90 ff.; Ibn Ḥajar, *Tahdhîb*, III, 140.

[24] The sacrificial animal should be slaughtered after prayer, but in the case of Abû Burdah Hâni' b. Niyâr, the animal he had slaughtered previously was accounted a valid sacrifice by the Prophet. This, however, is stated not to be a precedent. Cf. al-Bukhârî, *Ṣaḥîḥ*, IV, 21; *Concordance*, I, 329*b*, ll. 32 ff.

cases of Khuzaymah and Abû Burdah. Or, (it may be) al-Ḥajjâj reproached Salamah only because he was giving up his residence in Medina, as he was aware that emigration was no longer necessary after the Prophet's death. Salamah's reply was that it was more proper and better to avail himself of the Prophet's permission, who had distinguished him by this special permission only because (the Prophet) had some motive known to him(self) when he gave it.

In any event, the story does not imply that censure of desert (life) is meant by the expression "to become an Arab." It is known that the legal obligation to emigrate served the purposes of aiding and guarding the Prophet. It did not have the purpose of censuring desert (life). Use of the expression "to become an Arab," to condemn non-fulfillment of the duty (of emigration), is no indication that "becoming an Arab" is something blameworthy. And God knows better.

[5] *Bedouins are more disposed to courage than sedentary people.*

The [25] reason for this is that sedentary people have become used to laziness and ease. They are sunk in well-being and luxury. They have entrusted defense of their property and their lives to the governor and ruler who rules them, and to the militia which has the task of guarding them. They find full assurance of safety in the walls that surround them, and the fortifications that protect them. No noise disturbs them, and no hunting occupies them. They are carefree and trusting, and have ceased to carry weapons. Successive generations have grown up in this way of life. They have become like women and children, who depend upon the master of the I, 229
house. Eventually, this has come to be a quality of character that replaces natural (disposition).

The Bedouins, on the other hand, live separate from the community. They are alone in the country and remote from militias. They have no walls and gates. Therefore, they pro-

---

[25] Cf. Issawi, pp. 67 f.

vide their own defense and do not entrust it to, or rely upon others for it. They always carry weapons. They watch carefully all sides of the road. They take hurried naps only when they are together in company or when they are in the saddle. They pay attention to every faint barking and noise. They go alone into the desert, guided by their fortitude, putting their trust in themselves. Fortitude has become a character quality of theirs, and courage their nature. They use it whenever they are called upon or an alarm stirs them. When sedentary people mix with them in the desert or associate with them on a journey, they depend on them. They cannot do anything for themselves without them. This is an observed fact. (Their dependence extends) even to knowledge of the country, the (right) directions, watering places, and crossroads. The reason for this is the thing we have explained. At the base of it is the fact that man is a child of the customs and the things he has become used to. He is not the product of his natural disposition and temperament.[25a] The conditions to which he has become accustomed, until they have become for him a quality of character and matters of habit and custom, have replaced his natural disposition. If one studies this in human beings, one will find much of it, and it will be found to be a correct (observation).

"God creates whatever He wishes." [26]

I, 230 [6] *The reliance of sedentary people upon laws destroys their fortitude and power of resistance.*

Not everyone is master of his own affairs. Chiefs and leaders who are masters of the affairs of men are few in comparison with the rest. As a rule, man must by necessity be dominated by someone else. If the domination is kind and just and the people under it are not oppressed by its laws and restrictions, they are guided by the courage or cowardice that they possess in themselves. They are satisfied with the ab-

[25a] Cf. n. 21 to Ch. v, below.

[26] Qur'ân 3.47 (42); 5.17 (20); 24.45 (44); 28.68 (68); 30.54 (53); 39.4 (6); 42.49 (48).

sence of any restraining power. Self-reliance eventually becomes a quality natural to them. They would not know anything else. If, however, the domination with its laws is one of brute force and intimidation, it breaks their fortitude and deprives them of their power of resistance as a result of the inertness that develops in the souls of the oppressed, as we shall explain.

'Umar forbade Sa'd (b. Abî Waqqâṣ) to exercise such (arbitrary power) when Zuhrah b. Ḥawîyah took the spoils of al-Jâlinûs. The value of the spoils was 75,000 gold pieces. (Zuhrah) had followed al-Jâlinûs on the day of al-Qâdisîyah, killed him, and taken his spoils. Sa'd took them away from him and said, "Why did you not wait for my permission to follow him?" He wrote to 'Umar and asked 'Umar for permission (to confiscate the spoils). But 'Umar replied, "Would you want to proceed against a man like Zuhrah, who already has borne so much of the brunt (of battle),[27] and while there still remains so much of the war for you (to finish)? Would you want to break his strength and morale?" Thus, 'Umar confirmed (Zuhrah) in possession of the spoils.[28]

When laws are (enforced) by means of punishment, they completely destroy fortitude, because the use of punishment against someone who cannot defend himself generates in that person a feeling of humiliation that, no doubt, must break his I, 231
fortitude.

When laws are (intended to serve the purposes of) education and instruction and are applied from childhood on, they have to some degree the same effect, because people then grow up in fear and docility and consequently do not rely on their own fortitude.

For this (reason), greater fortitude is found among the savage Arab Bedouins than among people who are subject to laws. Furthermore, those who rely on laws and are dominated by them from the very beginning of their education and instruction in the crafts, sciences, and religious matters, are

[27] Or, more generally, "who has shown himself so courageous."
[28] Cf. aṭ-Ṭabarî, *Annales*, I, 2346.

thereby deprived of much of their own fortitude. They can scarcely defend themselves at all against hostile acts. This is the case with students, whose occupation it is to study and to learn from teachers and religious leaders, and who constantly apply themselves to instruction and education in very dignified gatherings. This situation and the fact that it destroys the power of resistance and fortitude must be understood.

It is no argument against the (statement just made) that the men around Muḥammad observed the religious laws, and yet did not experience any diminution of their fortitude, but possessed the greatest possible fortitude. When the Muslims got their religion from the Lawgiver (Muḥammad), the restraining influence came from themselves, as a result of the encouragement and discouragement he gave them in the Qur'ân.[29] It was not a result of technical instruction or scientific education. (The laws) were the laws and precepts of the religion, which they received orally and which their firmly rooted (belief in) the truth of the articles of faith caused them to observe. Their fortitude remained unabated, and it was
I, 232 not corroded by education or authority. 'Umar said, "Those who are not educated (disciplined) by the religious law are not educated (disciplined) by God." [30] (This statement expresses) 'Umar's desire that everyone should have his restraining influence in himself. It also expresses his certainty that the Lawgiver (Muḥammad) knew best what is good for mankind.

(The influence of) religion, then, decreased among men, and they came to use restraining laws. The religious law became a branch of learning and a craft to be acquired through instruction and education. People turned to sedentary life and assumed the character trait of submissiveness to law. This led to a decrease in their fortitude.

It has thus become clear that governmental and educational laws destroy fortitude, because their restraining in-

---

[29] *Talâ* "he recited." Cf. the term *matlûw*, p. 192 (n. 261), above, and p. 437 and 3:113, 284, below.

[30] Cf. 3:306, below.

fluence is something that comes from outside. The religious laws, on the other hand, do not destroy fortitude, because their restraining influence is something inherent. Therefore, governmental and educational laws influence sedentary people, in that they weaken their souls and diminish their stamina, because they have to suffer (their authority) both as children and as adults. The Bedouins, on the other hand, are not in the same position, because they live far away from the laws of government, instruction, and education. Therefore, Abû Muḥammad b. Abî Zayd,[31] in his book on the laws governing teachers and students (*Aḥkâm al-mu'allimîn wa-l-muta'allimîn*), said: "The educator must not strike a boy more than three times (in one punishment) as an educational measure." [32] (Ibn Abî Zayd) reported this remark on the authority of Judge Shurayḥ.[33] Certain scholar(s) argued in favor of the procedure mentioned, by referring to the threefold choking mentioned in the tradition concerned with the beginning of revelation.[34] This, however, is a weak argument. (The tradition about the) choking is not suitable proof, because it has nothing to do with ordinary instruction. God "is wise and knowing." [35]

[7] *Only tribes held together by group feeling can live in the desert.* I, 233

It should be known that God put good and evil into the nature of man. Thus, He said in the Qur'ân: "We led him

[31] Cf. p. 223, above.

[32] Cf. also 3:206, below. In the city of Ibn Khaldûn's ancestors, it was prescribed *ca.* 1100 that "an older child should not be struck more than five times, nor a small one more than three, and the severity of the blows should be according to the strength of the individual children to stand them." Cf. E. Lévi-Provençal, "Le Traité d'Ibn 'Abdûn," *Journal asiatique*, CCXXIV (1934), 214; tr. by the same, *Séville musulmane au début du XIIe siècle* (Islam d'hier et d'aujourd'hui, No. 2) (Paris, 1947), pp. 53 f.

[33] Shurayḥ lived in the seventh century and is said to have been appointed judge of al-Kûfah by 'Umar. Cf. J. Schacht, *The Origins of Muhammadan Jurisprudence* (Oxford, 1950), pp. 228 f.

[34] Cf. pp. 201 f., above. The story of the threefold choking is here understood as an educational measure, serving the purpose of teaching Muḥammad how to read the writing revealed to him by Gabriel.

[35] Qur'ân 6.18 (18), 73 (73); 34.1 (1).

along the two paths." [36] He further said: "And inspired (the soul) with its wickedness as well as its fear of God." [37]

Evil is the quality that is closest to man when he fails to improve his customs and (when) religion is not used as the model to improve him. The great mass of mankind is in that condition, with the exception of those to whom God gives success. Evil [38] qualities in man are injustice and mutual aggression. He who casts his eye upon the property of his brother will lay his hand upon it to take it, unless there is a restraining influence to hold him back. The poet thus said:

Injustice is a human characteristic. If you find
A moral man,[39] there is some reason why he is not unjust.

Mutual aggression of people in towns and cities is averted by the authorities and the government, which hold back the masses under their control from attacks and aggression upon each other. They are thus prevented by the influence of force and governmental authority from mutual injustice, save such injustice as comes from the ruler himself.

Aggression against a city from outside may be averted by walls, in the event of negligence,[40] a surprise attack at night, or inability (of the inhabitants) to withstand the enemy during the day. (Or,) it may be averted with the help of a militia of government auxiliary troops, if (the inhabitants are otherwise) prepared and ready to offer resistance.

The [41] restraining influence among Bedouin tribes comes from their *shaykhs* and leaders. It results from the great respect and veneration they generally enjoy among the people. The hamlets of the Bedouins are defended against outside en-

---

[36] Qur'ân 90.10 (10). [37] Qur'ân 91.8 (8). [38] Cf. Issawi, pp. 105 f.

[39] *'Iffah* is the term picked by translators of Greek texts into Arabic for σωφροσύνη.

The verse is by al-Mutanabbi'; cf. the appendix to the edition of his *Dîwân* (Beirut, 1882), II, 630, and ar-Râghib al-Iṣfahânî, *Muḥâḍarât*, I, 140.

[40] That is, a general state of unpreparedness.

[41] The remainder of this section was translated by R. A. Nicholson, *Translations of Eastern Poetry and Prose*, pp. 181 f.

emies by a tribal militia composed of noble youths of the tribe who are known for their courage. Their defense and protection are successful only if they are a closely-knit group [42] of common descent. This strengthens their stamina and makes them feared, since everybody's affection for his family and his group is more important (than anything else). Compassion and affection for one's blood relations and relatives exist in human nature as something God put into the hearts of men. It makes for mutual support and aid, and increases the fear felt by the enemy. I, 234

This may be exemplified by the story in the Qur'ân about Joseph's brothers. They said to their father: "If the wolf eats him, while we are a group, then, indeed, we have lost out." [43] This means that one cannot imagine any hostile act being undertaken against anyone who has his group feeling to support him.

Those who have no one of their own lineage (to care for) rarely feel affection for their fellows. If danger is in the air on the day of battle, such a one slinks away and seeks to save himself, because he is afraid of being left without support [44] and dreads (that prospect). Such people, therefore, cannot live in the desert, because they would fall prey to any nation that might want to swallow them up.

If this is true with regard to the place where one lives, which is in constant need of defense and military protection, it is equally true with regard to every other human activity, such as prophecy, the establishment of royal authority, or propaganda (for a cause). Nothing can be achieved in these matters without fighting for it, since man has the natural urge to offer resistance. And for fighting one cannot do without group feeling, as we mentioned at the beginning. This should be taken as the guiding principle of our later exposition.

God gives success.

---

[42] Here the text has *'aṣabîyah* "group feeling," though *'uṣbah* "group" would seem better.

[43] Qur'ân 12.14 (14).

[44] Cf. R. Dozy in *Journal asiatique*, XIV[6] (1869), 152 f.

I, 235 [8] *Group feeling results only from (blood) relationship or something corresponding to it.*

(Respect for) blood [45] ties is something natural among men, with the rarest exceptions. It leads to affection for one's relations and blood relatives, (the feeling that) no harm ought to befall them nor any destruction come upon them. One feels shame when one's relatives are treated unjustly or attacked, and one wishes to intervene between them and whatever peril or destruction threatens them. This is a natural urge in man, for as long as there have been human beings. If the direct relationship between persons who help each other is very close, so that it leads to close contact and unity, the ties are obvious and clearly require the (existence of a feeling of solidarity) without any outside (prodding). If, however, the relationship is somewhat distant, it is often forgotten in part. However, some knowledge of it remains and this causes a person to help his relatives for the known motive, in order to escape the shame he would feel in his soul were a person to whom he is somehow related treated unjustly.[46]

Clients and allies belong in the same category. The affection everybody has for his clients and allies results from the feeling of shame that comes to a person when one of his neighbors, relatives, or a blood relation in any degree (of kinship) is humiliated. The reason for it is that a client(-master) relationship leads to close contact exactly, or approximately in the same way, as does common descent. It is in that sense that one must understand Muḥammad's remark, "Learn as much of your pedigrees as is necessary to establish your ties of blood relationship." [47] It means that pedigrees

---

[45] Cf. Issawi, pp. 103 f. [46] Cf. Bombaci, pp. 446 f.

[47] Cf. *Concordance*, II, 238*b;* Ibn Abî Zayd, *Risâlah*, ed. L. Bercher (3d ed.), p. 326, where 'Umar is credited with the saying; F. Rosenthal, *A History of Muslim Historiography*, p. 27 (n. 3). The phrase *waṣala ar-raḥim* (*al-arḥâm*) has been understood to mean "to be kind and give presents to one's blood relatives." In the context where it occurs below, 2:145 (n. 761), one might think of such a translation, though it does not seem to be correct there. Here it would be impossible.

are useful only in so far as they imply the close contact that is I, 236
a consequence of blood ties and that eventually leads to mutual help and affection. Anything beyond that is superfluous.[48] For a pedigree is something imaginary and devoid of reality.[49] Its usefulness consists only in the resulting connection and close contact. If the fact of (common descent) is obvious and clear, it evokes in man a natural affection, as we have said. If, however, its existence is known only from remote history, it moves the imagination but faintly. Its usefulness is gone, and preoccupation with it becomes gratuitous, a kind of game, and as such is not permissible. In this sense, one must understand the remark, "Genealogy is something that is of no use to know and that it does no harm not to know." [50] This means that when common descent is no longer clear and has become a matter of scientific knowledge, it can no longer move the imagination and is denied the affection caused by group feeling. It has become useless.

And God knows better.

[9] *Purity of lineage is found only among the savage Arabs of the desert and other such people.*

This [51] is on account of the poor life, hard conditions, and bad habitats that are peculiar to the Arabs. They are the result of necessity that destined (these conditions) for (the Arabs), in as much as their subsistence depends on camels and camel breeding and pasturage. The camels are the cause of (the Arabs') savage life in the desert, since they feed on the shrubs of the desert and give birth (to their young ones) in the desert sands, as has been mentioned before.[52] The desert is a place of hardship and starvation, but to them it has become familiar and accustomed. Generations of (Arabs) grew
up in the desert. Eventually, they become confirmed in their I, 237
character and natural qualities. No member of any other

---

[48] The correct vocalization *mustaghnân* is indicated in C and D.
[49] Cf. p. 374, below.
[50] Cf. F. Rosenthal, *op. cit.*, p. 242.
[51] Cf. Issawi, pp. 104 f.
[52] Cf. p. 251, above.

nation was disposed to share their conditions. No member of any other race felt attracted to them. But if one of them were to find ways and means of fleeing from these conditions, he would not (do so or) give them up.[53] Therefore, their pedigrees can be trusted not to have been mixed up and corrupted. They have been preserved pure in unbroken lines. This is the case, for instance, with Muḍar tribes such as the Quraysh, the Kinânah, the Thaqîf, the Banû Asad, the Hudhayl, and their Khuzâ'ah neighbors. They lived a hard life in places where there was no agriculture or animal husbandry. They lived far from the fertile fields of Syria and the 'Irâq, far from the sources of seasonings and grains. How pure have they kept their lineages! These are unmixed in every way, and are known to be unsullied.

Other Arabs lived in the hills and at the sources of fertile pastures and plentiful living. Among these Arabs were the Ḥimyar and the Kahlân, such as the Lakhm, the Judhâm, the Ghassân, the Ṭayy, the Quḍâ'ah, and the Iyâd. Their lineages were mixed up, and their groups intermingled. It is known that people (genealogists) differ with respect to each one of these families. This came about as the result of intermixture with non-Arabs. They did not pay any attention to preserving the (purity of) lineage of their families and groups. This [54] was done only by (true) Arabs. 'Umar said: "Study genealogy, and be not like the Nabataeans of the Mesopotamian lowlands. When one of them is asked about his origin, he says: 'From such and such a village.' "[55] Furthermore, the Arabs of the fertile fields were affected by the general human trend toward competition for the fat soil and the good pastures. This resulted in intermingling and much mixture of lineages. Even at the beginning of Islam,
I, 238 people occasionally referred to themselves by their places of residence. They referred to the Districts of Qinnasrîn, of Damascus, or of the 'Awâṣim (the border region of northern

[53] But see above, p. 252. [54] Cf. Issawi, pp. 106 f.

[55] Cf. Ibn 'Abdrabbih, *'Iqd*, II, 37; Ibn 'Abd-al-Barr, *al-Inbâh 'alâ qabâ'il ar-ruwâh* (Cairo, 1350/1931–32), p. 43.

Syria). This custom was then transferred to Spain. It happened not because the Arabs rejected genealogical considerations, but because they acquired particular places of residence after the conquest. They eventually became known by their places of residence. These became a distinguishing mark, in addition to the pedigree, used by (the Arabs) to identify themselves in the presence of their amirs. Later on, sedentary (Arabs) mixed with Persians and other non-Arabs. Purity of lineage was completely lost, and its fruit, the group feeling, was lost and rejected. The tribes, then, disappeared and were wiped out, and with them, the group feeling was wiped out. But the (earlier situation) remained unchanged among the Bedouins.

God inherits the earth and whomever is upon it.

[10] *How lineages become confused.*

It is clear that a person of a certain descent may become attached to people of another descent, either because he feels well-disposed toward them, or because there exists an (old) alliance or client(-master) relationship, or yet because he had to flee from his own people by reason of some crime he committed. Such a person comes to be known as having the same descent as those (to whom he has attached himself) and is counted one of them with respect to the things that result from (common descent), such as affection, the rights and obligations concerning talion and blood money, and so on. When the things which result from (common) descent are there, it is as if (common descent) itself were there, because the only meaning of belonging to one or another group is that one is subject to its laws and conditions, as if one had come into close contact with it. In the course of time, the original descent is almost forgotten. Those who knew about it have passed away, and it is no longer known to most people. Family lines in this manner continually changed from one tribal group to another, and some people developed close contact with others (of a different descent). This happened both in pre-Islamic and in Islamic times, and between both

I, 239 Arabs and non-Arabs. If one studies the different opinions concerning the pedigree of the family of al-Mundhir[56] and others, the matter will become somewhat clearer.

The affair of the Bajîlah and 'Arfajah b. Harthamah is an(other) illustration. When 'Umar appointed 'Arfajah their governor, (the Bajîlah) asked ('Umar) to withdraw him, saying that he was a *nazîf*[57] among them, that is, one who had come to them from outside and attached himself to them. They asked that he appoint Jarîr (instead). 'Umar asked 'Arfajah about this, and he replied: "They are right, O Commander of the Faithful. I am from the Azd. I shed blood among my people, and joined (the Bajîlah)."[58] This shows how 'Arfajah had come to mix with the Bajîlah, had become of their skin, and was known as one having the same descent as they, to the extent that he could eventually become a candidate for leadership over them, (and would have) had someone not remembered the genealogical ramifications. Had they overlooked it and had (still) more time elapsed, (his foreign origin) would have been forgotten, and he would have been considered one of them in every respect.

This should be understood and pondered as one of God's ways with His creatures. Similar things occur frequently in our own times, and have always been frequent in former times.[59]

---

[56] The Lakhmids of al-Ḥîrah on the Euphrates.

[57] Bulaq has the freehand correction *lazîq*. *Nazîf* has no meaning that would be suitable here, according to the Arabic dictionaries. R. Dozy, *op. cit.* (n. 44, above), and also in *Supplément aux dictionnaires arabes*, II, 658a, called attention to the fact that aṭ-Ṭabarî has *nazî'* in reporting this story. Cf. aṭ-Ṭabarî, *Annales*, I, 2186, l. 14, and glossary, p. DIX. It seems that Ibn Khaldûn misread the word in aṭ-Ṭabarî or an intermediary source. The accusative *nazî'an* that appears in aṭ-Ṭabarî could easily be misread *nazîfan*.

[58] The story was referred to above, p. 55. Cf. also 2:39, below.

[59] Bulaq adds here another section, which appears only in the Tunis MS used by the editor of Bulaq, and which was dropped in all later texts, although reference is made to it at the beginning of the next section. It reads:

Among all those who share in a given group feeling,
leadership always remains vested in the particular
family to which it belongs.

It should be known that although each tribe and subtribe forms but a single (uniform) group because of their common descent, there exist among

[11] *Leadership over people who share in a given group feeling cannot be vested in those not of the same descent.*[60]

This is because leadership exists only through superiority, and superiority only through group feeling, as we have mentioned before.[61] Leadership over people, therefore, must, of necessity, derive from a group feeling that is superior to each individual group feeling. Each individual group feeling that becomes aware of the superiority of the group feeling of the leader is ready to obey and follow (that leader).

them special kinds of group feeling because of special relationships that constitute a closer kind of contact than common (general) descent. These may be, for instance, (the members of) one family, or the members of one tent, or brothers who are sons of one father. (People related in this way) are different from close or remote cousins. They are more firmly established in their particular descent, (but they still) share with other groups the common (general) descent. They feel affection for the people of their particular descent as well as for those of the common (general) descent. Their affection, however, is stronger in the case of the people of their particular descent because of the close contact.

Leadership is vested in one particular family among them, and not in the whole. Since leadership is the result of superiority, it (follows) necessarily that the group of the (particular) family in which (leadership is vested) must be stronger than that of all the other groups, in order to enable that (particular family) to gain superiority and, thus, full leadership for its members. If this is necessary, it is obligatory that leadership over (all others) always remain vested in the particular family having superiority over them. Were it to pass to outsiders and become vested in other groups of inferior power, they would not have full leadership.

Leadership is continuously transmitted within that (particular) family from one branch to another, but always to the strongest branch only, for reasons connected with the secret of superiority which we have mentioned. Social organization and group feeling may be compared to the (process of) mixture of the things that come into being. No mixture can come about in them if the elements are all equal to each other. One element must necessarily be superior. If not, the process of coming into being cannot materialize. [Cf. pp. 336 f., below.] This is the secret reason why superiority is a (necessary) condition in connection with (matters of) group feeling. It makes it obligatory for leadership to remain vested in a particular family, as we have established.

[60] In one of the comparatively rare references to the *Muqaddimah* in the *'Ibar*, Ibn Khaldûn refers to this chapter as proof of the spuriousness of the alleged Sassanian genealogy of the Bûyids; cf. *'Ibar*, III, 395. And again, in *'Ibar*, V, 436 f., and in VI, 7 f., he refers to it as an argument against the alleged descent of the Syrian tribe Âl Faḍl and their chief, Muhanna', from 'Abbâsah, the sister of ar-Rashîd. Cf. pp. 28 ff., above, and p. 272, below.

[61] In the deleted section which immediately preceded this one. Cf. n. 59.

Now, a person who has become attached to people of a common descent usually does not share the group feeling that derives from their common descent. He is merely attached to them.[62] The firmest connection he has with the
I, 240 group is as client and ally. This in no way guarantees him superiority over them. Assuming that he has developed close contact with them, that he has mixed with them, that the fact that he was originally merely attached to them has been forgotten, and that he has become one of their skin and is addressed as one having the same descent as they, how could he, or one of his forebears, have acquired leadership before that process had taken place, since leadership is transmitted in one particular branch that has been marked for superiority through group feeling? The fact that he was merely attached to the tribe was no doubt known at an earlier stage, and at that time prevented him (or rather, his forebears) from assuming leadership. Thus, it could not have been passed on by (a man) who was still merely attached (to the tribe). Leadership must of necessity be inherited from the person who is entitled to it, in accordance with the fact, which we have stated, that superiority results from group feeling.

Many leaders of tribes or groups are eager to acquire certain pedigrees. They desire them because persons of that particular descent possessed some special virtue, such as bravery, or nobility, or fame, however this may have come about. They go after such a family and involve themselves in claims to belong to a branch of it. They do not realize that they thus bring suspicion upon themselves with regard to their leadership and nobility.

Such things are frequently found among people at this time. Thus, the Zanâtah in general claim to be Arabs. The Awlâd Rabâb, who are known as the Ḥijâzîs and who belong to the Banû ʻÂmir, one of the branches of the Zughbah, claim that they belong to the Banû Sulaym and, in particular,

[62] Ibn Khaldûn once more uses the word *nazîf*.

to the Sharîd, a branch of the Banû Sulaym. Their ancestor is said to have joined the Banû 'Âmir as a carpenter who made biers. He mixed with them and developed a close contact with I, 241
them. Finally, he became their leader. He was called by them al-Ḥijâzî.

Similarly, the Banû 'Abd-al-Qawî b. al-'Abbâs of the Tûjîn claim to be descendants of al-'Abbâs b. 'Abd-al-Muṭṭalib, because they want to have noble descent (from the family of the Prophet), and hold a mistaken opinion concerning the name of al-'Abbâs b. 'Aṭîyah, the father of 'Abd-al-Qawî. It is not known that any 'Abbâsid ever entered the Maghrib. From the beginning of the 'Abbâsid dynasty and thereafter, the Maghrib was under the influence of the Idrîsids and the 'Ubaydid(-Fâṭimids), 'Alid enemies of the 'Abbâsids. No 'Abbâsid would have become attached to a Shî'ah.

Similarly, the Zayyânids, the 'Abd-al-Wâdid rulers (of Tlemcen), claim to be descendants of al-Qâsim b. Idrîs, basing their claim on the fact that their family is known to have descended from al-Qâsim. In their own Zanâtah dialect, they are called Ait al-Qâsim,[63] that is, Banû l-Qâsim. They claim that the Qâsim (after whom they are named) was al-Qâsim b. Idrîs, or al-Qâsim b. Muḥammad b. Idrîs. If that were true, all that can be said concerning that Qâsim is that he fled his own realm and attached himself to (the Zanâtah group of the 'Abd-al-Wâd). How, then, could he have gained complete leadership over them in the desert? The story is an error resulting from the name of al-Qâsim, which is very frequent among the Idrîsids. (The Zayyânids), therefore, thought that their Qâsim was an Idrîsid. (But after all,) they hardly need so spurious a genealogy. They gained royal authority and power through their group feeling, not through claims to 'Alid, 'Abbâsid, or other descent.

These things are invented by people to get into the good graces of rulers, through (sycophantic) behavior and through the opinions they express. Their (fabrications) eventually

---

[63] Berber *u*, pl. *ait*, "son."

become so well known as to be irrefutable. I have heard that Yaghamrâsin [64] b. Zayyân, the founder of the Zayyânid rule,
I, 242 when he was asked about (the alleged Idrîsid descent of his family), denied it. He expressed himself in the Zanâtah dialect as follows: "We gained worldly power and royal authority with our swords, not through (noble) family connections. The usefulness of (our royal authority for us) [64a] in the next world depends on God." And he turned away from the person who, in this way, had hoped to get into his good graces.

Another example is the claim of the Banû Sa'd, *shaykhs* of the Banû Yazîd of the Zughbah, to be descendants of (the Caliph) Abû Bakr aṣ-Ṣiddîq. Then, there is the claim of the Banû Salâmah, *shaykhs* of the Banû Yadlaltin (Idlelten) of the Tûjîn, that they belong to the Sulaym, as well as the claim of the Dawâwidah, *shaykhs* of the Riyâḥ, that they are descendants of the Barmecides.[65] We also hear that the Banû Muhanna', amirs of the Ṭayy in the East, claim to be descendants of the Barmecides. There are many such examples. The fact that these groups are the leaders among their peoples speaks against their claims to such pedigrees, as we have mentioned. Their common descent (with their people) must be pure, and they must enjoy the strongest possible group feeling (in their own tribe, to have gained the leadership). Were this taken into consideration, errors in this matter would be avoided.

---

[64] According to the vocalization in D, the name reads Yagh (a) mrâsin. The *Autobiography* suggests the vocalizations Yagha/imrâsa/in; cf. *Autobiography*, p. 453. Modern scholarship commonly uses the wrong form Yaghmu/orâsa/in. It seems to have been influenced by the occurrence of the name of Yaghmûr for the same man. But his name is also pronounced Ghamrasen, in modern Tlemcen, according to A. Bel in his edition of Yaḥyâ Ibn Khaldûn, *Histoire des Beni 'Abd el-Wâd* (Algiers, 1903/4), p. 157 (n. 3).

[64a] Cf. Surdon and Bercher, p. 26. Referring the Arabic pronoun to "the usefulness of (such a noble descent)" would imply that Yaghamrâsin was skeptical as to the religious merit of 'Alid descent.

[65] Cf. n. 60 to this chapter. A brief sketch of the history of the Faḍl, down to the present, is given in M. von Oppenheim, *Die Beduinen* (Leipzig, 1939), I, 350 ff.

The connection of the Mahdî of the Almohads with the 'Alid family should not be considered a case of this type. The Mahdî did not belong to the leading family among his people, the Harghah. He became their leader after he had become famous for his knowledge and religion, and by virtue of the fact that the Maṣmûdah tribe followed his call. Yet, he belonged to a (Harghah) family of medium rank.[66]

God knows the unseen and the visible.

[12] *Only those who share in the group feeling (of a group) can have a "house" and nobility in the basic sense and in reality, while others have it only in a metaphorical and figurative sense.*

This is because nobility and prestige are the result of (personal) qualities. A "house"[67] means that a man counts I, 243
noble and famous men among his forebears. The fact that he is their progeny and descendant gives him great standing among his fellows, for his fellows respect the great standing and nobility that his ancestors acquired through their (personal) qualities.

With regard to their growth and propagation, human beings can be compared to minerals. Muḥammad said: "Men are minerals. The best ones in pre-Islamic times are also the best ones in Islam, if they are understanding."[68] "Prestige" in its proper meaning refers to (family) descent.

We have explained that the advantage of (common) descent consists in the group feeling that derives from it and that leads to affection and mutual help. Wherever the group feeling is truly formidable and its soil kept pure, the advantage of a (common) descent is more evident (than else-

---

[66] Cf. pp. 54 f., above.

[67] *Bayt* in this sense has the pl. *buyûtât*. The word "house" was used in this sense in the ancient Near East. It was particularly well established in the old Persian Empire. All signs point to the fact that the Arabs derived their usage of the word in this particular sense from the Persian cultural orbit.

[68] Cf. *Concordance*, II, 110*b*, ll. 33 ff.; *Handbook*, p. 58*b*.

where), and the (group feeling) is more effective. It is an additional advantage to have a number of noble ancestors. Thus, prestige and nobility become firmly grounded in those who share in the group feeling (of a tribe), because there exists (in them) the result of (common) descent. The nobility of a "house" is in direct proportion to the different degrees of group feeling, because (nobility) is the secret of (group feeling).

Isolated [69] inhabitants of cities can have a "house" only in a metaphorical sense. The assumption that they possess one is a specious claim. Seen in its proper light, prestige means to the inhabitants of cities that some of them count among their forefathers men who had good (personal) qualities and who mingled with good people, and (that, in addition, they) try to be as decent as possible. This is different from the real meaning of group feeling, as group feeling derives from (common) descent and a number of forefathers. The terms "prestige" and "house" are used metaphorically in this connection, because there exists in this case a number of successive ancestors who consistently performed good deeds. This is not true and unqualified prestige.[70]

A "house" possesses an original nobility through group
I, 244 feeling and (personal) qualities. Later on, the people (who have a "house") divest themselves of that nobility when group feeling disappears as the result of sedentary life, as mentioned before,[71] and they mingle with the common people. A certain delusion as to their former prestige remains in their souls and leads them to consider themselves members of the most noble houses.[72] They are, however, far from that (status), because their group feeling has completely disappeared. Many inhabitants of cities who had their origins in

[69] That is, belonging to no tribe.

[70] Bulaq adds: "It is true that the term 'prestige' is correctly used in both cases according to conventional linguistic usage. It is an ambiguous term that is more appropriately used in some cases (than in others)."

[71] Cf., apparently, p. 267, above.

[72] The earlier texts add: "who represent (closely knit) groups."

(noble) Arab or non-Arab "houses" share such delusions.

The Israelites are the most firmly misled in this delusion. They originally had one of the greatest "houses" in the world, first, because of the great number of prophets and messengers born among their ancestors, extending from Abraham to Moses, the founder of their religious group and law, and next, because of their group feeling and the royal authority that God had promised and granted them by means of that group feeling. Then, they were divested of all that, and they suffered humiliation and indigence. They were destined to live as exiles on earth. For thousands of years, they knew only enslavement and unbelief.[73] Still, the delusion of (nobility) has not left them. They can be found saying: "He is an Aaronite"; "He is a descendant of Joshua"; "He is one of Caleb's progeny"; "He is from the tribe of Judah." This in spite of the fact that their group feeling has disappeared and that for many long years they have been exposed to humiliation.[74] Many other inhabitants of cities who hold (noble) pedigrees but no longer share in any group feeling, are inclined to (utter) similar nonsense.

Abû l-Walîd b. Rushd (Averroes) erred in this respect. He mentioned prestige in the *Rhetoric*, one of the abridgments of the books of the first science.[75] "Prestige," he states, "belongs to people who are ancient settlers in a town." He did not consider the things we have just mentioned. I should I, 245
like to know how long residence in a town can help (anyone to gain prestige), if he does not belong to a group that makes him feared and causes others to obey him. (Averroes,) in a way, considers prestige as depending exclusively on the

---

[73] Bulaq corrects the text to read: "subservience to unbelief."

[74] Cf. also p. 288 and 3:306, below.

[75] This strange expression seems to refer to the Aristotelian *Organon*. One is tempted to correct the text, with Bulaq, to "the First Teacher," the epithet by which Aristotle was commonly known; cf. 3:115, below. * The reference is to Averroes' *Talkhîṣ al-Khiṭâbah*, ed. ʿAbd-ar-Raḥmân Badawî (Cairo, 1960), p. 41. Cf. also Badawî, *Dawr al-ʿArab* (Beirut, 1965), pp. 115 ff.

number of forefathers. Yet,[76] rhetoric means to sway the opinions of those whose opinions count, that is, the men in command. It takes no notice of those who have no power. They cannot sway anyone's opinions, and their own opinions are not sought. The sedentary inhabitants of cities fall into that category. It is true that Averroes grew up in a generation (group) and a place where people had no experience of group feeling and were not familiar with the conditions governing it. Therefore, (Averroes) did not progress beyond his well-known (definition of) "house" and prestige as something depending merely on the number of one's ancestors, and did not refer to the reality of group feeling and its influence among men.

"God knows everything." [77]

[13] *"House" and nobility come to clients and followers only through their masters and not through their own descent.*

This is because, as we have mentioned before, only those who share in a group feeling have basic and true nobility. When such people take people of another descent as followers, or when they take slaves [78] and clients into servitude, and enter into close contact with them, as we have said, the clients and followers share in the group feeling of their masters and take it on as if it were their own group feeling. By taking
I, *246* their special place within the group feeling, they participate to some extent in the (common) descent to which (that particular group feeling belongs). Muḥammad thus said, "The client of people belongs to them, whether he is their client as a slave, or as a follower and ally." [79]

---

[76] That is, Averroes should have done better, since he discussed the matter in connection with rhetoric. A rhetorician ought not to concern himself with "ancient settlers in cities," because they do not count, and therefore cannot be confused with "people of prestige."

[77] Qur'ân 2.29 (27), etc.

[78] The form *'ibiddâ* used here is considered to designate specifically persons born in slavery.

[79] This is an important maxim in financial legislation. Cf. al-Bukhârî, *Ṣaḥîḥ*, IV, 290; *Handbook*, p. 148*a*, first entry under *mawlâ*.

His own descent and birth are of no help as regards the group feeling of (the master), since (that group feeling) has nothing to do with (his own) descent. The group feeling that belonged to (his own) family is lost, because its influence disappeared when he entered into close contact with that other family and lost contact with the men whose group feeling he had formerly shared. He thus becomes one of the others and takes his place among them. In the event a number of his ancestors also shared the group feeling of these people, he comes to enjoy among (these other people) a certain nobility and "house," in keeping with his position as their client and follower. However, he does not come to be as noble as they are, but remains inferior to them.

This is the case with clients of dynasties and with all servants. They acquire nobility by being firmly rooted in their client relationship, and by their service to their particular dynasty, and by having a large number of ancestors who had been under the protection of (that dynasty). One knows that the Turkish clients of the 'Abbâsids and, before them, the Barmecides, as well as the Banû Nawbakht, thus achieved "house" and nobility and created glory and importance for themselves by being firmly rooted in their relationship to the ('Abbâsid) dynasty. Ja'far b. Yaḥyâ b. Khâlid had the greatest possible "house" and nobility. This was the result of his position as a client of ar-Rashîd and his family. It was not the result of his own (noble) descent among the Persians. The same is the case with clients and servants under any dynasty. They have "house" and prestige by being firmly rooted in their client relationship with a particular dynasty and by being its faithful followers. Their original descent disappears (and means nothing), if it is not that of (the dynasty). It remains under cover and is not considered in connection with their importance and glory. The thing that is I, 247
considered is their position as clients and followers, because this accords with the secret of group feeling which (alone) produces "house" and nobility.

The nobility of (a client) is, in a way, derived from the

nobility of his masters, and his "house" is derived from what (his masters) have built. His own descent and birth do not help him. His glory is built upon his relationship as client to a particular dynasty, and upon his close contact with it as a follower and product of its education. His own original descent may have implied close contact with some group feeling and dynasty. If that (close contact) is gone and the person in question has become a client and follower of another (dynasty), his original (descent) is no longer of any use to him, because its group feeling has disappeared. The new (relationship) becomes useful to him, because (its group feeling) exists.

This applies to the Barmecides. It has been reported that they belonged to a Persian "house," the members of which had been guardians of the fire temples of (the Persians). When they became clients of the 'Abbâsids, their original (descent) was not considered. Their nobility resulted from their position as clients and followers of the ('Abbâsid) dynasty.

Everything else is unsupported and unrealistic delusions prompted [80] by undisciplined souls. (The facts of) existence confirm our remarks. "Most noble among you in God's (eyes) is he who fears God most." [81]

[14] *Prestige lasts at best four generations in one lineage.*[82]

It should be known that the world of the elements and all it contains comes into being and decays. This applies to both its essences and its conditions. Minerals, plants, all the animals including man, and the other created things come into being and decay, as one can see with one's own eyes. The same applies to the conditions that affect created things, and especially the conditions that affect man. Sciences grow up
I, 248 and then are wiped out. The same applies to crafts, and to similar things.

---

[80] D correctly indicates the active *tuwaswisu*.

[81] Qur'ân 49.13 (13).

[82] Cf. pp. 343 ff., below.

Prestige is an accident that affects human beings. It comes into being and decays inevitably. No human being exists who possesses an unbroken pedigree of nobility from Adam down to himself. The only exception was made for the Prophet, as a special act of divine grace to him, and as a measure designed to safeguard his true character.

Nobility originates in the state of being outside, as has been said.[83] That is, being outside of[84] leadership and nobility and being in a vile, humble station, devoid of prestige. This means that all nobility and prestige is preceded by the non-existence of nobility and prestige, as is the case with every created thing.

It reaches its end in a single family within four successive generations. This is as follows: The builder of the glory (of the family) knows what it cost him to do the work, and he keeps the qualities that created his glory and made it last. The son who comes after him had personal contact with his father and thus learned those things from him. However, he is inferior in this respect to (his father), in as much as a person who learns things through study is inferior to a person who knows them from practical application. The third generation must be content with imitation and, in particular, with reliance upon tradition. This member is inferior to him of the second generation, in as much as a person who relies (blindly) upon tradition is inferior to a person who exercises independent judgment.[85]

The fourth generation, then, is inferior to the preceding ones in every respect. This member has lost the qualities that preserved the edifice of their glory. He (actually) despises

---

[83] This apparently refers to some statement by others, not to a previous statement by Ibn Khaldûn.

[84] The root *kharaja* means "to go outside" and also "to be outside." The form used here usually means "going outside" or "departure." B actually has "departure toward leadership and nobility from a vile, humble station devoid of prestige." However, the preceding *khârijîyah* "state of being outside" or "an outsider" (cf. p. 376, l. 34, below), guarantees the accuracy of the above translation.

[85] "Blind reliance upon tradition" and "exercise of independent judgment" are important terms of Muslim legal scholarship.

(those qualities). He imagines that the edifice was not built through application and effort. He thinks that it was something due his people from the very beginning by virtue of the mere fact of their (noble) descent, and not something that resulted from group (effort) and (individual) qualities. For he sees the great respect in which he is held by the people, but he does not know how that respect originated and what the
I, 249 reason for it was. He imagines that it is due to his descent and nothing else. He keeps away from those in whose group feeling he shares, thinking that he is better than they. He trusts that (they will obey him because) he was brought up to take their obedience for granted, and he does not know the qualities that made obedience necessary. Such qualities are humility (in dealing) with (such men) and respect for their feelings. Therefore, he considers them despicable, and they, in turn, revolt against him and despise him. They transfer (political) leadership from him and his direct lineage to some other related branch (of his tribe), in obedience to their group feeling, as we have stated. (They do so) after they have convinced themselves that the qualities of the (new leader) are satisfactory to them. His family then grows, whereas the family of the original (leader) decays and the edifice of his "house" collapses.

This is the case with rulers who have royal authority. It also is the case with all the "houses" of tribes, of amirs, and of everybody else who shares in a group feeling, and then also with the "houses" among the urban population. When one "house" goes down, another one rises in (another group of) the same descent. "If He wants them to disappear, He causes them to do so, and brings forth a new creation. This is not difficult for God." [86]

The rule of four (generations) with respect to prestige usually holds true. It may happen that a "house" is wiped out, disappears, and collapses in fewer than four (generations), or

---

[86] Qur'ân 14.19 f. (22 f.); 35.16 f. (17 f.).

it may continue unto the fifth and sixth (generations), though in a state of decline and decay. The four generations can be explained as the builder, the one who has personal contact with the builder, the one who relies on tradition, and the destroyer. There could not be fewer.

The fact that prestige lasts four generations is considered (in statements discussed) under the subject of praise and glorification. Muḥammad said: "The noble son of the noble (father) of the noble (grandfather) of the noble (great-grandfather): Joseph, the son of Jacob, the son of Isaac, the son of Abraham." [87] This indicates that (Joseph) had reached the limit in glory.

In the Torah, there is the following passage: "God, your Lord, is powerful [88] and jealous, visiting the sins of the fathers upon the children unto the third and the fourth (generations)." This shows that four generations in one lineage are the limit in extent of ancestral prestige. I, 250

The *Kitâb al-Aghânî* [89] reports, in the story of 'Uwayf al-Qawâfî, that Khosraw asked an-Nu'mân whether there was among the Arabs a tribe that was nobler than other tribes. And when the answer was yes, he asked: "In what respect (does such greater nobility show itself)?" An-Nu'mân replied: "(In cases of men) with three successive ancestors who were leaders, and where the fourth generation, then, was perfect. The 'house' thus belongs to his tribe." [90] He looked for such people and found that the only ones that fulfilled the condition were the family of Ḥudhayfah b. Badr al-Fazârî, the house of Qays; the family of Ḥâjib b. Zurârah, the house of Tamîm; the family of Dhû l-Jaddayn, the house of

[87] Cf. al-Bukhârî, *Ṣaḥîḥ*, II, 352, and III, 262 f., and, for a very similar version of the same saying, II, 438, etc.

[88] De Slane here makes the important observation that the addition of "powerful" in Exod. 20:5 is found only in the Vulgate, which, therefore, must have been the ultimate source of Ibn Khaldûn's quotation.

[89] Cf. Abû l-Faraj al-Iṣfahânî, *Kitâb al-Aghânî*, XVII, 106 f.

[90] The text of the *Kitâb al-Aghânî* adds *fîhi*, which yields the better sense: "and the 'house' belonging to his tribe rests in him."

Shaybân; and the family of al-Ash'ath b. Qays, of the Kindah.[91] He assembled those clans and the families attached to them, and appointed impartial judges. Ḥudhayfah b. Badr stood up; then al-Ash'ath b. Qays, because of his relationship to an-Nu'mân; then Bisṭâm b. Qays of the Shaybân; then Ḥâjib b. Zurârah; and then Qays b. 'Âṣim. They made long speeches. Khosraw (finally) said: "Each one of them is a chieftain who occupies his proper place."

Those "houses" were the ones that enjoyed the greatest reputation among the Arabs after the Hâshimites. To them belonged also the house of the Banû ad-Dayyân,[92] of the Banû l-Ḥârith b. Ka'b, the house of the Yemen.

All this shows that prestige lasts at best four generations. And God knows better.

I, 251

[15] *Savage nations are better able to achieve superiority than others.*

It should be known that since, as we have stated in the Third Prefatory Discussion,[93] desert life no doubt is the reason for bravery, savage groups are braver than others. They are, therefore, better able to achieve superiority and to take away the things that are in the hands of other nations. The situation of one and the same group changes, in this respect, with the change of time. Whenever people settle in the fertile plains and amass [94] luxuries and become accustomed to a life of abundance and luxury, their bravery decreases to the degree that their wildness and desert habits decrease.

This is exemplified by dumb animals, such as gazelles, wild buffaloes (cows), and donkeys, that are domesticated.

---

[91] Bulaq reads here: "the family of Ḥâjib b. Zurârah; and the family of Qays b. 'Âṣim al-Minqarî, of the Banû Tamîm."

[92] For the Banû d-Dayyân, cf. Ibn Ḥazm, *Jamharat ansâb al-'Arab*, p. 391, where they are called the house of Madhḥij (a Yemenite tribe) and maternal uncles of (the first 'Abbâsid caliph) Abû l-'Abbâs as-Saffâḥ. Cf. also *Kitâb al-Aghânî*, XVII, 105.

[93] In the paragraph called thus (above, pp. 167 ff.), nothing of the sort is said. Ibn Khaldûn mentions the subject in the fifth section of this chapter, pp. 257 f., above.

[94] Cf. R. Dozy in *Journal asiatique*, XIV^{6} (1869), 153 f.

When they cease to be wild as the result of contact with human beings, and when they have a life of abundance, their vigor and violence undergo change. This affects even their movements and the beauty of their coat.[95] The same applies to savage human beings who become sociable and friendly.

The reason is that familiar customs determine human nature and character. Superiority comes to nations through enterprise and courage. The more firmly rooted in desert habits and the wilder a group is, the closer does it come to achieving superiority over others, if both (parties are otherwise) approximately equal in number, strength, and group (feeling).

In this connection, one may compare the Muḍar with the Ḥimyar and the Kahlân before them, who preceded them in royal authority and in the life of luxury, and also with the Rabî'ah who settled in the fertile fields of the 'Irâq. The Muḍar retained their desert habits, and the others embarked upon a life of abundance and great luxury before they did. I, 252
Desert life prepared the Muḍar most effectively for achieving superiority. They took away and appropriated what the other groups had in their hands.

The same was the case also with the Banû Ṭayy, the Banû 'Âmir b. Ṣa'ṣa'ah, and the Banû Sulaym b. Manṣûr[96] later on. They remained longer in the desert than the other Muḍar and Yemenite tribes, and did not have any of their wealth. The desert habits thus preserved the power of their group feeling, and the habits of luxury did not wear it out. They thus eventually became the most powerful (group) among (the Arabs). Thus, wherever an Arab tribe leads a life of luxury and abundance, while another does not, the one holding fast to desert life the longer will be superior to and more powerful than the other, if both parties are (otherwise) equal in strength and number.

This is how God proceeds with His creatures.

---

[95] Cf. pp. 178 f., above.

[96] This refers to the Arab tribes that invaded northwestern Africa in the eleventh century.

[16] *The goal to which group feeling leads is royal authority.*

This [97] is because, as we have mentioned before,[98] group feeling gives protection and makes possible mutual defense, the pressing of claims,[99] and every other kind of social activity. We have also mentioned before [100] that according to their nature, human beings need someone to act as a restraining influence and mediator in every social organization, in order to keep the members from (fighting) with each other. That person must, by necessity, have superiority over the others in the matter of group feeling. If not, his power to (exercise a restraining influence) could not materialize. Such superiority is royal authority (*mulk*). It is more than leadership. Leadership means being a chieftain, and the leader is obeyed, but he has no power to force others to accept his rulings. Royal authority means superiority and the power to rule by force.

When a person sharing in the group feeling [101] has reached
I, 253 the rank of chieftain and commands obedience, and when he then finds the way open toward superiority and (the use of) force, he follows that way, because it is something desirable. He cannot completely achieve his (goal) except with the help of the group feeling, which causes (the others) to obey him. Thus, royal superiority is a goal to which group feeling leads, as one can see.

Even if an individual tribe has different "houses" and many diverse group feelings, still, there must exist a group feeling that is stronger than all the other group feelings combined, that is superior to them all and makes them subservient, and in which all the diverse group feelings coalesce,

[97] Cf. Issawi, pp. 108 f. [98] Cf. p. 263, above.

[99] *Muṭâlabah* might be more simply translated "aggression," but it should be kept in mind that it is a legal term, translatable as "action." Cf. D. Santillana, *Istituzioni di diritto musulmano malichita*, II, 3, 554.

[100] Cf. pp. 91 f., above.

[101] Bulaq adds: "has reached a certain rank, he aspires to the next higher one (and so on). When he then. . ."

as it were, to become one greater group feeling. Otherwise, splits would occur and lead to dissension and strife. "If God did not keep human beings apart, the earth would perish." [102]

Once group feeling has established superiority over the people who share (in that particular group feeling), it will, by its very nature, seek superiority over people of other group feelings unrelated to the first. If the one (group feeling) is the equal of the other or is able to stave off (its challenge), the (competing people) are even with and equal to each other. (In this case,) each group feeling maintains its sway over its own domain and people, as is the case with tribes and nations all over the earth. However, if the one group feeling overpowers the other and makes it subservient to itself, the two group feelings enter into close contact, and the (defeated) group feeling gives added power to the (victorious) group feeling, which, as a result, sets its goal of superiority and domination higher than before. In this way, it goes on until the power of that particular group feeling equals the power of the ruling dynasty. Then, when the ruling dynasty grows senile and no defender arises from among its friends who share in its group feeling, the (new group feeling) takes over and deprives the ruling dynasty of its power, and, thus, obtains complete royal authority.

The power of (a given group feeling) may (also) reach its peak when the ruling dynasty has not yet reached senility. (This stage) may coincide with the stage at which (the ruling dynasty) needs to have recourse to the people who represent the various group feelings (in order to master the situation).
In such a case, the ruling dynasty incorporates (the people I, 254
who enjoy the powerful group feeling) among its clients whom it uses for the execution of its various projects. This, then, means (the formation of) another royal authority, inferior to that of the controlling royal authority. This was the case with the Turks under the 'Abbâsids,[103] with the Ṣinhâjah

[102] Qur'ân 2.251 (252).

[103] While the following two examples concern dynasties that made themselves independent, the first example is not quite of the same order. Ibn

and the Zanâtah in their relation to the Kutâmah, and with the Ḥamdânids in their relation to the (Fâṭimid) 'Alids and the 'Abbâsids.

It is thus evident that royal authority is the goal of group feeling. When (group feeling) attains that goal, the tribe (representing that particular group feeling) obtains royal authority, either by seizing actual control or by giving assistance (to the ruling dynasty). It depends on the circumstances prevailing at a given time (which of the two alternatives applies). If the group feeling encounters obstacles on its way to the goal, as we shall explain, it stops where it is, until God decides what is going to happen to it.

[17] *Obstacles on the way toward royal authority are luxury and the submergence of the tribe in a life of prosperity.*

The reason for this is that, when a tribe has achieved a certain measure of superiority with the help of its group feeling, it gains control over a corresponding amount of wealth and comes to share prosperity and abundance with those who have been in possession of these things (for a long time). It shares in them to the degree of its power and usefulness to the ruling dynasty. If the ruling dynasty is so strong that no one would think of depriving it of its power or sharing (its power) with it, the tribe in question submits to its rule and is satisfied with whatever share in the dynasty's wealth and tax revenue it is permitted to enjoy. Hopes would not go so high as to (think of) the royal prerogatives or ways to obtain the (royal authority. Members of the tribe) are merely concerned with prosperity, gain, and a life of abun-
I, *255* dance. (They are satisfied) to lead an easy, restful life in the shadow of the ruling dynasty, and to adopt royal habits in building and dress, a matter they stress and in which they take more and more pride, the more luxuries and plenty

---

Khaldûn himself considers the Turks usurpers of control over the 'Abbâsid rulers. The reference to the 'Alids (Fâṭimids) in connection with the Ḥamdânids also does not appear to be exactly to the point.

they obtain, as well as all the other things that go with luxury and plenty.

As a result, the toughness of desert life is lost. Group feeling and courage weaken. Members of the tribe revel in the well-being that God has given them. Their children and offspring grow up too proud to look after themselves or to attend to their own needs. They have disdain also for all the other things that are necessary in connection with group feeling. This finally becomes a character trait and natural characteristic of theirs. Their group feeling and courage decrease in the next generations. Eventually, group feeling is altogether destroyed. They thus invite (their) own destruction. The greater their luxury and the easier the life they enjoy, the closer they are to extinction, not to mention (their lost chance of obtaining) royal authority. The things that go with luxury and submergence in a life of ease break the vigor of the group feeling, which alone produces superiority. When group feeling is destroyed, the tribe is no longer able to defend or protect itself, let alone press any claims. It will be swallowed up by other nations.

It has thus become clear that luxury is an obstacle on the way toward royal authority. "God gives His kingdom (royal authority) to whomever He wants to give it." [104]

[18] *Meekness and docility to outsiders that may come to be found in a tribe are obstacles on the way toward royal authority.*

The [105] reason for this is that meekness and docility break the vigor and strength of group feeling. The (very fact) that people are meek and docile shows that (their group feeling) is lost. They do not become fond of meekness until they are I, *256*
too weak to defend themselves. Those who are too weak to defend themselves are all the more weak when it comes to withstanding their enemies and pressing their claims.

The Israelites are a good example. Moses urged them to

[104] Qur'ân 2.247 (248).

[105] Cf. Issawi, pp. 60 f.

go and become rulers of Syria. He informed them that God had made this their destiny. But the Israelites were too weak for that. They said: "There are giants in that country, and we shall not enter it until the giants have departed." [106] That is, until God has driven them out by manifesting His power, without the application of our group feeling, and that will be one of your miracles, O Moses. And when Moses urged them on, they persisted and became rebellious, and said: "Go you yourself and your Lord, and fight." [107]

The reason for (their attitude) was that they had become used to being too weak to offer opposition and to press claims.[108] (That is the meaning) required by the verse, and it must be interpreted in that manner. (This situation) was the result of the quality of docility and the longing to be subservient to the Egyptians, which the Israelites had acquired through many long years and which led eventually to the complete loss of their group feeling. In addition, they did not really believe what Moses told them, namely, that Syria would be theirs and that the Amalekites who were in Jericho would fall prey to them, by virtue of the divine decree that God had made in favor of the Israelites. They were unable to do (what they were asked to do) and felt too weak to do it. They realized that they were too weak to press any claims, because they had acquired the quality of meekness. They suspected the story their prophet told them and the command he gave them. For that, God punished them by obliging them to remain in the desert. They stayed in the desert between Syria and Egypt for forty years. They had no contact with civilization nor did they settle in any city,[109] as it is told in the Qur'ân.[110] This was because of the harshness the Amalekites in Syria and the Copts in Egypt had practiced against them. Thus, they thought themselves too weak to
I, *257* oppose them. From the context and meaning of the verse,

[106] Qur'ân 5.22 (25). [107] Qur'ân 5.24 (27).
[108] Cf. also p. 275, above, and 3:306, below.
[109] Bulaq adds: "and they did not mix with any human beings."
[110] Qur'ân 5.26 (29). Cf. also p. 132, above, and p. 344, below.

it is evident that (the verse) intends to refer to the implication of such a sojourn in the desert, namely, the disappearance of the generation whose character had been formed and whose group feeling had been destroyed by the humiliation, oppression, and force from which it had (just) escaped, and the eventual appearance in the desert of another powerful generation that knew neither laws nor oppression and did not have the stigma of meekness. Thus, a new group feeling could grow up (in the new generation), and that (new group feeling) enabled them to press their claims and to achieve superiority. This makes it evident that forty years is the shortest period in which one generation can disappear and a new generation can arise. Praised be the Wise, the Knowing One.

This shows most clearly what group feeling means. Group feeling produces the ability to defend oneself, to offer opposition, to protect oneself, and to press one's claims. Whoever loses (his group feeling) is too weak to do any of these things.

The subject of imposts and taxes belongs in this discussion of the things that force meekness upon a tribe.

A tribe paying imposts did not do that until it became resigned to meek submission with respect to (paying them). Imposts and taxes are a sign of oppression and meekness which proud souls do not tolerate, unless they consider (the payment of imposts and taxes) easier than being killed and destroyed. In such a case, the group feeling (of a tribe) is too weak for its own defense and protection. People whose group feeling cannot defend them against oppression certainly cannot offer any opposition or press any claims. They have submitted to humble (meekness), and, as we have mentioned before, meekness is an obstacle.

(An illustration of this fact) is Muḥammad's statement in the *Ṣaḥîḥ*,[111] on the subject of plowing. When he saw a plow-

[111] "In the *Ṣaḥîḥ*" is added in C *supra lineam*, and appears in the text of D. For the tradition, cf. al-Bukhârî, *Ṣaḥîḥ*, II, 67. Cf. also 2:335 f., below.

I, 258 share in one of the houses of the Anṣâr (in Medina), he said: "Such a thing never entered anyone's house save accompanied by humbleness." This is sound proof for (the contention) that payment of imposts makes humbleness necessary. In addition, the humbleness that is the result of paying imposts is accompanied by character qualities of cunning and deceit, because force rules (under such circumstances). According to the *Ṣaḥîḥ*,[112] the Messenger of God used to decry the payment of imposts. When he was asked about it, he said: "A man who has to pay imposts talks—and lies. He promises—and breaks his promise." When one sees a tribe humiliated by the payment of imposts, one cannot hope that it will ever achieve royal authority.

This makes clear that it is erroneous to assume that the Zanâtah in the Maghrib were sheep-breeding Bedouins who paid imposts to the various rulers of their time. As one can see, this is a serious error. Had such been the case, the Zanâtah would never have achieved royal authority and established a dynasty.

In this connection, one may compare the words of Shahrbarâz, the ruler of Derbend.[113] 'Abd-ar-Raḥmân b. Rabî'ah came upon him, and Shahrbarâz asked him for his protection with the (promise) that he would belong to him. On that occasion, (Shahrbarâz) said: "Today, I am one of you. My hand is in your hands. I am your sincere friend. You are welcome. God bless us and you. The poll tax we shall pay you will consist in our helping you and doing what you will. But do not humiliate us by (imposing the) poll tax. (Otherwise,) you would weaken us to the point of (becoming the prey of) your enemies." [114] This story sufficiently (supports) our preceding remarks.

[112] This tradition appears in the margin of C and in the text of D. Cf. al-Bukhârî, *Ṣaḥîḥ*, I, 214; *Concordance*, II, 65*b*, ll. 18 ff.

[113] Cf. n. 36 to Ibn Khaldûn's Introduction, above.

[114] Cf. aṭ-Ṭabarî, *Annales*, I, 2664. The event occurred in 22 [642/43]. Cf. also D. M. Dunlop, *The History of the Jewish Khazars* (Princeton, 1954), pp. 47 ff.

[19] *A sign of (the qualification of an individual for) royal authority is his eager desire to acquire praiseworthy qualities, and vice versa.* I, 259

Royal authority is something natural to human beings, because of its social implications, as we have stated.[115] In view of his natural disposition and his power of logical reasoning, man is more inclined toward good qualities than toward bad qualities, because the evil in him is the result of the animal powers in him, and in as much as he is a human being, he is more inclined toward goodness and good qualities. Now, royal and political authority come to man *qua* man, because it is something peculiar to man and is not found among animals. Thus, the good qualities in man are appropriate to political and royal authority, since goodness is appropriate to political authority.

We have already mentioned[116] that glory has a basis upon which it is built and through which it achieves its reality. (That basis) is group feeling and the tribal group (to which an individual belongs).

Glory also depends upon a detail that completes and perfects its existence. (That detail) is (an individual's personal) qualities. Royal authority is a goal of group feeling. Thus, it is likewise a goal of the perfecting details, namely, the (personal) qualities. The existence of (royal authority) without the (simultaneous existence of) the perfecting details would be like the existence of a person with his limbs cut off, or it would be like appearing naked before people.

The existence of group feeling without the practice of praiseworthy qualities would be a defect among people who possess a "house" and prestige. All the more so would it be a defect in men who are invested with royal authority, the greatest possible kind of glory and prestige. Furthermore, political and royal authority are (God's) guarantee to man-

[115] Cf. p. 284, above. [116] Cf. pp. 273 ff., above.

kind and serve as a representation of God among men with respect to His laws. Now, divine laws affecting men are all
I, 260 for their good and envisage the interests (of men). This is attested by the religious law. Bad laws,[117] on the other hand, all result from stupidity and from Satan, in opposition to the predestination and power of God. He makes both good and evil and predetermines them, for there is no maker except Him.

He who thus obtained group feeling guaranteeing power, and who is known to have good qualities appropriate for the execution of God's laws concerning His creatures, is ready to act as (God's) substitute and guarantor among mankind. He has the qualifications for that. This proof is more reliable and solid than the first one.

It has thus become clear that good qualities attest the (potential) existence of royal authority in a person who (in addition to his good qualities) possesses group feeling. Whenever we observe people who possess group feeling and who have gained control over many lands and nations, we find in them an eager desire for goodness and good qualities, such as generosity, the forgiveness of error, tolerance toward the weak, hospitality toward guests, the support of dependents, maintenance of the indigent, patience in adverse circumstances, faithful fulfillment of obligations, liberality with money for the preservation of honor, respect for the religious law and for the scholars who are learned in it, observation of the things to be done or not to be done that (those scholars) prescribe for them, thinking highly of (religious scholars), belief in and veneration for men of religion and a desire to receive their prayers, great respect for old men and teachers, acceptance of the truth in response to those who call to it, fairness to and care for those who are too weak to take care of themselves, humility toward the poor, attentiveness to the complaints of supplicants, fulfillment of the duties of the religious law and divine worship in all de-

[117] In what seems to be an intentional correction, Bulaq reads "human laws."

tails, avoidance of fraud, cunning, deceit, and of not fulfilling obligations, and similar things. Thus, we know that these are the qualities of leadership, which (persons qualified for royal authority) have obtained and which have made them deserving of being the leaders of the people under their control, or to be leaders in general. It is something good that God has given them, corresponding to their group feeling and superiority. It is not something superfluous to them, or something that exists as a joke [118] in connection with them. Royal authority is the good and the rank that most closely correspond to the group feeling they have. We thus know that God granted them royal authority and gave it to them. I, *261*

Vice versa, when God wants a nation to be deprived of royal authority, He causes (its members) to commit blameworthy deeds and to practice all sorts of vices. This will lead to complete loss of the political virtues among them. (These virtues) continue to be destroyed, until they will no longer exercise royal authority. Someone else will exercise it in their stead. This is to constitute (in addition) an insult to them, in that the royal authority God has given them and the good things He has placed at their disposal are taken away from them. "When we want to destroy a village, we order those of its inhabitants who live in luxury to act wickedly therein. Thus, the word becomes true for it, and we do destroy it." [119]

Upon close investigation, many instances of what we have said and outlined will be found among the nations of the past. God "creates whatever He wishes, and His is the choice." [120]

It should be known that a quality belonging to perfection, that tribes possessing group feeling are eager to cultivate and which attests to their (right to) royal authority, is respect for (religious) scholars, pious men, noble (relatives of the Prophet), well-born persons, and the different kinds of merchants and foreigners, as well as the ability to assign every-

---

[118] Cf. Qur'ân 23.115 (117). [119] Qur'ân 17.16 (17).
[120] Qur'ân 28.68 (68).

body to his proper station. The respect shown by tribes and persons (in control) of group feelings and families, for men of
I, 262 comparable nobility, tribal position, group feeling, and rank, is something natural. It mostly results from the (human) desire for rank, or from fear of the people of the person to whom respect is paid, or from a wish for reciprocal treatment. However, in the case of people who have no group feeling to make themselves feared, and who have no rank (to bestow) for which one might hope, there can be no doubt as to why they are respected, and it is quite clear what one wants (to find) through them, namely, glory, perfection in personal qualities, and total progress toward (a position of) political leadership. Respect for one's rivals and equals must exist in connection with the special [121] political leadership that concerns one's tribe and its competitors (and equals). Respect for excellent and particularly qualified strangers means perfection in general political leadership. The pious are thus respected for their religion; scholars, because they are needed for establishing the statutes of the religious law; merchants, in order to give encouragement (to their profession), so that (their) usefulness may be as widespread as possible. Strangers are respected out of generosity and in order to encourage (them) to undertake certain kinds (of activity). Assigning everybody to his proper station is done out of fairness, and fairness means justice. When people who possess group feeling have that, one knows that they are ready for general political leadership, which means (they are ready for) royal authority. God permits (political leadership) to exist among them, because the (characteristic) sign of (political leadership) exists among them. Therefore, the first thing to disappear in a tribe that exercises royal authority, when God wants to deprive the members of that tribe of their royal and governmental authority, is respect for these kinds of people. When a nation is observed to have lost (that respect), it should be realized that (all) the virtues have begun to go, and

[121] For the meaning of "special-general" in this connection, cf. below, n. 1 to Ch. III.

it can be expected that the royal authority will cease to exist in it. "If God wants evil to happen to certain people, nothing can turn it back." [122]

[20] *While a nation is savage, its royal authority extends farther.* I, 263

This is because, as we have said,[123] such a nation is better able to achieve superiority and full control, and to subdue other groups. The members of such a nation have the strength to fight other nations, and they are among human beings what beasts of prey are among dumb animals. The Arabs and the Zanâtah and similar groups, for instance, are such nations, as are the Kurds, the Turkomans, and the Veiled Ṣinhâjah.

These savage peoples, furthermore, have no homelands that they might use as a fertile (pasture), and no fixed place to which they might repair. All regions and places are the same to them. Therefore, they do not restrict themselves to possession of their own and neighboring regions. They do not stop at the borders of their horizon. They swarm across distant zones and achieve superiority over faraway nations.

One might compare in this connection what 'Umar is reported to have said when he received the oath of allegiance and arose to incite the people to the conquest of the 'Irâq. He said: "The Ḥijâz is your home only in as far as it is a pasturage. Those who dwell there have no power over it except in this respect. Where do (you) newcomers who emigrated (to Medina) stand with regard to God's promise, 'Travel about in the world'? [124] God promised it to you in His book for your inheritance, when He said, 'In order to give (the true religion) victory over all religions, even if the polytheists dislike it.' " [125]

---

[122] Qur'ân 13.11 (12). [123] Cf. pp. 282 f., above.

[124] Qur'ân 6.11 (11); 27.69 (71); 29.20 (19); 30.42 (41).

[125] Qur'ân 9.33 (33); 61.9 (9). Ibn Khaldûn's source is aṭ-Ṭabarî, *Annales*, I, 2160, *anno* 13. Cf. also 'Umar's speech in al-Mas'ûdî, *Murûj adh-dhahab*, IV, 197.

Another example is the condition of the ancient (pre-Islamic) Arabs, such as the Tubba's and the Ḥimyar. They are reported [126] to have marched from the Yemen to the Maghrib at one time, and to the 'Irâq and India at another
I, 264 time. No other nation except the Arabs ever did anything like that.

The condition of the Veiled (Ṣinhâjah) in the Maghrib is another example. When they aspired to royal authority, they swarmed out of their desert plains in the neighborhood of the Sudan, in the first zone, and overran the Spanish realm in the fourth and fifth zones, without any intermediate (stage).

Such is the case with savage nations. Their (dynasties), therefore, extend over a wider area and over regions farther from their (original) center (than do other nations).

God determines night and day.[127]

[21] *As long as a nation retains its group feeling, royal authority that disappears in one branch will, of necessity, pass to some other branch of the same nation.*

The reason for this is that (the members of a particular nation) obtain royal authority only after (proving their) forcefulness and finding other nations obedient to them. (Only a few) are then singled out to become the actual rulers and to be directly connected with the throne. It could not be all of them, because there is not enough room for all to compete (for leadership), and because the existence of jealousy cuts short the aspirations of many of those who aspire to high office.

Those who are singled out to support the dynasty indulge in a life of ease and sink into luxury and plenty. They make servants of their fellows and contemporaries and use them to further the various interests and enterprises of the dynasty. Those who are far away from the government and who

[126] "Are reported" is added in C *supra lineam* and in the text of D. In adding it, Ibn Khaldûn remembered the doubts he had expressed with regard to the historicity of the events, pp. 21 ff., above. Cf. also p. 360, below.

[127] Cf. Qur'ân 73.20 (20).

are thus prevented from having a share in it, remain in the shadow of the dynastic power. They share in it by virtue of their descent, (but) they are not affected by senility, because they remain far from the life of luxury and the things that produce luxury.

The (passing) days get the upper hand over the original group (in power). Their prowess disappears as the result of senility. (The duties of) the dynasty make them soft.[128] Time I, 265
feasts on them, as their energy is exhausted by well-being and their vigor drained by the nature of luxury. They reach their limit, the limit that is set by the nature of human urbanization (*tamaddun*) and political superiority.

Like the silkworm that spins and then, in turn,
Finds its end amidst the threads itself has spun.[128a]

At that moment, the group feeling of other people (within the same nation) is strong. Their force cannot be broken. Their emblem is recognized to be victorious. As a result, their hopes of achieving royal authority, from which they had been kept until now by a superior power within their own group, are high. Their superiority is recognized, and, therefore, no one disputes (their claim to royal authority). They seize power. It becomes theirs. Then, they have the same experience (their predecessors had) at the hands of those other groups within the nation that remain away from (the government). Royal authority thus continues in a particular nation until the force of the group feeling of (that nation) is broken and gone, or until all its groups have ceased to exist. That is how God proceeds with regard to life in this world. "And the other world, according to your Lord, belongs to those who fear God." [129]

[128] Paris has "grinds them," which is more expressive but not supported by the MSS.

[128a] Among related verses, the closest parallel is one by the famous poet Abû l-Fatḥ al-Bustî. Cf. Yâqût, *Irshâd*, ed. Margoliouth (E. J. W. Gibb Memorial Series, No. 6) (Leiden & London, 1907–27), I, 65; (Cairo, 1355–57), I, 163; al-Ghazzâlî, *Iḥyâʼ*, IV, 208.

[129] Qur'ân 43.35 (34).

This can be illustrated by what happened among the nations. When the royal authority of 'Âd was wiped out, their brethren, the Thamûd, took over. They were succeeded, in turn, by their brethren, the Amalekites. The Amalekites were succeeded by their brethren, the Ḥimyar. The Ḥimyar were succeeded by their brethren, the Tubba'5, who belonged to the Ḥimyar. They, likewise, were succeeded, by the Adhwâ'.[130] Then, the Muḍar came to power.

The same was the case with the Persians. When the Kayyanid[131] rule was wiped out, the Sassanians ruled after them. Eventually, God permitted them all to be destroyed by the Muslims.

The same was also the case with the Greeks. Their rule was wiped out and transferred to their brethren, the Rûm (Romans).

The same was the case with the Berbers in the Maghrib.
I, 266 When the rule of their first rulers, the Maghrâwah and the Kutâmah, was wiped out, it went to the Ṣinhâjah. Then it went to the Veiled (Ṣinhâjah), then to the Maṣmûdah, and then to the (still) remaining Zanâtah groups.

This is how God proceeds with His servants and creatures.

All this has its origin in group feeling, which differs in the different groups. Luxury wears out the royal authority and overthrows it, as we shall mention later on.[132] When a dynasty is wiped out, the power is taken (away) from (the members of that dynasty) by those people whose group feeling has a share in the (established) group feeling, since it is recognized that submission and subservience (by others) belong to (the established group feeling) and since people are used to the fact that (the established group feeling) has superiority over all other group feelings. (The same group feeling,) now, exists only in those people who are closely

[130] Like the Tubba's, the Adhwâ' (pl. of *dhû*) are a group of South Arabian rulers referred to in Muslim historical literature.

[131] Cf. n. 62 to Ibn Khaldûn's Introduction, above.

[132] Cf. pp. 340 ff., below.

related (to the outgoing dynasty), because group feeling is proportionate to the degree of relationship. (It goes on that way until,) eventually, a great change takes place in the world, such as the transformation of a religion, or the disappearance of a civilization, or something else willed by the power of God. Then, royal authority is transferred from one group to another—to the one that God permits to effect that change. This happened to the Muḍar. They gained superiority over nations and dynasties, and took power away from all the people of the world, after having themselves been kept out of power for ages.

[22] *The vanquished always want to imitate the victor in his distinctive mark(s), his dress, his occupation, and all his other conditions and customs.*

The[133] reason for this is that the soul always sees perfection in the person who is superior to it and to whom it is subservient. It considers him perfect, either because the respect it has for him impresses it, or because it erroneously assumes that its own subservience to him is not due to the nature of defeat but to the perfection of the victor. If that erroneous assumption fixes itself in the soul, it becomes a firm belief. The soul, then, adopts all the manners of the victor and assimilates itself to him. This, then, is imitation. I, 267

Or, the soul may possibly think that the superiority of the victor is not the result of his group feeling or great fortitude, but of his customs and manners. This also would be an erroneous concept of superiority, and (the consequence) would be the same as in the former case.

Therefore, the vanquished can always be observed to assimilate themselves to the victor in the use and style of dress, mounts, and weapons, indeed, in everything.

In this connection, one may compare how children constantly imitate their fathers. They do that only because they see perfection in them. One may also compare how almost everywhere people are dominated (in the matter of fashion)

[133] Cf. Issawi, pp. 53 f.

by the dress of the militia and the government forces, because they are ruled by them.

This goes so far that a nation dominated by another, neighboring nation will show a great deal of assimilation and imitation. At this time, this is the case in Spain. The Spaniards are found to assimilate themselves to the Galician nations in their dress, their emblems, and most of their customs and conditions. This goes so far that they even draw pictures on the walls and (have them) in buildings and houses. The intelligent observer will draw from this the conclusion that it is a sign of domination (by others). God has the power to command.[134]

In this light, one should understand the secret of the saying, "The common people follow the religion of the ruler." [135] (This saying) belongs to the subject under discussion. The ruler dominates those under him. His subjects
I, 268 imitate him, because they see perfection in him, exactly as children imitate their parents, or students their teachers.

God is wise and knowing.

[23] *A nation that has been defeated and come under the rule of another nation will quickly perish.*

The [136] reason for this may possibly lie in the apathy that comes over people when they lose control of their own affairs and, through enslavement, become the instrument of others and dependent upon them. Hope diminishes and weakens. Now, propagation and an increase in civilization (population) take place only as the result of strong hope and of the energy that hope creates in the animal powers (of man). When hope and the things it stimulates are gone through apathy, and when group feeling has disappeared under the impact of defeat, civilization decreases and business and other activities stop. With their strength dwindling under the impact of defeat, people become unable to defend themselves. They become the victims of anyone who tries to

[134] Cf. Qur'ân 13.31 (30); 30.4 (3); 82.19 (19).

[135] Cf. p. 58, above, and 2:123 and 306, below.

[136] Cf. Issawi, pp. 97 f.

dominate them, and a prey to anyone who has the appetite. It makes no difference whether they have already reached the limit of their royal authority or not.

Here, we possibly learn another secret, namely, that man is a natural leader by virtue of the fact that he has been made a representative (of God on earth). When a leader is deprived of his leadership and prevented from exercising all his powers, he becomes apathetic, even down to such matters as food and drink. This is in the human character. A similar observation may be made with regard to beasts of prey. They do not cohabit when they are in human captivity. The group that has lost control of its own affairs thus continues to weaken and to disintegrate until it perishes. Duration be- I, *269*
longs to God alone.

This may be illustrated by the Persian nation. In the past, the Persians filled the world with their great numbers. When their military force was annihilated in the days of the Arabs, they were still very numerous. It is said that Sa'd (b. Abî Waqqâṣ) counted (the population) beyond Ctesiphon. It numbered 137,000 (individuals), with 37,000 heads of families. But when the Persians came under the rule of the Arabs and were made subject to (oppression by) force, they lasted only a short while and were wiped out as if they had never been. One should not think that this was the result of some (specific) persecution or aggression perpetrated against them. The rule of Islam is known for its justice. Such (disintegration as befell the Persians) is in human nature. It happens when people lose control of their own affairs and become the instrument of someone else.

Therefore, the Negro nations are, as a rule, submissive to slavery, because (Negroes) have little (that is essentially) human and have attributes that are quite similar to those of dumb animals, as we have stated.[137]

Or,[138] there are those who by accepting slavery hope to obtain high rank or to get money or power. This was the

[137] Cf. p. 168, above.

[138] The rest of the section has little bearing upon the point Ibn Khaldûn intends to make here.

case with the Turks in the East, and with the Galician infidels and European Christians in Spain. Such people are customarily claimed by the dynasty for itself. Thus, they are not ashamed to be slaves, because they hope to be chosen for high position by the dynasty. And God knows better.

[24] *Arabs can gain control only over flat territory.*

This [138a] is because, on account of their savage nature, (the Arabs) are people who plunder and cause damage. They plunder whatever they are able to lay their hands on without having to fight or to expose themselves to danger. They then retreat to their pastures in the desert. They do not at-
I, 270 tack or fight except in self-defense. Every stronghold or (locality) that seems difficult (to attack), they bypass in favor of some less difficult (enterprise). They do not attack it. Tribes that are protected against (the Arabs) by inaccessible mountains are safe from their mischief and destructiveness. The Arabs would not cross hills or undergo hardship and danger in order to get to them.

Flat territory, on the other hand, falls victim to their looting and prey to their appetite whenever they (have the opportunity of) gaining power over it, when there is no militia, or when the dynasty is weak. Then they raid, plunder, and attack that territory repeatedly, because it is easily (accessible) to them. Eventually, its inhabitants succumb utterly to the Arabs and then they are pushed around by them in accordance with changes of control and shifts in leadership. Eventually, their civilization is wiped out. God has power over His creatures.

[25] *Places that succumb to the Arabs are quickly ruined.*

The [139] reason for this is that (the Arabs) are a savage nation, fully accustomed to savagery and the things that cause it. Savagery has become their character and nature.

[138a] For this and the following chapter, cf. J. Sauvaget, *Historiens arabes*, pp. 142–44.

[139] Cf. Issawi, pp. 55–58.

They enjoy it, because it means freedom from authority and no subservience to leadership. Such a natural disposition is the negation and antithesis of civilization. All the customary activities of the Arabs lead to travel and movement. This is the antithesis and negation of stationariness, which produces civilization. For instance, the Arabs need stones to set them up as supports for their cooking pots. So, they take them from buildings which they tear down to get the stones, and use them for that purpose. Wood, too, is needed by them for props for their tents and for use as tent poles for their dwellings. So, they tear down roofs to get the wood for that I, 271
purpose. The very nature of their existence is the negation of building, which is the basis of civilization. This is the case with them quite generally.

Furthermore, it is their nature to plunder whatever other people possess. Their sustenance lies wherever the shadow of their lances falls. They recognize no limit in taking the possessions of other people. Whenever their eyes fall upon some property, furnishings, or utensils, they take it. When they acquire superiority and royal authority, they have complete power to plunder (as they please). There no longer exists any political (power) to protect property, and civilization is ruined.

Furthermore, since they use force to make craftsmen and professional workers do their work, they do not see any value in it and do not pay them for it. Now, as we shall mention,[140] labor is the real basis of profit. When labor is not appreciated and is done for nothing, the hope for profit vanishes, and no (productive) work is done. The sedentary population disperses, and civilization decays.

Furthermore, (the Arabs) are not concerned with laws. (They are not concerned) to deter people from misdeeds or to protect some against the others. They care only for the property that they might take away from people through looting and imposts. When they have obtained that, they have no interest in anything further, such as taking care of

[140] Cf. 2:311 ff., below.

(people), looking after their interests, or forcing them not to commit misdeeds. They often level fines on property, because they want to get some advantage, some tax, or profit out of it. This is their custom. It does not help to prevent
I, 272 misdeeds or to deter those who undertake to commit (misdeeds). On the contrary, it increases (misdeeds), because as compared to getting what one wants, the (possible financial) loss (through fines) is insignificant.[141]

Under the rule of (the Arabs), the subjects live as in a state of anarchy, without law. Anarchy destroys mankind and ruins civilization, since, as we have stated, the existence of royal authority is a natural quality of man. It alone guarantees their existence and social organization. That was mentioned above at the beginning of the chapter.[142]

Furthermore, (every Arab) is eager to be the leader. Scarcely a one of them would cede his power to another, even to his father, his brother, or the eldest (most important) member of his family. That happens only in rare cases and under pressure of considerations of decency. There are numerous authorities and amirs among them. The subjects have to obey many masters in connection with the control of taxation and law. Civilization, thus, decays and is wiped out.

'Abd-al-Malik asked one Arab who had come to him on an embassy about al-Ḥajjâj. He wanted him to praise al-Ḥajjâj for his good political leadership (for the benefit of) civilization. But the Arab said: "When I left him, he was acting unjustly all by himself." [142a]

It is noteworthy how civilization always collapsed in places the Arabs took over and conquered, and how such settlements were depopulated and the (very) earth there turned into something that was no (longer) earth. The Yemen where (the Arabs) live is in ruins, except for a few cities. Persian civilization in the Arab 'Irâq is likewise com-

[141] Cf. p. 307, below.

[142] The reference possibly is to pp. 261 ff. and 284 ff., above.

[142a] He was preventing the Arabs from practicing their cherished lawlessness, and he alone was responsible for the oppressive rule of law. A closely related story is found in Ibn 'Abdrabbih, *'Iqd*, II, 77.

pletely ruined. The same applies to contemporary Syria. When the Banû Hilâl and the Banû Sulaym pushed through (from their homeland) to Ifrîqiyah and the Maghrib in (the beginning of) the fifth [eleventh] century and struggled there for three hundred and fifty years, they attached themselves to (the country), and the flat territory in (the Maghrib) was completely ruined. Formerly, the whole region between the Sudan and the Mediterranean had been settled. This (fact) is attested by the relics of civilization there, such as monu- I, 273
ments, architectural sculpture, and the visible remains of villages and hamlets.

God inherits the earth and whomever is upon it. He is the best heir.[143]

[26] *Arabs can obtain royal authority only by making use of some religious coloring, such as prophecy, or sainthood, or some great religious event in general.*

The [144] reason for this is that because of their savagery, the Arabs are the least willing of nations to subordinate themselves to each other, as they are rude, proud, ambitious, and eager to be the leader. Their individual aspirations rarely coincide. But when there is religion (among them) through prophecy or sainthood, then they have some restraining influence in themselves. The qualities of haughtiness and jealousy leave them. It is, then, easy for them to subordinate themselves and to unite (as a social organization). This is achieved by the common religion they now have. It causes rudeness and pride to disappear and exercises a restraining influence on their mutual envy and jealousy. When there is a prophet or saint among them, who calls upon them to fulfill the commands of God and rids them of blameworthy qualities and causes them to adopt praiseworthy ones, and who has them concentrate all their strength

[143] Cf. Qur'ân 21.89 (89).

[144] Cf. R. A. Nicholson, *Translations of Eastern Poetry and Prose*, pp. 182 f. Cf. Issawi, p. 58.

in order to make the truth prevail, they become fully united (as a social organization) and obtain superiority and royal authority. Besides, no people are as quick (as the Arabs) to accept (religious) truth and right guidance, because their natures have been preserved free from distorted habits and uncontaminated by base character qualities. The only (difficulty) lies in the quality of savagery, which, however, is easily taken care of and which is ready to admit good (qualities), as it has remained in its first natural state and remote from the ugly customs and bad habits that leave their impress
I, 274 upon the soul. "Every infant is born in the natural state," as is stated in the tradition that was quoted above.[145]

[27] *The Arabs are of all nations the one most remote from royal leadership.*

The [146] reason for this is that the Arabs are more rooted in desert life and penetrate deeper into the desert than any other nation. They have less need of the products and grain of the hills, because they are used to a tough and hard life. Therefore, they can dispense with other people. It is difficult for them to subordinate themselves to each other, because they are used to (no control) and because they are in a state of savagery. Their leader needs them mostly for the group spirit that is necessary for purposes of defense. He is, therefore, forced to rule them kindly and to avoid antagonizing them. Otherwise, he would have trouble with the group spirit, and (such trouble) would be his undoing and theirs. Royal leadership and government, on the other hand, require the leader to exercise a restraining influence by force. If not, his leadership would not last.

Furthermore, as we have stated before,[147] it is the nature of (the Arabs) not only to appropriate the possessions of other people but, beyond that, to refrain from exercising any (power of) arbitration among them and to fail to keep them

---

[145] Cf. p. 254, above.
[146] Cf. Issawi, pp. 59 f., and J. Sauvaget, pp. 145 f.
[147] For this paragraph, cf. pp. 303 f., above.

from (fighting) each other. When they have taken possession of a nation, they make it the goal of their rule to profit (from their position) by taking away the property of the members of that nation. Beyond that, they do not care to exercise any (power of) arbitration among them. They often punish crimes by fines on property, in their desire to increase the tax revenues and to obtain some (pecuniary) advantage. That is no deterrent (to crime). (Rather,) it is often an incentive (to crime), in view of the fact that incentives to commit misdeeds (may be very strong) and that, in the opinion of (the criminal), payment of a fine is insignificant, weighed against getting what he wants. Thus, misdeeds increase, and civilization is ruined. A nation dominated by the Arabs is in a state no different from anarchy, where everybody is set against the others. Such a civilization cannot last and goes quickly to I, *275*
ruins, as would be the case in a state of anarchy, as we have mentioned before.

For all these (reasons), the Arabs are by nature remote from royal leadership. They attain it (only) once their nature has undergone a complete transformation under the influence of some religious coloring that wipes out all such (qualities) and causes the Arabs to have a restraining influence on themselves and to keep people apart from each other, as we have mentioned.[148]

This is illustrated by the Arab dynasty in Islam. Religion cemented their leadership with the religious law and its ordinances, which, explicitly and implicitly, are concerned with what is good for civilization. The caliphs followed one after another. As a result, the royal authority and government of the Arabs became great and strong. When Rustum saw the Muslims assemble for prayer, he said: " 'Umar eats my liver. He teaches the dogs how to behave." [149]

Later on, the Arabs were cut off from the dynasty for generations. They neglected the religion. Thus, they forgot political leadership and returned to their desert. They were

---

[148] Cf. pp. 305 f., above.

[149] Cf. aṭ-Ṭabarî, *Annales*, I, 2291.

ignorant of the connection of their group feeling with the people of the ruling dynasty, because subservience and lawful (government) had (now) become strange to them. They became once again as savage as they had been before. The epithet "royal" was no longer applicable to them, except in so far as it (continued to) apply to the caliphs who were (Arabs) by race. When the caliphate disappeared and was wiped out, governmental power passed altogether out of their hands. Non-Arabs took over the power in their stead. They remained as Bedouins in the desert, ignorant of royal authority and political leadership. Most Arabs do not even know that they possessed royal authority in the past, or that no nation had ever exercised such (sweeping) royal authority as had their race. The dynasties of 'Âd and Thamûd, the Amalekites, the Ḥimyar, and the Tubba's testify to that
I, 276 statement, and then, there was the Muḍar dynasty in Islam, the Umayyads and the 'Abbâsids. But when the Arabs forgot the religion, they no longer had any connection with political leadership, and they returned to their desert origins. At times, they achieve superiority over weak dynasties, as is the case in the contemporary Maghrib. But their domination leads only to the ruin of the civilization they conquer, as we have stated before.

God is the best heir.[150]

[28] *Desert tribes and groups are dominated by the urban population.*

It [151] has been stated by us before [152] that desert civilization is inferior to urban civilization, because not all the necessities of civilization are to be found among the people of the desert. They do possess some agriculture at home, (but) they do not possess (all) the materials that belong to it, most of which (depend on) crafts. They do not have any

[150] Cf. Qur'ân 21.89 (89).
[151] Cf. Issawi, pp. 82 f.
[152] Cf. pp. 252 f., above.

carpenters, tailors, blacksmiths, or other (craftsmen whose crafts) would provide them with the necessities required for making a living in agriculture and other things.

Likewise, they do not have (coined) money (dinars and dirhams). They have the equivalent of it in harvested grain, in animals, and in animal products such as milk, wool (of animals), (camel's) hair, and hides, which the urban population needs and pays the Arabs money for. However, while (the Bedouins) need the cities for their necessities of life, the urban population needs (the Bedouins) for conveniences and luxuries. Thus, (the Bedouins) need the cities for the necessities of life by the very nature of their (mode of) existence. As long as they live in the desert and have not obtained royal authority and control of the cities, they need the inhabitants I, 277
(of the latter). They must be active in behalf of their interests and obey them whenever (the latter) ask and demand obedience from them.

When there is a ruler in the city, the submissiveness and obedience of (the Bedouins) is the result of the superiority of the ruler. When there is no ruler in the city, some political leadership and control by some of the inhabitants over the remainder must, of necessity, exist in it. If not, the civilization of the city would be wiped out. Such a leader makes (the Bedouins) obey him and exert themselves in behalf of his interests. He does so either by persuasion, in that he distributes money among them and lets them have the necessities they need from his city, which enables their civilization to subsist; or, if he has the power to do so, he forces them to obey him, even if he has to cause discord among them so as to get the support of one party, with the help of which he will then be able to overcome the remainder and thus force the others to obey him, since they fear the decay of their civilization as the result of (the unstable situation). (These Bedouins) often cannot leave the particular districts (where they live and go) to other regions, because all of them are (already) inhabited by (other) Bedouins who took them away (from someone) and kept others out. They have, therefore, no hope of survival except by being obedient to the city. Thus, they are of necessity dominated by the urban population.

God "exercises forceful domination over His servants." [153]

[153] Qur'ân 6.18 (18), 61 (61).

Chapter III

ON DYNASTIES, ROYAL AUTHORITY, I, 278
THE CALIPHATE, GOVERNMENT RANKS,
AND ALL THAT GOES WITH THESE THINGS.
THE CHAPTER CONTAINS BASIC AND
SUPPLEMENTARY PROPOSITIONS.

[1] *Royal authority and large[1] dynastic (power) are attained only through a group and group feeling.*

THIS[2] IS BECAUSE, as we established in the first chapter, aggressive and defensive strength is obtained only through group feeling which means (mutual) affection and willingness to fight and die for each other.

Now, royal authority is a noble and enjoyable position. It comprises all the good things of the world, the pleasures of the body, and the joys of the soul. Therefore, there is, as a rule, great competition for it. It rarely is handed over (voluntarily), but it may be taken away. Thus, discord ensues. It leads to war and fighting, and to attempts to gain superiority. Nothing of all this comes about except through group feeling, as we have also mentioned.

This situation is not at all understood by the great mass. They forget it, because they have forgotten the time when the dynasty first became established. They have grown up in settled areas for a long time. They have lived there for successive generations. Thus, they know nothing about what took place with God's help at the beginning of the dynasty. They merely notice that the coloring of the men of the dynasty is determined, that people have submitted to them, and that group feeling is no longer needed to establish their power. They do not know how it was at the beginning and what difficulties had to be overcome by the founder of (the dynasty). The inhabitants of Spain especially have forgotten group feeling and its influence, because so long a time has passed, and because as a rule they have no need of the power I, 279
of group feeling, since their country has been annihilated and is depleted of tribal groups.

God has power to do what He wishes.

---

[1] *'âmmah* "general," here and elsewhere refers to governmental power that is not restricted to a small unit, such as a tribe.

[2] Cf. Issawi, p. 109.

[2] *When a dynasty is firmly established, it can dispense with group feeling.*

The[3] reason for this is that people find it difficult to submit to large dynastic (power) at the beginning, unless they are forced into submission by strong superiority. (The new government) is something strange. People are not familiar with, or used to, its rule. But once leadership is firmly vested in the members of the family qualified to exercise royal authority in the dynasty, and once (royal authority) has been passed on by inheritance over many generations and through successive dynasties, the beginnings are forgotten, and the members of that family are clearly marked as leaders. It has become a firmly established article of faith that one must be subservient and submissive to them. People will fight with them in their behalf, as they would fight for the articles of faith. By this time, (the rulers) will not need much group (feeling to maintain) their power. It is as if obedience to the government were a divinely revealed book that cannot be changed or opposed. It is for some (good reason) that the discussion of the imamate is placed at the end of works dealing with the articles of faith, as if it were one of them.[4]

(The rulers) maintain their hold over the government and their own dynasty with the help, then, either of clients and followers who grew up in the shadow and power[5] of group feeling, or (with that) of tribal groups of a different descent who have become their clients.

I. 280 Something of the sort happened to the ʿAbbâsids. The group feeling of the Arabs had been destroyed by the time of the reign of al-Muʿtaṣim and his son, al-Wâthiq. They tried to maintain their hold over the government thereafter

---

[3] Cf. Issawi, pp. 109 f.

[4] Ibn Khaldûn refers to the numerous catechisms and creeds where the caliphate is discussed, usually near the end. Cf., for instance, al-Ashʿarî's *Kitâb al-Lumaʿ*, ed. and tr. R. J. McCarthy, *The Theology of al-Ashʿarî* (Beirut, 1953).

[5] *Wa-ʿizzi-hâ*, as in A, B, and C.

with the help of Persian, Turkish, Daylam, Saljûq, and other clients. Then, the Persians (non-Arabs) and clients gained power over the provinces (of the realm). The influence of the dynasty grew smaller, and no longer extended beyond the environs of Baghdad. Eventually, the Daylam closed in upon (that area) and took possession of it. The caliphs were ruled by them. Then (the Daylam), in turn, lost control. The Saljûqs seized power after the Daylam, and the (caliphs) were ruled by them. Then (the Saljûqs), in turn, lost control. Finally, the Tatars closed in. They killed the caliph and wiped out every vestige of the dynasty.

The same happened to the Ṣinhâjah in the Maghrib. Their group feeling was destroyed in the fifth [eleventh] century, or before that. Dynastic (power), but of decreasing importance, was maintained by them in al-Mahdîyah, in Bougie, in al-Qal'ah,[6] and in the other frontier cities of Ifrîqiyah. Frequently, some rival aspirant to royal authority would attack these frontier cities and entrench himself in them. Yet, they retained government and royal authority until God permitted their dynasty to be wiped out. Then the Almohads came, fortified by the strong group feeling among the Maṣmûdah, and obliterated all traces of the (Ṣinhâjah dynasty).

The same happened to the Umayyad dynasty in Spain. When its Arab group feeling was destroyed, the *reyes de taïfas* (small princes) seized power and divided the territory among themselves. In competition with each other, they distributed among themselves the realm of the (Umayyad) dynasty. Each one of them seized the territory under his control and aggrandized himself. (These rulers) learned of the relations that existed between the non-Arabs (in the East) and the 'Abbâsids. (Imitating them,) they adopted royal surnames and used royal trappings. There was no danger that anyone would take (the prerogatives they claimed) away from them or alter (the situation in this respect), be-

[6] The ancient capital of the Banû Ḥammâd, northeast of Msila.

I, 281 cause Spain was no (longer the) home of groups and tribes, as we shall mention. They went on in this way, (and it was) as Ibn Sharaf[7] described it:

> What makes me feel humble in Spain
> Is the use of the names Mu'taṣim and Mu'taḍid there.
> Royal surnames not in their proper place:
> Like a cat that by blowing itself up imitates the lion.

They tried to maintain their power with the help of clients and followers and with that of the Zanâtah and other Berber tribes which infiltrated Spain from the (African) shore. They imitated the way the (Umayyad) dynasty in its last stages had tried to maintain its power with their help, when the Arab group feeling weakened and Ibn Abî 'Âmir[8] obtained control of the dynasty. (These newcomers) founded large states. Each one of them had control over a section of Spain. They also had a large share of royal authority, corresponding to (that of) the dynasty they had divided up. They thus remained in power until the Almoravids, who shared in the strong Lamtûnah group feeling, crossed the sea. The latter came and replaced and dislodged them from their centers. They obliterated (all) traces of (the *reyes de taïfas*) who were unable to defend themselves because they had no (longer any) group feeling.

Such group feeling makes it possible for a dynasty to become established and protected from the beginning. Aṭ-Ṭurṭûshî thought that the military (strength) of a dynasty as such is identical with (the size of its) army that receives a fixed pay every month. He mentioned this in his *Sirâj al-*

[7] Muḥammad b. Muḥammad, d. 460 [1067/68]. Cf. *GAL*, I, 268; *Suppl.*, I, 473; C. Pellat in *Bulletin des études arabes*, VIII–IX (1948–49).

The verses, however, are not by Ibn Sharaf but by his contemporary Ibn Rashîq (see n. 23 to p. 10, above), who recited them in the presence of Ibn Sharaf. They are often quoted. Cf., for instance, Ibn Bassâm, *Dhakhîrah* (Cairo, 1364/1945), IV [1], 134; Ibn Sa'îd, *El Libro de las Banderas de los Campeones*, ed. and tr. E. García Gómez (Madrid, 1942), p. 101; Yâqût, *Irshâd*, VII, 96; al-Maqqarî, *Analectes*, I, 131 f. Cf. also p. 470, below.

[8] Cf. p. 61, above.

mulûk.[9] His statement does not take into consideration the (conditions obtaining at the) original foundation of large dynasties. It applies only to the later stages, after the dynasty has been established and after royal authority has become firmly anchored in a given family and its people have adopted (their) definite coloring. (Aṭ-Ṭurṭûshî) had personal contact only with a senile dynasty whose energy was exhausted and which had reverted to maintaining power with the help of I, 282
clients and followers, then hired servants for (its) defense. He had contact only with the small dynasties (the *reyes de taïfas*), at a time when the Umayyad dynasty was already in the state of (complete) dissolution, when its Arab group feeling was wiped out, and when each amir had (independent) control over his particular region. He lived under the administration of the Saragossans al-Musta'în b. Hûd and his son, al-Muẓaffar. They had no longer any group feeling left, because, for three hundred years, the Arabs had been dominated by luxury and had perished. Aṭ-Ṭurṭûshî thus saw only the kind of ruler who had (independent) control of royal authority to the exclusion of the families to which it belonged, and in whom the coloring of autocratic rule had been firmly established since the time of the dynasty('s power) and when a remnant of group feeling still existed. Therefore, his (royal authority) was not contested, and he could rely for maintenance of his power upon a soldiery with fixed pay. Aṭ-Ṭurṭûshî generalized the condition (observed by him) when he made the statement mentioned. He did not realize how a dynasty originally comes to power, nor that only those who share in a group feeling are able to accomplish (the formation of a dynasty). But this should be realized. It should be understood how God intended these things to be.

"God gives His kingdom (royal authority) to whomever He wants to give it." [10]

---

[9] The reference apparently is to Ch. XLV of the *Sirâj al-mulûk*, which deals with the relationship between ruler and army. See p. 122 of the ed. (Cairo, 1289/1872). For criticism of aṭ-Ṭurṭûshî, cf. also 2:87, below.

[10] Qur'ân 2.247 (248).

[3] *Members of a royal family may be able to found a dynasty that can dispense with group feeling.*

This is because the group feeling in which (a member of a royal family) shares may have much power over nations and races, and the inhabitants of remote regions who support his power may be obedient (to that family) and submissive. So, when such a person secedes, leaving the seat of his rule and the home of his might, and joins those inhabitants of remote regions, they adopt him. They support his rule and help him. They take care of establishing his dynasty on a
I, 283 firm basis. They hope that he will be confirmed in his family (rights) and take the power away from his kinsmen.[11] They do not desire to share in any way in his rule, as they subject themselves to his group feeling and submit to the coloring of material superiority firmly belonging to him and his people. They believe, as in an article of faith, in being obedient to (him and his people). Were they to desire to share his rule with him or to rule without him, "the earth would be shaken." [12]

That is what happened to the Idrîsids in Morocco and the 'Ubaydid(-Fâṭimids) in Ifrîqiyah and Egypt. Abû Ṭâlib's descendants had left the East and removed themselves from the seat of the caliphate, to go to remote regions of the Muslim realm. They aspired to deprive the 'Abbâsids of the caliphate whose coloring had (throughout the years) firmly established itself in the descendants of 'Abd-Manâf, first among the Umayyads and then among the Hâshimites ('Abbâsids). They seceded (from the ruling 'Abbâsid dynasty) in the western part of Islam and made propaganda for themselves. The Berbers supported their rule time after time. The Awrabah and Maghîlah (supported) the Idrîsids, and the Kutâmah, the Ṣinhâjah, and the Hawwârah (supported) the

---

[11] Bulaq adds: "and reward them for helping him by choosing them for royal ranks and positions, such as the wazirate, the army command, or the governorship of a frontier district."

[12] Qur'ân 99.1 (1).

'Ubaydid(-Fâṭimids). These (Berber tribes) cemented the dynasties of (the Idrîsids and 'Ubaydids) and firmly established their rule through the group support they gave them. They detached the whole Maghrib and then Ifrîqiyah from the realm of the 'Abbâsids. The influence of the 'Abbâsid dynasty grew steadily smaller and that of the 'Ubaydid (-Fâṭimids) larger. Eventually, the latter took possession of Egypt, Syria, and the Ḥijâz, and shared the Muslim empire half and half with the 'Abbâsids.[12a] Nonetheless, the Berbers who supported the dynasty submitted their own affairs to the 'Ubaydid(-Fâṭimids) and obeyed their rule. They merely vied for positions under them. They subjected themselves to the royal authority that had become the established coloring of the Hâshimites (the family of Muḥammad, the 'Alid-Fâtimids as well as the 'Abbâsids), and to the superiority over all nations of the Quraysh and the Muḍar. Royal authority, therefore, remained with their descendants down to (the time of) the complete destruction of Arab rule. I, 284

"God decides, and no one can change His decision." [13]

[4] *Dynasties of wide power and large royal authority have their origin in religion based either on prophecy or on truthful propaganda.*

This [14] is because royal authority results from superiority. Superiority results from group feeling. Only by God's help in establishing His religion do individual desires come together in agreement to press their claims, and hearts become united. God said: "If you had expended all the treasures on earth, you would have achieved no unity among them." [15] The secret of (this) is that when the hearts succumb to false desires and are inclined toward the world, mutual jealousy and widespread differences arise. (But) when they are turned toward the truth and reject the world and whatever is false,

---

[12a] Cf. p. 45, above, and p. 331, below.
[13] Qur'ân 13.41 (41).
[14] Cf. Issawi, p. 131.
[15] Qur'ân 8.63 (64).

and advance toward God, they become one in their outlook. Jealousy disappears. There are few differences. Mutual co-operation and support flourish. As a result, the extent of the state widens, and the dynasty grows, as we shall explain now.

[5] *Religious propaganda gives a dynasty at its beginning another power in addition to that of the group feeling it possessed as the result of the number of its (supporters).*

As[16] we have mentioned before, the reason for this is that religious coloring does away with mutual jealousy and envy among people who share in a group feeling, and causes
I, 285 concentration upon the truth. When people (who have a religious coloring) come to have the (right) insight into their affairs, nothing can withstand them, because their outlook is one and their object one of common accord. They are willing to die for (their objectives). (On the other hand,) the members of the dynasty they attack may be many times as numerous as they. But their purposes differ, in as much as they are false[17] purposes, and (the people of the worldly dynasty) come to abandon each other, since they are afraid of death. Therefore, they do not offer resistance to (the people with a religious coloring), even if they themselves are more numerous. They are overpowered by them and quickly wiped out, as a result of the luxury and humbleness existing among them, as we have mentioned before.[18]

This happened to the Arabs at the beginning of Islam during the Muslim conquests. The armies of the Muslims

---

[16] Cf. Issawi, pp. 131–33, and above, pp. 305 f.

[17] Whereas the truth is only one, and means unity of purpose. Cf., for instance, the saying attributed to Plato in al-Mubashshir b. Fâtik, *Mukhtâr al-ḥikam*, No. 227 (ed. Madrid, 1958, p. 158); cf. H. Knust, *Mittheilungen aus dem Eskurial*, p. 229: "Justice in something is one form, whereas injustice is many forms. Therefore it is easy to commit an injustice, and difficult to pursue justice. Justice and injustice are like hitting and missing (the target) in shooting. Hitting (it) requires practice and experience, while it does not require anything of the sort to miss."

[18] Cf., for instance, pp. 296 ff., above.

at al-Qâdisîyah and at the Yarmûk numbered some 30,000 in each case, while the Persian troops at al-Qâdisîyah numbered 120,000,[19] and the troops of Heraclius, according to al-Wâqidî, 400,000.[20] Neither of the two parties was able to withstand the Arabs. (The Arabs) routed them and seized what they possessed.

Another illustration is the Lamtûnah (Almoravid) and Almohad dynasties. In the Maghrib, there existed many tribes equaling or surpassing them in numbers and group feeling. However, their religious organization doubled the strength of their group feeling through (their) feeling of having (the right religious) insight [21] and (their) willingness to die, as we have stated, and nothing could withstand them.

This can also be illustrated (by the situation existing at the time) when the religious coloring changes and is destroyed. The power (of the ruling dynasty) is then wiped out. Superiority exists then merely in proportion to (the existing) group feeling, without the additional (power of) religion. As a result, the dynasty is overpowered by those groups (up to this time) under its control, that are equal or superior to it in strength. It had formerly overpowered the groups that had a stronger group feeling and were more deeply rooted in desert life, with the help of the additional power that religion had given it.

---

[19] Cf., p. 17, above.

[20] The very high figures given here and in some of the historical examples mentioned on the following pages, are not usually found in the old sources, such as aṭ-Ṭabarî, al-Mas'ûdî, etc. This might have warned Ibn Khaldûn against using them — had it been as easy for him to check the sources as it is for us.

The *Futûḥ ash-Sha'm*, a novelistic elaboration of the conquest of Syria ascribed to al-Wâqidî, speaks of four armies, the first three of which consisted of 100,000 knights each. This may have given rise to the figure of 400,000 mentioned by Ibn Khaldûn. However, Pseudo-Wâqidî also mentions 600,000 and 700,000 as the number of Heraclius' troops. Cf. *Futûḥ ash-Sha'm* (Cairo, 1354/1935), I, 102 f.

[21] *Istibṣâr*, as p. 320, above, and 2:134, below. The term, based on Qur'ân 29.38 (37), is quite frequently used in religious literature. In this passage one might be tempted to read *bi-l-intiṣâr* "through their willingness to win and die." However, in A, C, and D, where the word is provided with diacritical dots, it is *istibṣâr*.

I, 286 An illustration of this is the relationship of the Almohads with the Zanâtah. The Zanâtah were deeply rooted in the desert and more savage than the Maṣmûdah, but the Maṣmûdah had the religious call to follow the Mahdî. They took on (his religious) coloring. As a result, the strength of their group feeling increased many times over. Therefore, they were at first able to overpower the Zanâtah and to make them their followers, even though (the Zanâtah) were more strongly rooted in the desert and had a stronger group feeling than they. But (later on) when the Maṣmûdah lost their religious coloring, the Zanâtah rose up against them from every side and took their power away from them. "God has the power to execute His commands." [22]

[6] *Religious propaganda cannot materialize without group feeling.*

This [23] is because, as we have mentioned before, every mass (political) undertaking by necessity requires group feeling. This is indicated in the afore-mentioned [24] tradition: "God sent no prophet who did not enjoy the protection of his people." If this was the case with the prophets, who are among human beings those most likely to perform wonders, one would (expect it to apply) all the more so to others. One cannot expect them to be able to work the wonder of achieving superiority without group feeling.

It happened to the Sufi *shaykh* Ibn Qasî,[25] the author of the

---

[22] Qur'ân 12.21 (21).

[23] Cf. Issawi, pp. 133 f.; G. Surdon and L. Bercher, *Recueil de textes de sociologie*, pp. 59–61.

[24] Cf. p. 187, above, and p. 414, below. The earlier texts have "sound tradition." The word "sound" is deleted in C and does not appear in D at all.

[25] Aḥmad b. Qasî died in 546 [1151]. He started his revolt about ten years earlier. Cf. L. Massignon, *Recueil de textes inédits concernant l'histoire de la mystique en pays d'Islam* (Paris, 1929), pp. 102 f.; M. Asín Palacios, in his edition of Ibn al-'Arîf, *Maḥâsin al-majâlis* (Paris, 1933), p. 5; *'Ibar*, VI, 233 f.; de Slane (tr.), II, 184 f. He probably was a member of the Ibn Qasî family mentioned by Ibn Ḥazm, *Jamharat ansâb al-'Arab*, pp. 467 f. Cf. also *GAL, Suppl.*, I, 776, where his name is said to be Ibn Qasyî.

The title of his work refers to the Moses story in the Qur'ân 20.12 (12), which is given a mystical interpretation; cf. Ibn 'Arabî, *Futûḥât* (Bulaq,

Kitâb Khal' an-na'layn on Sufism. He rose in revolt in Spain and made propaganda for the truth shortly before the time when the propaganda of the Mahdî (of the Almohads) started. His followers were called *al-Murâbiṭûn*.[26] (Ibn Qasî) had some success, because the Lamtûnah (Almoravids) were preoccupied with their own difficulties with the Almohads. (But) there were no groups and tribes there to defend him. When the Almohads took over control of the Maghrib, he soon obeyed them and participated in their cause. He took the oath of allegiance to them at his stronghold, the fortress I, 287
of Arcos (de la Frontera). He handed his frontier province over to them and became their first missionary in Spain. His revolt was called the revolt of the *Murâbiṭûn*.

To this chapter belong cases of revolutionaries from among the common people and of jurists who undertake to reform evil (practices). Many religious people who follow the ways of religion come to revolt against unjust amirs. They call for a change in, and prohibition of, evil (practices) and for good practices. They hope for a divine reward for what they do. They gain many followers and sympathizers among the great mass of the people, but they risk being killed, and most of them actually do perish in consequence of their activities as sinners and unrewarded, because God had not destined them for such (activities as they undertake). He commands such activities to be undertaken only where there

---

1293/1876), I, 250 f. The work is contained in the Istanbul MS, Şehid Ali Paşa 1174 (written in 741 [1340]), fols. 1*a*–88*b*, where it is followed by Ibn 'Arabî's commentary, fols. 89*a*–175*b*. Only the commentary is contained in Aya Sofya 1879. The name Qasî is vocalized alternately with each of the three vowels in these MSS. * 'Afîfî in *Bull. Fac. Arts, Alexandria University*, XI (1957), 53–87.

The full title is *Kitâb Khal' an-na'layn wa-qtibâs al-anwâr min mawḍi' al-qadamayn*. The work should not be confused, as sometimes happens, with the *Kitâb khal' an-na'layn fî wuṣûl ilâ ḥaḍrat al-jam'ayn* by 'Abdallâh al-Bosnawî 'Abdî, d. 1054 [1644]. Cf. *GAL, Suppl.*, I, 793. MSS of the latter work are preserved in Istanbul Université, Arabic MS. 3164, and Nafiz (Süleymaniye) 503. Ḥâjjî Khalîfah, *Kashf aẓ-ẓunûn*, III, 172, mentions 'Abdî's work as a commentary on Ibn Qasî's work (?).

[26] Ibn Khaldûn has this word which is the same as the name of the Almoravids. However, Ibn Qasî's followers are said to have been called *Murîdûn* (mystic disciples).

exists the power to bring them to a successful conclusion. Muḥammad said: "Should one among you see evil activities, he should change them with his hand. If he cannot do that, he should change them with his tongue. And if he cannot do that, he should change them with his heart." [26a]

Rulers and dynasties are strongly entrenched. Their foundations can be undermined and destroyed only through strong efforts backed by the group feeling of tribes and families, as we have mentioned before. Similarly, prophets in their religious propaganda depended on groups and families, though they were the ones who could have been supported by God with anything in existence, if He had wished, but in His wisdom [27] He permitted matters to take their customary course.

If someone who is on the right path were to attempt (religious reforms) in this way, (his) isolation would keep him from (gaining the support of) group feeling,[28] and he would perish. If someone merely pretends to (achieve religious reforms) in order to gain (political) leadership, he
I, 288 deserves to be hampered by obstacles and to fall victim to perdition. (Religious reforms) are a divine matter that materializes only with God's pleasure and support, through sincere devotion for Him and in view of good intentions towards the Muslims. No Muslim, no person of insight, could doubt this (truth).

In Islam, the first person to start that sort of thing in Baghdad was a certain Khâlid ad-Daryûsh.[29] Ṭâhir had revolted. Al-Amîn was killed. Al-Ma'mûn in Khurâsân was slowed down in his advance toward the 'Irâq, and he ap-

[26a] Cf. Muslim, *Ṣaḥîḥ, Kitâb al-îmân;* Ibn al-Ukhuwwa, *Ma'âlim al-qurbah,* ed. R. Levy (E. J. W. Gibb Memorial Series, N.S. No. 12) (London, 1938), p. 18.

[27] The words "in His wisdom" are substituted in C and D for the concluding phrase, "God is wise and knowing," which the earlier texts have.

[28] Other translators have suggested a different translation: "(his) isolation from group feeling would cut him short."

[29] For the following events, cf. aṭ-Ṭabarî, *Annales,* III, 1008 ff. The role of Ibrâhim b. al-Mahdî (cf. p. 40, above, and pp. 430 f., below) is somewhat exaggerated by Ibn Khaldûn in retelling the story.

pointed 'Alî b. Mûsâ ar-Riḍâ, a descendant of al-Ḥusayn, successor to the throne. The 'Abbâsids showed their disapproval (of that move). They banded together in order to revolt and to renounce obedience to al-Ma'mûn and to choose some one else in his stead. Allegiance was sworn to Ibrâhîm b. al-Mahdî. Trouble broke out in Baghdad. The troublesome elements among the underworld and the soldiery were given a free hand against the decent citizens. They robbed the people and filled their pockets with loot, which they sold openly in the markets. The inhabitants turned for protection to the authorities, but these did not help them. The religious and good citizens, thereupon, united in order to stop the criminals and to put an end to their misdeeds. At that moment, a man named Khâlid ad-Daryûsh appeared in Baghdad. He appealed to the people to obey the law. Many responded to his call. They fought the troublesome elements and defeated them. Khâlid had them beaten and punished. After him, there appeared another man from among the populace of Baghdad,[30] by name Abû Ḥâtim Sahl b. Salâmah al-Anṣârî. He hung a copy of the Qur'ân around his neck, and appealed to the people to obey the law and to act in accordance with the Qur'ân and the Sunnah of the Prophet. High and low, I, 289
Hâshimites and others, all followed him. He established himself in the palace of Ṭâhir and took over the government office(s). He went about Baghdad, kept out all those who were frightening wayfarers, and put an end to the payment of protection money [31] to the underworld. When Khâlid ad-Daryûsh said to him that he (Khâlid) was not against the government, Sahl replied that he (for his part) was fighting

[30] The reading of the text *min sawâd ahl Baghdâd* seems doubtful. Ibn Khaldûn probably meant to say *min ahl Sawâd Baghdâd* "from the people of the Sawâd (lower Mesopotamia) of Baghdad." However, aṭ-Ṭabarî states that the man came from Khurâsân. In favor of the reading of the text, it may be noted that Ibn Khaldûn uses *sawâd* in the meaning of "people" below, 2:103, l. 4, and 2:300, l. 4.

[31] Aṭ-Ṭabarî graphically describes the procedure: "*Khafârah* means that someone goes to the owner of a garden and says to him: Your garden is under my protection (*khafar*). I shall keep away everyone who might want to do mischief there, and you are to pay me so much money each month."

all those who acted contrary to the Qur'ân and the Sunnah, whoever they might be. This happened in the year 201 [817]. Ibrâhîm b. al-Mahdî sent an army against (Sahl). He was defeated and captured, and his power quickly dissolved. He barely escaped with his life.

Later on, many deluded individuals followed that example. They took it upon themselves to establish the truth. They did not know that they would need group feeling for that. They did not realize how their enterprise must necessarily end and what they would come to. With respect to such people, it is necessary to adopt one of the following courses. One may either treat them, if they are insane, or one may punish them either by execution or beatings when they cause trouble, or one may ridicule them and treat them as buffoons.[32]

Some of these people allied themselves with the Expected Fâṭimid.[33] They pretended to be, either he himself, or one of his missionaries, despite their ignorance of everything concerning the Fâṭimid. Most men who adopt such ideas will be found to be, either deluded and crazy, or to be swindlers who, with the help of such claims, seek to obtain (political) leadership—which they crave and would be unable to obtain
I, 290 in the natural manner. They believe that such claims will be instrumental in bringing to them the fulfillment of their hopes. They do not consider the disaster that will overtake them in consequence. The trouble they create will speedily cause their death and bring their trickery to a bitter end.

At the beginning of this century, a man of Sufi leanings, by name at-Tuwayzirî, appeared in as-Sûs. He went to the Mosque of Mâssah [34] on the shore of the Mediterranean and pretended to be the Expected Fâṭimid. He was taking advantage of the common people's firm belief in predictions to the effect that the Fâṭimid was about to appear and that his

---

[32] Lit., "slapstick artists."
[33] Cf. pp. 408, 414, and 2:156 ff., below.
[34] Cf. p. 128, above.

mission would originate at that Mosque. A number of ordinary Berber groups were attracted to him like moths (to the flame).[35] Their chiefs then feared that the revolt might spread. The leader of the Maṣmûdah at that time, 'Umar as-Saksîwî,[36] secretly sent someone to him, who killed him in his bed.

Also at the beginning of this century, a man known as al-'Abbâs appeared among the Ghumârah. He made a similar claim. The lowest among the stupid and imbecile members of those tribes followed his blethering. He marched on Bâdis, one of the (Ghumârah) cities, and entered it by force. He was then killed, forty days after the start of his mission. He perished like those before him.[37]

There are many similar cases.[38] The mistake (they all make) is that they disregard the significance of group feeling (for success) in such matters. If deceit is involved, it is better that such a person should not succeed and be made to pay for his crime. "That is the sinners' reward." [39]

[7] *Each dynasty has a certain amount of provinces and lands, and no more.* I, 291

The [40] reason for this is that the group to which a given dynasty belongs and the people who support and establish it, must of necessity be distributed over the provinces and border regions which they reach and take into possession. Only thus is it possible to protect them against enemies and

---

[35] The attraction of moths to the flame is interpreted by the Arabs as indicating stupidity rather than eagerness or self-sacrifice. Cf. ath-Tha'âlibî, *Thimâr al-qulûb* (Cairo, 1326/1908), pp. 399 f. The latter interpretation, however, is that of Muslim mysticism.

[36] Cf. de Slane (tr.), *Histoire des Berbères*, II, 270 f. The Arabic text is missing in the edition of the *'Ibar*.

The story is repeated below, 2:197.

[37] This event, which took place at the end of the thirteenth century, is mentioned again, 2:197 f., below.

[38] Cf. also *'Ibar*, VI, 302; de Slane (tr.), II, 388.

[39] Qur'ân 5.29 (32); 59.17 (17).

[40] Cf. Issawi, pp. 127 f.

to enforce the laws of the dynasty relative to the collection of taxes, restrictions,[41] and other things.

When the (various) groups have spread over the border regions and provinces, their numbers are necessarily exhausted. This, then, is the time when the territory (of the dynasty) has reached its farthest extension, where the border regions form a belt around the center of the realm. If the dynasty then undertakes to expand beyond its holdings, it(s widening territory) remains without military protection and is laid open to any chance attack by enemy or neighbor. This has the detrimental result for the dynasty of the creation of boldness toward it and of diminished respect for it. (On the other hand,) if the group is a very large one and its numbers are not exhausted when distributed over border regions and territories, the dynasty retains the strength to go beyond the limit (so far reached), until its expansion has gone as far as possible.

The natural reason for this (situation) lies in the fact that the power of group feeling is one of the natural powers. Any power resulting in any kind of action must proceed in its action in such manner.[42]

A dynasty is stronger at its center than it is at its border regions. When it has reached its farthest expansion, it be-
I, 292 comes too weak and incapable to go any farther. This may be compared to light rays that spread from their centers, or to circles that widen over the surface of the water when something strikes it.

When the dynasty becomes senile and weak, it begins to

---

[41] The translators disagree as to who is to be restricted. De Slane: "to contain those who are defeated." Issawi: "to awe the population." Schimmel (p. 78): "to drive back enemies." The term used here is not common with Ibn Khaldûn, but it appears to refer to the restraining influence which is to be exercised upon the native population. The word *radʻ* used here occurs also elsewhere in the same sense in which Ibn Khaldûn preferably uses *wzʻ*. Cf., for instance, Ibn al-Ukhuwwa, *Maʻâlim al-qurbah*, p. 195, l. 19, or al-Mubashshir, *Mukhtâr al-ḥikam*, sayings of Socrates, Nos. 7 & 277(= ed. Badawî [Madrid, 1958], pp. 92 and 117).

[42] That is, it must follow its natural course. Each power can have only the effects depending on its inherent character.

crumble at its extremities. The center remains intact until God permits the destruction of the whole (dynasty). Then, the center is destroyed. But when a dynasty is overrun from the center, it is of no avail to it that the outlying areas remain intact. It dissolves all at once. The center is like the heart from which the (vital) spirit [43] spreads. Were the heart to be overrun and captured, all the extremities would be routed.

This may be observed in the Persian dynasty. Its center was al-Madâ'in (Ctesiphon). When the Muslims took over al-Madâ'in, the whole Persian empire dissolved. Possession of the outlying provinces of the realm was of no avail to Yazdjard.

Conversely, the center of the Byzantine dynasty in Syria was in Constantinople. When the Muslims took Syria away from the Byzantines, the latter repaired to their center in Constantinople. The loss of Syria did not harm them. Their rule continued there without interruption until God permitted it to be ended.[44]

Another example is the situation of the Arabs at the beginning of Islam. Since they were a very large group, they very quickly overran neighboring Syria, 'Irâq, and Egypt. Then, they kept on going, into Western India (as-Sind), Abyssinia, Ifrîqiyah, and the Maghrib, and later into Spain. They spread over many provinces and border regions, and settled in them as militiamen. Their numbers were exhausted by that expansion. No further conquests could be made by them, and the Muslim empire reached its farthest extension. Those borders were not passed, but the dynasty receded from them, until God permitted it to be destroyed. I, *293*

The situation of later dynasties was the same. Each dynasty depended on the numerical strength of its supporters. When its numbers were exhausted through expansion, no

---

[43] Cf. p. 74 (n. 5), and p. 210, above.

[44] The past tense is used here! The word "there" certainly does not refer to Syria, but to the Byzantine center in Constantinople. This anticipation of the fall of Constantinople may have something to do with traditions and predictions to that effect. Cf. 2:193, below.

further conquest or extension of power was possible. This is how God proceeds with His creatures.

[8] *The greatness of a dynasty, the extent of its territory, and the length of its duration depend upon the numerical strength of its supporters.*

The reason for this is that royal authority exists only through group feeling. Representatives of group feeling are the militiamen who settle in the provinces and territories of the dynasty and are spread over them. The more numerous the tribes and groups of a large dynasty are, the stronger and larger are its provinces and lands. Their royal authority, therefore, is wider.

An example of this was the Muslim dynasty when God united the power of the Arabs in Islam. The number of Muslims who participated in the raid against Tabûk, the Prophet's last raid, was 110,000,[45] (consisting of) Muḍar and Qaḥṭân horsemen and foot soldiers. That number was augmented by those who became Muslims after the (raid) and down to the time of the Prophet's death. When (all these people) then set out to seek for themselves the royal authority held by (other) nations, there was no protection against them or refuge. They were allowed (to take possession of) the realms of the Persians and the Byzantines who were the greatest dynasties in the world at that time, (as well as the realms) of the Turks in the East, of the European Christians and Berbers in the West (Maghrib), and of the
I, 294 Goths in Spain. They went from the Ḥijâz to as-Sûs in the far west,[46] and from the Yemen to the Turks in the farthest north. They gained possession of all seven zones.

One may also look at the Ṣinhâjah and Almohad dynasties and their relationship to the 'Ubaydid(-Fâṭimids) before them.

[45] Cf. also p. 352, below. Lower figures are given, for example, by Ibn Sayyid-an-nâs, *'Uyûn al-athar*, II, 216, who has 30,000 men and 10,000 horses.

[46] Cf. n. 110 to Ch. I, above.

The Kutâmah, supporters of the 'Ubaydid(-Fâṭimid) dynasty, were more numerous than the Ṣinhâjah and the Maṣmûdah. Consequently, their dynasty was larger. They took possession of Ifrîqiyah and the Maghrib, as well as of Syria, Egypt, and the Ḥijâz. One may also look at the later Zanâtah dynasty. Since the number of the Zanâtah was smaller than that of the Maṣmûdah, their royal authority fell short of that of the Almohads, because (the Zanâtah) were numerically inferior to the Maṣmûdah from the very start. One may also consider the situation of the two Zanâtah dynasties at this time, the Merinids and the 'Abd-al-Wâdids. The Merinids were numerically stronger than the 'Abd-al-Wâdids when they first seized power. Therefore, their dynasty was stronger and larger than that of the 'Abd-al-Wâdids. Time after time, (the Merinids) defeated (the 'Abd-al-Wâdids). It is said that the number of the Merinids at the beginning of their rule was three thousand and that of the 'Abd-al-Wâdids one thousand. However, (possession of) dynastic power with (its) life of ease and the (great) number of (its) followers increased their numbers.

Thus, the expansion and power of a dynasty correspond to the numerical strength of those who obtain superiority at the beginning of the rule. The length of its duration also depends upon it. The life of anything that comes into being depends upon the strength of its temper. The temper of dynasties is based upon group feeling. If the group feeling is strong, the (dynasty's) temper likewise is strong, and its life of long duration. Group feeling, in turn, depends on numerical strength, as we have stated.[47]

The real reason why (large dynasties last longer) is that when collapse comes it begins in the outlying regions, and I, 295 the large dynasty has many such provinces far from its center. Each defection that occurs necessarily requires a certain time. The time required (for collapse of the dynasty) will be long in such cases, because there are many provinces, each of

---

[47] Apparently, no specific passage is referred to here.

which collapses in its own good time. The duration of a large dynasty, therefore, is long.

This (fact) may be observed in the Arab Muslim dynasty. It lasted the longest of (all Muslim) dynasties, counting both the 'Abbâsids in the center and the Umayyads far away in Spain. Their rule collapsed only after the fourth [tenth] century.[48] The 'Ubaydid(-Fâṭimids) lasted about 280 years. The Ṣinhâjah dynasty did not last as long as that of the 'Ubaydid(-Fâṭimids), namely, from the time when Ma'add al-Mu'izz entrusted Ifrîqiyah to Buluggîn b. Zîrî in the year 358 [969], up to the time when the Almohads took possession of al-Qal'ah[49] and Bougie in the year 557 [1162]. The contemporary Almohad (Ḥafṣid) dynasty has lasted nearly 270 years.

Thus, the life of a dynasty depends upon (the number of) its supporters. "This is how God formerly proceeded with His servants."[50]

[9] *A dynasty rarely establishes itself firmly in lands with many different tribes and groups.*

The[51] reason for this is the differences in opinions and desires. Behind each opinion and desire, there is a group feeling defending it. At any time, therefore, there is much opposition to a dynasty and rebellion against it, even if the dynasty possesses group feeling, because each group feeling under the control of the ruling dynasty thinks that it has in
I, 296 itself (enough) strength and power.

One may compare what has happened in this connection in Ifrîqiyah and the Maghrib from the beginning of Islam to the present time. The inhabitants of those lands are

---

[48] The "Arab Muslim dynasty" comprises the 'Abbâsids and the Umayyads. Since, for Ibn Khaldûn, the 'Abbâsid dynasty as an independent power ended in the ninth/tenth century (cf., for instance, p. 351, below), he had to include the Spanish Umayyads, in order to give the "Arab Muslim dynasty" the longest duration of all Muslim dynasties.

[49] Cf. p. 315, above.

[50] Qur'ân 40.85 (85).

[51] Cf. Issawi, pp. 111–13.

Berber tribes and groups. The first victory of Ibn Abî Sarḥ [52] over them and the European Christians (in the Maghrib) was of no avail. They continued to rebel and apostatized time after time. The Muslims massacred many of them. After the Muslim religion had been established among them, they went on revolting and seceding, and they adopted dissident (Khârijite) religious opinions many times. Ibn Abî Zayd [53] said that the Berbers in the Maghrib revolted twelve times and that Islam became firmly established among them only during the governorship of Mûsâ b. Nuṣayr and thereafter. This is what is meant by the statement reported on the authority of ʿUmar, that "Ifrîqiyah 'divides' [54] the hearts of its inhabitants." The statement refers to the great number of tribes and groups there, which causes them to be disobedient and unmanageable. The ʿIrâq at that time was different, and so was Syria. The militia of the (ʿIrâq and Syria) consisted of Persians and Byzantines (respectively). All (the inhabitants) were a mixed lot of town and city dwellers. When the Muslims deprived them of their power, there remained no one capable of making a defense or of offering opposition.

The Berber tribes in the West are innumerable. All of them are Bedouins and members of groups and families. Whenever one tribe is destroyed, another takes its place and is as refractory and rebellious as the former one had been. Therefore, it has taken the Arabs a long time to establish their dynasty in the land of Ifrîqiyah and the Maghrib.

The same was the case in Syria in the age of the Israel- I, 297
ites. At that time, there existed (there) a very large number of tribes with a great variety of group feelings, such as the tribes of Palestine and Canaan, the children of Esau, the

[52] ʿUthmân's governor of Egypt, who tried to conquer Tripolitania shortly after 647.

[53] Cf. n. 333 to Ch. 1, above. The statement is repeatedly quoted in the *ʿIbar;* cf. VI, 12, 103, 110; de Slane (tr.), I, 28, 198, 215.

[54] This is a play on words, connecting Ifrîqiyah with the Arabic root *f-r-q* "to divide." Cf. also 3:474, below; al-Balâdhurî, *Futûḥ al-buldân,* p. 226.

Midyanites, the children of Lot, the Edomites, the Armenians[!], the Amalekites, Girgashites, and the Nabataeans from the Jazîrah and Mosul.[55] Therefore, it was difficult for the Israelites to establish their dynasty firmly. Time after time, their royal authority was endangered. The (spirit of) opposition (alive in the country) communicated itself to (the Israelites). They opposed their own government and revolted against it. They thus never had a continuous and firmly established royal authority. Eventually they were overpowered, first by the Persians, then by the Greeks, and finally by the Romans, when their power came to an end in the Diaspora. "God has the power to execute His commands."[56]

On the other hand, it is easy to establish a dynasty in lands that are free from group feelings. Government there will be a tranquil affair, because seditions and rebellions are few, and the dynasty there does not need much group feeling. This is the case in contemporary Egypt and Syria. They are (now) free from tribes and group feelings; indeed, one would never suspect that Syria had once been a mine of them, as we have (just) stated. Royal authority in Egypt is most peaceful and firmly rooted, because Egypt has few dissidents or people who represent tribal groups. Egypt has a sultan and subjects. (Egypt's) ruling dynasty consists of the Turkish rulers and their groups. They succeed each other in power, and the rule circulates among them, passing from one branch to another. The caliphate belongs in name to an 'Abbâsid, a descendant of the 'Abbâsid caliphs of Baghdad.

The same is the case in contemporary Spain. The group
I, 298 feeling of the ruler of (Spain), Ibn al-Aḥmar (the Naṣrids of Granada), was not strong or widespread to begin with. (The Naṣrids) belonged to one of the Arab houses that had supported the Umayyad dynasty, a few survivors of which remained. This situation came about as follows: When the Spaniards were no longer ruled by the Arab dynasty (of the

[55] Cf. p. 474, below. [56] Qur'ân 12.21 (21).

Umayyads) and the Lamtûnah and Almohad Berbers became their rulers, they detested this domination. Their oppression weighed heavily upon them, and their hearts were full of hate and indignation against (the new rulers).

Near the end of the (Almohad) rule, the Almohad lords handed over many of their strongholds to the abominable (Christian ruler), in order to gain his support for their attempts to capture the capital city of Marrakech. That caused remnants of the people in Spain who represented the ancient group feeling to unite. These were descendants of Arab houses who had to some degree kept away from urban civilization and the cities, and who were firmly rooted in military life. They included Ibn Hûd (of Saragossa), Ibn al-Aḥmar (of Granada), and Ibn Mardanîsh (of Valencia and Murcia), and others like them. Ibn Hûd seized power, made propaganda for the 'Abbâsid caliphate in the East, and caused the people to revolt against the Almohads. Allegiance to them was denounced, and they were driven out. Ibn Hûd thus became the independent ruler of Spain. Then, Ibn al-Aḥmar rose to power and opposed Ibn Hûd's propaganda. He made propaganda for Ibn Abî Ḥafṣ, the Almohad ruler of Ifrîqiyah, and seized power with the help of a group of relatives who were called "the chiefs." He needed no more people than these, because there were so few groups in Spain (at that time) possessing a government (*sulṭân*) and subjects. Ibn al-Aḥmar then sought support against the abominable (Christian ruler) from Zanâtah chieftains who came to him from across the sea. These Zanâtah chieftains became his associates in defense of the frontier regions and the manning of the garrisons.

Now, the Zanâtah (Merinid) ruler of the Maghrib had I, 299
hopes of gaining power in Spain. But these Zanâtah chieftains who were Ibn al-Aḥmar's associates defended him. His power, eventually, was firmly established. The people became used to his rule and could do nothing against him. He bequeathed his power to his descendants, who have held it down to the present. One should not think that he was with-

out group support. This was not so. He started out with a group, but it was a small one. However, it was sufficient for his needs, because there were few groups and tribes in (Spain) and, consequently, not much group feeling was needed there, in order to gain the upper hand over the Spaniards.

"God has no need of the worlds." [57]

[10] *By its very nature, the royal authority claims all glory for itself and goes in for luxury and prefers tranquillity and quiet.*[58]

As [59] to claiming all glory for itself, this is because, as we have mentioned before, royal authority exists through group feeling. Group feeling (such as leads to royal authority) is something composite that results from (the amalgamation of) many groups, one of which is stronger than all the others. Thus, (a group feeling) is able to overcome and gain power over (all the others), and, eventually, brings them all under its sway. Thus, social organization and superiority over men and dynasties come about. The secret here is that a group feeling extending over the entire tribe corresponds to the temper in the things that come into being. Temper is the product (of the mixture) of the elements. It has been explained in the proper place [60] that, when the elements are combined in equal proportions, no mixture can take place. One (element) must be superior to the others, and when (it exercises) its superiority over them, mixture

---

[57] Qur'ân 3.97 (92).

[58] This section is the consolidation of three sections, as the earlier texts presented the material. The second, entitled "Luxury belongs to royal authority by nature," begins on p. 338, l. 1 and the third, entitled "Tranquillity and quiet belong to royal authority by nature," begins on p. 328, l. 21. C still has the old division in the text but also contains corrections and slight changes made at the beginning of the original sections, and these are incorporated in the text of D.

[59] Cf. Issawi, pp. 114 f.

[60] This seems to be meant as a general reference to works on physics where the subject is treated. However, Ibn Khaldûn had made the same statement above (n. 59 to Ch. II) in an early stage of the text later deleted.

occurs. In the same way, one of the various tribal group feelings must be superior to all (others), in order to be able to bring them together, to unite them, and to weld them into 1, 300
one group feeling comprising all the various groups. All the various groups are then under the influence of the superior group feeling.

This highest group feeling can go only to people who have a "house" and leadership among (the tribe). One of those people must be the leader who has superiority over them. He is singled out as leader of all the various group feelings, because he is superior to all the others by birth. When he is singled out for (the position of leadership), he is too proud to let others share in his leadership and control over (the people) or to let them participate in it, because the qualities of haughtiness and pride are innate in animal nature. Thus, he develops the quality of egotism (*ta'alluh*), which is innate in human beings.

Moreover, politics requires that only one person exercise control. Were various persons, liable to differ among each other, to exercise it, destruction of the whole could result. "If there were other gods except God in the two (heaven and earth), they (heaven and earth) would have been destroyed." [61]

Thus, the aspirations of the various group feelings are blunted. People become tame and do not aspire to share with the leader in the exercise of control. Their group feeling is forced to refrain (from such aspirations). The leader takes charge all by himself, as far as possible. Eventually, he leaves no part in the power to anyone else. He thus claims all the glory for himself and does not permit the people to share in it. This may come to pass already with the first ruler of a dynasty, or it may come to pass only with the second or the third, depending on the resistance and strength of the various group feelings, but it is something unavoidable in a dynasty. This is how God proceeds with His servants.

---

[61] Qur'ân 21.22 (22).

As [62] to going in for luxury, this is because, when a nation has gained the upper hand and taken possession of the holdings of its predecessors who had royal authority, its prosperity and well-being grow. People become accustomed to a great number of things. From the necessities of life and a life of austerity, they progress to the luxuries and a life of comfort and beauty. They come to adopt the customs and
I, 301 (enjoy) the conditions of their predecessors. Luxuries require development of the customs necessary to produce them. People then also tend toward luxury in food, clothing, bedding (carpets), and household goods. They take pride in such things and vie with other nations in delicacies, gorgeous raiment, and fine mounts. Every new generation wants to surpass the preceding one in this respect, and so it goes right down to the end of the dynasty. The larger the realm ruled by a dynasty, the greater is the share of its people in these luxuries. The limit eventually to be reached is set for a particular dynasty by its own power and by the customs of its predecessors.

This is how God proceeds with His creatures.

As [63] to preferring tranquillity and quiet, this is because a nation obtains royal authority only by pressing its claims, having in mind the purpose of obtaining superiority and royal authority. When this purpose is accomplished, all efforts cease.

> I wondered at the busy efforts fate made in connection
> with my relationship with her.
> Then, when our relationship had ended, fate became
> quiet.[64]

---

[62] Cf. Issawi, p. 119.

[63] Cf. Issawi, pp. 120 f.

[64] The verses are by the seventh-century poet Abû Ṣakhr ʿAbdallâh b. Salm al-Hudhalî. Cf. Abû l-Faraj al-Iṣfahânî, *Kitâb al-Aghânî*, ed. R. Brünnow (Leiden, 1888), XXI, 143 f.; (Bulaq, 1285/1868), VIII, 172; (Cairo, 1345——/1927——), IX, 295. The poet bemoans his irrevocable separation from his beloved Laylâ.

When people have obtained the royal authority, they no (longer) do the tiresome chores they had been used to undertake while still in search of it. They prefer rest and quiet and tranquillity. Now they seek to enjoy the fruits of royal authority, such as buildings, dwellings, and clothing. They build castles and install running water.[65] They plant gardens and enjoy life. They prefer rest to tiresome chores. They take pride in clothing, food, household goods, and bedding (carpets), as much as possible. They get used to this (attitude) and pass it on to later generations. It continues to grow in their midst, until God permits His command to be executed.

[11] *When the natural (tendencies) of the royal authority to claim all glory for itself and to obtain luxury and tranquillity have been firmly established, the dynasty approaches senility.* I, 302

This [66] can be explained in several ways.

First: As we have stated, the (royal authority), by its very nature, must claim all glory for itself. As long as glory was the common (property) of the group, and all members of the group made an identical effort (to obtain glory), their aspirations to gain the upper hand over others and to defend their own possessions were expressed in exemplary unruliness and lack of restraint. They all aimed at fame. Therefore, they considered death encountered in pursuit of glory, sweet, and they preferred annihilation to the loss of (glory). Now, however, when one of them claims all glory for himself, he treats the others severely and holds them in check. Further, he excludes them from possessing property and appropriates it for himself. People, thus, become too lazy to care for fame. They become dispirited and come to love humbleness and servitude.

The next generation (of members of the dynasty) grows

---

[65] Cf. p. 250, above.

[66] Cf. Issawi, pp. 122–26.

up in this (condition). They consider their allowances the government's payment to them for military service and support. No other thought occurs to them. (But) a person would rarely hire himself out to sacrifice his life. This (situation) debilitates the dynasty and undermines its strength. Its group feeling decays because the people who represent the group feeling have lost their energy. As a result, the dynasty progresses toward weakness and senility.

Second: As we have said before, royal authority by its very nature requires luxury. People get accustomed to a great number of things. Their expenses are higher than their allowances and their income is not sufficient to pay for their expenditures. Those who are poor perish. Spendthrifts squander their income on luxuries. This (condition) becomes
I, 303 aggravated in the later generations. Eventually, all their income cannot pay for the luxuries and other things they have become used to. They grow needy. When their rulers urge them to defray the costs of raids and wars, they cannot get around it (but they have no money). Therefore, (the rulers) impose penalties on the (people) and deprive many of them of their property, either by appropriating it for themselves or by handing it over to their own children and supporters in the dynasty. In that way, they make the people too weak (financially) to keep their own affairs going, and their weakness (then reacts upon the ruler and) weakens him.

Also, when luxury increases in a dynasty and people's income becomes insufficient for their needs and expenses, the ruler, that is, the government, must increase their allowances in order to tide them over and remedy their unsound condition. The amount of tax revenue, however, is a fixed one. It neither increases nor decreases. When it is increased by new customs duties, the amount to be collected as a result of the increase has fixed limits (and cannot be increased again). And when the tax revenues must go to pay for recently increased allowances that had to be increased for everybody in view of new luxuries and great expenditures, the militia decreases in number from what it had been before the increase in allowances.[67]

Luxury, meanwhile, is still on the increase. As a result, allowances become larger, and the militia decreases in number. This happens a third and a fourth time. Eventually, the army is reduced to the smallest possible size. The result is that the military defense of the dynasty is weakened and the power of the dynasty declines. Neighboring dynasties, or groups and tribes under the control of the dynasty itself, become bold and attack it, and God permits it to suffer the destruction that He has destined for (all) His creatures.

Furthermore, luxury corrupts the character. (Through luxury,) the soul acquires diverse kinds of evil and sophisti- I, *304*
cated customs, as will be mentioned in the section on sedentary culture.[68] People lose the good qualities that were a sign and indication of (their qualification for) royal authority.[69] They adopt the contrary bad qualities. This points toward retrogression and ruin, according to the way God has (planned it) for His creatures in this connection. The dynasty shows symptoms of dissolution and disintegration. It becomes affected by the chronic diseases of senility and finally dies.

Third: As we have mentioned,[70] royal authority, by its very nature, requires tranquillity (and rest). When people become accustomed to tranquillity and rest and adopt them as character traits, they become part of their nature. This is the case with all the things to which one grows used and accustomed.

The new generations grow up in comfort and the ease of luxury and tranquillity. The trait of savagery (which former generations had possessed) undergoes transformation. They forget the customs of desert life that enabled them to achieve

[67] That is, since the allowances to be paid are higher than before, and the tax income has not increased, fewer men can be hired. Cf., further, 2:91 f., below.

[68] Cf. 2:293, below.

[69] Cf. pp. 291 ff., above.

[70] Cf. pp. 338 f., above.

royal authority, such as great energy, the habit of rapacity, and the ability to travel in the wilderness and find one's way in waste regions. No difference remains between them and ordinary city dwellers, except for their (fighting) skill [71] and emblems. Their military defense weakens, their energy is lost, and their strength is undermined. The evil effects of this situation on the dynasty show themselves in the form of senility.

People, meanwhile, continue to adopt ever newer forms of luxury and sedentary culture and of quiet, tranquillity, and softness in all their conditions, and to sink ever deeper into them. They thus become estranged from desert life and desert toughness. Gradually, they lose more and more of
I, *305* (the old virtues). They forget the quality of bravery that was their protection and defense. Eventually, they come to depend upon some other militia, if they have one.

An example of this is the nations whose history is available in the books you have. What I have said will be found to be correct and admitting of no doubt.

In a dynasty affected by senility as the result of luxury and rest, it sometimes happens that the ruler chooses helpers and partisans from groups not related to (the ruling dynasty but) used to toughness. He uses (these people) as an army which will be better able to suffer the hardships of wars, hunger, and privation. This could prove a cure for the senility of the dynasty when it comes, (but only) until God permits His command regarding (the dynasty) to be executed.

This is what happened to the Turkish dynasty in the East. Most members of its army were Turkish clients. The (Turkish) rulers then chose horsemen and soldiers from among the white slaves (Mamelukes) who were brought to them. They were more eager to fight and better able to suffer privations than the children of the earlier white slaves (Mamelukes) who had grown up in easy circumstances as a ruling class in the shadow of the government.

The same was the case with the Almohad (Ḥafṣid) dy-

[71] Cf. R. Dozy in *Journal asiatique*, XIV 6 (1869), 155.

nasty in Ifrîqiyah. Their rulers often selected their armies from the Zanâtah and the Arabs. They used many of them, and disregarded their own people who had become used to luxury. Thus, the dynasty obtained another, new life, unaffected by senility.

God inherits the earth and whomever is upon it.

[12] *Dynasties have a natural life span like individuals.*

It [72] should be known that in the opinion of physicians and astrologers, the natural life (span) of individuals is one I, *306*
hundred and twenty years, that is, the period astrologers call the great lunar year. Within the same generation, the duration of life differs according to the conjunctions. It may be either more or less than one hundred and twenty years. The life (span) of persons who are under some particular conjunction will be a full hundred years. Of others, it will be fifty, or eighty, or seventy years, accordingly as the indications of conjunctions noted by these observers may require. The life of a Muslim lasts between sixty and seventy years. This is stated in the *ḥadîth*.[73] The natural life span of one hundred and twenty years is surpassed only on the occasion of rare configurations and extraordinary positions on the firmament. Such was the case with Noah and with a few (individuals) among the peoples of ʿÂd and Thamûd.

The [74] same is the case with the life (span) of dynasties. Their durations may differ according to the conjunctions. However, as a rule no dynasty lasts beyond the life (span) of three generations.[75] A generation is identical with the average duration of the life of a single individual, namely,

---

[72] Cf. R. A. Nicholson, *Translations of Eastern Poetry and Prose*, pp. 183–85.

[73] Cf. *Concordance*, II, 398*b*, ll. 22 f.

[74] Cf. Issawi, pp. 117 f.

[75] Cf. pp. 278 ff., above. The following assumption of a period of forty years does not square with the remarks Ibn Khaldûn makes here about the length of human life, whether one translates "the average duration of life" or "middle life"—the latter a barely possible rendering, seemingly supported by the quotation from the Qur'ân and the discussion found 2:291 f., below.

forty years, (the time) required for growth to be completed and maturity reached. God said: "Until when he reaches his maturity and reaches the age of forty years. . . ." [76] Therefore, we have said that the (average) duration of the life of an individual is identical with the duration of a generation.

Our statement is confirmed by the significance of the (forty-year) sojourn of the children of Israel in the desert.[77] Those forty (years) were intended to bring about the disappearance of the generation then alive and the growth of another generation, (one) that had not witnessed and felt the humiliation (in Egypt). This is proof of the assumption that (a period of) forty years, which is identical with the (average) life of a single individual, must be considered the duration of a generation.

We have stated [78] that the duration of the life of a dynasty does not as a rule extend beyond three generations. The first generation retains the desert qualities, desert toughness, and
I, 307 desert savagery. (Its members are used to) privation and to sharing their glory (with each other); they are brave and rapacious. Therefore, the strength of group feeling continues to be preserved among them. They are sharp and greatly feared. People submit to them.

Under the influence of royal authority and a life of ease, the second generation changes from the desert attitude to sedentary culture, from privation to luxury and plenty, from a state in which everybody shared in the glory to one in which one man claims all the glory for himself while the others are too lazy to strive for (glory), and from proud superiority to humble subservience. Thus, the vigor of group feeling is broken to some extent. People become used to lowliness and obedience. But many of (the old virtues) remain in them, because they had had direct personal contact with the first generation and its conditions, and had observed

---

[76] Qur'ân 46.15 (14).
[77] Cf. pp. 132 and 288, above.
[78] Cf. pp. 278 ff., above.

with their own eyes its prowess and striving for glory and its intention to protect and defend (itself). They cannot give all of it up at once, although a good deal of it may go. They live in hope that the conditions that existed in the first generation may come back, or they live under the illusion that those conditions still exist.

The third generation, then, has (completely) forgotten the period of desert life and toughness, as if it had never existed. They have lost (the taste for) the sweetness of fame and (for) group feeling, because they are dominated by force. Luxury reaches its peak among them, because they are so much given to a life of prosperity and ease. They become dependent on the dynasty and are like women and children who need to be defended (by someone else). Group feeling disappears completely. People forget to protect and defend themselves and to press their claims. With their emblems, apparel, horseback riding, and (fighting) skill,[79] they deceive people and give them the wrong impression. For the most part, they are more cowardly than women upon their backs.
When someone comes and demands something from them, I, 308
they cannot repel him. The ruler, then, has need of other, brave people for his support. He takes many clients and followers. They help the dynasty to some degree, until God permits it to be destroyed, and it goes with everything it stands for.

As one can see, we have there three generations. In the course of these three generations, the dynasty grows senile and is worn out. Therefore, it is in the fourth generation that (ancestral) prestige is destroyed. This was stated before in connection with (the subject) that glory and (ancestral) prestige are restricted to four generations.[80] We have proved it with natural and evident arguments based on premises that we established before. The reader should consider that. As an impartial person, he should not disregard the truth.

---

[79] Cf. n. 71 to this chapter, above.

[80] Cf. pp. 278 ff., above.

Three generations last one hundred and twenty years, as stated before. As a rule, dynasties do not last longer than that many years, a few more or a few less, save when, by chance, no one appears to attack (the dynasty). When senility becomes preponderant (in a dynasty), there may be no claimant (for its power, and then nothing will happen), but if there should be one, he will encounter no one capable of repelling him. If the time is up, (the end of the dynasty) cannot be postponed for a single hour, no more than it can be accelerated.[81]

In this way, the life (span) of a dynasty corresponds to the life (span) of an individual; it grows up and passes into an age of stagnation and thence into retrogression. Therefore, people commonly say that the life (span) of a dynasty is one hundred years. The saying means the same as what (I have just explained).

One should consider this and derive from it a rule for finding the correct number of ancestors in a pedigree, if one is uncertain about it but knows the time interval that the
I, 309 pedigree covers. For each hundred years, one should figure three ancestors. If the result tallies with the total number of (ancestors indicated in the pedigree, it) is correct. If it is one generation short, there must be an error in the number of (ancestors indicated in the pedigree, and) there must be one (ancestor) too many in it. If (the result) indicates one generation too many, one (ancestor) must have been omitted (from the pedigree). In the same way, one may figure out the number of years, if one knows the correct number of ancestors.[82]

God determines night and day.[83]

---

[81] Cf. 2:124, below.

[82] Bulaq reads: ". . . if one knows the number of ancestors. If the reader considers (this rule), he will find it usually to be correct."

Ibn Khaldûn applied this idea to his own pedigree and came to the conclusion that it omitted quite a number of links; cf. *Autobiography*, p. 1. Cf. also above, p. lxvi (n. 80).

[83] Cf. Qur'ân 73.20 (20).

[13] *The transition of dynasties from desert life to sedentary culture.*

It should be known that these stages are natural ones for dynasties. The superiority through which royal authority is achieved is the result of group feeling and of the great energy and rapacious habits which go with it. As a rule, these things are possible only in connection with desert life. The first stage of dynasties, therefore, is that of desert life.

When royal authority is obtained, it is accompanied by a life of ease and increased opportunities. Sedentary culture is merely a diversification of luxury and a refined knowledge of the crafts employed for the diverse aspects and ways of (luxury). This concerns, for instance, food, clothing, building, bedding (carpets), utensils, and other household needs. Each one of these things requires special interdependent crafts serving to refine and improve it. (These crafts) increase in number with the (growing) variety of pleasures and amusements and ways and means to enjoy the life of luxury the soul desires, and (with the growing number of) different things to which people get used.

The [84] sedentary stage of royal authority follows the stage of desert life. It does so of necessity, as a result of the fact that royal authority is of necessity accompanied by a life of ease. In the sedentary stage and under (sedentary) conditions, the people of a given dynasty always follow the traditions of the preceding dynasty. They observe with their own eyes the circumstances (under which the preceding dynasty lived), and, as a rule, learn from them.

Something of the sort happened to the Arabs during the *1, 310*
conquest by which they came to rule the Persians and Byzantines and made their daughters and sons their servants. At that time, the Arabs had no sedentary culture at all. The story goes that when they were given a pillow they supposed

[84] Cf. Issawi, pp. 118 f.

it was a bundle of rags.[85] The camphor they found in the treasuries of the Persian king was used by them as salt in their dough. There are many similar things. The Arabs, then, enslaved the people of the former dynasties and employed them in their occupations and their household needs. From among them, they selected skilled masters of the various (crafts), and were in turn taught by them to handle, master, and develop them for themselves. In addition, the circumstances of the Arabs' life widened and became more diversified. Thus, they reached the limit in this respect. They entered the stage of sedentary culture, of luxury and refinement in food, drink, clothing, building, weapons, bedding (carpets), household goods, music, and all other commodities and furnishings. The same (perfection they showed) on their gala days, banquets, and wedding nights. In this respect, they surpassed the limit.

Looking at the reports of al-Mas'ûdî, aṭ-Ṭabarî, and other (historians) concerning the wedding of al-Ma'mûn to Bûrân, daughter of al-Ḥasan b. Sahl, one will be amazed.[86] They tell about the gifts Bûrân's father made to the retinue of al-Ma'mûn when the caliph came by boat to (al-Ḥasan's) house in Fumm aṣ-ṣilḥ to ask for Bûrân's hand. They tell about the expenditures for the marriage (settlement, *imlâk*) and the wedding gifts al-Ma'mûn gave her and the expenditures for the wedding. On the wedding day, al-Ḥasan b. Sahl gave a lavish banquet that was attended by al-Ma'mûn's retinue. To members of the first class, al-Ḥasan distributed

I, 311 lumps of musk wrapped in papers granting farms and estates

[85] This seems to refer to the treatment meted out by Bedouins to valuable cushions that belonged to the Persian commander, Rustum. According to the legend, they poked at them with their lances, thus ripping them open. Cf. Ibn aṭ-Ṭiqṭaqâ, *Fakhrî*, tr. C. E. J. Whitting (London, 1947), p. 77. C and D do not read *m-r-f-q*, but *m-r-q-q*; still, Issawi's suggestion that we read *muraqqaq* and translate "loaves of bread . . . parchment" is implausible. The story about the camphor also appears in Ibn aṭ-Ṭiqṭaqâ, p. 79.

[86] Cf. aṭ-Ṭabarî, *Annales*, III, 1081 ff.; al-Mas'ûdî, *Murûj adh-dhahab*, VII, 66 f. However, Ibn Khaldûn has many more details than aṭ-Ṭabarî and al-Mas'ûdî provide. For some further references to this often quoted story, cf. Jûrjîs 'Awwâd's edition of ash-Shâbushtî, *Diyârât* (Baghdad, 1951), p. 101 (n. 3).

to the holders. Each obtained what chance and luck gave him. To the second class, (al-Ḥasan) distributed bags each of which held 10,000 dinars. To the third class, he distributed bags with the same amount in dirhams. In addition to all this, he had already spent many times as much when al-Ma'mûn had stayed in his house. Also, al-Ma'mûn gave Bûrân a thousand hyacinths (rubies) as her wedding gift (*mahr*) on the wedding night. He burned candles of amber each of which weighed one hundred *mann* [87]—a *mann* being one and two-thirds pounds (*riṭl*). He had put down for her carpets woven with threads of gold and adorned with pearls and hyacinths. When al-Ma'mûn saw all this, he said, "That Abû Nuwâs is admirable! It is as though he had had this (situation and these carpets) before his eyes when he said, describing wine:

> As if its small and large shiny bubbles
> Were little pearls upon a ground of gold." [88]

One hundred and forty mule loads of wood had been brought three times a day for a whole year to the kitchen and were ready for the wedding night. All that wood was consumed that very night. Palm twigs were set alight by pouring oil on them. Boatmen were ordered to bring boats to transport the distinguished guests on the Tigris from Baghdad to the royal palaces in the city of al-Ma'mûn [89] for the wedding banquet. The boats prepared for that purpose numbered 30,000, and they carried people back and forth all day long. There were many other such things.

---

[87] How these stories gained in the telling is illustrated by the fact that another source has *riṭl* (pounds) instead of *mann* here. Cf. al-Khaṭîb al-Baghdâdî, *Ta'rîkh Baghdâd* (Cairo, 1349/1931), VII, 321.

[88] Cf. Abû Nuwâs, *Dîwân* (Cairo, 1898), p. 243. The verse is also quoted by grammarians. Cf. al-Ḥarîrî, *Durrat al-ghawwâṣ*, ed. H. Thorbecke (Leipzig, 1871), p. 46; Ibn Hishâm, *La Pluie de rosée*, tr. A. Goguyer (Leiden, 1887), p. 374.

[89] Ibn Khaldûn apparently has in mind the palace of al-Ma'mûn which, before him, had belonged to Ja'far al-Barmakî, and after him to al-Ḥasan b. Sahl. Cf. G. Le Strange, *Baghdad during the Abbasid Caliphate* (Oxford, 1900), p. 246.

A similar occasion was the wedding of al-Ma'mûn b. Dhî n-nûn in Toledo. It was described by Ibn Bassâm [90] in the *Kitâb adh-Dhakhîrah* and by Ibn Ḥayyân.

All these (people) had previously been in the first stage
I, 312 of desert life. They had been completely incapable of such things, because, in their low standard of life and their simplicity, they lacked both the means and people with technical ability. It has been said that al-Ḥajjâj gave a banquet on the occasion of the circumcision of one of his sons. He had one of the Persian landowners brought to him and asked him about the banquets the Persians had given (in former times). He asked him to tell him about the most lavish banquet he had ever attended. The reply was: "Yes, my Lord, I attended the banquet of one of the provincial governors (*marzbâns*) of the Persian king, given for the inhabitants of Fârs. He used golden plates on tables of silver, four (plates) to each (table). Each (table) was carried by four maidservants, and four persons were seated at each. After they had eaten, the four of them left with the table, the plates on it, and the maidservants." (When he heard that,) al-Ḥajjâj merely said, "Boy! Have some camels slaughtered and give the people to eat." He realized that he could not afford such sumptuousness as had once actually existed.

The allowances and gratuities the Umayyads gave (their followers) illustrate the point under discussion. In keeping with Arab desert custom, most of (their gratuities) consisted of camels. Then, in the 'Abbâsid, the 'Ubaydid(-Fâṭimid), and later dynasties, these gratuities, as one knows, came to be large sums of money, chests of clothes, and horses with their complete trappings.

The same situation prevailed among the Kutâmah in

---

[90] 'Alî b. Bassâm, d. 542 [1147/48]. Cf. *GAL*, I, 339; *Suppl.*, I, 579. Of the published portion of the *Dhakhîrah*, one passage contains a long description of a splendid festival on the occasion of the circumcision of al-Ma'mûn's grandson. Ibn Bassâm's source is Ibn Ḥayyân; cf. *Dhakhîrah* (Cairo, 1358——/1939——), IV [1], 99 ff. The wedding, however, does not seem to occur in the volumes published. The relevant section of Ibn Ḥayyân is not preserved; cf. n. 18 to Ibn Khaldûn's Introduction, above.

their relationship with the Aghlabids in Ifrîqiyah and the Banû Ṭughsh (Ikhshîdids) in Egypt, among the Lamtûnah in their relationship with the *reyes de taïfas* in Spain and also with the Almohads, and among the Zanâtah in their relationship with the Almohads, and so on.

Sedentary culture was always transferred from the preceding dynasty to the later one. The sedentary culture of the Persians was transferred to the Arab Umayyads and 'Abbâsids. The sedentary culture of the Umayyads in Spain was transferred to the Almohad and Zanâtah kings of the contemporary Maghrib. That of the 'Abbâsids was transferred,
successively, to the Daylam, to the Saljûq Turks, to the *I, 313*
Turks [91] in Egypt, and to the Tatars in the two 'Irâqs.

The larger a dynasty, the more important is its sedentary culture. For sedentary culture is the consequence of luxury; luxury is the consequence of wealth and prosperity; and wealth and prosperity are the consequences of royal authority and related to the extent of (territorial) possessions which the people of a particular dynasty have gained. All the (elements of sedentary culture) are, thus, proportionate to the (greater or smaller extent of) royal authority. Upon close and careful examination this will be found to be a correct statement as regards civilization and dynasties.[92]

God inherits the earth and whomever is upon it.

[14] *Luxury will at first give additional strength to a dynasty.*

The [93] reason for this is that a tribe that has obtained royal authority and luxury is prolific and produces many children, and the community grows. Thus, the group grows. Furthermore, a greater number of clients and followers is acquired. The (new) generations grow up in a climate of prosperity and luxury. Through them, (the dynasty) gains

---

[91] The earlier texts have "Turkish Mamelukes," but the word "Mamelukes" appears to have been crossed out in C and does not occur in D.

[92] "And dynasties" appears in the margin of C and in the text of D.

[93] Cf. Issawi, pp. 119 f.

in numbers and in strength, because a great number of groups form at that time as the result of the numerical increase. When the first and second generations are gone and the dynasty starts to become senile, its followers and clients cannot do anything on their own to put the dynasty and its royal authority on a firmer basis, because they never had authority of their own but were dependent on the men of (the dynasty) and (merely) supported it. When the roots are gone, the branches cannot be strong on their own, but disappear completely, and the dynasty no longer retains its former strength.

This is exemplified by what happened to the Arab dy-
I, 314 nasty in Islam. As we have stated,[94] the Arabs at the time of the Prophet and the early caliphs numbered approximately 150,000 Muḍar and Qaḥṭân (tribesmen). The life of luxury reached its climax in the dynasty. The (population) grew rapidly with the growth of prosperity. The caliphs acquired many clients and followers. Thus, the (original) number increased many times. It is said that during the conquest of Amorium, al-Mu'taṣim laid siege to the city with 900,000 men.[95] This number can hardly fail being correct, if one thinks of (the large size of) the Muslim militia of the border regions both far and near, in both the East and the West, and adds the soldiers directly in the service of the ruler, together with all the clients and followers.

Al-Mas'ûdî said: [96] "The descendants of al-'Abbâs b. 'Abd-al-Muṭṭalib were counted in the days of al-Ma'mûn, in order to give them pensions. They were found to number 30,000 men and women." It should be noted how great the number had become in less than two hundred years. It should be known that the increase was caused by the luxury and prosperity which the ('Abbâsid) dynasty had achieved and in which the new generations had grown up. Otherwise, the

[94] Cf. p. 330, above.

[95] Al-Mas'ûdî, *Murûj adh-dhahab*, VII, 135 f., has estimates ranging from 200,000 to 500,000.

[96] Cf. al-Mas'ûdî, VII, 59, where the figure is 33,000. Further references in A. Mez, *Die Renaissance des Islâms*, p. 146.

number of Arabs, as it had been in the beginning of the conquest, would not even remotely have (permitted) such an increase.

God is "the Creator, the Knowing One." [97]

[15] *The stages of dynasties. How the desert attitude differs among the people in the different stages.*[98]

It should be known that a dynasty goes through different stages and encounters new conditions. Through the conditions that are peculiar to a particular stage, the supporters of the dynasty acquire in that stage traits of character such as do not exist in any other stage. Traits of character are the natural result of the peculiar situations in which they are found.

The conditions and stages of a dynasty are as a rule no more than five (in number). I, 315

The first stage is that of success, the overthrow of all opposition, and the appropriation of royal authority from the preceding dynasty. In this stage, the ruler serves as model to his people by the manner in which he acquires glory, collects taxes, defends property, and provides military protection. He does not claim anything exclusively for himself to the exclusion of (his people), because (such an attitude) is what is required by group feeling, (and it was group feeling) that gave superiority (to the dynasty), and (group feeling) still continues to exist as before.

The second stage is the one in which the ruler gains complete control over his people, claims royal authority all for himself, excluding them, and prevents them from trying to have a share in it. In this stage, the ruler of the dynasty is concerned with gaining adherents and acquiring clients and followers in great numbers, so as to be able to blunt the

[97] Qur'ân 15.86 (86); 36.81 (81).

[98] The earlier texts had a different title, namely, "The stages of a dynasty and its varying conditions. The desert attitude of the people in the different stages." The old title is replaced in C by the new one, which then occurs in D.

aspirations of the people who share in his group feeling and belong to his group, who are of the same descent as he himself and have the same claim to royal authority as he has. He keeps them from power and bars them from the sources of (power). He stops them from getting to it, and, eventually, all the power is in the hands of his family. He reserves all the glory that he is building up to the members of his own house. He spends as much, or more, care to keep (his people) at a distance and to subdue them, as the first members of the dynasty expended in the search for power. The first (members of the dynasty) kept strangers away, and all the people who shared in their group feeling supported them in this. He, on the other hand, keeps (his) relatives away, and he is supported in this effort only by a very small number of people, who are not related to him. Thus, he undertakes a very difficult task.

The third stage is one of leisure and tranquillity in which the fruits of royal authority are enjoyed. (These fruits are) the things that human nature desires, such as acquisition of property, creation of lasting monuments, and fame. All the
I, *316* ability (of the ruler) is expended on collecting taxes; regulating income and expenses, bookkeeping and planning[99] expenditures; erecting large buildings, big constructions, spacious cities, and lofty monuments;[100] presenting gifts to embassies of nobles from (foreign) nations and tribal dignitaries; and dispensing bounty to his own people. In addition, he supports the demands of his followers and retinue with money and positions. He inspects his soldiers, pays them well, and distributes fairly their allowances every month. Eventually, the result of this (liberality) shows itself in their dress, their fine equipment, and their armor on parade days. The ruler thus can impress friendly dynasties and frighten hostile ones with (his soldiers). This stage is the last during

---

[99] Cf. p. 420 (n. 308), below.
[100] For *haykal*, cf. n. 172 to Ch. I, above.

which the ruler is in complete authority. Throughout this and the previous stages, the rulers are independent in their opinions. They build up their strength and show the way for those after them.

The fourth stage is one of contentment and peacefulness. The ruler is content with what his predecessors have built. He lives in peace with all his royal peers. He adopts the tradition of his predecessors and follows closely in their footsteps. He imitates their ways most carefully. He thinks that to depart from tradition would mean the destruction of his power and that they knew better (what is good for the preservation of) the glory they themselves had built.

The fifth stage is one of waste and squandering. In this stage, the ruler wastes on pleasures and amusements (the treasures) accumulated by his ancestors, through (excessive) generosity to his inner circle and at their parties. Also, he acquires bad, low-class followers to whom he entrusts the most important matters (of state), which they are not qualified to handle by themselves, not knowing which of them I, 317
they should tackle and which they should leave alone. (In addition,) the ruler seeks to destroy the great clients of his people and followers of his predecessors. Thus, they come to hate him and conspire to refuse support to him. (Furthermore) he loses a number of soldiers by spending their allowances on his pleasures (instead of paying them) and by refusing them access to his person and not supervising them (properly). Thus, he ruins the foundations his ancestors had laid and tears down what they had built up. In this stage, the dynasty is seized by senility and the chronic disease from which it can hardly ever rid itself, for which it can find no cure, and, eventually, it is destroyed. We shall explain that in connection with conditions to be discussed later on.[101]

God is the best heir.[102]

---

[101] Below, pp. 372 ff., and elsewhere.

[102] Cf. Qur'ân 21.89 (89).

[16] *The monuments of a given dynasty are proportionate to its original power.*[103]

The reason for this is that monuments owe their origin to the power that brought the dynasty into being. The impression the dynasty leaves is proportionate to (that power).

The monuments of a dynasty are its buildings and large (edifices, *haykal*). They are proportionate to the original power of the dynasty. They can materialize only when there are many workers and united action and co-operation. When a dynasty is large and far-flung, with many provinces and subjects, workers are very plentiful and can be brought together from all sides and regions. Thus, even the largest monument (*haykal*) can materialize.

Think of the works of the people of 'Âd and Thamûd, about which the Qur'ân tells.[104] Or, one should see with one's own eyes the Reception Hall of Khosraw (*Îwân Kisrâ*), that powerful achievement of Persian (architecture). Ar-Rashîd intended to tear it down and destroy it. He could not do so
I, 318 for all his trouble. He began the work, but then was not able to continue. The story of how he asked Yaḥyâ b. Khâlid for advice in that affair is well known.[105] It is worth noting that one dynasty was able to construct a building that another dynasty was not able to tear down, even though destruction is much easier than construction.[106] That illustrates the great difference between the two dynasties.

---

[103] The substance of this section is repeated below, 2:238 ff.

[104] Cf. pp. 25 ff., above, and, for the Thamûd, cf., for instance, J. Horovitz, *Koranische Untersuchungen*, pp. 103 ff.

[105] Cf. al-Mas'ûdî, *Murûj adh-dhahab*, II, 187 f. Ibn Khaldûn tells a similar story about al-Ma'mûn and Khâlid b. Barmak in *'Ibar*, III, 197. Cf. also 2:242 f., below.

[106] Cf. also 2:242 and 3:278, below, and al-Mas'ûdî, II, 154. According to Ibn Abî Ḥajalah at-Tilimsânî, *Sukkardân as-sulṭân* (Cairo, 1317/1899, in the margin of al-'Âmilî, *Mikhlâh*, and continued in the margin of p. 2 of the attached *Asrâr al-balâghah*, by the same 'Âmilî), p. 228, a legendary inscription on the pyramids read as follows: "We built them in sixty years. Let him who wishes, destroy them in six hundred years, for destruction is easier than construction."

II *a*. The Reception Hall of Khosraw in 1869

II *b*. The Reception Hall of Khosraw at the beginning of this century

III *a*. The Roman Bridge in Córdoba

III *b*. The Roman Aqueduct south of Carthage

One may also compare the Nave [107] of al-Walîd in Damascus, the Umayyad Mosque in Córdoba, the bridge over the river at Córdoba, and, as well, the arches of the aqueduct over which water is brought into Carthage, the monuments of Cherchel in the Maghrib, the pyramids of Egypt, and many other such monuments that may still be seen. They illustrate differences in strength and weakness that have existed among the various dynasties.

It should be known that all these works of the ancients were possible only through engineering skill and the concerted labor of many workers. Only thus could these monuments (*haykal*) and works be constructed. One should not think, as the common people do, that it was because the ancients had bodies larger in size than our own.[108] Human beings do not differ in this respect as much as monuments (*haykal*) and relics differ. Storytellers have seized upon the subject and used it to make exaggerated (fables). They have written stories in this vein about the 'Âd and the Thamûd and the Amalekites, which are complete lies. One of the strangest of these stories is about Og, the son of Anak, one of the Canaanites against whom the children of Israel fought in Syria. According to these storytellers, he was so tall that he took fish out of the ocean and held them up to the sun to be cooked.[109] To their ignorance of human affairs, the storytellers here add ignorance of astronomical matters. They believe that the sun is heat and that the heat of the sun is *I, 319*
greatest close to it. They do not know that the heat of the sun is (its) light and that (its) light is stronger near the earth (than it is near the sun) because of the reflection of the rays from the surface of the earth when it is hit by the light.

---

[107] The reference is apparently to the Mosque of al-Walîd, but to refer to it by *balâṭ* "nave" is unusual. "Palace" can hardly be meant here. Cf. also 2:262 f., below.

[108] Cf. also *'Ibar*, II, 23. Ibn al-Muqaffa' represents the opinion of the "common people" in the beginning of his *Durrah al-yatîmah*, in *Rasâ'il al-bulaghâ'* (Cairo, 1331/1913), p. 55.

[109] Cf. ath-Tha'labî, *Qiṣaṣ al-anbiyâ'*, in connection with the story of Moses and the sending out of spies to explore Palestine. (At p. 223 of a modern, undated Cairo text.) Cf. also B. Heller in *EI*, *s.v.* "'Ûdj."

Therefore, the heat here is many times greater (than near the sun). When the zone in which the reflected rays are effective is passed, there will be no heat there, and it will be cold. (That is) where the clouds are. The sun itself is neither hot nor cold, but a simple uncomposed substance that gives light.

Also, (the storytellers) say that Og, the son of Anak, was one of the Amalekites or Canaanites [110] who fell prey to the children of Israel when they conquered Syria. Now, even those of the children of Israel who at that time were the tallest in body, had bodies in size very like our own bodies. This is proven by the gates of Jerusalem. They were destroyed and have been restored, but their (original) shape and measurements have always been preserved. How, then, could there have been such a difference in size between Og and his contemporaries?

The error of (the storytellers) here results from the fact that they admired the vast proportions of the monuments left by nations (of the past), but did not understand the different situation in which dynasties may find themselves with respect to social organization and co-operation. They did not understand that (superior social organization) together with engineering skill, made the construction of large monuments possible. Therefore, they ascribed such monuments to a strength and energy derived by the peoples of the past from the large size of their bodies. But this is not so.

On the authority of the philosophers, al-Mas'ûdî expressed the following idea, whose only basis is in arbitrary (theorizing): [111] "When God created the world, the nature (element) that gives bodies their form was completely round [?] [112] and as strong and perfect as could be. Life lasted
I, 320 longer and bodies were stronger, because the nature (element) was then perfect. Death can come only through dis-

---

[110] Ibn Khaldûn appears to have corrected this statement later on. In C, "Amalekites" is crossed out in the text and replaced, in the margin, by "Canaanites," whereas D has "Canaanite Amalekites." Cf. also below, 2:240.

[111] Cf. al-Mas'ûdî, *Murûj adh-dhahab*, III, 376 f.

[112] Al-Mas'ûdî's text reads: "complete as to (its) large (numerical) size."

solution of the natural powers. When they are strong, life lasts longer. Thus, in the beginning, the world had (people whose) lives had their full duration and whose bodies were perfect. Because of the deficiency of matter it steadily deteriorated to its present condition, and it will not stop deteriorating until the time of (complete) dissolution and the destruction of the world."

This is an opinion that, as one can see, has only arbitrary (theorizing) as its authority. There is no natural or logical reason for it. We can see with our own eyes the dwellings and doorways of the ancients and the (construction) methods employed by them in producing their buildings, their monuments (*haykal*), their houses, and (other) dwellings such as the houses of the Thamûd, which were hewn out of solid rock, and they were small houses with narrow doors. Muḥammad indicated that those (rock dwellings) were the houses (of the Thamûd). He prohibited use of their water and (ordered that) the dough for which (the water) had been used be thrown out and (the water) poured on the ground. He said: "Do not enter the dwellings of those who wronged themselves. Only weep (in fear) lest the same misfortune that befell them befall you." [113] The same (reasoning) applies to the land of 'Âd, to Egypt, Syria, and all the other regions of the earth in the East and the West. The truth is what we have established.

Another (kind of) monument (to the greatness) of a dynasty is the way it handled weddings and (wedding) banquets, as we have mentioned in connection with the wedding of Bûrân and the banquets of al-Ḥajjâj and Ibn Dhî n-Nûn. All that has been mentioned before.[114]

Another monument (to the greatness) of a dynasty is the gifts it made. Gifts are proportionate to (the importance of

---

[113] Cf. al-Bukhârî, *Ṣaḥîḥ*, II, 349; *Concordance*, I, 212*a*, ll. 11 f. Cf. also 2:240, below.

The argument against the larger bodies of the Thamûd (although some exception is made for the 'Âd of South Arabia) was derived by Ibn Khaldûn from al-Mas'ûdî, III, 84, 377.

[114] Cf. pp. 348 ff., above.

a dynasty). (This rule) is operating even when the dynasty is close to senility. The aspirations of the members of the dynasty are proportionate to (the strength of) their royal authority and their superiority over the people. These aspirations remain with them until the final destruction of the dynasty.

One may compare the gifts Ibn Dhî Yazan presented to
I, 321 the Qurashite ambassadors. He gave each of them ten pounds (*riṭl*) of gold and silver and ten slaves and maidservants and one flask of ambergris. To 'Abd-al-Muṭṭalib, he gave ten times as much.[115] Ibn Dhî Yazan's realm, as it was located in the Yemen, was under the complete control of the Persians at that time. His (generosity), however, was caused by his high-mindedness, which stemmed from the royal authority that his family, the Tubba's, had possessed in the Yemen, and from the superiority they had once exercised over the nations of the two 'Irâqs, India, and the Maghrib.[116]

Also, when the Ṣinhâjah (Zîrids) in Ifrîqiyah presented gifts to an embassy sent them by the amirs of the Zanâtah, they gave them large sums of money and full chests of clothes and many fine pack horses. The *History* of Ibn ar-Raqîq [117] contains many stories of this kind.

The way the Barmecides gave allowances and gifts and spent their money was the same. Whenever they provided for a needy person, it meant property, high office, and prosperity for that person for ever after. It was not just an allowance that was spent in a day or sooner. There exist numerous stories in literature to this effect about (the Barmecides). All the (stories) reflect in the proper proportions the (power of the) dynasties (to which they relate).

When Jawhar al-Kâtib as-Ṣaqlabî, the general of the 'Ubaydid(-Fâṭimid) army, set out on his conquest of Egypt, he was provided by al-Qayrawân with a thousand loads of

---

115 Cf. (Pseudo-)Ibn Hishâm, *Tîjân*, pp. 306–310.

116 As to the extent of South Arabian domination, cf., however, pp. 21 ff., and 296, above.

117 Cf. p. 9 (n. 19), above.

money.[118] No dynasty today would be able to approach that.[119]

There exists in the handwriting of Aḥmad b. Muḥammad b. 'Abd-al-Ḥamîd a list showing the receipts of the treasury at Baghdad from all regions (of the realm) in al-Ma'mûn's day. I copied it from the book of Jirâb ad-dawlah: [120]

The Sawâd (Southern Mesopotamia)	Crops: 27,780,000 dirhams [121] Different kinds of revenue: [122] 14,800,000 dirhams	I, 322

[118] Cf. 2:283, below.

[119] None of the following documents, down to p. 368, l. 20, are found in C. C has a mark in the text indicating that something is to be inserted there. Possibly inserted slips were lost from the MS.

[120] *Jirâb ad-dawlah* means something like "public purse." It would seem to be the title of a book. However, an artist and littérateur called Aḥmad b. Muḥammad is known to have lived *ca.* 900, and to have been known under the name of Jirâb ad-dawlah. He wrote a book of jokes and anecdotes entitled *Tarwîḥ al-arwâḥ*. Cf. Ibn an-Nadîm, *Fihrist*, p. 153 of the Flügel ed., p. 218 of the edition, Cairo, 1348/1929–30. The work is also quoted by Ibn Abî Uṣaybi'ah, *'Uyûn al-anbâ'*, I, 181, l. 22, exactly as Ibn Khaldûn quotes it. There can be little doubt that this is the work referred to here. Like Ibn Ḥamdûn's *Tadhkirah*, it may have contained a large selection of interesting topics. A MS appears to be preserved in Paris, MS. Ar. 3527; cf. *GAL, Suppl.*, I, 599. It can be expected to solve the problem. Ibn Khaldûn certainly did not quote the work directly, but the exact source on which he drew cannot be named.

The list that follows is well known from a number of works. A comprehensive study of it was made by A. von Kremer, *Kulturgeschichte des Orients* (Vienna, 1875), I, 263 ff; cf., in particular, I, 356–59. Related material may be found also in Ibn Ḥamdûn, *Tadhkirah*, in the Topkapusaray MS. Ahmet III, 2948, Vol. XII, fols. 186 ff., as part of Ch. XLIX, which deals with history. The oldest and closest available parallel to Ibn Khaldûn's text is found in al-Jahshiyârî, *Wuzarâ'*, ed. H. von Mžik (Bibliothek arabischer Historiker und Geographen, No. 1) (Leipzig, 1926), fols. 179*a*–182*b*.

Von Kremer proved that the list does not date from the time of al-Ma'mûn but reflects a situation that existed *ca.* 785/86. The introductory remarks accompanying the list in al-Jahshiyârî show that although it was finally written down under al-Ma'mûn or later, its material goes back to the time of ar-Rashîd or somewhat earlier.

The variants found in al-Jahshiyârî are noted here only so far as they concern Ibn Khaldûn's text. Additional data, as found in some places in al-Jahshiyârî, are, as a rule, not indicated. In general, the few footnotes appended here are, of course, not meant to constitute a commentary on the text.

Cf. also R. Levy, *The Sociology of Islam* (London, 1931–33), I, 343–47, and B. Spuler, *Iran in früh-islamischer Zeit* (Wiesbaden, 1952), pp. 467 ff.

[121] Al-Jahshiyârî: 80,780,000.

[122] *Abwâb al-mâl* means "categories of income." Cf. A. Dietrich, *Arabische Papyri aus der Hamburger Staats- und Universitätsbibliothek* (Abhandlungen für die Kunde des Morgenlandes, No. 22,3) (Leipzig, 1937), p. 55.

		Najrânî cloaks: 200 Sealing clay: 240 pounds
	Kaskar	11,600,000 dirhams
	Tigris counties	20,800,000 dirhams
	Ḥulwân	4,800,000 dirhams
	Al-Ahwâz	25,000 dirhams [123] Sugar: 30,000 pounds
	Fârs	27,000,000 dirhams Rose water: 30,000 bottles Black raisins: 20,000 pounds
	Kirmân	4,200,000 dirhams Yemenite garments: 500 Dates: 20,000 pounds Cumin seeds: 1,000 pounds [124]
	Mukrân	400,000 dirhams
	Western India (Sind) and Neighboring Territories	11,500,000 dirhams Indian aloe wood: 150 pounds
	Sijistân	4,000,000 dirhams [125] Checkered [126] garments: 300 Sugar-candy: [127] 20,000 pounds
	Khurâsân	28,000,000 dirhams Silver ingots: 1,000
I, 323		Pack animals: 4,000

[123] Von Kremer corrects the figure to 25,000,000.

[124] Al-Jahshiyârî: 100.

[125] Al-Jahshiyârî: 4,600,000.

[126] The MSS have, indeed, the reading *al-m-'-t-b-h* that de Slane read *al-mu'attabah* and connected with a kind of silk called *al-'attâbî.* However, Dozy, in *Journal asiatique,* XIV[6] (1869), 155 f., preferred *al-mu'ayyanah,* which appears in Bulaq and which means "variegated by squares (lozenges), decorated with eye- or lozenge-shaped designs." The fact that the text of al-Jahshiyârî clearly has *al-mu'ayyanah* is definitely in favor of the latter reading.

[127] A discussion of the possible meaning of *al-fânîdh,* a preparation of sugar cane, was undertaken by P. Schwarz, "*Fânîḏ* und Verwandtes," in *Zeitschrift der Deutschen Morgenländischen Gesellschaft,* LXXIV (1920), 238–46. Cf. also Ibn al-Ukhuwwa, *Ma'âlim al-qurbah,* p. 106.

	Slaves: 1,000 head Garments: 27,000 Myrobalan: 30,000 pounds
Jurjân	12,000,000 dirhams Silk: 1,000 pieces [128]
Qûmis	1,500,000 dirhams Silver ingots: 1,000
Ṭabaristân, ar-Rûyân and Nihâwand [129]	6,300,000 dirhams Ṭabaristân carpets: 600 pieces Robes: 200 Garments: 500 Napkins: 300 Goblets: 300 [130]
ar-Rayy	12,000,000 dirhams Honey: 20,000 pounds [131]
Hamadhân	11,800,000 dirhams Pomegranate marmalade: 1,000 pounds [132] Honey: 12,000 pounds
The region between [!] [133] al-Baṣrah and al-Kûfah	10,700,000 dirhams
Mâsabadhân and ar-Rayyân [134]	4,000,000 dirhams

---

[128] Al-Jahshiyârî: *mann.*

[129] Instead of *Nihâwand*, one must read with al-Jahshiyârî, as von Kremer already suggested, *Dunbâwand.*

[130] Al-Jahshiyârî: 600.

[131] The honey item belongs to an entry dealing with Iṣfahân which follows but was omitted by Ibn Khaldûn. For ar-Rayy, al-Jahshiyârî has:

Pomegranates: 100,000
Peaches (*khawkh*): 1,000 pounds.

[132] Al-Jahshiyârî: *mann.*

[133] This is a bad but very understandable misreading in our text. Instead of *mâ bayn*, al-Jahshiyârî has the correct *mâhay*. The region referred to is that of Mâh-al-Baṣrah and Mâh-al-Kûfah, old Muslim names for Nihâwand and Dînawar. Cf. V. Minorsky in *EI*, *s.v.* "Nihâwand," and M. Streck in *EI*, *s.v.* "Dînawar."

[134] The place is doubtful. There is a Rayyân in the district of Kaskar—cf. Ibn Khurradâdhbih, *Kitâb al-Masâlik wa-l-mamâlik*, p. 12 (text), p. 8 (tr.)—but the name here may possibly be identical with *'-r-b-j-n* or the like, which

Shahrazûr	6,000,000 dirhams [135]
Mosul and environs	24,000,000 dirhams White honey: 20,000 pounds
Azerbaijan	4,000,000 dirhams
The Jazîrah and neighboring Euphrates districts	34,000,000 dirhams
Karaj [136]	300,000 dirhams
Jîlân	5,000,000 dirhams Slaves: 1,000 head [137] I, 324 Honey: 12,000 bags Falcons: 10 Robes: 20
Armenia	13,000,000 dirhams Embroidered carpets: 20 Variegated cloth: 580 pounds [138] Salted *Sûrmâhî* fish: [139] 10,000 pounds Herring: [140] 10,000 pounds Mules: 200 Falcons: 30
Qinnasrîn	400,000 dinars [141] Raisins: 1,000 loads

---

appears as an important city belonging to Mâsabadhân in Ibn Khurradâdhbih, p. 244 (text), p. 185 (tr.). There is also an ar-Radhdh near Mâsabadhân (cf. Yâqût, *Mu'jam al-buldân*, II, 775) which, however, is hardly meant here.

[135] Al-Jahshiyârî: "Shahrazûr and environs: 24,000,000."

[136] Ibn Khaldûn possibly read al-Karkh, but Persian Karaj and Mûqân are meant.

[137] Al-Jahshiyârî has no money item, only 100 slaves and some other products.

[138] Al-Jahshiyârî has "pieces," which goes better with *raqm* "variegated cloth," apparently meant here.

[139] The reading *sûr* is uncertain, but *mâhî*, in itself meaning "fish," is certainly correct. M. J. de Goeje considered *shûrmâhî* the correct reading. Cf. *Bibliotheca Geographorum Arabicorum* (Leiden, 1879), IV, 259 f.

[140] Ibn Khaldûn read something like *ṭurnuj*, which makes one think of *turunj* "citrus fruit." However, the correct reading, as de Slane suggested, is *ṭarîkh*, or *ṭirrîkh*, some kind of salted fish. Cf. A. Mez, *Die Renaissance des Islâms*, p. 410.

[141] Paris has 420,000. Al-Jahshiyârî gives the figure of 490,000 for both Qinnasrîn and the 'Awâṣim (northern Syrian border towns). He also adds an entry concerning Emesa.

Damascus	420,000 dinars
Jordan	96,000 dinars
Palestine	310,000 dinars Raisins: 300,000 pounds [142]
Egypt	1,920,000 dinars
Barca (Barqah)	1,000,000 dirhams
Ifrîqiyah	13,000,000 dirhams Carpets: 120
Yemen	370,000 dinars,[143] excluding garments
Ḥijâz	300,000 dinars

(End of the list)

Regarding Spain, reliable historians of (that country) have reported that 'Abd-ar-Raḥmân an-Nâṣir [144] left 5,000,000 dinars weighing altogether 500 hundredweight, in his treasuries.

I have seen in one of the histories of ar-Rashîd that in his day the income of the treasury was 7,500 hundredweight [145] each year.

Regarding [146] the 'Ubaydid(-Fâṭimid) dynasty, I have I, 325
read in the *History* of Ibn Khallikân, with reference to the

---

[142] According to al-Jahshiyârî, this amount came from all the districts of Syria together.

[143] Al-Jahshiyârî: 870,000.

[144] D adds: "the eighth (Spanish) Umayyad who was (the first to be) given the title of caliph."

[145] D adds: "of gold dinars."

[146] From here to p. 368, l. 20, the text is not found in Bulaq or A. It appears first on an inserted sheet in B and then in the text of D.

The first story appears in the texts of A and B in a shortened form: "Likewise, when the army commander al-Afḍal who controlled the 'Ubaydid(-Fâṭimids) in Egypt was killed, 600,000,000 [!] dinars and 250 *irdabbs* of dirhams were found (in his possession), as well as a proportionate amount of fabrics, household goods, precious stones for rings, and pearls. This is mentioned by army commander [147] al-Afḍal b. Badr al-Jamâlî who controlled the 'Ubaydid(-Fâṭimid) caliphs in Egypt, that when al-Afḍal was killed, 600,000 dinars and 250 *irdabbs* of dirhams were found in his treasury, as well as a correspondingly large amount of precious stones for rings, pearls, fabrics, household goods [147a], riding animals, and pack animals.

As for the dynasties of our own time, the greatest of them is that of the Turks in Egypt. It became important in the days of the Turkish ruler an-Nâṣir Muḥammad b. Qalâ'ûn. At the beginning of his rule, the two amirs, Baybars and Sallâr, had gained power over him, and Baybars had deposed him and occupied his throne, with Sallâr as his partner. Then, shortly after an-Nâṣir regained the rule, he seized (Baybars') partner Sallâr and cleaned out his treasury.[148] I have come across the inventory of that treasury and quote from it:

Ibn Khallikân in his *History*." Then the story is repeated, as it appears above, on the inserted sheet.

In D we find the same version as above, but at the end, after all the other documents have been quoted (below, p. 368, l. 20), we find the abrupt insertion of another version of the same story, which reads: "There was found (in the possession of) al-Afḍal 600,000,000 [!] gold dinars, 250 *irdabbs* of dirhams, 50,000 garments of brocade, 20,000 garments of silk, 30 animal (loads) of boxes of 'Irâqî gold, a bejeweled golden inkstand weighing (in value) 12,000 dinars, 100 nails of gold, each weighing 100 dinars, 500 boxes with robes, and a very large number of horses, mules, camels, slaves, *gâmûs* cows, other cows (*baqar*), sheep, and different kinds of victuals."

These later data are derived from Ibn Khallikân, *Wafayât al-a'yân*, tr. W. M. de Slane (Paris, 1843–71), I, 612 ff. (He was Aḥmad b. Muḥammad, 608–681 [1211–1282]; cf. *GAL*, I, 326 ff.; *Suppl.*, I, 561 f.) Apparently it was Ibn Khaldûn, and not someone else, who later added a slip containing a more accurate and complete quotation from Ibn Khallikân, which was inserted in D in the wrong place. Ibn Khallikân, incidentally, derived his information from the *Duwal al-munqaṭi'ah*, the historical work by 'Alî b. Ẓâfir al-Azdî (*GAL*, *Suppl.*, I, 553 f.).

147 The title of "army commander" actually belonged to al-Afḍal's father. Al-Afḍal perished in 515 [1121].

147a Or, possibly, "garments."

148 This refers to well-known events that took place in the years 1309–10. Ibn Taghrîbirdî, *an-Nujûm az-zâhirah* (Cairo, 1361/1942), IX, 17 f., 20 ff., quotes several authors in this connection. The list closest to Ibn Khaldûn's is that by al-Birzâlî, 665–739 [1267–1339]; cf. *GAL*, II, 36; *Suppl.*, II, 34 f. Cf. also al-Kutubî, *Fawât al-Wafayât*, I, 371 f.

Yellow hyacinths [149] and rubies [150]	4½ pounds
Emeralds	19 pounds
Diamonds and cat's-eyes for rings	300 large pieces
Assorted ring-stones	2 pounds
Round pearls, weighing from one *mithqâl* (1½ dirhams) to one dirham [151]	1,150 pieces
Coined gold	1,400,000 dinars
A pool full of pure gold	
Purses full of gold, discovered between two walls. It is not known how many there were.	
Dirhams	2,071,000
Jewelry	4 hundredweight

Also, a proportionately large amount of fabrics, household goods, riding animals, pack animals, (grain) crops, [152] cattle, male and female slaves, and estates. I, 326

Still later, we have the Merinid dynasty in Morocco. In their treasury, I came across an inventory in the handwriting of the Merinid minister of finance, Ḥassûn b. al-Bawwâq.[153] (The inventory states that) the property left by Sultan Abû Sa'îd in his treasury was over 700 hundredweight of gold dinars. He also had other property of a proportionately large amount. His son and successor, Abû l-Ḥasan, had even more than that. When he took possession of Tlemcen,[154] he found

[149] *Al-yâqût al-bahramân* is described as the best quality of *yâqût* (hyacinth, ruby) and as yellow rather than red. Cf. al-Bîrûnî, *al-Jamâhir fî ma'rifat al-jawâhir* (Hyderabad, 1355/1936–37), pp. 34 ff.

[150] For the "Badakhshânî hyacinths" mentioned here, cf. al-Bîrûnî, pp. 81 ff.

[151] "Dirham" is the reading of the MSS and al-Birzâlî, against the implausible "grain" of the Paris edition. The standard of weight in the pearl trade was the *mithqâl*. A pearl of the best quality, weighing one *mithqâl*, cost 1,000 dinars in 'Abbâsid times. Another quality brought half as much, and pearls of ordinary quality weighing one *mithqâl* cost ten dinars. Cf. al-Bîrûnî, pp. 129 ff. Needless to say, the prices of pearls varied greatly over the years.

[152] *Sic* B. Cf. also p. 368, l. 20, below. D reads *bighâl* "mules."

[153] MSS. B and D merely say ". . . in the handwriting of the Minister of Finance of the (Merinid) Sultan Abû Sa'îd." The name is found in the Paris edition. Abû Sa'îd reigned from 1310 to 1331, and Abû l-Ḥasan from 1331 to 1351, not long before Ibn Khaldûn's arrival in Fez.

[154] In 1337.

more than 300 hundredweight of gold in coins and (gold) jewelry, and a correspondingly large amount of other property in the treasuries of the Sultan of (Tlemcen), the 'Abd-al-Wâdid Abû Tâshfîn.

As to the Almohad (Ḥafṣid) rulers of Ifrîqiyah, I lived in the time of their [155] ninth ruler, Abû Bakr. He had seized [156] Muḥammad b. al-Ḥakîm, the commander of his armies, and had cleaned him out. He got forty hundredweight of gold dinars and a bushel of precious stones for rings, as well as pearls. He took an amount close to that in carpets from his houses, and a correspondingly large amount of estates and other possessions.

I was in Egypt in the days of al-Malik aẓ-Ẓâhir Abû Sa'îd Barqûq, who had seized power from the descendants of Qalâ'ûn, when he arrested his minister of the interior, the amir Maḥmûd,[157] and confiscated his property. The man charged with the confiscation informed me that the amount of gold he cleaned out was 1,600,000 dinars. There was in addition a proportionately large amount of fabrics, riding animals, pack animals, livestock, and (grain) crops.

I, 327 A [158] person who looks at these (data) should bear in mind the relative (importance) of the various dynasties. He should not reject (data) for which he finds no observable

[155] Ibn Khaldûn was born during the reign of Abû Bakr (1318–46). It is not quite clear how he figured the succession of the various Ḥafṣids, but he probably followed local Tunisian tradition in calling him the ninth, even if later on (2:17, below) he calls him the twelfth, and again (2:222, below), the tenth. E. de Zambaur, *Manuel de généalogie et de chronologie pour l'histoire de l'Islam* (Hannover, 1927), p. 74 f., lists him as the eleventh ruler, but it is obvious from the rather turbulent Ḥafṣid family relations that there could be differences over who was to be counted a legitimate ruler. For the numbering of the Ḥafṣids, cf. also below, 2:72, 101, 116, and 222.

Muḥammad b. al-Ḥakîm was Ibn Khaldûn's father-in-law; cf. p. xlv, above.

[156] *Nakaba* is a technical term for applying the *muṣâdarah,* meaning the removal of an official from office for the purpose of confiscating his property.

[157] This happened in 798 [1395/96], and the amir Maḥmûd died in 799 [1397]. Cf. Ibn Taghrîbirdî, *an-Nujûm az-zâhirah,* ed. W. Popper, in *University of California Publications in Semitic Philology,* V (1932–36), 568 f., 637. Ibn Taghrîbirdî speaks of about 1,400,000 dinars and 1,000,000 dirhams. Part of the money was deposited with Ibn Khaldûn. Cf. W. J. Fischel in *Studi orientalistici in onore di Giorgio Levi Della Vida* (Rome, 1956), I, 294.

[158] Issawi, pp. 33 f.

parallels in his own time. Otherwise, many things that are possible would (be considered impossible by him and) escape his attention.[159] Many excellent men, hearing stories of this kind about past dynasties, have not believed them. This is not right. The conditions in the world and in civilization are not (always) the same. He who knows a low or medium (level of civilization) does not know all of them. When we consider our information about the 'Abbâsids, the Umayyads, and the 'Ubaydid(-Fâṭimids) and when we compare what we know to be sound in it with our own observations of the less important dynasties (of today), then we find a great difference between them. That difference results from differences in the original strength of (those dynasties) and in the civilizations (of their realms). As we have stated before, all the monuments a dynasty (leaves behind it) are proportionate to the original strength (of that dynasty). We are not entitled to reject any such (information) about them. Much of it deals with matters that are extremely well known and obvious. Part of it is traditional information known through a continuous tradition. Part of it is direct information based upon personal observation of architectural monuments and other such things.

One should think of the various degrees of strength and weakness, of bigness and smallness, in the various dynasties as they are known through tradition, and compare that (information) with the following interesting story. In the times
of the Merinid Sultan, Abû 'Inân, a *shaykh* from Tangier, by I, 328
name Ibn Baṭṭûtah,[160] came (back) to the Maghrib. Twenty

[159] Lit., "your gullet would be too narrow to pick up things that are possible."

[160] Muḥammad b. 'Abdallâh, 703–779 [1304–1377]. Cf. *GAL*, II, 256; *Suppl.*, II, 365 f. It would seem that Ibn Khaldûn did not seek an opportunity to meet Ibn Baṭṭûṭah in person. In the story as he tells it, two different episodes were combined. In the *Travels*, Ibn Baṭṭûṭah speaks of celebrations and distribution of money in connection with the ruler's return from a journey, but it is in connection with a famine that he speaks of the gift of provisions to meet the population's needs for six months. Cf. *Les Voyages d'Ibn Batoutah*, ed. & tr. C. Defrémery and B. R. Sanguinetti (2d ed.; Paris, 1874–79), III, 238 and 373.

years before, he had left for the East and journeyed through the countries of the ʿIrâq, the Yemen, and India. He had come to the city of Delhi, the seat of the ruler of India, the Sultan Muḥammad Shâh.[161] (The ruler) esteemed Ibn Baṭṭûtah highly and employed him as Mâlikite judge in his domain. He then returned to the Maghrib and made contact with the Sultan Abû ʿInân. He used to tell about experiences he had had on his travels and about the remarkable things he had seen in the different realms. He spoke mostly about the ruler of India. He reported things about him that his listeners considered strange. That, for instance, when the ruler of India went on a trip, he counted the inhabitants of his city, men, women, and children, and ordered that their requirements for (the next) six months be paid them out of his own income. When he returned from his trip and entered (the city), it was a festive [162] day. All the people went out into the open country and strolled about. In front of (the ruler), in the crowd, mangonels were set up on the backs of pack animals.[163] From the mangonels, bags of dirhams and dinars were shot out over the people, until the ruler entered his audience hall.

Ibn Baṭṭûtah told other similar stories, and people in the dynasty (in official positions) whispered to each other that he must be a liar. During that time, one day I met the Sultan's famous wazir, Fâris b. Wadrâr. I talked to him about this matter and intimated to him that I did not believe that man's stories, because people in the dynasty were in general inclined to consider him a liar. Whereupon the wazir

---

[161] Muḥammad Shâh ruled from 1325 to 1351, and it was during his reign that Ibn Baṭṭûṭah was in Delhi. The earlier texts add: "He had contact with its ruler at that time, and it [= the capital, *wa-hiya* as in A and B, whereas Bulaq has *wa-huwa* "and he"] was Fîrûzgûh." This does not refer to Muḥammad Shâh's successor Fîrûz Shâh, but probably to the city which Fîrûz Shâh built near Delhi, and which was called, not Fîrûzgûh, but Fîrûzâbâd. The statement is not found in D. In C both names are found in the margin.

[162] For *yawm mashhûd*, an expression derived from Qur'ân 11.103 (105), cf. above, p. 46 (n. 139), and, for instance, Ibn al-Jawzî, *Muntaẓam*, VII, 278, l. 1. Cf. also p. 450, below.

[163] These, of course, were elephants.

Fâris said to me: "Be careful not to reject such information about the conditions of dynasties, because you have not seen such things yourself. You would then be like the son of the wazir who grew up in prison. The wazir had been imprisoned by his ruler and remained in prison several years. His son grew up in prison. When he reached the age of reason, he asked his father about the meat which he had been eating. (His father) told him that it was mutton, and he asked him what that was. When his father described a sheep to him in all details, (the son) said, 'Father, you mean, it looks like a rat?' His father was angry with him and said, 'What has a sheep to do with a rat?' The same happened later about beef and camel meat. The only animals he had seen in prison were rats, and so he believed that all animals were of the same species as rats."

I, 329

It often happens that people are (incredulous) with regard to historical information, just as it also happens that they are tempted to exaggerate certain information, in order to be able to report something remarkable. We stated this earlier at the beginning of the book.[164] Therefore, a person should look at his sources and rely upon himself. With a clear mind and straightforward, natural (common sense) he should distinguish between the nature of the possible and the impossible. Everything within the sphere of the possible should be accepted, and everything outside it should be rejected. (In using the word "possible") we do not have in mind "possible" in the absolute sense of what is intellectually possible. That covers a very wide range, so that it cannot be used to determine what is possible in actual fact. What we have in mind is the possibility inherent in the matter that belongs to a given thing. When we study the origin of a thing, its genus, (specific) difference,[165] size, and strength, we can draw conclusions as to (the possibility or impossibility) of the data (reported in connection with it). We ad-

---

[164] Cf. p. 19, above.

[165] Cf. p. 9 (n. 21), above.

judge to be impossible everything outside the sphere of (the possible, in this sense).

"Say: God, give me more knowledge."[166]

I, 330 [17] *The ruler seeks the help of clients and followers against the men of his own people and group feeling.*

It[167] should be known that, as we have stated, a ruler can achieve power only with the help of his own people. They are his group and his helpers in his enterprise. He uses them to fight against those who revolt against his dynasty. It is they with whom he fills the administrative offices, whom he appoints as wazirs and tax collectors. They help him to achieve superiority. They participate in the government. They share in all his other important affairs.

This applies as long as the first stage of a dynasty lasts, as we have stated.[168] With the approach of the second stage, the ruler shows himself independent of his people,[169] claims all the glory for himself, and pushes his people away from it with the palms (of his hands). As a result, his own people become, in fact, his enemies. In order to prevent them from seizing power, and in order to keep them away from participation (in power), the ruler needs other friends, not of his own skin, whom he can use against (his own people) and who will be his friends in their place. These (new friends) become closer to him than anyone else. They deserve better than anyone else to be close to him and to be his followers, as well as to be preferred and to be given high positions, because they are willing to give their lives for him, preventing his own people from regaining the power that had been theirs and from occupying with him the rank to which they had been used.

---

[166] Qur'ân 20.114 (113).

[167] Cf. Issawi, pp. 121 f.; G. Surdon and L. Bercher, *Recueil de textes de sociologie,* pp. 62 f.

[168] Cf. pp. 353 ff., above.

[169] Above, p. 353, using a slightly different preposition, the text reads: "gains complete control over his people."

In this (situation), the ruler cares only for his new followers. He singles them out for preference and many honors. He distributes among them as much (property) as (he does among) most of his own people. He confers upon them the most important administrative positions, such as the offices of wazir, general, and tax collector, as well as royal titles which are his own prerogative, and which he does not share (even) with his own people. (He does this) because they are now his closest friends and most sincere advisers. This, then, announces the destruction of the dynasty and indicates that I, 331
chronic disease has befallen it, the result of the loss of the group feeling on which the (dynasty's) superiority had been built. The feelings of the people of the dynasty become diseased as a result of the contempt in which they are held and the hostility the ruler (shows against them). They hate him and await the opportunity of a change in his fortune. The great danger inherent in this situation reverts upon the dynasty. There can be no hope it will recover from that illness. The (mistakes of the) past grow stronger with each successive generation and lead eventually to loss of the (dynasty's) identity.

This is exemplified by the Umayyad dynasty. For their wars and for administrative purposes, they had recourse to the support of Arabs such as 'Amr b. Sa'd b. Abî Waqqâṣ, 'Ubaydallâh b. Ziyâd b. Abî Sufyân, al-Ḥajjâj b. Yûsuf, al-Muhallab b. Abî Ṣufrah, Khâlid b. 'Abdallâh al-Qasrî, Ibn Hubayrah, Mûsâ b. Nuṣayr, Bilâl b. Abî Burdah b. Abî Mûsâ al-Ash'arî, Naṣr b. Sayyâr, and other Arab personalities. For a while [170] the 'Abbâsid dynasty, too, used the support of Arab personalities. But when the dynasty came to claim all the glory for itself and kept the Arabs from aspiring to administrative positions, the wazirate fell to non-Arabs and followers such as the Barmecides, the Banû Sahl b. Nawbakht,[171] and, later, the Bûyids, and Turkish clients such

[170] For *ṣadr* in this meaning, cf. 3:53 and 171, below.

[171] A reference to the Ṭâhirids is added in Bulaq, A, and Paris, but not in B or D. (This particular page is missing in my microfilm of C.)

as Bughâ, Waṣîf, Utâmish, Bâkiyâk (Bâyakbâk), Ibn Ṭûlûn, and their descendants, among other non-Arab clients. Thus, the dynasty came to belong to people other than those who had established it. The power went to people other than those who had first won it.

This is how God proceeds with His servants.

I, 332 [18] *The situation of clients and followers in dynasties.*

It should be known that followers in a dynasty occupy different positions in (the) dynasty depending on whether their close contact with the ruler is of old or of recent date. The reason for this is that the purpose of group feeling, which is defense and aggression, can materialize only with the help of a common descent. For, as we have stated before,[172] blood relations and other close relatives help each other, while strangers and outsiders do not. Client relationships[173] and contacts with slaves or allies have the same effect as (common descent). The consequences of (common) descent, though natural, still are something imaginary.[174] The real thing to bring about the feeling of close contact is social intercourse, friendly association, long familiarity, and the companionship that results from growing up together, having the same wet nurse, and sharing the other circumstances of death and life. If close contact is established in such a manner, the result will be affection and co-operation. Observation of people shows this to be so.

Something similar can be observed in connection with the relation between master and follower. Between the two, there develops a special closeness of relationship which has the same effect (as common descent) and strengthens the close contact. Even though there is no (common) descent, the fruits of (common) descent are there.

Whenever such a client relationship exists between a

---

[172] Cf. pp. 263 ff., above.
[173] Cf. Issawi, p. 105.
[174] Cf. p. 265, above.

tribe and its clients before the tribe has obtained royal authority, the roots of the relationship are more firmly intertwined, the feelings and beliefs involved are more sincere, and the relationship itself is more clearly defined, for two reasons.

First: Before (people obtain) royal authority, they are a model in their ways.[175] Only in the rarest cases is a distinction made between (common) descent and the client relationship. The position (of clients) is the same as that of close or blood relatives. However, if they choose followers after they have obtained royal authority, their royal rank causes them to make a distinction between master and client, and (another) I, 333
between close relatives and clients or followers. The conditions of leadership and royal authority require this in view of (existing) distinctions and differences in rank. The situation (of followers), therefore, is different. They are now on the same level as strangers. The close contact between (the ruler and his followers) weakens, and co-operation, therefore, becomes less likely. This means that followers are now less (close to the ruler) than they were before (the ruler obtained) royal authority.

Second: Followers from before (the time the ruler obtained) royal authority had the status of followers long before the dynasty (came to power).[176] It is, thus, no longer clear (to contemporaries) how the close contact (originally) came about. As a rule, it is supposed to be a case of (common) descent, and in this case the group feeling is strengthened. On the other hand, (follower relationships formed) after (the ruler has obtained) royal authority are of recent date and equally well known to most people. (The origin of) the close contact is clear, and it is clearly distinguishable from (common) descent. The group feeling, in the latter case, is weak in comparison with the group feeling that results from the client relationship that existed before the dynasty (came to power).

[175] Cf. p. 353, above.

[176] The text found in the MSS and Paris is meaningless. Instead of *ahluhu* one must read, with Bulaq, *'ahduhû*.

A look at (known) dynasties and other cases of (political) leadership will show this to be so. Follower relationships formed before leadership and royal authority were obtained, will be found to show a stronger and closer contact between masters and followers. The latter occupy the same position with their master as do his children, his brothers, and other blood relatives. On the other hand, follower relationships formed after royal authority and (political) leadership were obtained do not show the same close connection that exists in the first (group). One may observe this with one's own eyes.

At the end of their power, dynasties eventually resort to employing strangers and accepting them as followers. These people, however, do not acquire any such glory as the men who had become followers of the dynasty before (it came to power) were able to build up for themselves. Their (status as followers) is too recent in origin. Also, the destruction of the dynasty is impending. Therefore, they occupy a very low and humble position. In taking them on as followers and re-
I, 334 placing his old clients and original followers by them, the ruler is motivated by the fact that (his old clients and followers) have become overbearing. They show little obedience to him. They look at him in the same way as his own tribe and relatives do. Close contact existed between him and them for a very long time. They had grown up together with him, had had connections with his ancestors and older members of his family, and were aligned with the great men of his house. (Thus, they are familiar with him) and, as a result (of their familiarity with him), they become proud and overbearing towards him. This is the reason why the ruler comes to shun them and use others in their place. It has been only for a short time that he has come to care for these others and to use them as followers. Therefore, they do not attain positions of glory, but retain their position as outsiders.[177]

This is the case with dynasties at their end. As a rule, the words "followers" and "clients" are used for the first

---

[177] For *khârijîyah*, cf. n. 84 to Ch. II, above.

group. The more recent followers are called "servants" and "helpers."

"God is the friend of the believers." [178]

[19] *Seclusion* [178a] *of, and control over, the ruler (by others) may occur in dynasties.*

When royal authority is firmly established in one particular family and branch of the tribe supporting the dynasty, and when that family claims all royal authority for itself and keeps the rest of the tribe away from it, and when the children of (that family) succeed to the royal authority in turn, by appointment, then it often happens that their wazirs and entourage gain power over the throne. This occurs most often when a little child or a weak member of the family is appointed successor by his father or made ruler by his creatures and servants. It becomes clear that he is unable to I, *335*
fulfill the functions of ruler. Therefore, they are fulfilled by his guardian, one of his father's wazirs, someone from his entourage, one of his clients, or a member of his tribe. (That person) gives the impression that he is guarding the power of the (child ruler) for him. Eventually, it becomes clear that he exercises the control, and he uses the fact as a tool to achieve royal authority. He keeps the child away from his people. He accustoms him to the pleasures of his life of luxury and gives him every possible opportunity to indulge in them. He causes him to forget to look at government affairs. Eventually, he gains full control over him. He accustoms the (child ruler) to believe that the ruler's share in royal authority consists merely in sitting on the throne, shaking hands,[179] being addressed as Sire (*mawlâ*), and sitting with the women in the seclusion of the harem. All (exercise of the) actual executive power, and the personal handling and supervision of matters that concern the ruler, such as in-

---

[178] Qur'ân *3.68* (61).

[178a] In Muslim legal language, the Arabic term used refers to the guardianship of minors and incompetents.

[179] In confirmation of an appointment.

spection of the army, finances, and (defense of) the border regions, are believed (by the child ruler) to belong to the wazir. He defers to him in all these things. Eventually, the wazir definitely adopts the coloring of the leader, of the man in control. The royal authority comes to be his. He reserves it for his family and his children after him.

Such was the case with the Bûyids and the Turks, with Kâfûr al-Ikhshîdî [180] and others in the East, and with al-Manṣûr b. Abî 'Âmir in Spain.

It may happen that a ruler who is secluded and deprived of authority becomes aware of his situation and contrives to escape from it. He thus regains the royal authority for his family. He stops the person who has gained power over it, either by killing him or by merely deposing him. However, this happens very rarely. Once a dynasty has fallen into the hands of wazirs and clients, it remains in that situation. Rarely is it able to escape from it, because (such control by others) is mostly the result of living in luxury and of the fact that the royal princes have grown up immersed in prosperity.
I, *336* They have forgotten the ways of manliness and have become accustomed to the character traits of wet nurses, and they have grown up that way. They do not desire leadership. They are not used to exercising sole power, the prerogative of superiority. All their ambition requires is the satisfactions of pomp and having a great variety of pleasures and luxuries. Clients and followers gain superiority when the family of the ruler is in sole control over its people and claims all royal authority for itself to their exclusion. This is something that happens to dynasties of necessity, as we have stated before.[181]

These are two diseases of dynasties which cannot be cured, except in very rare cases.

"God gives His kingdom (royal authority) to whomever He wants to give it.[182]

---

[180] Kâfûr, who exercised control over Egypt in the last years of Ikhshîdid rule, died in 968.

[181] Cf. pp. 336 ff., above.

[182] Qur'ân 2.247 (248).

[20] *Those who gain power over the ruler do not share with him in the special title that goes with royal authority.*

This is because the first men to achieve royal and governmental authority at the beginning of the dynasty do so with the help of the group feeling of their people and with the help of their own group feeling which causes their people to follow (them) until they and their people have definitely adopted the coloring of royal authority and superiority. (The coloring,) then, continues to exist. Through it, the identity and persistence of the dynasty are assured.

Now, the person who gains superiority (over the ruler) may have a share in the group feeling that belongs to the tribe which has obtained royal authority or to its clients and followers. However, his group feeling still is comprised by, and subordinate to, the group feeling of the family of the ruler. He cannot (take on) the coloring of royal authority. Thus, in gaining control, he does not plan to appropriate royal authority for himself openly, but only to appropriate its fruits, that is, the exercise of administrative, executive, and all other power.[183] He gives the people of the dynasty the impression that he merely acts for the ruler and executes the latter's decisions from behind the curtain. He carefully I, 337
refrains from using the attributes, emblems, or titles of royal authority. He avoids throwing any suspicion upon himself in this respect, even though he exercises full control. For, in his exercise of full control, he takes cover behind the curtain the ruler and his ancestors had set up to protect themselves from their own tribe when the dynasty came into being. He disguises his exercise of control under the form of acting as the ruler's representative.

Should he undertake to adopt (any of the royal prerogatives), the people who represent the group feeling and tribe of the ruler would resent it [184] and contrive to appropriate

[183] For *ibrâm* and *naqḍ*, cf. above, n. 145 to Ibn Khaldûn's Introduction.

[184] *La-nafisahû 'alayhî* (A, C, and D: *ghalabahû* "would resent his superiority"?).

(the royal prerogatives) for themselves, to his exclusion. He has no definite coloring to (make him appear suited for the royal prerogatives) or cause others to submit to him and obey him. (Any attempt by him to appropriate the royal prerogatives) would, thus, instantly precipitate his doom.

Something of the sort happened to 'Abd-ar-Raḥmân b. al-Manṣûr b. Abî 'Âmir.[185] He aspired to share the title of caliph with Hishâm and his house. He was not satisfied with control of the executive power and the resulting forms (of honor) with which his father and brother had been satisfied. He sought to be entrusted with the caliphate by his caliph, Hishâm. The Marwânids (Umayyads) and the other Qurashites were furious to see him do that. They took the oath of allegiance to a cousin of the caliph Hishâm, Muḥammad (b. Hishâm) b. 'Abd-al-Jabbâr b. an-Nâṣir, and revolted against (the party of Ibn Abî 'Âmir). That caused the ruin of the 'Âmirid dynasty and the destruction of their caliph (Hishâm) al-Mu'ayyad. In (al-Mu'ayyad's) place, someone else from among the leaders of the dynasty was chosen, (and his house remained in power) down to the end of the dynasty and the dissolution of their pattern of royal authority.

God is the best heir.

[21] *The true character and different kinds of royal authority.*

I, 338 Royal [186] authority is an institution that is natural to mankind. We have explained before [187] that human beings cannot live and exist except through social organization and cooperation for the purpose of obtaining their food and (other) necessities of life. When they have organized, necessity requires that they deal with each other and (thus) satisfy (their) needs. Each one will stretch out his hand for whatever he needs and (try simply to) take it,[188] since injustice and ag-

[185] Called an-Nâṣir, d. 399 [1009]. Al-Manṣûr had another son, 'Abd-al-Malik al-Muẓaffar.

[186] Cf. Issawi, pp. 113 f.

[187] Cf. pp. 89 ff., above.

[188] Bulaq adds: "away from his fellow men."

gressiveness are in the animal nature. The others, in turn, will try to prevent him from taking it, motivated by wrathfulness [189] and spite and the strong human reaction when (one's own property is menaced). This causes dissension. (Dissension) leads to hostilities, and hostilities lead to trouble and bloodshed and loss of life, which (in turn) lead to the destruction of the (human) species. Now, (the human species) is one of the things the Creator has especially (told us) to preserve.

People, thus, cannot persist in a state of anarchy and without a ruler who keeps them apart. Therefore, they need a person to restrain them. He is their ruler. As is required by human nature, he must be a forceful ruler, one who (actually) exercises authority. In this connection, group feeling is absolutely necessary, for as we have stated before,[190] aggressive and defensive enterprises can succeed only with the help of group feeling. As one can see, royal authority of this kind is a noble institution, toward which all claims are directed, and (one) that needs to be defended. Nothing of the sort can materialize except with the help of group feelings, as has been mentioned before.

Group feelings differ. Each group feeling exercises its own authority and superiority over the people and family adhering to it. Not every group feeling has royal authority. Royal authority, in reality, belongs only to those who dominate subjects, collect taxes, send out (military) expeditions,[191] protect the frontier regions, and have no one over them who is stronger than they. This is generally accepted as the real meaning of royal authority.

There are people whose group feeling falls short of ac- I, 339
complishing (one or another of these things which constitute) part of (real royal authority), such as protecting the frontier regions, or collecting taxes, or sending out (military) ex-

---

[189] The θυμοειδές, one of the three parts of the soul according to Plato.

[190] Cf. pp. 89 ff. and 313, above.

[191] This, rather than "embassies," is the meaning of *bu'ûth*. Cf. R. Dozy in *Journal asiatique*, XIV 6 (1869), 156.

peditions. Such royal authority is defective and not royal authority in the real meaning of the term. This was the case with many of the Berber rulers of the Aghlabid dynasty in al-Qayrawân, and with the non-Arab (Persian) rulers at the beginning of the 'Abbâsid dynasty.

Then, there are people whose group feeling is not strong enough to gain control over all the other group feelings or to stop everyone, so that there exists an authority superior to theirs. Their royal authority is also defective, and not royal authority in the real meaning of the term. It is exercised, for instance, by provincial amirs and regional chieftains who are all under one dynasty. This situation is often found in far-flung dynasties. I mean that there are rulers of provincial and remote regions who rule their own people but also obey the central power of the dynasty. Such was the relationship of the Ṣinhâjah with the 'Ubaydid(-Fâṭimids); of the Zanâtah with the (Spanish) Umayyads at one time and with the 'Ubaydid(-Fâṭimids) at another; of the non-Arab (Persian) rulers with the 'Abbâsids; of the Berber amirs and rulers with the European Christians (in the Maghrib) prior to Islam; and of the rulers of the (old) Persian successor states with Alexander and his Greeks.

There are many such (examples), as, upon examination, will be found to be so. God "exercises forceful domination over His servants." [192]

[22] *Exaggerated harshness is harmful to royal authority and in most cases causes its destruction.*

It [193] should be known that the interest subjects have in their ruler is not interest in his person and body, for example,
I, 340 in his good figure, handsome face, large frame, wide knowledge, good handwriting, or acute mind. Their interest in him lies in his relation to them. Royal and governmental authority is something relative, a relationship between two

[192] Qur'ân 6.18 (18), 61 (61).

[193] Cf. Issawi, pp. 128–30.

things (ruler and subjects). Government becomes a reality when (there is a ruler who) rules over subjects and handles their affairs. A ruler is he who has subjects (*ra'âyâ*), and subjects are persons who have a ruler. The quality accruing to the ruler from the fact of his correlative relation with his subjects is called "rulership" (*malakah*).[194] That is, he rules them, and if such rulership and its concomitants are of good quality, the purpose of government is most perfectly achieved. If such rulership is good and beneficial, it will serve the interests of the subjects. If it is bad and unfair, it will be harmful to them and cause their destruction.

Good rulership is equivalent to mildness. If the ruler uses force and is ready to mete out punishment and eager to expose the faults of people and to count their sins, (his subjects) become fearful and depressed and seek to protect themselves against him through lies, ruses, and deceit. This becomes a character trait of theirs. Their mind and character become corrupted. They often abandon (the ruler) on the battlefield and (fail to support his) defensive enterprises. The decay of (sincere) intentions causes the decay of (military) protection. The subjects often conspire to kill the ruler. Thus, the dynasty decays, and the fence (that protects it) lies in ruins. If the ruler continues to keep a forceful grip on his subjects, group feeling will be destroyed, for reasons stated at the beginning.[195] The fence (which protects the dynasty) is torn down, for the dynasty has become incapable of (military) protection. (On the other hand,) if the ruler is mild and overlooks the bad sides of his subjects, they will trust him and take refuge with him. They (then) love him heartily and are willing to die for him in battle against his enemies. Everything is then in order in the state.

The concomitants of good rulership are being kind to I, *341*
one's (subjects) and defending them. The true meaning of royal authority is realized when the ruler defends his sub-

---

[194] It may be noted that the same word is used also as a technical term of quite a different meaning, namely, "habit." Cf. p. lxxxiv, above.

[195] Cf. pp. 314 ff., above.

jects. To be kind and beneficent toward them is part of being mild to them and showing an interest in how they are living. These things are important for the ruler in gaining the love of his subjects.

It should be known that an alert and very shrewd person rarely has the habit of mildness. Mildness is usually found in careless and unconcerned persons. The least (of the many drawbacks) of alertness (in a ruler) is that he imposes tasks upon his subjects that are beyond their ability, because he is aware of things they do not perceive and, through his genius, foresees the outcome of things at the start. (The ruler's excessive demands) may lead to his subjects' ruin. Muḥammad said: "Follow the pace of the weakest among you." [195a]

The Lawgiver (Muḥammad), therefore, made it a condition that the ruler not be too shrewd. The source for (this statement) is a story about Ziyâd b. Abî Sufyân.[196] When 'Umar deposed him (as governor) of the 'Irâq, he asked 'Umar why he had been deposed, whether it was because of his inability or his treachery. 'Umar replied that he had deposed him for neither of those reasons but because he disliked having people become the victim of his superior intelligence. This is (the source for the statement) that the ruler should not be too shrewd and clever, as were Ziyâd b. Abî Sufyân and 'Amr b. al-'Âṣ. For such (qualities) are accom-

[195a] "To follow the weakest among you" is the recommended procedure for the prayer leader. Cf. Ibn Ḥanbal, *Musnad* (Cairo, 1313/1895), IV, 217; al-Ḥâkim, *Mustadrak*, I, 199, 201.

[196] Ziyâd b. Abîhi, who was Mu'âwiyah's governor of the 'Irâq and is alleged to have been Mu'âwiyah's half brother, was born in the first year of the Hijrah and died in 53 [673]. Though a very young man at the time, he had some official positions and is supposed somehow to have acted as governor in al-Baṣrah in the last year of 'Umar's life. The historians report encounters between him and 'Umar in which he is depicted as a smart young man. However, our estimate of how accurate Ibn Khaldûn's story is must await discovery of its source.

In the absence of an express statement by the Prophet, a statement by 'Umar may be considered to express adequately the intention of the "Lawgiver" himself. But cf. p. 398, below, and the fact that Ibn Khaldûn, in using the term "lawgiver," occasionally thinks of it as a general term, not one restricted to the Lawgiver, Muḥammad.

panied by tyrannical and bad rulership and by a tendency to make the people do things that it is not in their nature to do. This will be mentioned at the end of the book.[197] God is the best ruler.

The conclusion is that it is a drawback in a political leader to be (too) clever and shrewd. Cleverness and shrewdness imply that a person thinks too much, just as stupidity implies that he is too rigid. In the case of all human qualities, the extremes are reprehensible, and the middle road is praiseworthy. This is, for instance, the case with generosity in I, *342*
relation to waste and stinginess, or with bravery in relation to foolhardiness and cowardice.[198] And so it is with all the other human qualities. For this reason, the very clever person is said to have the qualities of devils. He is called a "satan" or, "a would-be satan," and the like.

"God creates whatever He wishes." [199]

[23] *The meaning of caliphate and imamate.*

(As [200] explained,) the real meaning of royal authority is that it is a form of organization necessary to mankind. (Royal authority) requires superiority and force, which express the wrathfulness [201] and animality (of human nature). The decisions of the ruler will therefore, as a rule, deviate from what is right. They will be ruinous to the worldly affairs of the people under his control, since, as a rule, he forces them to execute his intentions and desires, which it may be beyond their ability (to do). This situation will differ according to the difference of intentions to be found in different generations. (But) it is for this reason difficult to be obedient to

---

[197] Cf. the beginning of section 23 and 2:103 ff., below?

[198] This theme dominates all Graeco-Muslim works on ethics. Cf., for instance, F. Rosenthal, "On the Knowledge of Plato's Philosophy in the Islamic World," *Islamic Culture*, XIV (1940), 416 ff.

[199] Qur'ân 3.47 (42), etc.

[200] Cf. Issawi, pp. 134–36; G. Surdon and L. Bercher, *Recueil de textes de sociologie*, pp. 64 f.

[201] Cf. n. 189 to this chapter, above.

(the ruler). Disobedience [202] makes itself noticeable and leads to trouble and bloodshed.

Therefore, it is necessary to have reference to ordained political norms, which are accepted by the mass and to whose laws it submits. The Persians and other nations had such norms. The dynasty that does not have a policy based on such (norms), cannot fully succeed in establishing the supremacy of its rule. "This is how God proceeded with those who were before." [203]

If these norms are ordained by the intelligent and leading personalities and (best) minds of the dynasty, the result will be a political (institution) on an intellectual (rational) basis. If they are ordained by God through a lawgiver who establishes them as (religious) laws, the result will be a political
I, 343 (institution) on a religious basis, which will be useful for life in both this and the other world.

This is because the purpose of human beings is not only their worldly welfare. This entire world is trifling and futile. It ends in death and annihilation. God says: "Do you think that we created you triflingly?" [204] The purpose (of human beings) is their religion, which leads them to happiness in the other world, "the path of God to whom belongs that which is in heaven and that which is on earth." [205] Therefore, religious laws have as their purpose to cause (human beings) to follow such a course in all their dealings with God and their fellow men. This (situation) also applies to royal authority, which is natural in human social organization. (The religious laws) guide it along the path of religion, so that everything will be under the supervision of the religious law. Anything (done by royal authority) that is dictated by force, superiority, or the free play of the power of wrathfulness, is tyranny and injustice and considered reprehensible by (the religious law), as it is also considered reprehensible by the

[202] D agrees with Bulaq in reading *al-'aṣabîyah* "group feeling," instead of *al-ma'ṣiyah* "disobedience."

[203] Qur'ân 33.38 (38), 62 (62).

[204] Qur'ân 23.15 (17).

[205] Qur'ân 42.53 (53).

requirements of political wisdom. Likewise, anything (done by royal authority) that is dictated (merely) by considerations of policy or political decisions without supervision of the religious law,[206] is also reprehensible, because it is vision lacking the divine light. "He for whom God makes no light has no light whatever." [207] The Lawgiver (Muḥammad) knows better than the mass itself what is good for them so far as the affairs of the other world, which are concealed from the mass itself, are concerned. At the Resurrection, the actions of human beings, whether they had to do with royal authority or anything else, will all come back to them. Muḥammad said: "It is your own actions that are brought back to you."

Political laws consider only worldly interests. "They know the outward life of this world." [208] (On the other hand,) the intention the Lawgiver has concerning mankind is their welfare in the other world.[209] Therefore, it is necessary, as required by the religious law, to cause the mass to act in accordance with the religious laws in all their affairs touching both this world and the other world. The authority to do so was possessed by the representatives of the religious law, I, *344*
the prophets. (Later on, it was possessed) by those who took their place, the caliphs.

This makes it clear what the caliphate means. (To exercise) natural royal authority means to cause the masses to act as required by purpose and desire. (To exercise) political (royal authority) means to cause the masses to act as required by intellectual (rational) insight into the means of furthering their worldly interests and avoiding anything that is harmful (in that respect). (And to exercise) the caliphate means to cause the masses to act as required by religious insight into their interests in the other world as well as in this world. (The worldly interests) have bearing upon (the in-

[206] "Without supervision of the religious law" is added by C in the margin.

[207] Qur'ân 24.40 (40). [208] Qur'ân 30.7 (6). [209] Cf. 2:138, below.

terests in the other world), since according to the Lawgiver (Muḥammad), all worldly conditions are to be considered in their relation to their value for the other world. Thus, (the caliphate) in reality substitutes for the Lawgiver (Muḥammad), in as much as it serves, like him, to protect the religion and to exercise (political) leadership of the world.

This should be understood and be kept in mind in the following discussion. God is wise and knowing.

[24] *The differences of Muslim opinion concerning the laws and conditions governing the caliphate.*[210]

We have (just) explained the real meaning of the institution of (the caliphate). It substitutes for the Lawgiver (Muḥammad) in as much as it serves, like him, to preserve the religion and to exercise (political) leadership of the world. (The institution) is called "the caliphate" or "the imamate." The person in charge of it is called "the caliph" or "the imam."

In [211] later times, he has (also) been called "the sultan," when there were numerous (claimants to the position) or when, in view of the distances (separating the different regions) and in disregard of the conditions governing the institution, people were forced to render the oath of allegiance to anybody who seized power.

The name "*imâm*" is derived from the comparison (of the caliph) with the leader (*imâm*) of prayer, since (the caliph) is followed and taken as a model like the prayer leader. Therefore (the caliphate) is called the "great imamate."

The name "caliph" (*khalîfah*) is given to the caliph, because he "represents" (*kh–l–f*) the Prophet in Islam. One

---

[210] Ibn Khaldûn's legal view regarding the history of the institution of the caliphate is expressed in connection with the case of an 'Abbâsid who claimed the caliphate before Timur in 1401. Cf. *Autobiography*, pp. 374 ff.; W. J. Fischel, *Ibn Khaldûn and Tamerlane*, pp. 40 f.

[211] The following paragraph is found in the margin of C and in the text of D. It embodies a strange and noteworthy concession to actual circumstances in the matter of Muslim political theory.

uses "caliph" alone, or "caliph of the Messenger of God." There is a difference of opinion concerning the use of "caliph of God." Some consider (this expression) permissible as derived from the general "caliphate" (representation of God) of all the descendants of Adam, implied in the verse of the Qur'ân, "I am making on earth a caliph," and the verse, "He made you caliphs on earth." [212] But, in general, it is not considered permissible to use (the expression "caliph of God"), since the verse quoted has no reference to it (in connection with the caliphate in the specific sense of the term). Abû Bakr forbade the use (of the expression "caliph of God") when he was thus addressed. He said, "I am not the caliph of God, but the caliph (representative, successor) of the Messenger of God." Furthermore, one can have a "caliph" (representative, successor) of someone who is absent, but not of someone who is present (as God always is). I, *345*

The position of imam is a necessary one. The consensus of the men around Muḥammad and the men of the second generation shows that (the imamate) is necessary according to the religious law. At the death of the Prophet, the men around him proceeded to render the oath of allegiance to Abû Bakr and to entrust him with the supervision of their affairs. And so it was at all subsequent periods. In no period were the people left in a state of anarchy. This was so by general consensus, which proves that the position of imam is a necessary one.

Some people have expressed the opinion that the necessity of the imamate is indicated by the intellect (rational reasons), and that the consensus which happens to exist merely confirms the authority of the intellect in this respect. As they say, what makes (the position of imam) intellectually (rationally) necessary is the need of human beings for social organization and the impossibility of their living and existing by themselves. One of the necessary consequences of social organization is disagreement, because of the pressure of

---

[212] Qur'ân 2.30 (28); 6.165 (165); 35.39 (37).

cross-purposes. As long as there is no ruler who exercises a restraining influence, this (disagreement) leads to trouble which, in turn, may lead to the destruction and uprooting of mankind. Now, the preservation of the (human) species is one of the necessary intentions of the religious law.

This very idea is the one the philosophers had in mind when they considered prophecy as something (intellectually) necessary for mankind. We [213] have already shown the incorrectness of (their argumentation). One of its premises is that the restraining influence comes into being only through
I, *346* a religious law from God, to which the mass submits as a matter of belief and religious creed. This premise is not acceptable. The restraining influence comes into being as the result of the impetus of royal authority and the forcefulness of the mighty, even if there is no religious law. This was the case among the Magians [214] and other nations who had no scriptures and had not been reached by a prophetic mission.

Or, we might say (against the alleged rational necessity of the caliphate): In order to remove disagreement, it is sufficient that every individual should know that injustice is forbidden him by the authority of the intellect. Then, their claim that the removal of disagreement takes place only through the existence of the religious law in one case, and the position of the imam in another case, is not correct. (Disagreement) may (be removed) as well through the existence of powerful leaders, or through the people refraining from disagreement and mutual injustice, as through the position of the imam. Thus, the intellectual proof based upon that premise does not stand up. This shows that the necessity of (the position of imam) is indicated by the religious law, that is, by general consensus, as we have stated before.

Some people have taken the exceptional position of stating that the position of imam is not necessary at all, neither according to the intellect nor according to the religious law. People who have held that opinion include the Mu'tazilah

---

[213] Cf. Issawi, pp. 102 f.; and pp. 92 f., above.
[214] Cf. n. 9 to Ch. I, above.

al-Aṣamm[215] and certain Khârijites, among others. They think that it is necessary only to observe the religious laws. When Muslims agree upon (the practice of) justice and observance of the divine laws, no imam is needed, and the position of imam is not necessary. Those (who so argue) are refuted by the general consensus. The reason why they adopted such an opinion was that they (attempted to) escape the royal authority and its overbearing, domineering, and worldly ways. They had seen that the religious law was full of censure and blame for such things and for the people who practiced them, and that it encouraged the desire to abolish them.

It should be known that the religious law does not censure royal authority as such and does not forbid its exercise. It merely censures the evils resulting from it, such as tyranny, injustice, and pleasure-seeking. Here, no doubt, we have forbidden evils. They are the concomitants of royal authority. I, 347
(On the other hand,) the religious law praises justice, fairness, the fulfillment of religious duties, and the defense of the religion. It states that these things will of necessity find their reward (in the other world). Now, all these things are concomitants of royal authority, too. Thus, censure attaches to royal authority only on account of some of its qualities and conditions, not others. (The religious law) does not censure royal authority as such, nor does it seek to suppress it entirely. It also censures concupiscence and wrathfulness[216] in responsible persons, but it does not want to see either of these qualities relinquished altogether, because necessity calls for their existence. It merely wants to see that proper use is made of them.[217] David and Solomon possessed royal authority such as no one else ever possessed, yet they were

[215] Al-Aṣamm is a rather conspicuous figure among the early Mu'tazilah who lived *ca.* 800. His opinion on the caliphate is also referred to by al-Mâwardî, *al-Aḥkâm as-sulṭânîyah,* at the beginning of the work where the rational necessity of the caliphate is discussed. Cf. pp. 3 f. of the edition, Cairo, 1298/1881. For the Khârijite views, cf. T. W. Arnold in *EI, s.v.* "Khalîfa."

[216] Cf. n. 189 to this chapter, above. [217] Cf. p. 415, below.

divine prophets and belonged, in God's eyes, among the noblest human beings (that ever existed).[218]

Furthermore, we say to them: The (attempt to) dispense with royal authority by (assuming) that the institution (of the imamate) is not necessary, does not help you at all. You agree that observance of the religious laws is a necessary thing. Now, that is achieved only through group feeling and power, and group feeling, by its very nature, requires (the existence of) royal authority. Thus, there will be royal authority, even if no imam is set up. Now, that is just what you (wanted to) dispense with.

If it has been established that the institution (of the imamate) is necessary by general consensus, (it must be added that the institution of the imamate) is a community duty [219] and is left to the discretion of all competent Muslims.[220] It is their obligation to see to it that (the imamate) is set up, and everybody has to obey (the imam) in accordance with the verse of the Qur'ân, "Obey God, and obey the Messenger and the people in authority among you." [221]

It [222] is not possible to appoint two men to the position (of imam) at the same time. Religious scholars generally are of this opinion, on the basis of certain traditions. Those traditions are found in the book, "On Leadership (*imârah*)," in the *Ṣaḥîḥ* by Muslim.[223] They expressly indicate that this is so.

---

[218] Cf. pp. 417 and 422.

[219] A "community duty" (*farḍ al-kifâyah*) is fulfilled when some members of the Muslim community comply with it, in contrast to "individual duties" (*farḍ al-'ayn*), such as the daily prayers, which every responsible (*mukallaf*) Muslim must carry out.

[220] Cf. Bombaci, pp. 447 f. The "competent" Muslims are those having authority and "executive power," as the Arabic term used here is usually rendered in this translation.

[221] Qur'ân 4.59 (62).

[222] The text from here to p. 394, l. 26, did not exist in the earlier stages of the *Muqaddimah*. It appears on an inserted sheet in B and is found in the margin of C and in the text of D.

[223] Cf. Muslim, *Ṣaḥîḥ* (Calcutta, 1265/1849), II, 193 ff., and esp. 312 and 307, where we find traditions such as: "If the oath of allegiance has been rendered to two caliphs, kill one of them," or another saying that the oath of allegiance to caliphs should be rendered to one at a time.

Others hold that (the prohibition against two imams) applies only to two imams in one locality, or where they would be close to each other. When there are great distances and I, *348*
the imam is unable to control the farther region, it is permissible to set up another imam there to take care of public interests.

Among the famous authorities who are reported to have held this opinion is Professor Abû Isḥâq al-Isfarâyinî,[224] the leading speculative theologian. The Imâm al-Ḥaramayn[225] also showed himself inclined toward it in his *Kitâb al-Irshâd.* The opinions of the Spaniards and Maghribîs often make it evident that they, too, were inclined toward it. The numerous religious scholars in Spain rendered the oath of allegiance to the Umayyads and gave the Umayyad 'Abd-ar-Raḥmân an-Nâṣir and his descendants the title of Commander of the Faithful. This title is characteristic of the caliphate, as we shall mention.[226] Somewhat later, the Almohads in the Maghrib did the same thing.

Some scholars have rejected (the possibility of more than one imam) with reference to the general consensus. This is no evident (proof), for if there existed a general consensus on the point, neither Professor Abû Isḥâq nor the Imâm al-Ḥaramayn would have opposed it. They knew better (than any one else) what the consensus meant. Indeed, the imam al-Mâzarî[227] and an-Nawawî[228] have been refuted[229] on the

---

[224] Cf. n. 256 to Ch. I, above.

[225] Abû l-Ma'âlî 'Abd-al-Malik b. 'Abdallâh al-Juwaynî, 419–478 [1028–1085]. Cf. *GAL*, I, 388 f.; *Suppl.*, I, 671 ff. The reference is to *Kitâb al-Irshâd* (Cairo, 1369/1950), p. 425.

[226] Cf. pp. 465 ff., below.

[227] The Mâlikite Muḥammad b. 'Alî, who was born *ca.* 453 [1061] and died in 536 [1141]. Cf. *GAL*, *Suppl.*, I, 663.

[228] Muḥyî-ad-dîn Yaḥyâ b. Sharaf, 631–676 [1233–1277]. Cf. *GAL*, I, 394 ff.; *Suppl.*, I, 680 ff.

[229] If the text is correct and I understand it correctly, Ibn Khaldûn means to say that al-Mâzarî and an-Nawawî also were inclined to admit two imams under certain circumstances, and any argument against them did not refer to the alleged existence of a general consensus in this matter, but had merely Muslim's traditions to go on. However, the text should possibly be corrected to *radda 'alayhi* or *radda 'alâ <Imâm al-Ḥaramayn> al-Imâm*, meaning that the imam al-Mâzarî and an-Nawawî refuted the Imâm al-Ḥaramayn (not

basis of the afore-mentioned evident sense of the traditions (in Muslim's *Ṣaḥîḥ*).

Certain more recent scholars have occasionally argued in favor of (a single imam) with the argument of mutual antagonism [230] referred to by the divine revelation in the verse, "If there were other gods except God in the two (heaven and earth), they (heaven and earth) would have been destroyed." [231] However, nothing of relevance in this connection can be deduced from the verse, because its (force as an) argument is in the field of the intellect. God called our attention to (the verse), so that we might have a rational proof of the oneness of God in which we are enjoined to believe, and so that, as a result, (this dogma) might be more firmly grounded. (On the other hand,) what we want to find out in connection with the imamate is why it is forbidden to set up two imams (at the same time), and that is something that belongs to the field of religious law and religious obligations (rather than to the field of the intellect). Thus, the (verse of the Qur'ân quoted) cannot be used for any deduction (in this connection), unless we establish it as belonging to the field of the religious law by the addition of another premise, namely, that (quite generally) from an increase in number there results corruption, and we are to keep away from anything that may lead to corruption. Then, (the verse) can be used for deductions in the field of religious law. And God knows better.

I, *349* The conditions governing the institution of (the imamate) are four: (1) knowledge, (2) probity, (3) competence, and (4) freedom of the senses and limbs from any defect that might affect judgment and action. There is a difference of

---

with reference to a general consensus but) with reference to the traditions.

The problem could easily be solved by finding out the opinions of al-Mâzarî and an-Nawawî in this matter from their works, but I have not had the opportunity to do so.

[230] Cf. 3:44, 63, and 144, below. [231] Qur'ân 21.22 (22).

opinion concerning a fifth condition, that is, (5) Qurashite descent.

(1) (The necessity of) knowledge as a condition is obvious. The imam can execute the divine laws only if he knows them. Those he does not know, he cannot properly present. (His) knowledge is satisfactory only if he is able to make independent decisions. Blind acceptance of tradition is a shortcoming, and the imamate requires perfection in (all) qualities and conditions.

(2) Probity (*'adâlah*) [232] is required because (the imamate) is a religious institution and supervises all the other institutions that require (probity). Thus, it is all the more necessary that (probity) be a condition required of (the imamate). There is no difference of opinion as to the fact that the (imam's) probity is nullified by the actual commission of forbidden acts and the like. But there is a difference of opinion on the question of whether it is nullified by innovations in dogma (made or adopted by the imam).

(3) Competence means that (the imam) is willing to carry out the punishments fixed by law and to go to war. He must understand (warfare) and be able to assume responsibility for getting the people to go (to war). He also must know about group feeling and the fine points (of diplomacy). He must be strong enough to take care of political duties. All of which is to enable him to fulfill his functions of protecting the religion, leading in the holy war against the enemy, maintaining the (religious) laws,[233] and administering the (public) interests.

(4) Freedom of the senses and limbs from defects or incapacitations such as insanity, blindness, muteness, or deafness, and from any loss of limbs affecting (the imam's) ability to act, such as missing hands, feet, or testicles, is a condition of the imamate, because all such defects affect the

---

[232] Cf. n. 107 to Ibn Khaldûn's Introduction, above.

[233] D has an addition referring to leadership in worldly affairs, which is also found in C but deleted there.

(imam's) full ability to act and to fulfill his duties. Even in the case of a defect that merely disfigures the appearance, as,
I, 350 for instance, loss of one limb, the condition of freedom from defects (remains in force as a condition in the sense that it) aims at perfection (in the imam).

Lack of freedom of action is connected with loss of limbs. Such a lack may be of two kinds. One is forced (inaction) and complete inability to act through imprisonment or the like. (Absence of any restriction upon freedom of action) is as necessary a condition (of the imamate) as freedom from bodily defects. The other kind is in a different category. (This lack of freedom of action implies that) some of (the imam's) men gain power over him, although no disobedience or disagreement may be involved, and keep him in seclusion. Then, the problem is shifted to the person who has gained power. If he acts in accordance with Islam and justice and praiseworthy policies, it is permissible to acknowledge (the imam). If not, the Muslims must look for help. (They must look to) persons who will restrain him and eliminate the unhealthy situation created by him, until the caliph's power of action is re-established.

(5) The condition of Qurashite origin is based upon the general consensus on this point that obtained in the men around Muḥammad on the day of the Saqîfah.[234] On that day, the Anṣâr intended to render the oath of allegiance to Sa'd b. 'Ubâdah. They said: "One amir from among us, and another from among you." [235] But the Qurashites argued against them with Muḥammad's statement, "The imams are from among the Quraysh." [236] They also argued that Muḥammad had exhorted them "to do good to (those of the Anṣâr) who do good, and leave unpunished those of them who do evil." [237] Now, (the Qurashites) said, if the leadership were

---

[234] The "hall" (*saqîfah*) of the Banû Sâ'idah, in which Abû Bakr's elevation to the caliphate was decided. Cf. also below, p. 403. For Sa'd b. 'Ubâdah, cf. K. V. Zetterstéen in *EI*, *s.v.*

[235] In addition to the historians, cf. also *Concordance*, I, 103*a*, ll. 6 f.

[236] Cf. *Handbook*, p. 109*a*.

[237] Cf. *Concordance*, I, 401*a*; III, 13*a*, ll. 6 ff.; Ibn Hishâm, *Sîrah*, p. 1007.

to be given to (the Anṣâr), the latter would not have been recommended (to their care as indicated in Muḥammad's statement). The Anṣâr bowed to these arguments and retracted their statement (just quoted), "One amir from among us, and another from among you." They gave up their intention to render the oath of allegiance to Sa'd. It is also well established by sound tradition that "this thing (the Muslim state) will always remain with this Qurashite tribe." [238] There are many other similar proofs.

However, the power of the Quraysh weakened. Their group feeling vanished in consequence of the life of luxury and prosperity they led, and in consequence of the fact that the dynasty expended them all over the earth. (The Qurashites) thus became too weak to fulfill the duties of the caliphate. The non-Arabs gained superiority over them, and I, *351*
the executive power fell into their hands. This caused much confusion among thorough scholars (with regard to Qurashite origin as a condition of the caliphate). They eventually went so far as to deny that Qurashite descent was a condition (of the imamate). They based themselves upon the evident sense (of certain statements), such as Muḥammad's statement, "Listen and obey, even should an Abyssinian slave, with (a head as black as) a raisin, be your governor." [239] This (statement), however, is no valid proof in connection with (the problem in question). It is just a hypothetical parable which, in an exaggerated form, is meant to stress the duty of obedience.

There [240] is also 'Umar's statement, "If Sâlim, the client of Abû Ḥudhayfah, were alive, I would appoint him,"—or: ". . . I would not have had any objection against him." [241]

---

[238] Cf. al-Bukhârî, *Ṣaḥîḥ*, II, 382; *Handbook*, pp. 128 f.

[239] This statement represents Khârijite doctrine. It is enumerated, together with a great number of related statements, by al-Muttaqî al-Hindî, *Kanz al-'ummâl* (Hyderabad, 1312/1894–95), III, 197, No. 2990.

[240] Cf. Bombaci, p. 448.

[241] According to the historians, 'Umar is supposed to have made this statement on his deathbed. Cf. aṭ-Ṭabarî, *Annales*, I, 2776 f.

Cf. al-Bâqillânî, *Tamhîd*, p. 179, where the objection is understood to refer to accepting Sâlim's advice. The biographers report that Sâlim acted

This statement also has nothing to do (with the problem in question). It is known that the opinion of one of the men around Muḥammad (such as 'Umar, in this particular case) does not constitute a proof. Furthermore, people's clients belong to them.[242] Sâlim's group feeling in his capacity as client was that of the Qurashites. And it is (group feeling) that is important when specific descent is made a condition (of the imamate). 'Umar had a high opinion of the caliphate. He thought, as he looked at it, that the conditions governing it were (all but) disregarded. Thus, he turned to Sâlim, because, in his opinion, the latter abundantly fulfilled the conditions governing the caliphate, including his client relationship which provided for group feeling, as we shall mention.[243] Only, a pure (Qurashite) descent was not there. ('Umar) considered it unnecessary, because the importance of descent lies solely in group feeling, and (group feeling) may result from a client relationship (such as that of Sâlim, as well as from common descent). The reason for 'Umar's (statement) was his desire to look after (the best interests of) the Muslims and to entrust their government to a man beyond reproach who (would not commit acts for which he, 'Umar,) would be held responsible.

Among those who deny that Qurashite descent is a condition (of the imamate) is Judge Abû Bakr al-Bâqillânî.[244] The Qurashite group feeling had come to disappear and dissolve (in his day), and non-Arab rulers controlled the caliphs. Therefore, when he saw what the condition of the caliphs was in his day, he dropped the condition of Qurashite origin (for the imamate), even though it meant agreeing with the Khârijites.

---

as prayer leader in the first days of Muslim settlement in Medina, but do not mention 'Umar's statement. Cf. al-Bukhârî, *Ta'rîkh*, II 2, 108; Ibn Sa'd, *Ṭabaqât*, III 1, 60–62; Ibn Ḥajar, *Iṣâbah*, II, 108 ff., No. 3049.

242 Cf. n. 79 to Ch. II, above.

243 This refers to the discussion that follows, of the importance of group feeling for the caliphate.

244 Al-Bâqillânî, *Tamhîd*, pp. 181 f., definitely considers Qurashite origin a condition of the caliphate.

Scholars in general, however, retain Qurashite descent as a condition (of the imamate). (They maintain that) the imamate rightly belongs to a Qurashite, even if he is too weak to handle the affairs of the Muslims. Against them is the fact that this involves dropping the condition of competence, which requires that (the imam must) have the power to discharge his duties. If (his) strength has gone with the disappearance of group feeling, (his) competence, too, is gone. And if the condition of competence be eliminated, that will reflect further upon knowledge and religion. (In this case, then, all) the conditions governing the institution (of the imamate) would no longer be considered, and this would be contrary to the general consensus. I, 352

We shall now discuss the wisdom of making descent a condition of the imamate, so that the correct facts underlying all those opinions will be recognized. We say:

All religious laws must have (specific) purposes and significant meanings of their own, on account of which they were made. If we, now, investigate the wisdom of Qurashite descent as a condition (of the imamate) and the purpose which the Lawgiver (Muḥammad) had in mind, (we shall find that) in this connection he did not only think of the blessing that lies in direct relationship with the Prophet, as is generally (assumed). Such direct relationship exists (in the case of Qurashite descent), and it is a blessing. However, it is known that the religious law has not as its purpose to provide blessings. Therefore, if (a specific) descent be made a condition (of the imamate), there must be a (public) interest which was the purpose behind making it into law. If we probe into the matter and analyze it, we find that the (public) interest is nothing else but regard for group feeling. (Group feeling) gives protection and helps people to press their claims. The existence of (group feeling) frees the incumbent in the position (of imam) from opposition and division. The Muslim community accepts him and his family, and he can establish friendly terms with them.

Now, the Quraysh were the outstanding, original, and

superior leaders of the Muḍar. Their number, their group feeling, and their nobility gave them power over all the other
1, 353 Muḍar. All other Arabs acknowledged that fact and bowed to their superiority. Had the rule been entrusted to anybody else, it may be expected that their opposition and refusal to submit would have broken the whole thing up. No other Muḍar tribe would have been able to sway them from their attitude of opposition and to carry them along against their will. The community would have been broken up. The whole thing would have been torn by dissension. The Lawgiver (Muḥammad) warned against that. He showed himself desirous to have them agree and to remove dissension and confusion from among them, for the sake of establishing close contact and group feeling and improved protection. (No dissension or confusion but rather) the opposite (could be expected to be the case), were the Quraysh to be in power. They were able, through superior force, to drive people into doing what was expected of them. There was no fear that anybody would oppose them. There was no fear of division. The Quraysh were able to assume the responsibility of doing away with (division) and of preventing people from (splitting up). Therefore, Qurashite descent was made a condition of the institution of (the imamate). The Quraysh represented the strongest (available) group feeling. (Qurashite descent of the imam,) it was thus (hoped), would be more effective (than anything else) in organizing the Muslim community and bringing harmony into it. When Qurashite affairs were well organized, all Muḍar affairs were likewise well organized. Thus, all the other Arabs obeyed them. Nations other than the Arabs submitted to the laws of the Muslim community. Muslim armies entered the most remote countries. That happened in the days of the conquests. It remained that way later on in the (Umayyad and ʿAbbâsid) dynasties, until the power of the caliphate dissolved and the Arab group feeling vanished. The great number of the Quraysh and their superiority over the Muḍar subtribes is known to

all diligent students of, and experts in, Arab history, biography, and relevant conditions. Ibn Isḥâq mentioned this in the *Kitâb as-siyar*, and (so did) other (authors).[245]

If it is established that Qurashite (descent) as a condition (of the imamate) was intended to remove dissension with the I, 354
help of (Qurashite) group feeling and superiority, and if we know that the Lawgiver (Muḥammad) does not make special laws for any one generation, period, or nation, we also know that (Qurashite descent) falls under (the heading of) competence. Thus, we have linked it up with (the condition of competence) and have established the over-all purpose of (the condition of) Qurashite (descent), which is the existence of group feeling. Therefore, we consider it a (necessary) condition for the person in charge of the affairs of the Muslims that he belong to people who possess a strong group feeling, superior to that of their contemporaries, so that they can force the others to follow them and the whole thing can be united for effective protection. (Such group feeling as a rule) does not comprise all areas and regions. Qurashite (group feeling), however, was all-comprehensive, since the mission of Islam, which the Quraysh represented, was all-comprehensive, and the group feeling of the Arabs was adequate to that mission. Therefore, (the Arabs) overpowered all the other nations. At the present time, however, each region has people of its own who represent the superior group feeling (there).

When one considers what God meant the caliphate to be, nothing more needs (to be said) about it. (God) made the caliph his substitute to handle the affairs of His servants. He is to make them do the things that are good for them and not do those that are harmful. He has been directly told so. A person who lacks the power to do a thing is never told

[245] Normally, the Arabic text would suggest the translation "*Kitâb as-siyar* and other (books)," which does not make much sense. The above translation is also suggested by C, which vocalizes *wa-ghayruhû*. Cf. p. 7 (n. 10), above. Ibn Isḥâq's work is usually referred to as the *Sîrah* (Biography of Muḥammad), but cf. also n. 1015 to this chapter, below.

directly to do it. The religious leader, Ibn al-Khaṭîb,[246] said that most religious laws apply to women as they do to men. However, women are not directly told (to follow the religious laws) by express reference to them in the text, but, in (Ibn al-Khaṭîb's) opinion, they are included only by way of analogical reasoning. That is because women have no power whatever. Men control their (actions), except in as far as the duties of divine worship are concerned, where everyone controls his own (actions). Therefore, women are directly told (to fulfill the duties of divine worship) by express reference to them in the text, and not (merely) by way of analogical reasoning.

Furthermore, (the world of) existence attests to (the necessity of group feeling for the caliphate). Only he who has gained superiority over a nation or a race is able to
I, *355* handle its affairs. The religious law would hardly ever make a requirement in contradiction to the requirements of existence.

And God, He is exalted, knows better.

[25] *Shî'ah tenets concerning the question of the imamate.*

It should be known that, linguistically, *Shî'ah* means "companions and followers." In the customary usage of old and modern jurists and speculative theologians, the word is used for the followers and descendants of 'Alî. The tenet on which they all agree is that the imamate is not a general (public) interest to be delegated to the Muslim nation for consideration and appointment of a person to fill it. (To the Shî'ah,) it is a pillar and fundamental article of Islam. No prophet[247] is permitted to neglect it or to delegate (the appointment of an imam) to the Muslim nation. It is incumbent

---

[246] Muḥammad b. 'Umar, 543 or 544 to 606 [1148/49 or 1149/50 to 1209/10]. He is more generally referred to as Fakhr-ad-dîn ar-Râzi. Cf. *GAL*, I, 506 ff.; *Suppl.*, I, 920 ff.

[247] Ibn Khaldûn speaks here of prophets in general (whether one reads *li-nabî* as in Bulaq or *li-n-nabî* as in the MSS), although it is Muḥammad who is primarily meant.

upon him to appoint an imam for the (Muslims). The imam cannot commit [248] sins either great or small. 'Alî is the one whom Muḥammad appointed. The (Shî'ah) transmit texts (of traditions) in support of (this belief), which they interpret so as to suit their tenets. The authorities on the Sunnah and the transmitters of the religious law do not know these texts. Most of them are supposititious, or some of their transmitters are suspect, or their (true) interpretation is very different from the wicked interpretation that (the Shî'ah) give to them.

According to (the Shî'ah), these texts fall into the two categories of express and implied statements.[249] An express statement, for instance, is the following statement (by Muḥammad): " 'Alî is master of those whose master I am." [250] As they say, such a position of master (mentioned in the tradition) applies only to 'Alî. 'Umar thus said to him: "You have become the master of all believers, men and women."

Another tradition of this sort is the following statement of (Muḥammad): "Your best judge is 'Alî." Imamate means exclusively the activity of judging in accordance with the divine laws. (The activity of) judging and being a judge is (what is) meant by "the people in authority" whom God requires us to obey in the verse of the Qur'ân: "Obey God, and I, 356
obey the Messenger and the people in authority among you." [251] Therefore, 'Alî and no other was arbitrator in the question of the imamate on the day of the Saqîfah.[252]

---

[248] Lit., "He is *ma'ṣûm*, has *'iṣmah*, against . . ."; cf. p. 185, above.

[249] Ibn Khaldûn found all this material in the relevant chapter of the heresiographers he mentions below, p. 414. Cf., for instance, ash-Shahrastânî, *Kitâb al-milal wa-n-niḥal*, ed. Cureton (London, 1842–46) p. 122 f.; tr. T. Haarbrücker (Halle, 1850–51), I, 184 ff.

[250] For the famous *ḥadîth* of Ghadîr Khumm, cf. I. Goldziher, *Muhammedanische Studien* (Halle, 1888–90), II, 116.

[251] Qur'ân 4.59 (62).

[252] Cf. p. 396, above. The decisive role of 'Alî in this matter is, of course, a Shî'ah view. Cf., for instance, al-Ya'qûbî, *Ta'rîkh*, ed. Houtsma (Leiden, 1883), II, 138, where 'Alî himself stopped the movement in his favor, or the *Risâlat as-Saqîfah* of Abû Ḥayyân at-Tawḥîdî, ed. I. al-Kaylânî, *Trois Epîtres* (Damascus, 1951).

Another statement of this sort is the following statement by (Muḥammad): "He who renders the oath of allegiance to me upon his life is my legatee and the man who will be in charge of this authority here after me." Only 'Alî rendered the oath of allegiance to him (in this manner).

An implied (argument), according to the Shî'ah, is the fact that the Prophet sent 'Alî to recite the *sûrat al-Barâ'ah* [253] at the festival (in Mecca) when it had (just) been revealed. He first sent Abû Bakr with it. Then it was revealed to Muḥammad that "a man from you,"—or: ". . . from your people"—"should transmit it." Therefore, he sent 'Alî to transmit it. As they say, this proves that 'Alî was preferred (by Muḥammad). Furthermore, it is not known that Muḥammad ever preferred anyone to 'Alî, while he preferred Usâmah b. Zayd [254] and 'Amr b. al-'Âṣ [255] to both Abû Bakr and 'Umar during two different raids. According to (the Shî'ah), all these things prove that 'Alî and no one else was appointed (by Muḥammad) to the caliphate. However, some of the statements quoted are little known, and others require an interpretation very different from that which (the Shî'ah) give.

Some (Shî'ah) hold the opinion that these texts prove both the personal appointment of 'Alî and the fact that the imamate is transmitted from him to his successors. They are the Imâmîyah. They renounce the two *shaykhs* (Abû Bakr and 'Umar), because they did not give precedence to 'Alî and did not render the oath of allegiance to him, as required by the texts quoted. The Imâmîyah do not take the imamates (of Abû Bakr and 'Umar) seriously. But we do not want to bother with transmitting the slanderous things said about

---

[253] *Sûrah* 9. Cf. Ibn Hishâm, *Sîrah*, p. 921.

[254] Just before the Prophet's death, Usâmah prepared an expedition to Syria, for which many of the old guard of Islam, including Abû Bakr and 'Umar, volunteered, but it did not come off. Cf. Ibn Hishâm, *Sîrah*, p. 999, and, with more detail, Ibn Sayyid-an-nâs, *'Uyûn al-athar*, II, 281 ff.

[255] The occasion was the raid of Dhât as-salâsil, in 629. Cf. Ibn Hishâm, *Sîrah*, p. 984; aṭ-Ṭabarî, *Annales*, I, 1604.

(Abû Bakr and 'Umar) by (Imâmîyah) extremists. They are objectionable in our opinion and (should be) in theirs.

Other (Shî'ah) say that these proofs require the appointment of 'Alî not in person but as far as (his) qualities are concerned. They say that people commit an error when they do not give the qualities their proper place. They are the Zaydîyah. They do not renounce the two *shaykhs* (Abû Bakr I, *357*
and 'Umar). They do take their imamates seriously, but they say that 'Alî was superior to them. They permit an inferior person to be the imam, even though a superior person may be alive (at the same time).[256]

The Shî'ah[257] differ in opinion concerning the succession to the caliphate after 'Alî. Some have it passed on among the descendants of Fâṭimah in succession, through testamentary determination (*naṣṣ*). We shall mention that later on. They (who believe this) are called the Imâmîyah, with reference to their statement that knowledge of the imam and the fact of his being appointed are an article of the faith. That is their fundamental tenet.

Others consider the descendants of Fâṭimah the (proper) successors to the imamate, but through selection (of an imam) from among the Shî'ah. The conditions governing (selection of) that imam are that he have knowledge, be ascetic, generous, and brave, and that he go out to make propaganda for his imamate. They (who believe this) are the Zaydîyah, so named after the founder of the sect, Zayd b. 'Alî b. al-Ḥusayn, the grandson of Muḥammad. He had a dispute with his brother Muḥammad al-Bâqir concerning the condition that the imam has to come out openly. Al-Bâqir charged him with implying that, in the way Zayd looked at it, their father Zayn-al-'âbidîn would not be an imam, because he had not come out openly and had made no prep-

---

[256] The Ismâ'îlîyah, on the other hand, were of the opinion that an inferior person could not be imam. Cf. W. Ivanow, *A Creed of the Fâṭimids* (Bombay, 1936), p. 41. Cf. also below, p. 432.

[257] On the Shî'ah sects, cf. also, briefly, *'Ibar*, III, 360 f.

arations to do so. He also accused him of holding Mu'tazilah tenets which he had learned from Wâṣil b. 'Aṭâ'. When the Imâmîyah discussed the question of the imamates of the two *shaykhs* (Abû Bakr and 'Umar) with Zayd, and noticed that he admitted their imamates and did not renounce them, they disavowed him and did not make him one of the imams. On account of that fact, they are called "Disavowers" (*Râfiḍah*).

Some (Shî'ah) consider as successors to the imamate, after 'Alî—or after his two sons, Muḥammad's grandsons (al-Ḥasan and al-Ḥusayn), though they disagree in this respect—(al-Ḥasan's and al-Ḥusayn's) brother, Muḥammad b. al-Ḥanafîyah, and then the latter's children. They are the Kaysânîyah, so named after Kaysân, a client of ('Alî's).[258]

There are many differences among these sects which we have omitted here for the sake of brevity.

I, 358 There are also (Shî'ah) sects that are called "Extremists" (*ghulâh*). They transgress the bounds of reason and the faith of Islam when they speak of the divinity of the imams. They either assume that the imam is a human being with divine qualities, or they assume that he is God in human incarnation. This is a dogma of incarnation that agrees with the Christian tenets concerning Jesus. 'Alî himself had these (Shî'ah) who said such things about him burned to death. Muḥammad b. al-Ḥanafîyah was very angry with al-Mukhtâr b. Abî 'Ubayd when he learned that al-Mukhtâr had suggested something along these lines concerning him. He cursed and renounced al-Mukhtâr openly. Ja'far aṣ-Ṣâdiq did the same thing with people about whom he had learned something of the sort.

Some (Shî'ah) extremists say that the perfection the imam possesses is possessed by nobody else. When he dies, his spirit passes over to another imam, so that this perfection may be in him. This is the doctrine of metempsychosis.

Some extremists stop (*w—q—f*) with one of the imams and do not go on. (They stop with the imam) whom they consider (to have been) appointed as the (last one). They (who

[258] Cf. C. van Arendonk in *EI, s.v.* "Kaisânîya."

believe this) are the Wâqifîyah. Some of them say that the (last imam) is alive and did not die, but is removed from the eyes of the people. As a proof for that (theory), they adduce the problem of al-Khiḍr.[259]

Something of that sort has been stated with regard to 'Alî himself. He is said to be in the clouds. The thunder is his voice, and lightning his whip.[260] Something similar has also been stated with regard to Muḥammad b. al-Ḥanafîyah. He is said to be in the Mountain of Raḍwâ in the Ḥijâz. The poet of (the sect holding that belief), Kuthayyir,[261] says:

Indeed, the Qurashite imams,
The champions of the Truth, are four, all alike:
'Alî and his three sons,
They are the grandsons of Muḥammad. To them, no obscurity is attached.
One grandson is the grandson of faith and piety.
Another was "removed" through Kerbelâ'.
And there is a grandson who will not taste death, until
He shall lead an army preceded by the flag.

---

[259] The word "problem, proposition" (*qaḍîyah*) is simplified in Bulaq to "story" (*qiṣṣah*). For the legend of al-Khiḍr, who gained eternal life, cf. A. J. Wensinck in *EI, s.v.* "al-Khaḍir." In connection with this passage, cf. also I. Goldziher, *Abhandlungen zur arabischen Philologie* (Leiden, 1899), II, LXIV.

[260] These opinions are ascribed to an alleged sect called as-Saba'îyah, after a certain 'Abdallâh b. Saba'. Cf., for instance, ash-Shahrastânî, *Kitâb al-milal wa-n-niḥal*, pp. 132 f.; tr. Haarbrücker, I, 200. Cf. also below, 2: 175.

[261] Cf. *GAL*, I, 48; *Suppl.*, I, 79; and 3:383 and 404, below. The verses are found in his *Dîwân*, ed. H. Pérès (Algiers & Paris, 1930), II, 185 ff. They are quoted not only in the heresiographers but also by many other authors with whose works Ibn Khaldûn was familiar, such as al-Mas'ûdî, *Murûj adh-dhahab*, V, 182; Abû l-Faraj al-Iṣfahânî, *Kitâb al-Aghânî*, VIII, 32 (Bulaq ed.); (Cairo, 1345——/1927——), IX, 14 f.; Ibn 'Abdrabbih, *'Iqd*, I, 203; II, 234. Cf. the references in the *Mukhtaṣar* of al-Baghdâdî's *Kitâb al-farq bayn al-firaq*, ed. P. K. Hitti (Cairo, 1924), p. 38.

The "grandsons" of the Prophet are al-Ḥasan, al-Ḥusayn, and Muḥammad b. al-Ḥanafîyah, according to the generally accepted interpretation. However, the last-mentioned was not a grandson of Muḥammad's. It is possible that the verses actually did not refer to Ibn al-Ḥanafîyah but to the alleged third son of Muḥammad's daughter Fâṭimah, al-Muḥsin, who died very young, and that they were later transferred to the historical personality of Ibn al-Ḥanafîyah.

He is "removed," and has not been seen among them
for a time,
In Raḍwâ, having with him honey and water.

I, 359 The extremist Imâmîyah, in particular the Twelvers, hold a similar opinion. They think that the twelfth of their imams, Muḥammad b. al-Ḥasan al-'Askarî, to whom they give the epithet of al-Mahdî, entered the cellar of their house in al-Ḥillah and was "removed" when he was imprisoned (there) with his mother. He has remained there "removed." [262] He will come forth at the end of time and will fill the earth with justice. The Twelver Shî'ah refer in this connection to the tradition found in the collection of at-Tirmidhî regarding the Mahdî.[263] The Twelver Shî'ah are still expecting him to this day. Therefore, they call him "the Expected One." Each night after the evening prayer, they bring a mount and stand at the entrance to the cellar where (the Mahdî is "removed"). They call his name and ask him to come forth openly. They do so until all the stars are out.[264] Then, they disperse and postpone the matter to the following night. They have continued that custom to this time.

Some of the Wâqifîyah say that the imam who died will return to actual life in this world. They adduce as a proof (for the possibility of this assumption) the story of the Seven Sleepers, the one about the person who passed by a village, and the one about the murdered Israelite who was beaten with the bones of the cow that (his people) had been ordered to slaughter, all of them stories included in the Qur'ân.[265] They further adduce similar wonders that occurred in the manner of (prophetical) miracles. However, it is not right to use those things as proof for anything except where they properly apply.

---

[262] Cf. pp. 412 ff., below. [263] Cf. 2:159 ff., below.
[264] Cf. R. Dozy in *Journal asiatique*, XIV 6 (1869), 156 f.
[265] Cf. *sûrah* 18 and Qur'ân 2.259 (261) and 2.67 ff. (63 ff.).

The (extremist Shî'ah) poet, as-Sayyid al-Ḥimyarî,[266] has the following verses on this subject:

When a man's head has become gray
And the barbers urge him to dye his hair,
His cheerfulness is gone and no longer there.
Arise, O companion, and let us weep for (our lost) youth.
What is gone of it will not return
To anyone until the Day of the Return,
Until the day on which people will return
To their life in this world before the Reckoning.
I believe that this is a true belief.
I do not doubt the Resurrection.
In fact, God has spoken about people
Who lived after they had decomposed and become dust.

The religious authorities (*imâms*) of the Shî'ah have themselves made it superfluous for us to bother with the arguments of the extremists, for they do not refer to them and thus invalidate the use (the extremists) make of their (arguments). I, 360

The Kaysânîyah consider (Muḥammad's) son Abû Hâshim successor to the imamate after Muḥammad b. al-Ḥanafîyah. They are therefore called the Hâshimîyah. Then, they split. Some of them transferred the imamate after Abû Hâshim to his brother 'Alî and then to 'Alî's son al-Ḥasan. Others thought that when Abû Hâshim died in the land of ash-Sharâh[267] upon his return from Syria, he appointed as his heir Muḥammad b. 'Alî b. 'Abdallâh b. 'Abbâs, who, in turn, appointed as his heir his son Ibrâhîm who is known as the Imam. Ibrâhîm appointed as his heir his brother 'Abdal-

---

[266] Ismâ'îl b. Muḥammad, d. 178 or 179 [794/95 or 795/96]. Cf. *GAL*, I, 83; *Suppl.*, I, 133.

[267] Cf. p. 133, above, and p. 420, below. Ibn al-Athîr, *Kâmil*, V, 25, *anno* 100, adds that this region belongs to the Belqâ' in Syria.

lâh b. al-Ḥârithîyah who got the surname of as-Saffâḥ, who, in turn, appointed as his heir his brother Abû Ja'far 'Abdallâh, who got the surname of al-Manṣûr. (The imamate) was then passed on to his children in succession through testamentary determination (*naṣṣ*) and appointment (*'ahd*), right down to the last of them. Such is the tenet of the Hâshimîyah who support the 'Abbâsid dynasty. Among them were Abû Muslim, Sulaymân b. Kathîr, Abû Salimah al-Khallâl, and other members of the (early) 'Abbâsid Shî'ah.[268] Their right to the power is often supported by the argument that their right goes back to al-'Abbâs. He was alive at the time of Muḥammad's death, and he had the best title to become Muḥammad's heir because of the group feeling attaching to paternal uncles (al-'Abbâs being the paternal uncle of Muḥammad).

The Zaydîyah consider the succession to the imamate in the light of their view concerning (the institution). (The imam) is chosen by competent [268a] Muslims and not appointed by testamentary determination (*naṣṣ*). They acknowledge as imams, 'Alî, his son al-Ḥasan, (al-Ḥasan's) brother al-Ḥusayn, (al-Ḥusayn's) son 'Alî Zayn-al-'âbidîn, and ('Alî's) son, the head of the Zaydîyah, Zayd b. 'Alî. Zayd came forth
I, *361* in al-Kûfah and made propaganda for the imamate. He was killed and his body exhibited in al-Kunâsah.[269] The Zaydîyah acknowledge the imamate of (Zayd's) son Yaḥyâ, as his (father's) successor. Yaḥyâ went to al-Khurâsân and was killed in al-Jûzajân [270] after he had appointed Muḥammad b. 'Abdallâh b. Ḥasan b. al-Ḥasan, (Muḥammad's) grandson, as his heir. Muḥammad is called "the Pure Soul" (*an-Nafs as-zakîyah*). He came forth in the Ḥijâz and took the surname of al-Mahdî. Al-Manṣûr's armies went against him. He was routed and killed. His brother Ibrâhîm was appointed his successor. He appeared in al-Baṣrah. With him was 'Îsâ b.

[268] Cf. also *'Ibar*, III, 100 ff.

[268a] Cf. n. 220 to this chapter, above.

[269] This happened in 122 [740]. Cf. also *'Ibar*, III, 98 ff. Al-Kunâsah is a part of al-Kûfah.

[270] Cf. also 2:210, below, and *'Ibar*, III, 104 f.

Zayd b. 'Alî. Al-Manṣûr himself, or his generals, went against him with the army. Both Ibrâhîm and 'Îsâ were routed and killed.[271] Ja'far aṣ-Ṣâdiq had told them all that (in advance). (His prediction) was considered one of Ja'far's acts of divine grace.[272]

Other (Zaydîs) assumed that the imam after Muḥammad b. 'Abdallâh, the Pure Soul, was Muḥammad b. al-Qâsim b. 'Alî b. 'Umar,[273] 'Umar being the brother of Zayd b. 'Alî. Muḥammad b. al-Qâsim came forth in aṭ-Ṭâliqân. He was captured and brought to al-Mu'taṣim, who imprisoned him. He died in prison.

Other Zaydîs say that the imam after Yaḥyâ b. Zayd was his brother 'Îsâ, who had participated with Ibrâhîm b. 'Abdallâh in his fight against al-Manṣûr. They consider his descendants the successors to the imamate. The impostor who appeared among the Negroes (Zanj during their revolt) considered him his ancestor. We shall mention that in connection with the history of the Zanj.[274]

Other Zaydîs say that the imam after Muḥammad b. 'Abdallâh was his brother Idrîs who fled to the Maghrib and died there.[r] His son Idrîs b. Idrîs seized power and laid out the city of Fez. His descendants succeeded him as rulers in the Maghrib, until they were destroyed, as we shall mention in connection with Idrîsid history.[275] Thereafter, the Zaydî I, 362
power became disorganized and remained so.

The missionary who ruled Ṭabaristân, al-Ḥasan b. Zayd b. Muḥammad b. Ismâ'îl b. al-Ḥasan b. Zayd b. al-Ḥasan, Muḥammad's grandson, as well as his brother, Muḥammad b. Zayd, also were Zaydîs. Zaydî propaganda was

---

[271] Ibrâhîm was killed at Bâkhamrâ in 145 [763]. Cf. Abû l-Faraj al-Iṣfahânî, *Maqâtil aṭ-Ṭâlibiyîn* (Cairo, 1368/1949), pp. 315–80.

[272] Cf. 2:203 and 209 f., below.

[273] Another "b. 'Alî" appears in A and B (apparently specifically marked in B as correct) and in C. In D it is deleted. The event mentioned happened in 219 [834]. Cf. Abû l-Faraj al-Iṣfahânî, *Maqâtil aṭ-Ṭâlibîyîn*, pp. 577 ff. Cf. also *'Ibar*, III, 257.

[274] Cf. *'Ibar*, III, 301 f.

[275] Cf. *'Ibar*, IV, 12 ff. Cf. also above, pp. 47 ff.

then continued among the Daylam by the (Ḥusaynid) an-Nâṣir al-Uṭrûsh. The Daylam accepted Islam from him. He was al-Ḥasan b. ʿAlî b. al-Ḥasan b. ʿAlî b. ʿUmar, the brother of Zayd b. ʿAlî. His descendants founded a dynasty in Ṭabaristân. They made it possible for the Daylam to obtain royal authority and control over the caliphs in Baghdad. We shall mention this in connection with the history of the Daylam.[276]

The Imâmîyah considered (the following) as successors to the imamate after ʿAlî al-Waṣî (the "Legatee") by appointment as heirs. ʿAlî's son al-Ḥasan, (al-Ḥasan's) brother al-Ḥusayn, (al-Ḥusayn's) son ʿAlî Zayn-al-ʿâbidîn, (ʿAlî's) son Muḥammad al-Bâqir, and (Muḥammad's) son Jaʿfar aṣ-Ṣâdiq. From there on, they split into two sects. One of them considers (Jaʿfar's) son Ismâʿîl as Jaʿfar's successor to the imamate. They recognize Ismâʿîl as their imam. They are called the Ismâʿîlîyah. The other considers (Jaʿfar's) son, Mûsâ al-Kâẓim, as Jaʿfar's successor to the imamate. They are the Twelvers, because they stop with the twelfth imam. They say that he remains "removed" until the end of time, as has been mentioned before.[277]

The Ismâʿîlîs say that the imam Ismâʿîl became imam because his father Jaʿfar appointed him (through *naṣṣ*) to be his successor. (Ismâʿîl) died before his father, but according to (the Ismâʿîlîs) the fact that he was determined by his father as his successor means that the imamate should continue among his successors. This is analogous to the story of Moses and Aaron.[278] As they say, Ismâʿîl's successor as imam was his son Muḥammad, the Concealed One (*al-Maktûm*).[279] He is the first of the hidden imams. According to the Ismâʿîlîs, an imam who has no power goes into hiding. His missionaries remain in the open, in order to establish
I, 363 proof (of the hidden imam's existence) among mankind.

[276] Cf. *ʿIbar*, III, 285, 366 f. Al-Uṭrûsh died in 304 [917].

[277] Cf. p. 408, above.

[278] Moses' vocation was continued by the descendants of Aaron, although Aaron died before Moses. Cf. also pp. 473 f., below.

[279] Cf. p. 45, above.

When the imam has actual power, he comes out into the open and makes his propaganda openly. As they say, after Muḥammad, the Concealed One, the hidden imams were: his son Ja'far al-Muṣaddiq, Ja'far's son Muḥammad al-Ḥabîb, the last of the hidden imams, and Muḥammad's son 'Ubaydallâh al-Mahdî. For him, open propaganda was made among the Kutâmah by Abû 'Abdallâh ash-Shî'î. People followed his call, and he brought al-Mahdî out of his confinement in Sijilmâsah. Al-Mahdî became the ruler of al-Qayrawân and the Maghrib. His descendants and successors ruled over Egypt, as is well known from their history.

The Ismâ'îlîs are called "Ismâ'îlîs" with reference to their recognition of the imamate of Ismâ'îl. They are also called "Bâṭinîs" with reference to their speaking about the *bâṭin*, that is, the hidden, imam. They further are called "heretics," because of the heretical character of their beliefs. They have an old and a new persuasion. Neo-Ismâ'îlî propaganda was made at the end of the fifth [eleventh] century by al-Ḥasan b. Muḥammad aṣ-Ṣabbâḥ. He ruled over certain fortresses in Syria and the 'Irâq.[280] His propaganda persisted there until the Turkish rulers in Egypt and the Tatar rulers in the 'Irâq destroyed it in their respective territories. The persuasion for which aṣ-Ṣabbâḥ made propaganda is mentioned in ash-Shahrastânî's *Kitâb al-milal wa-n-niḥal*.[281]

Among recent Shî'ah, the name of Imâmîyah is often restricted to the Twelvers. They acknowledge the imamate of Mûsâ al-Kâẓim b. Ja'far because his elder brother, the imam Ismâ'îl, had died while their father Ja'far was still alive. Ja'far then appointed Mûsâ (through *naṣṣ*) as imam. The imams after Mûsâ were 'Alî ar-Riḍâ, who was appointed by al-Ma'mûn as his successor (to the caliphate),[282] but died before al-Ma'mûn, so that nothing came of it. The imams after 'Alî, then, were ('Alî's) son Muḥammad at-Taqî,

[280] That is, the non-Arab 'Irâq, or western Persia.

[281] Muḥammad b. 'Abd-al-Karîm, d. 548 [1153]. Cf. *GAL*, I, 428 f.; *Suppl.*, I, 762 f. Cf. his *Kitâb al-milal wa-n-niḥal*, pp. 150 ff.; (tr.) I, 225 ff.

[282] Cf. pp. 434 f., below.

I, 364 (Muḥammad's) son 'Alî al-Hâdî, ('Alî's) son al-Ḥasan al-'Askarî, and (al-Ḥasan's) son Muḥammad, the Expected Mahdî, whom we have mentioned before.[283]

There are many divergences within each of these Shî'ah persuasions. However, the sects mentioned are the most prominent ones. For an exhaustive study of Shî'ah sects, one should consult the books on religions and sects (*al-milal wa-n-niḥal*) by Ibn Ḥazm,[284] ash-Shahrastânî, and others. They contain additional information.

"God leads astray whomever He wants to lead astray, and He guides whomever He wants to guide." [285]

[26] *The transformation of the caliphate into royal authority.*

It [286] should be known that royal authority is the natural goal of group feeling. It results from group feeling, not by choice but through (inherent) necessity and the order of existence, as we have stated before.[287] All religious laws and practices and everything that the masses are expected to do requires group feeling. Only with the help of group feeling can a claim be successfully pressed, as we have stated before.[288]

Group feeling is necessary to the Muslim community. Its existence enables (the community) to fulfill what God expects of it. It is said in (the sound tradition of) the *Ṣaḥîḥ*: "God sent no prophet who did not enjoy the protection of his people." [289] Still, we find that the Lawgiver (Muḥammad) censured group feeling and urged (us) to reject it and to leave it alone. He said: "God removed from you the ar-

---

283 Cf. p. 408, above.

284 'Alî b. Muḥammad, 384–456 [993–1064]. Cf. *GAL*, I, 399 f.; *Suppl.*, I, 692 ff.

285 Qur'ân 16.93 (95); 35.8 (9); 74.31 (34).

286 Cf. Issawi, p. 137; G. Surdon and L. Bercher, *Recueil de textes de sociologie*, pp. 66–73.

287 Cf. pp. 284 ff., above.

288 Cf. p. 284, above.

289 Cf. pp. 187 and 322, above.

rogance of the pre-Islamic times and its pride in ancestors. You are the children of Adam, and Adam was made of dust." [290] God said: "Most noble among you in God's (eyes) is he who fears God most." [291]

We also find that (the Lawgiver Muḥammad) censured royal authority and its representatives. He blamed them because of their enjoyment of good fortune, their senseless waste, and their deviations from the path of God. He recommended friendship among all Muslims and warned against discord and dissension.

It should be known that in the opinion of the Lawgiver (Muḥammad), all of this world is a vehicle for (transport to) I, *365*
the other world. He who loses the vehicle can go nowhere. When the Lawgiver (Muḥammad) forbids or censures certain human activities or urges their omission, he does not want them to be neglected altogether. Nor does he want them to be completely eradicated, or the powers from which they result to remain altogether unused. He wants those powers to be employed as much as possible for the right aims.[292] Every intention should thus eventually become the right one and the direction (of all human activities) one and the same. It was in this sense that Muḥammad said: "He who emigrates to God and His Messenger emigrates to God and His Messenger, but he who emigrates to gain worldly goods or to marry a woman emigrates to where he emigrates." [293]

The Lawgiver (Muḥammad) did not censure wrathfulness [294] in the intention of eradicating it as a human quality. If the power of wrathfulness were no longer to exist in (man), he would lose the ability to help the truth become victorious. There would no longer be holy war or glorification of the word of God. Muḥammad censured the wrathfulness that is in the service of Satan and reprehensible pur-

[290] Cf. *Concordance,* I, 7*b*, l. 32, and II, 190*b*, l. 28.

[291] Qur'ân 49.13 (13). [292] Cf. p. 391, above.

[293] Cf. al-Bukhârî, *Ṣaḥîḥ*, I, 23; *Concordance,* II, 357*a*, ll. 7 ff.

[294] Cf. pp. 381 and 391, above.

poses,[295] but the wrathfulness that is one in God and in the service of God, deserves praise. Such (praiseworthy) wrathfulness was one of the qualities of Muḥammad.

Likewise, when (the Lawgiver Muḥammad) censures the desires, he does not want them to be abolished altogether, for a complete abolition of concupiscence in a person would make him defective and inferior. He wants the desires to be used for permissible purposes to serve the public interests, so that man becomes an active servant of God who willingly obeys the divine commands.

Likewise, when the religious law censures group feeling and says: "Neither your blood relatives nor your children will be of use to you (on the Day of Resurrection)," [296] (such a statement) is directed against a group feeling that is used for worthless purposes, as was the case in pre-Islamic times. It is also directed against a group feeling that makes a person
I, *366* proud and superior. For an intelligent person to take such an attitude is considered a gratuitous action, which is of no use for the other world, the world of eternity. On the other hand, a group feeling that is working for the truth and for fulfillment of the divine commands is something desirable. If it were gone, religious laws would no longer be, because they materialize only through group feeling, as we have stated before.[297]

Likewise, when the Lawgiver (Muḥammad) censures royal authority, he does not censure it for gaining superiority through truth, for forcing the great mass to accept the faith, nor for looking after the (public) interests. He censures royal authority for achieving superiority through worthless means and for employing human beings for indulgence in (selfish) purposes and desires, as we have stated. If royal authority would sincerely exercise its superiority over men for the sake of God and so as to cause those men to worship God

---

[295] Bulaq adds: "When wrathfulness is for that purpose, it is reprehensible, . . ."

[296] Qur'ân 60.3 (3).

[297] Cf. pp. 322 ff., above.

and to wage war against His enemies, there would not be anything reprehensible in it. Solomon said: "O my Lord . . . give me royal authority, such as will not fit anyone after me." [298] He was sure of himself. (He knew) that, as prophet and king, he would have nothing to do with anything worthless.[299]

When 'Umar b. al-Khaṭṭâb went to Syria and was met by Mu'âwiyah in full royal splendor as exhibited both in the number (of Mu'âwiyah's retinue) and his equipment, he disapproved of it and said: "Are these royal Persian manners (*kisrawîyah*), O Mu'âwiyah?" Mu'âwiyah replied: "O Commander of the Faithful, I am in a border region facing the enemy. It is necessary for us to vie with (the enemy) in military equipment." 'Umar was silent and did not consider Mu'âwiyah to be wrong.[300] He had used an argument that was in agreement with the intentions of the truth and of Islam. If the intention (implied in 'Umar's remark) had been to eradicate royal authority as such, 'Umar would not have been silenced by the answer with which Mu'âwiyah (excused) his assumption of royal Persian manners. He would have insisted that Mu'âwiyah give them up altogether. 'Umar meant by "royal Persian manners" the attitude of the Persian rulers, which consisted in doing worthless things, I, 367
constantly practicing oppression, and neglecting God. Mu'âwiyah replied that he was not interested in royal Persian manners as such, or in the worthlessness connected with them, but his intention was to serve God. Therefore, ('Umar) was silent.

The same applies to the attitude of the men around Muḥammad towards abolishing royal authority and its conditions, and forgetting its customs. (The men around Mu-

---

[298] Qur'ân 38.35 (34). [299] Cf. pp. 391 f., above, and p. 422, below.

[300] The two basic stories from which the above version was evolved are contained in al-Balâdhurî's *Ansâb*. Cf. O. Pinto and G. Levi Della Vida, *Il Califfo Mu'âwiya I secondo il "Kitâb Ansâb al-Ashrâf"* (Rome, 1938), p. 159. Cf. also Ibn 'Abdrabbih, *'Iqd*, II, 236. For the use of the term *kisrawî*, cf. G. E. von Grunebaum, *Islam* (Menasha, Wis., 1955), p. 36.

ḥammad) were wary of the admixture of worthless things that might be found in (royal customs).

When the Messenger of God was about to die, he appointed Abû Bakr as his representative to (lead the) prayers, since (praying) was the most important religious activity. People were, thus, content to accept (Abû Bakr) as caliph, that is, as the person who causes the great mass to act according to the religious laws. No mention was made of royal authority, because royal authority was suspected of being worthless, and because at that time it was the prerogative of unbelievers and enemies of Islam. Abû Bakr discharged the duties of his office in a manner pleasing to God, following the Sunnah of his master (Muḥammad). He fought against apostates until all the Arabs were united in Islam. He then appointed 'Umar his successor. 'Umar followed Abû Bakr's example and fought against (foreign) nations. He defeated them and permitted the Arabs to appropriate the worldly possessions of (those nations) and their royal authority, and the Arabs did that.

(The caliphate), then, went to 'Uthmân b. 'Affân and 'Alî. All (these caliphs) renounced royal authority and kept apart from its ways. They were strengthened in this attitude by the low standard of living in Islam and the desert outlook of the Arabs. The world and its luxuries were more alien to them than to any other nation, on account of their religion, which inspired asceticism where the good things of life were concerned, and on account of the desert outlook and habitat and the rude, severe life to which they were accustomed. No nation was more used to a life of hunger than the Muḍar.
I, 368 In the Ḥijâz, the Muḍar inhabited a country without agricultural or animal products. They were kept from the fertile plains, rich in grain, because the latter were too far away and were monopolized by the Rabî'ah and Yemenites who controlled them.[301] They had no envy of the abundance of (those regions). They often ate scorpions and beetles. They were

[301] Cf. pp. 266 and 283, above.

proud to eat *'ilhiz*, that is, camel hair ground with stones, mixed with blood, and then cooked. The Quraysh were in a similar situation with regard to food and housing.

Finally, the group feeling of the Arabs was consolidated in Islam through the prophecy of Muḥammad with which God honored them. They then advanced against the Persians and Byzantines, and they looked for the land that God had truthfully promised and destined to them. They took away the royal authority of (the Persians and the Byzantines) and confiscated their worldly possessions. They amassed enormous fortunes. It went so far that one horseman obtained, as his share in one of the raids, about 30,000 gold pieces. The amounts they got were enormous. Still, they kept to their rude way of life. 'Umar used to patch his (sole) garment with pieces of leather.[302] 'Alî used to say: "Gold and silver! Go and lure others, not me!" [303] Abû Mûsâ [304] refrained from eating chicken, because chickens were very rare among the Arabs of that time and not (generally) known to them. Sieves were altogether non-existent among (the Arabs), and they ate wheat (kernels) with the bran.[304a] Yet, the gains they made were greater than any ever made by other human beings.

Al-Mas'ûdî [305] says: "In the days of 'Uthmân, the men around Muḥammad acquired estates and money. On the day 'Uthmân was killed, 150,000 dinars and 1,000,000 dirhams were in the hands of his treasurer. The value of his estates in Wâdî l-Qurâ and Ḥunayn and other places was 200,000 dinars. He also left many camels and horses. The eighth part I, 369

[302] Cf. al-Mas'ûdî, *Murûj adh-dhahab*, IV, 193; Ibn Kathîr, *Bidâyah*, VII, 134.

[303] Cf. al-Mas'ûdî, IV, 336.

[304] Abû Mûsâ al-Ash'arî, 'Abdallâh b. Qays, one of the most famous early Muslim politicians. Cf. below, p. 453.

[304a] An innovation shortly after the death of the Prophet allegedly was the use of sieves. Cf. al-Ghazzâlî, *Iḥyâ'*, I, 112; II, 3. Cf. also aṭ-Ṭabarî, *Annales*, I, 3032; * I. Goldziher, *Muh. Studien*, II, 25.

[305] Cf. his *Murûj adh-dhahab*, IV, 253–55. The quotation in Ibn Khaldûn is accurate but not literal. For the subject, cf. also Ibn Ḥamdûn, *Tadhkirah*, Ch. XLIX, MS. Topkapusaray, Ahmet III, 2948, Vol. XII, fol. 185*a*.

of the estate of az-Zubayr after his death amounted to 50,000 dinars. He also left 1,000 horses and 1,000 female servants. Ṭalḥah's income from the 'Irâq was 1,000 dinars a day, and his income from the region of ash-Sharâh [306] was more than that. The stable of 'Abd-ar-Raḥmân b. 'Awf contained 1,000 horses. He also had 1,000 camels and 10,000 sheep. One-fourth of his estate after his death amounted to 84,000. Zayd b. Thâbit left silver and gold that was broken into pieces with pickaxes, in addition to the (other) property and estates that he left, in the value of 100,000 dinars. Az-Zubayr built himself a residence in al-Baṣrah and other residences in Egypt and al-Kûfah and Alexandria. Ṭalḥah built one in al-Kûfah and had his residence in Medina improved. He used plaster, bricks, and teakwood. Sa'd b. Abî Waqqâṣ built himself a residence in al-'Aqîq, (a suburb of Medina). He made it high and spacious, and had balustrades put on top of it. Al-Miqdâd [306a] built his residence in Medina and had it plastered inside and out. Ya'lâ b. Munyah [307] left 50,000 dinars and estates and other things the value of which amounted to 300,000 dirhams." End of the quotation from al-Mas'ûdî.

Such were the gains people made. Their religion did not blame them for (amassing so much), because, as booty, it was lawful property. They did not employ their property wastefully but in a planned [308] way in (all) their conditions, as we have stated. Amassing worldly property is reprehensible, but it did not reflect upon them, because blame attaches
I, 370 only to waste and lack of planning, as we have indicated. Since their expenditures followed a plan and served the truth and its ways, the amassing (of so much property) helped

[306] Cf. pp. 133 and 409, above.

[306a] Miqdâd b. al-Aswad ('Amr), who is much less prominent than the preceding personalities, was an old Muslim. He died in 33 [653/54].

[307] Munyah is said to have been the name of Ya'lâ's mother, or of his grandmother (or a more remote female ancestor). The correct form is found fully vocalized in C. D has Munabbih, and A and B also suggest this wrong name. Ya'lâ's father was Umayyah.

[308] *Qaṣd*, from the meaning of "purposefulness" acquires the meaning of "moderation." Both meanings apply here. Cf. p. 354 (n. 99), above.

them along on the path of truth and served the purpose of attaining the other world.

Soon, the desert attitude of the Arabs and their low standard of living approached its end. The nature of royal authority—which is the necessary consequence of group feeling as we have stated[309]—showed itself, and with it, there came (the use of) superiority and force. Royal authority, as (the early Muslims) saw it, belonged in the same category as luxury and amassed property. (Still,) they did not apply their superiority to worthless things, and they did not abandon the intentions of the religion or the ways of truth.

When trouble arose between 'Alî and Mu'âwiyah as a necessary consequence of group feeling, they were guided in (their dissensions) by the truth and by independent judgment. They did not fight for any worldly purpose or over preferences of no value, or for reasons of personal enmity. This might be suspected, and heretics might like to think so. However, what caused their difference was their independent judgment as to where the truth lay. It was on this matter that each side opposed the point of view of the other. It was for this that they fought. Even though 'Alî was in the right, Mu'âwiyah's intentions were not bad ones. He wanted the truth, but he missed (it). Each was right in so far as his intentions were concerned. Now, the nature of royal authority requires that one person claim all the glory for himself and appropriate it to himself. It was not for Mu'âwiyah to deny (the natural requirement of royal authority) to himself and his people. (Royal authority) was a natural thing that group feeling, by its very nature, brought in its train. Even the Umayyads and those of their followers who were not after the truth like Mu'âwiyah felt that.[310] They banded together around him and were willing to die for him. Had Mu'âwiyah tried to lead them on another course of action, had he opposed *1, 371*
them and not claimed all the power for (himself and them),

---

[309] Cf. pp. 284 ff., above.

[310] Cf. Bombaci, p. 448.

it would have meant the dissolution of the whole thing that he had consolidated. It was more important to him to keep it together than to bother about (a course of action) that could not entail much criticism.

'Umar b. 'Abd-al-'Azîz used to say when(ever) he saw al-Qâsim b. Muḥammad b. Abî Bakr: [311] "If I had anything to say about it, I would appoint him caliph." Had he (really) wanted to appoint him as his successor, he could have done it, but he was afraid of the Umayyads who held the executive authority, for reasons mentioned by us. He was not able to take the power away from them, because to do so would have caused a split. All this was the consequence of the tendencies inherent in royal authority, as the necessary consequence of group feeling.

When royal authority is obtained and we assume that one person has it all for himself, no objection can be raised if he uses it for the various ways and aspects of the truth. Solomon and his father David had the royal authority of the Israelites for themselves, as the nature of royal authority requires, and it is well known how great a share in prophecy and truth they possessed.[312]

Likewise, Mu'âwiyah appointed Yazîd as his successor, because he was afraid of the dissolution of the whole thing, in as much as the Umayyads did not like to see the power handed over to any outsider. Had Mu'âwiyah appointed anyone else his successor, the Umayyads would have been against him. Moreover, they had a good opinion of (Yazîd). No one could have doubts in this respect, or suspect that it was different with Mu'âwiyah.[313] He would not have been the

---

[311] A grandson of the caliph Abû Bakr, who died between 720 and 730. For 'Umar's remark, cf. Ibn Sa'd, *Ṭabaqât*, V, 140, l. 12.

[312] Cf. pp. 392 f. and 417, above.

[313] The element of Mu'âwiyah's opinion concerning Yazîd is considered also below, pp. 431 and 434, though it makes the argument here nearly pointless. This fact would remain, were one to translate: ". . . the Umayyads would have been against him, even though they (might have) had a good opinion of him (personally). No one could have doubts in this respect or suspect that Mu'âwiyah had other (motives when he appointed Yazîd, but the preservation of harmony)." In favor of this translation, one may point to p. 432, l. 15, below, but there are reasons against it.

man to appoint Yazîd his successor, had he believed him to be (really) so wicked. Such an assumption must be absolutely excluded in Mu'âwiyah's case.

The same applies to Marwân b. al-Ḥakam and his son(s). Even though they were kings, their royal ways were not those of worthless men and oppressors. They complied with
the intentions of the truth with all their energy, except when I, 372
necessity caused them to do something (that was worthless). Such (a necessity existed) when there was fear that the whole thing might face dissolution. (To avoid that) was more important to them than any (other) intention. That this was (their attitude) is attested by the fact that they followed and imitated (the early Muslims). It is further attested by the information that the ancients had about their conditions. Mâlik used the precedent of 'Abd-al-Malik (b. Marwân) as argument in the *Muwaṭṭa'*.[314] Marwân belonged to the first class of the men of the second generation, and his excellence is well known.[315] The sons of 'Abd-al-Malik, then, came into power one after the other. Their outstanding religious attitude is well known. 'Umar b. 'Abd-al-'Azîz reigned in between them. He eagerly and relentlessly aspired to (follow) the ways of the first four caliphs and the men around Muḥammad.

Then came the later Umayyads. As far as their worldly purposes and intentions were concerned, they acted as the nature of royal authority required. They forgot the deliberate planning and the reliance upon the truth that had guided the activities of their predecessors. This caused the people to censure their actions and to accept the 'Abbâsid propaganda in the place of (the Umayyads'). Thus, the 'Abbâsids took over the government. The probity of the 'Abbâsids was outstanding. They used their royal authority to further, as far as possible, the different aspects and ways of the truth. (The early 'Abbâsids,) eventually, were succeeded by the

[314] Cf. J. Schacht, *The Origins of Muhammadan Jurisprudence*, pp. 167 f., but more can be said about Marwân in this connection. Cf. Schacht, pp. 114, 193, 195, 197, 200, and 221. Cf. also Ibn al-'Arabî, *Qawâṣim* (*al-'Awâṣim min al-qawâṣim*) (Cairo, 1371/1952), pp. 249 f.

[315] Bulaq reads: "who are known for their probity."

descendants of ar-Rashîd. Among them there were good and bad men. Later on, when the power passed to their descendants, they gave royal authority and luxury their due. They became enmeshed in worldly affairs of no value and turned their backs on Islam. Therefore, God permitted them to be ruined, and (He permitted) the Arabs to be completely deprived of their power, which He gave to others. "God does not do an atom of injustice." [316] Whoever considers the biographies of these caliphs and their different approaches to truth and worthlessness knows that what we have stated is correct.

I, 373 Al-Mas'ûdî [317] reports a similar judgment concerning the Umayyads on the authority of Abû Ja'far al-Manṣûr. "When al-Manṣûr's paternal uncles mentioned the Umayyads in his presence, he said, ' 'Abd-al-Malik was a tyrant who did not care what he did. Sulaymân was concerned only with his stomach and with sexual pleasure. 'Umar was a one-eyed man among the blind. Hishâm was their man." He continued: "The Umayyads continued to hold on to the power that had been established for them and to preserve it, and to protect the power that God had given them. They aspired to lofty matters and rejected base ones. Eventually, the power passed to their wasteful descendants who were only concerned with the gratification of their desires and with sinful pleasures. They were ignorant of God's attitude to sinners, and they felt safe from His punishment. At the same time, they prostituted the caliphate. They made light of the privileges of leadership and showed themselves too weak for political leadership. Therefore, God stripped them of their power. He humiliated them and deprived them of their prosperity."

"Then, 'Abdallâh b. Marwân was brought into the presence (of al-Manṣûr). He had fled from the 'Abbâsids and gone to the country of the Nubian king. He now told al-

[316] Qur'ân 4.40 (44).

[317] Cf. *Murûj adh-dhahab*, VI, 161–65. There are some omissions in the quotation but basically it is fairly literal. Cf. also Ibn 'Abdrabbih, *'Iqd*, II, 276. The story was also cited by Abû Ḥammû of Tlemcen, in his *Wâsiṭat as-sulûk* (Tunis, 1279/1862–63), p. 128.

Manṣûr about an experience he had had with that ruler. He said: I had been staying there a little while when their ruler came to me. He sat down on the ground, although I had valuable carpets spread out (to sit on).[318] I asked him what it was that prevented him from sitting upon our garments, and he replied, 'I am a ruler, and it behooves every ruler to humble himself before the greatness of God, since God has raised him (to his exalted position).' Then, he asked me why we drank wine, though it is forbidden in our Scripture. I replied: 'Our slaves and followers made bold to do that.' Then he asked why we permitted our animals to ride down the green crops, although destruction is forbidden us in our Scripture. I replied: 'Our slaves and followers did that in their ignorance.' Then, he asked why we wore brocade and gold and silk, although this was forbidden us in our Scrip- I, 374
ture. I replied: 'We lost our royal authority and accepted the help of non-Arab peoples who adopted our religion. They wore these things against our will.' The Nubian ruler, thereupon, reflected a while. He drew figures on the ground with his hand and said (to himself), 'Our slaves and followers and non-Arabs who adopted our religion . . .' Then he raised his head to me and said, 'It is not as you say. No, you are people who have declared (to be) permitted that which had been forbidden you by God. You committed deeds you had been forbidden to do. And you used your royal authority unjustly. Therefore, God stripped you of your power. He humiliated you because of your sins. God is taking a revenge which has not yet finished its full course. I am afraid that you will be punished while you are staying in my country, and that the punishment will then affect me, too. Hospitality lasts three (nights). Therefore, get yourself the provisions you need and leave my country.' Al-Manṣûr wondered (at that story) and reflected (some time about it)."

---

[318] *Busiṭat lî*, as in Bulaq and A (*busiṭa lî*), B, and C. D has *busiṭat lahû* which means "Valuable carpets had been spread out for him (to sit on)." This agrees with the printed text of al-Mas'ûdî, but is certainly a mistake as far as the Ibn Khaldûn tradition is concerned.

It has thus become clear how the caliphate is transformed into royal authority. The form of government in the beginning was a caliphate. Everybody had his restraining influence in himself, that is, (the restraining influence of) Islam. They preferred (Islam) to their worldly affairs, even if (the neglect of worldly affairs) led to their own destruction, while the mass (of the people, at least,) escaped.

When 'Uthmân was besieged in his house, al-Ḥasan, al-Ḥusayn, 'Abdallâh b. 'Umar, Ibn Ja'far,[319] and others came and offered to defend him. But he refused and did not permit swords to be drawn among Muslims. He feared a split and wanted to preserve the harmony that keeps the whole thing intact, even if it could be done only at the cost of his own destruction.

At the beginning of his (term of) office, 'Alî himself was advised by al-Mughîrah to leave az-Zubayr, Mu'âwiyah, and Ṭalḥah in their positions, until the people had agreed to render the oath of allegiance to him and the whole thing was consolidated. After that, he might do what he wanted. That was good power politics. 'Alî, however, refused. He
I, *375* wanted to avoid deceit, because deceit is forbidden by Islam. Al-Mughîrah came back to him the following morning and said: "I gave you that advice yesterday, but then I reconsidered and realized that it was not right and was not good advice. You were right." 'Alî replied: "Indeed, no. I know that the advice you gave me yesterday was good advice and that you are deceiving me today. However, regard for the truth prevented me from following your good advice (of yesterday)." [320] To such a degree were these early Muslims concerned with improving their religion at the expense of their worldly affairs, while we

---

[319] This was one of the three sons of 'Alî's brother, Ja'far b. Abî Ṭâlib, presumably Muḥammad, who was implicated in 'Uthmân's death, according to aṭ-Ṭabarî. Ibn Kathîr, *Bidâyah*, VII, 176, mentions 'Abdallâh b. az-Zubayr in this connection, but makes no reference to Ibn Ja'far.

[320] Cf. al-Mas'ûdî, *Murûj adh-dhahab*, IV, 299 ff.

Patch our worldly affairs by tearing our religion to pieces.
Thus, neither our religion lasts nor (the worldly affairs)
we have been patching.[320a]

It [321] has thus been shown how the form of government came to be royal authority. However, there remained the traits that are characteristic of the caliphate, namely, preference for Islam and its ways, and adherence to the path of truth. A change became apparent only in the restraining influence that had been Islam and now came to be group feeling and the sword. That was the situation in the time of Mu'âwiyah, Marwân, his son 'Abd-al-Malik, and the first 'Abbâsid caliphs down to ar-Rashîd and some of his sons. Then, the characteristic traits of the caliphate disappeared, and only its name remained. The form of government came to be royal authority pure and simple. Superiority attained the limits of its nature and was employed for particular (worthless) purposes, such as the use of force and the arbitrary gratification of desires and for pleasure.

This was the case with the successors of the sons of 'Abd-al-Malik and the 'Abbâsids after al-Mu'taṣim and al-Mutawakkil. They remained caliphs in name, because the Arab group feeling continued to exist. In these two stages caliphate and royal authority existed side by side. Then, with the disappearance of Arab group feeling and the annihilation of the (Arab) race and complete destruction of (Arabism), the caliphate lost its identity. The form of gov- I, *376*
ernment remained royal authority pure and simple.

This was the case, for instance, with the non-Arab rulers in the East. They showed obedience to the caliph in order to enjoy the blessings (involved in that), but the royal au-

[320a] The verse is ascribed to Abû l-'Atâhiyah by Ibn 'Abdrabbih, *'Iqd*, III, 285, and by ar-Râghib al-Iṣfahânî, *Muḥâḍarât*, I, 325. Other sources introduce it as a verse recited by the famous saint and mystic Ibrâhîm b. Adham. Cf. Ibn Qutaybah, *'Uyûn*, II, 330; al-Bayhaqî, *Maḥâsin*, ed. F. Schwally (Giessen, 1902), p. 390; al-Ghazzâlî, *Iḥyâ'*, III, 155.

[321] Cf. Issawi, pp. 137 f.

thority belonged to them with all its titles and attributes. The caliph had no share in it. The same was done by the Zanâtah rulers in the Maghrib. The Ṣinhâjah, for instance, had such a relationship with the 'Ubaydid(-Fâṭimids), and the Maghrâwah and also the Banû Yafran (Ifren) with the Umayyad caliphs in Spain and the 'Ubaydid(-Fâṭimids) in al-Qayrawân.

It is thus clear that the caliphate at first existed without royal authority. Then, the characteristic traits of the caliphate became mixed up and confused. Finally, when its group feeling had separated from the group feeling of the caliphate, royal authority came to exist alone.

God determines night and day.[322]

[27] *The meaning of the oath of allegiance.*

It [323] should be known that the *bay'ah* (oath of allegiance) is a contract to render obedience. It is as though the person who renders the oath of allegiance made a contract with his amir, to the effect that he surrenders supervision of his own affairs and those of the Muslims to him and that he will not contest his authority in any of (those affairs) and that he will obey him by (executing) all the duties with which he might be charged, whether agreeable or disagreeable.

When people rendered the oath of allegiance to the amir and concluded the contract, they put their hands into his hand to confirm the contract. This was considered to be something like the action of buyer and seller (after concluding a sale). Therefore, the oath of allegiance was called *bay'ah*, the infinitive of *bâ'a* "to sell (or buy)." The *bay'ah* was a handshake. Such is its meaning in customary linguistic terminology and the accepted usage of the religious law. It also is the meaning of *bay'ah* in the traditions concerning the oath of allegiance rendered to the Prophet on the night of

[322] Cf. Qur'ân 73.20 (20).
[323] Cf. G. Surdon and L. Bercher, *Recueil de textes de sociologie*, pp. 74 f.

al-'Aqabah and at the Tree,[324] and wherever else the word occurs.

The word is used for "oath of allegiance to the caliphs" and in *aymân al-bay'ah* "declarations (of loyalty) in connection with the oath of allegiance." The caliphs used to exact an oath when the contract was made and collected the declarations (of loyalty) from all Muslims. This then was called *aymân al-bay'ah* "declarations (of loyalty) in connection with the oath of allegiance." It was as a rule obtained by compulsion. Therefore, when Mâlik pronounced the legal decision that a declaration obtained by compulsion was invalid, the men in power (at the time) disliked (the decision) and considered it an attack upon the declarations (of loyalty) made in connection with the oath of allegiance. The imam (Mâlik), as a result, suffered his well-known tribulations.[325]

I, 377

The oath of allegiance that is common at present is the royal Persian custom of greeting kings by kissing the earth (in front of them), or their hand, their foot, or the lower hem of their garment. The term *bay'ah*, which means a contract to render obedience, was used metaphorically to denote this (custom), since such an abject form of greeting and politeness is one of the consequences and concomitants of obedience. (The usage) has become so general that it has become customary and has replaced the handshake which was originally used, because shaking hands with everybody meant that the ruler lowered himself and made himself cheap, things that are detrimental to leadership and the dignity of the royal position. However, (the handshake is practiced) by a very few rulers who want to show themselves humble and who, therefore, themselves shake hands with their nobles and with famous divines among their subjects.

This customary meaning of the oath of allegiance should

[324] The 'Aqabah was the place where Muḥammad met with the Medinese in preparation for his departure from Mecca. The so-called *Bay'at ar-riḍwân*, under the tree, took place in 627. Cf. Ibn Hishâm, *Sîrah*, p. 746.

[325] Cf. J. Schacht in *EI*, *s.v.* "Mâlik b. Anas."

be understood. A person must know it, because it imposes upon him certain duties toward his ruler and imam. His actions will thus not be frivolous or gratuitous. This should be taken into consideration in one's dealings with rulers.

God "is strong and mighty." [326]

[28] *The succession.*

It should be known that we have been discussing the imamate and mentioned the fact that it is part of the religious
I, 378 law because it serves the (public) interest. (We have stated) that its real meaning is the supervision of the interests of the (Muslim) nation in both their worldly and their religious affairs.[327] (The caliph) is the guardian and trustee of (the Muslims). He looks after their (affairs) as long as he lives. It follows that he should also look after their (affairs) after his death, and, therefore, should appoint someone to take charge of their affairs as he had done (while alive), whom they can trust to look after them as they had trusted him then.

(Such appointment of a successor) is recognized as part of the religious law through the consensus of the (Muslim) nation, (which says) that it is permissible and binding when it occurs. Thus, Abû Bakr appointed 'Umar as his successor in the presence of the men around Muḥammad. They considered (this appointment) permissible and considered themselves obliged by it to render obedience to 'Umar. Likewise, 'Umar appointed six persons, the remnant of the ten (men to whom Paradise had been guaranteed),[328] to be members of (an electoral) council (*shûrâ*), and he put it up to them to make the choice for the Muslims. Each one deferred to (the judgment) of the next man, until it was the turn of 'Abd-ar-

---

[326] Qur'ân 11.66 (69); 42.19 (18).

[327] Cf., for instance, pp. 387 and 399, above.

[328] The men of the *shûrâ* were 'Uthmân, 'Alî, Ṭalḥah, az-Zubayr, Sa'd b. Abî Waqqâṣ, and 'Abd-ar-Raḥmân b. 'Awf. Of the ten men to whom Paradise was guaranteed (cf. n. 165 to Ibn Khaldûn's Introduction, above), Sa'îd b. Zayd, usually considered to have been one of them, was also still alive when 'Uthmân became caliph.

Raḥmân b. ʻAwf. He applied his independent judgment and discussed the matter with the Muslims. He found that they agreed upon ʻUthmân and ʻAlî. He (himself) preferred ʻUthmân as the person to receive the oath of allegiance, because (ʻUthmân) agreed with him concerning the obligation to follow the example of the two *shaykhs* (Abû Bakr and ʻUmar) in every case, without making use of his independent judgment. Thus, ʻUthmân was confirmed, and it was considered necessary to obey him. A great number of the men around Muḥammad were present on the first and on the second (occasion).[329] None of them expressed the slightest disapproval. This shows that they were agreed upon the correctness of the procedure and recognized its legality. It is recognized that consensus constitutes proof.

No suspicion of the imam is justified in this connection, even if he appoints his father or his son his successor. He is trusted to look after the affairs of the Muslims as long as he lives. He is all the more responsible for not tolerating while he is (alive the possibility that there might arise evil) developments after his death. This is against those who say that (the imam) is suspect with regard to (the appointment of) his son or father, and also against those who consider him suspect with regard to (appointment of) his son only, not his father. In fact, he could hardly be suspected in this I, *379*
respect in any way. Especially if there exists some reason for (the appointment of a successor), such as desire to promote the (public) interest or fear that some harm might arise (if no successor were appointed), suspicion of the imam is out of the question.

This, for instance, was the case with Muʻâwiyah's appointment of his son Yazîd.[330] The action met with agreement of the people, and, therefore, is in itself an argument for the problem under discussion (namely, that the imam is not suspect with regard to whomever he might appoint). But

---

[329] That is, when the appointments of ʻUmar and of ʻUthmân were decided.

[330] Cf. pp. 422 f., above, and pp. 434 f., below.

Mu'âwiyah himself preferred his son Yazîd to any other successor, because he was concerned with the (public) interest of preserving unity and harmony among the people, (and realized that he could achieve this purpose only by appointing Yazîd), since the men who possessed executive authority, that is, the Umayyads, agreed at that time upon Yazîd. The Umayyads were then agreeable to no one except (Yazîd). The Umayyads constituted the core (group) of the Quraysh and of all the Muslims, and possessed superiority (Mu'âwiyah,) therefore, preferred (Yazîd) to anyone else who might have been considered more suited for the caliphate. He passed over the superior person in favor of the inferior one,[331] because he desired to preserve agreement and harmony, which is the more important thing in the opinion of the Lawgiver (Muḥammad). No other motive could be expected of Mu'âwiyah. His probity and the fact that he was one of the men around Muḥammad preclude any other explanation. The presence of the men around Muḥammad on that occasion and their silence are the best argument against doubt in this matter. They were not persons to tolerate the slightest negligence in matters of the truth, nor was Mu'âwiyah one of those who are too proud to accept the truth. They were all above that, and their probity precludes it. The fact that 'Abdallâh b. 'Umar avoided the issue must be ascribed to his general avoidance of participation in any business, whether permissible or forbidden. He is well known for this (kind of attitude). Ibn az-Zubayr was the only one left to oppose (Mu'âwiyah's) appointment, upon which the great mass had agreed. Small minorities of persons holding divergent opinions, it is well known, (are treated by jurists as not authoritative).

I, 380 After Mu'âwiyah, caliphs who were used to choose the truth and to act in accordance with it, acted similarly. Such caliphs included the Umayyads 'Abd-al-Malik and Sulaymân and the 'Abbâsids as-Saffâḥ, al-Manṣûr, al-Mahdî, and ar-

[331] Cf. p. 405, above.

Rashîd, and others like them whose probity, and whose care and concern for the Muslims are well known. They cannot be blamed because they gave preference to their own sons and brothers, in that respect departing from the Sunnah of the first four caliphs. Their situation was different from that of the (four) caliphs, who lived in a time when royal authority as such did not yet exist, and the (sole) restraining influence was religious. Thus, everybody had his restraining influence in himself. Consequently, they appointed the person who was acceptable to Islam, and preferred him over all others. They trusted everybody who aspired to (the caliphate) to have his own restraining influence.

After them, from Mu'âwiyah on, the group feeling (of the Arabs) approached its final goal, royal authority. The restraining influence of religion had weakened. The restraining influence of government and group was needed. If, under those circumstances, someone not acceptable to the group had been appointed as successor (to the caliphate), such an appointment would have been rejected by it. The (chances of the appointee) would have been quickly demolished, and the community would have been split and torn by dissension.

Someone asked 'Alî: "Why do the people disagree concerning you, and why did they not disagree concerning Abû Bakr and 'Umar?" 'Alî replied: "Because Abû Bakr and 'Umar were in charge of men like me, and I today am in charge of men like you." [331a] He referred to the restraining influence of Islam.

When al-Ma'mûn appointed 'Alî b. Mûsâ b. Ja'far aṣ-Ṣâdiq his successor and called him ar-Riḍâ, the 'Abbâsids greatly disapproved of the action. They declared invalid the oath of allegiance that had been rendered to al-Ma'mûn, and took the oath of allegiance to his uncle Ibrâhîm b. al-Mahdî.

[331a] Ibn Qutaybah, *'Uyûn*, I, 9, ascribes a similar remark to the caliph 'Abd-al-Malik b. Marwân, who said: "Be fair to me, O my subjects. You want me to act like Abû Bakr and 'Umar, while you do not act like the subjects of Abû Bakr and 'Umar. . . ."

I, 381 There was so much trouble, dissension, and interruption of communications, and there were so many rebels and seceders, that the state almost collapsed.[332] Eventually, al-Ma'mûn went from Khurâsân to Baghdad and brought matters back to their former conditions.

Such (differences as the one just cited between caliphate and royal authority) must be taken into consideration in connection with (the problem of) succession. Times differ according to differences in affairs, tribes, and group feelings, which come into being during those (times). Differences in this respect produce differences in (public) interests, and each (public interest) has its own particular laws. This is a kindness shown by God to His servants.

However, Islam does not consider preservation of (the ruler's) inheritance for his children the proper purpose in appointing a successor. The (succession to the rule) is something that comes from God who distinguishes by it whomsoever He wishes.

It is necessary in (appointing a successor) to be as well-intentioned as possible. Otherwise, there is danger that one may trifle with religious institutions.

God's is the kingdom (royal authority).[333] He gives it to those of His servants to whom He wants to give it.

There are some matters in this connection which need explanation.

First: There is the wickedness Yazîd displayed when he was caliph. One should beware of thinking that Mu'âwiyah could have known about it. Mu'âwiyah's probity and virtue were too great. While he lived, he censured Yazîd for listening to music and forbade him to do it, and (listening to music) is a lesser sin than (Yazîd's later wickedness) and is judged differently by the different schools.

When Yazîd's well-known wickedness showed itself, the men around Muḥammad disagreed about what to do with

---

[332] Cf. pp. 324 ff., above.

[333] Cf., for instance, Qur'ân 22.56 (55).

him. Some were of the opinion that they should revolt against him and declare the oath of allegiance that had been rendered to him invalid on account of (his wickedness). This was the attitude taken by al-Ḥusayn, 'Abdallâh b. az-Zubayr, and others. Others rejected that (course of action), because it threatened to stir up a revolt and to cause much bloodshed. In addition, (they knew that) they would be too weak to achieve success. Yazîd's strength at that time lay in the Umayyad group feeling and in the Qurashite majority who exercised all executive authority. It was they who controlled the group feeling of all the Muḍar. Thus, they possessed I, 382
greater strength than anyone else, and no resistance to them was possible. Therefore, (the above-mentioned persons knew that they) were not in a position to do anything against Yazîd. They prayed that he might find guidance or that they might be relieved of him. This was the course the majority of the Muslims followed. Both parties (of the opposition to Yazîd) used their independent judgment. Neither of them may be considered at fault. It is well known that all their intentions were determined by piety and championship of the truth. May God enable us to follow their model.

Second: There is the matter of the appointment of a successor by the Prophet. The Shî'ah claim that Muḥammad appointed 'Alî his heir. This is not correct. No leading transmitter of traditions has reported such a thing. It is stated in (the sound tradition of) the *Ṣaḥîḥ* that Muḥammad asked for ink and paper in order to write his will, and that 'Umar prevented it.[334] This clearly shows that (the appointment of 'Alî as successor) did not take place.

There also is the following statement by 'Umar, made after he had been stabbed and when he was asked about appointing a successor: "Were I to appoint a successor, it would be because someone who is better than I appointed a successor"—meaning Abû Bakr—"and were I not to appoint a successor, it would be because someone who is better

[334] Cf. al-Bukhârî, *Ṣaḥîḥ*, I, 41; *Handbook*, p. 161*a*.

than I did not" – meaning the Prophet.[335] And the men around Muḥammad were present and agreed with him that the Prophet [336] had not appointed a successor.

There is also the statement of 'Alî to al-'Abbâs. Al-'Abbâs invited 'Alî to go in to the Prophet (with him), and they both were to ask the Prophet how they stood with regard to being appointed as his successor. 'Alî, however, refused and said: "If he keeps us from (the caliphate), we cannot hope ever to get it." [337] This shows that 'Alî knew that Muḥammad had not made a will and had not appointed anyone his successor.

The doubt of the Imâmîyah in this matter is caused by
I, 383 the fact that they assume the imamate to be one of the pillars of the faith.[338] This is not so. It is one of the general (public) interests. The people are delegated to take care of it. If it were one of the pillars of the faith, it would be something like prayer, and (Muḥammad) would have appointed a representative (caliph), exactly as he appointed Abû Bakr to represent him at prayer. (Had he done so,) it would have become generally known, as was the case with the matter of prayer. That the men around Muḥammad considered the caliphate as something analogous to prayer and on the strength of that attitude argued in favor of Abû Bakr's caliphate, saying, "The Messenger of God found him acceptable for our religion. So, why should we not accept him for our worldly affairs?" [339] is merely another proof of the fact that no appointment of an heir had taken place. It also shows that the question of the imamate and succession to it was not as important then as it is today. Group feeling, which determines unity and disunity in the customary course of affairs, was not of the same significance then (as it was later

---

[335] As reported in all the historians. Cf., for instance, aṭ-Ṭabarî, *Annales*, I, 2777; Ibn Hishâm, *Sîrah*, p. 1010.

[336] The beginning of this sentence is not found in Bulaq and B, but appears in A, C, and D.

[337] Cf. *Handbook*, p. 1*b*.

[338] Cf. p. 402, above.

[339] Cf. also p. 450, below.

on). (At that time,) Islam was winning the hearts of the people and causing them to be willing to die for it in a way that disrupted the customary course of affairs. That happened because people observed with their own eyes the presence of angels to help them, the repeated appearance of heavenly messages among them, and the constant (Qur'ânic) recitation of divine pronouncements to them in connection with every happening. Thus, it was not necessary to pay any attention to group feeling. Men generally had the coloring of submissiveness and obedience. They were thoroughly frightened and perturbed by a sequence of extraordinary miracles and other divine happenings, and by frequent visitations of angels.[340] Such questions as that of the caliphate, of royal authority, succession, group feeling, and other such matters, were submerged in this turmoil the way it happened.

These helpful (circumstances) passed with the disappearance of miracles and the death of the generations that had *I, 384* witnessed them with their own eyes. The coloring mentioned changed little by little. The impression the wonders had made passed, and affairs took again their ordinary course. The influence of group feeling and of the ordinary course of affairs manifested itself in the resulting good and bad institutions. The (questions of) caliphate and royal authority and that of the succession to both became very important affairs in the opinion of the people. It had not been this way before. It should be noted how unimportant the caliphate was in the time of the Prophet, (so unimportant that) he did not appoint a successor to it. Its importance then increased somewhat during the time of the (early) caliphs because there arose certain needs in connection with military protection, the holy war, the apostasy (of Arab tribes after Muḥammad's death), and the conquests. The (first caliphs) could decide whether they would (appoint successors) or not. We mentioned this on the authority of 'Umar. Subsequently, as at the present time, the matter has become most important in connection with harmony in (military) protection and the

[340] Cf. p. 444, below.

administration of public interests. Group feeling has come to play a role in it. (Group feeling is) the secret divine (factor that) restrains people from splitting up and abandoning each other. It is the source of unity and agreement, and the guarantor of the intentions and laws of Islam. When this is understood, God's wise plans with regard to His creation and His creatures will become clear.[341]

Third: There are the wars that took place in Islam among the men around Muḥammad and the men of the second generation. It should be known that their differences concerned religious matters only, and arose from independent interpretation of proper arguments and considered insights. Differences may well arise among people who use independent judgment. Now, we may say that in the case of problems that are open to independent judgment, the truth can lie only on one side, and that he who does not hit upon it is in error. But, since it has not been clearly indicated by general consensus on which side (the truth lies), every side may be as-
I, *385* sumed to be right. The side that is in error is not clearly indicated, either. To declare all sides to be at fault is not acceptable according to the general consensus. Again, we may say that all sides have the true answer and that "everybody who uses independent judgment is right." [342] Then, it is all the more necessary to deny that any one side was in error or ought to be considered at fault.

The differences between the men around Muḥammad and the men of the second generation were no more than differences in the independent interpretation of equivocal religious problems, and they have to be considered in this light. Differences of the sort that have arisen in Islam include those (1) between 'Alî on the one hand, and Mu'âwiyah, as well as az-Zubayr, Ṭalḥah, and 'Â'ishah on the other, (2) between al-Ḥusayn and Yazîd, and (3) between Ibn az-Zubayr and 'Abd-al-Malik.

---

[341] The last sentence is not found in Bulaq or Paris.

[342] This is a well-known legal maxim. Cf. also J. Schacht, *The Origins of Muslim Jurisprudence*, p. 128.

(1) As for the case of 'Alî, (the following may be said:) When 'Uthmân was killed, the (important Muslims) were dispersed over the various cities. Thus, they were not present when the oath of allegiance was rendered to 'Alî. Of those who were present, some rendered the oath of allegiance to him. Others, however, waited until the people should come together and agree upon an imam. Among those who waited were, for instance, Sa'd (b. Abî Waqqâṣ), Sa'îd (b. Zayd), ('Abdallâh) b. 'Umar, Usâmah b. Zayd, al-Mughîrah b. Shu'bah, 'Abdallâh b. Salâm, Qudâmah b. Maẓ'ûn, Abû Sa'îd (Sa'd b. Mâlik) al-Khudrî, Ka'b b. 'Ujrah, Ka'b b. Mâlik, an-Nu'mân b. Bashîr, Ḥassân b. Thâbit, Maslamah b. Makhlad,[343] Fuḍâlah b. 'Ubayd, and other important personalities from among the men around Muḥammad. Those who were in the various cities also refrained from rendering the oath of allegiance to 'Alî and were in favor of seeking revenge for 'Uthmân, and so they left matters in a state of anarchy. Eventually, the Muslims formed an (electoral) council (*shûrâ*) to determine whom they should appoint. They suspected 'Alî of negligence when he kept silent and did not help 'Uthmân against his murderers, but they did not suspect him of having actually conspired against 'Uthmân. That would be unthinkable. When Mu'âwiyah openly reproached 'Alî, his accusation was directed exclusively against his keeping I, *386*
silent.

Later on, they had differences. 'Alî was of the opinion that the oath of allegiance that had been rendered to him was binding and obligatory upon those who had not yet rendered it, because the people had agreed upon (rendering the oath) in Medina, the residence of the Prophet and the home of the men around Muḥammad. He thought of postponing 'Uthmân's revenge until unity was established among the people and the whole thing was well organized. Then it would be feasible. Others were of the opinion that the oath of allegiance rendered to 'Alî was not binding, because the men around

[343] Or Mukhallad (?). Cf. Ibn Ḥajar, *Tahdhîb*, X, 148.

Muḥammad who controlled the executive power were dispersed all over the world and only a few had been present (when the oath to 'Alî was rendered). (They thought that) an oath of allegiance requires the agreement of all the men who control the executive power and that there was no obligation to confirm a person who had received it from others or merely from a minority of those men. (Thus, they thought that) the Muslims were at the time in a state of anarchy and should first seek revenge for 'Uthmân and then agree upon an imam. This opinion was held by Mu'âwiyah, by 'Amr b. al-'Âṣ, by the Mother of the Muslims, 'Â'ishah, by az-Zubayr and his son 'Abdallâh, by Ṭalḥah and his son Muḥammad, by Sa'd, by Sa'îd, by an-Nu'mân b. Bashîr, by Mu'âwiyah b. Ḥudayj, and by others among the men around Muḥammad who followed the opinion of those mentioned and who hesitated, as we have mentioned, to render the oath of allegiance to 'Alî in Medina.

However, the men of the second period after them agreed that the oath of allegiance rendered to 'Alî had been binding and obligatory upon all Muslims. They considered ('Alî's) opinion the correct one and clearly indicated that the error was on Mu'âwiyah's side and on that of those who were of his opinion, especially Ṭalḥah and az-Zubayr, who broke with 'Alî after having rendered the oath of allegiance to him, as has been reported. Still, it was not considered acceptable to declare both parties at fault, for such a thing is not done in
I, 387 cases of independent judgment. It is well known that such became the general consensus among the men of the second period as to one of the two opinions held by the men of the first period. 'Alî (himself), when asked about those who had died in the Battle of the Camel and the Battle of Ṣiffîn, replied: "By God, all of them who die with pure heart will be admitted by God to paradise." He referred to both parties. This remark was reported by aṭ-Ṭabarî and by others.[344]

The probity of none of these men should be doubted. No

[344] Cf. aṭ-Ṭabarî, *Annales*, I, 3167.

aspersion should be cast on them in this connection. It is well known who they were. Their words and deeds are models to be followed. Their probity is perfect, in the view of orthodox Muslim opinion. The only exception would be a statement by the Mu'tazilah with regard to those who fought 'Alî,[345] but no true believer pays attention to this statement or stoops to consider it seriously. He who looks at the matter impartially will find excusable, not only the differences among all the people (the Muslims) with regard to the affair of 'Uthmân, but also all the subsequent differences among the men around Muḥammad. He will realize that (these quarrels) were temptations inflicted by God upon the Muslim nation, while He vanquished the enemies of the Muslims and made the Muslims rulers of the lands and country of their enemies, and while they established cities in the border territories, in al-Baṣrah and al-Kûfah (the 'Irâq), in Syria, and in Egypt.

Most of the Arabs who settled in those cities were uncivilized. They had made little use of the Prophet's company and had not been improved by his way of life and manners, nor had they been trained in his qualities of character. Moreover, they had been uncivilized in pre-Islamic times, had been possessed by group feeling and overbearing pride, and had been remote from the soothing influence of the faith. When the (Muslim) dynasty came to be powerful, (these Arabs) were dominated by (Meccan) emigrants and (Medinese) Anṣâr, belonging to the Quraysh, the Kinânah, the Thaqîf, the Hudhayl, and the inhabitants of the Ḥijâz and Yathrib (Medina), who had been first to adopt the faith of Islam. They were scornful and disliked the situation. They I, 388
saw that they themselves possessed the older pedigree and the greater numerical strength, and that they had beaten the Persians and Byzantines. They belonged to such tribes as the Bakr b. Wâ'il, the 'Abd-al-Qays b. Rabî'ah, the Kindah and the Azd of the Yemen, the Tamîm and the Qays of the

[345] In general, the Mu'tazilah held to the theory that both parties were wrong. Cf. H. S. Nyberg in *EI*, *s.v.* "al-Mu'tazila."

Muḍar, among others. They grew scornful of the Quraysh and overbearing against them. They weakened in their obedience to them. They gave as the reason for their (attitude) the unjust treatment they received from them. They sought protection against them. They accused them (the Quraysh, etc.) of being too weak for military expeditions and of being unfair in distributing (the booty).

These complaints spread and reached the Medinese with their well-known attitude. They considered the matter important and informed 'Uthmân about it. He sent to the cities to get reliable information. He sent ('Abdallâh) b. 'Umar, Muḥammad b. Maslamah, Usâmah b. Zayd, and others. They noticed nothing in the (conduct of the) amirs (of the cities) that might call for disapproval, and found no fault with them. They reported the situation (to 'Uthmân) as they saw it. But the accusations on the part of the inhabitants of the cities did not stop. The slanderous stories and rumors grew continually. Al-Walîd b. 'Uqbah, the governor of al-Kûfah, was accused of drinking wine. A large number of Kûfians testified against him, and 'Uthmân punished him (as required by the religious law) and deposed him. Then, some of the people of those cities came to Medina to ask for the removal of the governors. They complained to 'Alî, 'Â'ishah, az-Zubayr, and Ṭalḥah. 'Uthmân deposed some of the governors, but the people still continued their criticisms. Then, Sa'îd b. al-'Âṣ, the governor of al-Kûfah, went on a mission (to 'Uthmân). When he returned, he was intercepted by (the Kûfians) on the road and sent back deposed. Then differences broke out between 'Uthmân and the men around Muḥammad
I, *389* who were with him in Medina. They resented his refusal to depose (his officials), but he did not want to (depose them) except for cause.

They then shifted their disapproval to other actions of ('Uthmân's). He followed his own independent judgment, and they did the same. Then, a mob banded together and went to Medina, ostensibly in order to obtain redress of their grievances from 'Uthmân. In fact, they thought of killing him. There were people from al-Baṣrah, al-Kûfah, and Egypt among them. 'Alî, 'Â'ishah, az-Zubayr, Ṭalḥah, and others took their side, attempting to quiet things down and to get 'Uthmân to accept their view of the situation. He deposed the governor of Egypt, and the people who had come to Medina left, but then, after having gone only a short distance, they came back. They had been deceived, they believed, by a forged letter which they had found in the hand of a messenger who was carrying it to the governor of Egypt. (The letter stated) that they were to be killed (upon their return to Egypt). 'Uthmân swore that (the letter was not genuine), but they said: "Let us have your secretary Marwân." Marwân, too, swore (that he had not written the letter). Then 'Uthmân said: "No more evidence is needed." Thereupon, however, they besieged 'Uthmân in his house. They fell upon him in the night when (his defenders) were not careful, and killed him. That opened the door to the (ensuing) trouble.

All the (persons involved in the affair of 'Uthmân) can be excused in connection with the occurrence. All of them were concerned with Islam and were not neglectful with regard to any aspect connected with the Muslim religion. After the event, they considered the matter and applied their independent judgment. God observes their circumstances. He knows these men. We can only think the best of them. What we know about their conditions, as well as the statements of the Speaker of the Truth (Muḥammad praising those men), require us to do so.

(2) As to (the case of) al-Ḥusayn, (the following may be said:) When the great mass of Yazîd's contemporaries saw his wickedness, the Shî'ah in al-Kûfah invited al-Ḥusayn to come to them, saying that they would take his side. Al-Ḥusayn was of the opinion that a revolt against Yazîd was clearly indicated as a duty, because of his wickedness. (That I, 390
duty, he felt,) was especially incumbent upon those who had the power to execute it. He felt that he had (that power) in

view of his qualifications and strength. His qualifications were as good as he thought, and better. But, regrettably enough, he was mistaken with regard to his strength. The group feeling of the Muḍar was in the Quraysh, that of the Quraysh in 'Abd-Manâf, and that of 'Abd-Manâf in the Umayyads. The Quraysh and all the others conceded this fact and were not ignorant of it. At the beginning of Islam, it had been forgotten. People were diverted by fearful wonders and by the Revelation, and by frequent visitations of angels in aid of the Muslims.[346] Thus, they had neglected their customary affairs, and the group feeling and aspirations of pre-Islamic times had disappeared and were forgotten. Only the natural group feeling, serving the purpose of military protection and defense, had remained and was used to advantage in the establishment of Islam and the fight against the polytheists. The religion became well established in (this situation). The customary course of affairs was inoperative, until prophecy and the terrifying wonders stopped. Then, the customary course of affairs resumed to some degree. Group feeling reverted to its former status and came back to those to whom it had formerly belonged. In consequence of their previous state of obedience, the Muḍar became more obedient to the Umayyads than to others.

Thus, al-Ḥusayn's error has become clear. It was, however, an error with respect to a worldly matter, where an error does not do any harm.[347] From the point of view of the religious law, he did not err, because here everything depended on what he thought, which was that he had the power to (revolt against Yazîd). Ibn 'Abbâs, Ibn az-Zubayr, Ibn 'Umar, (al-Ḥusayn's) brother Ibn al-Ḥanafîyah, and others, criticized (al-Ḥusayn) because of his trip to al-Kûfah. They realized his mistake, but he did not desist from the enterprise he had begun, because God wanted it to be so.

The men around Muḥammad other than al-Ḥusayn, in the
I, *391* Ḥijâz and with Yazîd in Syria and in the 'Irâq, and their fol-

[346] Cf. p. 437, above.

[347] And has no consequence upon one's welfare in the other world.

lowers, were of the opinion that a revolt against Yazîd, even though he was wicked, would not be permissible, because such a revolt would result in trouble and bloodshed. They refrained from it and did not follow al-Ḥusayn (in his opinion), but they also did not disapprove of him and did not consider him at fault. For he had independent judgment, being the model of all who ever had independent judgment. One should not fall into the error of declaring these people to be at fault because they opposed al-Ḥusayn and did not come to his aid. They constituted the majority of the men around Muḥammad. They were with Yazîd, and they were of the opinion that they should not revolt against him. Al-Ḥusayn, fighting at Kerbelâ', asked them to attest to his excellence and the correctness of his position. He said: "Ask Jâbir b. 'Abdallâh, Abû Sa'îd (al-Khudrî), Anas b. Mâlik, Sahl b. Sa'd, Zayd b. Arqam, and others." [348] Thus, he did not disapprove of their not coming to his help. He did not interfere in this matter, because he knew that they were acting according to their own independent judgment. For his part, he also acted according to independent judgment.

Likewise, one should not fall into the error of declaring that his murder was justified because (it also) was the result of independent judgment, even if (one grants that) he (on his part) exercised the (correct) [349] independent judgment. This, then, would be a situation comparable to that of Shâfi'ites and Mâlikites applying their legal punishment for drinking date liquor (*nabîdh*) [350] to Ḥanafites. It should be known that the matter is not so. The independent judgment of those men did not involve fighting against al-Ḥusayn, even if it involved opposition to his revolt. Yazîd and the men around him [351] were the only ones who (actually) fought

[348] Cf. aṭ-Ṭabarî, *Annales*, II, 329. The argument is that if al-Ḥusayn had disapproved of the attitude of these men, he would not have referred to their opinion of him as authoritative.

[349] The word "correct" is found in C but deleted there. It appears in D.

[350] Cf. n. 98 to Ibn Khaldûn's Introduction, above.

[351] That is, Yazîd's henchmen, who are to be distinguished from the men around Muḥammad who were with Yazîd.

against (al-Ḥusayn). It should not be said that if Yazîd was wicked and yet these (men around Muḥammad) did not consider it permissible to revolt against him, his actions were in their opinion binding and right. It should be known that only those actions of the wicked are binding that are legal. The (authorities) consider it a condition of fighting evildoers that any such fighting be undertaken with a just (*'âdil*) imam. This does not apply to the question under consideration.
I, 392 Thus, it was not permissible to fight against al-Ḥusayn with Yazîd or on Yazîd's behalf. In matter of fact, (Yazîd's fight against al-Ḥusayn) was one of the actions that confirmed his wickedness. Al-Ḥusayn, therefore, was a martyr who will receive his reward. He was right, and he exercised independent judgment. The men around Muḥammad who were with Yazîd [352] were also right, and they exercised independent judgment. Judge Abû Bakr b. al-'Arabî al-Mâlikî [353] erred when he made the following statement in his book *al-Qawâṣim wa-l-'Awâṣim:* "Al-Ḥusayn was killed according to the law of his grandfather (Muḥammad)." Ibn al-'Arabî fell into that error because he overlooked the condition of the "just (*'âdil*) imam" which governs the fighting against sectarians.

(3) Ibn az-Zubayr felt about his revolt as al-Ḥusayn had (about his). He was under the same impression (as al-Ḥusayn regarding his qualifications). But his error with regard to his power was greater (than that of al-Ḥusayn). The Banû Asad were no match for the Umayyads in either pre-Islamic or Islamic times. It does not apply in the case of Ibn Zubayr, as it does in the case of Mu'âwiyah against

---

[352] Who did not help al-Ḥusayn but did not do the actual fighting, the guilt for which rests only upon Yazîd and his henchmen.

[353] Muḥammad b. 'Abdallâh, 469–543 [1076/77–1148]. Cf. *GAL*, I, 412 f.; *Suppl.*, I, 632 f., 732 f. Cf. also below, n. 1123 to Ch. VI, and 3:303. The statement shocked some later scholars; cf. F. Rosenthal, *A History of Muslim Historiography*, p. 299. It is contained in the selection from Ibn al-'Arabî's work published under the title of *al-'Awâṣim min al-qawâṣim* (Cairo, 1371/1952), p. 232.

'Alî, that the error is expressly indicated to lie on his opponent's side. In (the case of Mu'âwiyah against 'Alî), the general consensus has decided the question for us.[354] In (the case of Ibn az-Zubayr), we do not have (a general consensus). The fact that Yazîd was in error was expressly indicated by the fact of Yazîd's wickedness, but 'Abd-al-Malik, who had to deal with Ibn az-Zubayr, possessed greater probity than anybody else. It is sufficient proof of his probity that Mâlik used 'Abd-al-Malik's actions as proof,[355] and that Ibn 'Abbâs and Ibn 'Umar rendered the oath of allegiance to 'Abd-al-Malik and left Ibn az-Zubayr with whom they had been together in the Ḥijâz. Furthermore, many of the men around Muḥammad were of the opinion that the oath of allegiance rendered to Ibn az-Zubayr was not binding, because the men who held the executive power were not present, as (they had been) when it was rendered to ('Abd-al-Malik's father) Marwân. Ibn az-Zubayr held the opposite opinion. However, all of them were using independent judgment and were evidently motivated by the truth, even though it is not expressly indicated to have been on one side. Our discussion shows that the killing of Ibn az-Zubayr did not conflict with the basic principles and norms of jurisprudence. I, *393*
Nonetheless, he is a martyr and will receive his reward, because of his (good) intentions and the fact that he chose the truth.

This is the manner in which the actions of the ancient Muslims, the men around Muḥammad and the men of the second generation, have to be judged. They were the best Muslims. If we permitted them to be the target of slander, who could claim probity! The Prophet said: "The best men are those of my generation, then those who follow them,"—repeating the latter sentence two or three times—"Then, falsehood will spread." [356] Thus, he considered goodness,

---

[354] Cf. p. 440, above. [355] Cf. p. 423, above.

[356] Cf. al-Bukhârî, *Ṣaḥîḥ*, II, 416; IV, 124. Cf. also F. Rosenthal, *op. cit.*, p. 256.

that is, probity, a quality peculiar to the first period and to the one that followed it.

One should beware of letting one's mind or tongue become used to criticizing any of (the ancient Muslims). One's heart should not be tempted by doubts concerning anything that happened in connection with them. One should be as truthful as possible in their behalf. They deserve it most. They never differed among themselves except for good reasons. They never killed or were killed except in a holy war, or in helping to make some truth victorious.

It should further be believed that their differences were a source of divine mercy for later Muslims, so that every (later Muslim) can take as his model the old Muslim of his choice and make him his imam, guide, and leader. If this is understood, God's wise plans with regard to His creation and creatures will become clear.

[29] *The functions of the religious institution of the caliphate.*

It [357] has become clear that to be caliph in reality means acting as substitute for the Lawgiver (Muḥammad) with regard to the preservation| of the religion and the political leadership of the world.[358] The Lawgiver was concerned with both things, with religion in his capacity as the person commanded to transmit the duties imposed by the religious laws to the people and to cause them to act in accordance with them, and with worldly political leadership in his capacity as
I, 394 the person in charge of the (public) interests of human civilization.

We have mentioned before that civilization is necessary to human beings and that care for the (public) interests connected with it is likewise (something necessary), if mankind is not to perish of neglect.[359] We have also mentioned before that royal authority and its impetus suffice to create (the

---

[357] Cf. G. Surdon and L. Bercher, *Recueil de textes . . .*, pp. 76–85.
[358] Cf. p. 388, above. [359] Cf. pp. 89 ff., above.

institutions serving) the (public) interest,[360] although they would be more perfect if they were established through religious laws, because (the religious law) has a better understanding of the (public) interests.

Royal authority, if it be Muslim, falls under the caliphate and is one of its concomitants. (The royal authority) of a non-Muslim nation stands alone. But in any case, it has its subordinate ranks and dependent positions which relate to particular functions. The people of the dynasty are given (particular) positions, and each one of them discharges (the duties of) his position as directed by the ruler who controls them all. Thus, the power of the ruler fully materializes, and he is well able to discharge his governmental (duties).

Even though the institution of the caliphate includes royal authority in the sense mentioned, its religious character brings with it special functions and ranks peculiar to the Muslim caliphs. We are going to mention the religious functions peculiar to the caliphate, and we shall come back later on to the functions of royal government.[361]

It should be known that all the religious functions of the religious law, such as prayer, the office of judge, the office of mufti, the holy war, and market supervision (*ḥisbah*) fall under the "great imamate," [362] which is the caliphate. (The caliphate) is a kind of great mainspring and comprehensive basis, and all these (functions) are branches of it and fall under it because of the wide scope of the caliphate, its active interest in all conditions of the Muslim community, both religious and worldly, and its general power to execute the religious laws relative to both (religious and worldly affairs).

(*The leadership of prayer*)

The leadership of prayer is the highest of (all) these functions and higher than royal authority as such, which, I, *395*
like (prayer), falls under the caliphate. This is attested by the

[360] Cf., for instance, pp. 386 ff., above.
[361] Cf. 2:1 ff., below.
[362] Cf. p. 388, above.

(circumstance) that the men around Muḥammad deduced from the fact that Abû Bakr had been appointed (Muḥammad's) representative as prayer leader, the fact that he had also been appointed his representative in political leadership. They said: "The Messenger of God found him acceptable for our religion. So, why should we not accept him for our worldly affairs?" [363] If prayer did not rank higher than political leadership, the analogical reasoning would not have been sound.

If this is established, it should be known that city mosques are of two kinds, great spacious ones which are prepared for holiday [364] prayers, and other, minor ones which are restricted to one section of the population or one quarter of the city and which are not for the generally attended prayers. Care of the great mosques rests with the caliph or with those authorities, wazirs, or judges, to whom he delegates it. A prayer leader for each mosque is appointed for the five daily prayers, the Friday service, the two festivals, the eclipses of (the sun and the moon), and the prayer for rain. This (arrangement) is obligatory only in the sense that it is preferable and better. It also serves the purpose of preventing the subjects from usurping one of the duties of the caliphs connected with the supervision of the general (public) interests. The (arrangement) is considered necessary by those who consider the Friday service necessary, and who, therefore, consider it necessary to have a prayer leader appointed.

Administration of the mosques that are restricted to one section of the population or to one quarter of the city rests with those who live nearby. These mosques do not require the supervision of a caliph or ruler.

The laws and conditions governing the office of (prayer leader) and the person entrusted with it are known from the law books. They are well explained in the books on administration (*al-Aḥkâm as-sulṭânîyah*) by al-Mâwardî [365] and

[363] Cf. p. 436, above.

[364] For *mashhûd*, cf. n. 139 to Ibn Khaldûn's Introduction, and n. 162 to this chapter, above.

[365] 'Alî b. Muḥammad, *ca.* 985–1058. Cf. *GAL*, I, 386; *Suppl.*, I, 668 f.

other authors. We shall not, therefore, mention them at any length. The first caliphs did not delegate the leadership of prayer. The fact that certain of the caliphs were stabbed in the mosque during the call to prayer, being expected (by the assassins to be there) at the prayer times, shows that the caliphs personally led the prayer and were not represented by others. This custom was continued by the Umayyads later on. They considered it their exclusive privilege and a high office to lead the prayer. The story goes that 'Abd-al-Malik said to his doorkeeper (*ḥâjib*): "I have given you the office of keeper of my door, (and you are entitled to turn away anyone) save these three persons: the person in charge of food, because it might spoil if kept back; the person in charge of the call to prayer, because he calls the people to God; and the person in charge of the mails, because delaying the mail might mean the ruin of the remote provinces."[366] I, *396*

Later, when the nature of royal authority, with its qualities of harshness and unequal treatment of the people in their religious and worldly affairs, made itself felt, (the rulers) chose men to represent them as prayer leaders. They reserved for themselves the leadership of prayer at certain times and on general (festive) occasions, such as the two holidays and the Friday service. This was for purposes of display and ostentation. Many of the 'Abbâsid and 'Ubaydid(-Fâṭimid) (caliphs) did this at the beginning of their respective dynasties.

(*The office of mufti*)

As to the office of mufti, the caliph must examine the religious scholars and teachers and entrust it only to those who are qualified for it. He must help them in their task, and he must prevent those who are not qualified for the office

---

[366] Cf. also 2:9, below. A related story is told about Ziyâd b. Abîhi, governor of the 'Irâq under Mu'âwiyah, by al-Jâḥiẓ; cf. *Fî l-ḥijâb*, ed. Ḥ. as-Sandûbî, in *Rasâ'il al-Jâḥiẓ* (Cairo, 1352/1933), p. 158. "The person in charge of the mails" is replaced there by the one in charge of a frontier region, and a fourth category is added, the person who comes at night and can, therefore, be expected to bring urgent news. Cf. also al-'Askarî, *Awâ'il*, Paris, MS. Ar. 5986, fol. 121*b*, and ar-Râghib al-Iṣfahânî, *Muḥâḍarât*, I, 130.

from (becoming muftis). (The office of mufti) is one of the (public) interests of the Muslim religious community. (The caliph) has to take care, lest unqualified persons undertake to act as (mufti) and so lead the people astray.

Teachers have the task of teaching and spreading religious knowledge and of holding classes for that purpose in the mosques. If the mosque is one of the great mosques under the administration of the ruler, where the ruler looks after
I, 397 the prayer leaders, as mentioned before, teachers must ask the ruler for permission to (teach there). If it is one of the general mosques, no permission is needed. However, teachers and muftis must have some restraining influence in themselves that tells them not to undertake something for which they are not qualified, so that they may not lead astray those who ask for the right way or cause to stumble those who want to be guided. A tradition says: "Those of you who most boldly approach the task of giving *fatwâs* are most directly heading toward hell." [367] The ruler, therefore, has supervision over (muftis and teachers) and can give, or deny, them permission to exercise their functions, as may be required by the public interest.

(*The office of judge*)

The office of judge is one of the positions that come under the caliphate. It is an institution that serves the purpose of settling suits and breaking off disputes and dissensions. It proceeds, however, along the lines of the religious laws laid down by the Qur'ân and the Sunnah. Therefore, it is one of the positions that belongs to the caliphate and falls under it generally.

At the beginning of Islam, the caliphs exercised the office of judge personally. They did not permit anyone else to function as judge in any matter. The first caliph to charge

---

[367] Cf. *Concordance*, I, 333*b*, l. 16. For the quotation and the preceding remarks, cf. also the last section of the sixteenth chapter of al-Mâwardî, *al-Aḥkâm as-sulṭânîyah*, p. 180. Cf., further, ar-Râghib al-Iṣfahânî, *Muḥâḍarât*, I, 80.

someone else with exercise of (the office of judge) was 'Umar. He appointed Abû d-Dardâ' [368] to be judge with him in Medina, he appointed Shurayḥ as judge in al-Baṣrah, and Abû Mûsâ al-Ash'arî as judge in al-Kûfah. On appointing (Abû Mûsâ), he wrote him the famous letter that contains all the laws that govern the office of judge, and is the basis of them. He says in it:[369]

> Now, the office of judge is a definite religious duty and a generally followed practice.
>
> Understand the depositions that are made before you, for it is useless to consider a plea that is not valid.
>
> Consider all the people equal before you in your court and in your attention, so that the noble will not expect you to be partial and the humble will not despair of justice from you.
>
> The claimant must produce evidence; from the de- I, 398
> fendant, an oath may be exacted.
>
> Compromise is permissible among Muslims, but not any agreement through which something forbidden would be permitted, or something permitted forbidden.
>
> If you gave judgment yesterday, and today upon reconsideration come to the correct opinion, you should not feel prevented by your first judgment from retracting; for justice is primeval, and it is better to retract than to persist in worthlessness.
>
> Use your brain about matters that perplex you and

[368] His name is said to have been 'Uwaymir b. Zayd. For Shurayḥ, cf. n. 33 to Ch. II, above, and for Abû Mûsâ, n. 304 to this chapter, above. For the three judges mentioned here, see also R. J. H. Gottheil's edition of al-Kindî, *The History of the Egyptian Judges* (Paris, etc., 1908), p. VI. Other sources give other names in this connection.

[369] For the document, which has been shown to be pseudepigraphical, cf. Gottheil, pp. VII f.; D. S. Margoliouth in *Journal of the Royal Asiatic Society* (1910), pp. 307–26; D. Santillana, *Istituzioni di diritto musulmano malichita*, II, 569; E. Tyan, *Histoire de l'organization judiciaire en pays d'Islam*, I, 23 f., 106–113. It is also quoted in Ibn Ḥamdûn, *Tadhkirah*, Topkapusaray, MS. Ahmet III, 2948, Vol. I, fols. 125*b*–126*a*; and Ibn Ukhuwwah, *Ma'âlim al-qurbah*, pp. 202 f. Cf., further, C. Pellat, *Le Milieu baṣrien et la formation de Ǧâḥiẓ* (Paris, 1953), pp. 283 f.

to which neither Qur'ân nor Sunnah seem to apply. Study similar cases and evaluate the situation through analogy with those similar cases.

If a person brings a claim, which he may or may not be able to prove, set a time limit for him. If he brings proof within the time limit, you should allow his claim, otherwise you are permitted to give judgment against him. This is the better way to forestall or clear up any possible doubt.

All Muslims are acceptable as witnesses against each other, except such as have received a punishment [370] provided for by the religious law, such as are proved to have given false witness, and such as are suspected (of partiality) on (the ground of) client status or relationship, for God, praised be He, forgives because of oaths [?] [371] and postpones (punishment) in face of the evidence.

Avoid fatigue and weariness and annoyance at the litigants.

For establishing justice in the courts of justice, God will grant you a rich reward and give you a good reputation. Farewell.

End of 'Umar's letter.

Although the personal exercise of the office of judge was to have been the task of (the caliphs), they entrusted others with it because they were too busy with general politics and too occupied with the holy war, conquests, defense of the border regions, and protection of the center. These were things which could not be undertaken by anyone else because of their great importance. They considered it an easy matter to act as judge in litigation among the people and, therefore,

---

[370] Lit., "received stripes as . . ."

[371] This translation is similar to the one given by Surdon and Bercher: "God forgives when sworn testimony is rendered." That is, oaths and evidence should be treated with the greatest respect, because they are considered decisive in God's eyes. However, we would expect the preposition *min* in this case, instead of *'an*. The other translators follow the simpler text of the other sources, reading "God alone knows the hidden thoughts."

had themselves represented by others in the exercise of (the office of judge), so as to lighten their own (burden). Still, they always entrusted the office only to people who shared in their group feeling either through (common) descent or their status as clients. They did not entrust it to men who were not close to them in this sense. I, 399

The laws and conditions that govern the institution (of the judiciary) are known from works on jurisprudence and, especially, from books on administration (*al-Aḥkâm as-sulṭânîyah*). In the period of the caliphs, the duty of the judge was merely to settle suits between litigants. Gradually, later on, other matters were referred to them more and more often as the preoccupation of the caliphs and rulers with high policy grew. Finally, the office of judge came to include, in addition to the settling of suits, certain general concerns of the Muslims, such as supervision of the property of insane persons, orphans, bankrupts, and incompetents who are under the care of guardians; supervision of wills and mortmain donations and of the marrying of marriageable women without guardians (*walî*) to give them away,[372] according to the opinion of some authorities; supervision of (public) roads and buildings; examination of witnesses, attorneys, and court substitutes,[373] to acquire complete knowledge and full acquaintance relative to their reliability or unreliability. All these things have become part of the position and duties of a judge.

Former caliphs had entrusted the judge with the supervision of torts.[374] This is a position that combines elements both of government power and judicial discretion. It needs a

[372] One of the fundamental requirements for marriage in Islamic law is that the bride must have a *walî*, usually the father or another close relative, to give her away. D adds another phrase before this, namely, "the marrying of marriageable Muslim girls," apparently because the word translated above as "marriageable women" (*ayâmâ*) was understood in its usual meaning of "widows."

[373] These are three classes of court officials, for whose appointment the judge is responsible.

[374] For the *maẓâlim*, cases for which the religious law does not provide, cf. p. xlviii, above.

strong hand and much authority to subdue the evildoer and restrain the aggressor among two litigants. In a way, it serves to do what the judges and others are unable to do. It is concerned with the examination of evidence, with punishments not foreseen by the religious law, with the use of indirect and circumstantial evidence, with the postponement of
I, 400 judgment until the legal situation has been clarified, with attempts to bring about reconciliation between litigants, and with the swearing in of witnesses. This is a wider field than that with which the judges are concerned.

The first caliphs exercised that function personally until the days of the 'Abbâsid al-Muhtadî. Often, they also delegated it to their judges. 'Alî,[375] for instance, (delegated torts) to his judge, Abû Idrîs al-Khawlânî;[376] al-Ma'mûn to Yaḥyâ b. Aktham;[377] and al-Mu'taṣim to Ibn Abî Du'âd.[378] They also often entrusted the judges with leadership of the holy war in summer campaigns. Yaḥyâ b. Aktham thus went on a summer campaign against the Byzantines in the days of al-Ma'mûn. The same was done by Mundhir b. Sa'îd,[379] judge under the Spanish Umayyad 'Abd-ar-Raḥmân an-Nâṣir. Making appointments to these functions was the task of the caliphs or of those to whom they entrusted it, such as a minister to whom full powers were delegated, or a ruler who had gained superiority.

(*The police*)

In the 'Abbâsid dynasty and in the dynasties of the Umayyads in Spain and under the 'Ubaydid(-Fâṭimids) in Egypt and the Maghrib, the control of crimes and imposition of

---

[375] Bulaq: 'Umar.

[376] His name is supposed to have been 'Â'idh-Allâh b. 'Abdallâh. Cf., for instance, Ibn Ḥajar, *Tahdhîb*, V, 85 ff.

[377] Cf. n. 101 to Ibn Khaldûn's Introduction, above. The campaign referred to is probably the one mentioned by aṭ-Ṭabarî, *Annales*, II, 1104, *anno* 216 [831].

[378] Aḥmad b. Abî Du'âd died in 240 [854]. Cf. aṭ-Ṭabarî, III, 1421.

[379] Born in 273 [886/87], Mundhir died in 355 [966]. Cf. Ibn al-Faraḍî, *Ta'rîkh 'ulamâ' al-Andalus* (Bibliotheca Arabico-Hispana, No. 8) (Madrid, 1890–92), II, 17 f.

punishments required by the religious law was also a special (task) and was delegated to the chief of police (*ṣâḥib ash-shurṭah*).[380] The police is another religious function that under these dynasties belonged to the positions connected with the religious law. Its field is somewhat wider than that of the office of judge. It makes it possible for suspects to be brought into court. It decides upon preventive punishments before crimes have been committed. It imposes the punishments required by the religious law where they are due, and determines compensation in cases of bodily injury where the law of talion applies. It imposes punishments not provided for by the religious law, and provides for corrective measures against those who did not execute the crimes (they planned).

The proper functions of the police and of torts were forgotten during the dynasties in which the nature of the cali- I, *401*
phate was no longer remembered. Torts were transferred to the ruler whether he had been delegated by the caliph to take care of them or not. The police function was split into two parts. One of them was that of taking care of suspects, imposing the punishments required by the religious law, and amputating (criminals condemned for crimes punished by the amputation of a limb), and seeing to it that the laws of talion were applied where appropriate. For these duties, the dynasties appointed an official who exercised his office in the service of the political (establishment) without reference to the religious laws. (That official) was sometimes called *wâlî* (governor), and sometimes *shurṭah* (police). The remaining (former police functions dealt with) punishments not provided for by the religious law and the imposition of punishments for crimes fixed by the religious law. They were combined with the functions of judge previously mentioned. They became part of the official duties of the office (of judge), and have so remained down to this time.

This position was taken away from the people who shared in the group feeling of the dynasty. When there was a re-

---

[380] Cf. 2:35 ff., below.

ligious caliphate, the caliph entrusted the function, since it was a religious office, only to Arabs or to clients—allies, slaves, or followers—who shared in their group feeling and upon whose ability and competence to execute the tasks they could rely.

When the character and appearance of the caliphate changed and royal and government authority took over, the religious functions lost to some degree their connection with (the powers in control), in as much as they did not belong among the titles and honors of royal authority. The Arabs later on lost all control of the government. Royal authority fell to Turkish and Berber nations. These caliphal functions, as far as their character and the group feeling that belonged to them was concerned, were even more remote from them (than from their predecessors). This was because the Arabs had been of the opinion that the religious law was their religion and that the Prophet was one of them and that his
I, 402 religious laws distinguished them in their thought and action from the (other) nations. The non-Arabs did not think that way. If they had some respect for (these functions) it was merely because they had become Muslims. Therefore, they came to entrust them to men outside their own group who had become familiar with (these functions) in the dynasties of former caliphs. Under the influence of the luxury of the dynasties to which they had been accustomed for hundreds of years, these people had forgotten the old desert period and desert toughness. They had acquired (the habits of) sedentary culture, luxurious customs, tranquillity, and lack of ability to take care of themselves. In the kingdoms that succeeded the (rule of the) caliphs, the functions of the caliphate became the prerogative of this kind of urban weakling. They were no longer exercised by people of prestige, but by persons whose qualifications were limited, both by their descent (which was different from that of the men in power) and by the (habits of) sedentary culture to which they had become accustomed. They were despised as sedentary people are, who live submerged in luxury and tranquillity, who have no

connection with the group feeling of the ruler, and who depend on being protected (by others). Their position in the dynasty derives from the fact that (the dynasty) takes care of the Muslim religious community and follows the religious laws, and that these persons know the laws and can interpret them through legal decisions (*fatwâ*). They have no standing in the dynasty because they are honored as personalities. Their standing merely reflects an affectation of respect for their position in the royal councils, where it is desired to make a show of reverence for the religious ranks. They do not have executive authority to make decisions in (these councils). If they participate in (the making of decisions), it is just as a matter of form, with no reality behind it. Executive authority in reality belongs to those who have the power to enforce (their decisions). Those who do not have the power (to enforce their decisions) have no executive authority. They are merely used as authorities on religious law, and their legal decisions (*fatwâ*) are accepted. This is indeed the fact. God gives success. I, 403

Some scholars think that this is not right, and that rulers who keep jurists and judges out of (their) councils act wrongly, since Muḥammad said, "The scholars are the heirs of the prophets." [381] However, it should be known that it is not as (such scholars) think.[382] Royal and governmental authority is conditioned by the natural requirements of civilization; were such not the case, it would have nothing to do with politics. The nature of civilization does not require that (jurists and scholars) have any share (in authority). Advisory and executive authority belongs only to the person who controls the group feeling and is by it enabled to exercise authority, to do things or not do them. Those who do not have group feeling, who have no control over their own affairs, and who cannot protect themselves, are dependent upon others. How, then, could they participate in councils, and why

[381] Cf. *Handbook*, p. 234a. One ought not to be surprised to find this tradition constantly quoted in scholarly works.

[382] Cf. 3:314 f., below.

should their advice be taken into consideration? Their advice as derived from their knowledge of the religious laws (is taken into consideration) only in so far as they are consulted for legal decisions (*fatwâ*). Advice on political matters is not their province, because they have no group feeling and do not know the conditions and laws which govern (group feeling). To pay honor to (jurists and scholars) is an act of kindness on the part of rulers and amirs. It testifies to their high regard for Islam and to their respect for men who are in any way concerned with it.

To understand Muḥammad's statement, "The scholars are the heirs of the prophets," it should be realized that the jurists of this time and of the recent past have represented the religious law mainly by ruling on ritual practices and questions of mutual dealings (among Muslims). They make (such rulings) for those who need them to be able to act in accordance with them. This has been the goal of (even) the
I, 404 greatest among (them). They are identified with (the religious law) only to a limited extent (and are known to be experts in it only) under certain conditions. The early Muslims, as well as pious and austere Muslims, on the other hand, represented the religious law in (all its aspects) and were identified with (all of) it and known to have had a thorough (practical) knowledge of its ways. People who represent the religious law without (recourse to the process of) transmission, may (be called) "heirs." Such, for instance, were the men mentioned in al-Qushayrî's *Risâlah*.[383] People who combine the two things [384] are religious scholars, the real "heirs," such as the jurists among the men of the second generation, the ancient Muslims, and the four imams,[385] as well as those who took them as models and followed in their steps. In the case of a Muslim who has only one of the two things, the better claim to be called an "heir" goes to a pious person

[383] Cf. n. 456 to Ch. VI, and 3:82, 85, and 102, below.

[384] That is, theoretical and practical knowledge.

[385] That is, the heads of the four juridical schools, not the first four caliphs.

rather than to a jurist who is not pious. The pious man has inherited a quality. The jurist who is not pious, on the other hand, has not inherited anything. He merely makes rulings for us as to how to act. This applies to the majority of contemporary (jurists) [386] "except those who believe and do good, and they are few." [387]

The position of official witness ('adâlah)

(The position of official witness) is a religious position depending on the office of judge and connected with court practice. The men who hold it give testimony—with the judge's permission—for or against people's (claims). They serve as witnesses when testimony is to be taken, testify during a lawsuit, and fill in the registers which record the rights, possessions, and debts of people and other (legal) transactions. This is the significance of the position.

We [389] have mentioned "the judge's permission" because people may have become confused, and (then) only the judge knows who is reliable and who not. Thus, in a way, he gives permission (and he does so only) to those of whose probity he is sure, so that people's affairs and transactions will be properly safeguarded.

The prerequisite governing this position is the incumbent's possession of the quality of probity (*'adâlah*) according to the religious law, his freedom from unreliability. Further- I, *405*
more, he must be able to fill in the (court) records and make

---

[386] Ergo, the jurists among our scholars cannot be called "heirs." Muḥammad's statement does not apply to them, and the rulers, therefore, are not acting wrongly if they do not consult them.

[387] Qur'ân 38.24 (23).

[388] In order to understand much of the discussion in this section, one must keep in mind the fact mentioned by Ibn Khaldûn only at the end, that *'adâlah* has come to mean two things. The one is "probity," considered as one of the conditions of the caliphate or other high office; cf. n. 107 to Ibn Khaldûn's Introduction, above, and n. 232 to this chapter. In that sense, *'adâlah* also means a person's reliability as a transmitter of traditions and as a religious scholar. The other usage is to designate the office of official witness, originally a "fair" (*'âdil*) man, one who possessed "probity" (*'adâlah*).

[389] This paragraph was added in the margin of C and is incorporated in the text of D.

out contracts in the right form and proper order and correctly, (observing) the conditions and stipulations governing them from the point of view of the religious law. Thus, he must have such knowledge of jurisprudence as is necessary for the purpose. Because of these conditions and the experience and practice required, (the office) came to be restricted to persons of probity. Probity came to be (considered) the particular quality of persons who exercise this function. But this is not so. Probity is one of the prerequisites qualifying them for the office.

The judge must examine their conditions and look into their way of life, to make sure that they fulfill the condition of probity. He must not neglect to do so, because it is his duty to safeguard the rights of the people. The responsibility for everything rests with him, and he is accountable for the outcome.

Once (official witnesses) have been shown clearly to be qualified for the position, they become (more) generally useful (to the judges). (They can be used) to find out about the reliability of other men whose probity is not known to the judges, because of the large size of cities and the confused conditions (of city life). (It is necessary to know their reliability) because it is necessary for judges to settle quarrels among litigants with the help of reliable evidence. In assessing the reliability of (the evidence), they usually count upon these professional witnesses. In every city, they have their own shops and benches where they always sit, so that people who have transactions to make can engage them to function as witnesses and register the (testimony) in writing.

The term "probity" (*'adâlah*) thus came to be used both for the position whose significance has just been explained and for "probity (reliability)" as required by the religious law, which is used paired with "unreliability." The two are the same, but still, they are different. And God knows better.

Market supervision (ḥisbah) *and mint*

The office of market supervisor (*ḥisbah*) is a religious
I, 406 position. It falls under the religious obligation "to command

to do good and forbid to do evil," which rests with the person in charge of the affairs of the Muslims. He appoints to the position men whom he considers qualified for it. The obligation thus devolves upon the appointee. He may use other men to help him in his job. He investigates abuses and applies the appropriate punishments and corrective measures. He sees to it that the people act in accord with the public interest in the town (under his supervision). For instance, he prohibits the obstruction of roads. He forbids porters and boatsmen to carry too heavy loads. He orders the owners of buildings threatening to collapse, to tear them down and thus remove the possibility of danger to passersby. He prevents teachers in schools and other places from beating the young pupils too much.[390] His authority is not restricted to cases of quarrels or complaints, but he (has to) look after, and rule on, everything of the sort that comes to his knowledge or is reported to him. He has no authority over legal claims in general but he has authority over everything relating to fraud and deception in connection with food and other things and in connection with weights and measures. Among his duties is that of making dilatory debtors pay what they owe, and similar things that do not require hearing of evidence or a legal verdict, in other words, cases with which a judge would have nothing to do because they are so common and simple. (Such cases,) therefore, are referred to the person who holds the office of market supervisor to take care of them.

The position of (market supervisor), consequently, is subordinate to the office of judge. In many Muslim dynasties, such as the dynasties of the 'Ubaydid(-Fâṭimids) in Egypt and the Maghrib and that of the Umayyads in Spain, (the office of market supervisor) fell under the general jurisdiction of the judge, who could appoint anyone to the office at discretion. Then, when the position of ruler became separated from the caliphate and when (the ruler) took general charge I, 407
of all political matters, the office of market supervisor became one of the royal positions and a separate office.

[390] Cf. n. 32 to Ch. II, above.

The mint [391]

The office of the mint is concerned with the coins used by Muslims in (commercial) transactions, with guarding against possible falsification or substandard quality (clipping) when the number of coins (and not the weight of their metal) is used in transactions, and with all else relating to (monetary matters.) Further, the office is concerned with putting the ruler's mark upon the coins, thus indicating their good quality and purity. The mark is impressed upon the coins with an iron seal that is especially used for the purpose and that has special designs (legends) on it. It is placed upon the dinar and the dirham after their proper weight has been established, and is then beaten with a hammer until the designs have been impressed upon the coin. This then indicates the good quality of the coin according to the best methods of melting and purification customary among the inhabitants of a particular region under the ruling dynasty. (The metal standard) is not something rigidly fixed but depends upon independent judgment. Once the inhabitants of a particular part or region have decided upon a standard of purity, they hold to it and call it the "guide" (*imâm*) or "standard" (*'iyâr*). They use it to test their coins. If they are substandard, they are bad.

Supervision of all these things is the duty of the holder of the office (of the mint). In this respect, it is a religious office and falls under the caliphate. It used to belong to the general jurisdiction of the judge, but now has become a separate office, as is the case with that of market supervision.

This is all that is to be said about caliphal positions. There were other positions that disappeared when the things
I, 408 that were their concern disappeared. Further, there are positions that became positions of rulers other than the caliph. Such are the positions of amir and wazir, and those concerned

---

[391] Cf. also 2:54 ff., below.

with warfare and taxation. They will be discussed later on in their proper places.

The position concerned with (prosecution of) the holy war ceased to exist when the holy war was no longer waged, save in a few dynasties which, as a rule, classify the laws governing it under the governmental (and not the caliphal) authority. Likewise, the office of marshal of the nobility consisting of relatives of the caliphs, whose descent gives them a claim to the caliphate or to an official pension, disappeared when the caliphate ceased.

In general, the honors and positions of the caliphate merged with those of royal authority and political leadership. This is the present situation in all dynasties.

God governs all affairs in His wisdom.

[30] *The title of "Commander of the Faithful," which is characteristic of the caliph.*

It was created in the period of the first four caliphs. This is because the men around Muḥammad and all the other early Muslims called Abû Bakr, when he received the oath of allegiance, "representative" (*khalîfah*, caliph) of the Messenger of God. This form (of address) was used until he died. Then, the oath of allegiance was rendered to ʽUmar who was appointed by (Abû Bakr), and people called ʽUmar "Representative of the Representative of the Messenger of God." However, they considered the title somewhat cumbersome. It was long and had a succession of genitives. (With successive caliphs,) that (style) would become longer and longer and end up as a tongue twister, and (the title) would no longer be distinct and recognizable because of the great number of dependent genitives. Therefore, they tried to replace the title by some other one appropriate to a (caliph). I, 409

The leaders of (military) missions used to be called "*amîrs*," a *faʽîl* (formation) connected with *imârah* (commandership). Before becoming Muslims, people used to call the Prophet "Amir of Mecca" and "Amir of the Ḥijâz." The men around Muḥammad also used to call Saʽd b. Abî Waqqâṣ

"Commander (*amîr*) of the Muslims," because he commanded the army at al-Qâdisîyah. (The army there) at that time was the largest agglomeration of Muslims (that existed).

Now, it so happened that one of the men around Muḥammad addressed 'Umar as "Commander of the Faithful" (*amîr al-mu'minîn*). People liked (this form of address) and approved it. Thus, they called 'Umar by (this title). It is said that the first to call him by this title was 'Abdallâh b. Jaḥsh.[392] According to others, it was 'Amr b. al-'Âṣ and al-Mughîrah b. Shu'bah. Again, according to others, it was a messenger [?] [393] who brought (the news) of victory from a (military) mission. He entered Medina and asked for 'Umar with the words, "Where is the Commander of the Faithful?" The men around ('Umar) heard this and liked it. They said: "Indeed, you give him the right title. He is truly the Commander of the Faithful." Thus, they called 'Umar (Commander of the Faithful), and this became his title among the people. The caliphs who succeeded him inherited the title as a characteristic which no other person shared with them. This was the case with all the Umayyads.

The Shî'ah used the title of Imam for 'Alî, ascribing to him the "imamate," which is a related expression for caliphate. (They called him Imam,) in order to display the novel theory that 'Alî was more entitled to lead the prayer (*imâmah*) than Abû Bakr. They restricted the title (of Imam) to ('Alî) and to those after him whom they considered his successors to the caliphate. All these men were called Imam

---

[392] Actually, Ibn Jaḥsh—who died at Uḥud in 625—is said to have himself been addressed as "Commander of the Faithful" during a raid he made in the year preceding his death. Cf. Ibn Sa'd, *Ṭabaqât*, III [1], 63, ll. 15 f. The stories about the introduction of the title vary greatly. It is even said that Muḥammad addressed 'Umar as "Commander of the Faithful." Cf. Ibn Kathîr, *Bidâyah*, VII, 137.

[393] Possibly *barîd*. I do not know of any Burayd in this context. However, according to al-'Askarî, *Awâ'il*, Paris, MS. Ar. 5986, fols. 75*b*–76*a*, one of two messengers involved in this story was Labîd b. Rabî'ah (apparently, the famous poet). Ibn Khaldûn's source may have had Labîd or some other proper name in this place.

as long as their propaganda for them was clandestine. But when they eventually seized power (openly), they changed the title of their successors to that of Commander of the Faithful. This was done by the 'Abbâsid Shî'ah. They had always called their leaders Imam down to Ibrâhîm, for whom *I, 410* they came out into the open and unfurled the banner of war. When (Ibrâhîm) died, his brother as-Saffâḥ was called Commander of the Faithful. The same was the case with the extremist Shî'ah in Ifrîqiyah. They always called their leaders, who were descendants of Ismâ'îl, Imam, until 'Ubaydallâh al-Mahdî came to power. They continued to call him, and also his son and successor Abû l-Qâsim, Imam. But when their power was secure, their successors were called Commander of the Faithful. The same was the case with the Idrîsids in the Maghrib. They called Idrîs, and also his son and successor Idrîs the Younger, Imam. This is (Shî'ah) procedure.

The caliphs inherited the title of Commander of the Faithful from each other. It became a characteristic of the ruler of the Ḥijâz, Syria, and the 'Irâq, the regions that were the home of the Arabs and the center of the Muslim dynasty and the base [394] of Islam and Muslim conquest. Therefore, (it was no longer distinctive) when the ('Abbâsid) dynasty reached its flowering and prime, (and) another style of address gained currency, one that served to distinguish them from each other, in as much as the title of Commander of the Faithful was one they all had. The 'Abbâsids took surnames such as as-Saffâḥ, al-Manṣûr, al-Mahdî, al-Hâdî, ar-Rashîd, and so on, and thus created a sort of cover to guard their proper names against abuse by the tongues of the common people and protect them against profanation. (They continued with that custom) down to the end of the dynasty. The 'Ubaydid(-Fâṭimids) in Ifrîqiyah and Egypt followed their example.

The Umayyads refrained from that (for a long time). The

---

[394] *Aṣl,* as in A, C, and D. Bulaq and B have *ahl* "people."

earlier Umayyads in the East had done so, in keeping with their austerity and simplicity. Arab manners and aspirations had not yet been abandoned in their time, and (the Umayyads) had not yet exchanged Bedouin characteristics for those of sedentary culture. The Umayyads in Spain also refrained from such titles, because they followed the tradition of their ancestors. Moreover, they were conscious of their
I, 411 inferior position, since they did not control the caliphate which the 'Abbâsids had appropriated, and had no power over [395] the Ḥijâz, the base of the Arabs and Islam, and were remote from the seat of the caliphate around which the group feeling (of the Arabs) centered. By being rulers of a remote region, they merely protected themselves against the persecution of the 'Abbâsids. Finally, however, at the beginning of the fourth [tenth] century, the (Umayyad) 'Abd-ar-Raḥmân the Last [396] (III) an-Nâṣir (b. Muḥammad) b. al-amîr 'Abdallâh b. Muḥammad b. 'Abd-ar-Raḥmân II, appeared on the scene. It became known how greatly the liberty of the caliphate in the East had been curtailed and how the clients of the 'Abbâsids had taken control of the dynasty and had achieved complete power to depose, replace, kill, or blind the caliphs. 'Abd-ar-Raḥmân III, therefore, adopted the ways of the caliphs in the East and in Ifrîqiyah: He had himself called Commander of the Faithful and assumed the surname of an-Nâṣir-li-dîn-Allâh. This custom, which he had been the first to practice, was followed and became an established one. His ancestors and the early (Umayyads) had not had it.

This situation prevailed down to the time when Arab group feeling was completely destroyed and the caliphate lost its identity. Non-Arab clients gained power over the 'Abbâsids; followers (of their own making) gained power over the 'Ubaydid(-Fâṭimids) in Cairo; the Ṣinhâjah gained

[395] "The caliphate . . . power over" appears in the margin of C and in the text of D.

[396] There were, however, other Umayyads called 'Abd-ar-Raḥmân after an-Nâṣir.

power over the realm of Ifrîqiyah; the Zanâtah gained power over the Maghrib; and the *reyes de taïfas* in Spain gained power over the Umayyads. (Each of) these (groups) took over part of (the caliphate). The Muslim empire dissolved. The rulers in the West and the East adopted different titles. Formerly, they had all been called by the name of *Sulṭân.*

The non-Arab rulers in the East were distinguished by the caliphs with special honorific surnames indicating their subservience and obedience and their good status as officials. (Such surnames included) Sharaf-ad-dawlah, 'Aḍud-ad- I, 412
dawlah, Rukn-ad-dawlah, Mu'izz-ad-dawlah, Naṣîr-ad-dawlah, Niẓâm-al-mulk, Bahâ'-al-mulk, Dhakhîrat-al-mulk, and so on.[396a] The 'Ubaydid(-Fâṭimids) used also to distinguish the Ṣinhâjah amirs in that manner. When these men gained control over the caliphs, they were satisfied to keep these surnames and did not adopt caliphal titles out of deference to the institution and in order to avoid any usurpation of its peculiar characteristics, as is customary among those who gain power and control (over an existing institution), as we have stated before.[397] However, later on, the non-Arabs in the East strengthened their grip on royal authority and became more and more prominent in state and government. The group feeling of the caliphate vanished and dissolved completely. At that time, these non-Arabs were inclined to adopt titles that were characteristic of royal authority, such as an-Nâṣir and al-Manṣûr. This was in addition to the titles they had previously held and which indicated that they were no longer clients and followers through the fact that they were simply combinations with *dîn* (religion), such as Ṣalâḥ-ad-dîn, Asad-ad-dîn, and Nûr-ad-dîn.[397a]

The *reyes de taïfas* in Spain, who had a powerful grip on

[396a] These surnames may be translated as follows: Honor of the Dynasty, Strong Arm of the Dynasty, Pillar of the Dynasty, Champion of the Dynasty, Defender of the Dynasty, Order of the Kingdom, Splendor of the Kingdom, Treasure of the Kingdom, etc.

[397] Cf. p. 379, above, and 2:11, below.

[397a] That is, Welfare of the Religion, Lion of the Religion, and Light of the Religion.

(the caliphate) by virtue of the fact that they shared in its tribal group feeling, divided up and distributed among themselves the caliphal titles. They had themselves called an-Nâṣir, al-Manṣûr, al-Mu'tamid, al-Muẓaffar, and so on. Ibn Sharaf criticized them for this in these verses:

What makes me feel humble in Spain
Is the use of the names Mu'taṣim and Mu'taḍid there.
Royal surnames not in their proper place:
Like a cat that by blowing itself up imitates the lion.[398]

The Ṣinhâjah restricted themselves to the display titles that the 'Ubaydid(-Fâṭimid) caliphs had given them, such as
I, 413 Naṣîr-ad-dawlah, Sayf-ad-dawlah,[399] and Mu'izz-ad-dawlah. They kept to this (even) when they exchanged the 'Ubaydid(-Fâṭimid) propaganda for that of the 'Abbâsids. Later on, as the distance between them and the caliphate grew, they forgot the period of (the caliphate). They forgot these titles and restricted themselves to the name of Sultan. The same was the case with the Maghrâwah rulers in the Maghrib. The only title they adopted was that of Sultan, in accordance with Bedouin custom and desert austerity.

At the time when the name of the caliphate had become extinct and its influence non-existent, the Lamtûnah (Almoravid) ruler Yûsuf b. Tâshfîn made his appearance among the Berber tribes in the Maghrib. He became the ruler of both shores. He was a good and conservative man who, consequently, in order to comply with all the formalities of his religion, wished to submit to the caliphal authority. He addressed himself to the 'Abbâsid al-Mustaẓhir and sent to him two *shaykhs* from Sevilla as his ambassadors, 'Abdallâh b. al-'Arabî and ('Abdallâh's) son, Judge Abû Bakr.[400] They

[398] Cf. p. 316, above.

[399] Sayf-ad-dawlah is added in C and D.

[400] For Abû Bakr, cf. n. 353 to this chapter, above. He and his father, 'Abdallâh b. Muḥammad, left on the pilgrimage in 485 [1092], and visited Baghdad twice, once before the pilgrimage and once afterwards; they performed the pilgrimage in 489 [1096]. It must have been in 1097/98, during

were to transmit the oath of allegiance to (al-Mustaẓhir) and were to ask him to appoint and invest Ibn Tâshfîn as ruler over the Maghrib. They returned with the caliphal appointment of Ibn Tâshfîn as ruler over the Maghrib and with (permission to) use the caliphal style in dress and flag. In (the document, the caliph) addressed (Ibn Tâshfîn) as "Commander of the Muslims," [401] in order to honor and distinguish him. Ibn Tâshfîn, therefore, took that as his title. Others say that he had been called "Commander of the Muslims" before that, out of deference to the high rank of the caliphate, because he and his people, the Almoravids, practiced Islam and followed the Sunnah.

The Mahdî (of the Almohads) followed upon the (Almoravids). He made propaganda for the truth. He adopted the tenets of the Ash'arites and criticized the Maghribîs for having deviated from them by returning to the ancestral tradition of rejecting allegorical interpretation of explicit statements of the religious law, a rejection that leads to (anthropomorphism),[402] as is known from the Ash'arite school. He called his followers Almohads (champions of the strict oneness of God), displaying (by the choice of that name) his disapproval (of anthropomorphism). He followed the opinion of the 'Alids with regard to "the Infallible Imam" [403] who must exist in every age and whose existence preserves the order of the world. (Al-Mahdî) was at first called Imam, in accordance with the afore-mentioned Shî'ah practice with regard to the title of their caliphs. The word *al-ma'ṣûm* (infallible) was linked (with Imam) to indicate his tenet concerning the infallibility of the Imam. In the opinion of his followers, he was above the title of Commander of the Faith- I, 414

their second stay in Baghdad, that Ibn Tâshfîn commissioned them to act as his ambassadors to al-Mustaẓhir (1094–1118). 'Abdallâh died on their return trip in 493 [1099]. Cf. Ibn Farḥûn, *Dîbâj*, pp. 281 f. For the embassy, cf. also *'Ibar*, VI, 188; de Slane (tr.), II, 82.

[401] And not the caliphal title "Commander of the Faithful," which the Almoravids did not use.

[402] The word "anthropomorphism" is expressly added in Bulaq.

[403] For *ma'ṣûm*, *'iṣmah*, cf. pp. 185 and 403, above.

ful. (To avoid this title) was in accordance with the tenets of the old Shî'ah, and (he also avoided it), because to use it meant sharing it with the foolish young descendants of the caliphs who were alive in the East and the West at that time. 'Abd-al-Mu'min, who was appointed successor to (the Mahdî), did adopt the title of Commander of the Faithful. His successors, the caliphs of the Banû 'Abd-al-Mu'min, followed his example, and so did their successors, the Ḥafṣids in Ifrîqiyah.[404] They appropriated it exclusively as their own, since their *shaykh*, the Mahdî, had made (religious) propaganda (justifying the use of) that (title) and since the power belonged to him and to his friends (clients) who succeeded him and to nobody else, because Qurashite group feeling had completely ceased to exist. Thus, (the use of the title) came to be their custom.

When governmental (authority) in the Maghrib lapsed and the Zanâtah took power, their first rulers continued the ways of desert life and simplicity and followed the Lamtûnah (Almoravids) in using the title of Commander of the Muslims, out of deference to the high rank of the caliphate. They rendered obedience, first to the caliphate of the Banû 'Abd-al-Mu'min, and afterwards to that of the Ḥafṣids. The later (Zanâtah) rulers aspired to the title of Commander of the Faithful, and are using it at this time to comply fully with royal aspirations and the ways and characteristics of royal authority. "God has the power to execute His commands." [405]

I, 415 [31] *Remarks on the words "Pope" and "Patriarch" in the Christian religion and on the word "Kohen" used by the Jews.*

It [406] should be known that after the removal of its prophet, a religious group must have someone to take care of it. (Such a person) must cause the people to act according to the religious laws. In a way, he stands to them in the

---

[404] "In Ifrîqiyah" is added in the margin of C and is in the text of D.
[405] Qur'ân 12.21 (21). [406] Cf. Issawi, pp. 136 f.

place (*khalîfah*, caliph) of their prophet, in as much as (he urges) the obligations which (the prophet) had imposed upon them. Furthermore, in accordance with the afore-mentioned [407] need for political leadership in social organization, the human species must have a person who will cause them to act in accordance with what is good for them and who will prevent them by force from doing things harmful to them. Such a person is the one who is called ruler.

In the Muslim community, the holy war is a religious duty, because of the universalism of the (Muslim) mission and (the obligation to) convert everybody to Islam either by persuasion or by force. Therefore, caliphate and royal authority are united in (Islam), so that the person in charge can devote the available strength to both of them [408] at the same time.

The other religious groups did not have a universal mission, and the holy war was not a religious duty to them, save only for purposes of defense. It has thus come about that the person in charge of religious affairs in (other religious groups) is not concerned with power politics at all. (Among them,) royal authority comes to those who have it, by accident and in some way that has nothing to do with religion. It comes to them as the necessary result of group feeling, which by its very nature seeks to obtain royal authority, as we have mentioned before,[409] and not because they are under obligation to gain power over other nations, as is the case with Islam. They are merely required to establish their religion among their own (people).

This is why the Israelites after Moses and Joshua remained unconcerned with royal authority for about four hundred years.[410] Their only concern was to establish their religion. The person from among them who was in charge of their religion was called the Kohen. He was in a way the I, *416*

---

[407] Cf. pp. 92 and 380 f., above.

[408] That is, toward religion (caliphate) and politics (royal authority).

[409] Cf. pp. 284 ff., above. [410] *'Ibar*, II, 88, has "three hundred."

representative (caliph) of Moses. He regulated the prayers and sacrifices of the Israelites. They made it a condition for (the Kohen) to be a descendant of Aaron, as it had been destined for him and his children by divine revelation.[411] For (supervision of the) political matters which naturally arise among human beings, the Israelites selected seventy elders who were entrusted with a general legal authority. The Kohen was higher in religious rank than they and more remote from the turbulent legal authority. This continued to be (the situation among the Israelites) until the nature of group feeling made itself fully felt and all power became political. The Israelites dispossessed the Canaanites of the land that God had given them as their heritage in Jerusalem and the surrounding region, as it had been explained to them through Moses. The nations of the Philistines, the Canaanites, the Armenians [!],[412] the Edomites, the Ammonites, and the Moabites fought against them. During that (time), political leadership was entrusted to the elders among them. The Israelites remained in that condition for about four hundred years. They did not have any royal power and were annoyed by attacks from foreign nations. Therefore, they asked God through Samuel, one of their prophets, that He permit them to make someone king over them. Thus, Saul became their king. He defeated the foreign nations and killed[413] Goliath, the ruler of the Philistines. After Saul, David became king, and then Solomon. His kingdom flourished and extended to the borders of the Ḥijâz and further to the borders of the Yemen and to the borders of the land of the Romans (Byzantines). After Solomon, the tribes split
I, 417 into two dynasties. This was in accordance with the necessary consequence of group feeling in dynasties, as we have mentioned before. One of the dynasties was that of the ten tribes in the region of Nablus, the capital of which is Samaria

[411] Bulaq: "since Moses left no offspring." Cf. also p. 412, above.

[412] Cf. p. 334, above.

[413] The subject of the active verb is Saul, though Ibn Khaldûn was aware that Saul did not kill Goliath personally, but "had him killed." Cf. *'Ibar*, II, 95.

(Sabasṭiyah),[414] and the other that of the children of Judah and Benjamin in Jerusalem.[415] Nebuchadnezzar, the king of Babylon, then deprived them of their royal authority. He first (dealt with) the ten tribes in Samaria (Sabasṭiyah),[416] and then with the children of Judah in Jerusalem. Their royal authority had had an uninterrupted duration of a thousand years. Now he destroyed their temple, burnt their Torah, and killed their religion. He deported the people to Iṣfahân [417] and the 'Irâq. Eventually, one of the Persian Kayyanid (Achaemenid) rulers brought them back to Jerusalem, seventy years after they had left it. They rebuilt the temple and re-established their religion in its original form with priests only. The royal authority belonged to the Persians.

Alexander and the Greeks then defeated the Persians, and the Jews came under Greek domination. The Greek rule then weakened, and, with the help of (their) natural group feeling, the Jews rose against the Greeks and made an end to their domination over them. (Jewish) royal authority was in charge of their Hasmonean priests. (The Hasmoneans) fought the Greeks. Eventually, their power was destroyed. The Romans defeated them, and (the Jews) came under Roman domination. (The Romans) advanced toward Jerusalem, the seat of the children of Herod, relatives by marriage of the Hasmoneans and the last remnant of the Hasmonean dynasty. They laid siege to them for a time, finally conquering (Jerusalem) by force in an orgy of murder, destruction, and arson. They laid Jerusalem in ruins and exiled (the Jews) I, 418
to Rome and the regions beyond. This was the second destruction of the temple. The Jews call it "the Great Exile."

---

[414] As indicated in this and the following two notes, Ibn Khaldûn originally had some rather incorrect geographical information in his earlier text, which he corrected later. In C the corrections are applied in the text or in the margin. In D they appear incorporated in the text. Originally the text here had "the Jazîrah and Mosul."

The Arabic form of Samaria, Sebaste, is vocalized *Ṣubuṣṭiyah* in C.

[415] The earlier text added: "and Syria."

[416] "In Samaria" is an addition of C and D.

[417] For this legend concerning the origin of the Jewish settlement in Iṣfahân, cf. W. J. Fischel in *The Joshua Starr Memorial Volume*, pp. 112 f.

After that, they had no royal authority, because they had lost their group feeling. They remained afterwards under the domination of the Romans and their successors. Their religious affairs were taken care of by their head, called the Kohen.

The Messiah (Jesus) brought (the Jews) his religion, as is known. He abolished some of the laws of the Torah. He performed marvelous wonders, such as healing the insane [418] and reviving the dead. Many people joined him and believed in him. The largest group among his following were his companions, the Apostles. There were twelve of them. He sent some of them as messengers (Apostles) to all parts of the world. They made propaganda for his religious group. That was in the days of Augustus, the first of the Roman emperors, and during the time of Herod, the king of the Jews, who had taken away royal authority from the Hasmoneans, his relatives by marriage. The Jews envied (Jesus) and declared him a liar. Their king, Herod, wrote to the Roman Emperor, Augustus, and incited him against (Jesus). The Roman Emperor gave (the Jews) permission to kill him, and the story of Jesus as recited in the Qur'ân occurred.[419]

The Apostles divided into different groups. Most of them went to the country of the Romans and made propaganda for the Christian religion. Peter was the greatest of them. He settled in Rome, the seat of the Roman emperors. They [420] then wrote down the Gospel that had been revealed to Jesus, in four recensions according to their different traditions. Matthew wrote his Gospel in Jerusalem in Hebrew. It was translated into Latin by John, the son of Zebedee, one of (the Apostles). (The Apostle) Luke wrote his Gospel in

[418] Bulaq has "the blind and the lepers," which looks very much like a correction by the editor of Bulaq, because Qur'ân 3.49 (43) and 5.110 (110) mentions the blind and the lepers, whereas no mention is made in it of the insane.

[419] This refers to the docetist idea of Jesus' death, as expressed in Qur'ân 4.157 (156).

[420] For the following discussion of the Jewish and Christian Scriptures, cf. *'Ibar*, II, 148.

Latin for a Roman dignitary. (The Apostle) John, the son of Zebedee, wrote his Gospel in Rome. Peter wrote his Gospel in Latin and ascribed it to his pupil Mark. These four recensions of the Gospel differ from each other. Not all of it is pure revelation, but (the Gospels) have an admixture of the words of Jesus and of the Apostles. Most [421] of (their contents) consists of sermons and stories. There are very few laws in them. I, 419

The Apostles came together at that time in Rome and laid down the rules of the Christian community. They entrusted them to Clement, a pupil of Peter, noting in them the list of books that are to be accepted and in accordance with which one must act.

(The books which) belong to the old religious law of the Jews are the following:

The Torah, which consists of five volumes.
The Book of Joshua.
The Book of Judges.
The Book of Ruth.
The Book of Judith.[422]
The four Books of Kings.
The Book of Chronicles.[423]
The three Books of Maccabees, by Ibn Gorion.[424]

---

[421] Originally, Ibn Khaldûn had said "all." He corrected "all" to "most" in C, and "most" is found in the text of D.

[422] The MSS have *Yahûdhâ* "Judah," but there can be no doubt that the Book of Judith is meant.

[423] The MSS do not agree about the name of Chronicles. It seems that the original text in C was *b–r–y–w–m–y–n*, while A has *b–r–y–'–m–w–m–y–n*. This is easily explained as a corruption of *b–r–<l–y>–b–w–m–y–n* Paraleipomena.

[424] The reference to the alleged authorship of the Books of the Maccabees by Joseph b. Gorion (Pseudo-Josippon), is not found in *'Ibar*, II, 148, and, incidentally, appears in C only in the margin. It should be noted that the Arabic text of the *History of the Jews* by Pseudo-Josippon is occasionally called "Book of the Maccabees." Cf. the edition of the Ethiopic version by Murad Kamil, *Zênâ Ayhûd* (New York, 1937), pp. xvi ff., and J. Wellhausen, "Der arabische Josippus" in *Abhandlungen der Kgl. Gesellschaft der Wissenschaften zu Göttingen*, philol.-his. Kl., N.F., I 4 (1897), 3. Cf. now W. J. Fischel, "Ibn Khaldûn and Josippon," in *Homenaje a Millás-Vallicrosa* (Barcelona, 1954), I, 596.

The Book of Ezra, the religious leader.
The Book of Esther [425] and the story of Haman.
The Book of Job the Righteous.
The Psalms of David.
The five Books of David's son, Solomon.
The sixteen Prophecies of the major and minor prophets.
The Book of Jesus, the son of Sira, the minister of Solomon.

(The books of) the religious law of Jesus that was received by the Apostles are the following:

The four recensions of the Gospel.
The Book of Paul which consists of fourteen epistles.
The Katholika (General Epistles) which consist of seven epistles, the eighth being the Praxeis (Acts), stories of the Apostles.
The Book of Clement which contains the laws.
The Book of the Apocalypse (Revelation) which contains the vision of John, the son of Zebedee.

I, *420* The attitude of the Roman emperors toward Christianity varied. At times, they adopted it and honored its adherents. At other times, they did not recognize it and persecuted its adherents and killed and exiled them. Finally, Constantine appeared and adopted Christianity. From then on, all (the Roman emperors) were Christians.[426]

The head of the Christian (community) and the person in charge of (Christian religious) institutions is called Patriarch. He is their religious head and the representative (caliph) of the Messiah among them. He sends his delegates and representatives to the remote Christian nations. They are called "bishop," that is, delegate of the Patriarch. The man who leads the prayers and makes decisions in religious matters is called "priest." The person who withdraws from society and

[425] The MSS read *Ûshîr*. This may represent a misreading *Osther* for Esther.
[426] Cf. also 2:261, below.

retires into solitude for worship is called "monk." The latter usually seek solitude in (monastic) cells.

The Apostle Peter, the chief Apostle and oldest of the disciples, was in Rome and established the Christian religion there. Nero, the fifth Roman emperor, killed him.[427] Successor to Peter at the Roman see was Arius.

Mark the Evangelist spent seven years in Alexandria and Egypt and the Maghrib making propaganda. After him came Ananias, who was called Patriarch. He was the first Patriarch there. He appointed twelve priests to be with him, and it was arranged that when the Patriarch died, one of the twelve should take his place, and one of the faithful [428] be elected to take his place as the twelfth priest. Thus, the patriarchate fell to the priests.

Later on, dissension broke out among the Christians with regard to the basic principles and articles of their religion. They assembled in Nicea in the days of Constantine, in order to lay down (the doctrine of) true Christianity. Three hundred and eighteen bishops agreed upon one and the same doctrine of Christianity. They wrote it down and called it "the Creed." They made it the fundamental principle to *I, 421*
which they would all have reference. Among the things they set down in writing was that with respect to the appointment of the Patriarch as the head of Christianity, no reference should be made to the independent judgment of the priests, as Ananias, the disciple of Mark, had prescribed. That point of view was abolished. The Patriarch was to come from a large group and to be elected by the leaders and chiefs of the believers. It has been so ever since. Later on, other dissensions arose concerning the basic principles of Christianity. Synods concerned with regulating (the religion), were assembled, but there was no dissension with regard to the basic principles (of the method of selecting the Patriarch). It has remained the same ever since.

---

[427] Bulaq adds: "together with other patriarchs and bishops." This may have been the old text, and Ibn Khaldûn later took the words out, because he remembered that patriarchs and bishops did not yet exist at that time.

[428] *Wâḥidun*, as in the MSS.

The Patriarchs always appointed bishops as their delegates. The bishops used to call the Patriarch "Father," as a sign of respect. The priests similarly came to call the bishop "Father," when he was not together with the Patriarch, as a sign of respect. This caused confusion in the use of the title over a long period, ending, it is said, with the Patriarchate of Heraclius in Alexandria. It was considered desirable to distinguish the Patriarch from the bishop in the matter of respect (shown to him by style of address). Therefore, the Patriarch was called "Pope," that is, "Father of fathers." The name (of "Pope") first appeared in Egypt, according to the theory expressed by Jirjis b. al-'Amîd [429] in his *History*. It was then transferred to the occupant of the most important see in (Christianity), the see of Rome, which was the see of the Apostle Peter, as we have mentioned before. The title of Pope has remained characteristic of the see of Rome down to this day.

Thereafter, there were dissensions among the Christians with regard to their religion and to Christology. They split into groups and sects, which secured the support of the various Christian rulers against each other. At different times there appeared different sects. Finally, these sects crystallized into three groups, which constitute the (Christian) sects. Others have no significance. These are the Melchites, the Jacobites, and the Nestorians. We do not think that we should blacken the pages of this book with discussion of their dogmas
I, 422 of unbelief. In general, they are well known. All of them are unbelief. This is clearly stated in the noble Qur'ân. (To) discuss or argue those things with them is not up to us. It is (for them to choose between) conversion to Islâm, payment of the poll tax, or death.

Later on, each sect had its own Patriarch. The Patriarch

---

[429] Al-Makîn, *ca.* 1205–1273. Cf. *GAL*, I, 348; *Suppl.*, I, 590. G. Graf, *Geschichte der christlichen arabischen Literatur* (Studi e Testi No. 133) (Città del Vaticano, 1947), II, 348 ff. Although the second part of al-Makîn's *History* (which contains the Muslim period) has been known since the seventeenth century, the first part of the work, where the above quotation may be expected to occur, has not yet been published.

of Rome is today called "Pope." He is of the Melchite persuasion. Rome belongs to the European Christians. Their royal authority is established in that region.

The Patriarch of the (Christian) subjects [430] in Egypt is of the Jacobite persuasion. He resides among them. The Abyssinians follow the religion of (the Egyptian Christians). The Patriarch of Egypt delegates bishops to the Abyssinians, and these bishops arrange religious affairs in Abyssinia. The name of "Pope" is specially reserved for the patriarch of Rome at this time. The Jacobites do not call their patriarch "Pope." The word (Pope) is pronounced *Pappa.*

It is the custom of the Pope with respect to the European Christians to urge them to submit to one ruler and have recourse to him in their disagreements and agreements, in order to avoid the dissolution of the whole thing. His purpose is to have the group feeling that is the strongest among them (concentrated upon one ruler), so that (this ruler) has power over all of them. The ruler is called "Emperor" (*Emperador*), with the middle letter [431] (pronounced somehow) between *dh* and *ẓ*. (The Pope) personally places the crown upon the head of (the emperor), in order to let him have the blessing implied (in that ceremony). The emperor, therefore, is called "the crowned one." Perhaps that is the meaning of the word "emperor."

This, briefly, is our comment on the two words Pope and Kohen.

"God leads astray whomever He wants to lead astray, and He guides whomever He wants to guide." [432]

[CHAPTER III IS CONTINUED IN VOLUME 2]

---

[430] Lit., "those who have entered the covenant (*'ahd*)." This word is used as a technical term for Christians (and Jews) who have accepted the restrictions placed upon them by the so-called "covenant of 'Umar."

[431] The reference is to the *d/t*. The Arabic text here is not quite clear. Perhaps we should translate: "with the (foreign) letter (pronounced somehow) in the middle between *dh* and *ẓ*." Cf. also as-Silafî, *Mu'jam*, MS (photograph), Cairo, *ta'rîkh* 3932, p. 379, who refers to the name *Ẓunuh*, also spelled *Ẓûnuh* or *Dhûnuh*, and explains it as meaning "master" in "Roman."

[432] Qur'ân 16.93 (95); 35.8 (9); 74.31 (34).

Printed in the USA
CPSIA information can be obtained
at www.ICGtesting.com
LVHW072129151123
763991LV00007B/212

9 789390 804740